A POSTCOLONIAL COMMENTARY
ON THE NEW TESTAMENT WRITINGS

Edited by

Fernando F. Segovia
and R. S. Sugirtharajah

Other titles in the series

THE BIBLE AND POSTCOLONIALISM, 13

t&t clark

Published by T&T Clark
A Continuum imprint
The Tower Building, 11 York Road, London SE1 7NX
80 Maiden Lane, Suite 704, New York, NY 10038

www.continuumbooks.com

First published 2007

British Library Cataloguing-in-Publication Data
A catalogue record for this book is available from the British Library

ISBN-10: 0-567-04563-3 (hardback)
ISBN-13: 978-0-567-04563-8 (hardback)

Typeset by CA Typesetting Ltd, www.publisherservices.co.uk
Printed on acid-free paper by Biddles Ltd, King's Lynn, Norfolk

CONTENTS

ACKNOWLEDGMENTS

This volume has been made possible due to the assistance and support of a good number of people, to whom we are deeply indebted and most thankful. First and foremost, to all those who kindly accepted the invitation to serve as contributors to the project. Second, to Dean James Hudnut-Beumler of the Divinity School at Vanderbilt University for his unreserved backing of the project and much-appreciated support toward editorial expenses. Third, to the Revd James A. Metzger, who, as a doctoral student in New Testament and Early Christianity within the Graduate Department of Religion at Vanderbilt University, served as editorial assistant for the project, for his superb editing of the project. Finally, to the staff of T&T Clark International, especially Mr Dominic Mattos, who oversaw the entire editorial process, and to Dr Mark Newby, who was responsible for the final editorial preparation of the manuscript – their assistance proved invaluable and was deeply appreciated.

CONTRIBUTORS

Efraín Agosto, Hartford Theological Seminary, Hartford, Connecticut, USA

Jennifer G. Bird, Greensboro College, Greensboro, North Carolina, USA

Ralph Broadbent, University of Birmingham, Birmingham, United Kingdom

Virginia Burrus, The Theological School, Drew University, Madison, New Jersey, USA

Allan Dwight Callahan, Seminário Teológico Batista de Nordeste, Bahia, Brazil

Warren Carter, St. Paul's School of Theology, Kansas City, Missouri, USA

Neil Elliott, United Theological Seminary, New Brighton, Minnesota and Metropolitan State University, St. Paul, Minnesota, USA

Richard A. Horsley, University of Massachusetts Boston, Boston, Massachusetts, USA

Cynthia Briggs Kittredge, Episcopal Seminary of the Southwest, Austin, Texas, USA

Tat-siong Benny Liew, Pacific School of Theology, Berkeley, California, USA

Stephen D. Moore, The Theological School, Drew University, Madison, New Jersey, USA

Muriel Orvillo-Montenegro, The Divinity School, Silliman University, Dumaguete City, Philippines

Rohun Park, Graduate Department of Religion, Vanderbilt University, Nashville, Tennessee, USA

Jeremy H. Punt, Faculty of Theology, University of Stellenbosch, Stellenbosch, Republic of South Africa

Sharon H. Ringe, Wesley Theological Seminary, Washington, DC, USA

Elisabeth Schüssler Fiorcnza, The Divinity School, Harvard University, Cambridge, Massachusetts, USA

Fernando F. Segovia, The Divinity School, Vanderbilt University, Nashville, Tennessee, USA

Abraham Smith, Perkins School of Theology, Southern Methodist University, Dallas, Texas, USA

R. S. Sugirtharajah, University of Birmingham, Birmingham, United Kingdom

Sze-kar Wan, Andover-Newton Theological Seminary, Newton, Massachusetts, USA

Gordon Zerbe, Canadian Mennonite University, Winnipeg, Canada

INTRODUCTION:
CONFIGURATIONS, APPROACHES, FINDINGS, STANCES

Fernando F. Segovia

The present commentary constitutes, on various counts, a landmark achievement in the trajectory of postcolonial biblical criticism: it contains highly integrative critical analysis of all the writings of the New Testament; it brings together a highly diverse representation of critical faces and voices; and it reveals a highly expansive deployment of critical frameworks and responses. A previous volume in this series on The Bible and Postcolonialism (Stephen D. Moore and Fernando F. Segovia (eds), *Postcolonial Biblical Criticism: Interdisciplinary Intersections* [London and New York: T&T Clark International, 2005]) has already traced the overall path of postcolonial criticism, its origins and developments, in biblical studies, in the light of other poststructuralist and ideological approaches in the discipline. In this introduction, therefore, I should like to pursue a comparative analysis of the different contributions in terms of four fundamental areas of discussion in postcolonial inquiry. These are as follows: (1) configurations, the envisioned meaning and scope of the postcolonial as such; (2) approaches, the particular mode of interpretation adopted as well as the specific line of development undertaken; (3) findings, the range of positions advanced with regard to the perceived interaction between the socio-religious arena of the unfolding Christian texts and communities and the socio-political realm of the Roman Empire; and (4) stances, the relationship between critic and findings. Such an exercise should, it is my hope, bring an overarching sense of the volume as a whole – without doubt, a daunting collection of immense breadth and incredible richness.

Meaning and Scope of Postcolonial Criticism

Matthew

For Warren Carter, the Gospel of Matthew constitutes a postcolonial text and Rome qualifies as an imperial power, provided that such terms are properly defined and used. Considerable attention is devoted, therefore, to the meaning and scope of the postcolonial. To begin with, a variety of common and established approaches in postcolonial inquiry – the chronological, the geographical, the economic – are pronounced inappropriate for Matthew and its context. For example, in contrast to a sequential understanding of the postcolonial as involving a 'once' of domination and a 'now' of liberation, in light of the global process of decolonization that took place in the mid-twentieth century, the world of Matthew knows of no such transition or experience. The Gospel does not come from the world of the now-liberated, coming to terms with the colonial legacy of silencing and external representation, nor does it belong to the world of the once-dominant, engaged in producing imperial representations of the other. Similarly, distinct from a spatial understanding of the colonial as the implantation of settlements in foreign lands, the world of Matthew was not that of a *colonia*. To be sure, there were *colonia* of retired soldiers elsewhere in Syria, and Roman legions were stationed in Antioch itself, but no such settlement was ever established by Rome in Antioch, the likely location of the Gospel. Lastly, in contrast to a Leninist understanding of the imperial as the highest stage of capitalism, the world of Matthew lacks a systematic and centralized exploitation of foreign resources by a state for economic self-gain. Rome certainly sought economic benefits, but in no way can it be characterized along the lines of a capitalist empire of the nineteenth century. Thus, Carter argues, the key to an appropriate postcolonial analysis of Matthew and its context lies in a more expansive notion of imperialism, where the imperial is seen as taking on different forms and working from different motivations throughout history.

Central to such a concept is the element of 'power over', as exercised by one group over another in any number of ways. Postcolonial analysis would then address the whole of this 'imperializing experience', in all of its different variations as well as from imposition to aftermath. Such analysis would include, in effect, the means, the dynamics, the impact and the legacy of imperialization, with special attention to textual and cultural expressions. Only in this broad sense would postcolonial analysis apply to Matthew and its context: Rome would stand as an example of imperialism – a dominating metropolitan centre with 'power over' others; the Gospel would represent a postcolonial text – a textual product from a context of interaction between imperial culture and local culture. Such analysis would focus precisely on this interaction and thus highlight the reality and experience of imperialization as expressed in Matthew.

Postcolonial analysis would also be applicable to Matthew in terms of two other contexts. On the one hand, a postcolonial focus on Matthew would extend to the use of the Gospel in the concomitant expansion of Western imperialism and the Christian religion in the eighteenth and nineteenth centuries. Why the Western expansion of the fifteenth through to the seventeenth centuries is bypassed is not clear. On the other hand, a postcolonial inquiry would also attend to the use of the Gospel within contemporary ecclesial contexts, as Christians seek to avoid the language, worldview and practices of imperialism today. While the former dimension is not pursued, the latter is, by way of conclusion.

Mark

Tat-siong Benny Liew does not specify the force or reach of the term 'post-colonial' as such and hence does not pursue the question of meaning and scope; at the same time, however, he does characterize the Gospel of Mark as a colonial text and his own approach to it as a postcolonial reading. With regard to the Gospel, he speaks of a twofold colonial dimension: first, as a writing coming from a 'turbulent time of colonial politics' (either before or after the destruction of the Jerusalem temple in 70 CE in the first Judaeo–Roman War); second, as part of the 'colonizing can(n)on' of the West throughout its period of colonial expansion. With regard to his own reading, a twofold postcolonial dimension is again cited: first, by foregrounding – taking a cue from Norman Cohn – the link between apocalyptic and colonialism, yielding a view of Mark as an apocalyptic writing immersed in politics; second, by distinguishing such an approach from that of Western scholarship in general, pointing to the latter's failure to pursue this connection given its traditional identification with Rome, antagonism toward Judaism, and separation of religion and culture.

Luke-Acts

Virginia Burrus's approach to meaning and scope in postcolonial inquiry is swift and to the point: such analysis is highly fruitful for reading Luke-Acts and thoroughly sound for approaching the Roman Empire. With regard to the text, she points to three specific features as particularly inviting in this regard: (1) the evident concern of Luke-Acts with power relations between centre and periphery, defined in geopolitical terms as Rome and those under imperial rule – a concern further identified at work in terms of social class (rich/poor), social space (urban/rural), ethnic/racial boundaries (Jew/Gentile), religious space (Jerusalem temple/land of Israel); (2) the universalizing and transcultural perspective adopted by Luke-Acts – a world that imitates the reach of the Greek and Roman Empires and where 'travellers' as well as encounters between 'social "others" ' and 'ethnic "strangers" ' abound; (3) the ambiguities and ambivalences present throughout Luke-Acts – traits marked, following Homi Bhabha, as highly distinctive of the postcolonial condition, and hence of postcolonial literature, and directly responsible for the critical and transforming power of such literature. Indeed, Burrus adds, the lack of postcolonial analysis on Luke-Acts can only be explained on the grounds of the newness of the approach itself or as a result of the well-known ambiguity of Luke's political stance, yielding quite varied interpretations of the work as 'radically subversive' or 'skillfully accommodationist'. With regard to context, while readily acknowledging (following Robert Young) that imperialism and colonialism are not to be conflated as systems of domination, Burrus argues that contemporary theories of 'colonialism, neocolonialism, and postcoloniality' can properly account for Rome's impact, cultural as well as economic, on its subjugated peoples. Consequently, she specifies, the term 'postcolonial' is used not in chronological fashion (the aftermath of colonialism) but in reference to the 'critical potentialities' present within given frameworks of colonialism and imperialism.

John

The realm of the geopolitical constitutes, for Fernando Segovia, the central problematic of postcolonial inquiry, specifically the differential relationship of power at work in imperial–colonial frameworks, involving domination by the core and subordination of the periphery. In a prolegomenon on key issues of method and theory in postcolonial analysis, he begins by addressing the question of meaning and scope, drawing on postcolonial theory to move on to biblical criticism.

Segovia develops the force of the postcolonial by means of three standard approaches to the import of the prefix 'post' and thus the sense of 'coming after' operative in such approaches regarding the relationship between the colonial and the postcolonial. Two of these, he argues, subscribe to a historical–political understanding of the term as a period of time, differentiated by point of departure: the postcolonial as signifying what follows upon either the imposition or the termination of colonization. The third is said to follow a social-psychological understanding of the term as a state of mind, whether collective or individual: the postcolonial as marking the emergence of critical awareness regarding the problematic of colonization. Segovia himself opts for this last approach: the post-colonial as 'conscientization' in the midst or face of a geopolitical relationship of domination and subordination. Such conscientization, he argues, is imperative in the critic but not in the text. While the text may or may not exhibit critical awareness regarding such a problematic within the imperial–colonial formation in question, it is the presence of such awareness in the critic, within his/her own imperial–colonial framework, that leads to its foregrounding in the text.

Segovia also examines the reach of the postcolonial by way of various standard approaches to the demarcation of its historical and cultural parameters. The range in question is outlined as follows: from an exclusive focus on imperial–colonial formations of the West in the nineteenth or twentieth centuries; through a broadening of this focus historically, via the extension to Western formations of the sixteenth to eighteenth centuries, or culturally, through the incorporation of non-Western formations during the period in question; to an inclusive consideration of such formations across history and culture. His own choice is for this last, expansive approach. Consequently, he regards the raising of the postcolonial problematic as most appropriate for biblical criticism, given the presence and relevance of imperial–colonial frameworks for texts and critics alike, although with due attention to the varying components and dynamics of the different formations in question.

In both regards Segovia specifies what the writing of a postcolonial commentary on the Gospel of John entails. With respect to scope, such analysis is granted and viewed as encompassing both text and reader, each within their respective imperial–colonial frameworks. With regard to meaning, the following specifications are offered: first, the Gospel itself is classified as a 'postcolonial' writing, given its critical awareness of geopolitical power within the Roman Empire; second, as reader, Segovia characterizes his position as 'postcolonial', in light of his own conscientization regarding the deployment of geopolitical power in his context; lastly, the reading of the Gospel advanced is described as 'postcolonial', given its foregrounding of the imperial–colonial problematic in the text.

Romans

One finds in Neil Elliott's contribution no explicit consideration of the force or reach of the concept of the postcolonial. One does find references, largely dispersed and unconnected, to figures and elements of postcolonial theory, so that, while the meaning and scope of postcolonial inquiry are not pursued as such, its application to the texts of early Christianity and the context of Rome is viewed as appropriate and revealing, even imperative. In fact, one detects in Elliott a decidedly multidimensional approach, variously deployed in the commentary itself, to postcolonial analysis in the study of Christian origins.

A first level of attention, most prominent throughout, concerns the textual production of early Christianity. Thus, invoking Edward Said, Elliott argues for the need to foreground the imperial context of Paul and his letters. Similarly, in approaching the letters themselves, Elliot further highlights various areas of particular interest to a postcolonial reading: the presence of common themes of imperial culture; the representation of peoples and lands as both in need and search of domination; and the employment of terms whose political connotations evoke the theological vision of Rome. Lastly, calling upon Frantz Fanon and James C. Scott, Elliott paints a picture of the colonial situation in terms of control and resistance. A second level of attention, not as pervasive but decisive as a point of departure, addresses the interpretation of early Christianity in the Western tradition. Here he points to traditional unconcern with the context of Roman imperialism in the reading of Romans and a corresponding obsession with the letter as a theological brief – the 'cornerstone' of Pauline theology. In the process, he argues, the immediate setting and aim of the letter are put aside and obscured. A final level of attention, intimated by way of conclusion, deals with the use of Romans in the face of contemporary manifestations of imperial domination.

1 and 2 Corinthians

Familiarity with postcolonial criticism is evident in Richard Horsley's contribution, but no formal discussion of meaning or scope is to be found. In fact, recourse to postcolonial theory as such is mostly by way of brief and scattered references to certain concerns or representatives. One such invocation serves as point of departure for the commentary. Horsley sees postcolonial criticism, a discourse specifically associated with 'fields' of literary criticism, as involving the reading of 'colonial' and 'anti-colonial' as well as 'postcolonial' literatures in their 'colonial/imperial' and 'neo-imperial' contexts, respectively. As such, he argues, this type of analysis is pertinent to biblical studies in two respects: first, with regard to the use of the Bible and the discipline of biblical criticism within the modern imperial cultures of the West; second, in terms of the biblical texts themselves within a variety of imperial cultures, including that of Rome in the case of early Christian texts in general and the Pauline Letters in particular. Actually, as the definition already suggests, such analysis is relevant in a third respect as well, left largely undeveloped here: reading and critical practices within the present context of 'neo-imperialism of global capitalism'.

To begin with, Horsley argues, the modern role of the Bible and biblical criticism as 'colonial literature' must be acknowledged and foregrounded. Not only did the Bible serve as an inspiration for Western imperialism, but also, as the 'focal agenda' behind Christian missionary movements, it secured a place among the colonized territories and peoples. Indeed, it is in this regard, Horsley ventures, that postcolonial biblical criticism will have its greatest impact. At the same time, biblical criticism, whose emergence and development in the nineteenth and twentieth centuries parallels the 'heyday of Western imperialism', not only focused on the theological rather than the political–economic, given the Western relegation of religion to the private sphere, but also largely bypassed or romantically idealized the imperial context of Rome, given its own unreflected linkage with Western imperialism. Consequently, Horsley adds, the role of imperial contexts in the production of the biblical texts must be acknowledged and foregrounded as well, as he himself proceeds to do in the case of Paul and the letters to the Corinthians. Thus, against a Paul fashioned, invoking Edward Said, in the spirit of orientalism – a Paul who was used to justify both European imperial and Christian missionary expansionism, a Paul who functioned as the catalyst in the break away from the 'political and parochial' particularism of Judaism and the turn toward a 'universal and spiritual' religion open to Gentiles, and a Paul who was used to support, along the lines of the deutero-Pauline letters, the system of slavery and the subordination of women – the anti-imperial Paul, the Paul who stood in opposition to the Roman system of domination and set about organizing a movement among the subjugated of the empire, should be highlighted.

Galatians
Sze-Kar Wan specifically classifies his commentary as 'postcolonial' and has recourse to the language of the imperial and the colonial throughout, but he does not entertain the question of meaning and scope in postcolonial criticism directly. In both regards, therefore, the underlying positions have to be traced and surfaced. His stance on reach emerges as broad-based, while that on force emphasizes the dynamic of struggle, of pressure from the centre and response from the periphery, within the phenomenon of empire.

Regarding meaning, the 'postcolonial' classification certainly applies to both the text and the reception of Galatians. In terms of interpretation, the scholarly tradition is portrayed as 'heavily colonized' by critics steeped in Reformation theology and its dominant lens of justification by faith, yielding a view of both letter and author as in 'ideological captivity'. Such confinement is twofold: a theological approach in search of 'dogmatic dicta' and 'timeless truths', and an essentialistic representation of Judaism as monolithic and devoid of tension. The result is evident: a 'Jesus-movement' in Galatia conceived in the abstract, disembodied and dehistoricized; a Paul envisioned – even within the new perspective on Paul as a Jewish writer – in binary disjunction, as either Jewish or Christian. In contrast, Wan's postcolonial reading sets out to concretize and complicate: dismantling the theological encasement by foregrounding ethnicity as construction and rupturing the binomial Jewish–Christian by muddying the construction of Judaism as well as Christianity, signified by quotation marks around both terms ('Jewish' and 'Christian'). In terms of analysis, the letter is contextualized, both by way of Judaism and ethnicity, as a text 'marked by... experience in the empire', in which players and positions reflect the 'constant impingement' of empire and attempt to 'construct a vision in response' – a text immersed and participating in a complex clash of narratives. Wan's approach to meaning, consequently, follows the path of conscientization. Regarding reach, conceptual tools borrowed from a wide range of postcolonial theory – the pattern of material and discursive dominance and subjection between centre and periphery; the concept of interstitial space marked by doubleness (Bhabha); the practice of colonial worldling (Spivak); the distinction between settler and occupation colonies – are applied to the analysis of both text and context in a direct fashion. Wan's approach to scope, therefore, is crosscultural and transhistorical.

Ephesians

Although certainly aware of the multiplicity of methods at work in postcolonial criticism and explicitly designating her own approach as 'postcolonial', Jennifer Bird does not set forth in principle what such analysis signifies or covers; its force and range must be secured, therefore, from the way in which she goes about her task. Regarding meaning, a sense of the political, writ large, clearly lies at the heart of what the postcolonial involves. From the start she notes the lack of critical attention given – whether by way of insouciance or rejection – to the political tenor and vision of Ephesians, yielding a consistent spiritualized interpretation of the letter. Regarding scope, a broad sense of what the postcolonial embraces prevails, given the concern for both the texts of early Christianity and their interpretive traditions. Thus, she attributes the absence of the political in Ephesians not to the letter as such, a text characterized as profoundly political in its own right, but rather to the critical tradition. Given such conception and extent of the postcolonial, one would anticipate an even broader historical as well as cultural application in Bird, but the point is neither pursued nor alluded to further.

In light of such critical consensus, Bird's response is threefold. First of all, she argues, recent scholarship on the early Christian movement renders impossible the reading of its texts without a 'political lens' – without attention to their context within the Roman Empire and their engagement with its imperial ideologies. In fact, Ephesians itself is said to advance a counter-empire of its own in the face of Rome. In addition, she continues, in setting aside the political dimension of early Christian texts, the standard interpretation lays bare its own conflicted character – on the surface, seemingly apolitical; at bottom, upholding rather than transforming the status quo through such depoliticization. Consequently, a postcolonial reading of Ephesians and its project of a counter-empire is deemed imperative. Lastly, the political reading of the early Christian texts, she specifies, should have the aim of liberation in mind – seeking to move beyond imperial ideologies and thus be applicable not only to the initial context of composition but also to the different contexts of interpretation, including her own. Therefore, the proposed postcolonial reading of Ephesians and its counter-empire is specifically qualified as a 'critique', not simply a determination of its political stance but also a pointed evaluation of such a stance in the light of liberation.

Philippians
In explicit conversation with postcolonial theory, Efraín Agosto is directly forthcoming on the meaning and scope of postcolonial analysis. Drawing on Georg Gugelberger, he adopts an oppositional view of such criticism: the postcolonial optic focuses on the impact of imperialism upon the colonized and seeks to reinsert the voices of the latter 'back into history'; in so doing, it encompasses within its angle of vision both the texts of hegemony and the texts of subordination. Moreover, such an approach is said to apply in any context of imperial domination and thus, in principle, across history and culture. Consequently, Agosto regards a postcolonial optic as quite appropriate for biblical criticism, with his own interest focused on the texts of early Christianity in general, the letters and figure of Paul in particular, and the Letter to the Philippians most concretely.

Such application, Agosto explains, is actually threefold. First, it concerns the texts themselves, insofar as they emerge from the context of Roman imperial domination. In effect, Paul's communities were founded in imperial 'colonies' of the eastern Mediterranean, including Philippi, and thus Philippians reflects and addresses the situation of one such 'subject' congregation. Second, it involves the tradition of academic criticism, given its development in the context of Western imperial domination. As such, approaches to and interpretations of the Bible produced throughout the modern era of Western expansionism stand in need of critical reassessment. Third, it has to do with the contemporary criticism among the children of colonization, in light of the enduring effects of Western imperial domination over the non-Western world. These new voices bring, given their unique position within the system of domination, an alternative and necessary perspective to the critical task. At all levels, Agosto points out, criticism must take into account the impact of imperialism as well as the reaction to such domination. His own proposal in this regard addresses not just Philippians within its Roman context but also his own reading of the letter within his context as an heir of colonization.

Colossians

There are numerous references to postcolonial reading in Gordon Zerbe and Muriel Orevillo-Montenegro's contribution, but no explicit discussion regarding meaning and scope. From these various expositions, however, it is possible to put together a broad picture of what such analysis entails and encompasses. The entire discussion is conducted in terms of biblical criticism, with a focus on Colossians itself, but within the context of Paul and his mission and the Pauline correspondence as a whole. From the point of view of meaning, the proposed postcolonial reading may be described as contextual, ideological and dialogical. First, it is a reading grounded in the authors' location and experience in the Philippines and contrasted with the dominant tradition of interpretation in the West. Within the Philippines itself, moreover, this reading is further located in a context of struggle, on the side of social transformation with a vision of social justice and cultural integrity. Second, as such, it is a reading concerned not so much with the standard Western tradition of searching after historical questions (authorship, community situation, tradition) or religious content (spiritual meaning) but rather with issues of a cultural, social and political nature. Third, it is a reading committed to ideological critique of texts and interpretations in the light of such struggle and such issues. This it does by seeking to establish whether such texts and interpretations promote or confront the project of colonialism – its 'intentions and assumptions', its 'ideologies and patterns' – in their respective contexts. In terms of scope, therefore, the postcolonial reading envisioned involves a variety of texts produced in colonial contexts: the biblical texts themselves – the Letter to the Colossians; modern interpretations of the West – critical and missionary readings of Colossians; contemporary interpretations inside as well as outside the West – critical and ecclesial readings of Colossians.

1 and 2 Thessalonians

In Abraham Smith's contribution there is attention to both force and reach in postcolonial analysis, mostly within the ambit of postcolonial biblical criticism but with reference to postcolonial studies as well. Indeed, he begins with a series of affirmations about postcolonial criticism in general, from which he then proceeds to a consideration of meaning and scope in postcolonial biblical criticism as such. First, postcolonial analysis is defined in wide historical terms as encompassing the 'whole complex of imperialism' – from the actual process of 'colonization', through the stage of resistance for the sake of 'political independence', to the emergence of 'neocolonialism'. Second, although none of these terms is defined, 'colonialism' is, following the distinction of Kathleen O'Brien Wicker into 'historical' (political, economic and social domination) and 'discursive' (psychological domination through appeals to authority); however, its relationship to the other terms is not specified. Finally, postcolonial analysis is further said to focus on 'constructions' of the 'other'. Against this backdrop, then, Smith takes up the question of force and reach in biblical 'postcolonial interrogation'.

Regarding meaning, he explains, biblical critics set out to trace 'the shadow of imperialism', historically as well as discursively, 'within and beyond' the biblical texts. In so doing, he adds, they highlight the question of power relations in the representation of 'the other'. Regarding scope, such tracing is said to admit of various 'interrelated types of criticism': analysing the imperial shadow in the history of interpretation; examining the 'anti-imperialist stances' of the texts; and critiquing 'imperialist tendencies' within the texts regardless of any 'tacit overtures or explicit claims' against colonization in them. For Smith, therefore, postcolonial criticism involves: (1) a sustained focus on strategies of domination and constructions of 'the other' in imperial–colonial frameworks – that is, its force; and (2) attention to the biblical texts as well as to their reception histories (scholarly as well as popular) – that is, its reach. Given the broad definition of the postcolonial, one would suspect that Smith would have no difficulty in extending such analysis in transhistorical as well as crosscultural fashion. Finally, the conclusion makes it clear that this foregrounding of domination and construction of the other does have, although untheorized, the 'creation of a just world' as a goal.

Pastoral Letters

Evidently in dialogue with postcolonial studies, sharply described as 'perhaps more complex and convoluted' than biblical studies in its 'further reaches', Ralph Broadbent approaches the issue of meaning in postcolonial criticism in direct but hesitant fashion, citing the 'risk of oversimplification' in the face of such discursive breadth. This he does in terms of focus and objective: postcolonial criticism deals with power and hierarchy 'within imperial settings' and does so with contestation in mind. At the same time, the question of scope is not raised as such. It is clear, nevertheless, from his reading of the letters – viewed, in agreement with mainstream scholarship, as pseudonymous and hailing from the second or third generation of Christianity (90–120 CE) – that postcolonial criticism addresses both the biblical texts within the context of the Roman Empire and critical interpretations of these texts within modern and contemporary imperial–colonial frameworks, with a special focus in his case on commentators from the time or legacy of the British Empire. Given the emphasis on biblical studies, it is impossible to tell whether Broadbent would grant greater transhistorical or transcultural application to postcolonial analysis.

Philemon

Allan Callahan's position on the force and reach of postcolonial inquiry is not explicitly formulated but can be inferred from the argument as a whole. Its meaning is framed in terms of the development of modern Western colonialism, with a twofold emphasis on the settlement of foreign territories and the needs of political economy. Its scope emerges as wide-ranging, comprehending any situation of colonialism, from antiquity to modernity to the present.

With regard to meaning, Callahan begins by outlining two variations in modern colonialism: dependent colonies, in which the transplanted minority relies on the oppressed indigenous majority as the source of surplus labour; and settler or creole colonies, in which the transplanted minority effects a permanent displacement of the indigenous population and turns to importation as the source of surplus labour. While the former scenario is said to provide the framework for the 'guerrilla theoreticians' of foundational postcolonial discourse, the latter is appropriated as his own, with specific reference to the United States – a settler colonialism 'with colour', racialized and relying on the importation of Africans as slaves. The resultant postcolonial reading, he explains, presents two distinguishing traits: it must acknowledge the colonial legacy as ongoing, so that no reading is possible without reference to colonialism and its effects; it must choose between an anticolonial and a neocolonial orientation, that is, between opposition to and advancement of the colonialist project. His own brand he situates squarely within the first camp: a foregrounding of colonialism throughout in order to reject it and all readings in support of it.

In terms of scope, the stance adopted comes across as applicable, in principle, across colonial situations. Such is certainly the case with regard to the history of interpretation of the Letter to Philemon. Thus, the standard reading of Philemon is characterized as 'imperialist' throughout, from its beginnings in late antiquity, through its invocation in the United States and the New World, to its regular assessment in contemporary criticism. Such is the case as well with regard to the text itself within Roman colonialism, given not only the reference to 'moments' in the letter that point toward an anti-colonial stance but also a historical interpretation of it in direct opposition to its standard reading.

Hebrews

Informed in general by postcolonial studies, but in close dialogue with postcolonial biblical criticism, Jeremy Punt considers at length the question of force in postcolonial analysis while bypassing that of reach. His point of departure in this regard is a twofold affirmation: the ongoing phenomenon of imperial–colonial frameworks today and the continued collusion of the biblical texts and their histories of reception in such frameworks. Thus, he declares, not only are the forces of imperialism, neocolonialism and eurocentrism 'alive and well' in the world, but also the 'legitimating and totalizing' discourse of the Bible and its interpretive histories are to be found at work in such 'hegemonies of imperialism'. Against this contemporary backdrop, then, the task of postcolonial criticism is unveiled.

In terms of meaning, Punt characterizes postcolonial criticism as deconstructive, constructive and postmodernist. It is deconstructive insofar as it highlights the 'entanglement' between colonization, its discourse and practice, and the Bible, its writings and readings. Such foregrounding has two distinctive objectives: problematizing the 'co-optation' of texts for hegemonic purposes and searching the texts for suppressed or distorted voices. It is constructive insofar as it seeks an 'alternative hermeneutics' in opposition to colonial biblical interpretation. Toward this end, it turns to the resources of the local, allowing for a reading 'on our own terms' and 'from our own specific location', without, however, deifying the local in the process. It is postmodernist insofar as it lays no claim to 'objective', 'final and prescriptive', 'exhaustive' meaning in interpretation and rules out no other 'exegetical or hermeneutical' approach. Rather, it emphasizes throughout the role of construction and contextualization – the real reader and social location – in interpretation, avoiding thereby becoming an imperial model in its own right. In terms of scope, it becomes clear from the discussion that, for Punt, the lens of postcolonial analysis includes the biblical texts as well as their reception histories, but it cannot be established whether he would allow for more extensive application across history and culture.

In sum, against a traditional biblical criticism deeply implicated in imperial–colonial frameworks, Punt advances a postcolonial model. Its traits can no longer be, following Kathleen O'Brien Wicker, those of colonial criticism: a patriarchal lens; the view of Christianity as either the one and true or even a superior religion; identification with the political postures of the texts as theologically justified; the disqualification of texts on the grounds of orthodoxy and heresy; and the decontextualization of textual content. Rather, postcolonial criticism should be marked by accountability in the use of texts, the promotion of geopolitical liberation, encouraging global diversity alongside appreciation of the local and the native, and the pursuit of liberating strategies of interdependence in a globalized world. In the end, Punt presents his own postcolonial reading of Hebrews as contextual, emerging from postcolonial Africa in general and post-apartheid South Africa in particular; and perspectival, reflecting his own diasporic and hybrid status as Afrikaner – an indigenous white with no other home and embodying a 'variety of traditions and contexts'.

James

While Sharon Ringe calls the Letter of James a 'postcolonial' voice, describes its standard interpretation as 'colonized' and regards this voice as relevant to any situation of 'imperial challenges', she does not address theoretically what postcolonial analysis signifies or comprehends. The discussion proceeds entirely within the confines of biblical criticism, with undeviating focus on the letter. Yet, her operative understanding of the force and reach of such criticism can be construed on the basis of her repeated invocations of the category 'postcolonial' and related terms. As far as meaning is concerned, postcolonial analysis is regarded as political and oppositional. It is political insofar as it has foremost in mind the contexts of 'imperial domination' behind biblical texts and their interpretations as well as the reactions of both texts and interpretations to such contexts. It is oppositional insofar as it reserves the denomination 'postcolonial' to those texts and interpretations that react by way of resistance to imperial contexts. Such resistance, Ringe specifies, can take two forms, with the first as possibly leading to the second: resistance by way of critique and resistance by way of alternative proposal. As far as scope is concerned, postcolonial analysis is viewed as applicable to the biblical text – the Letter of James, its history of interpretation – the dominant reading of James across a variety of discourses (ecclesial and academic, secular and others, scholarly), and its ongoing reception history – the world of contemporary interpretation, broadly understood, including her own. As such, postcolonial analysis is envisioned as extending across historical periods within the Western world, from antiquity through the present. At the same time, given Ringe's position that the postcolonial stands for opposition in any situation of imperial domination, such analysis emerges, in principle, as universally applicable across culture and history.

1 Peter

There is pointed and sophisticated attention in Elisabeth Schüssler Fiorenza's contribution to matters of theory and method in postcolonial criticism. Among them, the question of meaning is entertained directly, while that of scope indirectly. Both come to light in her articulation of a critical feminist postcolonial analysis. Indeed, the various components of this designation provide a ready key in both regards.

What such criticism entails is clear from the juncture of critical feminist interpretation and postcolonial interpretation. The former approach, already well established, stands as foundation for the present one. As such, this project is described as 'interpretation', since it does not require the ability to read as condition, only conscientization and critical analysis; 'critical', insofar as it involves systemic analysis of structures and ideologies; and 'feminist', because it examines the system of kyriarchal domination (lord, slave-master, father, husband, elite male) and does so with emancipation in mind. What renders this approach 'postcolonial' is a matter of emphasis. In effect, the present project foregrounds the 'colonial–imperial' dimension in the systemic analysis of kyriarchal domination, within which such a dimension constitutes one of multiple layers of domination. Thus, Schüssler Fiorenza declares, critical feminist analysis and critical feminist postcolonial analysis are 'practically identical'.

Two further considerations are in order with regard to meaning. First, against any claims of identity politics and any invocation of essential difference between a dominant or 'Western' and a subaltern or 'Third World' feminism, the proposed approach qualifies as properly postcolonial, given its critical and feminist orientation. Although advanced from the perspective of a 'white Western feminist', it is in principle no less 'postcolonial' than any other; at the same time, it does not exclude from critical attention the question of social location. Second, against a conception of feminism as focused exclusively on women and gender, the proposed approach adopts the category of 'wo/men' to signify that it is attentive to all voices of the 'submerged' under the different layers of kyriarchal domination and hence inclusive of women and men.

What such criticism attends to can be discerned in, as well as extrapolated from, the discussion. In practice, it involves the biblical text (the letter of 1 Peter, classified as a pseudonymous writing from the end of the first century CE) as well as scholarly interpretations of the text (the dominant exegetical tradition characterized as 'malestream', written by Euro-American Christian academicians). This is the actual focus of the analysis. In theory, given her modulation of the term 'interpretation' and definition of 'kyriarchal system', it would ultimately encompass all interpretations of the text, beyond the scholarly and the written, as well as all contexts of kyriarchal domination, across history and culture. Such is the potential focus of analysis.

2 Peter

There is no recourse in Cynthia Briggs Kittredge's contribution to postcolonial studies and hence no engagement with the question of force and reach in postcolonial analysis. The discussion is conducted solely in terms of biblical criticism, with a sustained focus on 2 Peter and critical approaches to it. A sense of what such criticism means and includes is possible on the basis of her various assertions regarding its concerns and aims. In terms of meaning, postcolonial criticism is presented as contextual–perspectival, from below and contestatory. Thus, a postcolonial critic is described as someone grounded in a 'specific' context (social, historical, theological) and raising questions from this 'particular' perspective. Consequently, she argues, it is by definition a highly diverse type of criticism. Further, the context in question is characterized as one of subordination, so that a postcolonial critic is also someone who stands defined as 'other' and deprived of a role as 'subject and actor' in history. Given such a context, a postcolonial critic is also presented as someone who challenges texts in terms of their rhetorical strategies and the ramifications of such strategies within the dynamic of domination/subordination. In terms of scope, Briggs Kittredge simply allows, without further discussion, for the application of postcolonial analysis to 2 Peter, and thus to the biblical texts and the historical context of Rome. Yet, from the definition of what this approach entails, one could readily argue for a vision of broad application on her part – in effect, whenever a location of subordination and a stance of contestation are present.

Throughout, it should be noted, Briggs Kittredge mentions feminist criticism and postcolonial criticism in the same breath. For her such approaches belong together but are not hyphenated. The two approaches are clearly differentiated, as signified by her own self-description as a feminist scholar both situated within the Western tradition and challenged by the questions of postcolonial critics. What brings them together, then, is their perceived common situation of subordination and contestation; what sets them apart, is the distinctive nature of their respective contexts and challenges.

Johannine Letters

The appeal to postcolonial studies in R. S. Sugirtharajah's contribution is pervasive and substantial: from the initial identification of colonial discursive traits in the letters; through the subsequent exposition of the ideological framework advanced as akin to a colonial scenario, representation of the religious world constructed as influenced by Buddhism and thus hybridized, surfacing of postcolonial discursive traits, and espousal of a contrapuntal reading involving Buddhist textual traditions; to the concluding description of the letters as marked by ambivalence. Such recourse to the literary and conceptual apparatus of postcolonialism extends to the question of meaning but not that of scope in postcolonial analysis.

The force of postcolonial criticism is defined as oppositional, 'repairing of colonial misrepresentation and defamation', and committed, 'engaging in the struggle for a better world'. With regard to the letters, Sugirtharajah points out various dimensions of such criticism: counteracting the binary thinking developed by the author; pursuing a contrapuntal reading of the letters alongside Buddhist texts, with a view of the two religious traditions as complementary and hence the aim of making connections between them; siding with their emphasis on a praxis of truth, justice and love. The reach of postcolonial criticism, as one can gather from his approach to the letters, emerges as broad. To begin with, Sugirtharajah deals with the biblical text, its history of interpretation, and, in keeping with the goal of contrapuntal reading, other texts from the various contexts in question, ancient or modern. In addition, he clearly views the discursive characteristics of coloniality and postcoloniality as transhistorical, and there is no reason to think otherwise with respect to culture as well.

Jude

While characterizing his approach to Jude as a 'postcolonial' reading and a reading 'with decolonization in mind', Rohun Park does not take up the issues of meaning and scope in postcolonial analysis and thus provides no explicit location of his reading project within a critical spectrum in either regard. Further, while invoking terms such as 'colonialism' and 'neocolonialism' and adding that 'colonialism', like 'imperial power relations', has never come to an end but rather has undergone various transmutations, he does not draw on postcolonial studies for a definition of such terms and concepts, focusing instead on a conjunction between politics and religion ('colonizing desires' and 'religious symbols and structures' or 'cultic ritual systems') identified as operative in imperial–colonial frameworks throughout. The discussion proceeds, consequently, by way of current affairs and biblical criticism. As a result, Park's position on the force and scope of the postcolonial can only be established, and tentatively at that, from the actual line of argumentation. Regarding meaning, he clearly views postcolonial criticism as oppositional – a strategy for decolonization, as he puts it. His aim is to expose this working alliance between colonization and religion in order to work against it, to break it apart, in the interest of the colonized. Such a project, further described as an exercise in 'alternative hermeneutics', is designed to approach cultic ritual systems in 'more liberating' fashion by allowing the call of God to filter through the layer of imperial domination in the lives of 'colonial subjects and postcolonial subjects'. Regarding scope, Park clearly regards postcolonial criticism as applicable across history and culture. Thus, he ranges from the ancient world of Rome to the modern and postmodern world of the twentieth and twenty-first centuries. Similarly, within this latter period, he deals with Asia by way of Japan and Korea as well as the West by way of the United States. In sum, for Park postcolonial analysis emerges as contestatory in character and wide-ranging in application.

Revelation
There is in Stephen Moore's contribution extensive recourse to postcolonial theory, in matters both minor and central: application of the distinction between 'settler' and 'occupation' colonization to describe the Roman pattern, with a focus on Asia Minor; use of the concept of hegemony, as advanced by Antonio Gramsci, to account for the durability and efficiency of Roman administration in the province of Asia; appeal to the rhetorical device of catachresis, as revisioned by Gayatri Spivak, to capture the basic stance of Revelation toward Roman presence and power; deployment of the categories of ambivalence, mimicry and hybridity, all derived from the conceptual repertoire of Homi Bhabha, to pursue key dimensions and ramifications of Revelation's basic posture toward Rome; invocation of the concept of strategic essentialism, as proposed by Spivak, to provide a functional explanation for the binomial political strategy adopted by Revelation. In sum, Moore's reading is imbued with postcolonial studies, in line with the goal of opening a 'supplementary space' in the long-standing analysis of Revelation's 'relations to empire' by means of engagement with 'postcolonial theory or discourse'.

Yet, interestingly enough, one finds in Moore no formal consideration of force and reach in postcolonial analysis, both of which can only be supplied from the reading itself. With respect to meaning, Moore lists a variety of 'phenomena' under the postcolonial umbrella: colonialism, imperialism, decoloniza-tion, globalization, neocolonialism. Of these, only 'imperialism' is defined: the set of mutually constitutive ideologies (political, economic, racial/ethnic, religious and so forth) within a metropolitan centre that 'impel' its annexation of distant territories and 'determine' all subsequent relations. Thus, for Moore, postcolonial criticism is concerned with all the different dimensions involved in the dynamics and mechanics of imperial–colonial frameworks. With respect to scope, the swift translation of models from contemporary theory to the study of early Christianity within the Roman Empire signals a decided tendency toward broad application.

Approach and Argument in Postcolonial Criticism

Matthew

In light of his position on meaning and scope in postcolonial inquiry, with its call for a consideration of the 'imperializing experience' as a whole (means, dynamics, impact and legacy of 'power over'), Carter's approach to Matthew has both cultural production and material matrix in mind. At the same time, the balance tips clearly toward the text rather than the context, for within an 'imperializing experience' he immediately highlights the diversity of textual and cultural expressions for special attention. For Carter, therefore, Matthew constitutes one such expression: a text emerging from a particular interaction of imperial culture and local culture, the imperial world of Rome, and enmeshed, actively so, in its 'nexus of power relationships and societal structures'. In effect, texts both reflect and intervene in contexts, and Matthew is no exception. Consequently, Carter proceeds to analyse both the Roman imperial system and the Matthean literary production.

The historical context, though tied closely to the city of Antioch and the province of Syria, is ultimately universalized. The argument is explicitly made that, should such an attribution be incorrect and should its composition have taken place elsewhere, the systemic analysis of Roman power offered would still apply, given its 'pervasive' nature. As a result, such analysis is at once comprehensive and broad: on the one hand, it takes into account various dimen-sions of the Roman presence (administrative structures, political economy and socio-economic conditions, military deployment, cultural manifestations, reli-gious practices); on the other hand, it presents all such facets not as distinctive of Syria but rather as empire-wide. The Matthean text is examined through extended analysis of two narrative features, plot and character. The plot, said to provide the action that holds the narrative together, is pursued in terms of six major sections, each assigned a specific role and purpose in the development of the plot. Jesus' character is identified as the fulcrum of the action: he challenges and alienates the Jerusalem elite through his attack on societal structures as contrary to God, is crucified by a coalition of the local elite and the Roman governor, and is raised by God. Such analysis foregrounds the political stance subscribed to by Matthew within the imperial context of Rome.

Mark

Liew's reading of Mark is decidedly focused on text rather than context and thus on cultural production rather than material matrix. Texts, he argues, not only reflect history and culture but also create them. Thus, while situating Mark squarely within the colonial context of its time, it is Mark's rhetorical constructions of such a context that are analysed. For this purpose, Liew adopts the organizing filter of a 'politics of time'. To begin with, following Peter Osborne, he accepts a close relationship between politics and temporality: constructions of modernity led to constructions of time (the 'present' of the West as the 'future' of all others) and constructions of colonial politics ('development' as imperative). Then, following Stephen O' Leary, he sees apocalyptic rhetoric as involving the interplay of time, authority and evil, to which mixture he adds the element of gender, given his conviction that women function as signifiers of both colonial oppression and postcolonial resistance. With this theoretical framework in place, Liew proceeds to examine the politics of apocalyptic time in Mark by way of a threefold development, namely, as conveyed through its rhetorical constructions of authority, agency (human ability to resist evil and bring about change) and gender.

Luke-Acts

In principle, as her position regarding the suitability of postcolonial inquiry for both the text of Luke-Acts and the context of Rome indicates, Burrus is open to analysis of cultural production and material matrix alike. In practice, it is the text of Luke-Acts on which she focuses, almost exclusively. With regard to context, two comments are in order. First, although the appropriateness of a postcolonial literary approach attentive to textual indeterminacy and instability is deemed 'especially promising' with respect to Luke-Acts, given its ambiguities and ambivalences, a historical approach sensitive to the 'polyglot' character of the colonial context of antiquity as well as the neocolonial context of postmodernity is readily granted. Second, in the analysis of Luke-Acts, references to context, while approached as discursive representations within the Lucan framework, are also expanded by comments about the extra-textual nature of such context, thus placing the Lucan representations in broader view. The material matrix does not disappear altogether, therefore, but does yield to cultural production as overriding focus.

Such predominant focus on the text is pursued by foregrounding the ideological stance and literary art of Luke-Acts. With respect to ideological thrust, Burrus calls attention to the political and economic framework of Luke-Acts as conveyed by Luke, approached by way of theories of empire and resistance. It is here that one finds the filling out of Lucan representations by reference to extra-textual information. The procedure is clear: a composite of Lucan ideology is put together through a sequential consideration of key texts from the Gospel and Acts and then read in the light of Michael Hardt and Antonio Negri's view of empire and James C. Scott's approach to resistance. With respect to literary artistry, Burrus highlights Luke's heightened self-awareness as a writer, his conscious use of and position toward a set of broader literary practices, and the novelistic aspects of Luke-Acts, approached through theories of the novel and postcoloniality. The procedure is similar: a composite of Lucan art, viewed from a variety of categories (time and space, language, border encounters), is drawn through the invocation of key texts from the Gospel and Acts and subsequently read through the lens of Mikhail Bhaktin's view of the novel and Homi Bhabha's approach to postcolonial literature. In the end, these two dimensions of Luke-Acts emerge as closely related given their pronounced use of ambiguity.

John

In his prolegomenon on matters methodological and theoretical, Segovia raises the issue of subject matter directly within the section on 'terrain'. Postcolonial criticism, he argues, should address material foundations as well as cultural expressions. Both foci, moreover, should be envisioned and pursued in comprehensive fashion: the cultural as involving the whole of textual as well as non-textual production; the material as ranging across the various dimensions of society. Such joint attention, furthermore, is in order at both the level of composition, the production of John as text, and of interpretation, the consumption of John by way of readings and readers. In the commentary itself, however, Segovia restricts himself to textual analysis. Two grounds are adduced: first, a critic may opt for emphasis on one or the other pursuit, provided that such a move is surfaced and justified; second, and more significantly, the lack of evidence regarding the composition of John and thus the high degree of abstraction present in any consideration of its proximate context. Yet, the material matrix does not disappear altogether. The study approaches the text as an active intervention in its social and cultural context, with attention to the latter as represented in the text.

Such textual analysis Segovia undertakes through a study of Johannine 'reality' as constructed by the Gospel. Such representation of 'all that is' is examined from three literary standpoints: (1) the story or temporal sequence of events abstracted from the narrative, pursued in terms of three overarching stages and seen as conveying a postcolonial proposal; (2) the opening or 'prologue' of the narrative, examined in light of key figures and dynamics introduced and described as advancing a postcolonial alternative; (3) the plot or causal sequence of events deployed by the narrative, developed in terms of its generic casting as a life of Jesus, yielding a threefold division, and its literary recourse to the journey motif, yielding a complex travel structuration, all presented as delineating a postcolonial programme. In the end, therefore, for Segovia the Gospel constitutes and is approached as a literary, rhetorical and ideological product.

Romans

The tight connection drawn by Elliott between text and context, between the Letter to the Romans and the imperial framework of Rome, signals combined attention to cultural production and material matrix. The letter is used as point of entry throughout and thus becomes the main focus of attention. On the one hand, its rhetoric is used to lay out the historical context, distant as well as proximate, from which the letter emerges and to which it is addressed; this context is further amplified by extra-textual references to the dynamics of Roman imperialism. On the other hand, its rhetoric is also used to lay bare the strategic response offered by Paul to the Romans in the light of the context envisioned and the dynamics identified. For Elliott, therefore, the text discloses, as in traditional historical criticism, both historical setting and theological aim, now properly expanded and corrected by a postcolonial optic of attention to empire.

Such combined attention to text and context is sustained and systematic. To begin with, the addressees and intent of the letter are named – Gentile Christians in Rome, in the face of emerging anti-Judaism among such congregations. Such circumstances are explained by recourse to context: long-standing Roman prejudice toward the Jews, most recently expressed by way of expulsion from Rome through the edict of Claudius. Then, the central message of the letter is summarized – an ethic of 'mutual interdependence' embracing higher-status and lower-status Christians, accompanied by a corresponding distinction between the present status of Israel and its ultimate status in the light of God's covenant. This message is similarly placed in context: the return of impoverished Jewish Christians to Rome, the adoption of Roman ethnocentrism toward the vanquished (the Jews), and the patronage system of the empire based on status. Further, the stance of the letter vis-à-vis the empire is unveiled – total inversion of imperial ideology by way of a different Lord, an alternative universal vision encompassing all nations, and a contrasting project of justice. This stance is also placed in context: the claims and representations of the Roman emperors as well as the actual practices of the empire. Lastly, the nature of Paul's mission is examined – his expressed obligation to all nations, including the vanquished and the barbarian, and in particular Israel, whose covenantal promises are reaffirmed with a view toward God's action in the future. This conception is set in context as well: Rome's hierarchical vision of all peoples under its power and the Roman subjection of Israel.

1 and 2 Corinthians

Given the definition of postcolonial criticism adopted – the study of literatures from imperial contexts in the light of such contexts – Horsley's approach embraces cultural production, the various components of the Corinthian correspondence brought together in the present 1 and 2 Corinthians, as well as their material matrix, the imperial setting of this correspondence in both local and general fashion, that is, with respect to the city of Corinth itself as well as the Roman system as a whole. This combined emphasis on text and context, moreover, is balanced: the context is drawn as immediate backdrop for the composition of this series of ad hoc communications on the part of Paul, while the various communications in question are interpreted directly against this backdrop. Cultural production and material matrix are thus used to point to and enlighten one another in sustained and systematic fashion.

A depiction of the historical context provides the point of entry. It is a picture drawn in broad terms: the imperial record of Rome in the eastern Mediterranean, including the destruction of Corinth in 146 BCE and its restoration as a Roman colony in 44 BCE; the record of resistance to Rome among 'Israelite peoples' in Palestine (peasant revolts, prophetic and messianic renewal movements, apocalyptic expectations); the character of the 'Jesus-movement' as a renewal movement of Israel against Jerusalem and imperial rule; the character of the Jewish diaspora as a partly self-governing community through assemblies and variously assimilated to the dominant culture; the early adhesion of diaspora Jews, including Paul, to the anti-imperial Jesus-movement; the status of Corinth as a commercial centre and cosmopolitan city – the centre of imperial influence and control in Greece, where the emperor cult featured prominently and a circle of elite families flourished as beneficiaries of the imperial patronage system while most of the population remained in severe economic marginalization. Out of this context, Horsley argues, emerges Paul and, with him, a 'master-narrative' of opposition to Rome: a vision of history and providence as channelled not through Rome but through Israel, not through the emperor but through Jesus, in whom the promises of Abraham for Israel and all nations have been fulfilled and whose triumphal return is imminent. In the light of this complex historical context and radical vision of Paul, then, the letters are read. It is a reading that proceeds in sequential fashion: a beginning focus on 1 Corinthians, in internal sequential fashion as well, with analysis of its major sections from beginning to end; a subsequent focus on 2 Corinthians, in terms of continuing issues in the communities. It is also a reading that pays particular attention to rhetorical design and aims, as well as political and economic concerns and postures, with further explication of the context interspersed throughout.

Galatians

As applied to the letter, the main focus of the commentary, Wan's postcolonial reading entails a sense of Galatians as a concrete response to the contingencies of empire and thus calls for contextualization, which, given the pivotal role assigned to 'ethnic tension' in the letter, is carried out in terms of ethnicity in general and Judaism in particular. As such, the reading proffered is at once concerned with material matrix and cultural production. The context, clearly coming to the fore in the text, is put together from a variety of sources, including Galatians itself; the text, distinctly set against the context, is approached as a strategic option within it. By way of introduction to such a dual pursuit, Wan offers a theorization of the concept of 'ethnicity' at work throughout. This he does via an essentialist–constructivist spectrum, with decided predilection on his part for the latter pole and its view of all ethnic categories as 'inherently stable' and 'forever in flux'. This position is described as true both today and, indeed 'even more' so, in the first century.

Wan turns first to a delineation of the material matrix of the letter. This he unfolds in narrowing fashion: first, outlining competing definitions of Jewish identity at work in the first century in light of the given axis – with the book of *Jubilees* and Philo of Alexandria representing essentialism and constructivism, respectively; second, locating such rival visions within the 'Christ-following' sect of Judaism – marked, not at first but subsequently, by Paul at Antioch and the 'pillars' in Jerusalem; finally, situating the conflict in Galatians along such lines as well – with a view of Paul as representative of the universalizing position and of his interlocutors as adherents to the primordialist stance. Wan then undertakes a literary analysis of Galatians as a cultural product. Here he unpacks Paul's construction of a 'new discourse' for the 'new movement', revolving around three postulates: a new colonial self – autonomous and hybrid, paralleling and displacing the centrality of Jerusalem; a new ethnos – a new creation, defined as 'in-Christness', encompassing all Jews and Gentiles without distinction; and a new authority structure – a vision of himself as a 'new patriarch' within an 'emerging colony'.

In the end, however, it should be noted that, despite this undeniable sequence of argumentation, context and text are used throughout to configure and enlighten one another.

Ephesians

By its very nature, Bird's 'primary' insight into Ephesians as advancing a counter-empire in the face of Rome – a political project involving a sustained exercise in mimicry whereby the heavenly empire of God is constructed along the lines of the earthly empire of Caesar – calls for attention to cultural production as well as the material matrix. To establish such a pattern of imitation, she proceeds to examine, in comparative fashion, the image of God's counter-empire elaborated by the letter and the vision of Rome's empire offered through its discourses and practices – in effect, a twofold focus on text and context.

This task is pursued by way of three key dimensions of the letter's political project. First, the imperializing rhetorics of the letter as a whole. Here a wide net is cast: from the foundational reinscription of empire in the heavenly realms of God with Christ as its ruler; through a variety of devices and references (building metaphors to describe the community as the temple for the worship of God; the seal of the Spirit as the stamp of empire; the unity between Jews and Gentiles brought about by Christ, yielding the citizenship of all within the empire; the gnosticizing ascription of 'fulness' and special knowledge to the community; and the sense of the movement as global); to the very exercise of writing itself as a means of asserting community control and submission. Second, the socio-political exhortations conveyed by the household codes, with the calls for fear and obedience on the part of wives and slaves as well as the invocation of unequal gender images to characterize the relationship between Christ as ruler and the community as ruled (his body and bride). Finally, the concluding appeal to battle imagery to depict the proper life and conduct of the community in the world. All such terminology, Bird argues, involves religio-political claims and should be taken as such rather than spiritualized. In each case, therefore, she shows how what is claimed of God's counter-empire in the letter finds a basis, *mutatis mutandis*, in what is claimed of Rome's empire. Thus, while the text is accorded primacy of focus in analysis, the context is invoked throughout, so that in the end both serve to illumine one another.

Philippians
As the study of imperial domination, with its twofold focus on the effects of imperialism and the responses of the subjugated, postcolonial analysis involves, for Agosto, attention to the material matrix, the imperial context in question, as well as cultural production, the texts produced within such a context, whether from the side of domination or that of subordination. This is true at all three levels of inquiry identified. Such is certainly the case here with regard to his analysis of both Philippians itself, the primary focus of inquiry, and his own reading of the letter.

What Agosto advances, therefore, is a conjoined approach to text and context: attention to the Philippian situation and the imperial order as well as attention to the letter as a letter. Thus, analysis of one dimension always has the other in view, with mutual referencing and illumination as a result. The text serves as the point of departure. To begin with, then, Philippians is analysed as a rhetorical communication, marking the various components of its argumentative structure and highlighting its strategic concerns and aims. The latter are identified as follows: overall friendly disposition; composition from prison, with death as a real possibility; exhortation to unity in the face of conflict and opposition, grounded in the moral example of various leaders; reference to a network of financial support. Subsequently, the Philippian context – both in its local, communitarian and its general, imperial dimension – is examined in terms of various central aspects foregrounded in the letter. These are as follows: the nature of the prison system as well as the causes and conditions of Paul's imprisonment; the representation of community leadership in opposition to the model of imperial leadership; the vision of a heavenly citizenship for the community in the face of the promise and benefits of Roman citizenship; the development of a Christian model of underground economy vis-à-vis the Roman model of top-down and margins-to-centre political economy.

Colossians

In light of the call for attention to cultural, social and political issues in interpretation, against the predominantly historicizing and spiritualizing interpretations of the West, one can readily conclude that Zerbe and Orevillo-Montenegro are interested in both context and text in postcolonial analysis. To be sure, the primary emphasis here is on cultural production – not only Colossians itself but also its reception history. Thus, the letter is analysed in terms of the three perspectives identified as central to postcolonial reading: the cultural angle – an attack on alternative religious beliefs and practices; the social angle – recourse to a programme of hierarchical order in order to secure identity and cohesion; the political angle – proclamation of a Christ victorious over all powers. Similarly, its history of interpretation is examined in terms of how such perspectives fare in a variety of reading frameworks: traditional criticism, common missionary practice, emancipatory critical approaches. At the same time, a focus on the material matrix is evident throughout, though in passing fashion: delineation of theological and hermeneutical programmes and their ramifications in the Philippines, references to the missionary enterprise of colonialism and its consequences, unpacking of the community situation, information about the Roman imperial order. At all levels of inquiry, the text functions as point of entry into the context, in itself developed both in light of the text in question and independently of it.

1 and 2 Thessalonians

The initial description of postcolonial analysis in general readily reveals Smith's interest in both material matrix and cultural production. Not only is such analysis said to encompass the phenomenon of 'imperialism' across its various historical phases, but also the phenomenon of 'colonialism' (howsoever related to 'imperialism') as defined entails consideration of both text (discursive) and context (historical). The ensuing description of postcolonial biblical criticism as attentive to the discursive and historical dimensions of the 'imperial shadow' in texts and beyond confirms such combined interest in literary texts and historical contexts. Smith's own approach to the Thessalonian letters takes to heart such a call for joint analysis of cultural production and material matrix.

The literary text functions as the point of entry for the exercise as a whole. Thus, Smith begins with 'summaries' of each letter which are meant to serve as a foundation for a postcolonial reading in terms of strategies of domination and constructions of the 'other'. These summaries involve descriptions of the rhetorical strategies deployed and constructions of the community situations in question in the light of such strategies. Here, then, the twofold focus is beyond question. The literary text continues to play the leading role through the postcolonial reading and its 'interrogative lens'. This Smith pursues in three stages, the first two of which are directly relevant to the discussion. To begin with, he traces the shadow of empire in scholarly as well as popular readings of Paul in general and the Thessalonian letters in particular. These reception histories are closely linked to their respective historical contexts. Both interpretive traditions, Smith concludes, 'obstruct' the political and anti-imperial dimension of the Pauline Letters. Consequently, and in keeping with recent revisionist readings of Paul in this regard, Smith undertakes a reading of the letters as texts of opposition and resistance to the imperial order of Rome. This he does by foregrounding various strategies of resistance at work in the letters: the recourse to apocalyptic traditions, the development of alternative 'assemblies', the critique of accommodationist practices. In each case, Smith situates the rhetorical and ideological strategies of the letters squarely within their historical context, whether of the empire in general or of Thessalonica in particular. Again, the twofold focus is without question. For Smith, therefore, cultural production and material matrix shed light on one another and should be pursued concomitantly.

Pastoral Letters

In principle, given his definition of postcolonial criticism as concerned with power and hierarchy and as oppositional in mode, Broadbent stands open to analysis of both material matrix and cultural production. His comments regarding the application of such criticism to the Pastorals confirm such openness. With regard to the letters, he raises the question of the community situation behind them and why they reacted to Rome as they did. With regard to mainstream scholarship, particularly in the British context, he declares outright that the critical tradition, as revealed by its hermeneutical choices, was keen on supporting empire and the 'power and authority' of the elite in control. In practice, however, Broadbent's focus rests primarily on the literary text rather than on the historical context. Indeed, his representation of the contexts behind both the letters and the critical tradition is directly derived from his analysis of these texts. In the case of the Pastorals, he argues for a deliberate brake on egalitarian impulses present within the community. In the case of mainstream scholarship, he posits fundamental agreement with the hierarchical impulses of empire. Such analysis of power and hierarchy proceeds by foregrounding key passages from the letters having to do with the attitude of colonial subjects, the condition of slavery, the role of women, and the qualifications for male leadership in the community.

Philemon

In principle, given his position on the multidimensionality of both the colonial experience and the postcolonial optic, it is clear for Callahan postcolonial inquiry involves historical context and textual production; in practice, however, it is the discursive element that is foregrounded, while the material element is identified but not pursued, in such analysis.

The importance of the material matrix is beyond question. Indeed, Callahan is very much concerned with the question of political economy, its character and postulates, in colonial contexts. Thus, slavery is identified as the 'most important' power relation at work in the colonialist project of Rome, while a similar exploitation of surplus labour is surfaced as the primary power relation behind the colonialist project of Western modernity, in both its dependent (oppression of indigenous labour) and its settler (importation of labour) variations, with recourse to 'colour' slavery as marking the project in the Americas as a whole and the United States in particular. Interestingly, while speaking of the colonial legacy as a *sine qua non* of contemporary interpretation, Callahan does not address the question of political economy in the present global context. The significance of cultural production lies, then, in its mode of relation toward the material base. Thus, Callahan proposes, texts are to be examined on whether they serve to foster or counter the project of colonialism, whether they function as 'imperialist' or 'neocolonial', therefore, or 'anti-colonial'. In biblical criticism such analysis proceeds at various levels: the biblical text itself, written within a colonial context – such as the Letter to Philemon in Roman colonialism; the reading of this text in other colonial contexts – such as the standard interpretation of Philemon from late antiquity through to modern criticism; the reading of this text in the context of ongoing colonial legacy – such as the contemporary interpretation of Philemon, including his own.

Hebrews

Various aspects of postcolonial analysis as envisioned by Punt call attention to both the material matrix and cultural production: the collusion posited between imperial–colonial frameworks, ancient and modern, and the Bible, its writings and critical tradition; the emphasis on global diversity with its corresponding focus on the local and the native; the pivotal role assigned to social location and the real reader in interpretation, yielding a 'polyphonic hermeneutics'; and the aim of liberation at a geopolitical level. Such joint attention is readily confirmed by his twofold characterization of Hebrews as an example of 'contextual theology' and of his reading of Hebrews as contextual and perspectival. Yet, it is analysis of the literary text that prevails, with analysis of the historical context provided mostly by way of background information or present-day application.

Thus, for example, Punt's description of his own location and perspective as an Afrikaner in post-apartheid South Africa is not expanded beyond its basic summary as a diasporic and hybrid existence, while the general context of postcolonial Africa is invoked at various points, but with no systematic or interlacing analysis. Similarly, there are recurrent allusions to historical Christianity and contemporary globalization, but again in largely intermittent and unconnected fashion. Lastly, not much information is given regarding the context of Hebrews itself, whether by way of the community situation, characterized as profoundly 'diasporic' and of 'desperate urgency', or the Roman imperial–colonial framework, which remains quite in the background throughout.

In contrast to such relative absence of the material matrix, the focus on the text of Hebrews is sustained and comprehensive. Punt examines a wide variety of theological topics, ten in all, deemed particularly relevant to a postcolonial reading: the projection of a Christian dualism, the exalted identification of Jesus Christ, the themes of diaspora and rest, the issues of sin and atonement, the concept of the Word of God, the question of faith and eschatology, the figures of Abraham and Sarah and the question of discipline. Interspersed throughout this exposition of theological strategies one finds references to historical context – the world of Rome and of the later Western empires, the world of subsequent Christianity, the world of today in general and of Africa in particular. This focus on the text does extend to the critical tradition on Hebrews, and expansively so, but largely in *ad locum* fashion; for the most part, therefore, the discussion remains centred on Hebrews itself.

James

Ringe's view of postcolonial criticism as political and oppositional, whereby resistance to imperial projects on the part of texts and interpretations is foregrounded, logically demands joint attention to cultural production and the material matrix, and that is indeed the case. Thus, with respect to James, she points to its context of Roman imperial domination as an 'indispensable... backdrop' for critical analysis. Such a judgment cannot but apply as well to its dominant history of interpretation, given the charge of 'colonization' of the letter as a result; however, neither such reception nor its underlying context(s) of imperial domination constitute a focus of inquiry here. These elements are mentioned as constitutive for postcolonial analysis, especially in light of their impact on the common reading of James and their 'interception' of its postcolonial voice, but not pursued. In this combined focus on cultural production and material matrix, the letter serves as the point of departure throughout. First, by way of the community situation identified at work behind the letter – a distortion of Pauline theology that reflects the values of the 'surrounding culture of empire' with nefarious consequences for community life. Then, in terms of central thematic concerns of the letter that crystallize the nature and consequences of such imperial values in response to the community problematic – economic, linguistic and ideological issues. In each category, as the contrast between the values of the empire and the values of the gospel is developed, Ringe introduces pointed information regarding both the imperial context and the community situation. As a result, text and context are read alongside one another – the former as entry point, the latter as backdrop.

1 Peter

From her delineation of critical feminist postcolonial criticism, with its call for analysis of the structures and discourses of kyriarchal systems of domination, it is clear that Schüssler Fiorenza has material matrix and cultural production in mind. In this regard, however, she makes an important distinction between the context as represented by the text and the context submerged by the text. The dynamics involved in such a distinction and bifocal attention can be readily unpacked by following her exposition of the fundamental methodological components at work in the proposed approach.

Four such components are identified in all. To begin with, the approach is decidedly rhetorical in orientation. Not, however, along the formalist lines of 'classical-rhetorical' or 'literary-rhetorical' analysis, where the text functions as a means of communication, but rather along the ideological lines of Edward Said, with a view of the text as 'embedded in power relations' – the text as a 'field of power and action'. Further, following Chela Sandoval, the approach examines this 'worldly' embeddedness of the text in pyramidal as well as horizontal fashion, borrowing from the conjunction of such power relations in the political economy of capitalist globalization. As a result, the power relations embodied in the text are viewed as both kyriarchal and networking, since kyriarchal domination yields a multiplicity of structures that intersect and heighten one another. In addition, following Sandoval again, the approach analyses the text-as-embodied with a counter-vision of 'democratics', grounded in a 'methodology of the oppressed' and a stance of 'dissident consciousness'. In so doing, it seeks to read 'against the kyriocentric grain' by searching for voices behind that of the author, submerged by the text and its rhetorics – a reading concerned with the 'historical agency of wo/men'. Finally, for the actual execution of the approach, a fourfold procedure is outlined: (1) establishing the socio-religious location of both author and addressees, (2) uncovering the power relations inscribed in the text, (3) reconstructing the rhetorical strategies of the text, (4) reconstructing the voices and arguments submerged by the text. Throughout, the text serves as point of departure, with information about the context extracted from the text and amplified from a variety of other sources, primary or secondary. Text and context thus shed light on one another, with the text (the rhetorical response) having the lead role, since the context (the rhetorical situation) can no longer be directly accessed but only reconstructed from the text (as 'fitting' response).

This approach, as her commentary shows, is clearly regarded as applicable to both the text and its history of interpretation, although the centre of attention remains the former. Furthermore, although the reception history envisioned is in principle broadly conceived, the centre of attention also remains academic criticism and its dominant tradition of 'malestream' exegesis. Thus, Schüssler Fiorenza draws a crucial distinction between 'malestream' exegetical and feminist emancipatory analysis: the former, which fails to problematize its own socio-religious situation of neutrality and objectivity, fails to observe as well the distinction between the rhetorics of the text and the rhetorics of the context. As a result, it allies itself, out of its unreflected and unquestioned position within a kyriarchal system of domination, with the rhetorical perspective advanced by the biblical text and hence its underlying kyriarchal vision, with similar ramifications for dissident voices within systems of kyriarchal dominations in both past (continued submersion) and present (ongoing submersion). Given such a working alliance, feminist emancipatory analysis cannot but offer a critical systemic analysis of structures and ideologies at work in both texts and interpretations.

2 Peter

Given her representation of postcolonial criticism as contextual and perspective, indeed from below and oppositional, one would expect from Briggs Kittredge a joint analysis of cultural production and material matrix. While that may well be the case in principle, and I suspect that it is, the point is not made here as such. The focus of the discussion remains throughout on the text of 2 Peter and its rhetorical strategies as well as on the interpretation of such strategies in the scholarly literature. The historical context is but briefly considered by way of the community situation, which is used in turn to explain the reason for the deployment of such strategies in particular. Following a most succint portrayal of the community problematic, therefore, Briggs Kittredge foregrounds the three strategies in question (construction of authority, institution of a canon, polemical self-definition) and then proceeds to contrast the readings offered of such strategies by feminist and postcolonial critics with those advanced by other critical approaches. The discussion throughout is thus discursively oriented, so that even the context of empire does not surface in the analysis of the letter itself or its various interpretive traditions.

Johannine Letters

As conveyed by his definition of postcolonialism as discursively oppositional (correcting misrepresentation and defamation) and ethico-politically committed (struggling for a better world), both cultural production and material matrix prove significant for Sugirtharajah. Yet, it is the text that draws by far the greater attention. Analysis of the historical context involves a consideration of the community situation behind the letters and the multireligious situation in the Mediterranean world, with not much amplification in either case. The community context revolves around a 'schism', a 'great dissension' regarding the 'person and work' of Christ between the author (viewed as 'possibly' the same for all three and identified as 'probably' John the Elder) and a dissident party, possibly Hellenistic in background, who deny not that Jesus was a human being but who do question the attribution of exalted claims to Jesus, including that of the promised Messiah. The multireligious context focuses on the presence of Mahayana Buddhism in urban centres of the Mediterranean and its influence on

Gnosticism as well as on the Johannine community and its religious worldview. Analysis of the literary text, in contrast, is more thorough, pointing out the many colonial traits evident in the author's rhetorical and ideological strategy as well as a number of postcolonial traits similarly discernible, which allow room for a partial contrapuntal reading of the letters. The commentary's structural design follows this latter sequence: exposition of colonial traits; unfolding of postcolonial traits, with contrapuntal expansion; final evaluation of the letters in the light of such a combination of traits.

Jude

In foregrounding the intersection of politics and religion, colonizing projects and ritual systems, in imperial–colonial frameworks, Park subscribes in principle to combined analysis of cultural production and material matrix. This joint critical attention comes across clearly in his approach to recent imperial–colonial contexts. The various texts considered – the visits of Japanese prime ministers to the war-dead memorial, the theological pronouncements of the US president on both the country and his own figure, and the missionary enterprise of US churches in Korea – are all set, albeit briefly so, against their respective historical contexts. Such joint critical attention proves quite evident as well in his reading of Jude within the context of the Roman Empire. In two ways, actually. On the one hand, by way of general context, in terms of the politico-religious collusion at work in Roman imperial religion, strategically extended to the provinces with ramifications for society and culture alike – the emperor as master and lord, divinely appointed and favoured. On the other hand, more concretely and at greater length, in terms of the community situation presupposed and addressed by the letter – a conflict involving local believers and outside 'intruders', in which the politico-religious collusion operative throughout the empire plays a part as well. Park's actual approach to Jude proceeds in two stages: first, drawing on the letter itself, he reconstructs the community problematic in question; then, he reads the letter as a response to this problematic. In this reading he highlights rhetorical design and flow: a close, sequential reading following the major structural divisions outlined and showing how the various argumentative strategies, with particular emphasis on 'articulations of faith' and 'criteria advanced for acknowledging falsehood … and finding spiritual orientation and worship', relate to the conflict at hand. For Park, therefore, text and context stand as closely interrelated, both shedding light on one another; at the same time, it is the text that plays the pivotal role throughout, with information about the context mainly derived from the text itself, though from other sources as well.

Revelation

Moore's approach to postcolonial analysis as attending to a variety of phenomena in imperial–colonial contexts (from imperialism and colonization to decolonization and neocolonialism to globalization) and as including a variety of mutually constitutive ideological frameworks (from the political and eco-nomic to the ethnic–racial and religious) leads to critical consideration of material matrix and cultural production alike. This twofold focus is structurally embodied within the commentary itself: a first part concentrates on the historical context of the Roman Empire, in general as well as with respect to Asia Minor and the westernmost province of Asia; the second part focuses on the rhetorical and political strategy of Revelation in light of the context outlined. In so doing, Moore tips in the direction of the text, but not overwhelmingly so.

The exposition of the context, a 'fleshing out of the socio-political context', is multidimensional: the tradition of colonization in Asia Minor – a heavily Hellenized region readily absorbed by the 'consummately' Hellenized Romans; the pattern of Roman colonization both in general and in Asia – an 'occupation' model (foreign administration of a majority indigenous population) involving urban communities of Roman citizens (mostly composed of military veterans and few in number relative to the indigenous population), self-governing and serving as centres of administration over assigned surrounding territory; the mode of Roman governance in Asia – domination not by military force (ungar-risoned province) but by 'hegemony' or consent of the indigenous through the incorporation of local urban elites, in competition with one another for impe-rial recognition and benefits within a provincial infrastructure of cities; and the symbolic omnipresence of the imperial cult in Asia – a key channel for the ethos of competition among the urban elites. The exposition of the text reads it against this backdrop: a 'catachrestic' response involving the appropriation and redeployment of Roman imperial rule. Revelation emerges thereby as a 'stunning' example of anti-imperial resistance literature: a 'consummately counter-hegemonic' work that foretells the destruction of the Roman Empire, describes its imperial cult as a monstrosity in service of Satan, and advances a Christian Empire instead (God as emperor, Jesus Christ as co-regent and the Christian communities as priests of the imperial cult). This grand rhetorical and political strategy of resistance Moore unfolds through close reading of selected key sections of the work.

Christian Church and Roman Empire in Postcolonial Criticism

Matthew

As a text emerging from and enmeshed in a context of interaction between imperial culture and local culture, where Rome is the wielder of power-over, Carter situates Matthew within an imperialized local culture and hence among the ranks of the subordinated and the marginalized. As a 'silenced provincial' and a 'voice on the margins', the discourse of Matthew, he specifies, is that of an individual or a collectivity who 'writes back' in challenge of Rome. For Carter, therefore, Matthew stands as a text of opposition. As such, it provides a view of life in the margins of empire, revealing in the process modes of imperial subjugation as well as modes of local resistance. At the same time, Carter hastens to point out, resistance in local cultures can vary considerably. Indeed, in the interaction between the local and the imperial, a complex process of negotiation is always at work. The outcome of this process, as it is presented, ranges over a broad spectrum, which could be summarized as follows: from outright submission (accommodation, complicity, cooperation, co-optation), through tactical ambiguity (protective compliance, mimicry, disguised resistance), to open protest and confrontation (non-violent or violent). As an oppositional text, Matthew emerges as a conflicted text, a mixture of confrontation and co-optation – open challenge to Rome, in keeping with the principles of Rome. To wit: the Gospel defies, on the one hand, the imperial values of Rome through the figure and teachings of Jesus; the Gospel couches, on the other hand, the local role and values of Jesus in the concepts and language of the empire. In opposing the existing power-over of Rome, consequently, Matthew enacts the alternative power-over of Jesus.

All aspects of the Gospel, then, reflect this conflicted stance of resistance and imitation, from the literary genre adopted to the theological formulations advanced. All are shown to have an imperial underside, yielding a mirror image of a similar claim on Rome's part. Such is the case with the turn to biography, a vehicle for the presentation of leading figures in the empire (whether for praise or censure): Matthew presents a compromised Jesus, a 'provincial peasant' at once crucified by the empire for defiance of its values and launching an imperial project of his own – a coming empire of God, ultimately overcoming in violent triumph. Such is also the case with the depiction of God and Jesus: God's sovereignty over creation, history and human beings bears all the marks of imperial sovereignty – acceptance or punishment; Jesus' ministry as part of God's saving work follows the theological claims of Rome – uniqueness, with no room for competitors; Jesus' divine presence recalls the global reach and beneficial character ascribed to imperial rule – assurance of triumph and validation of worldwide mission as well as a promise of blessings, for the poor in spirit and in a future world; the extent of Jesus' authority matches that of Rome – absolute power over the past, the present and all things. Such is further the case with the construction of the world as binary: the stance adopted toward the reign of Satan, in control of all empires and in coalition with leadership groups, duplicates that of Rome toward its rivals – elimination for being too evil; the view of the world as a place of sins and in need of redemption by Jesus recreates the imperial division of time – the 'before' and 'after' of Rome; the alternative societal experience advanced by Jesus (promise of blessings for all, celebration of inclusion, bias towards the non-elite) embodies imperial divisiveness – by no means inclusive, gendered and with blessings for the community only. In this parallelism of Rome and Matthew, Carter sees a perfect example of Homi Bhabha's concept of mimicry at work: while the Gospel mocks and threatens imperial power, accounting for Jesus' crucifixion, it also lays claim to imperial counter-mastery, to be effected through Jesus' eschatological return. In sum, as he aptly puts it, the Gospel is both a product of and productive of imperial power.

Mark

For Liew, Mark's politics of apocalyptic time are at once radical and imitative, embodying a profoundly conflicted vision of life within a colonial context. At the heart of it, one finds the expectation of an imminent intervention of God in history, which shall bring to an end the present evil age, under the dominion of Satan, and usher in a new and perfect age, the kingdom of God. This kingdom is proclaimed and unleashed, as an attack on Satan, by Jesus, God's only Son and unique representative. Such a fundamental vision of life moulds the Gospel's construction of authority, agency and gender. With regard to authority, Jesus is depicted as replacing all traditional authority – not only political, Jewish and Roman alike, but also wealth, family, ethnicity, rituals and traditions, and the desire for power. However, in so doing, Liew points out, Mark sets up a new supreme authority and hierarchical structure, centred on Jesus and representing a new system of inclusion and exclusion, with violence and destruction for the latter. In terms of agency, neither Jesus nor his followers are presented as able to effect lasting change in the world; such change, according to Mark, can only come about as a result of God's action. Consequently, Liew observes, human beings have but one choice, to serve God or Satan, and the former option implies a life of suffering and martyrdom. With regard to gender, Jesus is portrayed as forming a new family in the world. Yet, Liew notes, within such a family women continue to play a traditional role under Jesus' authority and as Jesus' followers, obedient to male authority and confined to home and family.

In the light of such findings, Liew concludes, the anti-colonial vision of Mark ends up reproducing, within the Christian community, central elements of colonial politics under Rome: rigid central authority, utter human powerlessness in the face of evil and patriarchal gender relations. Thus, what at first sight appears to be a radical intervention in colonial politics under the empire turns out to be, upon closer inspection, a mirror imitation of such politics within the community in opposition to the empire.

Luke-Acts

Burrus's analysis of ideological stance and narrative art in Luke-Acts identifies ambiguity as a key feature of the text. Politically, first of all, Luke is at pains to situate the story of Jesus and his followers within the world of Roman/Judaean politics and its complex web of power mediation. In so doing, Luke emphasizes the dastardly role of the priestly elite of Judaea, downplays the role of the Romans and their Herodian allies by portraying the benign effects of such rule, and creates a space for a kingdom of God with a 'global' community of believers. From the perspective of Hardt and Negri's analysis of postmodern empire – an empire with no Rome, with decentred political sovereignty and glo-balized economic incorporation – Luke's envisioned kingdom is seen as simi-larly inclusive and dangerous: a space without boundaries where distinctions between the imperial and the colonial become irrelevant, a 'counter-empire'. From the perspective of Scott's analysis of resistance – appropriation of the public transcript of domination by the subjugated as a strategy of resistance – Luke's envisioned kingdom is seen, even if totalizing in its own right, as sub-versive: using the values of Rome to question the policies of Rome, such as the execution of an 'innocent' figure like Jesus. In the end, Burrus argues, while the influence of Rome emerges as rather benign, no mediator of Rome is depicted in positive light. Economically, then, Luke also takes great pains to situate the story of Jesus and his disciples within the world of Roman/Judaean economic relations and its imperial system of taxation and patronage. In the process, Luke adopts a twofold strategy: an idealistic past in which the radicalism of Jesus and his early followers prevails in the face of the imperial tax burden, with denunciations of exploitation and poverty and calls for justice and sharing; a pragmatic present where accommodation and paternalism rule, with espousal of the patronage system and philanthropy in mind. In the end, Burrus concludes, it is impossible to judge how subversive Luke-Acts actually proves regarding the political economy of Rome.

Artistically, Luke follows the rise of novelistic writing that flourishes upon the advent of the empire and the profound dislocation that it brings about. This is a genre where the boundaries between history and fiction become blurred and where cultural difference vis-à-vis both Rome and others is in constant negotiation along ever-changing borderlines. It is a genre, therefore, that ques-tions the hegemony of the empire as well as any monolithic version of truth or history. This is true, first of all, of its relationship to time and space. Drawing on Bakhtin, the novel is described as a parody of genres, where conventions are exposed and subverted at once. Temporally, Luke-Acts not only rewrites earlier gospel accounts and adds a book of Acts but also provides no closure to its own story: the past of Jesus is brought into dialogue with the present of ministry in the empire, in itself quite open-ended, since the fate of Paul in Rome is left in suspension. Spatially, Luke-Acts presents a gravitating centre in Jerusalem for both Paul and Jesus that no longer exists and ultimately shifts that centre to a Rome that fails to materialize: the result (invoking Bhabha) is a 'flawed imita-tion' of imperial expansionism – the reconquest of the world through a story. Second, it is also true of the novel's relationship to language. Again drawing on Bakhtin, the novel is described as having a polyglot consciousness. Thus, Luke-Acts places multiple languages in dialogue: the experience of the Spirit, the use of direct speech, the marking of such speech as angelic, inspired or scrip-tural. Such heteroglossia cannot be contained and might even signal (invoking Bhabha) a movement toward the 'in-between' space of 'hybridity'. Finally, it is true as well of boundary negotiation. Luke-Acts' mission of evangelization emerges as highly complex and unstable: a tale of conversion, a critique of colonization, a resistance to empire – all highly compromised in the end. In sum, ambivalence rules in Luke-Acts, whether in the ideological or the artistic plane.

John

For Segovia the Gospel of John emerges as an outright and searing postcolonial text – a text whose story emplaces a proposal of absolute challenge, whose opening strikes a chord of absolute otherness, and whose plot traces a programme of absolute opposition. At some undetermined point in some undetermined location, he argues, John casts a critical eye upon the imperial–colonial framework of Rome roundabout. Such a gaze is said to yield utter condemnation of Roman dominion and power alongside a radical vision of divine power and dominion. Such a gaze is further said to comprehend not only imperial Rome and its colonial minions but ultimately all religio-political frameworks in the world. Its judgment is unsparing: all lies under the rule of Satan. Its alternative is totalizing: salvation lies only in the rule of God. This kingdom of God is made known, within the kingdom of Satan, by the Son of God, the Word sent by the Father and humanized in Jesus, and his disciples – the children of God sent by Jesus and divinized by the Spirit. This rule of God the Gospel presents as follows: breaking out in outlying territories of the Roman Empire – lands and peoples associated with the Jewish ethnos; issuing forth from a provincial deity – the God of Judaism, claimed as the one and true God; irrupting through the words and deeds of a provincial subject – Jesus of Nazareth, Messiah of the Jews and Saviour of the world; and enduring beyond him via provincial followers of all sorts – Jews and non-Jews alike re-born as children of God.

In the narrative, Segovia continues, this vision of the Gospel emerges as a conflict between the two worlds constitutive of Johannine reality – the world above of God and the world below of Satan. A myth of beginnings presents the this-world of flesh as created by the other-world of spirit. Prior to the sending of the Word, however, the two worlds stand in stark but passive opposition to one another. With the arrival of the Word in Jesus, such opposition turns into outright conflict, yielding rejection and hostility, and builds up to a decisive climax, the death/resurrection of Jesus and the triumph/defeat of Satan. After the glorification of Jesus the Word, active opposition continues by way of his followers, now subject to rejection and violence as well. A myth of fulfilment anticipates a 'last day' whereupon this opposition between the two worlds will come to an end.

In this overall scenario, Segovia points out, the disciples of Jesus – those who have come to believe in his claims and have thereby undergone regeneration by the Spirit as children of God – constitute, in the wake of Jesus, a clearing of space, a colony, of the other-world in the this-world. In this outpost of the empire of God, light and life, grace and truth, are to be found. Within it, the children of God give witness to the rule of God and the example of Jesus, with love and service toward one another. At the same time, he adds, this site of enlightenment and resistance within the empire of Satan, this colonial settlement from above, proves complex as well as ambiguous. On the one hand, decidedly unstable: not only hated and tormented from the outside, but also subject to removal and destruction from the inside. On the other hand, uncomfortably imperial: condemning and demonizing whatever lies outside, while deploying hierarchy and obedience inside. In sum, a remarkable postcolonial intervention of absolute challenge, otherness and opposition, ultimately beholden 'perhaps... much too much' to the imperial–colonial formation of Rome and Satan 'for its own good'.

Romans

In Romans Elliott finds a decidedly anti-imperial text, second only to Revelation in the corpus of the New Testament. This oppositional stance is expressed in both local and general terms: not only with respect to the local Christian communities in the city of Rome, therefore, but also with regard to the Christian mission and presence throughout the dominion of Rome.

In the case of Rome itself, the community dynamics among Christian believers are said to move against the backdrop of the return of Christian Jews to the city after the rescission under Nero of the edict of banishment of 49 CE. Gentile Christians, now predominant in such communities (the 'strong'), stand in danger of falling prey to a view of Jewish Christians, dispossessed and dishonoured as they are (the 'weak'), through the filter of Roman ethnocentrism in general and anti-Judaism in particular – the 'stumbling' of Israel and 'boasting' over Israel. In the face of such developments, in a situation where contempt and resistance are seemingly flourishing, Paul counters the imperial practices and claims of Roman supremacy through a call for mutual obligation, a 'preferential option for the powerless', and a defence of the continuing validity of God's promises to Israel despite all appearances to the contrary. In the case of the empire, the dynamics of the Christian mission and message are set against the background of the design and project of Rome. In the face of a Roman discourse of power and subjugation, Paul offers a counter-discourse: in lieu of the emperor, Jesus as the Son of God; in lieu of imperial global reach, a commission to bring all nations under the 'obedience of faith'; in lieu of imperial policies of subjection and terror and claims to piety and justice, a coming triumph of God and a coming era of justice; in lieu of a vanquished Israel and a tortured creation, liberation from slavery.

1 and 2 Corinthians

In the eyes of Horsley, the letters to the Corinthians reflect and convey Paul's vision of imperial opposition, derived from the Jesus-movement of Palestine and transplanted to the peoples and territories of the eastern Mediterranean, including Corinth. This counter-imperial vision bears a master narrative, a personal mission, and a plan of action. To begin with, the ruling narrative brings about a radical displacement of Roman claims in favour of Christian claims. In effect, it was through Israel, a subject people of Rome, and through Jesus, a provincial rebel leader executed by Rome, that the course of history and the hand of providence moved. Indeed, God's vindication of Jesus through resurrection and exaltation as 'Lord of the world' signified the fulfilment of the Abrahamic promises, so that in Jesus, and through his movement – the blessings of God would flow on both Israel and on all peoples of the world. Further, through Jesus' return the power of Rome would be brought low and the power of God would be triumphantly established. Second, the appointed mission bestows on Paul a universal role as 'lead apostle' to non-Israelite peoples. He it was who would spearhead the offer of God's blessings in Jesus throughout the subject peoples of the empire. Lastly, the strategic plan of action puts into effect an 'international' movement of resistance against Rome. Among the subjugated of Rome, Paul's task would be that of organizing a network of local cells, in the style of a 'labour movement or anti-colonial movement', that would stand together as an alternative society – in charge of its own affairs, marked by an egalitarian ideal regarding membership, with exclusive loyalty to God, given to care for one another, and in pursuit of a horizontal sharing of resources. Corinth, a city to which Paul devoted considerable time, was one such target of Paul's movement, mission and narrative.

At the same time, Horsley points out, as with other cells of the movement, not all proved smooth in Corinth. On the one hand, a variety of important issues – ranging from the communitarian to the social, the moral to the confessional – arose after Paul's departure; on the other hand, a number of dissenting viewpoints emerged as well, in opposition to Paul. Such concerns and stances were brought to his attention by letters from the community, and these he proceeded to address in his own various letters to the community. Behind such developments, Horsley adds, stood above all a view of wisdom, grounded in Hellenistic Jewish mystical theology, as the means to attain immortality of the soul, knowledge of the divine and spiritual enlightenment. In the face of Roman domination, Paul regarded such emphasis on personal 'spiritual transcendence' not only as disruptive of community solidarity but also as contrary to God's fulfilment of history in Jesus and against Rome. Such wisdom, therefore, Paul countered with his own wisdom of counter-imperial resistance, grounded in the crucifixion and vindication of Jesus. Two final comments are in order. First, it is impossible to tell, Horsley admits, what the ultimate outcome of these interchanges were in the case of the fledgling Corinthian community. Second, Paul's ideal of an alternative society, Horsley further acknowledges, was compromised in some respects, such as, for example, a certain regression regarding the equality of men and women and too great an accommodation in the direction of the language and concepts of the wisdom faction in Corinth.

Galatians

At the core of the crisis in Galatians, Wan proposes, lies a fundamental struggle over ethnic identity and relations, revolving around the criteria for admission of the Galatians, as 'Gentiles', into the Jesus-movement, 'Jewish' in origins and composition: should the requirements of the Mosaic law be observed or not? Among the 'Jesus-followers' themselves, there is profound disagreement: Paul, on the one hand, argues in opposition; Antioch–Jerusalem, on the other hand, argues in favour. Both crisis and responses, Wan argues, should be set against the background of empire, with Rome as impinging centre and Jerusalem as resistant periphery. In the process, both responses emerge as 'survival strategies' within Judaism as a minority group within the Roman Empire. This scenario Wan elaborates at various levels of application, from the general to the concrete.

At the widest level, Jerusalem (signified by the 'temple administrators') is said to develop, in reaction to the dominant power and discourse of Rome, a totalizing discourse and power of its own. Such an exercise in 'mimicry' and 'worlding' relies on the following principles: first, a myth of homogeneity is used to flatten 'Gentiles' and 'Jews' alike, while a myth of difference is invoked to separate such constructs into a binomial opposition; second, a 'classic' colonial pattern of domination is established with Jerusalem as centre and Jewish communities elsewhere as peripheries. Thereby, not only is the homogeneity advanced by Rome called into question but also its position as centre relegated to the periphery. Within Judaism itself, moreover, various positions develop regarding identity and outsiders: toward one end, a primordialist view according to which Gentiles can be received only through full integration; toward the other end, a universalizing position where integration is worked out by insiders and outsiders in an 'interstitial' space.

At the intermediate level, this situation is seen as replicated within the 'Jesus-movement': Jerusalem (signified by the 'pillars') functions as the centre, undertakes the establishment of 'colonies' throughout by way of the missions and expects obeisance and tribute from such settlements. When the admission of Gentiles into the movement becomes problematic in Antioch, with Paul opting for a universalizing position and others espousing an essentialist position, Jerusalem first sides with Paul but then, subsequently, goes back on such an agreement, resulting in the creation of a Jerusalem–Antioch alliance. At a concrete level, this situation is said to be replicated in Galatians: against emissaries of the Jerusalem–Antioch stance, who call for full submission to the Mosaic law, Paul defends his stance, forged in the 'hybridity' of diaspora and agreed to by Jerusalem, demanding faith in Christ without the requirements of the law.

For Wan, therefore, the controversy that surfaces in Galatians is not at all between 'Jewish' and 'Christian' but within the circles of a Jewish 'sect' whose constitutive parties view faith in Jesus as the Christ as an essential requirement for membership but disagree on the need for other requirements.

These competing positions, moreover, subscribe to the overall resistant strategy adopted by Judaism as a minority group in the face of imperial contingencies and yielding a counter-hegemonic domination of its own. The parting of the ways comes on the issue of admission of Gentiles, such as the Galatians, as Jesus-followers. Within this envisioned state of affairs, Wan portrays Paul as realizing from the start how the flow of Gentiles into the new movement would result in ambivalence and prepared for such a development accordingly. In sum, all 'Christian' sides in Galatians are 'Jewish', messianic, anti-imperial as well as totalizing and colonizing, but in different ways and with different consequences.

Ephesians

Bird regards the political project of Ephesians as highly complex: a vision at once oppositional, positing a conflict of empires between that of Caesar and that of God, and hybrid, involving a thorough linguistic and conceptual intermingling of such empires. On the one hand, the counter-empire constructed is decidedly spiritualized, given its location in the heavenly realms, yet such a move should be seen as by no means apolitical but rather as sharply political. Indeed, the sense of 'citizenship' in the heavenly empire of God ultimately renders allegiance to Rome inconsequential, leading to submission to the worldly empire of Caesar for the sake of avoiding persecution and preserving peace. On the other hand, the construction of this spiritual counter-empire emerges as ultimately dependent on the material empire. As a result, the heavenly empire ends up duplicating the worldly in structure and dynamics, with similar ramifications for insiders and outsiders. The result, Bird argues, is an escapist and imitative political project. To wit: a Christian imperial order, set in the heavenly realms of God and under the rulership of Christ, which (1) at once relativizes and bows to the Roman imperial order and (2) at once distantiates itself from and incorporates within itself the Roman imperial order.

For the community in the face of Rome, the ramifications of this imperial order are numerous and profound. Bird draws them in terms of all three dimensions of the project examined.

The first is the imperializing rhetoric at work. First and foremost, in the heavenly counter-empire, at the right hand of God, sits the exalted and all-powerful Christ as ruler, having triumphed over all powers and with all peoples subject to him. In this 'household of God' the community stands as 'citizens', holding sway over all the powers of oppression, marked as God's own by the seal of the Spirit and assured of their promised salvation and inheritance. Among them, Jews and Gentiles, Jesus as supreme ruler has established unity and peace. Theirs too is a sharp awareness of 'fulness' and 'special knowledge' that sets them off from all outside. Theirs as well is a keen consciousness of belonging to an international movement as opposed to all outsiders. All this Ephesians conveys to the community as a 'material manifestation' of its counter-imperial ideology.

The second is the household codes adopted. Both the instructions for wives and slaves and the portrayal of the community as body and bride of Christ reinforce the sense of a 'household of God' whose lives are solely for the glory of the counter-emperor.

The third is the call to battle issued. Such military imagery further conveys the sense of the 'household of God' as the army of the counter-emperor, ready to inflict violence upon their enemies and oppressors.

In the end, Bird argues, such a portrayal of life, its beliefs and practices, within the Christian imperial order is both positive and problematic. Without doubt, given their situation within the Roman Empire, such a vision of belonging to a higher political order is bound to bring consolation and reassurance to the community. At the same time, such a sense of belonging shifts the eyes of the community away from the material to the spiritual realm, making way for a view of the worldly empire as immaterial and of their own relationship to it as one of tactical subordination for the sake of preserving life and peace. In sum, a counter-empire that is both escapist and hybrid.

Philippians
The Christian community founded by Paul at Philippi – a politically and economically prosperous '*colonia*', renamed in honour of Augustus in 31 BCE by the emperor himself as a reward for loyalty – constitutes, in Agosto's eyes, an 'alternative society', set up by Paul in opposition to the claims and practices of Rome and facing opposition from the outside as a result. This community, Agosto continues, is also experiencing dissension from the inside, ultimately grounded as well in this counter-imperial project of Paul.

This vision of an alternative society is readily evident in the systematic transformation of imperial ideology at work throughout the letter: the proclamation of a different 'good news' about another 'Lord', Jesus Christ; the representation of this 'Lord' not as one in search of glory and honour but rather as divesting himself of such for the sake of others; the further representation of this 'Lord' as exalted by God and as returning in triumph; the definition of honour and glory for the community in terms of both a righteousness attained through faith in this 'Lord' and of citizenship in terms of a world other than that of Rome. Given their adherence to such principles and practices, the Christian community finds itself facing the same type of opposition as Paul, who is himself confronting the hardships and uncertainties of jail as a result of such a vision. At the same time, and by no means unrelated to such a vision and its consequences, conflict has erupted within this alternative society. Indeed, there are those who question Paul's leadership precisely because of his imprisonment. Other disputes, such as that between Euodia and Syntyche, threaten disruption as well. In the face of such a precarious situation, Paul's response is to seek steadfastness and unity through self-giving, always with the welfare of others in mind, following the example of Jesus Christ, that of Timothy and Epaphroditus, and his very own.

Such self-giving clearly includes the mobilization of financial assistance for those in need, whether in prison, as in the case of Paul himself, or in other struggling communities – in other words, a movement of resources within the Christian network of communities along horizontal rather than vertical lines. In the face of opposition from without and conflict from within, therefore, the Philippian community is to remain firm and united as an 'alternative society' in opposition to the empire – under its 'Lord', following the moral path of its leaders, and with their eyes set on their citizenship in the heavens.

Colossians

A central task of postcolonial reading, as postulated by Zerbe and Orevillo-Montenegro, is to determine whether, within a context of colonialism, texts promote or contest the colonial order. Such ideological analysis of texts is conceived not in terms of a binomial opposition but rather along the lines of a spectrum. Within such a spectrum, Colossians is placed toward the middle – an 'ambivalent text', with tendencies in both directions. This 'hybrid' position is established on the basis of the letter's cultural, social and political stance. For this inquiry the community situation serves as point of departure, opening the way to these various perspectives of the text and ultimately, through them, to its position vis-à-vis the colonial context. This community situation is sharply put: in Colossians Paul (the issue of authorship is not addressed) is faced with an internal crisis on the part of a community not founded by him. In effect, 'rival teachers' have introduced 'alternative' beliefs (intermediary cosmic powers) and practices (circumcision, special festivals, rules for drinking and eating, asceticism, mystical experiences). The letter seeks, therefore, to reassert the 'apostolic' authority of Paul in this 'wayward' community, enjoining a normative understanding of beliefs and practices and enhancing social identity and cohesion within the community as well as with other Pauline communities.

From a cultural perspective, the letter is said to advance 'Christological absolutism': Christ is represented as supreme over all other powers, religious and political alike. From a social perspective, it is said to assert 'hierarchical order', most clearly at work in the household code: the status quo is upheld through religious legitimation and to the detriment of the powerless (slaves, women, children). From a political perspective, the letter is said to proclaim Christological triumphalism: Christ is represented as 'unmasking' and 'shaming' the powers – actually created 'in, through and for' him – through his crucifixion. Such positions, the authors reflect, prove ultimately ambiguous: while embodying the oppositional views of a 'minority movement' struggling for survival within the context of Rome, they ultimately construct a colonial framework of their own, marked by expansionism and exclusivism. Indeed, the authors add, not only can interpretation go in such a direction, but it has done so repeatedly. Consequently, postcolonial analysis stands in need of ideological critique at this point, having foregrounded the stance of the text and its ramifications.

1 and 2 Thessalonians

Given his commitment to trace the discursive and historical 'shadow of empire' in the biblical 'texts and beyond' and the pursual of this commitment through analysis of the strategies of domination and constructions of the 'other' present in the letters, the relationship between the Christian community and the imperial order emerges as quite prominent in Smith. As point of entry in this regard, Smith relies on the rhetorical and ideological strategies of the letters as well as the community situations inferred from such strategies.

On the one hand, he argues, 1 Thessalonians – dated to 50 or 51 CE and explicitly ascribed to Paul, following consensus opinion – makes use of military imagery and group distinctiveness to urge the 'assembly' to remain faithful ('to stand firm') to the 'apocalyptic gospel' preached by Paul, characterized by the expectation of an imminent parousia. Behind this rhetoric, Smith points out, stands hostility to the community on the part of its former neighbours and the lure of its former ways. On the other hand, he continues, 2 Thessalonians – seemingly accepted as pseudonymous, in keeping with majority opinion, but with no date provided – also appeals to group cohesion and military 'diction' and with the same purpose in mind of warning the 'assembly' to remain faithful ('to stand firm') to the apocalyptic traditions handed down by 'established apostolic authorities, now marked, however, by a projection of the parousia into an unspecified future and the deployment of apocalyptic details. Behind such rhetoric, Smith explains, lies not only ongoing hostility from the surroundings – not necessarily in Thessalonica itself, he cautions, but with 'likely' familiarity with 1 Thessalonians on the part of the addressees – but also the emergence of 'enthusiastic apocalypticists' within the community, whom the author sets out to counter through such expanded apocalyptic expectations and corresponding directives toward involvement in everyday life.

Then, over and beyond their close link to the underlying community situations, Smith proceeds, relying on the work of James C. Scott, to analyse such strategies as concrete expressions of resistance and opposition to the imperial order. The invocation of apocalyptic traditions, for example, may be seen as embodying a critique of the rulers and values of 'this age', in light of the extensive recourse in the letters to imperial imagery and terminology. Similarly, against a background of resistance to Rome by way of both local armed conflicts and 'alternative philosophical movements', the formation of Christian 'assemblies' such as those at Thessalonica as sites of communal participation, broad membership and a 'reformatory ethic' may be viewed as amounting to a profound questioning of the dominant values of imperial society. Lastly, various aspects of the letters – such as the emphasis on salvation through Jesus and the exhortations toward self-reliance within the community – may be read as critiques of the local elite, given the accommodationist impulses at work revolving around imperial honours. These strategies, therefore, Smith uses to foreground the question of domination and construction of the other in the

Thessalonian letters vis-à-vis the Roman Empire, giving rise thereby to a view of the letters as sharply political and anti-imperial documents, in direct contrast to their standard interpretation in both the scholarly and the popular histories of reception.

Pastoral Letters

With respect to the relations envisioned by the Pastorals between the Christian communities and the Roman Empire, Broadbent's sustained focus on both letters and interpretations should be kept in mind. In both cases, a distinction is made between the ideological stance advanced by the texts, biblical and critical, and the historical contexts in question, where other ideological options are in evidence and could have been invoked.

Regarding the Pastorals, Broadbent posits a sharp difference between the community situation behind the letters and the community response urged by the letters. The rhetorical stance advocated reveals, on all issues foregrounded, an 'accommodating attitude' to the imperial order, usually accounted for in the literature as a deliberate choice in the face of persecution and death. The letters thus call for submission to hierarchical authority on the part of imperial subjects, slaves and women. In so doing, the letters further present male leadership as normative and define its constitutive characteristics accordingly: proper and efficient management of the household; respectability outside the community; absence of love of money (implying wealthy status). The historical context reveals claims for greater participation on the part of women and slaves, 'possibly' as a result of a Pauline egalitarian model of community. Such developments, Broadbent suggests, the author – alongside other prominent male members of the community – set out to arrest through the strategy of accommodation to imperial norms. This, he continues, was the result of not only outside pressure, fear of imperial retribution, but also internal pressure, fear that their own power as wealthy men in authority would be undermined by such developments.

Regarding the Western critical tradition, and the British one in particular, Broadbent shows, through specific hermeneutical decisions and observations, how commentators side with the ideological stance of the letters (for submission and against egalitarianism) as a way of upholding imperial order and norms in their own contexts. Such commentators, Broadbent observes, do not hesitate in applying the accommodating message of the Pastorals to their own contexts, taking a stand thereby against any options for egalitarianism present in such contexts.

From a postcolonial perspective, therefore, Broadbent posits in both the Pastorals and its interpreters a decision for accommodation to empire over against any option for resistance available in their respective contexts. In both cases, moreover, he attributes such a conscious choice to the self-interest of the male authors as members of the elites in question, who stand in outright opposition to any surrender of their own political, class and gender privileges in the name of egalitarianism.

Philemon

Following the division drawn between texts of advocacy and texts of contestation in the face of political economy in colonialism, Callahan contrasts the values and practices that mark both sets of texts. On the side of advancement, the system of exploitation is promoted: a myth of 'radical alterity' – a dialectical structure involving the 'superordinate' colonial self over against the 'subordinate' colonial other; a rhetoric of entitlement – an authoritarian stance demanding obedience from the other and yielding a discourse of rights; and recourse to coercion – the use or threat of violence against the colonial other in order to secure compliance and defend rights. On the side of opposition, agency without exploitation is promoted: a call for 'solidarity'; a rhetoric of indebtedness, producing a discourse of justice; and recourse to persuasion.

From his own anti-colonialist perspective, it is this latter programme that Callahan finds at work in the Letter to Philemon. In effect, the Paul that stands behind Philemon is viewed as an 'organizer' of 'Jesus-communities' in the Greek-speaking eastern Mediterranean, who, in the face of a situation involving a rupture among members, adopts a strategy embodying anti-colonial values and practices toward its resolution. This dispute, Callahan argues, has nothing to do with slavery: Onesimus and Philemon stand to one another not as slave and master but as blood brothers who have fallen apart. Consequently, Paul's attempt at reconciliation does not address in any way the issue of slavery within the Christian community but the status of two brothers as colleagues in the gospel. Such reconciliation, moreover, is grounded on a solidarity of love, a rhetoric of relationship and intimacy among those working together in the project of the gospel, and a recourse to appeals and commendations.

Hebrews

The relationship between the Christian community and the Roman Empire does not figure very prominently in Punt, nor do relations within the community itself. The discussion centres rather on the character and objective of Hebrews – an anonymous Christian homily, bearing epistolary features, dated to the second generation of Christianity but with a post-70 CE date left open – as a diasporic and hybrid text.

Hebrews, Punt argues, offers a representation of Jesus, in the light of Jewish tradition in general and the Moses tradition in particular, as the 'great high priest' who inaugurates a new covenant through his death and resurrection. Toward this end, he continues, Hebrews draws, in 'syncretistic' fashion, on a great variety of religious and philosophical traditions, from the Hellenistic to the Jewish to the early Christian. In the process, these traditions are reappropriated and redeployed with a different goal in mind: to assist believers – described as

'Hellenistic-oriented' and 'dissenting-Hebrew' Christians – in overcoming 'the stranglehold of past traditions' and adjusting to 'fresh movements of God in a fast-changing world'. For Punt, therefore, Hebrews offers, in the face of a Christian life seen as profoundly diasporic, a hybrid contemporization of belief in Jesus as Son of God for its day and age. Such a version of the gospel, Punt concludes, constitutes a call to 'persistent, unwavering faith', conveyed not in 'traditional garb' but in a 'with-it' translation understandable to and relevant for its addressees.

In sum, from the point of view of Punt's own diasporic location and hybrid perspective, Hebrews emerges as an exercise in contextual theology in which the 'Christ-event' undergoes creative reformulation, given new developments in the situation of the Christian community, by drawing upon multiple resources from such a situation – a hybrid response to a diasporic Christian life.

James

At the heart of the community problematic behind James, which involves a fundamental disagreement regarding the relationship between community and empire, lies, according to Ringe, a 'distortion' of Pauline theology whereby the elements of faith and ethics, inseparable in Paul, have been divorced from one another. This separation has come about as a result of surrender to the attraction of imperial ideology and its values (competition, domination) and has led, in turn, to the loss of individual and community integrity. More pointedly, such adoption of 'alien' values has brought about a fissure in the community especially along class lines, as community members who have prospered under the imperial system mistreat, in keeping with the values of the system, other members below them in wealth and power. In response, James – a pseudony-mous letter from the turn of the first century CE – offers a 'corrective' affirming, in line with Paul, the coherence of faith and ethics. For James, the community, a 'diasporic' people (literal or metaphorical) under political domination from the outside, stands in danger of cultural domination from the outside as well. Consequently, Ringe argues, James sets before them a fundamental choice between the wisdom of God and the wisdom of the world, in which there can be no separation between belief and conduct. Thus, to belong to the community means to place faith and action under the values of God and against the values of the world, so that the Christian life emerges as a 'radical alternative' marked by faith in Jesus and a love grounded in acts of justice, following the teachings of Jesus.

What such Christian life entails in detail is fleshed out through analysis of the letter's economic, linguistic and ideological vision. In terms of economics, over against the imperial message of prosperity, James underscores the fragility of wealth and points to God as the sole source of true security. With respect to the Christian community, the letter challenges any attitude toward wealth in league with the imperial project: favouritism toward the rich is decried, God's 'option for the poor' is upheld, and the wealthy are accused of oppression. In terms of discourse, over against imperial manipulation of language in the service of domination, James emphasizes the crucial role of language in an integrated life of faith. With the Christian community in mind, the letter urges a use of language contrary to that of the imperial project: in the interest of cohesion and wholeness, matched by correspondence in action, and avoiding competition for honour and status. In terms of ideology, over against imperial imposition of unity and pursuit of greed and competition, James proposes single-minded devotion to the wisdom of God. With respect to the Christian community, the letter calls for unity and values at variance with the imperial project: personal and social integrity at all levels in terms of faith and ethics as defined by God and proclaimed by Jesus.

1 Peter

As a writing that classifies its addressees as 'resident aliens', locates them in a province of the Roman Empire (Asia Minor), and describes them as 'marginalized' and subject to 'harassment' and 'suffering', Schüssler Fiorenza sees 1 Peter as a text that 'invites' postcolonial or decolonizing interpretation. Such interpretation, following the fourfold method outlined for critical feminist postcolonial analysis, sets out to contrast the rhetorical stance adopted by the author and the rhetorical stance open to other voices in light of the socio-religious situation common to all within the context of the Roman Empire and its kyriarchal system of domination – a situation involving, therefore, the religio-cultural world as well as the socio-political order. The end result is a view of the letter as in fundamental alliance, given its position of limited accommodation to empire, with the ethos of kyriarchal domination.

The context shared by author and addressees is portrayed in sharp colonial–imperial terms. Thus, 1 Peter is described as a circular letter sent from colonial subjects living in Rome, at the centre of empire ('Babylon'), to colonial subjects living in Asia Minor (Pontus, Galatia, Cappadocia, Asia, Bithynia), whether such territories are understood as geographical areas or, more probably, actual provinces. Further, all colonial subjects in question, inscribed sender and recipients alike, are identified as self-consciously within diaspora Judaism, including the large numbers of Gentile converts likely present in their ranks. These two designations prove crucial for the demarcation of the situation in common. First, as colonial subjects, the inscribed recipients form part of a region, Asia Minor, long marked by imperial domination: to begin with, as a result of Hellenistic colonization of the local kingdoms, which introduced Hellenistic social and cultural institutions; then, by way of Roman colonization of the Hellenized kingdoms, which readily conformed such institutions to the norms of Roman society and culture. This pattern of domination brought about a profound social division: on the one hand, an aristocratic upper class and a new middle class made up of colonial settlers and Hellenized elites; on the other, the working and lower classes consisting of the masses of indigenous peoples. Within such a context, the privileged classes, propertied and educated, functioned as guarantors of unity and stability in the empire. Second, as diasporic Jews, the inscribed recipients, who would otherwise have formed part of the settler middle class, stood out by virtue of their lifestyle, their religion and their history of resistance against Rome.

As a communication between colonial subjects of the Jewish diaspora, Schüssler Fiorenza argues, 1 Peter keenly reflects such status. Thus, the inscribed recipients are characterized as follows: 'transients' ('migrants', 'foreigners') – exiles away from home; 'resident aliens' ('noncitizens', 'settlers', 'colonials') – second-class citizens subject to social and cultural exclusion as well as exposed to suspicion and hostility. Such status readily accounts, in turn, for their representation as suffering and marginalized. Indeed, as colonial subjects and diasporic Jews, such status, Schüssler Fiorenza adds, would have been greatly impacted upon, in the aftermath of the Roman–Jewish War, by their designation as 'messianic' Jews (*christianoi*) – 'revolutionary messianists undermining the dominant society'.

Against this backdrop, then, the inscribed author is said to send, invoking both Petrine (directly, by way of authorship) and Pauline (indirectly, by way of genre) authority, a 'letter of advice and admonition' to messianic Jewish communities of Asia Minor in which an overall rhetorical strategy of 'good conduct and sub-ordination' is urged upon the inscribed recipients. In so doing, the author portrays the communities in exalted terms of divine election and love (a royal priesthood, a holy nation, a temple of the spirit). The author further addresses them as both 'household of God', in which God stands as the paterfamilias and father of Jesus Christ and they as his 'obedient children' and 'brotherhood' (gender inclusive), among whom an ethic of love toward insiders and a code of honour toward outsiders are to prevail. These two designations prove essential to a delineation of the rhetorical stance deployed. First, in the course of Hellenistic and Roman colonization, a discourse of household management unfolds in Asia Minor (and the Mediterranean as a whole) in which the stability of the 'household' emerges as crucial to that of the empire. Such stability, centred in the leading social classes, worked to counteract egalitarian tendencies within Graeco-Roman society and involved 'ethical mitigation' of the absolute power of the paterfamilias through an ethos of fidelity, cooperation and proper relations based on fear and love. Second, within this context, the term 'brotherhood' was appropriated by religious and political associations (such as *collegia* and mystery cults) to convey, in contrast to the household, an ethos of collegiality and solidarity. As such, these associations were regarded as problematic to imperial stability and kept under close watch.

In describing the Christian communities along the lines of 'household of God' and 'brotherhood', Schüssler Fiorenza argues, the inscribed author imports a colonial–imperial model of governance and conduct. In the face of ongoing exclusion and harassment, the communities are urged to show, at once, 'honourable behaviour' toward all outside (slave wo/men are to endure harsh treatment from their masters in patient suffering, freeborn wives are to persevere in the conversion of their husbands, all messianists are to obey the authorities and the emperor) and 'constant love' toward all inside (unity of spirit, mutual sympathy, brotherly/sisterly love, compassion, humble minded-ness). To promote this twofold goal, the author marshalls a three-pronged argumentative strategy: (1) suffering, presented as a way of life inseparable, given the example of Jesus the Messiah, from being Christian and doing good – a theological interpretation along moralizing or naturalizing lines; (2) election and honour, offered as a way of dealing with social disgrace through engagement, following the example of Christ, in honourable conduct – a theological borrowing of the cultural ethos; and (3) subordination, advanced as a call for submission within and without the community, with special emphasis on freeborn women and wo/men slaves – a theological adoption of the rhetoric of subjection. Consequently, Schüssler Fiorenza concludes, 1 Peter represents a 'Christianizing' of the kyriarchal system of domination in light of the adverse socio-religious situation. In effect, a stance of limited accommodation to empire in the face of hostility from the world – in the end, a decidedly colonizing rather than anticolonial stance.

2 Peter

The problematic at play behind 2 Peter – classified as a pseudonymous work written toward the end of the first century CE – is crystallized by Briggs Kittredge as involving a fundamental questioning of Jesus' promised return among some members of the community. In response, the letter, attributed to the apostle Peter, brings together a pointed combination of generic features: in part testamentary, in which the author appeals to tradition and mounts an attack on the 'false teachers and prophets' in question as wicked and immoral; in part exhortative, in which the author appeals to Scripture for proof that God stands over the wicked in judgment. Three rhetorical strategies are identified as central in such a response. First, the letter advances a monolithic model of authority and leadership, invoking the unity of tradition and the eyewitness of Peter. On the one hand, the author constructs a uniform line of tradition from the prophets, through Jesus, to the apostles; in this construction, moreover, Peter and Paul stand in unity as 'models and heroes' of the church. On the other hand, the author claims privileged authority as a witness of Jesus' transfiguration, given the restriction of this experience to three apostles. Second, the letter develops a canon of Scripture, marking certain writings in particular – among them the letters of Paul and Peter – as authoritative. Moreover, given its use of the testament form, the letter further marks itself as the end of the Petrine tradition. Third, the letter unleashes a bitter tirade against the false teachers and prophets, resorting to highly vituperative language and engaging in a dehumanization and demonization of the opposition. For Briggs Kittredge, such strategies are not without consequence.

Johannine Letters

One finds in Sugirtharajah's contribution a displacement of the 'colonial scenario' or imperial–colonial framework under investigation: from the relationship between the Christian communities and the Roman Empire to that between two segments of the community in conflict – a faction represented by the author and a faction embodied by the opposition. The one exception in this regard is his description of the author's representation of Jesus as the 'imperial Christ' – far more than the Jewish Messiah expected, indeed the 'Saviour of the world', and, as such, a new emperor in place of the Roman emperor; this insight, however, remains undeveloped. Sugirtharajah proceeds to show instead how the letters – 1 John as a circular letter; the other two as personal letters – deploy a colonizer–colonized strategy to deal with the conflict and the opposition.

Rhetorically, this strategy has recourse to a series of standard features of colonial discourse: rejection of diversity and discussion (espousal of 'unvarying and exclusive truth'), language of intolerance (branding of the opposition as 'sons of Satan' and 'antichrists') and an arsenal of hermeneutical strategies. The latter include a claim to authority as eyewitness (establishing credibility), insistence on the authenticity of the message (preserving the original message), designation of supporters as God's people (legitimizing both their power and their role as judges in theological disputes), advancing a highly exalted image of Christ (calling for total allegiance), restricting hospitality (denying food and lodging to theological dissidents) and employing flattery and threat (playing up to supporters and warning opponents). Ideologically, the strategy denies a 'voice' to the other, either speaking to them or on their behalf. Toward this end, two moves are foregrounded, both designed to maintain tight control over the community: setting up a binary opposition between the two parties (two kinds of reality) and addressing the community as children (father–child relationship).

In the end, the 'colonial scenario' is clear: a local and divided Christian community, in which the author (alongside those who stand with him) takes on the role of 'colonizer', while casting the dissidents (alongside the 'majority' who have gone over to their side) in the role of 'colonized'. At the heart of this scenario, there stands the figure of Jesus: for the 'colonizer', Jesus as the imperial Christ, with emphasis on his incarnation and sacrificial death of atonement; for the 'colonized', a human Jesus devoid of such exalted claims, hence their identification as 'antichrists'.

Jude

The situation underlying and addressed by Jude involves, according to Park, a sharp conflict between two different parties within a Christian community, its original members and newcomers from outside, revolving around the introduction by the latter among the former of a different set of beliefs and practices. This situation Park further portrays as pitting a standing local community in the Jewish-Christian tradition against a band of intruders (seemingly of Gentile extraction) in accord with Graeco-Roman culture. For Park, therefore, this is a conflict bearing strong, though indirect, imperial–colonial connotations.

As reconstructed from the letter, the outsiders, described from the outset as 'ungodly', emerge for Park as 'itinerant teachers or prophets' of the sort common in early Christianity. Their beliefs and practices are further presented as in opposition to the received apostolic tradition. Thus, they are said to deny the exclusive lordship of Jesus Christ, submitting to other lords or even demanding worship of themselves; to slander the angels; and to depict themselves, presumably on the basis of their charismatic authority, as the truly spiritual. Similarly, they are said to be marked by moral laxity and idolatrous worship and to look out only for themselves. This party Park sees as espousing 'some sort of religious and cultural assimilation' to the dominant Graeco-Roman culture. In the process, they are wreaking havoc in the community, luring followers from among the locals into their ranks. As conveyed by the letter (classified as a pseudonymous letter of exhortation written in the late first century CE), Park portrays the author as writing an urgent response, in which a variety of rhetorical strategies are deployed to counteract such developments: affirming the sole authority of Jesus as Lord and Master; providing ethical instructions for living in keeping with Jesus' lordship; warning the community, in particular those who have wandered away, about the falsehood of all such claims and the destruction forthcoming upon such intruders and their followers. Throughout, Park observes, a Jewish-Christian definition of faith and life prevails, most evident perhaps in the extended recollection of figures from the past, both disobedient angels and erring Israelites, who suffered punishment as a result of their sinful intercourse with unbelieving Gentiles.

Behind this conflict, therefore, Park posits the presence of the imperial order and the power of imperial religion. While the 'intruders' stand for accommodation, Jude urges resistance. For Jude, it is not the emperor who is 'master' and 'lord', wielder of supreme power over his subjects and head of the imperial order, but Jesus Christ, in keeping with the exclusive lordship of the God of Israel. For Jude, moreover, it is not the emperor who is divinely appointed and favoured, following the collusion of politics and religion in the empire, but Jesus Christ, in whom God has acted in history. Such a God, Jude reminds his addressees, has acted in the past, bringing judgment upon those who deviate from the true path, and will act again in the future – a note of consolation and warning.

Revelation

Despite Moore's classification of Revelation as a work of resistance against Rome, yielding a binomial opposition between existing Roman imperial rule and envisioned Christian imperial rule, the actual relationship signified by Revelation between the empire of Rome and the empire of God, and hence between Roman authority and Christian community, emerges as profoundly conflicted. At a surface level, the end result of its grand catachrestic strategy is evident. In its radical displacement and replacement of the Roman Empire by a Christian Empire, through appropriation, Revelation sets up an unyielding 'metaphysical and moral opposition' between the two imperial realms. Such separation is and must remain absolute. At a deeper level, however, a further result of such catachrestic strategy becomes evident as well. In retaining the Roman model of empire through redeployment in the Christian model of empire advanced, Revelation remains utterly dependent on Rome, reinscribing rather than opposing empire.

This conflict at the heart of Revelation Moore pursues through Bhabha's critique of dichotomization in imperial–colonial relations. First, such relations seek, through imposition, the replication of the colonizer – 'mimicry'; this goal, however, is never perfect, for the colonized is never an exact copy nor does the colonizer so desire it, lest the distinction between the two collapse, and the goal prove dangerous in the end, ever threatening to turn into parody or mockery. Mimicry, Moore argues, is 'endemic' to Revelation. While the book parodies Rome as a pale imitation of the divine realm, it is actually the divine realm that is described in terms of Rome, and thus Rome remains the ultimate authority. Second, such relations are grounded not in opposition but in simultaneous attraction and repulsion – 'ambivalence'. Revelation's utter rejection of Rome, Moore points out, is severely compromised by its imitation of Rome. Third, such relations create not a fusion of independent cultures but an in-between space in which cultures are never pure but always impure – 'hybridity'. Revelation's determination to remain distinct and pure, according to Moore, is severely compromised by the presence of the Nicolaitans, assimilationists to imperial culture, and thus impurity within. In the end, Moore concludes, the binary opposition fiercely established by Revelation emerges as fundamentally parasitic on Rome, an imitative and infiltrated Christian Empire. What thus seemed at first glance like a consummate work of resistance turns out to be, upon closer inspection, a supreme example of reinscription, in which empire and counter-empire emerge as but mirror images of one another.

Interpretive Findings and Critical Stance

Matthew
Postcolonial reading does not stop for Carter with critical analysis of the text in the light of its imperial context. Such a task calls for two further moves, similarly important and imperative. The first is not pursued in this study for reasons of space: attention to the use of Matthew in the era of Western imperial expansion, given the accompanying expansion of Christianity. The second is addressed at length: evaluation of Matthew as a production from within an imperial context in order to avoid any possible repetition of imperial concepts,

terminology or practices of the text in the contemporary world. While only the latter move is explicitly identified with church-based readers, those who look to the Gospel for 'guidance and formation', both presuppose such ecclesial context, within which Carter clearly locates himself. In this regard, given his reading of Matthew as a highly conflicted text – an 'impure subject', at once in resistance to and complicity with empire – Carter argues for a reading posture of suspicion rather than idealization.

The critical principles underlying such a posture are well outlined. First and foremost, holding both dimensions of the text together in reading, the contestation as well as the replication of Roman power. Second, employing the critique of empire offered by the Gospel against its own imperial project and practices: intimidation and coercion of the disciples into submission, expectation of a violent victory of God over all rivals, erection of privilege by means of an 'us-versus-them' division. Lastly, using a theological affirmation of the Gospel – the image of a God who is predominantly 'merciful and life-giving' to all in the present – against itself: the image of God's reign in the future as 'violent, coercive and punitive' for those outside. The practical implications of a reading from suspicion are also well delineated: examining the claim of imperial benefit, tracing any elements of coercion and destruction; questioning the claim to exclusivity in the dispensation of God's justice, looking for signs of such justice among all peoples and in all texts; examining all structures, societal and ecclesial alike, attentive to signs of exploitation; and challenging the language of empire, imagining new ways of describing God's merciful and life-giving ways.

Mark
Of the various assumptions identified by Liew as underlying his reading, two are to the point here. First, the reading of Mark advanced is described as neither positivist nor idealizing, but rather as one caught up in its own politics of time. It is a reading, therefore, that grants a complex relationship between ancient text and the reader's perspective – it denies any finding of unchanging 'truths' in Mark. Whatever 'truths' are found, Liew notes, derive from and are tied to the various locations and interests of its readers, so that Mark speaks in 'multiple voices'. Second, such a reading is said to call for interaction on the part of the reader(s). It is a reading that posits a critical relationship between ancient text and the reader's perspective – it denies any view of the 'truths' in Mark as 'timeless'. Whatever the 'truths' in question are, Liew argues, political critique is of the essence, so that Mark, and its rhetorical constructions, is always subjected to critical appraisal. In the end, however, Liew's critique of Mark remains deliberately indirect. Afraid of 'defeating [his] own postcolonial logic', seemingly by supplying a sustained response of his own, he poses, in the spirit of Jacques Lacan's psychoanalytic style, a series of questions without answers.

Luke-Acts

Burrus does not raise the issue of dialogue with or evaluation of the text as interpreted on the part of the critic. However, she does envision, in general terms, a recourse to and use of the text in the world of the twenty-first century. The character of Luke-Acts as both an anti-imperialist and a postcolonial text emerges as particularly relevant for such an exercise. The exercise itself presupposes a twofold grounding. On the one hand, a fundamental similarity between the imperial context of Rome and our imperial context of today. Thus, the political complexity and universalizing ambitions of Rome are said to resemble – in keeping with the analysis of Michael Hardt and Antonio Negri – our own 'globalizing, postmodern "neo-empire" ' much more than the imperial models of modern Europe. On the other hand, there is also an imperative of resistance to empire today. Consequently, Luke's insight into and strategy within its own imperial context stand as valuable resources for contemporary readers, given the imperial similarities and the critical mandate in question.

First of all, while the ambiguities of Luke-Acts lie beyond resolution, there is no doubt that the work does contain a distinctly anti-imperialist vein. Unfortunately, this aspect of Luke-Acts has been seriously underplayed in the scholarly literature, largely as a result of the subtlety and ambivalence of this critique. In light of Luke's keen 'attunement' to the power and project of Rome, such anti-imperialism, Burrus argues, must be surfaced in full, in all of its ambivalence and subtlety, with our own 'project of resistance' to empire in mind. Second, while a postcolonial historical approach is by no means ruled out, a literary approach sensitive to textual indeterminacy and instability brings out the nature of Luke-Acts as a ' "hybrid" novelistic' text, full of ambiguities and ambivalences. Behind these, such an approach further reveals a vigorous process of negotiation and contestation of identity at work, in the borders of cultural difference and as a result of colonial resistance. Again, in light of Luke's reading of Rome, its control and programme, such a site of 'emergent political possibilities', Burrus argues, may stand us in good stead for our project of resistance. In the end, therefore, although a critical assessment of Luke-Acts is not undertaken, it would be fair to say that Burrus holds a positive view of this text as a work of resistance within an imperial setting, indeed exemplary for contemporary readers.

John

Various working principles underlie Segovia's position on the text–reader relationship in postcolonial analysis, all coming to expression within the prolegomenon on method and theory. To begin with, in unpacking meaning and scope, two general principles are set forth: postcolonial criticism as applicable to ancient texts and modern readers alike in light of their respective imperial–colonial frameworks; postcolonial enlightenment on the part of readers as a point of departure. Further, in dealing with terrain, a third general principle is outlined: a call for combined material and cultural attention to both texts and readers. Lastly, in the section on mode, two specific principles are added regarding his own approach: it is constructivist – related in close but complex fashion to his location and agenda as reader, thus allowing for a multiplicity of other postcolonial interpretations of the Gospel; and it is interactive – demanding critical discussion and evaluation, with such dialogue extending not only to the geopolitical stance advanced with regard to the Gospel but also to other postcolonial interpretations of such a stance.

In the commentary, however, Segovia limits himself to exposition of the Gospel's geopolitical stance, with neither interaction with it nor attention to other readings and readers. This failure to pursue such dimensions of postcolonial analysis, advanced as fundamental to the task, is directly attributed to the constraints of the assignment and declared essential for the future. In a closing reflection, Segovia refers to such critical dialogue as imperative and ineluctable, especially for those who have the Gospel as a religious and ecclesial legacy, among whom he situates himself. He also goes on to posit two other pressing tasks: an ongoing nuancing and refining of the postcolonial vision constructed in the light of narrative details and close conversation with other ideological discourses (feminist, queer, minority, materialist).

Romans

There is in Elliott's contribution no explicit critical interaction with the text of Romans, so that the call for postcolonial attention to the reading of Romans within the context of present-day imperialism remains unpursued. At the same time, there is no doubt that Elliott is in profound agreement and sympathy with Paul's stance vis-à-vis Rome. This can be readily inferred from both his evaluation of the traditional interpretation of the letter in the West and his concluding observations on Rom. 13.1-7.

Thus, at present, Elliott argues, a 'fundamental ideological struggle' rages within Pauline studies regarding the interpretation of Christian origins. On one side, there is the array of traditional readings of Paul and especially Romans in highly theological terms, with three main approaches ('dogmatic–apologetic') in evidence: the soteriological (the offer of God's salvation, in the face of universal human sinfulness), the universalistic (a charter of universalism, in the face of Jewish particularism or ethnocentrism) and the sociological (defence of freedom from the law for Gentiles, in the face of Judaizing pressures). On the other side, one finds a view of Paul and Romans in highly political terms, with emphasis on the context of Rome: an imperial power marked by a military machine of enormous might and a political economy based on large-scale exploitation.

Within this battle, Elliott's option for the latter, political approach is unreserved. However, within this line of interpretation, where Romans emerges as a fully fledged oppositional text with a message against both Roman ethnocentrism in the light of the Christian communities of Rome and Roman ideology in the face of the Christian mission as a whole, Rom. 13.1-7 gives pause. This admonition of subjection to the governing authorities, Elliott readily admits, would seem to undermine beyond redemption Paul's oppositional discourse and turn his eschatological rhetoric into a flight of fancy. Such pause is but momentary. What Rom. 13.1-7 exhibits, Elliott argues, is hard realism on the part of Paul in the face of the colonial situation. As such, the text is to be read not against the binary framework of Franz Fanon (revolution or accommodation) but the everyday resistance scenario of James C. Scott (multiple acts of insubordination, including the appropriation of public symbols). In effect, Rom. 13.1-7 represents a 'survival strategy' in the face of Roman power: not a call for accommodation to empire, but a call for caution, for eschatological realism, in the defiant pursuit of the Christian message and mission.

In the end, therefore, there can be little doubt that Elliott views Paul's stance in Romans as highly relevant for today as well. Indeed, his final sentence clearly points the way in this regard: in our own contemporary striving for liberty as children of God, in a similar situation of imperial domination, the letter offers 'important guidelines'.

1 and 2 Corinthians

Horsley undertakes no critical evaluation of 1 and 2 Corinthians as interpreted. As a result, there is no direct glimpse as to how postcolonial criticism, as defined, functions today. That it is applicable, there is no question. He explicitly defines the contemporary world as a new imperial order, characterized as follows: at the base, a political economy constituted by 'multinational, global capitalism'; at work, a system whereby which the economic resources of the poorer nations are drained through the financial policies of such bodies as the World Bank or the International Monetary Fund, resulting in greater impoverishment; on guard, a 'policing' structure maintained by the power of the American military. This new order, moreover, is explicitly likened to that of Rome, both in terms of a centralized political economy and the draining of resources from subject peoples. What the reading of the Bible and the doing of biblical criticism entail in such a context emerges indirectly but forcefully. Indeed, Horsley's reading of Paul shows that he finds himself in sympathy with the counter-imperial vision projected. The evidence in this regard is substantial.

First, he argues strongly for a separation of the genuine letters from the pseudonymous letters, the radical Paul from the 'conservative' Paul. This latter Paul, brought into accommodation with the imperial order, became the 'establishment' Paul, in the light of which all the letters were read. The result was a 'subordinationist' Paul, used to argue on behalf of slavery, the subjection of women and imperial–colonial relations. Similarly, Horsley looks with favour upon the collection organized by Paul as an 'international' movement of economic resources along 'horizontal' rather than 'vertical' lines, comparing the latter in the process to the policies carried out by the World Bank or the IMF. Finally, he has no patience for the type of position espoused by the wisdom opposition at Corinth, as conveyed by Paul in 1 Corinthians. Their view of *Sophia* as the means and content of salvation, with its corresponding claims to immortality of soul and transcendent spiritual status, he characterizes as a 'personal' spirituality akin to the 'new age' spirituality of today, highly detrimental to cooperation and solidarity in the community. In the face of Rome, Horsley clearly sides with Paul's view of the crucifixion as the fulfilment of history and the end of the imperial order. In fact, he finds fault with Paul for giving in too much in language and symbols to the opposition in 2 Corinthians, in light of the evident failure of 1 Corinthians to stem the tide; in so doing, Horsley observes, Paul has moved 'halfway' toward the spiritualization of 'his gospel' evident in Colossians and Ephesians.

Galatians

At no point in his postcolonial reading of Galatians, a task involving both letter and reception history, does Wan raise the question of critical engagement; as a result, no formal position is forthcoming regarding the reader–text relationship and the responsibilities of criticism in such a project. At the same time, the commentary does offer insights into what the overall parameters of such a stance on his part might be.

Such is more clearly the case with respect to the interpretive tradition. Thus, Wan indicts the vestigial obsession with matters theological and dogmatic, with its lens of justification and its abstract approach to the crisis, to the detriment of the imperial context and its clash of narratives – the script imposed by Rome and the script offered in resistance by Jerusalem. Wan further indicts the sharp disjunction drawn between Judaism and Christianity, even within the new perspective on Paul, to the detriment of the complex discussion regarding Jewish identity in the face of empire and its narrative.

In terms of reception history, therefore, for Wan a postcolonial reading is one that seeks to move beyond prevailing theological and essentialist categories to bring out the concreteness of empire and its ramifications for ethnic identity and relations. With respect to critical findings, the situation is more opaque. On the one hand, there is no doubt that Wan favours a constructivist approach to ethnicity, whether in the present or in the past, thus tipping his hand toward the diasporic position of Paul rather than the essentialist stance of Jerusalem–Antioch. On the other hand, it remains unclear how he would ultimately come down on his evaluation of both positions as privileging 'Judaism' (howsoever conceived) vis-à-vis the 'Gentiles' within the empire, since both responses are said to constitute variations of a discursive 'imperial' narrative of its own, positing a different centre in the face of Rome. In terms of textual analysis, therefore, for Wan a postcolonial reading is one that seeks to displace stable and unchanging categories of identity construction to emphasize flux instead in all such constructions, though the extent to which such a task should be pressed remains uncertain.

Ephesians

In defining postcolonial reading as a 'critique' with liberation as aim, Bird adopts a position of active critical engagement between reader and text. For her, it is not sufficient simply to establish the political stance of a text; critical evaluation of such a stance and its ramifications must follow. This critical position she grounds in her own social location, both as a woman in a field of study dominated by men and as a Christian with an ecclesial background that includes mainstream liberalism and an intervening 'turn' in conservative fundamentalism. The driving hope behind such a critique, and hence the nature of the liberation in mind, is identified as an altogether different conception and use of power, marked by sharing-with rather than domination-over. Its ultimate goal, then, is the development of 'liberative spaces' and 'new ways of being' toward an alternative understanding of community for all. This critique is brought to bear on Ephesians and its political project of a counter-empire of God.

The critique is applied to all three dimensions of the letter analysed. In the case of the imperializing rhetorics, the evaluation is biting. With regard to the foundational reinscription of empire, not only does the portrait of the exalted and all-powerful Christ weaken the humanity of Jesus and his identification with the weak, but also the vision of the community as 'citizens' of the 'household of God' holding sway over all powers turns the oppressed into the oppressors. The status of peace and unity established by Christ among all citizens of God's household not only rides on conquest and obedience but also signifies woe to those outside. The claim to fullness and special knowledge on behalf of the community leads to escapism in the face of injustice and oppression. The consciousness of a worldwide community brings about distantiation from, as well as demonizing of, outsiders. Finally, the use of writing signifies a desire for control and subordination of the community. Second, with respect to the household codes, the evaluation is also quite harsh. On the one hand, the directives concerning wives and slaves not only import fear and control into the community but also single out those who, given their central role in the economics of the household, prove the greatest threat to the imperial order. On the other hand, the turn to somatic and bridal images to describe the relationship between ruler and ruled further imports into the community a thoroughly androcentric and patriarchal perspective. Lastly, the call to battle receives a sharp critique as well. The deployment of military imagery inscribes a sense of aggression and violence within the community.

In short, for Bird, Ephesians merely replaces one system of power and domination with another: ultimately, a counter-empire, even if spiritual and heavenly, remains an empire. As such, from the standpoint of liberation, both the letter and its critical tradition are found wanting. Both stand in need of 'liberationist subversion', therefore, if we are to move imperial ideologies and dynamics: the text, insofar as its political project reinscribes imperial power and domination and its strategy of submission to Rome in order to secure peace and avoid persecution yields indifference regarding social change; the standard interpretation, insofar as it not only fails to enter into critical engagement with the letter but also regards it as apolitical. For 'glimmers of hope' to prevail, Bird concludes, a postcolonial critique is of the essence in both respects.

Philippians
In keeping with his call for multidimensional postcolonial analysis, including what is described as the imperative need for interpretation of the texts by the children of the colonized in order to render a 'better, more complete' reading, and his own self-description as one such critic, Agosto openly acknowledges that his reading of the letter proceeds from his own experience of colonization and enters into critical interchange with the reading advanced in the light of such experience. This he does, he further explains, as a 'Latino' child of colonization – a member of a non-Western minority in the United States, born in the country of parents from the colonial possession of Puerto Rico, taken over in the course of the Spanish–American War (1898). From this Latino perspective, therefore, Agosto approaches the central points surfaced in the text and analysed in the context. In each and every case, he views the letter as highly relevant for the contemporary context of imperial domination.

The factor of prison and imprisonment opens the way to a consideration of the use of prison in modern and contemporary imperial systems of domination. For such comparative analysis, Agosto draws on figures from both the United States and Puerto Rico. The question of proper community leadership, marked by counter-imperial values of service and sacrifice, connects readily with the development of leaders from within marginalized Latino communities. Such leaders, Agosto notes, follow neither the credentials nor the expectations of the broader society. The issue of citizenship, heavenly vis-à-vis Roman, is seen as paralleling the ongoing situation of Puerto Rico. Here, Agosto points out, the extension of US citizenship has brought undeniable economic advantages as well as a keen loss of identity. Lastly, the emplacement of an underground economy among the communities of Paul in the midst of an oppressive Roman economy brings up the question of church responsibility in the midst of global capitalism and its oppressive consequences for many throughout the world. Such alternative economies, Agosto argues, while perhaps not very effective on a grand scale, signify nonetheless a much-needed and subversive approach. At this point, a brief point of criticism surfaces in Agosto: while Paul did not raise a more fundamental challenge to imperial economic oppression, in all likelihood as a result of his eschatological expectations, there is no reason why the children of the colonized should not do so today.

Colossians

Zerbe and Orevillo-Montenegro view critical interaction with texts as a central task of postcolonial analysis. Upon establishing the orientation of a text within the spectrum of promotion–opposition vis-à-vis colonialism, therefore, ideological critique is imperative. Such critique here is undertaken by way of the history of interpretation of Colossians, ultimately leading to a critical exchange with the text itself. In light of the proposed character of Colossians as a hybrid text, a text with tendencies in both directions, the authors point out both how the letter has been commonly interpreted in favour of colonialism and how it can be read in opposition to it.

The record of colonial promotion stands clear. Culturally, first of all, its advocacy of Christological absolutism has resulted in the rejection of indigenous religious beliefs and practices by the colonial missionary enterprise, a stance still in evidence today among certain pastors in the Philippines. Such absolutism, moreover, Western criticism has viewed favourably as resistance to error on the part of Paul, with no discussion of the religious and cultural issues involved. Second, socially, the letter's espousal of hierarchical order – with only a minor softening of the distinctions advanced (men are to love, parents are not to provoke children, masters are to treat slaves justly) – has placed it on the side of androcentrism, patriarchalism and classism. Such hierarchy, again, Western criticism has used to argue that Christianity favours 'transformation from within' or to conclude that Paul's legacy is one of 'fundamental conservatism', refraining from any critique whatsoever. Lastly, politically, the letter's espousal of Christological triumphalism has given way to endorsement of the ruling powers and the project of civilizing and Christianizing the subjugated, both positions in recent evidence as well in the Philippines. Such triumphalism, once again, Western criticism has approached by way of spiritualization, without concrete political reference. As a result, the authors point out, Colossians – along with the Pauline corpus as a whole – has not featured prominently in the struggle for social transformation, in the Philippines or elsewhere.

At the same time, the authors hasten to add that, while such a deconstructive reading is indispensable, an emancipatory reading is not only possible, given the letter's ambivalence, but very much in order, given the high status ascribed to the Scriptures in the Philippines. Fundamental in this regard is the contrast drawn between historical context and contemporary context: Christianity as a minority religious movement struggling to survive in the face of highly attractive alternatives; Christianity as a colonial religion, expansionist and exclusivist in nature, wedded to materialism (capitalism) and eliminating alternatives. In this light, the promotional side of Paul can be understood in historicizing fashion, while the oppositional side can be foregrounded in light of later developments and interpretations. Toward this end, a broad variety of strategic moves in reading the letter is offered, all meant to bring forth the emancipatory side of Colossians.

1 and 2 Thessalonians

Given his commitment to trace the shadow of empire in the biblical texts and the critical tradition through analysis of 'anti-imperialist' as well as 'imperialist' tendencies present in their strategies of domination and constructions of the 'other', critical dialogue emerges as imperative in Smith's contribution. Such dialogue is undertaken with the goal in mind of working toward a just world, although what this vision implies is not formally addressed.

From the discussion one can infer that at heart it involves breaking down power relations of domination, including those having to do with untoward constructions of the 'other'. Such interaction can be readily observed at work with regard to both the letters and their 'effective history' or tradition of interpretation.

Concerning interpretation, Smith points out how the scholarly tradition as well as the popular tradition 'obscure' and 'obstruct' the political thrust of the letters. On the one hand, the academic reception has been ruled, from its beginnings, by two driving representations of Paul: first, within the framework of Protestant–Catholic debates, the 'bold proclaimer' of justification by faith, against a Judaism essentialized as a 'religion of merits'; second, within the framework of Western racial discourse, the 'creator' of a 'superior' (universal) religion, against a Judaism categorized as 'inferior' (parochial). On the other hand, the popular reception has been marked, in the North Atlantic in general and the United States in particular, by a representation of Paul as a preacher of the end-times: the purveyor of a 'millennialist, Manichaean' discourse. The Thessalonian letters in particular, Smith points out, have played a significant role in this latter popular tradition, serving as the source for the belief in a coming 'rapture' and the speculation regarding the identity of the 'antichrist'. Both developments, he adds, have played a major role in the mythic identification of the US as a 'nation uniquely chosen by God'. Against such reception histories, Smith brings out the highly anti-imperial thrust of the letters, especially in terms of apocalyptic discourse.

Concerning the letters, Smith shows how, despite their strong anti-imperial stance, they remain complicit with the imperial project in the way they 'reinscribe' within the Christian 'assemblies' the 'hierarchical arrangement of social relations' in the empire. In effect, by turning to invective in the construction of the 'other', the authors deploy standard androcentric critiques in their denunciations of sexual depravity, greed and lack of discipline in the community. Thus, for example, the letters rail against ignorance of God, immorality and greed as qualities associated with outsiders. In so doing, moreover, the letters espouse an 'ethic of self-mastery' in which self-control is viewed as a masculine trait. Similarly, the letters address their readers as 'faithful military recruits' in order to set them apart from the lack of order and discipline that mark those outside. Consequently, Smith concludes, the letters reveal an 'internal rhetoric of othering' based on the imperial 'rhetoric of othering'.

In sum, from the point of view of creating a just world, the letters emerge as highly ambiguous texts: obscured by the shadow of empire in their histories of reception in the West, exhibiting strong anti-imperial impulses in the face of empire, and betraying strong imperial impulses in its own strategies of domination and construction of the other. Yet, such analysis is precisely what is needed: examination of power relations 'wherever they exist'.

Pastoral Letters

In keeping with his definition of postcolonial criticism as contestatory of power and hierarchy in imperial settings as well as his sustained attention to texts and interpretations, Broadbent engages in sharp critical dialogue with both the letters and the critical tradition. This interaction is pursued throughout. With regard to the Pastorals, he argues that the strategy of accommodation should be seen as directly related to the gender and class interests of the wealthy male elites in the Christian communities, for whom the emulation of 'the hierarchical rules of empire' prove most beneficial. With regard to criticism, he consistently exposes the geopolitical links at work between 'subsequent interpreters' and 'modern imperial projects', most particularly in the British context, in their sustained identification with and espousal of the strategy of imperial accommodation advocated by the Pastorals, all in support of the imperial project as 'beneficial to its imperial subjects'. Such interaction finds its sharpest moment in his concluding reflections. In the case of the critical tradition, such espousal of power and hierarchy, he observes, has had untold consequences for the native subjects of empire, for women and slaves, and for the poor working classes at the heart of empire. In the case of the Pastorals, he wonders, whether the proper path to follow should be removal from the canon or preservation with full consciousness of their 'internal flaws' and conservative reception.

Philemon

Callahan's project of a postcolonial reading of anti-colonialist orientation, grounded as it is in a problematization of the colonial legacy in the United States and calling as it does for evaluation in terms of advancement of, or opposition to, the colonialist project, clearly calls for critical dialogue for texts produced in colonial contexts. Such interchange he does not pursue with the Letter to Philemon as interpreted, since he finds it in full accord with the programme of contestation that he himself favours. Such critique he does undertake, however, with respect to the sustained and systematic interpretation of the letter as the 'Pauline mandate' for the justification and preservation of slavery as the mode of production in colonialism from Christian antiquity (John Chrysostom) through Western Christendom (Cotton Mather and Alonso de Sandoval) to biblical criticism (*The Oxford Annotated Bible*). According to this interpretation, Onesimus is a runaway slave whom Paul returns to his master, Philemon, with an appeal for reconciliation; thus, in effect, not only did Paul not question the power relation of slavery but he actually stood for the obedience of slaves to their masters. This line of interpretation Callahan characterizes as 'colonialist' throughout and rejects, aligning himself squarely in the process with those African American slaves who reacted to this reading in anti-colonialist fashion. In contrast to predominant Christian tradition, therefore, Callahan draws up a dissenting tradition: from Paul, to slave interpretations, to his own version.

Hebrews

Various central features ascribed to postcolonial analysis by Punt establish a basic need for critical dialogue with the text: from its deconstructive side, the surfacing of political–textual collusion and the quest for voices silenced or misrepresented; from the constructive side, the emphasis on diversity and the local; from the postmodernist side, the foregrounding of contextualization and construction in criticism. Other features advanced by way of contrast to colonial analysis heighten the need for such dialogue: the call for accountability; the stress on polyphonic hermeneutics; the search for liberating strategies of interdependence; and, above all, the promotion of geopolitical liberation. This interaction Punt carries out by analysing the manifold ramifications of the diasporic-hybrid exercise in contextual theology unveiled in Hebrews through the lens of the ten theological strategies deployed by the letter. Such interaction is ultimately grounded on a contextualization model like that attributed to Hebrews: to render the 'gospel message', and certainly Hebrews itself, comprehensible to and relevant for this day and age.

As he proceeds through the different theological topics, Punt offers an ongoing critique of these strategies from a variety of perspectives: former and ongoing projects of colonization, past and present collusion of Christianity in colonization, the contemporary situation of globalization and its untoward consequences for so many, the postcolonial conditions of his own African continent. In every instance such critique is offered with the goal of liberation in mind, in all of its various aspects. In the process, the highly commendable exercise in contextual theology offered by Hebrews is shown to have a highly objectionable underside as well. Thus, while Hebrews is found to offer a 'valuable perspective' on the need for continuous reinterpretation of Jesus Christ, it is also found to be implicated in 'imperialist endeavours', both within its own historical context and by way of its 'reception history' in other contexts of Christianity. From the perspective of 'Christian faith in the third millennium', Punt concludes, postcolonial criticism can and does offer a 'valuable hermeneutical strategy' for surfacing hegemonic complicity as well as liberating strands in the biblical texts.

James

Ringe's description of the postcolonial voice and of postcolonial analysis as resistance to imperial domination entails critical engagement with the text: both the biblical text and its history of interpretation. Here such engagement proceeds by way of the dominant tradition of reading James rather than the letter itself, since Ringe finds herself in fundamental agreement with the vision of James, once removed from the governing ambit of its interpretation. In effect, Ringe argues, in accord with Elsa Tamez, James has been 'intercepted' by its reception history: its postcolonial voice of opposition to empire in its context has been 'colonized' by ecclesial and theological elites – given their captivity to the 'doctrinal norm' of Paul in Romans; by secular and other authorities – in light of their rejection of the letter's social and economic vision; and by the critical tradition – given its exclusive focus on historical questions and its dismissal of the letter's theological value. Thus, Ringe's postcolonial reading of James recovers, or liberates, the postcolonial voice of James: an author who is not opposed to Paul as such but to a distortion of Paul and who advances, grounded in the union of faith and ethics, both a radical critique of imperial reality and values and a substitute reality and values in Jesus. In so doing, Ringe affirms, the author calls on the 'moral authority' of James and the traditions of Jesus himself, thus embodying 'the core of the gospel' in the face of impe-rial domination and community surrender. Ultimately, this oppositional voice of James, with its deployment of the 'inherently destabilizing values' of the gospel, is regarded as central to any situation of empire, including the present, in which she herself stands together with James.

1 Peter

As called for by the objectives and mechanics of postcolonial feminist biblical interpretation, Schüssler Fiorenza undertakes a critical analysis of the rhetorical stance – the rhetorical strategies and power relations inscribed – adopted by the inscribed author of 1 Peter in light of the socio-religious situation unveiled. In so doing, as further called for by her project, she pursues as well a critical analysis of the 'malestream' tradition of interpretation regarding the letter. In both respects the critique is quite sharp: with regard to the letter, because of its colonizing rhetorical strategy – its Christianization of the ethos of kyriarchal imperial domination; and with regard to scholarship, because of its historicizing and objectivist stance, which results in continued colonization – its implicit identification with the rhetorical strategy of the letter and legitimation of its kyriarchal relations of power and dominance. For this twofold critique, the fundamental point of departure lies in imagining a different rhetorical stance than that of the inscribed author within the common socio-religious situation identified.

What is required, Schüssler Fiorenza proposes, is an interpretation 'against the grain', going against the hegemonic rhetorical project of the letter and bring-ing to the surface voices submerged by such a project. The proposed counter-interpretation seeks to construct a historical consciousness of resistance and to give voice to the argumentative strategies of such resistance on the part of the submerged. In other words, to conceive of an alternative response to the situation of suffering and marginalization on the part of the communities – messianists, freeborn wives and slave wo/men. Its lines are clearly drawn. Such a response would have opposed the accommodation to the kyriarchal order urged by the inscribed author and entertained instead – along the lines of the vision supplied in the pre-Pauline fragment of 2 Corinthians 6.14–7.1 – separation from Gentile society and resistance to imperial culture. Such separatism would have been seen as in order given their radical change in status (from 'migrants' and 'resident aliens' to the lofty titles of 'royal priesthood', 'holy nation' and 'temple of the Spirit') and as a means of reducing harassment and exclusion. Such a response would have argued for just treatment rather than patient suffering on the part of slave wo/men and for running away in case of harsh treatment, for divorce on the part of freeborn wives in case of failure to convert their husbands, and for no obeisance to Roman authorities on the part of all messianists. In the end, Schüssler Fiorenza adds, the accommodationist proposal advanced by the inscribed author might be seen as coming from the 'owner and patron' class of the Christian community based in the metropolis, whose interests were perceived as undermined by such a possible emancipatory vision arising from the inscribed recipients in the provinces.

For Schüssler Fiorenza, moreover, foregrounding such tensions within the Christian communities and searching for submerged voices and visions behind 1 Peter further constitutes an exercise in resistance and emancipation in the face of malestream interpretation – a tradition that not only makes no distinction between the hegemonic strategy of the author and other possible strategies of dissidence within the community but also further marginalizes the voices of dissidence in contemporary scholarship. In the end, this hegemonic tradition of interpretation ends up aligning, by commission or omission, with the kyriarchal system of domination as envisioned by 1 Peter and opposing a radical democratic equality as envisioned by critical feminist postcolonial interpretation.

2 Peter

Quite in keeping with her description of postcolonial analysis as from below and contestatory, characteristics shared with feminist criticism, Briggs Kittredge enters into critical dialogue with the rhetorical strategies uncovered in 2 Peter and critical interpretations of such strategies. Such interchange is given a further grounding as well: insofar as these strategies form part of Scripture and are received as such by the Christian community, their influence remains significant at all times and hence their ramifications must be carefully scrutinized. This she does, quite explicitly, as a member of a Christian community for whom the text holds – in the light of its canonical status, its liturgical use and its history of interpretation – 'special status and authority'.

With regard to the uniform model of tradition and authority laid out, while traditional theologians and critics might tend to identify with its élan and its leaders, feminist criticism emphasizes its omission of women's leadership and advances instead an alternative model involving conflict between a 'male authority' tradition and a 'spirit/prophecy' tradition. Such reconstruction of historical models leads, Briggs Kittredge argues, to a variety of theological options: identification with silenced voices, formulation of new theological positions, abandonment of constructs involving an idealized past. Such concerns regarding the search and usage of the past, she adds, apply to postcolonial criticism as well. With respect to the demarcation of a scriptural canon, feminist criticism emphasizes instead the liberation of women and marginalized groups. Together, Briggs Kittredge points out, both criticisms reject the canons imposed on them and struggle to develop their own voices. In particular, postcolonial critics have questioned the very idea of a canon as such, arguing instead for parallel reading of canons from diverse religions. With regard to the use of polemics, Briggs Kittredge asserts, while mainstream scholars have sought to interpret such language in historical context, feminist as well as postcolonial critics question the very use of 'othering' language in light of their own experience at the hands of the dominant. In sum, the rhetorical strategy of 2 Peter regarding authority, canonicity and demonization prove clearly unacceptable for feminist as well as postcolonial criticism.

Johannine Letters

Given his view of postcolonial criticism as oppositional and committed, Sugirtharajah stands resolutely for critical interaction with the text. Moreover, given his view of postcolonial criticism as expansive in scope, such interaction applies in principle as well to the history of interpretation as well as to any texts invoked in contrapuntal reading. This latter dimension is in evidence but briefly, when he paints the Western critical tradition as engaged in a 'hermeneutics of denial', following the 'eurocentric habit' of looking only toward the Jewish and Hellenistic milieux of the Christian writings in general and the Johannine writings in particular. The interaction envisioned proceeds in various ways.

- First, through a sustained critical exposé of the colonial rhetorical and ideological components of the letters.
- Second, by way of recurrent references to the presence of such devices in recent times: the invocation of the term 'axis of evil' by US President George W. Bush (language of intolerance); the subjugation of countries and cultures in the name of an imperial Christ (exalted images of Jesus); the use of famine as a weapon against opponents (denial of hospitality); political and religious division of the world into 'with us' and 'against us' today (reliance on flattery and threat); wide appeal to dualistic thinking in the contemporary world (construction of binary opposition).
- Third, through a contrapuntal reading based on the postcolonial rhetorical and ideological components of the letters, all related to the influence of Buddhist religious thought: discovery of a 'Buddhized' concept of God

(made present only in the exercise of human love); evaluation of the concept of love as restricted (in light of a Buddhist love that encompasses all creation and extends to the unliked); parallel insistence on ethical involvement (a search for truth, justice and love).

- Finally, and most explicitly, in a concluding evaluation of the letters as ambivalent, given the mixture of 'imperial intentions' and 'praxiological impulses'. On the one hand, Sugirtharajah finds in the letters highly objectionable features: a project of colonization on the part of a self-appointed chosen people of God involving hegemonic control of truth and manipulation of power. On the other hand, he points to highly redeeming features as well: a hybridized religious tradition, against any claim of isolation and purity, and a joint display of theorizing and involvement, against any bypassing of ethico-political engagement. There is no doubt, therefore, where Sugirtharajah stands on this score: against any and all 'imperial intentions'. There is no doubt either as to where he sees politics and religion going: toward bifurcation of the world into good and evil.

Jude

Without question, Park's project of reading for decolonization calls for critical interaction with texts, especially given the collusion posited between the political and the religious in imperial–colonial frameworks. Such dialogue is pursued with the goal in mind of developing 'alternative ways of thinking and acting' in order to 'reorder' views of the past, the present and the future 'among colonial and postcolonial subjects', so that the call of God can pierce the layer of imperial domination. Thus, Park places his project as in continuity with the efforts of both *Minjung* Christian theology and *Minjung* Buddhist activism in Korea, in the 1970s and 1980s respectively. Such interaction with Jude reveals a twofold result: fundamental acceptance of the community situation as advanced by the letter and corresponding identification with its author's rhetorical strategy and ideological position over against the 'intruders'.

Toward this end, Park draws upon the imagery and moral of a sermon by Jung Young Lee, a Korean theologian, with a twofold story of marginalization and dominance – at the level of narration and at the level of recollection – involving the unwanted presence of a dandelion. The story itself is straightforward. At the level of narration, removal of a dandelion leads to reflection on marginalization, in which Lee identifies himself with the dandelion, and then a decision to let it multiply, as one of God's creatures in God's world. At the level of recollection, a dandelion is plucked from a lawn by the landowner so that grass can spread evenly throughout, decides upon coming back to suppress its identity and become like the grass, and in the end, highly frustrated, resolves to show its identity again. The moral is also straightforward: the marginalized are part of God's creation and should be allowed to flourish in God's world. In applying the sermon to the community situation behind Jude, Park turns the story of the dandelion into an allegory: in the face of relentless pressure from 'intruders' in league with dominant Graeco-Roman culture – the expansive green grass, under the ultimate power and authority of the Roman emperor – the landowner, a Jewish-Christian community in possession of traditional Christian beliefs and practices does belong to and should grow in God's world – the unwanted yellow dandelion.

In the end, such outright identification with the argumentative strategy and political stance of the letter yields Park's own attitude toward politico-religious collusion in imperial–colonial frameworks: resistance to domination and subordination through liberation of cultic space from the exploitation of colonization; affirmation of God's presence in the world and of existence for all in God's world; and looking out for others rather than oneself.

Revelation

There is in Moore's contribution no explicit grounding or call for critical conversation with the text within the task of postcolonial criticism. Yet, behind his analysis of the relations of Revelation to empire, a definite though subdued critique can be discerned. This critique surfaces straightaway in the introduction, when, in opening up a space for postcolonial criticism, he notes that the proposed focus on empire is by no means a 'novel gesture' in the scholarly literature. On the one hand, traditional scholarship has read the book as 'the most uncompromising attack' on both Rome and collusion with Rome; on the other hand, liberation critics have not only placed empire at the centre of their reading but also have used the book as a tool against ancient and contemporary empires. Both positions will be ultimately called into question by Moore's postcolonial reading à la Bhabha. The critique reappears in the discussion regarding the concept of ambivalence and its relevance for Revelation. This relation of simultaneous repulsion and attraction, Moore observes, is evident in the book's duplication of the Roman imperial ethos in its own proposed Christian imperial ethos. Through such absorption of its antithetical opposition, he adds, Revelation foreshadows the turning of Christianity into Rome in the Constantinian and post-Constantinian periods. Again, both the traditionalist and liberationist positions are profoundly called into question thereby. As an attack on Rome and a foundation for an attack on all imperial–colonial frameworks, Revelation, Moore would counter, is severely flawed.

The critique comes to a climax in the concluding reflections on Revelation as a 'Book of Empire'. First, it is given unreserved expression. In Constantinian Christianity, Moore declares, the parasitic inversion of the Roman Empire in the Christian empire comes to actual historical expression, a 'monstrosity' beyond the imagination of the seer yet in line with the work's fatal flaw: an empire that is both 'Roman and Christian at one and the same time'. Further, it is expanded to encompass the whole of Christian theology. Any construction of God or Christ, Moore comments, that draws on imperial ideology does not shatter imperial rule but rather reproduces it on a transcendental plane: it is not a discourse of resistance, except as a move of 'strategic essentialism' in the face of a desperate situation, but rather of reinscription. Yet, the lack of non-imperial terms and concepts in contemporary Christian theology pointedly shows the profound impact of such ideology on Christian imagination. Thus, Moore concludes, for Christian theology to be 'intellectually as well as ethically adequate', it stands in need of what Revelation cannot provide: a construction of the divine realm 'as empire writ large'. In the end, therefore, not only is the interpretive tradition of Revelation indicted, traditionalist and liberationist alike, but also all of Christian theology. Presumably, Moore would invoke such a criterion of evaluation in all postcolonial biblical criticism.

Concluding Comment

The preceding comparative analysis reveals that, behind what I characterized in the introduction as a collection of incredible breadth and immense richness, lies a complex site of contending definitions and contrasting paths, varying findings and diverging encounters. Indeed, in all four fundamental areas of discussion, from configurations through approaches and findings to stances, the volume provides a comprehensive and decisive spectrum of opinion, which can serve as a most adequate critical framework not only for the examination of any and all previous work but also for the pursuit of any and all future work in postcolonial biblical criticism. In conclusion, therefore, I find it most proper to reiterate my description of the project as a landmark achievement, providing a lens with which to organize and scrutinize the past as well as to inform and guide the future.

THE GOSPEL OF MATTHEW

Warren Carter

Is a postcolonial reading of Matthew possible, and, if so, what might it contribute? I begin by addressing this question and elaborating some perspectives and critical sensibilities of postcolonial reading. I then sketch the nexus of power relationships and societal structures of the Roman imperial world that the Gospel of Matthew is enmeshed in, emerges from, contests and in some ways imitates. In relation to this perspective and context, I examine the Gospel's plot and characters and main theological claims. I conclude with a brief consideration of some of the challenges that postcolonial inquiry might present for reading Matthew in contemporary (Western) ecclesial contexts.

Postcolonial Perspectives

Are the reading perspectives or 'optic' that the term 'postcolonial' betokens applicable to Matthew's Gospel? The starting point concerns the much-debated meaning of 'post'. The prefixed preposition reflects the location of much contemporary discussion that wrestles with the continuing legacy of post-Enlightenment, European colonialism, the post-1940s period of 'decolonization' or the official relinquishing of formal control by the colonial power, the emergence of 'independent' nations and the rise of newer forms of global economic and cultural imperialism (often called 'neocolonialism').

Matthew clearly does not belong to this world in which the once colonized now confront their colonial legacy of silenced voices and (mis)represented identities. It is a first-century text, and its world is dominated by Roman imperial power. There is no chronological sequence comprising the 'once' of Roman domination and the complex 'now' of liberation. Moreover, Matthew is not a 'centrist' or Western text that originates with the powerful and that performs their tasks of creating representations of the other, with which postcolonial work has been so concerned.

Further, the world from which Matthew originates, probably centred on Antioch in Syria, is not only not 'post-colonial' (in a chronological sense), it is not even colonial if the term is understood as the 'implanting of settlements on foreign territory'. In the Roman world, the term 'colonial', at least in its most basic meaning, refers to one of Rome's numerous ways of spreading its influence, namely, by establishing '*colonia*' or settlements of retired soldiers in territory that it controlled. In Syria, Rome established *colonia* of veterans, for instance, at Berytus, Heliopolis and Ptolemais. While Rome stationed legions in Antioch and recruited from the local population, it did not establish *colonia* in Antioch (though the emperor Caracalla conferred the status of 'colony' on Antioch in 212 CE). Matthew's world is not colonial in this sense.

But is it imperial? Some have argued that imperialism, understood particularly in exploitative economic terms as 'the highest stage of capitalism' (Lenin), is not an applicable term for Rome's world, since Rome did not enact the systematic, state-administered exploitation of resources for economic gain evidenced by nineteenth- and twentieth-century capitalist empires. The term 'imperialism' would, then, be anachronistic for Rome's world.

This line of thinking, though, has some obvious difficulties. Imperialism, 'the practice, the theory, and the attitudes of a dominating metropolitan center ruling a distant territory', to use Edward Said's definition (1993: 9), has taken different forms and motivations in human history. To declare one expression (nineteenth-century capitalism) to be the normative form by which to assess – and invalidate – all other expressions fails because of the arbitrary nature of the exercise. While Rome was not a nineteenth-century capitalist empire, its elite certainly knew numerous ways of being a 'dominating metropolitan center', including gaining economic benefit from patron–client relations and involvement in trade, investment, control of land, slave labour, taxes and rents.

If the term 'postcolonial' is understood, then, in very literal ways, it is not appropriate for Matthew's Gospel. The term, however, connotes much more expansive understandings that suggest postcolonial perspectives offer important strategies for engaging Matthew's Gospel. Postcolonial scholarship often understands 'postcolonial' to embrace the investigation of the whole of the imperializing experience in its diverse forms from its imposition to its aftermath. Central to these imperial situations is the experience of 'power over', the power of one group dominating another in numerous arenas. Postcolonialist inquiry, then, concerns primarily not a temporal focus nor a chronological sequence nor a solitary means of exerting control, but a critical investigation that centres on much more extensive and complex issues, namely, the means, dynamics, impact and legacy of imperialization, especially the diverse textual and cultural expressions that emerge from imperial contexts. Matthew is such an expression, the product of the interaction of imperial culture and local cultural experience and practices. It expresses a silenced provincial, a voice on the margins who contests and embraces Roman power.

Three dimensions of this investigation of imperial social formation and cultural production are especially applicable to Matthew. Since Matthew originates in the world of Roman power, one area involves an examination of the interaction between the Gospel and the empire as evidenced by the

Gospel (sections 2–4 below). Postcolonial interpretation of this Gospel places the reality of imperialization at its centre, understanding Matthew to be a text that emerges from a particular context of subordination as the discourse of a subjugated, imperialized person (and group?) who 'writes back' to challenge Roman power. The Gospel offers the contingency of lived imperial experience on the margins, attesting both modes of subjugation and modes of resistance in an oppositional yet co-opted text.

Second, since the expansion of Christianity often accompanied (and sanctioned) the worldwide imperial expansion of various European powers in the eighteenth and nineteenth centuries, postcolonial perspectives would also investigate the Gospel's role in recent imperialism and its aftermath. This investigation may well uncover interpretations of Matthew that legitimate (for example, the influence of the worldwide mission in 28.18-20) as well as resist imperialization. (Space limitations prevent discussion of this dimension here.)

Third, contemporary readers in ecclesial contexts who engage the Gospel for guidance and formation must carefully and critically evaluate this text that emerges from imperial circumstances so as not to perpetuate imperial practices, mindset and language (section 5 below). The second and third areas represent the phenomenon whereby a text emerging from, yet protesting, contexts of subordination becomes a means of effecting subordination.

In relation to investigation of the first dimension (Matthew and Roman power), the Gospel's origin among the subordinated and marginalized offers some promising insight. Since imperialism often masks its imposition of far-reaching control, disguises the tyrannical nature of its power relations, and silences local and dissenting voices, postcolonial perspectives have the task of unmasking and revealing the various means by which this imperial control takes effect. The ruling power, usually centred in an urban context, asserts its superior power over local populations and land (and sea) in diverse ways to gain control of minds, bodies, resources, societal interactions, cultural expressions, institutions, media, the past and future, and so forth. The central and minority elite benefits at the expense of the marginalized non-elite in the dispersed geographical regions. At the heart of postcolonial discussion is consideration of the experience, strategies and effects of power – political, economic, societal, cultural, religious, military. This analysis of the means by which power is exerted, control disguised and wealth extracted from the subordinated unveils the exploitation and oppression that comprise the long-lasting cost and destructive human face of subjugation. As the product of interaction between imperial power and local experience, Matthew depicts various aspects of the experience of subjugation.

Moreover, postcolonial perspectives are also concerned to redress the imperializer's self-focus and expedient representations of the imperialized by setting the imperialized's cultural history, experience and voices at the centre. A significant element of this task involves the various complex evaluations formulated by local populations as they, silenced by imperialization, negotiate imperial power. While resistance usually accompanies the exertion of power (Foucault), it cannot be assumed to be instantaneous, universal and/or mono-lithic. Local evaluations of imperial power include self-benefiting accommo-dation, complicity, cooperation and/or co-optation, self-protective compliance, mimicry, calculated and disguised forms of resistance (often by peasants), open protest (non-violent and violent) that directly confronts the ruling power. This 'catalogue' is not to suggest that provincials chose one means of interac-tion, but rather it is to illustrate a range of simultaneous interactions. Matthew is an oppositional text, yet it evidences complex negotiation with the imperial status quo.

The Gospel's genre – ancient biography – attests this diverse and complex negotiation. Roman biographies such as Tacitus' *Agricola* concentrated on leading figures such as emperors and generals, parading, celebrating and rein-forcing imperial values of political and military domination either for direct imitation or by censure (as often in Suetonius' *Lives*). The Gospel employs features of this genre, such as focus on a key person, his teaching and way of life. However, its celebration of the life, actions and teachings of a provincial peasant crucified by the empire employs the genre to defy and resist imperial values. Yet, it also imitates imperial values and engages in imperialistic practice by presenting his teaching in imperial language ('the good news of the empire', 4.23) and conceptualization (the coming violent universal triumph of God's reign over all opponents, 24.27-31).

The chosen genre significantly shapes the expression of opposition and accommodation. As an ancient biography, Matthew focuses on the external actions and teachings of its main character in the Roman imperial context. The Gospel, though, pays little attention to internal psychological and emotional dimensions. These latter dimensions have been prominent in some postcolonial discussions of imaginative literary texts, especially in explorations of identity and the representations of the imperializer and the imperialized (hybridiza-tion, mimicry, assimilation, agency) forged in (post)colonial contexts. Clearly, Matthew as an ancient biography does not offer access to the inner psycho-logical dimensions of characterization that have often been so important in postcolonial explorations of nineteenth- and twentieth-century novels, as well as of lived imperial experience (e.g., Fanon, Bhabha). Negotiated opposition. though, is not confined to one genre or to the private or inner sphere. This ancient text offers other dimensions, especially of the more public sphere, that require examination.

The Gospel locates Jesus' ministry in the context of Roman imperial power. Its focus on his actions, teachings and interactions, especially his conflict with the Jerusalem elite, allies of Rome, displays various dimensions of his engage-ment with, imitation yet critique of, and alternative to, imperial power and the world it creates. Similarly the Gospel's theological formulations in areas such as theology, Christology, soteriology, ecclesiology and eschatology are influenced by the imperial world, while shaping the Gospel's own imperial-imitating system of dominating power and sovereignty. The Gospel is a product of imperial power and productive of its own imperial system of power.

Such negotiations of imperialization disqualify overly simple binaries of domination and subjugation, exploitation and deprivation, power and resistance, oppression and injustice, good and bad – as apt as they often seem to be. Such simplicity is deficient not only because imperial control is experienced in different ways by groups of differing societal status (and not always as something to be resisted) but also because imperial control is effected not only through force, intimidation and spin, but also through complex and disguised means such as alliances, client-kings, interdependence, patronage, calculated benefits and self-beneficial euergetism. These strategies often benefited the subordinated in some ways, thereby mixing gift with obligation, benefits with exploitation, appreciation with resentment, complicity with coercion, enablement with dependency, to create ambivalence and ambiguity in the subordinated's experience of the dominant power. Reg, the fictional leader of the People's Front of Judaea and a staunch opponent of Roman control in the movie *Life of Brian*, expresses the ambiguity of complicity in oppositional practices by conceding (in a list that also reflects his creator's socialization) that the Romans have provided 'better sanitation, medicine, education, irrigation, public health, roads, freshwater systems, baths and public order'. Contemporary studies have noted the ambiguous roles of African mission schools that were a means of imperial control (imposing Western language/culture and silencing local languages for example) while simultaneously productive of power in providing educated leaders who articulated dissent, organized protest and subsequently led independent states.

My task, then, consists of a brief study of Matthew's Gospel as a text that is enmeshed in, emerges from, and contests, the nexus of power relationships and societal structures of the Roman imperial world. Matthew is a complex text not only because it is produced by and productive of worlds of power but also because of the ambiguities and complicities it attests in negotiating its imperial context. It mirrors imperial realities, even while it contests them. It protests imperial power, even while it imitates imperial structures, language and ways of being. It advocates an alternative identity and way of life, even while recognizing a continuing accommodated existence. It envisages the future and violent triumph of God's power and empire over Rome (24.27-31), even while it forms a community that renounces violence (5.43-44) and structures that embody 'power over' others (20.25-26). Such ambiguities reflect the pervasive hold of imperial power, the continual attempts to negotiate daily existence within it, the struggles to resist it, the Hebrew Bible and Jesus traditions evoked to sustain the engagement, and the indomitable human spirit that imagines alternative ways of being human. We should not be surprised to find such imprints on a text that is produced from the nexus of power relationships and societal structures of the Roman imperial world and that is productive of a world dominated by God's sovereignty and power pictured as the empire of God.

What is surprising is that much Matthaean scholarship has not engaged the Gospel in relation to Roman imperial power. Rather, Matthew has been read in relation to an isolated Jewish world, notably a dispute with a local synagogue community and especially its leadership. Various factors account for this restricted reading strategy that has neglected the Gospel's interaction with Roman imperial power. Spurred by the discovery of the Dead Sea Scrolls, scholarly attention in the second half of the twentieth century has often concentrated on first-century Judaisms. Graduate Schools training the next generation of scholars have perpetuated this focus, to the neglect of the Graeco-Roman world. Also influential have been twentieth-century Western notions of religion as privatized and individualized experience of a spiritual nature that is separated from socio-political dynamics and physical–material realities.

Among others, these factors have shaped a reading strategy for Matthew that views the Gospel only as a religious text, concerned only with spiritual matters and a religious dispute with another religious group, the synagogue. This limited reading strategy artificially and falsely separates the religious from the socio-political, the spiritual from the material, the individual from the societal, the synagogue building from the synagogue/Jewish community, and the Jewish community from the larger socio-political context of the Roman Empire. To fight over interpretations of Torah, for example, is to fight over claims to possess the past and envision present societal interaction and structure. To fight with the temple-based Jerusalem leaders is to fight with those who also must negotiate Roman power, allying with it to preserve their own status and power, while selectively representing traditions that are often contestive of imperial power.

To attend to the interaction between Matthew's Gospel and the Roman Empire, then, is not to ignore or dismiss the Gospel's interaction with a synagogue community. The synagogue community is equally embedded in the Roman world. One key point of interaction involves the likely conflicts with synagogue leaders. The existing evidence suggests that synagogue leaders were defined not by specialized, vocational training and skills (analogous to contemporary clergy) but within a Graeco-Roman euergetistic framework that required significant wealth, power and societal status to effect group benefaction and representation. They are not primarily religious officials with religious duties (in the modern sense), but (sub)community leaders embedded in and representative of a euergetistic and doxic society.

A further point of compatibility between the leaders and the empire occurs in that such elite roles suggest investment in maintaining the unjust societal status quo and the elite's 'power over' vision of society. To conflict with synagogue leaders, for example, over matters of Sabbath observance (12.1-14) or *korban*

(15.1-20), in which questions of the welfare of much of society are involved, is to struggle over societal visions and the interpretation of the traditions that sustain them. In both scenes the leadership figures defend interpretations and practices that uphold unjust societal practices that harm most of the population. Similarly, to struggle over the assertions that Jesus manifests God's saving presence (1.21-23), reign (4.17) and will (e.g., 4.18–7.29) is not simply a dispute over Jesus' identity as God's agent (Christ and Son, 1.1; 3.17). It is a struggle over who has the right to shape societal order (9.3; 12.2, 38; 16.1-4; 21.23-27), to name it as unjust, to articulate that from which this unjust world needs saving, to determine what salvation looks like, and to envisage what sort of societal order God's reign and will might create. That is, the struggle with synagogue leaders is not a restricted religious dispute over a few doctrinal niceties or matters of obtuse practice. Rather, it is a struggle with those invested in, allied with, and representative of an unjust societal order that Rome oversees for the elite's benefit and that the Gospel declares to be contrary to God's purposes. Postcolonial perspectives are interested in unmasking the imperial structures, practices and visions in which Matthew is enmeshed, by which it is shaped, and to which it articulates resistance, as well as in identifying the alternative world and the world of (imperial-imitating) power that the Gospel creates.

The Roman Imperial System

It is by no means clear where and when Matthew's Gospel was written. Several factors, though, suggest that Antioch in Syria in the decade of the 80s CE is a reasonable guess. In terms of location, the earliest citations of material unique to Matthew in writings associated with Antioch in Syria (Ignatius of Antioch, *The Didache*), the surprising reference to 'Syria' in 4.24 that Matthew adds in the context of a focus on Galilee (compare Mk 1.28, 39), and the prominent place of Peter in both the Gospel and Antioch (compare Gal. 2.11-14) make Antioch a reasonable guess. (Because of pervasive Roman power, none of the following analysis would be incorrect if another location could be established.) In terms of date, the Gospel's use of sources Q (a tradition expanding through 40s to 60s CE) and Mark (probably written around 70 CE), its interpretation of the Roman destruction of Jerusalem in 70 CE as God's punishment (21.12-13, 19, 41-43; 22.7), and its discussion of the tax levied by Rome on Jews after 70 CE for the temple of Jupiter Capitolinus in Rome (17.24-27) point to a post-70 date. Some passing of time is necessary to allow for the synagogue dispute to develop, suggesting a date in the 80s or possibly the 90s for the writing of Matthew's Gospel.

Antioch had its beginnings in imperial power. It was established under the guidance of Zeus by Seleucus I around 300 BCE and named after his father. Roman control had been established in 64 BCE when Pompey, taking advantage of declining Seleucid power, turned the area into the province of Syria with

Antioch as its capital. Roman power was imposed without direct military action through alliances with local ruling elites, permitting their continued rule over Antioch and surrounding territory through the city council (accessible only to elite males) but under Roman supervision and taxation exercised through the governor of Syria. In laying one experience of imperial power upon another, Roman control exemplifies what has been called the palimpsestic nature of imperial power (Bhahba).

Through the first century CE, numerous displays of Roman power in Antioch advertised Roman control, creating and reinforcing its societal order. Several emperors (and future emperors) visited Antioch. Just prior to the writing of Matthew's Gospel, Vespasian (emperor from 69–79 CE), assembled troops in Antioch in 66, marching them south against Judaea and levying Syrian corn and other goods for their supplies (Josephus, *JW* 3.8, 29; 5.520). As emperor, Vespasian visited Antioch again in 69, where the oath of allegiance was administered to his troops and he addressed citizens in the theatre (*JW* 3.29; 4.630). His son Titus, the victorious general in the siege of Jerusalem in 70 and emperor from 79 to 81, displayed Roman military power when he visited Antioch with captured prisoners and booty from the Jerusalem temple in 70–71. He quelled riots against Jews in the city and refused the demand to withdraw their protections (*JW* 7.100-111).

Antioch was the residence of the governor of Syria, who was responsible for representing Roman power by raising taxes, maintaining public order, improving buildings, roads and so forth, deciding legal matters on regular tours throughout the province, and influencing local government. The governor and his small staff along with their allies in Antioch were members of the 2 to 3 per cent of the empire's population that comprised the ruling elite, in whom were concentrated enormous levels of wealth, power and status. The wealth of this ruling elite was based largely in their control of the means of production, namely land with access to cheap labour either through slavery or hiring day labourers. The elite also engaged in some commercial and trade activity. Sale of production secured wealth, while taxes (foundational to the empire's functioning, Tacitus, *Annals* 13.50) and rents (often paid in kind) transferred wealth from the non-elite (about 97 per cent of the population), as did loans and foreclosures. Wealth was conspicuously displayed, and a network of power and social honour was secured and extended through acts of patronage and calculated and self-serving euergetism (the ostentatious practice of giving benefits of money or services to a community or group, such as funding a building or food handout or entertainment, thereby receiving social honour for oneself, obligating and subordinating the so-called beneficiaries, and securing the hierarchical status quo).

Some three or four legions were stationed in Antioch. Approximately 20,000 troops in a city of around 150,000 ensured great visibility for Roman power. The regular use of these troops through the century, especially to intervene in disputes to the south in Galilee, Samaria and Judaea, contributed to the myth of Rome's superior fighting abilities, equipment and strategies, and exerted a significant subjugating influence. Their presence also meant a significant tax burden in levying supplies for provisions and equipment, and in the practice of *angareia*, the requisitioning of animals, labour and lodging (5.41). Antiochenes thereby experienced on a daily basis the burdensome and oppressive price of Pax Romana. Tacitus masks the complexity of imperial engagement when he claims with explicit reference to Antioch that 'the provincials ... enjoyed association with' the soldiers (*Hist.* 2.80).

Various buildings such as the governor's headquarters and tax and financial records offices proclaimed Roman power over the societal order. They also functioned as objects of violent protest. A fire in the late 60s destroyed the marketplace, magistrates' quarters, record office and law courts. Given the volatile situation in Judaea, some Jews were blamed, but according to Josephus the fire turned out to have an economic not ethnic motivation, being 'the work of some scoundrels who under the pressure of debts, imagined that if they burnt the market place and the public records they would be rid of all demands' (Josephus, *JW* 7.54-62). Statues represented and made present powerful Roman figures, such as the emperors Tiberius and Vespasian. Gates depicted Roman power, such as a gate on Antioch's main street built by Tiberius depicting Romulus and Remus, Rome's legendary founding figures.

Coins, the handheld billboards of Rome's world, also announced Rome's claims. Images of emperors and various gods and goddesses proclaimed Rome to have been chosen by the gods – such as Jupiter, Victoria (victory) or Pax (peace) – to be agents of the gods' will and purposes. After the defeat of Jerusalem and its temple in 70 CE, for instance, Judaea Capta coins were issued, depicting Judaea as a subdued and bound female figure overpowered by Rome's military might personified by a (male) soldier. After 70 CE, the emperor Vespasian also added a tax on Jews that he used to rebuild and maintain the temple of Jupiter Capitolinus in Rome, reinforcing their identity as a conquered people who continued to be punished for rebellion against Rome and its gods, forced to acknowledge the triumph of Jupiter's will over Israel's God (Josephus, *JW* 7.218).

Though specific evidence for Antioch is very thin, it is likely that some form of the imperial cult existed in Antioch promoted by both local elite figures and Roman representatives. Tiberius had renovated the temple of Jupiter and perhaps had installed an image of himself. In various provincial centres, local elites had initiated shrines, images and temples and encouraged prayers, sacrifices, feasting and parades to honour emperors. It is most likely that celebrations of Rome's founding, of an emperor's birthday and of military victories, for instance, took place in Antioch.

There was another daily experience of Rome's exploitative rule in Antioch and its surrounding territory, namely, the harsh socio-economic conditions under which much of the population lived, as the elite extracted wealth from them through taxes and rents. Between the elite and the non-elite existed a vast gap in terms of wealth, power and status. There was no middle class, though a few people, often lacking power and status, could, through trade, patronage or inheritances, gain considerable wealth. The non-elite, despised by the elite, comprised farmers of small landholdings (either free or lease holders), skilled and unskilled artisans, traders, day labourers and slaves (of varying skills). Most of the population lived at near subsistence level, experiencing regular food shortages due to rents, taxes, weather, crop failure, high prices, marketeering, poor distribution and so forth, though at times they knew some surplus. Some estimates for pre-industrial cities identify 4 to 8 per cent of the population as incapable of providing food and shelter for themselves, 20 per cent in permanent crisis because of low wages and price fluctuations, and 30 to 40 per cent (artisans, shopkeepers) who for short periods fell below subsistence levels.

Food production, distribution and consumption were shaped by and expressive of these relationships of power. While the Mediterranean diet, comprising staples such as cereals, olives, wine and beans, was potentially healthy, actual diet determined by factors such as available quantities, affordability, lack of diversity, poor quality and geographical location meant that malnutrition was widespread. Diseases of both nutritional deficiency (eye diseases, rickets or limb deformity, painful bladder-stones) and of contagion (malaria, dysentery, diarrhoea, cholera, typhus) accompany malnutrition and poverty. Living conditions for many were marked by overcrowding, noise, squalor, garbage, human excrement, conflicts, poor water supply, animals, crime, fire, flooding from the Orontes river, lack of personal hygiene, etc. While a very few could by various means secure significant wealth, some surplus and security, most were intent on daily survival with no aspirations or opportunity to improve their lot.

Matthew's Gospel emerges from, is enmeshed in, addresses, imitates and contests this world of late first-century Antioch shaped by Roman imperialism, while constructing an alternative world of power and sovereignty identified as the kingdom/empire of God.

Matthew's Plot and Characters in Postcolonial Perspective

There has, surprisingly, been relatively little discussion of the Gospel's plot, since many studies have preferred to examine aspects of the Gospel's thought, thereby missing the fundamental action that holds the Gospel together. The Gospel's plot centres on its main character Jesus, crucified as king of the Jews by an alliance of the Jerusalem leadership and Pontius Pilate, Rome's governor and raised by God on the third day. Through his actions and teachings, Jesus challenges and alienates the elite over their societal structure as contrary to God's purposes, is crucified by them and is raised by God. The Gospel is a committed narrative, located among the subjugated, negotiating existence in relation to Roman power and employing theological perspectives from Israel's traditions to interpret the experience. I will briefly explore the unfolding and main contours of this plot through each of the Gospel's six sections.

First Section (1.1–4.17)

The Gospel contextualizes the significance of Matthew's Jesus in the opening genealogy not in conventional imperial terms of wealth, power and elite status, but in relation to God's just purposes (1.1-17). These purposes, evoked by the genealogy, were previously manifested and enacted not in the mighty Roman Empire but in the small and often subjugated (see 1.11-16) nation of Israel. As God's anointed (Messiah, 1.1, 16-17), Jesus continues God's promise to Abraham (not to Rome) to bless all the nations of the earth with life (Gen. 12.1-3), not just the powerful, wealthy elite and allies of Rome. He inherits the promises made to David (not Rome) of a just reign that will last forever (2 Samuel 7) and that will embody justice and righteousness for all, not domination and exploitation by a few (Psalm 72). These purposes, underway but as yet unfinished, embrace male and female (the five women named in 1.3, 5, 16), Jew and Gentile (Babylon), the giants of the tradition (1.1) including powerful kings (1.6-11), and those whom the tradition has largely forgotten (1.13-15).

In this context, God initiates the story of Jesus through Mary's conception by the Holy Spirit (1.18, 20, 25). The action is culturally disruptive in marginalizing the betrothed Mary (see Sir. 23.22-26; Wis. 3.16-19; 4.3-6) and in requiring Joseph's counter-cultural marriage to her. The subsequent narrative will frequently locate God's actions away from established centres of power and in disruptive and counter-cultural acts. The angel sent from God names the newly conceived child 'Jesus' and declares his life's work (1.21). His greatness does not consist of military conquest, huge land acquisition, great wealth and self-serving exploitation, but of 'saving people from their sins', punished by Rome in the conquest of Jerusalem in 70 CE (22.7). In doing so, Jesus manifests God's saving purposes as Emmanuel (1.23). Jesus' commission to manifest God's saving presence indicates that the present world under Roman control is contrary to God's purposes, despite Rome's claims to be the world's saviour.

Jesus' commission evokes three Hebrew Bible traditions that in turn elaborate the anti-imperial nature of his commission. First, the name Jesus, the Greek form of the Hebrew name Joshua, evokes God's purposes of liberating the people from Egyptian slavery and landlessness by overcoming the Canaanites (ironically, by dispossessing them of land) in leading the people into the land promised by God. Second, the commission 'to save his people from their sins' resembles the concluding verse of Psalm 130 (130.8). The Psalm seeks God's deliverance for Israel from 'trouble', namely God's deliverance from their punishment for sin. The Psalm identifies Israel's present circumstances as punishment by an imperial power, turns worshippers to God, reassures them of God's covenant loyalty, exhorts them to hope in God and assures them that

God's salvation or liberation is at hand in defeating the oppressor. Third, in designating Jesus 'Emmanuel' in 1.23, Matthew cites Isa. 7.14, in which God offers to King Ahaz and Judah, threatened by Assyrian and Israelite imperial aggression, a sign of continuing life and God's presence in the form of a new-born child named Emmanuel. Isaiah 7–9 depicts God's opposition to imperial powers, God's use of them to punish the people and God's destruction of them in saving or liberating the people from them. Significantly in using the name Emmanuel for Jesus, 1.23 applies to him a common designation for emperor and kings (*deus praesens/epiphanes*), thereby disputing their claims to manifest divine presence by claiming it for Jesus.

These three intertextual links elaborate central dimensions of what is involved in Jesus' commission of manifesting God's saving presence. God's purposes are not narrowly individualistic, religious, spiritual, unrelated to or unconcerned with human socio-political circumstances. Rather, God's purposes manifested in Jesus continue to be about the task of transforming human existence in all its dimensions. They confront and resist that which is contrary to God's purposes, especially imperial powers and their misuse of power and imposition of false and oppressive societal structures. Yet, in imitation of imperial ways of being, the Gospel envisages the defeat of such power and the victorious establishment of God's empire, God's just and life-giving purposes for all creation. Moreover, the evoking of the three texts as witnesses to Jesus' commission continues Matthew's imperialist attempt, initiated with the genealogy, to lay claim to Israel's past in order to sustain his Christological agenda.

Jesus' birth takes place in Bethlehem (2.1), a place that recalls David's kingly power (1 Samuel 16; see Mt. 1.1) but is marginal to Jerusalem, the current centre of imperial power represented by Herod, 'king of the Jews' and Rome's loyal puppet king, ally and agent (Josephus, *AJ* 15.387; 16.311). In the characteriza-tion of Herod, ch. 2 offers a subordinate's representation of an imperial figure as a tyrant. The eastern magi, priests with access to centres of power but renowned for their destabilizing predictions, astrological knowledge and magical powers, ask the politically tactless and disruptive question, 'Where is the one born king of the Jews?' Threatened, King Herod secures his power and guards against any challenge by responding with standard tyrannical practices: alliances with Jerusalem's leadership (2.4-6), subterfuge (2.7), intelligence gathering (2.5-7), covert operations (2.8), deception and disinformation (2.8, 'spin') and murder-ous military violence against his own people (2.16-18).

However, the narrative reveals that Herod's power, despite its murderous reach, is not total. God temporarily thwarts Herod's plans to kill Jesus by inter-vening in dreams, warning the faithful magi not to report Jesus' whereabouts to Herod (2.12), and directing Joseph to take Mary and Jesus to Egypt (2.13, 19). Yet, three times the death of Herod, the one who seeks Jesus' death, is mentioned (2.15, 19, 20). He dies while Jesus lives. Yet, God's thwarting of imperial power is only partial, since, while it saves Jesus from Herod, Herod murders the baby boys around Bethlehem (2.16-18) and Herod's son Archelaus 'rules in the place of his father Herod' (2.22).

The magi exhibit a different response. Unlike the hostile Herod and the Jerusalem leaders who supportively maintain their alliance with Herod, the magi bravely and determinedly seek out Jesus and pay him homage (2.11, the verb commonly designates political loyalty and submission to a king). Their gift-giving recalls texts like Ps. 72.10-11 and Isa. 2.1-4; 60.4-11 that envision the imperially imitative establishment of God's just purposes over all the nations. Gentiles bring gifts such as gold in acts of recognition, willing submission and worship.

Chapter 3 jumps an unspecified number of years to the activity of a new oppositional character, the prophet John the Baptist (3.1-12). In a marginal location, dressed in clothing that evokes the prophet Elijah who confronted King Ahab and Jezebel (2 Kgs 1.8; see 1 Kgs 16.29–21.29), living a lifestyle of scarcity that contrasts with the excess of the elite, employing a dramatic sign-action emphasizing repentance and cleansing, and warning of imminent judgment on life contrary to God's purposes, John calls people to a changed way of life. He rebukes the Jerusalem leadership (3.7-10) and testifies to Jesus' ministry as effecting blessing and destruction.

John baptizes Jesus (3.13-17) in a scene that further underlines Jesus' disturbing commission. Jesus' task to 'fulfill all righteousness/justice' (3.15) manifests God's saving presence and covenant purposes (1.21-23). In doing so, Jesus is revealed by the spirit's presence, the opened heaven and God's own words to be God's 'beloved son' (3.17). The image of 'son', frequently used of emperors to associate them with previous great figures such as Augustus, designates in the biblical tradition either an individual (the king, Ps. 2.7; the servant who suffers imperial violence, Isaiah 40–55; the wise person, Wisdom 2) or the people (Hos. 11.1), who in intimate relationship with God participate in God's imperial work of manifesting God's just and liberating purposes for a world saved from imperial power.

Chapter 4 tests Jesus' identity and commission in a cosmic context. The temptation narrative reveals the cosmic power Satan, who is opposed to God's purposes and in the three temptations seeks sovereignty over Jesus. While several temptations offer good ends (bread in 4.3; Jesus' worldwide dominion in 4.9), they come at the price of Jesus' allegiance to Satan's purposes, not to God's purposes. Citing passages of covenant loyalty from Deuteronomy 6–8, Jesus remains steadfast to God as God's Son or agent (4.3, 5). Significantly, the third temptation (4.8-10) reveals the extent of Satan's power, who claims to have control of 'all the empires of the world'. This boast allies Rome and Satan, depicting the devil as the power behind the throne and Rome as the devil's agent, belittling Rome's propaganda claim to be the chosen agent of Jupiter and the gods and deframing/framing Rome's empire as diabolical and opposed to

God's just purposes. This regrettable demonization of Rome will subsequently extend in the narrative to Rome's allies, the Jerusalem leadership (see 16.1, 4). Jesus' commission to manifest God's saving presence embraces the cosmic and the political, the societal and the individual.

The closing scene of this first narrative section summarizes Jesus' commission (4.12-16). A brief and vague reference to John's arrest, elaborated later in 14.1-12, has Jesus move from Nazareth (2.23) to Capernaum in Galilee, not to withdraw from danger but to begin his commission in its midst. The use of a further citation from Isaiah 7–9 (see 1.23) concerning Assyria and Israel's imperial threat to Judah identifies the area by the tribal names Zebulun and Naphtali to emphasize that this is land given by God to the people and that Roman control contravenes God's purposes. 'Galilee under the Gentiles', under Roman control, a place of darkness and death, usurps God's sovereignty, violates God's will and challenges God's purposes. Yet, light, a common image for God's creation (Gen. 1.3-5) and salvation (see Ps. 27.1), is about to dawn in the person of Jesus, God's Son or agent, commissioned to manifest God's saving presence (1.21-23). This is good news for most of the population but bad news for Rome and its allied ruling elite, the Jerusalem leadership.

Second Section (4.17–11.1)

While the first section has established Jesus' commission, it has not indicated *how* Jesus will manifest God's saving presence in the midst of Roman imperialism. Israel's traditions offered several paradigms of resistance in negotiating imperial power: armed (1 Maccabees), unarmed (Daniel), strategic accommodation (Jeremiah), alternative community (Qumran), divine intervention (Ben Sirach, Masada, *Psalms of Solomon*), eschatological judgment (*1 Enoch*), messianic intervention (*2 Baruch, 4 Ezra*). The narrative will locate Jesus in this diversity, depicting Jesus' non-violent enactment of his commission in the present through his words and actions, creating an alternative community and practices in the midst of Rome's empire until his future return to destroy Roman power.

Jesus' public ministry begins with an announcement of his central theme, that God's reign or empire has come near (4.17). The reference to God's empire evokes God's sovereignty over the created realm (Psalms 45; 47) and the history of God's intervention on Israel's behalf to assert God's rule and to save or redeem the people from (imperial) powers that oppose God's purposes (e.g., Isa. 52.7, Babylon). The term thus summarizes Jesus' commission to manifest God's saving presence (1.21-23). Jesus' subsequent actions and words will demonstrate God's empire, God's saving presence, at work in creating a different world.

First, Jesus disrupts the Roman socio-economic order by calling two sets of brothers from their household fishing business contracted to Rome to constitute an alternative community with a new focus ('follow me') and a new mission ('fish for people') (4.18-22). It is among the lowly and often despised, such as fishermen, that God's reign, presence and salvation are encountered.

Second, Jesus manifests God's empire in preaching the 'good news of the kingdom' (4.23). Again, the term 'good news' is ambiguous, evoking imperial propaganda claims in celebrating an emperor's birthday or accession (thereby maintaining the harsh societal order) as well as Hebrew Bible traditions that celebrate the assertion of God's reign in saving people from imperial power such as Babylon's empire (Isa. 40.9; 52.7; 61.1).

Third, Jesus enacts what is presented as the transformative power of God's empire in healings (4.23-25). Though Roman propaganda claimed to have healed a sick world and blessed it with abundance, the Roman world, like the Gospel, was peopled with sick folk. For much of the population (peasant farmers, skilled and unskilled artisans), poor hygiene, food shortages, poor nutrition, contaminated water supply, hard work, anxiety, diseases from nutritional deficiency and contagion by infectious diseases, overcrowding in cities, injuries from work, all resulted in numerous 'diseases and pains' (4.22). Satan's hold on the empires of the world (4.8) is also evidenced in demoniacs under the control of demons (4.24; see 13.38). Moreover, some social scientists and medical experts have identified demonic possession, paralysis and muteness as common responses to the trauma of invasive, imperial, socio-political, military and economic acts. Jesus' healings reveal that Rome's imperial power is hazardous for people's health and contrary to God's purposes. The healings confront the destructiveness of Rome's order, display the transformative power of God's empire, and anticipate the final and full establishment of God's purposes for wholeness. These purposes have been revealed previously, for example, in Isaiah's visions of life marked by health and wholeness when God's reign is established in full (Isa. 26.19; 29.18-19; 35.5-6; 61.1). Other eschatological texts contemporary with Matthew envisage a similar new order (*2 Bar.* 29.5-8; 73.1-5; *4 Ezra* 8.53).

Jesus' preaching of God's empire (4.23) is elaborated in the Sermon on the Mount (chs 5–7), the first of five collections of Jesus' teaching that reveal God's purposes and will (chs 10, 13, 18, 24–25). The sermon instructs the newly called disciples on the identity and lifestyle shaped by God's empire. God's reign creates a communal life marked by:

- God's blessing found not among the privileged, wealthy and powerful, but among the desperate (literally) poor, the non-elite without resources, options and hope, whose poverty is reversed and to whom is promised access to resources, notably land (5.3-6).
- Social actions that enact mercy, justice (doing right) and God's wholeness (peace, not Pax Romana), and provoke retaliation (5.7-12).
- Transforming mission, not retreat or passivity (5.13-16).
- Actions that enact Jesus' interpretations of God's will revealed in the Decalogue and its expanding traditions concerning murder, adultery, divorce, oaths, non-violent resistance and love for neighbours including enemies (5.17-48).

- Actions that enact mercy and justice through benefiting those in need (not the elite euergetistic practice of enhancing one's honour), prayer and fasting that means not only abstinence from food but doing justice (Isa. 58.3-14: food, clothing, housing, setting free; 6.1-18).
- Trust in God and pursuit of the justice of God's reign, which will mean enough food, drink and clothing for all, not the pursuit of wealth (6.19-34).
- Community relations that provide support for a minority and alternative community (7.1-12).
- Awareness that the goal of counter-cultural and alternative discipleship is participation in the future completion of God's purposes (7.13-27).

In a series of scenes, chs 8–9 elaborate aspects of Jesus' ministry that enact God's reign and confront the world created by Roman power and its Jerusalem allies. Healings dominate, especially of the socially marginal, such as lepers, slaves, women, demoniacs, the paralysed. The healings, often effected through faith or trust in Jesus' power (but note 8.28-34), offer people of supposedly no social significance in the elite-dominated societal structure new physical life (e.g., 8.1-4), participation in a new community (e.g., 9.9-13), encounter with God's saving presence (e.g., 9.2-8) and anticipation of the completion of God's purposes (e.g., 8.11-12). Jesus also exhibits God's sovereign power over a centurion, interestingly represented as dependent and submissive to Jesus but who understands Jesus' authority as analogous to his own authority in the imperial system (8.5-13). The scene evidences the impact of the subjugated on the imperialist power. Jesus exerts God's sovereignty over the sea (8.23-27), contesting claims that Rome and/or the emperor ruled the sea (Philostratus refers to the emperor Domitian as 'master of lands and seas and nations', *Apollonius* 7.3). The scene in 8.28-34, the exorcism of the two tomb-living men whose cast-out demons cause a herd of pigs to destroy themselves in the sea, functions as a satirical political cartoon. The devil has been linked to the Roman Empire in 4.8 with Satan's boast to control 'all the empires/kingdoms of the earth' (4.8). The two hostile demoniacs in a graveyard embody the violence and death of the empire under Satan's control (8.28). In the exorcism Jesus overcomes this power alliance. The pig was the symbol of the 10th Fretensis Legion stationed in Syria and prominent in the destruction of Jerusalem in 70 CE. With the demons entering the pigs, the scene not only reveals (again) the alliance of Satan and Rome but also emphasizes Jesus' greater power in sending the demons and pigs into the sea (under his control, 8.23-27). The drowning in the sea recalls the destruction of the Egyptians pursuing the Israelites in the exodus and offers an analogous, coded depiction of Rome's anticipated demise at Jesus' return (24.27-31). Jesus also continues to call people to join his community as followers (9.9).

Jesus summarizes the situation of 'Galilee under the Gentiles'/Rome as 'harassed and helpless, like sheep without a shepherd' (9.36). The vocabulary represents people under Roman rule enacted through its local-elite allies as oppressed, downtrodden and beaten-up. The image of a shepherd commonly denoted rulers and leaders. By evoking the prophetic denunciation of Israel's leaders as shepherds who rule 'with force and harshness' and benefit themselves as they deprive the sheep of food and clothing and make them sick (see Ezekiel 34), Matthew's Jesus negatively represents and denounces the Jerusalem-based leaders of the societal order that he resists and begins to transform in these actions.

In ch. 10, the second of Jesus' five major instructional addresses, Jesus elaborates his call to the disciples to 'fish for humans' (4.19) and to be a transformative mission community (5.13-16). He extends his own mission demonstrated in chs 8–9 by commissioning his disciples to join in the merciful (see 9.13) task of contesting the status quo through proclaiming the kingdom/empire of God, healing the sick, raising the dead, cleansing the lepers and casting out demons (10.7-8). This mission assumes that the world under Roman rule is not as God intends it. Unlike Rome's Jupiter-given mission to 'rule the nations with your power' (Virgil, *Aeneid* 6.851-53), Jesus' mission extended through the disciples benefits its recipients with merciful and transforming power, new life, health and community. However, like Rome's mission, it employs the same image of empire (10.7), comes with the same price of recognizing God's all-embracing sovereignty that does not tolerate dissent (10.13-15, 32), and labels its enemies in negative terms (10.17-18). In commissioning the disciples to participate in this mission, Jesus does not permit them to flee their society nor naively accept it as it is. Mission is not optional but integral to the community's existence. Jesus warns disciples that because their mission is contestive, confrontive and divisive (10.34-39), the imperial and synagogal status quo will not warmly welcome it but will resist it and persecute disciples (10.16-25). Jesus labels this missional way of life the way of the cross (10.38), imitative of Jesus' life and death because it threatens the empire's societal vision that furthers the elite's power, greed and status. His missional community, though, refuses to be intimidated into compliance and is at cross-purposes with the empire.

Third Section (11.2–16.20)
While the first section establishes Jesus' identity as God's agent commissioned to manifest God's transformative saving presence in the Roman world (1.1–4.16) and the second section demonstrates how Jesus carries out this commission to establish God's rule or empire in his words and actions (4.17–11.1), the third section emphasizes people's responses to Jesus' identity and commission manifested in his words and actions (11.2–16.20). Some are receptive, some hostile.

The opening scene frames the issue as disciples from John, hearing of what Jesus was doing, ask Jesus about his identity. Jesus responds by interpreting his healing work in terms of Isaiah's vision of the establishment of God's reign (11.2-6). When God's reign is established, there is wholeness and health as the destructive impact of imperial rule is reversed (Isa. 35.5-6). Jesus goes on to note a negative response to both John and Jesus that is sometimes violent (11.12-13) and frequently dishonouring. It does not understand Jesus' identity (11.18-19) and despises his alternative social order based on mercy not social status, wealth and power (11.19). As with any empire, God's judgment inevitably falls on those who reject God's purposes (11.20-24).

In language imitative of claims made for the emperor, Jesus asserts God's sovereignty and the revelation of God's purposes to the powerless (11.25-27). Jesus again invites those who are wearied and burdened by the taxing demands of Rome and its Jerusalem allies to find in him rest, a frequent Hebrew Bible image for the absence of imperial rule. Yet, like numerous empires, he claims his yoke, a common image for imperial rule and control, is kind or good (11.28-30). Again, in presenting God's empire, the Gospel ironically imitates the language and claims of that which it resists.

In contrast to the invited powerless, the powerful reject Jesus' claimed revelation of God's purposes. Two scenes depict Jesus' conflict with leaders over interpretation of appropriate ways to observe the Sabbath. The Jerusalem leaders, represented by the Pharisees, urge strict abstaining from work that includes not procuring food (12.1-8) and no healing (12.9-14). Jesus resists such unjust practices by claiming that acts of mercy honour the Sabbath. The leaders' response is to initiate plans to kill this threat to their power and societal order (12.14). Israel's traditions are again co-opted to interpret the action. Like those who suffer victoriously at the hands of Babylon's power while serving God, Jesus' commitment to justice and life-giving mercy brings about his suffering yet eventual victory (12.15-21, quoting Isa. 42.1-4). An exorcism demonstrates Jesus' power over Satan's realm (including Rome's empire, 4.8), provoking another lengthy debate with the leaders about his identity (12.22-45). They are unable to accept that God has commissioned him or that he manifests God's reign (12.28), but attribute his work to Satan (12.24). Jesus mocks them by showing that this charge makes no sense and by charging that they, not he, embody the devil's evil purposes (12.34, 39; see 6.13). By contrast, an alternative community is emerging based not on conventional criteria of birth, ethnicity, status, wealth and power, but on response to God's purposes revealed in Jesus and in the active doing of God's will (12.46-50).

In ch. 13, in a series of seven parables that employ comparisons to illuminate God's empire, Jesus accounts for the division that his ministry is effecting. While often employing images from everyday village and agricultural practices, he depicts a reign that is simultaneously cosmic and political, individual and eschatological. God's reign is God's initiative, resisting Rome, opposed to and by Satan, causing division, disrupting and disturbing existing commitments and structures. It is at work in strange ways that are often unconventional, apparently inconsequential, hidden, coexistent with evil and injustice, and as yet incomplete (13.24-30, 31-32, 36-43). While a minority welcomes it with joy and makes it their priority (13.3-9, 18-23, 44-45), others are deceived by Satan or overcome by other human commitments so that they miss the opportunity to participate in the, as yet future, accomplishment of God's purposes (13.18-22, 36-43).

Chapters 14–16.12 continue this intermingling of revelations of God's reign in Jesus' actions (often contesting Roman claims), negative responses from leadership groups and positive responses from various figures. For instance, in two feeding scenes (14.13-21; 15.32-29), Jesus feeds hungry people, demonstrating the anticipated abundance and fertility that will mark the final establishment of God's reign (Isa. 25.6-10). Despite Rome's propaganda claims that the gods had provided such abundance through Rome's rule, food shortages were common and undernourishment pervasive. Jesus' powerful act and related healings (14.34-36; 15.29-31) critique and expose Roman claims, while revealing food shortages and sickness to be contrary to God's will. In 14.22-33, in calming a storm and walking on water, he again demonstrates that God's sovereignty extends even to the sea (see 8.23-27), again disputing claims that Rome was 'ruler of lands and seas and nations' (Juvenal, *Sat.* 4.83-84).

Opposition is evident in struggles over questions of societal order and over who has the right to determine how society will be shaped. Herod Antipas, Rome's ally and ruler of Galilee, beheads John for criticizing his incestuous marriage (14.1-12; see 4.12). Jesus again collides with the Jerusalem leadership's interpretations of the tradition because he considers them to validate unjust practices (15.1-20). Jesus responds to their accusation that his disciples do not observe handwashing by accusing them of upholding it and other purity requirements while enriching the temple at the expense of the elderly and ignoring moral and just actions. He declares their leadership, and hence the societal order over which they preside, to not be from God (15.13-14). He responds to their request for a sign that would legitimate his claim to reveal God's will by demonizing them, linking them with the devil in testing him (see 4.1, 3) and in being evil (6.13), and by warning disciples against their teaching or interpretation as corruptive and corrosive (16.6).

Yet there are also positive responses. The disciples remain with Jesus, though they struggle to grow in faith and understanding (14.22-33; 15.15-20; 16.5-12). A Canaanite woman overcomes cultural, ethnic, political, economic, religious and gender barriers in confronting Jesus' excluding focus on Israel's covenant privileges to gain healing and inclusion in God's purposes for herself and daughter (15.21-28). The final scene summarizes the section's emphasis on discerning Jesus' identity. Peter repeats the confession made by all disciples (14.33), agreeing with God's perspective on Jesus and confessing him to be God's agent, 'the Messiah, the Son of the living God' commissioned to manifest God's saving presence and reign (16.16; see 1.1; 3.17). In turn, Jesus commissions Peter to a key role in the community that shares his confession ('on this rock'). This inclusive community, not the elite assembled in city councils, has the task of resisting Satan's work (including Rome's empire, 4.8) and interpreting and implementing Jesus' revelation of God's purposes (16.13-20).

Fourth Section (16.21–20.34)

The fourth section marks a significant new focus on the consequences of Jesus' commission: his collision with the elite and subsequent death and resurrection. The disciples' understanding of Jesus as God's commissioned agent (Christ and Son of God, 16.16) is incomplete and inadequate (hence Jesus' command to silence in 16.20) until they understand that his commission means his death and subsequent vindication by God (16.21). Five times in this section Jesus announces that his mission of manifesting God's saving purposes and reign/ empire will inevitably ('must', 16.21) draw him to Jerusalem in conflict with the centre of elite power in Judaea and Galilee. His challenge to the leadership groups and status quo means their certain retaliation and his death by crucifixion at the hands of an elite alliance of the Jerusalem leadership and the Roman governor (16.21; 17.12, 22-23; 20.17-19, 28). As with numerous prophets before him, including John (14.1-12) and other opponents of Rome's order throughout the empire, Jesus' death exhibits the empire's intolerance of dissent, opposition and advocates of alternative societal order.

Crucifixion was in the first century a distinctly Roman form of execution. It embraced immense physical pain, societal humiliation, marginalization and political rejection. It was used for those who threatened Rome's order and control: rebellious foreigners, violent criminals and brigands, as well as slaves who revolted. True to the Roman notion that the punishment should fit the social status of the criminal, it was not used for Roman citizens except for those who committed treason. Crucifixion was usually carried out in public places to deter non-compliant behaviour. Jesus' crucifixion indicates an accurate elite perception that his words, actions and followers pose a significant threat to their power.

His death, however, is not their triumph and his defeat, since God will raise him from the dead (16.21; 17.23; 20.19). God confirms Jesus' announcement in the transfiguration with a direct declaration (repeating 3.17) and a vision of the glorified Jesus (17.1-8). His disciples struggle to understand, as Peter argues with Jesus and Jesus links him with Satan for resisting God's purposes (16.22-23). With little faith, they fail to exorcize the epileptic boy (17.14-20), despite Jesus' commission to them (10.8), and when Jesus repeats his crucifixion announcement, they are deeply distressed (17.23).

Yet, Jesus' crucifixion is not an isolated act. While he outlines his own crucifixion, he instructs his disciples that they too must live the way of the cross as opponents of the Roman order (16.24). Jesus' previous teaching, such as in the Sermon on the Mount, has already described something of this counter-cultural and contestive way of life (chs 5–7). He will elaborate it in the following chapters.

The strange scene about the 'didrachma' tax and the coin in the fish's mouth contributes to this instruction (17.24-27). The way of the cross does not mean, for example, violent revolt but requires, and as James Scott has shown is typical of peasant protest, calculated and self-protective, non-violent resistance (see 5.38-48). After the destruction of Jerusalem and its temple in 70 CE, the emperor Vespasian co-opted a tax formerly paid by Jews to the Jerusalem temple (Josephus, *JW* 7.128; Dio Cassius 65.7.2). The tax punitively marked Jews as a conquered people subject to Roman power. Adding insult to injury, Vespasian used the tax to rebuild and maintain the temple of Jupiter Capitolinus, the god who had blessed Rome and Vespasian in defeating Jerusalem and its God. Walking the way of the cross does not mean withholding this tax, an action that would be viewed as open rebellion and bring harsh reprisal. Rather, Roman power is negotiated by Jesus reframing the payment of the tax. Fish were subject to imperial control through taxes on their catch and distribution, but the Gospel has exhibited God's sovereignty over fish and sea (7.10; 8.23-27; 14.13-33; 15.32-39). The provision of the coin for Vespasian's tax in a fish's mouth asserts God's provision of the tax (17.27). The tax is to be paid, but for disciples the act signifies not Rome's sovereignty (as taxes were supposed to do) but God's greater sovereignty. The way of the cross means at times self-protective, calculated, symbolic acts of defiance and compliance that remind disciples of their greater allegiance and anticipate God's ultimate victory over Rome (24.27-31).

In addition, ch. 18, Jesus' fourth teaching discourse, emphasizes active caring relationships among disciples (18.1-14), practices of reproof and reconciliation (18.15-20), and forgiveness (18.21-35) to sustain the difficult and challenging way of the cross.

In chs 19–20, as Jesus travels from Galilee to Jerusalem, he instructs the disciples on a further dimension of the way of the cross. The reign or empire of God, like most empires, shapes households that appropriately reflect its primary values. Since Aristotle, such (elite) households had been envisaged as hierarchical, patriarchal and androcentric. They comprise three sets of relationships focused on the head male as husband who rules over wife, father who rules over children, and master who rules over slaves. In addition, this male was responsible for managing the household's wealth. Systematically Jesus deconstructs this elite household pattern to create contrasting, more inclusive and egalitarian patterns among disciples. Husbands and wives participate in a 'one flesh' existence (19.3-12); all disciples are children (19.13-15, no parents); wealth is not to secure the household's status and power but is to be redistributed, as in Jubilee traditions, to meet the needs of the poor (19.16-30); all disciples are slaves like Jesus in serving each other (20.17-28, no masters). A parable of a householder with large landholdings and vineyards demonstrates its fundamental equality (20.11-16), and the healing of two blind men reassures disciples of God's transformative power that enables disciples to live the counter-cultural way of life expressive of God's reign, which comprises the way of the cross (20.29-34).

Fifth Section (21–27)

Chapters 21–27 are set in Jerusalem and narrate Jesus' final challenge to the ruling elite centred in the temple. They reject his challenge and, in alliance with the Roman governor Pilate, crucify him.

Jesus enters Jerusalem in a procession that parodies the imperial mindset and practices of Roman entry processions involving elite figures such as emperors, governors and generals (21.1-17). Such processions incorporated standard elements – the central figure with entourage of supporters or prisoners; entry into a city; welcoming crowds, hymns, speeches; worship in a temple – to secure recognition of and submission to Roman power. However, Jesus' entry on a donkey, not a war-horse, is about God's empire not Rome's. The reference to the Mount of Olives (21.1), the citation of Zech. 9.9 in 21.5, and Jesus' transportation (donkey, 21.2-7) evoke the scene in Zechariah 9–14 of God's entry to Jerusalem to establish God's reign in salvation from and judgment on God's enemies. Again, the Gospel imitates what it resists to present God's purposes. The tree branches (21.8) evoke celebration of the Maccabaean victory over 'the yoke of the Gentiles' in the second century BCE (1 Macc. 13.41, 51), while Psalm 118, quoted in v. 9, is associated with the Passover celebration of the liberation from Egypt. Jesus' entry takes the form of subversive street theatre to proclaim God's judgment on, and liberation of the people from, Roman power, as well as to anticipate the establishment of God's reign.

Jesus enters the temple, the centre of the Jerusalem elite's power, and attacks their temple economy, societal order and political power (21.12-17). Crucial for this scene is the realization that religion, politics, economics and societal order are not separate entities. With collections of various offerings and tithes/taxes, its management of large landed estates, its purchase of necessary supplies and its role in celebrating central festivals, the temple and those who administered it exercised enormous political and economic power and maintained a hierarchical societal order. They functioned, though, under Rome's supervision. The chief priest was appointed by the Roman governor (Josephus, *AJ* 18.33-35; 20.197) and the chief priestly garments were kept in the Antonia fortress under Roman control (*AJ* 18.90-95; 20.6-14). Josephus identifies the chief priests as 'the leadership of the nation' (*AJ* 20.249-51). Jesus' attack on the moneychangers, crucial for the functioning of the temple, is not an attack on 'empty ritual' but an attack, as his interpretive comment in v. 13 makes clear, on the economic oppression that the temple leadership enacts. In accusing them of making the temple a 'den for robbers/bandits', Jesus quotes from Isa. 56.7 and Jeremiah 7. The former text celebrates God's salvation for creating an inclusive community accessible to all the nations and marked by justice. The latter text condemns corrupt leaders for violently oppressing the poor while appealing to the temple for legitimacy and security. Most interpreters see the scene as presenting Matthew's theological interpretation of Rome's destruction of the temple in 70 CE, expressing God's will to punish such unjust and exploitative leadership.

Jesus' subsequent actions reinforce his critique and contrasting vision. The cursed, withered fig tree symbolizes judgment (21.18-20; Jer. 6.12-13). His alternative community brings wholeness to the broken (21.14), creates opposition from the powerful (21.15-16), comprises the powerless and vulnerable (21.16) and is marked by prayer and faith (21.18-20). The Jerusalem leadership challenges Jesus' legitimacy to do these things only to find their own legitimacy challenged by his response (21.23-27; see 9.36; 12.34; 15.12-13; 16.5-12; 20.25-26).

In chs 21–25, Jesus continues this attack. First, three parables (21.28–22.14) employ landowning situations to depict the leaders as greedy and unjust. They fail to enact God's purposes and welcome God's agent (Jesus the Son), for which they are under God's judgment exercised in the fall of Jerusalem in 70 CE by God's agent and, ironically, their ally, Rome (22.7). The leaders want to arrest him but do not because of the crowds (21.45-46).

Second, in a series of conflict scenes, Jesus disputes their interpretations and practices of Torah by which they sustain their unjust societal order. He betters them, thereby shaming them, in three verbal exchanges. Pharisees and Herodians try to 'entrap' him by having him forbid paying taxes to Rome, an act of treasonous disloyalty that would be open defiance of Rome (21.15-22). Jesus' answer, 'Render to Caesar what is Caesar's and to God what is God's' (22.21), employs ambiguity, a traditional weapon of the weak, to avoid their public trap, while also expressing opposition to Rome. Jesus relativizes the payment of tax in relation to (greater) loyalty to God. Moreover, by focusing on the coin bearing the emperor's image (a violation of the Torah's prohibition of images, Exod. 20.1-6; Deut. 8.5), he requires people to 'give back' to Rome not that which represents Rome's eternal order blessed by the gods (as Rome claims) but that which violates God's will and invites God's judgment. Pharisees and Sadducees ask further questions about resurrection and patriarchy (22.23-33) and about what is central to the tradition of Torah (22.34-40). Jesus' responses confront dominant imperial values by claiming the end of patriarchal power and systems (epitomized in the empire that identified the emperor as the *pater patriae*, the father of the fatherland). By citing Moses in 22.37-39, he makes love central to relationship with God and to societal order. His command to 'love your neighbour as yourself' (22.39, citing Lev. 19.18) evokes Leviticus 19's extensive vision of just and caring social relationships that they fail to enact. He challenges them to recognize his identity as the Messiah, the one commissioned by God to manifest God's saving presence and reign and attested by Moses, but they cannot. Verbally out-sparred and shamed, they did not 'dare to ask him any more questions' (21.41-46).

Third, in a very troublesome chapter, Jesus curses, or evokes judgment on, the leaders (notably the scribes and Pharisees) for the societal order they administer as allies with the Jerusalem priesthood and Rome. The chapter has been falsely and hatefully read as a cursing of all Jews. It is located in the Gospel as part of Jesus' conflict with the temple-based Jerusalem leadership (chs 21–27). It reflects the pronounced post-70 hostility toward and conflict with synagogue leaders as allies of Rome's hierarchical societal order. The chapter also employs stereotypical polemic used by various Jewish (and Gentile) groups to distinguish themselves from others and to identify and attack an enemy. Throughout, Jesus attacks and rejects societal practices that are hierarchical, dominating and honour-seeking (23.1-12), excluding (23.13-15), inattentive to God's purposes, notably the covenant values of justice, mercy and faithfulness (23.16-24), masking of greed, hypocrisy and lawlessness (23.25-28), and rejecting of God's agents (23.29-36). Again, the chapter ends by linking this unjust leadership behaviour with God's judgment enacted by Rome's destruction of Jerusalem in 70 CE, but it adds a further dimension: this judgment and punishment are not God's final word (23.37-39).

Fourth, in chs 24–25, Jesus' fifth and final teaching discourse, Jesus elaborates God's final act of judgment in ending the unjust societal order over which these leaders and their Roman allies preside, and in establishing God's reign in full. The action centres on Jesus' return or parousia (24.3, 27, 37, 39. Lat. *adventus*), a term that can designate both the arrival of an imperial figure and the presence of God. The time between Jesus' resurrection and coming is difficult for disciples. Jesus challenges them to mission, faithfulness, non-violent resistance and hopeful anticipation (24.3-26).

Jesus' spectacular return is described as a battle in 24.27-31 in language rich in imperial and biblical significance. The eagle, symbolic of numerous imperial powers in the biblical tradition and especially of Rome, is 'gathered with the corpse' as Rome's army, a key instrument of imperialization, is defeated. Loss of light (24.29) commonly signifies judgment (Amos 5.20; Ezek. 32.7-8). Here it especially denotes 'lights out' time for the celestial divinities of the sun, moon and stars that Rome claimed sanctioned their rule. God's salvation means the ingathering of Jews and Gentiles. Again, the scene mirrors violent imperial practices and dominating mindset to present the universal triumph of God's empire. Chapters 24–25 conclude with a series of parables that exhort faithfulness and watchfulness as well as active discipleship expressed in deeds of transformative mercy, in readiness for this final judgment exercised by Jesus the Son of Man (24.36–25.46). The term Son of Man evokes Dan. 7.13-14 in which God destroys human empires and gives 'everlasting dominion... and kingship that will never be destroyed' to one 'like the Son of Man'.

After such public proclamations and challenge, the ruling elite has little option but to remove this threat to their power and societal order. The elite conspire to kill Jesus (26.3-5), ironically in accord with his predictions (e.g., among many, 16.21; 20.17-19). They do so with the aid of one of his disciples, Judas, who, consistent with Jesus' prediction during the Passover meal of such betrayal (26.17-30), facilitates Jesus' arrest for 30 pieces of silver (26.14-16, 47-56) before committing suicide (27.3-10). Jesus is tried before the Jerusalem council, presided over by the chief priest Caiaphas, for his actions against the temple and for claiming to be the agent of God's purposes as 'the Christ the Son of God' and as the powerful 'Son of Man'. They denounce him for blasphemy, but, since religious power is political power, his blasphemy is treason in that it claims God's sanction for his own ruling role over against them (26.57-68). Their condemnation requires the assent of their ally, the Roman governor Pilate, to carry out the death penalty.

Roman governors, usually appointed from the elite ranks of the equestrians, were wealthy and powerful men entrusted with the self-serving and largely unaccountable task of securing Roman interests. Contrary to impossible scholarly interpretations that claim Pilate is weak (or even neutral!) and has his arm twisted to act against Jesus, the narrative (from a subordinated provincial) represents Pilate to be powerful and astute in working with his Jerusalem allies and in manipulating the crowd to protect Roman interests. He quickly condemns Jesus in 27.11-14 for being 'king of the Jews', a title that Rome entrusted only to carefully chosen and loyal allies and client-kings (Herod, ch. 2). Since Rome has not designated Jesus king of the Jews, his claim amounts to insurrection. This so-called 'trial' represents a massive power differential, as the wealthy, powerful, high-born, educated, high-status Roman Pilate confronts and condemns the poor, powerless, low-born, low-status, provincial Jesus.

Pilate then skilfully assesses how much support Jesus has, and how much unrest the death of a kingly pretender might provoke, with a series of questions to the crowd (27.15-26). Manipulated by the Jerusalem elite, this particular Jerusalem crowd (not all Jews) calls for Jesus' crucifixion and the release of a more popular prisoner, Barabbas. Pilate consents, washing his hands, claiming to yield to and execute the crowd's demands. He denies his own responsibility, while placing responsibility on them, which, tragically but typically in imperial situations where the subjugated internalize the imperialists' worldview, they accept (27.25).

The narrative, however, does not participate in the (white)washing, preferring to represent and expose Pilate's power-protecting deception. Hence, it removes Pilate's mask and reveals the self-serving nature of Roman 'justice' that hides behind claims of enacting the public wishes, when it in fact accomplishes its own goals. The narrative lays bare Pilate's ways of operating as the callous and calculated ways in which the elite further their own interests: his alliance with the Jerusalem leadership (27.2); Judas' conclusion that the sending of Jesus to Pilate means he is already condemned (before the 'trial' takes place, 27.3); Pilate's quick decision about Jesus as king of the Jews (27.11-14); his polling of the crowd (27.15-23); the manipulation of the crowd by his allies, the Jerusalem elite (27.20); the calculated release of a 'popular' prisoner (and less dangerous? Barabbas' crime is not identified, 27.21); his apparent consent to the crowd's wishes manipulated by the elite to accomplish their purposes (27.22-23). What Pilate cannot see, but what the narrative also makes clear, is that in such actions he sows the seed of his own demise in God's judgment (see 24.27-31).

After mocking Jesus' kingly pretensions, soldiers crucify Jesus (27.27-54). Ironically, they proclaim Jesus' identity as king with an identifying sign on the cross (27.37). Despite the continued mocking (27.38-44), and reflecting the influence of the subjugated on the imperialists, at least one Roman soldier recognizes that Jesus was God's Son or agent (27.27-54). Some women followers of Jesus from Galilee, including perhaps the woman who anointed Jesus for burial (26.6-13), remain with him at the cross, and a disciple, Joseph, buries Jesus (27.55-61). Their actions contrast with the male disciples, who have shown themselves to be especially faithless and unwilling to walk the way of the cross (16.24). Both Judas and Peter betray Jesus, despite the latter's boast that he would never do so (26.31-35, 69-75). They sleep when Jesus asks them to watch and pray (26.36-46). They flee when Jesus is arrested (26.56). By the end of ch. 27, imperial power has done its best/worst, successfully employing the death penalty to remove a threat to its societal order, and economic, political and religious power. Jesus' commission to manifest God's saving presence and empire seems to have come to naught. Imperial power is safe. The Jerusalem elite and Pilate take extra steps in resorting to military measures to seal and guard Jesus' tomb to counter reports of Jesus' prediction that God would raise him on the third day (27.62-66).

Sixth Section (28.1-20)

The final chapter is short but monumental in representing the limits of Roman power. Set on the third day after Jesus' death, women at Jesus' tomb await Jesus' predicted resurrection (16.21, and others). With an accompanying earthquake that represents divine power and presence, an angel from God reveals an empty tomb. In this place of God's life-giving power, the Roman guards, representatives of Rome's military might, are rendered 'like dead men' (28.4). The angel announces, with a passive construction to denote divine action, that Jesus 'has been raised' and commissions the women to proclaim this resurrection message to the disciples along with the instruction to meet Jesus in Galilee. As they depart, the women encounter Jesus who repeats their commission (28.1-10).

The empire has exerted its life-and-death power in crucifying Jesus, but it is not able to keep Jesus dead and thwart God's purposes and reign. Chapter 28 thus presents the empire's verdict on Jesus as a treasonous 'wannabe' king worthy only of crucifixion as wrong because it is contrary to God's verdict of Jesus as God's agent (3.17). The chapter, as well as the whole Gospel, functions as a counter-narrative to contest Roman claims.

Meantime, the guards have awakened sufficiently to inform the Jerusalem elite (28.11-15). They resort immediately to damage control, comprising bribery and spin in creating an alternative claim that the disciples stole Jesus' body. The scene encapsulates the world of imperial lies and hostility whose power has been shown to be both death-bringing and limited in the crucifixion and resurrection of Jesus.

The final scene of the Gospel describes a meeting in Galilee between Jesus and the disciples (28.16-20). Unable to keep Jesus dead, the empire cannot control his presence and continuing influence in 'Galilee under the Gentiles'/ Rome. In claiming to have been given 'all authority in heaven and earth' by God, Jesus participates in God's reign over heaven and earth (11.27), shown in the raising of Jesus to be superior to Rome's claims to world dominion and to Satan's claimed control of 'all the empires of the world' (4.8). This authority will, in imitation of Rome's imperial power, be definitively exercised in his return and judgment over Rome (24.27-31).

In the meantime, Jesus commissions the community of disciples of Jews and Gentiles to engage in a worldwide mission that teaches and lives Jesus' teaching. This mission and community parallel and contrast Rome's worldwide mission and societal order. Various authors (Virgil, Seneca, Martial, Statius, Josephus) claimed Rome to have been divinely commissioned to extend its power over the nations. Like the Roman Empire, Jesus' community has a worldwide mission that demands allegiance and extends divine power. Both claim to engage in just and life-giving missions. Jesus' community, however, does not have a military mission. Nor does it recognize Jupiter's role or Rome's right to determine human destiny. In asserting God's sovereignty and rule (4.17; 11.25), it claims God's purposes to be all powerful, and victorious in the return of Jesus (24.27-31). As Emmanuel (1.23), Jesus promises his continuing presence with his disciples in this counter-cultural and confrontive mission until the completion of God's purposes (28.20). Where does Jesus go? Verse 19 suggests he joins God in heaven, in imitation of the imperial practice of apotheosis in which a dead emperor (or member of his family) ascends into the heavens with the gods.

Matthaean Theology in Postcolonial Perspective

Central to this reading of Matthew is the paradox that the Gospel imitates what it resists. As much as it resists the domination of the Roman Empire, it replicates it in the proclamation of the victorious establishment of God's empire that overpowers Rome and its allies. This victory is demonstrated in Jesus' resurrection, which outpowers their imposition of death, and is foreshadowed in his return to establish God's reign in full over defeated and destroyed Rome, symbolized by the fallen eagles and corpses (24.27-31). In announcing the triumph of God's empire over Rome, Matthew ultimately employs the imperial and destructive 'power over' model in presenting God's final salvation. Moreover, as much as the Gospel resists the societal experience of the Roman Empire marked by hierarchy, patriarchy and exclusion, it imitates aspects of it in the formation of an alternative, privileged, community of disciples of Jesus that alone encounters

God's 'fatherly' saving presence and rule and is defined over against the rest of society. This dynamic of repudiation yet replication, of dissent yet duplication, of critique yet complicity, pervades the Gospel's plot and theological world-view, requiring readers, especially committed readers in ecclesial traditions, to adopt an ambivalent 'yes/no' reading stance, simultaneously listening to and talking back to, owning and disowning (parts of), Matthew.

This 'imitation of empire' is evident in every theological category that the Gospel employs: theology, anthropology, Christology, hamatology, soteriology, eschatology, ecclesiology, ethics. For example, the languaging and conceptu-alizing of the Gospel's central theological claim, the 'kingdom/empire of the heavens', employs imperial language and mindset denoting domination, oppres-sion, violence, hierarchy, patriarchy, injustice and elitism. What role do these connotations play in the use of this language to articulate the assertion of God's saving presence, rule and purposes in the words, actions, death, resurrection and return of Jesus and in the community committed to him?

In the context of Rome's empire, the claim of God's reign/empire expresses fundamental convictions about God, notably the assertion of God's sovereignty as 'Lord of heaven and earth' (11.25) and as 'Father' (6.9). This sovereignty is attested in God's sustaining of creation (5.45) and previous guiding of Israel (1.1-17), including the revelation of God's will and purposes (5.17-48) and of God's saving work of redeeming the people from imperial powers such as Egypt and Babylon (chs 1–2). Manifested there as God's life-giving and liberat-ing work, it is also exerted through Jesus' call to people to 'follow me' (4.18-22) as a claim of human ownership, thereby creating, as imperial allegiance does, a new identity and way of being. That is, God's sovereignty embraces all of creation, human history and individuals. In classic imperialist style, it is a 'take it or pay the penalty' sovereignty that embraces human destiny. It imposes eschatological condemnation of being cast into the 'furnace of fire' for those who do not welcome God's sovereignty or rule over them (13.41).

God's saving work continues to be revealed in Jesus' ministry, also pre-sented in terms parallel with and imitative of Rome's elitist and excluding imperial theological claims. Various writers (Virgil, Seneca, Statius, Silius Italicus) announce the gods' choice of Rome and the emperor as their agent to manifest their presence, will and blessings. Matthew similarly presents Jesus as God's chosen agent, the Christ, the Son of God, conceived by God's initiative (1.18-25), commissioned before birth (1.21-23), witnessed to by the Scriptures (1.22-23; 2.6, 15; and many others), preserved by divine interven-tion from Rome's murderous ally Herod (ch. 2), witnessed to by the prophet John (3.1-12) and blessed by God as 'my beloved Son' (3.13-17; 17.1-8). Matthew rivals Rome in the imperial strategy of claiming unique agency, thereby disqualifying any competition.

Like Rome, Matthew claims, Jesus also manifests divine presence. The claim is first made in 1.23 by evoking and claiming Isaiah 7–9 where the manifestation of God's presence in a new-born threatens imperial power, signalling divine triumph over imperial aggressors. In 28.20, it validates the worldwide mission of the community to make disciples of all nations. Rome also exercises a worldwide mission, 'to rule the nations with your power' (Virgil, *Aeneid* 6.851-53). In this context, Jesus announces (5.3-12) and enacts (chs 8–9) blessing on those whom he encounters, especially (in contrast to Rome) on the 'poor in spirit', the materially poor who with little hope and few resources know the devastating power of imperial greed. Drawing on visions such as those of Isaiah for a world free from domination by the nations and now under God's rule, he also envisages a blessed future world marked by wholeness and release from disease and brokenness (11.2-5), by abundance of food and fertility as all gain access to resources like land in a new heaven and earth (14.13-21; 15.32-39), by justice, mercy, peace and faithfulness (5.3-12; 23.23). With such visions, Jesus resembles the claims of numerous empires and rulers who typically promote their rule as beneficial for all, while critiquing Rome for failing to be so.

Throughout his ministry, Matthew's Jesus exerts absolute authority over most areas of human life. As imperialists have frequently done, Matthew claims the past, reworking Israel's traditions to serve his own purposes. In an act of revisionist writing, he reinterprets Israel's history to point to Jesus (1.22-23; 2.5-6, 15, 17-18; 4.14-16; 8.17; and others). Claiming texts that often resisted imperialism and spoke of God's redemption from it (e.g., Isaiah 7–9, 52–53), he continues their anti-imperial claims to express his own opposition. He co-opts these authoritative traditions to legitimize his own Christological agenda.

Likewise, Matthew's Jesus exerts absolute authority over the present. He claims human allegiance (4.18-22), banishes sickness and demons (4.23-25), determines how people should think (5–7), claims the definitive interpretation of God's will over against tradition and contemporary interpreters (5.17-48; and others), offers the definitive interpretation of the Scriptures (1.22-23; 4.15-16; 8.17; and others), calms the sea (8.23-27), enacts the destruction of Rome (8.28-34), forgives sin (9.2-8), raises the dead (9.18-26), constitutes a community that mirrors the empire's 'us and them' division based now not on birth, status, power and wealth but on believing in/following him (10.11-23, 34-39), commissions it to extend his authority in mission (10; 28.16-20), enacts the destruction of the temple, the centre of the Jerusalem leadership's power (21.12-17), announces eternal damnation on opponents, especially societal leaders (23), envisages the destruction of Rome in a final battle (24.27-31) and the condemnation of a (significant?) part of humanity in the final judgment (25.31-46). Not surprisingly, after exhibiting authority over death in his resurrection, he claims the totalizing power of empires, 'all authority has been given to me in heaven and earth' (28.18), and promises (threatens?) continual supervision and knowledge of their lives, 'I am with you always' (28.20). In attributing such all-encompassing authority to Jesus, the Gospel mirrors and replaces one system of absolute authority with another.

This revelatory work and assertion of God's ruling authority is necessary because of the dualistic or binary way in which the Gospel constructs the present world. Satan is presented as challenging God's sovereignty, claiming control of all the empires of the world (4.8), and establishing its own reign in the midst of God's world by securing the loyalty of empires and humans who are agents for Satan's opposition to God's purposes (13.38-39, see the numerous demoniacs encountered in the Gospel). The Gospel claims that in controlling the empires of the world, a special alliance exists between Satan and leadership groups such as Rome's allies, the Jerusalem elite, who, with Pilate, crucify Jesus. It discredits these leaders by identifying them with characteristics of Satan, namely, being 'evil' (6.13; 12.34; 16.4) and 'tempting' (4.1, 3; 16.1; 19.3) or resisting God's purposes, while presenting itself as the beacon of righteousness.

The two empires coexist in the present in conflictual struggle (13.24-30, 37-40). The present is not the time for a definitive cosmic division. Jesus' exorcisms redeem individuals from the power of Satan as the reign of God is manifested (12.28). Likewise, Satan assails those committed to Jesus, exerting continual opposition to the community of disciples (16.16) and at times influencing their behaviour so that they oppose God's purposes (16.22-23). The coexistence of the two empires, though, does not last forever. Again, in imperial style, the Gospel confidently claims the elimination of its rivals and opponents in the certain, future, demise of both Satan (13.39-42) and Rome (24.27-31), deemed to be (again in imitation of Rome's imperial practices) too rebellious and evil to live.

In addition to presenting the world as being under Satan's control, the Gospel also styles it as a place of sins from which people need saving by Jesus (1.21). That is, Matthew employs a typical imperial 'before' and 'after' paradigm to present the 'before' as evil and the 'after' as a transforming experience effected by God's reign. These sins comprise primarily, but not exclusively, the leadership of the elite and the unjust societal order that they impose for their own advantage at the expense of the rest (9.36; 15.1-20; 20.25-28). Based in the temple and allied with Rome (21–27), this order contravenes God's purpose (20.25-26). Its opposition to Jesus and to God, expressed in its crucifixion of Jesus, is impotent because Jesus' death and resurrection, along with his life, effect 'forgiveness of sins' (9.1-8; 26.26-28). The term 'forgiveness' expresses release and is the same term used for the Year of Jubilee in Leviticus 25 to denote social and economic justice and transformation, removing societal injustice such as slavery, debt and land accumulation.

The alternative societal experience that Jesus requires of disciples also evidences the impact of empire. In resisting conventional hierarchical and patriarchal social patterns, Jesus offers this community identities that participate in his own, namely slaves (20.25-28) and children (19.15-18; see 2; 3.17). Such images for the whole community based in their solidarity with Jesus point to a significant societal alternative and suggest some deconstruction of imperial norms of power. Yet, while domination is forbidden to disciples, Jesus retains it, exercising it in naming and defining their identity as well as in choosing for disciples subservient roles marked by marginalization and powerlessness, thereby offering illusory solidarity. While 'power over' is forbidden to disciples, God and Jesus exercise it as 'Father' (6.9; 23.9), as teacher (10.24-25) and as 'instructor/ master' (23.10). Further, while violence is forbidden to disciples in their interaction with Rome's world (5.38-48; Jesus foregoes it, 26.52-53), Jesus and God retain its use for the final violent and forcible establishment of God's empire (24.27-31).

A similar dynamic exists around membership in this community. Jesus proclaims that God bestows life-giving blessings on all, ironically described in very bifurcated terms as the evil and the good, the righteous and the unrighteous (5.45). Beginning with the genealogy, the Gospel seems to celebrate the inclusion of women and men, Jews and Gentiles, the powerful and the powerless in God's purposes, in stark contrast to imperial 'inclusion' of the (predominantly male) wealthy, powerful and high-status, to the exclusion of the rest. Jesus seems committed to merciful inclusiveness, welcoming despised fishermen, tax-collectors and sinners to his circle (4.18-22; 9.9-13). Yet, his central community of 12 disciples comprises only men, and a woman has to better (shame?) him in verbal contest in order to gain benefits (15.21-28). Jesus' mission shows a profound bias toward the non-elite and little patience or mercy for the elite, whom he strongly condemns (9.36; 15.12-13; 23). However, it is not plain-sailing for the non-elite either, since only those who commit to Jesus are welcome now and in the eschatological divide (10.32-42). That is, Matthew has replicated imperial divisiveness, replacing some of its criteria (wealth, power), redefining others (status), maintaining some (androcentricity?) and adding the definitive criterion of commitment to Jesus for determining who is in and out. Matthew imitates the imperial insistence on boundaries and borders to define a privileged social/eschatological entity to the exclusion of the rest.

In this dualistic and privileging 'us versus them' formulation, Matthew employs typical features of imperial practices that parallel Rome's strategies. These standard features include: claims of divine sanction, a dualistic societal division of the good and the bad that is mirrored by and reinforced with a cosmic dualism, attempts to exert control by defining 'the other' in negative (and demonic) terms, defining the present (or past) as inadequate/inferior and in need of saving, frequent claims of violent punishment on those who resist God's empire in order to intimidate and coerce compliance, and the claim that the asserted reign is benign and beneficial for all. As Homi Bhahba has observed, such counter-imperial mimicry leads to mockery of, and menace to, the imperial power, hence Jesus' crucifixion. Yet, it also leads to claims of counter-mastery that Matthew locates in God's violent, eschatological victory forcibly imposed with Jesus' return.

Ecclesial Matthew: A Text of Justice?

Clearly, to use postcolonial jargon, there can be no idealization of Matthew's text. Its assertion of resistance to imperial paradigms is undoubted yet not univocal, since it replicates the 'power over' mentality of empires, duplicates hierarchical structures, creates a privileged community, and employs threats of eschatological violence and punishment (torture?) to bully people into submission to and compliance with God's purposes. It is an impure subject, complicit with empire, produced by and producing imperial power, enmeshed in and reflective of Rome's world.

Yet, this text from a subjugated provincial also contests and protests Roman power. It exposes the injustice and destructive nature and impact of Roman rule in revealing its demonic commitments, in the brutal use of power by the various rulers who appear in the text, in its pervasive hierarchies, in its numerous encounters with the victims of empire (the sick, diseased, incapacitated, mute, hungry and powerless), in the economic scenarios – especially of parables – depicting the harmful practices of the wealthy and powerful, in the destructive teaching and practices legitimated by the Jerusalem elite, in the scenes involving taxation, in the warnings against wealth, in the crucifixion narrative. With its presentation of Jesus as one who in his death absorbs imperial violence rather than employs violence against it, the Gospel momentarily breaks the cycle of violence and depicts the power of the weapons of the weak as an alternative strategy. It provides glimpses of something of an alternative societal order that is inclusive, merciful, non-violent, protective of the weak, genuinely structured for the good of all, committed to wholeness, oriented to the loving pursuit of the good of the other (service) in reciprocal practices, providing all with just access to resources necessary to sustain good life.

To notice both dimensions of this text, to engage and be engaged by such a text, requires a hermeneutics of suspicion. The exposure of Roman injustice and of the devastating impact of its reign is laudable; the Gospel's imitation of imperial practices and mindset is not. Aspects of the Gospel's alternative societal experience give life; other aspects maintain death.

Empires have always tried to hold the elements of benefit and punishment, mercy and compliance, gratefulness and submission, cooperation and coercion together. Frequently the former are magnified not to reduce but to disguise and hide the latter. Empires like Rome's – and Matthew's – always claim that their rule is benign and beneficial for all (Pax Romana), while holding the literal big stick to punish those who do not show appropriate grateful submission.

One strategy for readers of Matthew is to employ the Gospel's critique of imperialism against the Gospel's (and our own?) imperialist hopes for God's violent triumph. The Gospel trains its readers to be suspicious of the people-subjugating, health-destroying, death-bringing, coercion-oriented powers of empire. While the Gospel levels its critique against Roman imperial practices (e.g., 20.25-26), readers can employ the same critique against the Gospel itself. This is not to say that the Gospel knows no self-critique. Numerous times it warns disciples against complacency, carelessness, distraction, disobedience, arrogance, co-option and usurping God's role of exercising eschatological judgment to determine who participates in God's blessing and who does not (7.1-5, 24-27; 13.19-23; 22.11-14). Yet, even here imperial influence is evident, since the Gospel employs the imperial means of intimidation and coercion, bullying disciples into faithful and sustained living. It also continues to perpetrate the imperial structure in maintaining the violent victory of God over all opponents. Further, it also maintains the privileged 'us versus them' division.

The Gospel perhaps contains the seeds of its own critique. It is adamant that in the present God's predominant (not exclusive because punishment is operative in the present, 22.1-10) way of being is life-sustaining and merciful. It openly affirms God's indiscriminate, merciful and life-giving blessing for all regardless of their moral disposition or commitment to Jesus (5.45). It repeatedly asserts God's disposition to mercy (9.13; 12.7). Yet, it does not extend this affirmation about God's *present* work to all of God's *future* purposes. That is, in representing the future imposition of God's reign as violent, coercive and punitive for the non-compliant, it creates a profound discontinuity with its presentation of God's merciful and life-giving actions in the present.

What would it mean for reading Matthew to trust this affirmation about God's present merciful and life-giving work and extend it to God's future workings? Is it possible to maintain human freedom in and accountability to God's purposes and authority without casting them in terms of coercion and violent destruction for noncompliance? While the Gospel seems to swamp mercy and freedom with harsh accountability, coercive authority and destructive punishment, is it possible to conceive of God's indiscriminate mercy as the all-embracing and determinative category for the present *and* the future and as extending to all people while allowing those who do not wish to participate the freedom not to do so without violent divine consequences?

One implication of trusting the affirmation about God's merciful saving presence would be to examine the claim of imperial benefit. Rome's claims to have, for example, blessed the world with abundance, fertility and plenty, or with desirable Pax are readily assessed in terms of the poverty, food shortages, poor health and excessive taxation experienced by most of the empire's residents. The Gospel negatively (and rightly) evaluates and exposes Rome's rule in part by attending to its actual consequences, who benefits and who is harmed, thereby exposing a massive disconnection between its claim and reality. The destructive and harmful ways in which Roman power was experienced, depicted on every page in the Gospel, cannot be dismissed as merely the attempts of one empire to outdo another. Such consequences are measurable and observable. However, the

Gospel requires comparable examination for itself and its committed readers. Affirmations of God's saving presence as life-giving and merciful need similar attention to formulations of coercion and destructive consequences as well as to lived demonstrations.

A second implication is to question the Gospel's exclusive claim that only Jesus and his community enact God's justice. The Gospel's advocacy of God's indiscriminate benefits for all (5.45) invites precisely this critique of privileging the community of disciples and, by extension, of privileging this text. The impact of looking for signs of God's transformative and life-giving work among all people and in non-biblical texts is to dismantle something of the 'us and them' boundary.

A third implication of trusting this affirmation about God's present merciful purposes for the future involves the continual scrupulous examination of ecclesial and societal structures. Constant vigilance and watchfulness are the basis for resisting conventional imperial-imitating ways marked by exploitation and acquisition.

Finally, while attention to the larger conceptualization, structures and practices of empires is a constant, there is also the challenge of language. While the Gospel employs the linguistic formulation 'the empire/reign/kingdom of God/ the heavens', contemporary committed readers do not have to be so confined but are invited to re-imagine and re-language God's merciful and life-giving ways of working.

BIBLIOGRAPHY

Alföldy, G.
    1988   *The Social History of Rome* (Baltimore: The Johns Hopkins University Press).
Ashcroft, B., G. Griffiths and H. Tiffin (eds)
    1995   *The Post-colonial Studies Reader* (London and New York: Routledge).
Bhabha, H.
    1994   *The Location of Culture* (London: Routledge).
Carter, W.
    2000   *Matthew and the Margins: A Sociopolitical and Religious Reading* (Maryknoll, NY: Orbis Books).
    2001   *Matthew and Empire: Initial Explorations* (Harrisburg, PA: Trinity Press International).
    2003   *Pontius Pilate: Portraits of a Roman Governor* (Interfaces; Collegeville, MN: Liturgical Press).
    2003   'Are There Imperial Texts in the Class? Intertextual Eagles and Matthaean Eschatology as "Lights Out" Time for Imperial Rome (Matthew 24:27-31)', *Journal of Biblical Literature* 122: 467–87.
Castle, G. (ed.)
    2001   *Postcolonial Discourses: An Anthology* (Oxford: Blackwell).
Donaldson, L. (ed.)
    1996   *Postcolonialism and Scriptural Reading* (Semeia, 75; Atlanta: Scholars Press).

Fanon, F.
  1968   *The Wretched of the Earth* (New York: Grove).
Garnsey, P.
  1999   *Food and Society in Classical Antiquity* (Cambridge: Cambridge University Press).
Garnsey, P. and R. Saller
  1987   *The Roman Empire: Economy, Society, and Culture* (Berkeley: University of California Press).
Hanson, K. C. and D. E. Oakman
  1998   *Palestine in the Time of Jesus: Social Structure and Social Conflict* (Minneapolis: Fortress Press).
Harrison, N.
  2003   *Postcolonial Criticism: History, Theory and the Work of Fiction* (Oxford: Polity/Blackwell).
Huskinson, J. (ed.)
  2000   *Experiencing Rome: Culture, Identity, and Power in the Roman Empire* (London: Routledge).
Lenski, G.
  1984   *Power and Privilege: A Theory of Social Stratification* (Chapel Hill: University of North Carolina Press).
Mattingly, D. J. (ed.)
  1997   *Dialogues in Roman Imperialism: Power, Discourse, and Discrepant Experience in the Roman Empire* (Journal of Roman Archaeology Supplementary Series, 23; Portsmouth: Rhode Island).
Mongia, P. (ed.)
  1996   *Contemporary Postcolonial Theory: A Reader* (London: Arnold).
Moore-Gilbert, B.
  1997   *Postcolonial Theory: Contexts, Practices, Politics* (London: Verso).
Said, E.
  1993   *Culture and Imperialism* (New York: Alfred Knopf).
Schwarz, H. and S. Ray (eds)
  2000   *A Companion to Postcolonial Studies* (Oxford: Blackwell).
Scott, J.
  1980   *Domination and the Arts of Resistance* (New Haven: Yale University Press).
  1985   *Weapons of the Weak: Everyday Forms of Peasant Resistance* (New Haven: Yale University Press).
Segovia, F. F.
  2000   *Decolonizing Biblical Studies: A View From the Margins* (Maryknoll, NY: Orbis Books).
Sugirtharajah, R. S.
  2002   *Postcolonial Criticism and Biblical Interpretation* (Oxford: Oxford University Press).
Sugirtharajah, R. S. (ed.)
  1998   *The Postcolonial Bible* (Postcolonialism and the Bible, 1; Sheffield: Sheffield Academic Press).
Webster, J. and N. J. Cooper (eds)
  1996   *Roman Imperialism: Post-Colonial Perspectives* (Leicester Archaeology Monographs, 3; Leicester: University of Leicester Press).

Whittaker, C. R.
    1993   'The Poor', in A. Giardina (ed.), *The Romans* (Chicago: University of Chicago
                Press): 272–99.
Williams, P. and L. Chrisman (eds)
    1994   *Colonial Discourse and Post-Colonial Theory* (New York: Columbia Univer-
                sity Press).

THE GOSPEL OF MARK

Tat-siong Benny Liew

Realizing the intricate relationships between cultural forms and social practices, contemporary postcolonial inquiries are keen to 'provincialize' rather than universalize human knowledge (Chakrabarty 2000). Let me 'provincialize' my comments on Mark by specifying four assumptions at the start. First, my post-colonial criticism is not a return to 'nativism'. Frantz Fanon pointed out over 40 years ago that 'nativism' and 'assimilationism' are apparent opposites operating under the same 'regionalist and separatist' logic of colonialism (1963: 94). Thus, my comments will intentionally refer to scholars of the geopolitical West to argue for (and demonstrate) the reality of intercultural dynamics. Second, I grant as a given the messy and tangled relationship between one's stake in the present and her study of the past. No one can offer a positivist account of Mark's meaning. We perceive certain 'truths' of an ancient text through the lens of our personal commitments and current investments. Third, my commitments and investments are characterized by a diasporic sensibility that 'make[s] room for reciprocal critique and multiple commitments' (Cheung 1997: 10). I refuse to idealize anything or any book, including the Gospel of Mark. Rather than looking at Mark in any monolithic way, I understand its cultural power to rest precisely on its ability to speak in multiple voices. Finally, I believe that literary texts do more than simply reflect history and culture; they also create them. Mark's rhetorical constructions will therefore be my focus.

Orientation

Peter Osborne has recently suggested that constructions of modernity involved a certain construction of time, which in turn constructed the colonial politics of the modern period (1995). According to Osborne, this 'politics of time' entailed a diachronic ordering of synchronic time, in which the 'presents' of the geopolitical West were taken to be the 'futures' of the 'rest'. The resulting need for 'development' and 'progress' (on the part of the geopolitical 'non-West') thus became the rationale for modern colonial discourse. Although Osborne's study focuses on post-Enlightenment philosophy in Europe, I find his notion regarding temporality and politics helpful for a postcolonial reading of Mark.

Many scholars have pointed out the apocalyptic emphasis (the belief in an imminent divine intervention in history to bring about a new and perfect age) within the Second Gospel. Mark's story of Jesus opens with a scriptural 'quotation' regarding God's coming visit (1.2-3), and Mark's Jesus opens his mouth for the first time with a message about the nearness of God's kingdom (1.15). For Mark, this Jesus, or the coming kingdom, is about an aggressive assault on Satan. Not only does Jesus engage Satan in solo combat in an apocalyptic setting of wild beasts and angels immediately after his baptism (1.12-13), his exorcisms (1.21-28, 32-34, 39; 5.1-20; 9.14-29) are identified as plunderings of Satan's household (3.23-27). Mark keeps alluding to this imminent kingdom and typifies it as both powerful and eternal (9.1; 10.29-30; 14.62). Within the Gospel there is also the so-called 'Little Apocalypse' (ch. 13), the significance of which is evidenced by a couple of not-so-subtle addresses to its readers (13.14, 37). Given its generous use of the adverb 'immediately' as well as the conjunction 'and', even the form of the Gospel communicates a sense of urgency, or a shortness of time.

Norman Cohn's study of the roots of ancient Jewish apocalyptic understanding has hinted at the potential connection between ancient Jewish apocalyptic and colonial politics (1993). This connection becomes more cogent for Mark considering the tacit agreement by Markan scholars that Mark was written during a turbulent time of colonial politics (either immediately before or after the Romans destroyed the temple in 70 CE). Since its canonization, Mark's apocalyptic story has continued its involvement in colonial politics as the Bible becomes a colonizing can(n)on across the globe. Traditional studies of Mark from the First World have, however, generally (dis)missed this colonial connection. Because of the West's conventional identification with Rome, its habitual antagonism against Jewish cultures and its grandiloquent separation of politics and religion, Markan studies tend to focus on either first-century religious conflicts between Jews and Christians or other contemporary questions of 'faith'.

Stephen D. O'Leary has suggested that apocalyptic rhetoric involves the interplay between time, authority and evil (1994). His insight, however, leaves out one important factor. Regardless of what one thinks of Julia Kristeva's 'women's time' and its relations to linear temporal understandings, she does point to the entanglements between time and gender politics (1986; see also Keller 1997). Given the connections between (apocalyptic) time and (colonial) politics, I do not think it is incidental that authority, evil (or human ability to resist evil and bring about progressive social change) and gender have all been topics of much discussion within postcolonial inquiries. In what follows, I will examine what Mark's politics of apocalyptic time has to say about these three topics.

Authority

Jewish Authorities in Mark

The question of authority is conspicuous in Mark for the number of times as well as the scenarios in which the word appears in the Gospel. 'Authority' is highlighted in Mark's first healing miracle (1.21-28) and first controversy story (2.1-12). Although 1.21-28 is undeniably a healing story, its 'frame' (1.21-22, 27-28) indicates that the healing serves to validate Jesus' authority over and above that of the scribes. Likewise, 2.1-12 centres on Jesus' authority to forgive sins and the scribes' self-condemnation by charging Jesus with blasphemy. What we see in these two stories is basically Jesus replacing the scribes as a reliable mediator of divine wisdom, divine forgiveness and divine power. With the next four controversies (2.13–3.6), Mark expands Jesus' opponents to include various factions of the Jewish leadership and escalates their problem from one of weakness to one of wickedness. It is one thing to be lacking in authority or understanding (1.22; 2.6-7), it is quite another to plot a murder on a Sabbath that is meant for doing good and saving life (3.4, 6).

The word 'authority' appears again in 11.27-33, where various factions of the Jewish authorities question the origin of Jesus' authority. In response, Jesus poses a counter-question, whether they would attribute John's baptism to heaven or humanity. While the divine origin of Jesus' authority is already made clear in his baptism (1.9-11), the Jewish leaders' refusal to answer Jesus' counter-question also clarifies that their authority is dependent on human beings. As 11.32 explains, they do not dare answer Jesus, because 'they were afraid of the crowd' (see also 11.18; 14.2).

This controversy regarding the origin of Jesus' authority does not, however, end at 11.33. Linked by Mark's habitual 'and' (12.1), the story continues in 12.1-12, or what is traditionally known as the parable of the Wicked Tenants. If the first half (11.27-33) betrays the human origin, and thus the weakness, of the Jewish authorities, its second half, as the traditional heading suggests, focuses again on their wickedness as usurpers and murderers. As a result, Jesus promises in the parable that God will do three things: God will come, God will destroy the Jewish authorities and God will transfer their positions of leadership to others. Although the parable is so explicit that the Jewish authorities realize its sting, they simply walk away from Jesus, because, Mark tells us yet once more, 'they were afraid of the crowd' (12.12).

The Jewish leaders in Mark have actually entertained a third possible origin of Jesus' authority. Back in 3.20-30, some scribes have accused Jesus of exorcising by Beelzebul or Satan. Blaspheming the Holy Spirit that has descended into Jesus (1.10) as 'an unclean spirit', they have, of course, condemned themselves to eternal punishment (3.29-30). But what Jesus says then in his own defence, he ends up enacting in his cleansing of the temple (11.15-19), and thus ironically indicts the Jewish authorities for Satanic associations.

Notice the parallels between what Jesus says 'in parables' (3.23) after the accusation of his acting by Satanic authority and what he does in the temple before the other interrogation about the source of his authority. He talks about 'entering' Satan's 'house' in 3.27, and we find Jesus 'entering' the temple, which he later specifies as a 'house' that originally belonged to God (11.17). He talks about 'driving out' demons in 3.23, and he begins to 'drive out' those who are buying and selling in the temple in 11.15. He talks about 'ransacking' Satan's 'goods' and 'house' in 3.27, and in 11.15-16 he is 'overturning' furniture, and stopping the movement of any 'goods' through the temple.

This reading of 3.20-30 and 11.15-19 is consistent with 1.21-28, where Jesus' very first visit to a synagogue is met with the protest of a demon, thus leading to his first exorcism within 'their' synagogue (1.23). This episode insinuates that Jesus will not find synagogues particularly welcoming, because they are dwelling places of demons (see also 3.1-6). If Mark presents the Jewish temple and synagogues as Satan's 'breeding ground', Mark further designates the Jewish leaders as Satan's 'feeding ground'. Like the 'hard ground' in the parable of the Sower (4.1-20), where Jesus' gospel seeds are immediately snatched by Satan, Jewish authorities maintain the same view towards Jesus from beginning to end. When they come on the scene for the very first time, they accuse Jesus of blasphemy (2.1-12); when the Jewish council finally condemns Jesus to die, its charge against him is still blasphemy (15.53-65). In Mark's depiction, Jewish leaders are weak, wicked and, perhaps most condemnatory of all, demonic.

Mark's attack on the Jewish authorities is certainly not limited to these passages. Jesus' first miraculous feeding in Mark, for instance, contrasts Jesus' compassion and the Jewish leaders' failure to shepherd and care for the people (6.34). This particular problem of the Jewish leaders has already been illustrated in the immediately preceding episode, when King Herod agrees to behead John the Baptizer because of a whimsical promise he has made at his birthday banquet (6.14-29). Jesus' willingness to place human needs above ritual laws, on the other hand, has already occasioned many controversies (2.13–3.6). This contrast is underscored again in another controversy between Jesus' two feeding miracles (7.1-23). This controversy starts because Jesus' disciples eat without washing their hands in accordance with 'the tradition of the elders'. In response, Jesus calls his inquisitors 'hypocrites' and countercharges them for placing rituals and traditions before human needs. As part of his counter-attack, Jesus gives the example of how the Jewish authorities disregard God's intentions by teaching people to plead financial commitment to God in extenuation of neglecting ageing parents.

The second feeding miracle opens with a similar statement emphasizing Jesus' compassion on the people (8.2). The bulk of the 'Jewish-leadership bashing', however, is found in the ensuing boat trip (8.11-21), with Jesus issuing a direct warning against their 'leaven' or influence. When the disciples mistake his warning for a reprimand against their negligence to bring bread, Jesus reminds them of the two miraculous feedings. Without doubt, the feedings should have reminded the disciples of Jesus' supernatural ability to provide an overabundant food supply, thus making their worry over bread superfluous. These two feedings, however, should also present a vivid contrast between Jesus' concern with human welfare and the Jewish leaders' emphasis on legalism. Their set of mixed-up priorities may well be the 'leaven' against which the disciples should be on the lookout.

Roman Authorities in Mark

One may question if Mark is in effect promoting a form of anti-Judaism, given his critical re-presentations of the Jewish leaders. Mark is, however, equally critical of non-Jewish authorities, which, in both the text and context of Mark, turn out inevitably to be Roman imperialists. In response to the squabble over the request for the next-best seats in God's kingdom, Mark's Jesus corrects his disciples by denouncing the type of rule Gentiles (read Roman) practice as oppressive and authoritarian and authors a new understanding that features servanthood and sacrifice (10.35-45). In Jesus' last passion prediction, the Gentiles are identified as the ones who will, in cooperation with the Jewish leaders, torment and kill Jesus (10.33). Likewise, both Gentile and Jewish leaders are listed side by side as those who will hound the disciples in the 'apocalyptic discourse' (13.9).

The projection of the passion prediction is, of course, confirmed in the passion narrative (14.1–15.47). This section of Mark is full of parallels. Not only does Mark parallel the death of John the Baptizer and that of Jesus, he also parallels Herod and Pilate. Both occupy an official position that gives them power to decide on the fate of a 'God-sent'. Both are intrigued by their prisoner in a somewhat favourable manner: Herod is both puzzled and delighted by what the Baptizer has to say (6.20), while Pilate is amazed by Jesus' silence (15.5). Like Herod, Pilate realizes that the accused standing before him is not guilty (6.19-20; 15.10, 14), but lacks the strength to do the right thing. Instead, both succumb to 'people-pressure' and sentence an innocent person to death on an occasion of festivity (6.21, 26-28; 15.6, 14-15).

Mark's assault on the Roman authorities is further demonstrated by another double parallel. After Jesus' parallel trial before the high priest and Pilate, both the Roman soldiers and the Jewish leaders spit on him, strike him and ridicule him (14.65; 15.19-20). This double parallel does not only implicate both Jewish and Roman leaders, it further suggests a collaborative relationship between them when it comes to Jesus. Indeed, such a relationship may be connoted in the controversy regarding paying taxes to Caesar (12.13-17), since the controversy means to catch Jesus in a dilemma where he has to choose between offending Jewish or Roman sensibility. Jesus' reply ('Return to Caesar what belongs to Caesar, and return to God what belongs to God', 12.17), however, contains another implicit challenge against the Romans. The passage is clear that the denarius is what belongs to Caesar, but the immediately preceding controversy (12.1-12) has also specified that what belongs to God is a vineyard that God created and that God is expecting a proper share of its produce. Whether one interprets the vineyard as Israel or the world (or both), Rome's colonization of Israel and its status as the main imperial power of the time place the

Romans as tenants who, in spite of their apparent control over the vineyard, are ultimately accountable to God. Their participation in the abuse and murder of Jesus (10.33-34; 15.1-24) as well as the prediction that they will do the same to persecute Jesus' disciples (13.9) clearly mark them as part of the present, wicked tenants whom God will come to remove and destroy in due time.

Twice within the Gospel of Mark (9.33-37; 10.13-16), Jesus uses children as an object lesson to teach his disciples that their service and sacrifice should benefit those who have little or no power in society. This teaching comes with a stern warning that failure to do so will lead to a fate more regrettable than drowning in the sea (9.42-48). In light of the negative evaluation Jesus makes regarding the way Gentiles or Romans use power (10.42-43), this warning may intimate a certain apocalyptic terror that will await the Romans.

In fact, Mark's apocalyptic rhetoric provides a basis to further nuance his charges against the Jewish leaders. Since ancient Jewish apocalyptic writers, in the interest of self-preservation, tend to level their attacks at a more benign target than the Roman imperialists themselves, it is possible that Mark's verbal assault on the Jewish authorities is a similar tactic of 'scapegoating'.

Anti-Authority in Mark

In addition to his criticisms of Jewish and Roman authorities, Mark's discontent with the ruling powers of his day can be seen by the way he identifies and situates Jesus' faithful followers. Those who respond favourably to Jesus – like the leper (1.40-45), the tax-collectors and sinners (2.13-17), the Gerasene demoniac (5.1-20), the woman who has been haemorrhaging for 12 years (5.25-34), the Syrophoenician woman (7.24-30), the blind beggar called Bartimaeus (10.46-52) or the unnamed woman who anoints Jesus with a jar of expensive nard (14.3-9) – tend to come from the lower strata, if not the margins, of society. In contrast, Mark gives the comic yet tragic assessment that camels will have a better chance of going through the eye of a needle than the wealthy and powerful entering the kingdom (10.25).

Mark's polemic against those in power is represented as a politics of (apocalyptic) time. For Mark, change will take place at the parousia. The idea that the heavenly convulsion described in 13.24-25 signifies a socio-political commotion is not only supported by the emphasis on wars in 13.7-8 but also by the 'end-time judgment' that Mark's Jesus implies in 8.38, 12.9, 36 and 14.61-62. Although the warnings of judgment in chs 12 and 14 are directed at Jewish authorities, the fact that Mark has a military officer of imperial Rome confessing to 'the (crucified) King of the Jews' (15.39) shows that Mark has in mind an anti-imperial 'shake-up'.

Mark's apocalyptic emphasis is also related to other challenges that he makes against various forms of traditional authorities. Mark's Jesus is willing to override customary familial obligations on the basis of one's commitment to the 'good news'. When his mother and siblings attempt to place a 'restraining order' on his activities, Jesus responds by treating them as 'outsiders' and talks about a new family that is based on one's decision to do God's will rather than one's blood ties (3.21, 31-35; see also 10.29). The fact that this change in familial relations is connected with Mark's apocalyptic understanding can be seen in the 'apocalyptic discourse' as well as Jesus' encounter with the Sadducees. Disintegration of natural family relations, caused by mutual betrayal, is given as a sign of the apocalypse (13.12); likewise, Jesus' response to the Sadducees contains an implicit critique of their failure to move beyond traditional understandings of marriage and family in light of the resurrection (12.25).

With faithful obedience to God replacing heredity as the new basis of 'familial relations', the traditional barrier between Jews and Gentiles also becomes a thing of the past. Mark's apocalyptic promise of a racially or ethnically inclusive eschatological community (13.10, 27) is already echoed in Jesus' ministry. Welcoming those who come to him from beyond Galilee (3.7-12), as well as going beyond Galilee to minister himself (5.1; 6.45; 7.24, 31), Mark's Jesus models his promise that the gospel is to be preached to the entire world (14.9). Judging from the scriptural quotation that the temple should be 'a house of prayer for all the nations' (11.17), cultic exclusivity is also a major reason behind Jesus' cleansing of the temple.

In addition to family and ethnicity, oppressive rituals and traditions represent another form of established powers that Mark's Jesus comes to demolish. Much to the dismay of the Jewish leaders, Jesus consistently ignores and violates their established laws, whether they have to do with cultic cleanliness (1.40-44; 2.15-17; 7.1-23), fasting (2.18-22) or the Sabbath (1.21-31; 2.23-3.6). As an explanation to those who are puzzled by his unconventional and non-conforming actions, Jesus gives three metaphors – fasting in the bridegroom's company at a wedding feast, sewing a piece of new cloth on an old garment and storing new wine in old wineskins – to illustrate the incompatibility of a new age and a set of old laws (2.18-22).

Mark's anti-authority stance is also evident in his criticisms against the desire for power. Mark is obviously dissatisfied with the Jewish leaders about many things, but his arguably most direct and public denunciation of them centres on their craving for glory and honour (12.38-40). While their lust for power will drive them to persecute Jesus and his followers, this same lust will cause Jesus' own followers to falsify Jesus' messianic claim (13.6, 21-22). In fact, a constant source of contention between Jesus and his disciples is the latter's obsession with splendour and power (8.31-33; 9.5, 33-38; 10.23-27, 35-45). Whether by way of betrayal (14.42-45), flight (14.50-52) or denial (14.54, 66-72), the disciples' failure during Jesus' passion demonstrates the incongruence of the gospel and self-enhancement.

The failure of the disciples may be yet another segment of Mark's anti-authority stance. Personally called (1.16-20; 3.13), individually named (3.16-19) and collectively designated as the 'Twelve' and, in some manuscripts, 'apostles' (3.14, 16), they are marked by Mark as Jesus' special companions and representatives (3.14-15) who are privy to Jesus' private instruction (4.33-34; 9.28-29; 13.3-4). As the Gospel unfolds, however, their roles as disciples are often played, and replaced, by other, unexpected figures. The first person who preaches the gospel in addition to Jesus is the Gerasene demoniac instead of the so-called 'disciples' (5.19-20). While a storm overwhelms these Twelve with faithless fear (4.35-41), a woman who has been haemorrhaging for 12 years and a father of a 12-year-old girl have faith to overcome sickness and death (5.21-43). Accounts of Jesus curing people of demonic possession (7.24-30; 9.14-28), deafness (7.31-37) and blindness (8.22-26; 10.46-52) immediately before and within Mark's 'on-the-way' section (8.22–10.52) are alternated with episodes in which Jesus finds it impossible to do the same for his disciples (8.14-21; 8.31–9.13; 9.30-49; 10.13-16; 10.32-45). Almost immediately after the disciples' failure at exorcism (9.14-29), we hear of another successful exorcist whom they try to exclude (9.38-41). Immediately before Judas makes his deal to betray Jesus for money (14.10-12), we read of an unnamed woman who anoints Jesus with a jar of expensive nard despite others' objection (14.3-9). As the other disciples flee and deny Jesus (14.50-52, 66-72), Simon of Cyrene becomes the one who bears the cross (15.21), Joseph of Arimathea the one who provides the burial (15.42-46) and a group of women the ones who follow Jesus all the way to the tomb (15.40-41, 47; 16.1-2). Talking to his disciples, Mark's Jesus makes a statement that also aptly describes their downfall: 'many who are first will be last, and the last first' (10.31; see also 9.35). Considering the special status already granted the Twelve in Paul's epistles (1 Cor. 15.5; Gal. 1.17-19), the way Mark puts them among the 'fall guys' is certainly in line with his promise of an apocalyptic rearrangement of power.

New Authority in Mark

Despite Mark's anti-authority and barrier-breaking rhetoric, he is more concerned with the categories of authority than its constitution. This can be seen from the way he derides the traditional and hollow authority of the Jewish leaders but delights in the new and substantial authority of Jesus in the first healing miracle and the first controversy story of the Gospel (1.21-28; 2.1-12).

The authority of Mark's Jesus is closely related to the authority of the Hebrew Scriptures. Time after time, Mark presents Jesus as one who can quote and expound Scripture to justify his own teachings and actions, whether the issue at hand concerns the Sabbath (2.23-28), his practice of speaking in parables (4.10-12), ritual cleanliness (7.1-8), responsibility to parents (7.9-13), the acceptability of divorce (10.2-12), the assurance of eternal life (10.17-22), the operation of the temple (11.15-17), the credibility of resurrection (12.18-27), the first commandment (12.28-31), the relationship between David and the Messiah (12.35-37) or the apocalypse (13.24-27). Mark is careful to point out that the way Jesus uses and interprets Scripture is recognized as valid by the crowd (11.18; 12.37) as well as by the scribe who questions him about the 'first commandment' (12.32-33). At the same time, however, Mark indicates that this Jesus is much more than a master scribe who understands Scripture; he is, in fact, its very fulfilment. In addition to Jesus' own references to Scripture as a prophecy of his upcoming suffering and ultimate glory (9.12-23; 12.10-11; 13.26; 14.21, 27, 48-49, 62; 15.33), Mark also has 'many' chanting the 'hosanna chorus' at Jesus' entry into Jerusalem (11.8-10) and thus identifying Jesus as the promised Messiah. Of course, at the broader narrative level – that of the implied author or narrator – this entire story about Jesus begins itself with a scriptural allusion to Isaiah (1.1-3).

Perhaps two scenes best underscore Mark's Jesus as the very fulfilment of Jewish Scripture. The first is the parable of the Wicked Tenants (12.1-11), which asserts that Jesus will conclude the succession of servant-prophets sent by God to re-establish God's claim of ownership of the vineyard. The other, Jesus' transfiguration (9.2-8), though sequentially earlier, is actually more forceful in making this point. Initially, Moses and Elijah greet the transfigured Jesus. After Peter rashly proposes to make 'three tents' or 'dwellings' for the conversation partners, three things happen: a cloud overcomes them, a heavenly voice announces that Jesus is God's 'beloved Son' and one to be listened to, and Moses and Elijah disappear from the scene altogether. The disappearance of Moses and Elijah after this command to 'listen' signifies that Peter should not have placed Moses, Elijah and Jesus as equals. Granted that Moses and Elijah are respectively the great lawgiver and the great prophet of the Hebrew Scriptures, the Son's appearance fulfills and brings with him the authoritative interpretation of that tradition.

The authority of Mark's Jesus, then, is ultimately dependent on his status as God's beloved Son and heir. Mark has effectively positioned one story at the beginning of the Gospel (Jesus' baptism, 1.9-11), one at the middle (Jesus' transfiguration, 9.2-8) and one at the end (Jesus' crucifixion, 15.33-40) to declare Jesus as God's Son, but Mark's consummate touch in making Jesus' status special and his authority absolute may be found in one little word that he tucks away in the parable of the wicked tenants to qualify this 'beloved Son': 'the owner still had *one* other person, a beloved son' (12.6; emphasis mine). In other words, there is no other heir than Jesus; he is God's last authorized agent, God's one and only regent. This claim of singularity is, of course, an effective ideological weapon that leads to absolutism by allowing no comparison or competition.

This status allows Jesus to 'author' his own assumptions, arguments and pronouncements in many controversy stories that his opponents may not even share or accept. Rather than just being subjected to the authority of Hebrew Scriptures, Jesus becomes his own authority to give pronouncements that ask for decision without discussion. In fact, his authority is so absolute that he has the freedom and flexibility to override the instructions that he himself gives to others to follow. While Jesus chides the scribes for exploiting the livelihood of poor widows (12.40-44), asks a rich man to sell all he owns so that he can give the money to the poor (10.17-22) and sends the Twelve out on a mission like minimalists both in terms of personal belongings taken and charity sought (6.7-13), he allows an undistinguished woman to anoint him at a leper's house with a jar of expensive nard that could have been sold for money to help the poor (14.3-9). He faults the Pharisees and the scribes for neglecting their parents with the excuse of the *korban* offering (7.9-13), yet Jesus himself justifies his decision to ignore and shame his mother and siblings on the basis of a higher calling from God (3.31-35). Similarly, he forbids his disciples to exclude another exorcist because, he says, the exorcist is exorcizing in Jesus' name (9.38-40); at the same time, he reserves for himself the right to decide people's 'proximity' to the kingdom (12.34) and to identify 'false' prophets, even if they are also performing miracles in his name (13.21-22).

Jesus' status as God's only Son and heir in Mark's Gospel results in yet another hierarchical community structure. Despite the familial terms Mark uses to describe the community of Jesus, Jesus' family is not devoid of its own pecking order. Alongside his language of brotherly and sisterly relations, we also find within Mark's Gospel the language of hierarchy that undercuts his egalitarian ideals. At the end of the 'apocalyptic discourse' (13.34-37), Jesus describes his household in terms of a 'lord' who 'authorizes' his 'servants' and 'commands' his 'doorkeeper' to various tasks before he goes on a trip. Since the parable begins and concludes with the warning that one should stay alert and awake (13.32, 35-37), the imagery is that of an institution where vertical structure and the threat of punishment are all accepted modes of operation. Jesus is at the pinnacle of the hierarchy of his household, just as the Gentile or Roman rulers are at the pinnacle of their hierarchy of power, 'lording over' and 'exercising authority over' (10.42) those who rank below them. Although Mark's Jesus forbids his disciples to treat each other in this manner and sets himself up as the model of a different way of relating (10.43-45), this is the kind of language that Mark uses to describe Jesus' interaction with his disciples (3.14-15; 6.7-8; 8.15).

With Jesus on the throne, his disciples are often reduced to, borrowing Patrick Brantlinger's phrase for coloured characters in British literature, ' "sidekick" roles, as the loyal satellites – virtually personified colonies' (1988: 57) of the Messiah. To keep a safe distance between himself and the 'madding crowd', Jesus tells the disciples to go and get a boat for him to teach in (3.9). As the disciples strain at the oars, Jesus takes a nap in the stern (4.38). When there are miraculous feedings to be performed, the disciples are the ones who assume the ushering role of seating people, the table-waiting role of distributing food and the janitorial role of picking up crumbs (6.39, 41, 43; 8.6-8; see also 8.19-20). In the latter part of the Gospel, they continue to act as Jesus' 'gofers': they are sent by Jesus to go for Bartimaeus (10.49), to go for the colt in the next village (11.1-7) and to go for the Passover preparation in the city (14.12-16).

If familial language does not exclude oppressive and dominating relations, the conspicuous absence of the word 'father' in Jesus' expositions of the new family (3.33-35; 10.28-30) also does not necessarily imply the dismantling of authority or hierarchy. After all, Mark's Jesus reintroduces an authoritative 'father' figure for both himself and his disciples in the person of God, who has the last say on honour and shame (8.38), forgiveness (11.25), the time of the apocalypse (13.32) and what happens and does not happen (14.36). Even if doing God's will makes one a mother or sibling of Jesus, one must remember that within Mark's Gospel, God's will is arbitrated by and fulfilled in Jesus, the 'beloved Son' and 'heir' of God (1.11; 9.7; 12.6-7). Jesus' new definition of 'family' does not automatically eliminate the interplay of power and subordination; quite to the contrary, power always resides with the one who has the authority to define.

'Children' is another familial term that Mark uses. According to Mark's Jesus, his followers should welcome and incorporate 'children' (9.36-37) in their midst and, at the same time, be 'child-like' (10.13-16). In other places, we find Mark's Jesus referring to his disciples as 'the sons of the bridal party' (2.19) and the Jewish people as 'children' (7.27). Once, Jesus addresses his disciples directly as 'children' (10.24). Even if one understands 'children' as a symbol for something else, like those who occupy a marginal position in society, infantilization is still an insulting form of patronization at best and an extreme form of victimization at worst.

Because of Jesus' unique and authoritative status, those who criticize him are 'guilty of an eternal sin' (3.29). Similarly, Jesus instructs his disciples to demonstrate formally their rejection of those who reject them in their mission (6.10-11). When a disciple, Peter, rejects Jesus' first passion prediction, he instantly becomes 'Satan', since he does not share the mind or obey the thoughts of Mark's Jesus (8.33). Not only do these crude methods of polarization further fuel the absolute authority of Mark's Jesus, they also lead to a duplication of the insider–outsider binarism.

As the above episodes intimate, Mark's Gospel operates on a rather straightforward equation: those who respond favourably to Jesus, the authoritative interpreter and fulfilment of God's will, are 'in'; those who do not are 'out' (8.38). Granted that this new criterion is opened to people of all heritages and ethnicities and that the stories of the disciples and the 'other exorcist' show that one's status as an 'insider' may involve a few surprising twists, understanding and following Jesus is still a prerequisite for inclusion. The result, therefore, is not inclusiveness, but the validation of a new criterion that is based on one's response to Jesus rather than other conventional measures.

Mark's duplication of the insider–outsider binarism also involves violent destruction of those 'outside' when the 'ins' and 'outs' become clear and absolute at Jesus' parousia. We have seen already how, with Jesus reappearing in power and in judgment (8.38–9.1; 12.9, 36; 13.26; 14.61-62), the parousia will bring about a realignment of socio-political power and the full establishment of God's reign, the 'wicked' authorities will be destroyed, and the temple built by 'indiscriminating builders' will be dismantled. In other words, the 'outsiders' who 'ousted' Jesus will, in turn, be 'ousted'. Mark actually has in mind something worse than a 'tit-for-tat' policy; as his Jesus declares, 'What measure you measure with, it will be measured against you, *with added proportion*' (4.24; emphasis mine). The horror of this 'interest-incurring' repayment of violence is reflected in Jesus' comment regarding his betrayer, that 'it would have been better for that man if he had not been born' (14.21). Elsewhere, he talks about his eschatological judgment as an experience that is worse than drowning and mutilation, for it involves the torture of 'never-dying' worms and 'ever-burning' fire (10.42-48).

Presenting an all-authoritative Jesus who will eventually annihilate all opponents and all other authorities, Mark's utopian, or dystopian, vision, in effect, duplicates the colonial non-choice of 'serve-or-be-destroyed'. This non-choice is, in turn, based on another colonial rationalization that Mark shares, namely, that certain people have proven to be too barbaric, too evil or too underdeveloped to be given autonomy, or even the right to live. Despite the Gospel's invocation of the Deity and its rhetoric that polarizes things divine and human (8.33; 11.30), it, like most human power systems, promotes 'a hierarchical, punitive, and tyrannical concept of ruler and ruled, while claiming that it was all for the best' (Sinfield 1992: 167).

Mark's politics of parousia supports the use of power, then, at the same time as it expresses dissatisfaction with the present political power. Actually, power is also a word that would nicely summarize how Mark understands and presents Jesus' authority. Although the word 'authority' is first used in association with Jesus' first public teaching (1.21-22), what we find in that pericope is not the content of Jesus' teaching but the account of Jesus' first healing miracle (1.23-26). Correspondingly, when those who witness the miracle echo in amazement how Jesus' teaching is coupled with authority, their statement contains not a recapitulation of what Jesus teaches but a reiteration of the exorcism (1.27).

Three observations can be made from this pericope. First, Mark makes Jesus' teaching inseparable from Jesus' miracles – the (unknown) content of Jesus' teaching is known by his ability to heal, or his command over unclean spirits. Second, that power to perform miracles, or the ability to have his commands obeyed, is understood to be Jesus' authority. Third, concluding from the above, what Jesus has to teach is his power to do miracles. In other words, his message is his authority.

Mark restates these same points in the controversy story about Jesus healing a paralytic (2.1-12). Like the pericope concerning the healing of the man with the unclean spirit, Mark ties Jesus' healing of the paralytic together with Jesus' teaching, the content of which may seem muddled at first glance. The unspoken questions of the scribes and the ensuing response from Jesus make it clear that the controversy or the point that Jesus wants to teach or get across is his author-ity – more specifically, his authority to forgive sins. To prove his authority, Jesus performs his miracle-working power. He gives the paralytic a 'three-point' command: the paralytic is to stand, pick up his mat and walk home. To the amazement of all, his command is obeyed point by point.

This Markan understanding of authority as power can also be seen in other miracle and controversy stories, where, for example, Jesus overpowers death (5.35-43) and nature (4.35-41; 6.45-51) until people say 'he has done all things well' (7.37), or where Jesus overwhelms his challengers until 'no one dared to ask him any question any more' (12.34). Although it works in opposite direc-tions, this same understanding (authority as power) underlies both the Baptizer's deference to Jesus and the Nazarenes' rejection of him. The Baptizer's statement that he is not worthy to untie Jesus' sandals is sandwiched by two statements about Jesus' power: Jesus' superior strength and Jesus' baptism with the Holy Spirit (1.7-8). On the other hand, the Nazarenes are so convinced of Jesus' humble family background (6.2-3) that they conclude that Jesus' miracles must not be real, because the same assumption, put in negative terms, means that people without authority do not have real power.

Despite people's opposition and Jesus' crucifixion, Mark's understanding of Jesus and of authority remain the same. In fact, Mark's understanding of authority as power becomes obvious in the dramatic events associated with the parousia. According to Mark, the parousia is God's ultimate show of force (and authority) through Jesus. This event, which is often associated with the word 'power' (9.1; 13.26; 14.61-62), will right all wrongs with the annihilation of the 'wicked'. I, for one, tend to think that Jesus' resurrection and return would be enough to undo his murder literally and establish his special place. Yet for Mark, such a scenario, which may solicit from some a somewhat contrite response similar to Herod's when he thinks John the Baptizer has come back to life in the person of Jesus (6.14), is not enough of a demonstration of authority. Authority is (over)power(ing). It demands the submission of everybody, and thus also the annihilation of those who do not submit. In other words, vindi-cation must become vindictive. The problem is that by defeating power with more power, Mark is, in the final analysis, no different from the 'might-is-right' ideology that has led to colonialism, imperialism and various forms of suffering and oppression. Mark's Jesus may have replaced the 'wicked' Jewish–Roman power, but the tyrannical, exclusionary and coercive politics goes on.

Agency

Life within Limits

Mark's Jesus begins his public ministry, preaching about God's coming kingdom and calling for repentance and change, after the alarming note that John the Baptizer has been arrested (1.14-15). Although the Baptizer's baptism of repentance and forgiveness has obviously resulted in more show than substance, Mark seems to provide enough early clues that Jesus is a different kind of agent and that he can make a difference that the Baptizer cannot. After all, Mark has already had the Baptizer clarify that Jesus is 'stronger', because, as Jesus' baptism confirms, Jesus can baptize people with the Holy Spirit rather than water (1.7-8). Mark also parades Jesus' 'strength' right from the start: after having four fishermen leave their careers or their families 'immediately' upon hearing Jesus' call, Mark details four healing stories that lead not only to Jesus' instant stardom but also to people glorifying God, as well as five controversy stories in which Jesus so overwhelmingly defeats his opponents that they have to resort to the possibility of murder (1.14–3.6).

As Mark alerts us to the hard-heartedness and murderous intent of the Jewish leaders, he continues to show a Jesus who is enlarging his mission. First, his influence is no longer limited to Galilee (3.7-8). Second, Jesus is formally establishing a personal entourage who will also serve as his emissaries (3.13-19).

It is at the end of this roster of disciples that Mark hints at another obstacle to Jesus' mission. Besides the Jewish leaders, there is a traitor within by the name of Judas (3.19). This piece of information, given right before Jesus' own statement that divided kingdoms and divided households cannot stand (3.24-25), casts an ominous shadow over the future of Jesus' mission. On the other hand, Jesus' claim that exorcisms are not possible without the binding of Satan (3.23-27) seems to confirm that, if Satan is a 'strong man', Jesus is the 'stronger' one (1.7), who will be able to fulfil his calling as God's authorized agent of change.

As we follow the narrative sequence of the Gospel, the external and internal threats that surface against Jesus in ch. 3 begin to loom larger and larger. The 'key' parable that opens ch. 4 discloses that Jesus' word will not bring about any lasting difference in most people (4.13-20). Jesus cannot change the Twelve. He can calm a storm, but he cannot help the disciples to overcome fear with faith or understand his identity (4.35-41). Originally called by Jesus, the 'stronger one' (1.7) with the authority to exorcize (3.14-15), the disciples turn out to be without strength to do the very thing they are called to do (9.14-18). All the private tutorials with Jesus notwithstanding, the Twelve end up fearing people (and thus denying and forsaking Jesus) rather than fishing for people as Jesus has intended (1.17).

Mark's ironic twist on the development of the disciples as well as his straightforward account of how many (especially the authorities) misunderstand and reject Jesus weaken our impression of human agency in a colonial world. The way Jesus' family, thinking that he has gone mad, goes out to restrain him is really not too different in their disapproval of Jesus' mission from the scribes who come down from Jerusalem to accuse Jesus of demonic possession (3.21-22). Similarly, he is rejected by the people at Gerasa (5.14-17) as well as his hometown folks at Nazareth (6.1-6). The crowd that is attracted rather than affronted by his miracles turns out to be a fair-weather group. In the passion narrative, we find them collaborating with the Jewish authorities to arrest, accuse and afflict Jesus (14.43, 55-59; 15.6-15).

Concerning Jesus' relationship with the authorities, what happens in Jerusalem is almost an exact replication of what happens in Galilee. While his words and deeds in Galilee result in the authorities first charging him with blasphemy (2.6-7) and then plotting to kill him (3.6), his increasingly aggressive assault on the authorities in Jerusalem causes the authorities to resort to a vicious scheme immediately (12.12; 14.1), and then accuse him of blasphemy (14.63-64). The major difference is, of course, that what remains a plot in Galilee becomes a reality in Jerusalem – Jesus is violently put to death.

It is one thing to realize that Mark's Jesus cannot do too much with the disciples (who are fearful dimwits) and the authorities (who are diehard reactionaries), it is quite another to see that Jesus is also limited in what he can do with those he heals. The leper, whom Jesus dismisses with a solemn caution that he not say anything about Jesus' role in his recovery, ends up dismissing Jesus' warning and severely inhibiting Jesus' freedom of movement (1.43-45). Those who bring a deaf man to Jesus in the Decapolis also disregard Jesus' command to silence after Jesus heals their friend; in fact, Mark's language almost implies an intentional defiance on their part: 'but the more he ordered them [to tell no one], the more exceedingly they proclaimed' (7.36).

About midway through the Gospel, we find Jesus succumbing to the reality that his mission is going to be a failure. On his way towards Jerusalem, this one who first appears as an independent and confident visionary with overpowering wisdom and might is suddenly talking about his own suffering and death as a 'necessity' (8.31; see also 9.31; 10.33-34). As Mark's Jesus explains it in the parable of the Wicked Tenants (12.1-11), the resistance to repentance and change is so strong that it surprises even God, who makes the fatal miscalculation that the beloved Son would command a respect from the wicked tenants that the previous servants could not. Jesus' experiences and encounters with people have now led him to identify his own future with the past failure of the new Elijah or John the Baptizer (9.12-13). Like the Baptizer, then, Jesus is 'handed over'. He appears before the socio-politically powerful and is crucified, because the authority having jurisdiction over him does not have the courage to stand up against 'people-pressure' (14.41, 53-65; 15.1-15).

While the parable of the Wicked Tenants (12.1-11) succinctly shows that what Jesus experiences is basically a repetition of what many of God's servants have previously gone through, the apocalyptic discourse (13.1-37) makes it clear that Jesus' faithful should not expect to fare any better. Like Jesus, they will be 'handed over'; they will be beaten, tried before the authorities and even betrayed to death. After all, if the authorities of this world do not even allow God's only beloved Son to pass over death at a time when they are commemorating the gracious Passover of God (14.1), why will they be kinder or gentler to Jesus' followers at any other time? This inevitability of failure, suffering and death is also confirmed by Jesus' earlier announcement that, in order to follow him, his would-be followers must be prepared to take up the cross and lose their lives (8.34-37). This same point is made in a more subtle way when Mark 'sandwiches' the account of the Baptizer's murder (6.14-29) between the Twelve heading out for mission (6.7-13) and their subsequent return and report to Jesus (6.30). Being God's agents for change may bring about a measure of initial success (6.12-13), but ultimately death and failure await those who follow Jesus on this path.

Despite the miracles and fanfare associated with Jesus' appearance as God's beloved Son, Jesus cannot bring his disciples to understanding or those in power to repentance and change. In the end, the single most important action of his earthly life is negative rather than positive: he drinks his bitter cup and lets himself be crucified by his enemies. He breathes his last, and his mission fails. If anything, Jesus' death calls attention to the huge gap between vision and agency. What he envisions, he cannot implement. The opposing power is too strong, and this same helplessness will haunt his followers.

Hints about Hindrances
Mark attributes our inability to effect positive change to, first of all, isolation and alienation. Although Mark's Jesus pictures a new family made up of those who do the will of God (3.31-35) and sends his disciples out in pairs (6.7), he lives and dies an isolated individual. Misunderstood by his own family (3.20-21), rejected by his own hometown (6.1-6) and misunderstood as well as rejected by his own disciples (4.41; 6.51; 8.14-21, 31-33; 9.32; 10.32; 14.10-11, 32-46, 51-52, 66-72), his last words in the Gospel were the lonesome ones he utters while dying on the cross: 'My God, my God, why have you forsaken me?' (15.34). The faithful ones in Mark – like the Gerasene demoniac (5.1-20), the woman who has been haemorrhaging for twelve years (6.25-34), or the unnamed woman who anoints Jesus at Bethany (14.3-9) – tend to come and go also as lone rangers. In Mark's world, lasting change cannot be made, because agents of change are inevitably solitary pilgrims. As Jesus tells his disciples in the 'apocalyptic discourse', treachery and betrayal are constant possibilities (13.5-6, 12, 21-22), and they will be hated by all (13.13).

In relation to isolation and alienation, Mark's emphasis on treachery and betrayal brings out another hindrance to change: the fickleness and unreliability of human beings. Mark's Gospel is full of such examples, but perhaps the best one has to do with John the Baptizer, whose shift from prophet to prisoner is just as sudden and unexpected as his later transition from being protected to being beheaded by Herod (1.4-5, 14; 6.14-29).

Mark explains this human tendency to vacillate, and the general human inability to bring about change, in terms of two different but closely related human emotions: the fear of loss and the lust for gain. King Herod, having made the impetuous promise that he would give his daughter whatever she asks, decides to go against his better judgment and grant her request for the Baptizer's head, because he is afraid of losing face in front of his guests (6.26). Likewise, Peter, having promised that he would rather die than deny Jesus (14.31), ends up reversing his choice and denies Jesus, because he is afraid of losing his life (14.66-72). It is exactly the same fear that causes the other disciples to forget their vow of loyalty and bravery and flee (14.31, 50-52). There is also the rich man who leaves Jesus 'grieving' (10.22), because he is afraid of losing his wealth.

On the other hand, Judas offers to betray Jesus to attempt a gain. After the Jewish leaders promise him a monetary reward, the deal is made (14.10-11). Judas is, of course, not the only disciple whose want for gain has caused him to struggle with Jesus and impede him from doing God's will. While only James and John have the nerve to plead with Jesus for the next-best seats of his kingdom (10.35-37), all the disciples vie with each other for power and prominence (9.33-34; 10.41).

The division between a fear of loss and a lust for gain becomes murky when it comes to the authorities that bring about Jesus' death. Pilate's decision 'to satisfy the crowd' and have Jesus crucified, despite his knowledge of Jesus' innocence and his attempt to release him (15.6-10, 14-15), reflects the unequal but unstable power relations of colonialism. His choice for political expediency nonetheless exposes his chief concern to preserve and/or enhance his own political career. The same is true of the Jewish leaders who bring Jesus to Pilate with a variety of trumped-up charges. Mark already has Jesus disclose and denounce their obsession with glory and power (12.38-40), and now he specifies again that the Jewish leaders are persecuting and prosecuting Jesus 'because of jealousy' (15.10). Challenged by Jesus but unwilling to relinquish the power they have come to enjoy, and for which they have an insatiable appetite, they decide to get rid of him by deceit and violence. Or, putting it in terms of the parable of the Wicked Tenants, they murder the heir because, first, they do not want to lose any share of their produce (12.2) and, second, they are greedy for an inheritance that is not rightfully theirs (12.7).

Ultimately, Mark relegates the above problems, as well as Jesus' failure, to the sorry state of the world, because for Mark, faith is a prerequisite rather than a product of miracles. The 'unbelief' of the Nazarenes handicaps Jesus' ability to perform miracles (6.5-6), and miracles occur in decreasing number but with increasing complexity as the Gospel progresses with more and more references to people's resistance to Jesus. An apocalyptic worldview is, after all, one in which the present is still under the evil control of Satan. Even if Jesus is able to 'bind' this 'strong man' in their initial encounter in the desert (1.12-13; 3.27), Satan turns out to have enough strength left to devour all of God's agents of change, including God's only beloved Son.

Mark has already 'disclosed' these factors that work against Jesus and human agency in the parable of the Sower (4.1-20). As Jesus explains (if we may reverse his order), three quarters of people who encounter God's call will not make any genuine change because of their desire for wealth or other worldly things (4.18-19), their fear of the difficulty and pain involved (4.16-17) and the sway of Satan (4.15). Nevertheless, Mark is confident that the kingdom of God, though temporarily hidden, will be disclosed or become manifest in the future (4.22).

Sending or Saving
The last two parables in ch. 4 (4.26-32) promise that given time, despite an outward appearance that may look discouraging, the kingdom will come in its fullness. Since the parable of the Sower has already hinted at the supernatural cause behind human futility, the manifestation and the magnitude of God's future kingdom will have to be dependent on the Deity. Accordingly, 4.26-29 makes no remark of the sower's labour. The sower simply, almost carelessly, 'throws' or 'scatters' the seed and goes to sleep; without the sower's toil or know-how, 'the ground bears fruit automatically' until it is ripe for harvest. In the second parable, the sower is not even mentioned. The mustard seed, once sown, just germinates and grows until it 'becomes greater than all the [other] vegetable plants' (4.32).

The inadequacy of human agency to bring about change, then, turns into the 'dispensability' of human endeavour within Mark. What gets emphasized in the certainty of change is a mysterious and automatic process known only to, and done only by, God. As Mark's Jesus, commenting on the kingdom and the difficulty associated with it, reminds us, 'with people it is impossible, but not with God; for all things are possible with God' (10.27; see also 14.36). As the parable of the Wicked Tenants also shows, the only one who can act and do something about the presumably desperate situation is the owner (12.1-11). The fact that Jesus, commenting on God's direct divine intervention, stresses that only God knows the final day and the final hour (13.32) is yet another indication that final change and deliverance are beyond the control of any human and solely in the hands of God.

With God as the single constructive actor in history, human characters in Mark are no longer subjects or agents of positive change. Although the early part of the Gospel seems to emphasize how agents are sent to do God's work, that emphasis gradually gives way to how God will do what God's agents cannot do, as well as how God will save the faithful. Mark starts with a 'quote' from the Hebrew Scriptures about God 'sending' (1.2) a messenger to prepare God's way; as soon as Jesus is baptized, the Holy Spirit immediately 'sent out' (1.12) Jesus to encounter Satan. Jesus, in turn, 'sent out' (1.43) the cleansed leper, who ends up proclaiming the word despite Jesus' command of silence. Finally, there are two references to Jesus' programme to 'send' (3.14; 6.7) the disciples on mission trips. After Jesus' first passion prediction (8.31), however, there is only one genuine reference to God's 'sending' programme (9.37). Furthermore, the word 'send' is used in the parable of the Wicked Tenants to point out the futility of that 'sending' programme. Not only do the wicked tenants beat and kill the agents sent by God, they also send them back, devoid of result, and sometimes of life (12.2-6, 8).

The word 'save', on the other hand, appears only three times (3.4; 5.23, 34) before Jesus' first passion prediction (8.31) but turns up nine times in the last eight chapters of Mark (8.35; 10.26, 52; 13.13, 20; 15.30, 31). More importantly, almost every single one of these nine references to salvation highlights the impossibility of salvation through human effort and/or God's gracious power to save.

This emphasis on being saved (by God) constructs human beings as objects that are acted upon rather than subjects who act. In Mark, human beings actually have no original agency or original autonomy, except the choice to serve either of the true actors of history: God and Satan. That choice, moreover, affects only individual destiny but not the final course of history. In Mark, Satan's hold on this world has proven to be so strong and human agency so weak that God has determined to resort to a direct and violent intervention in the near future (9.1; 12.1-11). This intervention will bring salvation to some and destruction to others; either way, human beings remain objects instead of subjects of agency.

The strong hold of Satan and the lack of human agency also mean that, in the present, the choice to serve God is a choice to suffering and martyrdom (8.34-38; 10.29-30, 39; 13.9-23). Mark's Jesus is, of course, the perfect model of such a choice. Instead of struggling for anything original, he accepts his God-given identity as the 'beloved Son' to encounter Satan (1.9-12); when it becomes obvious that his mission is doomed to fail, Jesus surrenders, once again, to the new course God has ordained (8.31; 9.31; 10.33-34; 14.32-42). It is only within these terms of acceptance and surrender that Mark's Jesus is able to act. Whereas he knows that Judas will betray him, he makes no effort to prevent the betrayal from taking place except with what may, at most, function as an indirect verbal warning (14.17-21). In the same way, Jesus makes no attempt to resist his arrest, although someone with him does take a pretty good swing at it and chops off a capturer's ear (14.41-49). When he is given the opportunity to defend himself before both the high priest and Pilate, he remains stoic and largely silent; when he does speak, what he says serves to convict rather than acquit him (14.60-64; 15.2-5). Even when he is offered a mixed drink of alcohol and myrrh (something akin to a modern painkiller) on the cross, he rejects it, and endures the crucifixion without 'watering down' any of its pain. Jesus' strength lies in his willingness to endure the 'necessity' (8.31) of suffering and death. Maybe it is her demonstration of a similar 'futile' or 'fatalistic faithfulness' that prompts Jesus to place the unnamed woman at Bethany in such high regard (14.3-9). With no capacity to avert the violent death that awaits Jesus, she honours him by preparing his body for burial with a jar of expensive nard. As Mark's Jesus puts it, what is memorable about this woman is the fact that 'she did what she could' (14.8).

For Mark, suffering and death are the hallmarks of faithful discipleship. Judging from the way Mark's Jesus concludes his teaching on 'servanthood leadership' with the example of how he sacrifices his life (10.43-45), one may gather that martyrdom not only assures salvation (13.9-13) but is also the 'service' that would make one 'first' (10.44) in the kingdom. Besides, human sufferings (especially martyrdom) constitute a form of induced labour that will move God to quicken the birth process of the 'new world order'. The beatings and killings of a succession of God's servants and finally the murder of the heir compel God to do with force what God's agents cannot do with words (12.1-11). As Mark's Jesus declares, God will mercifully shorten the days of suffering 'because of the elect' (13.20). In losing their lives, Jesus' followers not only ensure for themselves the future reward of eternal life (8.34–9.1; 10.30) but also expedite the receiving of that reward.

Mark suggests, then, that incapacity and suffering are essential components of colonial subjectivity. To be a colonial subject is to be powerless and defence-less, being vulnerable to suffering, and to live daily in the shadow of death. In Mark, the agency of change belongs to God and is largely beyond the reach of human hands. Even the promise that human suffering will accelerate the coming of the kingdom is followed by the reminder that timing the end is an executive decision that only God can make (13.19-20, 32).

Chronology and Geography

Mark's view of human agency is connected not only with his apocalyptic under-standing of time but also his representation of space and human mobility. In the beginning, Jesus seems to have a clear sense and firm control of his direction. After a succession of rather rapid movements, Jesus finds himself a rising star with the rising sun of a brand new day in Capernaum (1.14-37). Sought by everybody, Jesus decides to leave Capernaum to preach in the adjoining towns, because, as he declares, 'I came out for this purpose' (1.38). Although this state-ment seems to communicate autonomy and purpose, the words 'came out' take us back to the happenings before Jesus came to Galilee. What we find is Jesus' baptism in the River Jordan (1.9-11) and, even more significantly, how the Holy Spirit 'sent him out' (1.12) to encounter Satan in the desert. Not only does this extremely brief account establish Satan as the arch-rival of Jesus' mission, it also introduces an invisible force that may be piloting Jesus' every movement. In fact, Mark dissipates the firm control of direction that Jesus seems to inti-mate in 1.38 rather quickly and consistently. In the very next episode (1.40-45), we already find Jesus' mobility being hampered by his beneficiary; because of some free publicity, courtesy of the healed leper, Jesus has to stay in the out-skirts rather than going into various towns as he had intended. When Jesus spe-cifically asks to be taken across the lake to Gerasa, he has to turn back because his demoniac-calming and swine-drowning miracle makes people nervous and they ask him to leave (5.14-21). When he is back on the other side, his trip to

Jairus' house is interrupted by the haemorrhaging woman (5.21-35). After he finally finishes his business at Jairus' home and returns to his hometown (6.1-6), the unbelief of the Nazarenes pushes him away. For the remainder of the Gospel, there is no mention of Nazareth again.

Upon the disciples' return from mission, the gathering throngs cause Jesus to treat the disciples to a retreat (6.30-31). Even that plan, however, is interrupted. The desert place they choose turns into a gathering place immediately upon their arrival. Instead of resting, Jesus and the disciples find themselves involved in another teaching session as well as another miraculous act (6.32-44).

If this double change of plans seems complicated, the next trip that Jesus and the disciples make seems even more puzzling. Immediately after the first miraculous feeding in the desert, Mark's Jesus has Bethsaida, a town across the lake, clearly set as his destination (6.45). Following a boat trip that is compounded by a natural storm and Jesus' 'walking-on-water' stunt, Mark has them landing at Gennesaret rather than Bethsaida (6.53). They do not reach Bethsaida until 8.22, after an extensive and (geographically speaking) senseless 'detour' that takes them through Tyre (7.24), Sidon (7.31) the Decapolis (7.31) and Dalmanutha (8.10). Even within this 'detour', for which Mark offers no explanation, Jesus' plan for a little 'hide-out' in Tyre is frustrated by an unwanted seeker (7.24-27).

Mark's Jesus is always on the move, but his movements before his trip up to Jerusalem (8.31) often seem coerced or haphazard. His destinations are spontaneously decided, repeatedly diverted and sometimes involve detours that hardly resemble a planned trail. In addition to God's commission to proclaim the gospel in various places (1.12, 38), where Jesus goes is more dependent on other peoples' (re)actions and chance than his own decision. Thus, his movements seem more like those of a drifter or vagabond who wanders out of 'necessity', which may be understood in divine, human and/or fortuitous terms. Long before Jesus is physically arrested (14.46), he has already been subjected to a less conspicuous but equally confining form of arrest that governs and inhibits his comings and goings.

In comparison, Jesus' trip to Jerusalem seems planned and, methodologically and geographically speaking, sensible. Before we credit Jesus with autonomy and agency over this trip, however, we must remember that Jesus has already characterized this trip as a 'necessity' (8.31) in his first passion prediction. Whether this 'necessity' relates to Satan's control over this world and/or God's permissive will (12.6-8; 14.35-36), Jesus' steps are still circumscribed and mapped out for him.

In Mark, movement by necessity is hardly a personal frustration of Jesus. Sometimes people travel a long distance to reach Jesus, and many do so out of need or necessity (1.32-33, 40; 2.3-4; 3.8, 10-11; 5.22-27; 6.54-56; 7.25, 32; 8.22; 9.14-18). In addition, there are other human factors that make people go places where they do not choose. John the Baptizer is arrested and imprisoned by Herod (1.14; 6.17); Simon of Cyrene is 'forced' (15.21) to carry Jesus' cross to Golgotha by the Romans. Summing up the constraints and control that the Jewish and Roman authorities have over people with the verb 'hand over' (13.9, 11), Mark is adamant that what happens to the Baptizer and Simon of Cyrene will also befall all of God's faithful.

Gender

Domestic Women

My comments on gender do not arise out of a 'benevolent' attempt to include women but rather out of the conviction that women define colonial oppression and postcolonial resistance. Not only does Mark's Jesus never call any female character personally to leave her family to follow him, as he does with Simon, Andrew, James and John (1.16-20), Mark usually presents women in relation to their roles as mothers, wives or daughters. In other words, in typical Roman fashion, women are associated with their domestic duties. While others have applauded Mark's representation of the Syrophoenician woman (7.24-30), I want to suggest that the episode actually betrays an alliance between sexism and ethnocentrism. Not only does the episode confirm home and family as the arena where women may find a place and have a voice, it further acknowledges non-Jewish females as second-class citizens.

Those who affirm this Markan pericope generally do so on three bases: it is revolutionary for the Syrophoenician woman to leave her own home (a woman's assigned territory) to seek out a man for a favour; she enters into a verbal duel with Jesus, wins and gets her request; and with her reply, she becomes an agent or a catalyst, who helps Jesus understand the inclusive nature of his mission. Notice, however, that Mark has her encounter with Jesus happen rather privately inside a 'house' (7.24) or a home. Her request also has to do with home and family; it concerns her demon-possessed daughter rather than something that she desires for herself or her town. Like Jairus before her (5.22-23), she falls at Jesus' feet and asks for the healing of a daughter. Rather than simply granting her request as he does with Jairus, however, Mark's Jesus adds insult to her injury by referring to her and her daughter as 'dogs' who have no right to consume the 'children's' food. Ethnicity alone cannot be the issue here, because Jesus has already healed the Gerasene demoniac (5.1-13) and has just blurred the distinction between Jews and non-Jews in the immediately preceding episode (7.1-23). Gender also cannot be the issue here by itself, because Jesus has already healed three women: Simon's mother-in-law (1.29-31), Jairus' daughter (5.21-24, 35-43) and the haemorrhaging woman (5.25-34). Moreover, Jesus has made it clear that his new family does include 'sisters' (3.35). Two things clearly discriminate in this particular request: the requestor for Jesus' healing is a woman rather than a man; and the potential recipient of Jesus' healing is not just a female, she is a 'Greek, a Syrophoenician' female. It is true that the Syrophoenician woman, by virtue of her quick wit, is able to move Jesus and secure health for her daughter, but she does so at a great price. Instead of arguing with Jesus that she and her daughter are also children with equal rights and equal shares in God's kingdom, she simply affirms that 'dogs' do receive 'trickled-down' benefits from the 'children'. Her acquiescence results in another healing miracle by Jesus, but it is also the only healing miracle in Mark that Jesus performs without ever meeting the 'healee'. Is this 'remote-controlled' healing, a step removed from the personal visit that Jesus made to Jairus' house, the equivalent of a piece of 'falling crumb'?

Mark's confinement of female subjects to home and family matters can also be seen by the way he links the scribal exploitation of widows directly with widows' 'houses' (12.40) and has the woman anointing Jesus 'in the house of Simon the leper' (14.3). In fact, women who seem independent in Mark – the Syrophoenician woman, the poor widow who makes an offering in the temple, the woman who anoints Jesus and the haemorrhaging woman – share an important common factor: the absence of a male figure in their lives. Once a female character is associated with a male figure in Mark's Gospel, she either loses her independence or has to work indirectly through her man. Simon acts as his mother-in-law's spokesman, while she behaves as his household servant (1.30-31). Herodias, on the other hand, cannot gratify her desire to kill the Baptizer because of Herod's protection; she can only manipulate behind the scenes (6.19-28).

Mark asserts the importance of having a man in a woman's life with another commonality that the Syrophoenician woman, the poor widow, the woman who anoints Jesus, and the haemorrhaging woman share: without a man, they are all targets of (male) harassment or exploitation. The Syrophoenician woman is insulted by Jesus the widow is exploited by the temple system, the woman who anoints Jesus is 'scolded' and 'bothered' (14.5-6) by some onlookers and the haemorrhaging woman is taken advantage of by doctors. Even the haemorrhaging woman, who without asking for anybody's permission claims healing for herself in a public place, is finally seen trembling and kneeling to give a full account of her healing to Jesus (5.33). Calling her 'daughter' (5.34), Jesus incorporates her into his family and establishes himself as her spokesman, provider and protector, as Jairus is to his daughter (5.21-24, 35-43). As Jesus' imperative of permission ('you may go in peace', 5.34) further evidences, this woman is once again placed under the direction of a man.

Not only does Jesus' new family not free women from obligations of home and family, it also does not deliver them from male domination. They must be obedient to God, the 'Father' and to Jesus, God's authorized agent or regent. Even if one dismisses Jesus' designation of the haemorrhaging woman as 'daughter' to be merely a term of endearment, Mark's Jesus will repeatedly remind us that God is the 'father figure' of his new family (8.38; 11.25; 13.32; 14.36), and as such patriarchy remains unchallenged.

My argument that Jesus' so-called 'new' family is (to switch the terms of Jesus' metaphor) but a case of 'old wine' put into 'new wineskins' (2.22) can also be seen in the exchange between Jesus and the Sadducees concerning resurrection (12.18-27). Patriarchy and property are, of course, the core issues within the levirate marriage scenario given by the Sadducees, yet Jesus' answer does not signify the end of patriarchal marriage. Jesus' pronouncement that people will no longer marry after the resurrection must be placed alongside his self-designation as 'the bridegroom' (2.19-20), and his analogy of humans in heaven as angels must be read in light of Mark's other references to angels (1.13; 8.38; 13.27, 32). For Mark, Jesus is the new patriarch who marries and owns everybody in heaven, and everybody will be serving Jesus as Simon's mother-in-law does the night she is healed (1.29-31). In Mark's Gospel, patriarchy never dies; women will only be subjects at home and will always be subjected to the men and the needs of the family.

Model Women

The connection between women and service (1.31; 15.41) has caused some to contend that women are 'model disciples' in Mark's Gospel. In contrast to the male disciples, these women already understand and possess the quality with which Mark's Jesus chooses to characterize his followers as well as his own life and ministry (9.35; 10.41-45). The woman who anoints Jesus at Bethany (14.3-9), for example, has been lauded as both one who assumes the traditionally male prophetic role to consecrate Jesus for his divinely appointed task and one who, in contrast to Peter's mere verbal acknowledgment (8.27-33), understands Jesus' suffering messiahship. Unlike the male disciples who end up betraying, deserting or denying Jesus (14.43-52, 66-72), several women follow Jesus to the cross as well as to the tomb (15.40-41, 47; 16.1-2).

If women make up Mark's 'model minority', they are also kept at the margins by Mark. Mark, therefore, professes rather than protests women's oppression. In addition to what I have said about women as family subjects, Mark's women tend to assume 'mop-up' and 'back-up' roles. Mark specifies that the woman at Bethany is anointing Jesus' body in anticipation of its burial and further qualifies her act not as a 'prophetic sign-action' (Schüssler Fiorenza 1989: xiii, xiv) but as one of resignation ('she did what she could', 14.8). Unable to stop the plot for Jesus' life, what she does is akin to cleaning up the ashes of an unjust situation. That is indeed what the women have come to the tomb to do. Not only do they come with spices to anoint Jesus' corpse (16.1), their worry over the tombstone indicates that they do not come with any expectation of a miracle (16.3). They are not there out of faith in Jesus' promised resurrection but out of duty. They are there to clear the remaining business. Anointing the dead is conventionally a Jewish woman's responsibility. Mark is only reinscribing the traditional prescriptions for women's activities in both scenarios.

The sudden appearance of these women at the cross and at the tomb – after the failure of the male disciples and as Mark's narrative comes to a close – confirms women's roles as consummate alternates. Like Simon's mother-in-law (1.29-31) and Jairus' wife (5.40), these women stay in the house and in the background, doing what they do without a name and without a voice until the men are, for one reason or another, unavailable. Only as men's substitutes or replacements will women be given the room to operate outside the home and in the frontline. As I have mentioned earlier, women who seem to have travelled and acted somewhat independently in Mark are not identified with any male association. 'From a distance' (15.40), which Mark uses to describe the way several women observe Jesus' crucifixion, may well be an apt description of the way they have always followed and served Jesus. When Jesus and his male disciples are in Galilee and then on the way to Jerusalem, these women are kept invisible, out of the way, until the male disciples have fallen away. Even more damaging to the 'model minority' thesis is Mark's decision to have these perennial 'mop-ups' fail at their call to 'back-up' the disciples. Having been shown the empty tomb and told to go and tell the good news of Jesus' resurrection and imminent reappearance – by who else but a 'young man' (16.5) – these 'replacement disciples' become fearful and flee without saying anything to anyone (16.8). Instead of presenting women as the 'model minority', Mark presents them as inadequate male surrogates, who prove to be incapable of serving as 'back-ups' in the affairs of men.

Trafficking Women

Gayle Rubin has written about an injury peculiar to women with what she terms 'traffic in women' (1975). Rubin suggests that women are often the building blocks on which homosocial communities of men are established. Through their activities, or their being given in marriage (by men to men), male-dominant kinship networks are formed and reinforced. That is exactly what Mark does with Simon's mother-in-law (1.29-31). Jesus has just started his ministry; in fact, Jesus has just finished his very first miraculous act with his 'first disciples' (Simon, Andrew, James and John) by his side (1.16-28). It is also the very first time that Jesus and these disciples have a retreat together away from the crowd. After Jesus miraculously rids Simon's mother-in-law of her fever, Mark has her playing the (expected) role of the perfect hostess. Moreover, Mark is very clear that she does not serve only Jesus, but also 'them' (1.31). The picture that Mark paints, then, has one woman (Simon's mother-in-law) doing all the work and taking care of all the chores, so that five grown men (Jesus, Simon, Andrew, James and John) can rest, interact and socialize together.

Note also that Herod's birthday banquet is restricted to 'his great men and officers and the chief men of Galilee' (6.21). Even his wife, Herodias, cannot participate, which explains why her daughter has to run in and out the banquet hall to talk to each of her parents in turn (6.24-25). The daughter is also not there to participate in the banquet; she only goes into the banquet hall to dance (10.22). Like the food served on the banquet table and like Simon's mother-in-law who serves (food) in Simon's house, her role is to facilitate the bonding among men.

This commodification of women may also explain why in Mark John the Baptizer condemns the 'wife swapping' between Herod and his brother Philip (6.17-18), while Jesus does not utter a critical word about the levirate marriage custom itself when the Sadducees bring it to his attention (12.18-27). The levirate marriage passes a 'son-less' widow to her brother-in-law to assure the continuity of both family name and property, as well as to fortify men as proper subjects and women as male properties and exchange objects. Judging from the grudge Herodias holds against John the Baptizer (6.19), she obviously prefers to be married to Herod rather than staying with Philip. Herodias' desire to intervene in this male business of women exchange, then, may be the first reason she draws such condemnations from Mark and Mark's interpreters. Furthermore, she disrupts the female 'conduit' that is supposed to solidify male relations and benefit male participants. Not only does her 'behind-the-scenes' manipulation create discord between Herod and John the Baptizer, she also participates in reaping a share of the benefit – she gets her revenge (6.27-28).

Likewise, Mark makes it clear that the women disciples at the tomb are not equals of the failed men disciples. These women's (back-up) roles are limited to the restoration of the broken bond between Jesus and his (male) disciples, for these women are never told what the resurrection has to do with them on Mark's first Easter morning. They are only told to 'go, tell his disciples and Peter' (16.7) that a reunion is awaiting the male disciples at Galilee. These women disciples are, in other words, called to be mere channels, so that they can help renew a brotherly bond to which they remain marginal. Mark incorporates these named women disciples in the end of his Gospel in such a way that he secures their subordinate status even while portending, or pretending, their importance.

Since women are trafficked as building blocks of male bonding, they are also blamed for the break-up of male relationships. The women's inability to say what the young man told them to tell (16.7-8) threatens the restoration of the (male) disciples and their reunion with Jesus. On the other hand, the already thin cords between John the Baptizer and Herod as well as between Jesus and Peter are broken when Herodias and the servant girl of the high priest speak their own minds (5.24-28; 14.66-72). Women, as a result, find themselves in a 'lose-lose' situation within Mark: they are either passive channels of male bonding or active culprits of male discord.

Questions

My reading of what Mark's (colonial) politics of (apocalyptic) time has to say on the subjects of authority, agency and gender actually involves another 'politics of time'; namely, the indispensable political critique in light of historical time. Taking time or historicity seriously, I must appraise the actions and attitudes that Mark endorses and excludes rather than assuming them to be timeless truths.

As I mentioned at the beginning, knowledge and power constitute each other. To problematize the often unequal relations between a knowing specialist and an unknowing patient, Jacques Lacan supposedly ended all his psychoanalytic sessions with questions without answers. To avoid defeating my own non-colonial logic as Mark did his, I will likewise end my postcolonial comments on Mark with questions in place of the traditional 'conclusions'. What have we inherited from Mark's understanding of authority, agency and gender? How do we want to differ from Mark in our own understanding of these subjects? Do the acknowledgment and articulation of these differences actually mark the difference between a postcolonial and a neocolonial reading of Mark? If this study of Mark demonstrates that 'the colonization of consciousness and the consciousness of colonization' (Comaroff and Comaroff 1992: 236) are ongoing processes, what does that mean to our understanding of social change? Instead of presuming that all hybrids are necessarily and equally liberating, do we not need to give greater specificity to our postcolonial theorizing of 'hybridity'?

BIBLIOGRAPHY

Brantlinger, Patrick
    1988   *Rule of Darkness: British Literature and Imperialism, 1830–1914* (Ithaca, NY: Cornell University Press).

Chakrabarty, Dipesh
    2000   *Provincializing Europe: Postcolonial Thought and Historical Difference* (Princeton, NJ: Princeton University Press).

Cheung, King-Kok
    1997   'Re-viewing Asian American Literary Studies', in King-Kok Cheung (ed.), *An Interethnic Companion to Asian American Literature* (New York: Cambridge University Press): 1–36.

Cohn, Norman
    1993   *Cosmos, Chaos, and the World to Come: The Ancient Roots of Apocalyptic Faith* (New Haven: Yale University Press).

Comaroff, John and Jean Comaroff
    1992   *Ethnography and the Historical Imagination* (Boulder, CO: Westview).

Fanon, Frantz
    1963   *The Wretched of the Earth* (trans. Constance Farrington; New York: Grove).

Gandhi, Leela
    1994   *Postcolonial Theory: A Critical Introduction* (New York: Columbia University Press).

Keller, Catherine
    1997   'The Breast, the Apocalypse, and the Colonial Journey', in Charles B. Strozier and Michael Flynn (eds), *The Year 2000: Essays on the End* (New York: New York University Press): 42–58.

Kristeva, Julia
    1986   'Women's Time', in Hazard Adams and Leroy Searle (eds), *Critical Theory since 1965* (Tallahassee: University Press of Florida): 469–84.

Liew, Tat-Siong Benny
    1999   *Politics of Parousia: Reading Mark Inter(con)textually* (Leiden: E. J. Brill).

Myers, Ched
    1992   *Binding the Strong Man: A Political Reading of Mark's Story of Jesus* (Maryknoll, NY: Orbis Books).

O'Leary, Stephen D.
    1994   *Arguing the Apocalypse: A Theory of Millennial Rhetoric* (New York: Oxford University Press).

Osborne, Peter
    1995   *The Politics of Time: Modernity and Avant-Garde* (New York: Verso).

Rubin, Gayle
    1975   'The Traffic of Women: Notes on the Political Economy of Sex', in Rayne R. Reiter (ed.), *Toward an Anthropology of Women* (New York: Monthly Review): 157–210.

Schüssler Fiorenza, Elisabeth
    1989   *In Memory of Her: A Feminist Theological Reconstruction of Christian Origins* (New York: Crossroad).

Sinfield, Alan
    1992   *Faultlines: Cultural Materialism and the Politics of Dissident Reading* (Berkeley: University of California Press).

Tolbert, Mary Ann
    1989   *Sowing the Gospel: Mark's World in Literary-Historical Perspective* (Minneapolis: Fortress Press).

The Gospel of Luke and The Acts of the Apostles

Virginia Burrus

Luke-Acts is notably preoccupied with power, pulsing with the energy of charged exchanges between centre and periphery – rich and poor, urban and rural, Jew and Gentile, the Jerusalem temple and the land of Israel, Rome and those subjugated under imperial rule. The perspective of Luke-Acts is, moreover, not only distinctly universalizing (Acts 1.8) but also explicitly transcultural (Acts 2.5-13), a fact that has made it extraordinarily difficult to tie its author to a specific social or geographic location. The ambitious narrative, exceeding the limits of the gospel genre by overflowing into a second volume, mimics the reach of the empires of both Alexander and Augustus. Fanning out from the Palestinian matrix of Jesus' movement to span the eastern Mediterranean and finally extending as far west as Rome itself, the text maps a terrain traversed by the passages of travellers and marked by meetings between social 'others' and ethnic 'strangers'. On such grounds alone, Luke's work would seem to provide rich opportunities for a thoroughgoing postcolonial analysis. If few have yet taken up the challenge of such an analysis, it is not only because of the relative newness of this theoretical-hermeneutical approach within biblical studies but also (one suspects) because of the haunting ambiguity of Luke's political stance. Symptomatically, Luke-Acts has been interpreted with passionate persuasiveness both as radically subversive and as skilfully accomodationist in relation to the forces of imperialism and colonialism.

Beginning by surveying the political and economic contexts invoked and critically interrogated by Luke-Acts, this commentary will attempt to situate Luke's ideological position within the framework of recent theories of empire and resistance. Admittedly, the systems of domination constituted by imperialism and colonialism respectively cannot be simply conflated (Young 2001: 15–19, 25–29). Nonetheless, the economic and cultural effects of Roman imperialism on subjugated peoples are frequently well described by current theories of colonialism, neocolonialism and postcoloniality (Sugirtharajah 2002: 24–28). The collusion of imperialism with colonialism in the case of the Roman Empire – and thus the relevance of a 'postcolonial' critique of that empire – will here be assumed. In this context, the term 'postcolonial' clearly does not indicate a stage 'after colonialism' but rather points toward critical potentialities already available within the structures of colonialism and imperialism (Sugirtharajah

2002: 12–13). This commentary will finally also explore possibilities for reading Luke-Acts as an instance of postcolonial literature precisely on the basis of its frequently perplexing ambiguities and ambivalences. As contemporary critics (most notably, Bhabha) have argued, ambivalence toward the cultural authority of the colonizer is not only characteristic of the 'postcolonial condition' but also the source of much of its critical – and critically transforming – power.

Luke-Acts and Empire: Collaboration versus Resistance

Rome and Its Political Brokers

More than any of the other gospel writers, Luke is concerned to place the narrative of Jesus and his followers into the broader context of Roman/Judaean politics, in part by appropriating the literary conventions of historiographic prose. (In this respect, his work invites comparison with that of his Jewish contemporary Josephus.) The events immediately prior to Jesus' conception are described as occurring 'in the days of Herod, king of Judaea' (Lk. 1.5), and Jesus' birth is placed in the time of the first census ordered by Caesar Augustus 'when Quirinius was governor of Syria' (Lk. 2.1-2). From the start, then, readers are reminded of the political circumstance of early first-century Judaea, ruled by the Herodians, a Judaized Idumaean dynasty that had come to power through the patronage of Rome, profiting directly from the rise of Roman military influence in the region (Schwartz 2001: 38–39, 42–48). The formidable influence of the Romans is marked in Luke's text both by the imposed power of taxation conveyed by the census and by the presence of a Roman governor (and thus the threat of Roman military forces) in the neighbouring province of Syria.

Luke's account of the preaching of John the Baptist, leaping a chronological gap of some three decades, is introduced by a still more elaborate political roster: 'In the fifteenth year of the reign of Tiberius Caesar, Pontius Pilate being governor of Judaea, and Herod being tetrarch of Galilee, and his brother Philip tetrarch of the region of Ituraea and Traconitis, and Lysanias tetrarch of Abilene, in the high-priesthood of Annas and Caiaphas, the word of God came to John the son of Zechariah in the wilderness' (Lk. 3.1-2). The reader is thereby alerted to the swift pace of political change in the region. Following the death of Herod in 4 BCE, the former kingdom of Judaea – which had, since the days of Hasmonaean expansionism, included territory beyond Judaea proper – was partitioned, with Judaea itself being placed under the direct control of a Roman governor, while Galilee and other surrounding areas ('tetrarchies') were left at least nominally under the rule of Herod's heirs. Luke also signals the presence of another group of significant players in Judaean politics, namely, the members of the leading priestly families.

Although the cast of characters will continue to shift, throughout Luke-Acts events are informed by the complex dynamics of power circulating between the various mediating 'brokers' of imperial dominion – governors and military tribunes, centurions and soldiers, representing direct Roman presence in the region; ambiguously 'Jewish' tetrarchs and client kings dependent on Roman support; and the 'native' priestly elite who control the temple cult of Jerusalem and thereby also exert influence over the land of Israel more generally, exercising a degree of independence in matters of local politics but also necessarily collaborating (however ambivalently) with both the Herodians and the Roman governors, who exercise the power of appointment to the high priesthood. The Roman emperors themselves, it might be noted, are purely off-stage presences in Luke's narrative – as in the lives of most subjects of empire.

The two 'trial' scenes that occur near the ends of the Gospel and Acts, respectively, provide the clearest view of Roman/Judaean politics as Luke interprets them. He is at pains to show that popular opposition to Jesus and his followers is orchestrated by the Jerusalem ruling elite, typically described by Luke as 'the chief priests and scribes' (Cassidy 1978: 452–54; Cassidy 1983).

In the Gospel, it is the priestly members of the 'council' of Jerusalem who initially arrest and interrogate Jesus (Luke 22) and then bring him to the governor Pontius Pilate for a political trial, proclaiming, 'We found this man perverting our nation, and forbidding us to give tribute to Caesar, and saying that he himself is Christ a king' (Lk. 23.2). After briefly questioning Jesus, Pilate states curtly that he finds no grounds for prosecution, but the members of the council insist: 'He stirs up the people, teaching throughout all Judaea, from Galilee even to this place' (Lk. 23.5). Learning that Jesus is a Galilaean, Pilate sends him on to Herod Antipas, the tetrarch of Galilee, who happens to be in Jerusalem at the time (Lk. 23.7). Possibly Pilate is here observing protocol while also trying to avoid dealing with a bothersome complaint; he is likely also testing the political waters. Luke, who uniquely includes the role of Herod in Jesus' trial, does not comment on the governor's motives in referring Jesus to Herod; unlike Mark and Matthew, he does not even leave him 'wondering' about Jesus' passive demeanour (cf. Mk 15.5; Mt. 27.14). Perhaps Pilate's actions speak for themselves in Luke's text.

Luke has already recounted Herod's imprisonment of John the Baptist, who had enraged the tetrarch by publicly rebuking him 'for Herodias, his brother's wife, and for all the evil things that Herod had done' (Lk. 3.19). However, his treatment of Herod's relationship to Jesus is more ambiguous. When Herod first hears of Jesus' teaching and healings, he is depicted as rather more curious than menacing: '"John, I beheaded; but who is this about whom I hear such things?" And he sought to see him' (Lk. 9.9). Certain Pharisees subsequently warn Jesus that Herod intends to kill him, but it is not immediately clear whether the reader is expected to trust this rumour, despite its inherent plausibility (Lk. 13.31). Indeed, when Herod receives Jesus from Pilate, Luke's description again emphasizes his curiosity: 'he was very glad, for he had long desired to see him, because he had heard about him, and he was hoping to see some sign done by him' (Lk. 23.8). Herod, unlike Pilate, questions Jesus at length. Jesus, who has said little enough to Pilate, says nothing at all to Herod, seemingly preferring to sustain a noble silence in the face of what remains, despite Herod's apparent openness, a hostile political interrogation (Lk. 23.9). The chief priests and scribes continue to repeat their accusations in Herod's presence, and Herod finally loses patience with Jesus, who has not only refused to answer his questions but also failed to impress him with any display of miraculous powers. The tetrarch and his soldiers now subject Jesus to elaborately contemptuous treatment, and Herod sends him back to Pilate, dressed in splendid attire that implicitly mocks Jesus' supposed claims on kingship (Lk. 23.10-11). Perhaps Luke intends us to read in Herod's gesture mockery of the priests as well as Jesus: it is, after all, they who assertively position the Galilaean peasant as a would-be king. At any rate, the tetrarch has clearly adopted the cautious ploy of deferring to the Roman governor by returning Jesus to him, clothed in an ambiguous message. The strategy proves successful. Luke reports ominously that 'Herod and Pilate became friends with each other that very day, for before this they had been at enmity with each other' (Lk. 23.12).

Pilate now renders his judgment, proclaiming his decision to release Jesus: 'I did not find this man guilty of any of your charges against him; neither did Herod, for he sent him back to us' (Lk. 23.14-15). The sentence predictably produces an outcry of protest on the part of the chief priests and rulers. (Possibly we are even meant to infer that this was Pilate's intention all along.) They request that he instead release Barabbas, who has been sentenced for inciting a riot in Jerusalem as well as for murder, and that he crucify Jesus in his place – thereby implying that Jesus is a still more dangerous political criminal than Barabbas (Lk. 23.18-19). Having by now not only tested public opinion but also demonstrated his own power to grant or withhold political favours, Pilate concludes negotiations by conceding magnanimously to the desires of the mob and its leaders: 'Jesus he delivered up to their will' (Lk. 23.25).

As Jesus hangs on the cross, the Jewish rulers scoff at him. Roman soldiers repeat their mockery, as does one of the two 'criminals' crucified with Jesus (having presumably, like Barabbas and Jesus, been sentenced for political offences, though it should be noted that Luke avoids the more pointedly political label of 'bandit' found in both Mark and Matthew [Lk. 23.32-33; cf. Mk 15.27; Mt. 27.38]). The second criminal, however, passes prophetic judgment on all the mockers, tetrarch, priests, soldiers and criminal alike: 'This man has done nothing wrong' (Lk. 23.41). His words echo with greater fervour (and far less irony) the initial, dismissive judgment of the Roman governor: 'I find no crime in this man' (Lk. 23.6). They are echoed in turn by the awestruck Roman centurion who has witnessed the omens that accompany Jesus' death: 'Certainly this man was innocent!' (Lk. 23.47). (The figure of a 'converted' centurion will be repeated in Acts 10 in the tale of Cornelius, a God-fearing centurion of the Italian cohort; the centurion at the cross also recalls the 'faithful' centurion of

Lk. 7.1-10.) Jesus, Luke insinuates, can lead even a Roman military officer to see the injustice of a governor's judgment.

What does the repeated insistence on Jesus' 'innocence' imply? Most Lukan scholars (following Conzelmann) have interpreted it to mean that Jesus is, in Luke's view, in fact a dutiful subject of Rome, innocent of the charges brought against him – namely, leading the Jews astray, forbidding tribute to Caesar and claiming that he is Christ, a king (with Walaskay [1983] offering a particularly extreme version of the argument for a pro-Roman Lukan perspective, Walton [2002] exemplifying a mediating position). Yet, Luke's subtle but persistent ambivalence toward both Pilate and Herod renders it more likely that Luke intends his readers to understand that, although these charges are at least partly accurate, Jesus is nonetheless being persecuted wrongfully, according to the justice of God's kingdom (Schmidt 1983). This latter, politicizing interpretation is implicitly supported by the words of the crucified criminal who has proclaimed Jesus' innocence: 'Jesus, remember me when you come into your kingdom'. Here as elsewhere, Jesus responds enigmatically by slyly side-stepping language of kingship: 'Today you will be with me in Paradise' (Lk. 23.42-43).

Acts continues the pattern established in the Gospel, positioning the direct representatives of Rome ambiguously, while placing blame for the persecution of Jesus and his followers most squarely on the shoulders of the priestly elite of Jerusalem. Emphasis is on the frequently miraculous success of the apostles in evading the attempts of the priestly rulers to arrest, imprison and execute them (e.g., Acts 4.1-22; 5.17-42; 6.8–8.3). Interestingly, however, both Pilate and Herod are now clearly lumped with all the others who persecuted Jesus (Acts 4.27), and the death of a subsequent Herodian client king, Herod Agrippa, who was responsible for the killing of James the brother of John (Acts 12.2), is recorded with grim satisfaction: 'An angel of the Lord smote him, because he did not give God the glory; and he was eaten by worms and died' (Acts 12.23). Moreover, whereas the Gospel initially presents the Pharisees negatively as the opponents of Jesus, Acts showcases the wisdom of the Pharisee Gamaliel, who on one occasion persuades the council of priests to leave to God the punishment of rebellions initiated by men like Theudas, Judas of Galilee or Jesus (Acts 5.34-40); later, Pharisaic members of the Jerusalem council will be depicted as supporting Paul (Acts 23.9). Nonetheless, such complications do not altogether disrupt the pattern of subtly downplaying the agency of the Romans and their Herodian collaborators while blaming the priests and their allies, a pattern that culminates in the account of the final trial(s) of Paul.

Although Paul's activity as a teacher, like Jesus', has lain largely outside Judaea, like Jesus he insists on returning to Jerusalem, knowing that political opposition awaits him there. The reader receives the distinct impression that Luke is, once again, making the most of his opportunity to stage a political showdown, and indeed he will repeat the markedly ambivalent performance more than once. The anticipated opposition to Paul initially takes the form of mob violence instigated by Jews from Asia Minor, resulting in the interven- tion of the Roman military tribune, who arrives with soldiers and centurions to restore peace to the streets by arresting and torturing Paul in order to extract a confession (Acts 21.27–22.22). When the tribune realizes that Paul is a Roman citizen and thus not liable to the usual forms of physical punishment inflicted by Roman officials, he unbinds him and takes him to the 'chief priests and all the council' to discover the nature of the charges against him (Acts 22.23-30). The meeting results in conflict within the council and a resurgence of violence against Paul, so that the tribune removes Paul to the relative safety of a Roman prison (Acts 23.10).

As the threats on Paul's life grow still more acute, the tribune transfers him to the custody of the Roman governor Felix, stationed in Caesarea – an event that allows Luke to replay the staging of Paul's trial. The governor, who is married to the Jewish Drusilla, listens attentively to the high priest's charge that Paul is a political agitator among the Jews and ringleader of the 'sect of the Nazarenes' as well as to Paul's defence, but he defers judgment in such a controversial matter. Indeed, two years later, when Felix's term of office expires, Paul is still a prisoner, although living in relative comfort (Acts 24). The new governor, Festus, reopens the trial for a third performance. This time, Paul appeals his case to Caesar himself, and Festus agrees to send him to Rome (Acts 25.6-12). In the meantime, the Herodians Agrippa and Bernice, who have arrived in Cae- sarea to pay their respects to the new governor, hear of Paul's case and express interest in meeting with him and learning more of the charges against him (Acts 25.12-27). Paul's speech provokes Festus' irritation. King Agrippa is, however, more favourably impressed: 'This man is doing nothing to deserve death or imprisonment', he proclaims, in yet another ambivalent echo of Pilate's initial judgment of Jesus (Acts 26.31).

Paul, however, has appealed to Caesar and to Caesar he now must go, facing the not inconsiderable dangers of a difficult sea journey with uncanny serenity (Acts 27.1–28.14). Having finally reached Rome, he meets (once again) with mixed response from the local Jewish community yet continues his teaching to the Gentiles. 'And he lived there two whole years at his own expense, and wel- comed all who came to him, preaching the kingdom of God and teaching about the Lord Jesus Christ quite openly and unhindered': thus, the last, enigmatic line of Luke's history (Acts 28.30-31). Paul, the prisoner of Rome, now seems freer than he ever was in Jerusalem or the other cities of the eastern Mediter- ranean, where he met routinely with rejection and political persecution. If Luke knows the tradition of the apostle's execution in the imperial capital city, he does not choose to report it. Indeed, Paul never meets the emperor in Luke's text; his trial reaches no conclusion.

Has the story of Jesus' harsh execution by the Romans as a political crimi- nal thus been converted by Luke into a celebration of the benign effects of an imperial regime that, according to his account, both mitigates the brutality of the 'native' priestly elite of Judaea and opens up providential space for an effectively 'global' ('transnational') community of believers? It is nearly impossible simply to contradict such an interpretation and even more difficult to deny its ominous political implications. Ominous, first of all, in relation to the fourth-century conversion of the Roman emperors to Christianity, which seemed to confirm that the kingdom of God and the empire of Rome were not, in fact, incompatible regimes – were perhaps even mirror images of one another. Ominous as well in relation to our own 'postmodern' era, when a European-based colonialism begins to give way to a globalized economy that effectively decentres political sovereignty and 'progressively incorporates the entire global realm within its open, expanding frontiers', as vividly described by Michael Hardt and Antonio Negri (2000: xii). If, as Hardt and Negri also observe, 'our postmodern Empire has no Rome' (2000: 317, writing, admittedly, prior to the US response to '9/11'), the same might be said for Luke's vision of the kingdom: Rome, ultimately superseding Jerusalem in his narrative, has become less a 'place' than an unbounded space of expansive inclusiveness in which the distinctions between Jew and Gentile, emperor and subject, colonizer and colonized are finally rendered irrelevant.

To be sure, Hardt and Negri find in ancient Christianity less an anticipation of the postmodern empire than 'an enormous potential of subjectivity' that 'offered an absolute alternative' to the empire of Rome (2000: 21). In this respect, ancient Christianity prefigures Hardt and Negri's own, equally absolute vision of 'counter-Empire, an alternative political organization of global flows and exchanges... that will one day take us through and beyond Empire' (2000: xv; see Sugirtharajah 2002: 32 on the 'two varieties of globalization'). Yet, the close resemblance of 'counter-empire' to 'empire', evidenced in the ease with which the Christian discourse of counter-empire became, within a few centuries, the discourse of the Roman Empire (Cameron 1991), may call for a more ambivalent assessment of the 'enormous potentiality' of totalizing eschatologies, whether Christian or neo-Marxist (see Liew 1999).

At the same time, it should not be denied that Luke-Acts carries a message of political subversion. The subversiveness of the text may lie less, however, in the extent to which it opposes the totalizing claims of one empire – the Roman – with the totalizing claims of another – God's Kingdom – than in the very ambivalence that has earned Luke his reputation as an apologist for Rome. Not unlike Josephus, Justin or other Jewish and Christian 'apologists', Luke has, in the act of laying claim to the political values of Rome, used those same values to interrogate the oppressive policies of empire, thereby wedging open room within which a persecuted people might manoeuvre. As James C. Scott has argued, the appropriation by subjugated populations of the terms of the 'public transcript' by which their oppressors legitimate their own rule is often best read not as a sign that the people have simply been brainwashed (as is the claim of

Gramsci's theory of hegemonic incorporation) but rather as an indication of a strategy of resistance: 'Many radical attacks initiate in critiques within the hegemony – in taking the values of ruling elites seriously, while claiming that they (the elites) do not' (1990: 106).

Luke has, in effect, authoritatively defined the limits of 'proper' governance by invoking shared values, most notably the values that inform a legal system that is, on the surface, concerned to discern 'truth' and deliver 'just' sentences rather than execute 'innocent' men. Herod Agrippa's grotesque fate serves as a particularly sharp condemnation of those rulers who transgress propriety. Yet, none of the Roman governors or client rulers is finally presented by Luke in a positive light: to the extent that their influence is marked as relatively benign, this is positioned as the indirect result of their strategic passivity, reflecting a desire to maintain 'peace' among a subjugated population. Indeed, one might even read Luke's treatment of such figures as subtle encodings of double messages 'in which ideological resistance is disguised, veiled, and masked for safety's sake' (Scott 1990: 137).

Luke's depiction of Herod is here particularly instructive. Although his account of Jesus' trial is frequently read as letting Herod as well as Pilate off the hook, this is by no means the only possible reading. The Lukan Jesus' silence in the face of Herod's interrogation takes on a distinctly tricksterish cast when we see that it forces Herod not only to expose his own ignorance and brutality but also inadvertently to confess Jesus' true status by clothing him in robes fit for a king; in this respect, Jesus' role in Luke's Gospel is continuous with broader traditions of martyrdom. Moreover, Luke's inclusion of Herod in the trial of Jesus uncovers the complex webs of ambivalent alliance through which imperial power is exercised, while also rendering the Roman governor Pilate even more centrally responsible for Jesus' death than is the case in any of the other Gospels. (It is no accident that there is no 'washing of hands' in Luke's Gospel; cf. Mt. 27.24.) Finally, whether or not he intended it, through his very vilifying depiction of the 'chief priests and scribes' and the mob violence of the people of Jerusalem, Luke has painted a poignant picture of the drastically divisive effects of empire on those societies forced to accommodate themselves to the conditions of foreign rule.

The Economics of Empire

Luke's economic interests are perhaps as prominent as his political interests, nor are the two sets of interests unrelated, for it is Roman taxation that ultimately pressures the provincial economy of Palestine to the point of near collapse (and eventually to the point of outright revolt). 'Is it lawful for us to give tribute to Caesar, or not?' is the question famously put to Jesus in this Gospel, as in others. The question is clearly a set-up, but Jesus stays one step ahead of his interlocutors, who are, according to Luke, 'spies' sent by the priests and scribes, seeking an excuse to accuse Jesus before Pilate. Jesus asks them to show him a coin and tell him whose likeness and inscription it bears. The answer, of course, is 'Caesar's'. Jesus responds: 'Then render to Caesar the things that are Caesar's, and to God the things that are God's' (Lk. 20.22-26). Many contemporary readers, like the spies themselves, find themselves acutely disappointed (albeit for different reasons) by this apparently 'apolitical', even 'politically incorrect', reply. Later in Luke's Gospel the priests will shift the script, informing Pilate that they have found Jesus 'forbidding us to give tribute to Caesar' (Lk. 23.2). Either this is an outright lie and Jesus, with his eyes focused on purely 'spiritual' goods, in fact has no objection to imperial taxation, or (more likely) Jesus' initial answer is indeed as cleverly devious – as deliberately duplicitous – as Luke's recounting of the exchange implies, not least by emphasizing the frustration of the spies: 'And they were not able in the presence of the people to catch him by what he said'. The most literal reading is perhaps also the most radical, namely, that Jesus is implicitly advocating a return of the coin itself, in a covert, yet thoroughgoing, denunciation of the imposed Roman monetary economy on which imperial exploitation is based. At the very least, Jesus is leaving open a loophole (perhaps a very wide loophole) in the shape of the possibility that the rightful demands of God's kingdom might conflict with those of Caesar's (Cassidy 1978: 55–61; Horsley 2003: 99; but see the dissenting view of Sugirtharajah 2002: 89–90). The message remains, however, strategically veiled in ambiguity.

Less ambiguous is Luke's representation of Jesus' humble birth (Lk. 2.3-20; cf. Matthew 1–2), lending contextual resonance to the uncompromising language of Mary's Magnificat – 'He has filled the hungry with good things, and the rich he has sent empty away' (Lk. 1.53), and of Jesus' own citation of Isaiah – 'He has anointed me to preach good news to the poor' (Lk. 4.18), both texts found uniquely in the Lukan Gospel. Luke's rendering of the Beatitudes is also notably attuned to the social injustice of poverty: 'Blessed are you poor, for yours is the kingdom of God. Blessed are you that hunger now, for you shall be satisfied... But woe to you that are rich... Woe to you that are full now' (Lk. 6.20-21, 24-25). Matthew, in telling contrast, spiritualizes the message: 'Blessed are the poor in spirit, for theirs is the kingdom of heaven... Blessed are those who hunger and thirst for righteousness, for they shall be satisfied' (Mt. 5.3, 6). Similarly clear in their critical focus on economic injustice are cautionary parables like that of the rich fool 'who lays up treasure for himself, and is not rich toward God' (Lk. 12.21) or of the rich man who feasts sumptuously while the poor Lazarus hungers (Lk. 16.19-31), as well as the approving narrative of Zacchaeus, the prosperous tax-collector who gives half his wealth to the poor and promises to restore fourfold the amount to any he has defrauded (Lk. 19.8), all also uniquely Lukan texts. The problematic relation between the rich and the poor and the crushing weight of poverty on both the urban and rural populations are recurring themes in the Gospel.

Acts, in turn, features a well-known depiction of early Christian 'communism': 'And all who believed were together and had all things in common; and they sold their possessions and goods and distributed them to all, as any had need' (Acts 2.44-45); and: 'Now the company of those who believed were of one heart and soul, and no one said that any of the things which he possessed was his own, but they had everything in common' (Acts 4.32). Those in possession of real estate – always the primary source of wealth in the Roman Empire – sell their property and bring the proceeds to the apostles to distribute according to need, Luke repeats, so that there are no longer either landholders or poor among them (Acts 4.34-37). The ominous tale of Ananias and Sapphira, who secretly hold back some of their wealth after selling their property, resulting in their sudden and dramatic deaths, both hints at the strains on the community and conveys Luke's own strident views (Acts 5.1-11). Luke seems partly to mask another instance of conflict in the communal paradise – 'the Hellenists murmured against the Hebrews because their widows were neglected in the daily distribution' (Acts 6.1) – by swiftly moving on to describe its resolution through the appointment of seven men charged, by the laying on of hands, with the duty of just food distribution (Acts 6.2-6).

There are thus good reasons to view Luke as the advocate of justice for the economically exploited. However, throughout both Gospel and Acts depictions of relations of patronage carry a more ambiguous message, raising the possibility that Luke's attitude toward the poor is rather more paternalistic and his vision of economic reform rather less radical than the above-cited texts might at first suggest (Oakman 1991). Indeed, in the view of many scholars, Luke's writings are best understood as addressed to the philanthropic rich (a view shared, to varying degrees, e.g., by Blomberg, Karris, Pilgrim, Schottroff and Stegemann). In fact, they are rather literally thus addressed, for the two-volume work is dedicated to one Theophilus, presumably Luke's patron, whom Luke graces with the honourific title of 'excellency' (Lk. 1.3-4; Acts 1.1).

Among the most interesting references to economic patronage in the Gospel is the description of the female disciples of Jesus: 'And the twelve were with him, and also some women who had been healed of evil spirits and infirmities: Mary, called Magdalene, from whom seven demons had gone out, and Joanna, the wife of Chuza, Herod's steward, and Susanna, and many others, who provided for them out of their means' (Lk. 8.2-3). Though many modern interpreters (including feminist critics, e.g., Schaberg 1992) have depicted these women as grateful 'helpers' (as if constituting a sort of precursor to the modern 'women's auxiliary'), an ancient reader would certainly have recognized them as patrons with sufficient wealth at their disposal to offer support to the band of itinerant teachers, who are thereby implicitly positioned as the 'clients' or social dependants of the women. To be sure, the initial reference to Jesus' healings highlights the economy of exchange in which Jesus also appears as a patron to the women who benefit from his spiritual powers. Yet, such an exchange does not simply invert the social hierarchy. Nor does it merely even the balance, producing an egalitarian community. On the one hand, social clients are typically expected to offer services to their patrons in return for which they are granted economic or political protection. On the other hand, to the extent that the Gospel's claims for Jesus' powers add up to rather more than the usual services rendered by clients (to say the least), the result is a tense leveraging of competing axes of patronage within the nascent Christian community (Moxnes 1991). This situation is likely more directly reflective of Luke's own late first- or early second-century urban context than of conditions in early first-century Palestine, though such complex relations of economic and 'spiritual' patronage would also not have been alien to Jesus' context.

Acts, especially the latter half of the text, which deals with Paul's missionary journeys and the spread of Christianity outside Judaea, is keenly attuned to the role of the economically privileged urban elites, women as well as men, in supporting – or refusing to support – the itinerant Christian teachers. We have already seen how Acts depicts Paul (in marked contrast to the stubbornly silent Jesus) as eager to present his case to potential patrons at the highest levels – the Roman governors Felix and Festus, the Herodian rulers Agrippa and Bernice and finally the emperor himself. Prior to these accounts, Luke has repeatedly staged the scene of Paul entering a new city and confronting the local powers that be. At Paphos in Cyprus, Paul gains the support of a Roman proconsul whom he converts to Christianity (Acts 13.12). In Pisidian Antioch, on the other hand, the jealousy of the local Jews leads them to incite 'the devout women of high standing and the leading men of the city' to stir up a persecution of Paul and Barnabas (Acts 13.50). In Thessalonica, 'a great many of the devout Greeks and not a few of the leading women' support Paul and Silas (Acts 17.4). In Beroea, again we are told that 'not a few Greek women of high standing as well as men' are converted (Acts 17.12). Paul is reported to have friends among the Asiarchs (city benefactors) of Ephesus (Acts 19.31). Such references, which amount to a kind of ostentatious name-dropping, indicate Luke's desire to show that the Christian teachers have support of urban patrons of high social standing. That he repeatedly signals the presence of women among these patrons in part reflects the historical realities of ancient Mediterranean society, in which the privileges of social class and economic power frequently outweigh the hierarchy of gender. Other references to female householders and benefactors of more modest means include Martha (Lk. 10.38-42), Sapphira (Acts 5.1-12), Tabitha (Acts 9.36-42), Mary the mother of John (Acts 12.12), Lydia (Acts 16.14-15, 40) and Priscilla (Acts 18). Individual male patrons appear rather less frequently in comparison.

In fact, elite women seem often to have been more open to the teachings of new religious movements than were the men of their class. Yet, Luke's selective focus on female patronage may also reflect a subtler rhetorical strategy. If evidence of elite patronage is in itself a source of political capital for the Christian movement, evidence of elite female patronage has a particular message to convey, in an imperial culture that invests heavy significance in domestic figures of womanly influence. Where a man's political reputation could be tainted by accusations that he was susceptible to the attractions of a seductress who might tempt him to betray his public duty, it could also be buttressed by demonstrations that he acquiesced to the influence of a virtuous woman whose moral rectitude could be counted on to strengthen his resolve in the performance of that same duty (Cooper 1996; Matthews 2001). The exercise of female influence, essentially familial in its idealization, exceeds the bounds of the family as soon as it becomes a public image. Women with resources are women with potentially widespread influence as patrons; as rhetorical figures appearing in ancient texts, they are therefore also highly charged emblems of social power, exercised either positively or negatively on the public acts of men. Thus, in emphasizing the role of female patrons, Luke is able both to honour and to instruct the women as well as the men in his audience on how to be properly generous benefactors, while also buttressing the reputation of Christianity by enabling its men to go public under the influence of the right kind of women.

Luke's view of economic relations finally presents an even more mixed message than does his view of Roman politics. His Jesus proclaims a more radical (and arguably, via his ambiguous opposition to Roman taxation, also an explicitly anti-imperial) economic platform than does the Jesus of any other gospel-writer, a message underlined by Luke's depiction of the 'communism' of the earliest Christians in Jerusalem. Yet, as he brings his history ever closer to the narrative present, Luke seems to allow the radicalism of Jesus and his earliest followers to slip into an irretrievable past, leaving his readers to follow his lead in responding more pragmatically to the realities of economic patronage that structure the socio-political relations of the ancient Roman world. Indeed, at times he appears to be centrally concerned merely with securing the right patrons and with converting those patrons to new levels of generosity in the age-old competitive pursuit of social honour. He does this, however, in large part by challenging his readers with the depiction of an enviably ascetic 'golden age' when wealthy Christians voluntarily embraced poverty and no one hungered. How thoroughgoing a subversion of the top-heavy Roman economy he ultimately advocates is a question that is finally extremely difficult to answer. Luke's very hesitations and apparent inconsistencies may point to an important fact, namely, that it is even more difficult and dangerous to question the invisible economic infrastructure of empire than to question the public face of its political leadership.

Luke-Acts as Literature: Postcolonial Ambivalence

Luke as Novelist
Luke's self-awareness regarding his own authorial role distinguishes him rather sharply from the authors of other New Testament texts. This is clearest in the dedicatory prefaces to both the Gospel and Acts but is also subtly signalled by

the emphasis placed on texts and textual interpretation throughout Luke-Acts (Robbins 1991). If Luke positions himself as a writer consciously participating in a broader web of literary practices, then we must take seriously both those practices and his particular self-placement in relation to them. Specifically, attunement to the 'novelistic' aspects of Luke's work will open up possibilities for a distinctly postcolonial reading of his literary corpus.

Genre, however, remains a disputed issue with regard to Luke-Acts. This is partly because 'genre' was itself a moving target during the early imperial period, which witnessed a veritable explosion in the production of prose narrative, a practice of writing that not only defied traditional generic classification but also seemed intentionally to subvert the distinction between history and fiction, truth and lies. As Glen Bowersock notes, 'the overt creation of fiction as a means of rewriting or even inventing the past was a serious business for many of the ancients, and for us the enormous increase in fictional production of all kinds during the Roman empire poses major questions of historical interpretation' (1994: 13). Indeed, as Bowersock hints, it appears that the historical advent of the Roman Empire and the consequent experience of cultural and political dislocation largely accounts for the prominence of novelistic writing in this period as well as for the blurring of boundaries between history and fiction that characterizes such writing. The world had become at once far larger and much smaller. Cultural difference – not only the difference between 'Romans' and 'others' but also the differences between those 'others' – was constantly being negotiated along shifting borderlines of competition and attraction, emulation and repudiation. When the empire spoke, its subjects 'talked back', and frequently they did so by telling stories that subtly (or not so subtly) questioned the hegemony of Rome, in part by questioning the 'truth' or stability of any encompassing monolithic version of 'history'.

Mikhail Bakhtin suggests that the novel is best understood not as a genre but rather a parody of genres; it both exposes generic conventions as such and plays subversively with those same conventions. Among the features of novelistic literature that he highlights is the particular relationship of the novel to time. Unlike the epic, which effects closure by inscribing distance between an idealized past and the present, 'the novel comes into contact with the spontaneity of the inconclusive present; this is what keeps the genre from congealing. The novelist is drawn toward everything that is not yet completed' (1981: 27). Luke-Acts has frequently been read as an instance of 'epic' historicizing (most recently and explicitly by Bonz 2000) on the grounds that its author, by supplementing the Gospel with a second, distinctly historiographic volume, consigns the ministry of Jesus and his earliest followers to a distant, idealized past, while also gracing the Christians with a respectable ethno-literary pedigree. Yet, such a reading, while not without its merits, still misses something important, namely, the way in which Luke plays with the barely congealing conventions of the gospel 'genre' precisely by producing the supplemental book of Acts.

Luke's awareness of rewriting earlier accounts is already announced (even hyperbolically staged) in the preface to the Gospel: 'Inasmuch as many have undertaken to compile a narrative of the things which have been accomplished among us... it seems good to me also, having followed all things closely for some time past, to write an orderly account for you, most excellent Theophilus' (Lk. 1.1-3). It is with the addition of Acts, however, that Luke renders not only the 'many' prior gospels but even his own Gospel incomplete while also refusing to finish the story.

For starters, the initial 'summary' of the first volume does not easily map onto the volume itself: the events of one day's encounter with the risen Jesus (Luke 24) have now stretched to include forty days of extended conversation (Acts 1.3) – itself a sign of things to come. As the narrative continues to grow, metamorphizing the Galilaean ministry of Jesus into the evangelization of the Roman Empire itself, the reader's sense of time shifts dizzyingly. The past is not merely safely distanced: its distance – its temporal 'otherness' – is brought into dialogue with an ambiguously open-ended present. The novelistic present is literally open-ended, for, as we have already seen, Acts comes to a halt without actually concluding. The reader who 'knows' that Paul is martyred in Rome is refused the satisfaction of closure. In its place is offered the pleasure of suspension within a story without end. It is, as we have also already seen, an ever-shifting tale of imperial domination and ambivalent resistance. Paul's narrative both does and does not repeat the narrative of Jesus. Our own readerly narratives both will and will not repeat the narratives of Jesus and Paul. History does not come to a close: the past continues to be rewritten. In this respect, Luke-Acts betrays its affinities with more recent postcolonial novels that 'deliberately set out to disrupt... notions of "history" and the ordering of time' by running 'history aground in a new and overwhelming space which annihilates time and imperial purpose. Received history is tampered with, rewritten, and realigned from the point of view of the victims of its destructive progress' (Ashcroft, Griffiths and Tiffin 2002: 33).

Temporal dislocations are, moreover, matched by and interwoven with spatial displacements in Luke's narrative, as in other novelistic literature (see Ashcroft, Griffiths and Tiffin 2002: 'A major feature of post-colonial literatures is the concern with place and displacement' [p. 8]). If Jerusalem and its temple constitute a centre of gravity toward which the itinerant ministries of both Jesus and Paul are eventually (and, in Paul's case, repeatedly) drawn, it is a centre that no longer exists. This is not only the case because Luke and his early readers 'know', as we also 'know', that the temple was destroyed by the Romans in 70 CE. It is also the case because the meandering travelogue of Acts has finally veered drastically off-centre. Or rather, it has veered toward a different centre, namely, the capital city of the Roman emperor himself. Yet, 'Rome' refuses to stabilize, even as its emperor fails to show his face. Have the readers, with Paul, 'colonized' (by evangelizing) Rome, only to discover that the emperor has no clothes? To borrow the terms of postcolonial theorist Homi Bhabha, perhaps the Christian 'mimicry' of imperial expansionism has here revealed itself to be 'at once resemblance and menace', disrupting the authority of imperial discourse in a 'scene of colonial power, where history turns to farce and presence to "a part" ' (1994: 86, 91). In place of the totalizing history of empire and the presence of the emperor himself, we are offered a strategically flawed imitation, the unfinished narrative of a mobile provincial, a hybrid subject born 'Roman' but also born elsewhere, a prisoner of Rome but also 'unhindered' in the capital city, who sets out to reconquer the world by telling a story – Jesus' story, his own story. But, above all, *Luke*'s story.

Hybridity and Heteroglossia

As significant as its relationship to time and place is the novel's relationship to language, dubbed by Bakhtin 'polyglossia', 'heteroglossia' or 'hybridization', which he understands as a reflection of a 'polyglot consciousness' resulting from layered histories of conquest and colonization that produce complex intersections of cultures. Novelistic literature, argues Bakhtin, does not preserve a single cultural–linguistic heritage but always places multiple languages in dialogue: 'The novelistic hybrid is *an artistically organized system for bringing different languages in contact with one another*, a system having as its goal the illumination of one language by means of another, the carving out of a living image of another language' (1981: 361; emphasis in the original).

Luke thematizes such 'heteroglossia' explicitly in the well-known account of Pentecost. When all of the disciples of Jesus are gathered in one place, the sound of a 'mighty wind' fills the house where they have assembled and 'tongues of fire' rest on each one, as Luke describes it. Filled by the Holy Spirit, they begin 'to speak in other tongues (*heterais glossais*)' (Acts 2.1-4). The first wonder is, then, a wonder of speech, of alien, and thus denaturalized, speech: the disciples find not their own but 'other' hot tongues in their mouths, which have become hollowed (hallowed) spaces housing 'a living image of another language'. The second wonder is a wonder of comprehension. Present are Jews 'from every nation under heaven', yet to their surprise, 'each one heard them speaking in their own language' (Acts 2.5-6). The moment teeters toward the would-be 'monoglossia' attempted by a virtual UN miracle of simultaneous translation: 'Were not all those who are speaking Galilaeans? And how is it that we hear each of us in his own native tongue?' (Acts 2.7-8). And yet, translation is never exact precisely because languages will not relinquish their differences. The text continues to invoke a clamour of exotically 'native languages': 'Parthians and Medes and Elamites and residents of Mesopotamia, Judaea and Cappadocia, Pontus and Asia, Phrygia and Pamphylia, Egypt and the parts of Libya belonging to the Cyrene, and visitors from Rome, both Jews and proselytes, Cretans and Arabians, we hear them telling us in our own tongues the mighty works of God' (Acts 2.9-11). The scene is marked as carnivalesque when those participating are mocked as 'drunken'

(Acts 2.13). If they are drunk, however, they are drunk on the exhilarating spirit of heteroglossia itself, charged by the energy of an excess of fiery tongues. Citing the prophet Joel (and thus still speaking with the tongue of another), Peter proclaims: 'And in the last days it shall be, God declares, that I will pour out my spirit upon all flesh, and your sons and your daughters shall prophesy, and your young men shall see visions, and your old men shall dream dreams' (Acts 2.17).

Pentecost functions as a metonym for Luke's pervasive, and distinctly dialogic or hybridizing, practice of citing direct speech. By opening up the book of Acts to linguistic interpenetration, Luke's account of Pentecost also repeats the trick by which he has already opened his Gospel. Such direct speech is 'other-tongued' (heteroglossal) not only because it is not delivered in Luke's own narrative voice, not only because it issues from many different voices, but also because it is marked as coming from elsewhere, uttered from the mouths of angels, borne on the breath of inspiration, cited from the text of the Scriptures. In the Gospel, the angel Gabriel addresses Zechariah, announcing John's birth (Lk. 1.13-17). Zechariah, who is not initially a receptive listener, is struck dumb, but speech withheld is eventually translated into a written text, cited by Luke – 'His name is John' (Lk. 1.20, 63) – which releases Zechariah's tongue in a stream of inspired prophecy (Lk. 1.67-79). In an enfolded doublet, Mary too is addressed by the angel as well as by Elizabeth, imparting news of the birth of Jesus. She responds with a hymn of prophetic praise and celebration (Lk. 1.26-55). An angel addresses shepherds (Lk. 2.10-14), Simeon prophesies in the temple (Lk. 2.29-35), as does Anna, though her words are not reported (Lk. 2.36-38) and John delivers his sharp-edged prophecies (Lk. 3.7-17). All this before Jesus' ministry has even begun.

Attentiveness to Luke's 'redactional' interests should not distract from the significance of his stylistic choices. Luke is present as 'author' not merely in the narrative or theological frame within which he places prophetic speech – a frame that indeed seeks to 'control' or even 'discipline' such speech (as frames inevitably do). Luke is present (and also, paradoxically, absent) as 'author' equally in his mobilization of a heteroglossia that cannot finally be contained. Nor, therefore, can Lukan heteroglossia be reduced – or inflated – to a single, inclusive 'Spirit' of truth. Speech in Luke-Acts remains textured by contingency, split or doubled by the awareness of other 'tongues', spaces and temporalities. Perhaps, if we listen very closely, we can even discern in the text a movement toward what Bhabha names a 'third' or an 'in-between' space of ambivalent signification 'that may open the way to conceptualizing an *inter*national culture, based not on the exoticism of multiculturalism or the *diversity* of cultures, but on the inscription and articulation of culture's *hybridity*' (1994: 38; emphasis in the original).

Borderland Translations
More local readings of two selected narrative episodes from Acts will provide another window onto the complexity of Luke's novelistic art, while also allow-

ing us to consider further his concept of 'mission' – necessarily problematic from a postcolonial perspective, given the long history of explicitly colonialist Christian evangelizing, in which the reception of Acts has played no small part.

In Acts 8.26-40, we meet a figure native to a land that lies beyond even the boundaries embraced by the linguistic plenitude of Pentecost – an Ethiopian, in fact, hailing from the very 'end of the earth' (see Acts 1.8; Martin 1989). We never learn his name, but other identity markers proliferate almost bewilderingly. He is not only an Ethiopian but also a eunuch, minister to 'the Candace', queen of the Ethiopians, 'in charge of all her treasure'. He is, furthermore, a Jew, it would appear, for he is returning from a pilgrimage to Jerusalem. This is, then, an alluringly exotic personage, not only presumably black-skinned (Martin 1989) but also implicitly feminized, even arguably 'queered', because he is a eunuch but also because of his proximity to a 'queen' and her wealth. His access to luxury is further signalled by the fact that he is riding in a chariot and is in possession of a personal copy of the writings of the prophet Isaiah. He is also, then, educated, perhaps even 'wise': Ethiopia was known for its wise men. (A later novel, Heliodorus' *Ethiopian Story*, represents the wisdom of the Ethiopian 'gymnosophists', or 'naked sages', who were advisors to the king and queen, as eclipsing even that of the widely renowned Egyptian sages.)

The Ethiopian's path is intersected by Philip, a Greek-speaking Jew from the circle of Jerusalem Christians who has just completed a more or less successful mission to the Samaritans, a liminal people closer to home. 'More or less' successful, because it appears that the baptism Philip brought was lacking the crucial seal of the Spirit, requiring a supplemental visit from Peter and John to perform the laying on of hands (Acts 8.12-17). If Philip's status in relation to the Galilaean apostles is thus slightly ambiguous, he does have the attentions of 'an angel of the Lord', who has instructed him to go to the desert road between Jerusalem and Gaza, where he sees the Ethiopian. It is 'the Spirit' who gives Philip his next cue: 'Go up and join this chariot'. Trotting alongside the chariot, perhaps craning his neck awkwardly upward, Philip is at a distinct social and physical disadvantage, but this does not deter him. The Ethiopian is evidently reading aloud (as was the typical practice in antiquity), which gives Philip (who may or may not be able to read) the opportunity to ask whether he understands what he is reading. The Ethiopian apparently takes this conversational opener as just that, for he responds graciously, first with an implicit invitation – 'How can I, unless someone guides me?' – and then with an explicit invitation for Philip to join him in the chariot. (It is, perhaps, simply too wildly improbable that this yokel jogging in the desert could be addressing the chariot-borne minister of the queen of Ethiopia patronizingly.)

Since Philip has indicated interest in the text, the Ethiopian now presents him with the hermeneutical question over which he is puzzling. He has been reading the following passage: 'As a sheep led to the slaughter or a lamb before its shearer is dumb, so he opens not his mouth. In his humiliation justice was denied him. Who can describe his generation? For his life is taken up from the earth' (Isa. 53.7-8). 'About whom, pray, does the prophet say this, about himself or about someone else?' queries the Ethiopian. It is, of course, the perfect opportunity for Philip, who knows exactly to whom the passage refers and is only too eager to tell his companion all about Jesus. The Ethiopian is not only receptive, but actively enthusiastic. As they pass some water – fine luck, in the desert! – he asks Philip, 'What is to prevent my being baptized?' (He, of course, does not know of Philip's imperfect record with the Samaritans, but perhaps that is just as well.) Then: 'And he commanded the chariot to stop, and they both went down into the water, Philip and the eunuch, and he baptized him'. The structure of this sentence is intriguing, for although it is clear from the context that it must be Philip who baptizes the eunuch, the grammar wobbles ambiguously: the *eunuch* commands, *both* go down, *he* baptizes *him*. Has the Ethiopian given up his commanding position of agency in the sentence or not? The ambiguity breaks the surface of the next sentence: 'and when they came up out of the water, the Spirit of the Lord caught up ...' not the baptized Ethiopian (as we might have expected) but the baptizer 'Philip' – 'And the eunuch saw him no more, and went on his way rejoicing'. The Ethiopian continues on his chosen path, but it is Philip who has been most powerfully changed, it would seem. (He has in fact been translocated to another town, in a rather bizarre concluding twist.)

Though it initially seems to have all the right ingredients – 'authoritative interpreter of God's word converts receptive native' – this exotic tale finally resists employment as a typical colonialist narrative of mission and conversion. Timely nudges from supernatural figures notwithstanding, the exchange, unlike Philip's evangelizing of Samaria, has the trappings of a chance encounter. The Ethiopian has travelled to Jerusalem to worship, but he meets Philip not in the city itself but in the desert outside the city – a distinctly liminal zone, a space of passages. Philip for his part has not planned to be there at all. Neither of them is, then, exactly at home, least of all the Ethiopian, but it is he who offers Philip the hospitality of his chariot, even as Philip offers him the common ground of an exegetical conversation. The Ethiopian – black Jew, castrated man – is a split subject, and then some. Clearly, Philip's social and cultural superior, he is nonetheless too queer a character to function like other figures of patronage in Luke's text. Yet, Philip too is marked by ambivalence, a Greek-speaking Jew in Jerusalem, a not quite successful Christian missionary to the not quite Jewish Samaritans. Rising together from the baptismal waters (where it is not clear who has actually baptized whom), the two meet, however fleetingly, at the transformative borderlines of already hybridized subjectivities.

Acts 16.11-40, in contrast, conforms more closely to the anticipated colonial script, with Paul, missionary par excellence, in firm control of events. Macedonian Philippi – a Roman colony, as Luke carefully notes – is the site of the apostle's encounter with Lydia, a God-fearing merchant who seems to personify the new, foreign, and distinctly 'Roman' territory that Paul sets out to conquer and re-colonize through his evangelism (Staley 1999; building on Dube 2000). Alluring in her understated power, the silent Lydia (who never speaks in the text) is also seductively receptive in her femininity: 'the Lord opened her heart to give heed to what was said by Paul'. She and her household are baptized and she insists that Paul and his companions stay in her home.

The brief account of this quietly hospitable convert is, however, noisily interrupted and thereby complicated by the story of a slave girl who possesses a spirit of pythonic prophecy that profits her masters greatly, we are told. In Luke's narrative, the spirit also, however, conveys a cryptic message that profits her masters not at all. Following in Paul's wake for several days, the girl cries out: 'These men are servants of the Most High God, who proclaim to you the way of salvation'. Whether this is an expression of her hopes (salvation) or her fears (yet another conquering god) remains unclear. Oddly enough, Paul is irritated, apparently hearing in the slave girl's repetitious proclamation not a convert's witness but a spirit's mockery. His patience finally snaps, and he commands that the spirit leave the girl. The silenced girl herself evaporates from the text at this point, but not without leaving a number of unanswered questions behind. Ambivalent prophetess of a 'native' Greek cult – for none other than the prestigious Delphic oracle is signalled by the reference to a 'pythonic' spirit – the woman whom we meet wandering the streets of a Roman colony has already been enslaved by masters who exploit her gift. Has Paul 'liberated' this feminine figure of colonized Greece from her 'Roman' masters by freeing her from the possession of the spirit? Or has he conquered her already bound spirit by depriving her of her prophetic powers, leaving the territory clear for his own God's occupation?

We might wonder as well why her story is embedded in the tale of Lydia (which is not yet quite complete). The 'good woman' is doubled by the 'bad woman': these figures of feminized nativity do not merely contrast but also collude, standing closely on either side of the boundary of 'conversion', combining forces to articulate 'the ambiguous relationship of the colonizer to the colonized' and to enact multiple crossings and recrossings of ambivalent borderlands (Staley 1999: 130). In the end, both women have been silenced, whether rendered compliant or effectively dead to the narrative. On the other hand, and from another perspective, both are remarkably resilient. Each has already crossed many borders: Lydia reaches the Roman colony from Thyatira and the slave girl, at least symbolically, hails from Delphi. If Lydia manoeuvres the dangers of the borderland with quiet competence, the slave girl's urgent – yet barely coherent – warnings haunt its margins and gaps.

The figure of Paul reiterates the ambivalence of the doubled figures of women: split (not least in his relationship to the two women) between the subjection of the colonized and collusion with the forces of a missionary (counter-)colonization, he too is positioned as a hybrid subject in Luke's narrative. It is crucial that

Paul's intervention to release the girl from the spirit that binds her to slavery leads to his own stripping, beating and imprisonment, not in this case at the instigation of Jews (as is the usual Lukan pattern) but rather at the instigation of the girl's 'Roman' masters on the grounds of his very Jewishness: 'These men are Jews and they are disturbing our city. They advocate customs which it is not lawful for us Romans to accept or practice.' Paul's subsequent miraculous release from prison both mimics and is mocked by the slave's ambiguous (merely spiritual?) 'liberation' – or, alternatively, her dispossession by Paul himself. Indeed, Paul gains his freedom by distinctly tricksterish means, his clever double-talk, which culminates with the invocation of his Roman citizenship, resulting in the drama of a public shaming of the very civic magistrates who have initially shamed and injured him. When Luke represents Paul as saucily prolonging this momentary turning-of-the-tables by insisting on going to visit Lydia before finally leaving town, he also tightens the weave of a narrative that leaves missionary, patroness and prophetess positioned together (albeit also positioned differently) in a shared borderland, thereby further complicating (though by no means eliding) the significations of gender.

The story of Paul and the two women of Philippi is thus not *simply* a triumphal apologetic that unapologetically aligns a masculinized missionary Christianity with the cultural and political powers of empire and colonialism. Even this brief consideration of Acts 16 exposes the complexity and instability of the text. Luke's critique of the Greek slave girl's exploitation by her Roman masters (a bondage doubled by Paul's own imprisonment through the intervention of those same masters) conveys a broader critique of Roman colonization, yet this critique (whether Luke intends it or not) is also shadowed by insinuations that Paul, in the name of his God, has himself come to exploit the already colonized territory personified in the doubled figures of female receptivity and resistance. Paul's own resistance to the leadership of the Roman colony is likewise complicated by his appeal to the privilege of his Roman citizenship to effect that very resistance. The most promisingly 'postcolonial' spaces in this 'missionary' text are opened by the distinctly hybrid figures of the two women, but they are spaces of menace as well as hope.

'Postcolonial' Luke?

The ambiguities of Luke's ideological stance cannot simply be resolved into clarities, yet we have seen that Luke-Acts may nonetheless yield distinctly anti-imperialist interpretations. Indeed, the political subversiveness of the text has been seriously underestimated by most, though not all, scholars. This is at least partly due to a widespread misreading of Luke's 'apologetic' strategy that misses the subtlety of its critique. Surfacing the Lukan critique, while also acknowledging not only its subtlety but also its ambivalence, may be of particular importance for our own projects of resistance to empire. For Luke, more than almost any other biblical writer (the most obvious exception being the author of Revelation), is attuned to the political complexity and universalizing ambitions of a Roman Empire that perhaps bears even more resemblance than do the colonialist regimes of modern Europe to the globalizing, postmodern 'neo-empire' of the twenty-first century.

But is an 'anti-imperialist' reading also a 'postcolonial' reading? The answer depends, of course, above all on one's definition of the postcolonial. In part because of the 'literariness' of Luke-Acts itself, a literary approach to postcoloniality that is sensitive to textual indeterminacy and instability has seemed especially promising. (Though a 'historical' approach is not thereby simply eschewed: here too resonances between the polyglot colonial or neocolonial contexts of late antiquity and postmodernity are implicitly invoked.) In particular, initial forays into reading Luke-Acts as a 'hybrid' novelistic text have allowed us to perceive precisely in many of Luke's ambiguities and ambivalences the lively negotiations and contestations of identity taking place at the ever-shifting borders of cultural difference articulated on the field of colonial resistance. Luke-Acts becomes, on such a reading, not merely a source of political critique, but also a site of emergent political possibility.

BIBLIOGRAPHY

Ashcroft, Bill, Gareth Griffiths and Helen Tiffin
    2002   *The Empire Writes Back: Theory and Practice in Postcolonial Literatures* (2nd edn; London: Routledge).

Bakhtin, M. M.
    1981   *The Dialogic Imagination: Four Essays* (trans. C. Emerson and M. Holquist; Austin: University of Texas Press).

Bhabha, Homi K.
    1994   *The Location of Culture* (London: Routledge).

Blomberg, Craig L.
    1999   *Neither Poverty Nor Riches: A Biblical Theology of Material Possessions* (Grand Rapids: Eerdmans).

Bonz, Marianne Palmer
    2000   *The Past as Legacy: Luke-Acts and Ancient Epic* (Minneapolis: Fortress Press).

Bowersock, Glen W.
    1994   *Fiction as History: Nero to Julian* (Berkeley: University of California Press).

Cameron, Averil
    1991   *Christianity and the Rhetoric of Empire: The Development of Christian Discourse* (Berkeley: University of California Press).

Cassidy, Richard J.
    1978   *Jesus, Politics, and Society: A Study of Luke's Gospel* (Maryknoll, NY: Orbis Books).
    1983   'Luke's Audience, the Chief Priests, and the Motive for Jesus' Death', in R. J. Cassidy and P. J. Scharper (eds), *Political Issues in Luke-Acts* (Maryknoll: Orbis Books): 145–67.

Conzelmann, Hans
    1961   *The Theology of St. Luke* (New York: Harper).

Cooper, Kate
    1996   *The Virgin and the Bride: Idealized Womanhood in Late Antiquity* (Cambridge: Harvard University Press).

Dube Shomanah, Musa W.
    2000   *Postcolonial Feminist Interpretation of the Bible* (St. Louis: Chalice).

Hardt, Michael and Antonio Negri
    2000   *Empire* (Cambridge: Harvard University Press).

Horsley, Richard A.
    2003   *Jesus and Empire: The Kingdom of God and the New World Disorder* (Minneapolis: Fortress Press).

Karris, R. J.
    1978   'Poor and Rich: The Lukan *Sitz im Leben*', in C. H. Talbert (ed.), *Perspectives on Luke-Acts* (Danville, VA: Association of Baptist Professors of Religion): 112–25.

Liew, Tat-Siong Benny
    1999   'Tyranny, Boundary and Might: Colonial Mimicry in Mark's Gospel', *Journal for the Study of the New Testament* 73: 7–31.

Martin, Clarice J.
    1989   'A Chamberlain's Journey and the Challenge of Interpretation for Liberation', *Semeia* 47: 105–35.

Matthews, Shelly
    2001   *First Converts: Rich Pagan Women and the Rhetoric of Mission in Early Judaism and Christianity* (Stanford: Stanford University Press).

Moxnes, Halvor
    1991   'Patron-Client Relations and the New Community in Luke-Acts', in J. H. Neyrey (ed.), *The Social World of Luke-Acts* (Peabody, MA: Hendrickson Publishers): 241–68.

Oakman, Douglas E.
    1991   'The Countryside in Luke-Acts', in J. H. Neyrey (ed.), *The Social World of Luke-Acts* (Peabody, MA: Hendrickson Publishers): 151–79.

Pilgrim, Walter E.
    1981   *Good News to the Poor: Wealth and Poverty in Luke-Acts* (Minneapolis: Augsburg).

Robbins, Vernon K
    1991   'The Social Location of the Implied Author of Luke-Acts', in J. H. Neyrey (ed.), *The Social World of Luke-Acts* (Peabody, MA: Hendrickson Publishers): 305–32.

Schaberg, Jane
    1992   'Luke', in C. A. Newsom and S. H. Ringe (eds), *Women's Bible Commentary* (Louisville, KY: Westminster/John Knox Press): 275–92.

Schmidt, Daryl
    1983   'Luke's "Innocent" Jesus: A Scriptural Apologetic', in R. J. Cassidy and P. J. Scharper (eds), *Political Issues in Luke-Acts* (Maryknoll, NY: Orbis Books): 111–21.

Schottroff, Luise and Wolfgang Stegemann
    1986   *Jesus and the Hope of the Poor* (trans. M. J. O'Connell; Maryknoll, NY: Orbis Books).

Schwartz, Seth
2001   *Imperialism and Jewish Society, 200 B.C.E. to 640 C.E.* (Princeton, NJ: Princeton University Press).

Scott, James C.
1990   *Domination and the Arts of Resistance: Hidden Transcripts* (New Haven: Yale University Press).

Staley, Jeffrey L.
1999   'Changing Woman: Postcolonial Reflections on Acts 16:6-40', *Journal for the Study of the New Testament* 73: 113–35.

Sugirtharajah, R. S.
2002   *Postcolonial Criticism and Biblical Interpretation* (Oxford: Oxford University Press).

Walaskay, Paul W.
1983   *'And So We Came to Rome': The Political Perspective of St. Luke* (Cambridge: Cambridge University Press).

Walton, Steve
2002   'The State They Were in: Luke's View of the Roman Empire', in Peter Oakes (ed.), *Rome in the Bible and the Early Church* (Carlisle: Paternoster Press): 1–41.

Young, Robert
2001   *Postcolonialism: An Historical Introduction* (Oxford: Blackwell).

THE GOSPEL OF JOHN

Fernando F. Segovia

The Gospel of John has played a rather prominent role in postcolonial biblical criticism (Dube 1996, 1998, 2000; Dube and Staley 2002) – relatively speaking, of course, given the still incipient character and limited output of such criticism. Such attention proves, upon closer examination, quite understandable. The Gospel is a writing in which a postcolonial problematic is both prominent and pervasive. A text primarily religious in character, to be sure, but also a text with strong geopolitical preoccupations and ramifications.

Without question, the Gospel stands as a pre-eminent example of religious writing. It is a text with a driving focus on matters human and divine. Its tale involves classic elements of such writing: a realm of spirit and deities – an 'other-world'; a realm of matter and human beings – a 'this-world'; and a pattern of interaction between such realms – the complex web of relations that mark the coexistence and engagement of these two 'worlds'. The Gospel further stands, however, as a writing with decidedly political overtones. It is a text that conveys, in and through such religious concerns and pursuits, a sharp sense of the political. Not only in the general sense that all writing, of whatever ilk and genre, inevitably reflects and addresses, in any number of ways, the political context within which it comes to be, macro or micro, but also in the pointed sense that such a context, howsoever conceptualized and formulated, is specifically foregrounded and problematized by a writing. This the Gospel does at various levels and by way of conflict, all ultimately and closely interrelated: the local or 'national', by way of regional conflict among various groupings within the area of colonial Palestine; the global or 'international', in terms of geopolitical conflict between the colonial and the imperial within the framework of the Roman Empire; the cosmic or 'transworldly', through mythical conflict between suprahuman powers within the conception of reality as a whole.

The Gospel advances a view of Jesus and his group of followers as in conflict, in light of their religious beliefs and practices, with the ruling circles of colonial Palestine, the overseeing masters of imperial Rome, and the overarching ruler of the demonic this-world. Such a conflict bears broader, even universal, dimensions. To begin with, it reaches beyond the ranks of the elite to the masses of the people, whether in Palestine or throughout the empire. In addition, it further encompasses, in principle, all political frameworks and all ethnic groupings beyond the borders of Rome. It is thus a conflict that impinges ultimately on all human beings in the this-world. It is, therefore, a conflict profoundly religious as well as profoundly political.

As such, the Gospel of John is a text bent on claiming and exercising power – in fact, absolute power – in both the religious and political spheres at once. It invalidates and displaces all existing institutions and authorities, values and norms, ideals and goals, while promoting and emplacing alternative authorities and institutions, norms and values, goals and ideals. Such a project the Gospel conceives and articulates from within the imperial–colonial framework of Rome and, in so doing, highlights and scrutinizes the differential relationship of power operative within such a context. In sum, a postcolonial text.

It is this geopolitical problematic and project that I seek to capture in this postcolonial commentary. I shall begin by setting forth a set of basic principles behind postcolonial criticism as I envision it, continue with a postcolonial reading from a variety of different perspectives, and conclude with a critical summary of the Gospel's geopolitical agenda.

Postcolonial Criticism: A Prolegomenon

Given the extensive, complex and sharp discussions within postcolonial studies regarding all aspects of postcolonial reality and inquiry, the constitutive components of postcolonial analysis are neither self-evident nor unproblematic. Any such exercise in criticism should, therefore, not only specify but also unpack the underlying principles at work. The present commentary is no exception. What follows, then, are various theoretical and methodological considerations that inform and guide the task at hand (Segovia 2005). These touch on such fundamental issues as the meaning, the scope, the subject and the mode of postcolonial analysis. In each case a summary of the critical discussion is followed by a placement of the project within the given spectrum. Thereby the specific nature of the commentary is properly grounded and demarcated.

Meaning of Postcolonial Inquiry

A first area of discussion concerns the meaning of postcolonial analysis. The critical bearings in this regard are well established and revolve around the signification attributed to the temporal prefix 'post' and hence the force of the term 'postcolonial' as such. The issue may be summarized as follows: if the postcolonial represents *what comes after* the colonial, following the base etymological meaning of the term, what precisely is the force of the prefix 'after' and the nuance of the expression 'coming after'? Put differently, what is the relation at play between the colonial and the postcolonial? More to the point, what do such concepts point to and convey?

Two major lines of argumentation, yielding three positions in all, can be readily outlined. On the one hand, a historical–political understanding of the term views the 'postcolonial' as a period of time. Within this first approach two variations are to be found. In the first case, by far the more common, the postcolonial is taken to represent *what comes after* a process of decolonization and hence the end of colonialism. In the second case, the postcolonial is said to constitute *what comes after* a process of colonization and thus the onset of colonialism. In this approach, therefore, the historical–political expanse of the postcolonial varies considerably: the second variation proves far more extensive than the first, both preceding and encompassing the whole of it. On the other hand, a social-psychological understanding of the term regards the 'postcolonial' as a state of mind. Within this second approach, the postcolonial marks the problematization, whether by a group or an individual, of the unequal relationship of power at work in imperial–colonial formations. In this approach, consequently, the social-psychological lens of the postcolonial emerges as independent of actual historical–political conditions: it can surface within a context of colonialization or fail to emerge within a context of decolonization. My own preference is for a social-psychological understanding: conscientization, collective or personal, in the midst or face of a geopolitical relationship of domination and subordination.

What, then, does it mean to write a 'postcolonial' commentary on John? This is a question to be pursued at two different levels of application: composition and interpretation. To begin with, an observation regarding the task in general. At the level of criticism, the reader, in light of her/his own awareness regarding the presence and dynamics of an uneven geopolitical relationship of power (or set of such relationships) in his/her own context, proceeds to foreground such a relationship of domination and subordination in the text, given its origins within an imperial–colonial formation. At the level of writing, the text may or may not reveal, within the imperial–colonial framework in question, a similar consciousness regarding the geopolitical relationship at work. Thus, a postcolonial commentary on John calls for the reader but not the Gospel to be 'postcolonial'. Now, a comment on the present undertaking in particular. With regard to John, I believe that the Gospel does constitute a 'postcolonial' writing – a text that reveals critical awareness of geopolitical power within the Roman Empire. With regard to myself as reader, I would characterize my approach to the Gospel as 'postcolonial' – a reader with critical consciousness of the geopolitical problematic in his own historical and ongoing context plus a reading that highlights such a problematic in the Gospel of John within its own imperial–colonial context.

Scope of Postcolonial Inquiry

A second point of discussion has to do with the scope of postcolonial analysis. Here the critical lines are neither firmly set nor explicitly debated, so that the discussion remains throughout much too general and unreflective in tone. The issue may be crystallized as follows: is the range of postcolonial analysis to be conceived in expansive or restricted fashion? More concretely, should the problematic be extended across historical distance as well as cultural difference to include within its purview imperial–colonial formations across historical periods and cultural domains? Further, is postcolonial analysis to be seen, in principle or in practice, as a comparative or local inquiry?

Despite the vagueness and imprecision of the overall discussion, a number of parameters can nonetheless be discerned. First, the literature deals, by and large, with the Western imperial–colonial formations from the late eighteenth century through the mid-twentieth century in general and with the British Empire in particular. When this focus is critically grounded, which is not often the case, it is on the basis of a principle of uniqueness: a conjunction of modernity and capitalism renders the imperial–colonial formations of the West, with the United Kingdom as a salient and pacesetting example, unique vis-à-vis all other such formations. Second, not infrequently mention is also made of previous formations within the context of the West, from the sixteenth through to the mid-eighteenth centuries, thus reaching across historical distance. Third, occasionally mention is made as well of similar formations outside the West, across both culture and history, though for the most part in terms of modernity. Finally, far more rarely the literature further refers to imperial–colonial formations as a common, if not constant, phenomenon, extending beyond modernity all the way to antiquity, across history and culture, although with decided emphasis on Greece and (above all) Rome, both generally presented as foundational for the later Western empires. My own preference is for a broad scope in application, transhistorically as well as cross-culturally.

In this light, then, what does the writing of a 'postcolonial' commentary on John assume? In coming to terms with this question, two issues prove helpful. The first involves the question of universality and specificity; the second, the tools of analysis to be employed.

The first issue may be posed as follows: are imperial–colonial formations across history and culture essentially the same, radically different or somewhere in between, a combination of similarities and differences? The present exercise obviously grants the relevance and significance of the postcolonial problematic for both the contemporary world and the ancient world, that is, for reader and text alike. It foregrounds and problematizes the location and perspective of both text and reader within their respective imperial–colonial frameworks. It opts without question, therefore, for a broad range in application. At the same time, I do not view the dynamics of such formations as the same throughout, universally present across historical periods and cultural domains. Rather, I would argue for specificity as of the essence in both – or howsoever many – worlds. In fact, I see contextualization as imperative not only with respect to the different formations in question but also within each formation, insofar as conditions can and do vary widely across different times or areas within the same framework. In the end, therefore, the exercise does grant the possibility of differences and similarities in both discourse and praxis between – or among – different frame-works, all to be duly acknowledged and analysed.

The second issue may be formulated as follows: is recourse to postcolo-nial theory a *sine qua non* in the study of imperial–colonial formations across history and culture? The present exercise obviously grants the value of such a discursive framework for postcolonial analysis. At the same time, I would hold that the foregrounding and problematization of the geopolitical relation-ship can be approached by other means and in other terms as well. Ultimately, therefore, I would argue that the use of postcolonial theory, while not only most appropriate but also most fruitful, is not indispensable. I would further add that recourse to such theory, when invoked, should be in neither sketchy nor uncriti-cal fashion. Far too often the theoretical agent or angle in question is advanced without a sense of discursive context or critical dialogue; in other words, the filter invoked and deployed remains totally or insufficiently critiqued as filter, with a discursive history and perspective of its own.

Terrain of the Postcolonial Inquiry

A third area of discussion involves the terrain of postcolonial analysis. In this respect the critical formations are distinctly drawn and have even assumed, at times, the character of battlelines. The issue may be defined as follows: what is the subject matter of postcolonial inquiry, howsoever conceived in terms of meaning or scope? Put more broadly, should its object be envisioned as limited or comprehensive? More to the point, what areas of concern and study does its critical gaze encompass?

Three general postures can be distinguished in all. To begin with, postcolo-nial analysis may devote itself, primarily if not solely, to the cultural production of imperial–colonial formations. The actual object of inquiry can vary markedly: from the circumscribed, involving literary studies and its various components, to the expansive, comprehending the whole of textual production and even non-textual production. The emphasis here is on issues of representation, yielding a predominantly theoretical and universalist enterprise, heavily indebted to post-structuralist thought. In contrast, postcolonial analysis may pursue, primarily if not solely, the material matrix of imperial–colonial frameworks. The actual object of inquiry can vary widely as well: from the economic, to the political, to the social. The stress here is on issues of historical context, leading to a largely mate-rialist and localized endeavour, heavily indebted to social theory and, especially, neo-Marxist thought. It is from this particular end of the critical spectrum, above all, that severe challenges have been launched against the other pole, making for some rather acrimonious moments in postcolonial studies. Lastly, a middle ground – in principle, if not always in application – is not uncommon, calling for engagement with both material matrix and cultural production in postcolonial analysis. My own preference is for a combined and inclusive approach, with due attention given to cultural expressions as well as material foundations.

Against this background, then, what does the writing of a 'postcolonial' commentary on John address? This question of terrain, like the previous one of meaning, should also be pursued at a twofold level of application, composition and interpretation. It is the former, the realm of the text, that I should like to entertain at this point; the latter, the realm of the reader, I shall take up in the next section on mode.

To begin with, a comment about the task in general. In principle, I would argue, a postcolonial commentary on the Gospel should keep in mind the material matrix as well as cultural production: the world out of which the writing emerges, as conveyed by other sources, and the world as advanced by the writing itself. The operative principle in this regard would be that texts not only presuppose and reflect their contexts but also construct and engage such contexts: they constitute, therefore, active interventions rather than faithful reproductions of the cultural and social realms in question. In practice, however, such a combined approach remains an ideal, on two counts. At a most basic level, there is always the question of emphasis in interpretation: a critic may choose to emphasize, for whatever reasons, either the material or the cultural dimension. From this perspective, as long as such an emphasis is properly highlighted and grounded, there is no reason why it should not be put into effect. At a more substantial level, there is also the question of a fundamental dearth of information regarding the constitutive components of proximate context (*inter alia*: place of origin, time of writing, identity of authorship, circumstances of composition, reception of text), all of which remain the subject of intense debate and beyond resolution. From this perspective, any discussion of the material matrix remains perforce at a very high level of abstraction throughout, occluding thereby the full character of the text as a social and cultural intervention. An observation, then, on the concrete task at hand. In the present commentary on John, I will deal specifically with the text as a moment of cultural expression within the imperial–colonial framework of the Roman Empire. My focus will thus be on the world of the narrative: the world constructed – aesthetically crafted, strategically arranged and politically moulded – by the text. I shall pursue the problematic of terrain, therefore, in terms of the Gospel as a literary, rhetorical and ideological product.

Mode of Postcolonial Inquiry

A final point of discussion deals with the mode of postcolonial analysis. In this matter the critical groupings stand clearly demarcated and can ultimately be traced to, and described in, terms of critical stands taken, explicitly or implicitly, with respect to two fundamental debates in literary criticism, namely, the production of meaning within the relationship between text and reader and the nature of the interaction between reader and text. The issue can be formulated as follows. On the one hand, does postcolonial analysis imply recovery or construction of meaning? Put more concretely, what is the role assigned to the reader in the process of establishing the geopolitical stance of a text within an imperial–colonial framework? Does the reader retrieve or re-create meaning with regard to the text? On the other hand, does postcolonial analysis call for exposition or for engagement? Put more pointedly, what is the role to be espoused by the reader toward the geopolitical stance of a text advanced?

With regard to the first dimension, the critical spectrum can range from the passive and unidimensional to the active and multidimensional. From the former perspective, the task of postcolonial analysis would be that of uncovering and surfacing the given geopolitical stance of a text, with minimal agency on the part of the reader in the formulation of such a stance. The result is a view of meaning as unidimensional (in the text) and of criticism as passive (recovery). From the latter perspective, the task of postcolonial analysis would consist in putting together and arguing persuasively for a particular view of a text's geo-political stance, with a view of such stance as related in highly complex fashion to the reader's own context and perspective. The result is a view of meaning as multidimensional (a text and many readers) and of criticism as active (construc-tion). With regard to the second dimension, the critical spectrum can extend from a posture of neutral presentation to one of critical dialogue. In the former approach, the task of postcolonial criticism would demand no critical evaluation of a text's geopolitical stance on the part of the reader. The result is a view of the reader as expositor. In the latter approach, the task of postcolonial criticism would require critical engagement with the text's geopolitical stance on the part of the reader. The result is a view of the reader as interlocutor. My preference is for both a constructive view, with allowance for active participation by the reader and the production of plural positions, and a dialogical view, with a call for critical engagement by the reader, of postcolonial analysis.

With this in mind, then, what does the writing of a 'postcolonial' commentary on the Gospel of John convey? To begin with, its envisioned slant is not one of objectivism but of partiality. Insofar as I hold to a middle position regarding the production of meaning, with actually more than a gentle nod toward the reader pole in this regard and hence a controlling view of the reader in the process of interpretation, I view the commentary as one reading of the Gospel's geopoliti-cal stance, closely intertwined with my own location and perspective as reader. I make no claims to a final and definitive reading of John, that is, to the discov-ery and recovery of the Gospel's original and intended position in this regard. In fact, I hold firmly to a multiplicity of readings, both existent and potential, regarding such a stance. In addition, the slant envisioned is one of interaction. Insofar as I subscribe to a view of the reader as interlocutor rather than specta-tor, I see critical dialogue with the reading constructed and advanced as impera-tive and not just a desideratum. Indeed, such dialogue I would extend to the multiplicity of readings concerning such a stance constructed and advanced. It should be clear, therefore, that I make no special allowance in this regard for the character of the Gospel as a biblical text: not only do I see its meaning as always refracted in the light of its multiple readers and readings, I also see all such meaning as subject to discussion and evaluation.

Given this delineation of the task at hand, a couple of further observations regarding mode are in order. In light of the partial slant attributed to the commentary, and the position that the meaning I construct and advance in the process is related to my own location and perspective as a reader, a critical reading of such factors is essential. This would apply to all readers, certainly. Given the strictures of space, it is impossible to do so here: suffice it to say that I rely on the principles set forth elsewhere regarding a theology of the diaspora and a hermeneutics of otherness and engagement. Similarly, in view of the interactive slant posited of the commentary, and the position that critical engagement with the meaning constructed and advanced is of the essence, such dialogue should occupy a central role in this assignment. Given the limitations of space, again, it proves impossible to do so here: suffice it to say that I shall do so in future, as I come to terms, and necessarily so, with the implications of my reading. Thus, what is granted in principle must, in practice, be deferred to other times and venues by way of a division of labour.

A Final Word: Nomenclature

With the working principles behind the present commentary on John duly identified and elaborated within the critical context of various constitutive facets of postcolonial analysis, a final comment, I find, is in order. The above discussion regarding postcolonial analysis has had recourse throughout, as will the commentary to follow, to the designation 'imperial–colonial framework', whereby a structural correlation is established between 'imperialism' and 'colonialism' as constitutive components of the same geopolitical phenomenon. These terms and concepts are neither self-evident nor unproblematic. Such juxtaposition on my part signifies, in agreement with Ania Loomba (1998: 1–7), a conjunction of political power and geographical space: 'imperialism' as referring to whatever has to do with the dominant centre and 'colonialism' as pointing to whatever has to do with the subordinated periphery. For me, therefore, there can be no imperialism without colonialism and no colonialism without imperialism.

A Postcolonial Reading of the Gospel

The proposed focus on the world of the narrative and its representations of the material matrix within which the Gospel functions as an intervention may be pursued in any number of ways. I should like to do so by foregrounding the construction of reality, by which term I mean the whole of existence or all that is, as conceptualized and deployed by the Gospel. Thus, I shall highlight the setting of John or the spatial and temporal circumstances in which the events of the narrative take place (see Prince 1987: 86–87). Such reality, I would argue, involves a threefold configuration: the projection of a removed, indiscernible non-material or spiritual world; the givenness of a roundabout, manifest material or fleshly world; the attribution of a complex network of relations between such worlds, at once disparate and interlaced.

As setting, Johannine reality may be further described as follows. With regard to mode of disclosure, it is to be found scattered through the narrative, though with a prominent and grounding contiguous description at the outset, where its main components are immediately outlined. From the point of view of function, it may be classified as utilitarian and symbolic – each element not only has a role to play in the action but also reflects the fundamental conflict at work. With respect to manner of constitution, it may be variously characterized: quite salient – readily available, not at all in the background; thoroughly consistent – yielding an altogether coherent and harmonious picture; fairly precise – though not without significant gaps in information; and objectively presented – set forth by an omniscient narrator, confirmed and expanded by a most reliable protagonist, yet not accessible to all.

This Johannine view of reality I shall unpack, toward a postcolonial reading, from three different yet related angles of inquiry: the overall story, its crucial beginning, the unfolding plot.

To begin with, I shall examine the story of the Gospel or narrative of events in temporal fashion. I shall approach it by way of its major and framing components, each of which marks a specific and defining phase in the chronological succession of events, showing how each anchors and shapes the pivotal, all-encompassing and multidimensional conflict embodied in Jesus and his movement. In so doing, I shall expand on my characterization of the Gospel as an eminently religious text with strong political overtones, a text bent on claiming and exercising power within the imperial–colonial context of Rome, and thus on its character as a postcolonial writing. In the setting of the stage, therefore, the Gospel puts forth a postcolonial proposal.

Thereupon, I shall turn to the beginning unit of the Gospel. I shall analyse it in terms of the central figures and dynamics identified in reality, pointing out how the various resulting relationships account for and anticipate the fundamental conflict engendered by Jesus and his followers. This unit, I have argued, functions as an ideal point of entry into and key summary of the world of the narrative and its creation of reality (Segovia 2002: 33–35). In the process, I would add, the unit further provides a first and grounding glimpse of the Gospel's geopolitical vision and programme. Thus, I shall use it as a foundational point of departure for the political and religious project advanced by the narrative. Through its opening salvo, then, the Gospel launches a postcolonial alternative.

Lastly, I shall take up the plot of the Gospel or narrative of events in causal fashion. I shall approach it by highlighting two formal elements of the Gospel: its genre as an ancient biography of Jesus and its appropriation of the journey motif as a central element in structuration. The plot, I have argued, develops in sustained and systematic fashion the driving conflict unleashed by Jesus and his disciples – from gradual emergence, through rapid intensification, to varied resolution, both proximate (intra-narrative) and ultimate (extra-narrative) (Segovia 1991). As a result, I would submit, the plot rounds out in careful and detailed fashion the initial geopolitical reflection conveyed by the opening unit. Consequently, I shall draw on it to show how the religious and political project of the Gospel unfolds through the narrative. In plotting Jesus, therefore, the Gospel outlines a postcolonial programme.

First Angle of Inquiry
Setting the Stage: Conflict and Resolution – A Postcolonial Proposal

The story of the Gospel – what might be generally described as the full sequence of events in chronological arrangement as reconstructed by readers from the narrative (Prince 1987: 91) – may be summarized in terms of three distinct and overarching phases. These divisions may, in turn, be further seen as providing the basic framework for John's distinctive foregrounding and problematization of the geopolitical relationship of power within the imperial–colonial formation of Rome. They may be described as follows: (1) the primordial erection of a two-tiered reality in unquestionable though unexplained conflict; (2) the detailed account of a climactic clash within this bipolar and divided reality, involving the two tiers in question and yielding an initial twofold resolution of the conflict; (3) an envisioned portrayal of reality beyond this confrontation as in continuing and unremitting conflict, with the two tiers in question still at odds, and the anticipation of a final twofold resolution – the first, temporary and fully described; the other, definitive and largely unexplained. As such, the middle phase functions as a hinge in the story, with the first phase as the preparation for it and the last phase as the aftermath of it. By means of the story, then, the Gospel sets up a radical postcolonial proposal – a challenge of absolute power.

Reality as Bipolar and Divided

The Gospel posits two spatial and temporal realms or domains of reality, juxtaposed in stark contrast: a world 'above' – the removed world of spirit; a world 'below' – the roundabout world of flesh. This contrast is further solidified and accentuated through the application of a series of metaphorical oppositions to describe such worlds: light and darkness, life and death, truth and falsehood, grace and sin. In addition, within this two-tiered and conflicted construction of reality, the Gospel presents the other-world as not only preceding the this-world but also giving rise to it: the world 'above' as anterior and creating, the world 'below' as posterior and created. The resultant relationship of creation and estrangement, however, is not pursued. Thus, the crucial question of how the this-world, which comes to be through the agency of the other-world, comes to stand in alienation from this other-world is never addressed. As a result, why these two realms of reality come to embody such radical opposition to one another – a spiritual world marked by light, life, truth and grace; a material world stamped by darkness, death, falsehood and sin – receives no proper explication and remains an unfilled and perplexing gap in the story.

These two domains of reality are further assigned different supreme powers or authorities in charge: God, the Father, as master of the world above; Satan, the evil one, as ruler of the world below. These sovereigns are portrayed as attended by subordinate delegates or representatives in their respective levels of reality: in the world above, God is accompanied by the Word and the Spirit; in the world below, Satan stands behind all ruling powers, as exemplified by those featured in the narrative: the Judaean 'state' or 'nation' and its governing classes, signified by the high priest, the council and a shifting configuration of leading groups; the Roman Empire and its Caesar, represented by Pontius Pilate as procurator of Judaea. The provenance and dominion of Satan remain, however, similarly unexplained. Hence, the key question of how the evil one comes to be and to rule over the this-world, brought into being by the other-world, is never entertained. Consequently, why these two domains come to represent such a radical disjunction in reality – in the world 'above', what is good; in the world 'below,' what is evil – is never addressed and constitutes another open and frustrating silence in the story.

A Climactic Confrontation in Reality

These instruments from the different realms of reality encounter and clash with one another when the world of God intrudes in the world of Satan. From the world above, God sends the Word, his Son and creative agent, into the world below, taking on in the process a variety of identities and roles: a human being – Jesus, a Jew from Nazareth in Galilee; a special messenger to the Jews – the awaited Messiah of Judaism, and the sole revealer of God to all peoples and 'nations' – the Saviour of the world. In the world below, Satan offers, in return, opposition to Jesus, the Word, throughout: against his person – promoting hatred among the populace and directly infiltrating the group of followers in order to hand him over to his colonial and imperial enemies; against his mission – bringing about, as Father of the Jews, widespread rejection and hostility through Judaea and Galilee; and against his message or revelation – working through colonial and imperial authorities toward investigation and refutation, seizure and condemnation, torture and execution. This climactic confrontation yields two immediate resolutions: on the one hand, a seeming victory of Satan over God, in light of the radical termination of the mission through death and burial – a surface resolution; on the other hand, a definitive triumph of God over Satan, in light of the radical success of the mission through resurrection and glorification – a depth resolution.

Ultimately, to be sure, given the definitions of the two domains of reality, the ramifications of this confrontation emerge as universal: all human beings

– whether in Judaea, other territories of Palestine, or among the other 'nations' and peoples of the empire; indeed, whether inside the Roman imperial order or beyond – face, through the sending and intervention of the Word, a radical choice between the world above and the world below. An option for God through acceptance of Jesus signifies reception of the Spirit from the other-world, becoming children of God – in possession of eternal life (light, life, truth, grace) – and a final dwelling with Jesus and God in the other-world. An option for Satan through rejection of Jesus means abiding in the flesh of the this-world, continuing as children of Satan in the this-world – devoid of eternal life (mired in darkness, death, falsehood, sin) – and ultimate exclusion from the household of God and Jesus in the other-world. A final word is in order in this regard. To what extent such an option for or against Jesus remains entirely up to the agency of human beings remains, in the end, highly ambiguous. For the most part, the Gospel seems to presuppose the possibility of choice among human beings; at times, however, such choice comes across as, so to put it, pre-determined through prior birth from God or belonging to God. Such ambiguity constitutes yet another gaping and baffling gap in the story.

Bipolar Reality in Ongoing Division

The defining clash between the two realms of reality endures beyond Jesus' departure from the world below and return to the world above, thus accounting for the portrayal of a reality in continuing conflict. Such confrontation takes place through Jesus' group of followers, both immediate and to come, upon whom God sends the Spirit, the holy Spirit of truth, in another intervention from the world above in the world below. Thus, to opt for God through belief in Jesus means to relate to one another in the way of Jesus, to undertake the spread of Jesus' message and revelation in the this-world and to undergo the same fate as Jesus in so doing. The result is clear: belonging to Jesus in mutual love, ventur-ing into the world as messengers of Jesus and undergoing hatred and death in the this-world. Similarly, to opt for Satan through unbelief in Jesus signifies to stand with one another in the way of Satan, to resist the dissemination of Jesus' words and works throughout and to inflict the same fate on Jesus' followers as on Jesus. Again, the result is clear: belonging to the world in mutual love, opposing the messengers of Jesus throughout and visiting hatred upon them by way of persecution and death.

Such continuing conflict yields two resolutions: first, the glorification or divinization of the followers through reunion with Jesus, the Word, and abiding with God, in God's mansion, in the other-world – a temporary resolution; second, a return of Jesus to the this-world, at a time classified as 'the last day', and thus a further intervention from the world above – a definitive resolution. However, the actual dynamics and consequences of this second coming remain elusive: the outcome envisioned for Satan (its ruler), his attending representa-tives (the different polities and ruling elites), his children at large (all those who do not believe in Jesus) and even creation itself (the world of flesh and site of his rule) is left unaddressed. Thus, while the ultimate liberation of Jesus' followers from estrangement is established through spatial translation to the world above, the ultimate situation of the world below upon the return of Jesus endures as one more and disturbing omission in the story. Do the oppositions finally collapse? Does the alienation come to an end? Is there a return to the primal condition of a world above only, with the utter destruction of the world below? Is the creative agency of the Word totally reversed at the end via a similarly destructive agency? On such questions the Gospel remains silent and the story inconclusive.

Gospel as Postcolonial Proposal

Against a story comprising such framing components, the postcolonial problematic offered by the Gospel is pointed and striking: with Jesus and his movement, religious conflict rules, and behind it lies political conflict – focusing, all-engulfing, multi-sided conflict – at the cosmic level, between God, sovereign of the world above, and Satan, sovereign of the world below – at the global level, between Jesus, Word of God and Saviour of the world, and the imperial rulers of Rome – at the local level, between Jesus, Word of God and Messiah of the Jews, and the colonial elite of Judaea. Given such parameters, this is a conflict that draws in all of humanity, not just those in Judaea or elsewhere in Palestine, or among the other nations and peoples of the empire, but also all political frameworks outside the empire. No one remains untouched. All are forced to choose – although, again, such a choice may amount to no more than an 'unmasking' rather than a 'becoming', depending on the degree of agency actually attributed to human beings in the process – between status as children of God through Jesus and status as children of Satan against Jesus. Such, then, is the power that the Gospel claims to hold: bringing down all established dominions and allegiances and substituting an alternative dominion and allegiance, all in the midst of a firmly entrenched and immensely powerful imperial–colonial formation. Truly a postcolonial proposal.

Second Angle of Inquiry
Opening Salvo: Prologue as Grounding Vision – A Postcolonial Alternative

The beginning unit of the Gospel – generally delineated as 1.1-18, a delimitation with which I stand in agreement, and traditionally referred to as its 'prologue', a designation that I find acceptable as well – may be seen as both a formal introduction to and a tactical entrée into the narrative, providing, respectively, a narrative of origins for John's biographical account or life of Jesus and a grounding imaginary for John's vision of reality. In both regards, narrative world and field of vision alike, the unit may be further seen as a key summary of the work as a whole.

Its characteristics as a literary, ideological and rhetorical product may be summarized as follows. Artistically, a threefold structuration by way of inclusion may be posited: (1) a first section offers an initial description of the relationship between God and the Word (vv. 1-2), (2) the middle section pursues, in narrowing fashion, the relationship between the Word and the world below (vv. 3-17): from all of creation (v. 3), to the sphere of human beings (vv. 4-13) and to the circle of God's children (vv. 14-17) and (3) the final section returns to and expands upon the initial description of the relationship between God and the Word (v. 18). Politically, a variety of interrelated and interdependent central tenets may be outlined: (1) a vertical chain of command operative both between worlds (above over below) and within each world, resulting in a set ethos of hierarchy and obedience, (2) a stance of extreme othering toward the outside and outsiders, giving way to harsh condemnation of all social and cultural dimensions of the this-world and (3) a total denial of all other approaches to and claims on the divine, yielding absolute control of access to and knowledge of God. Strategically, a concomitant expository and polemical objective may be detected: lengthy critique of all standing established realities alongside lengthy exposition of the proposed alternative reality.

The opening salvo of the Gospel emerges, therefore, as a carefully arranged, keenly targeted and skilfully argued composition. Within it, moreover, a foundational postcolonial reflection takes place – a critical surfacing and awareness of the imperial–colonial framework in question. Such conscientization may be summarized by way of the set of constitutive components identified as undergirding the reality or setting of the Gospel: the other-world envisioned, the this-world acknowledged and the web of relations established between such worlds. With the prologue, therefore, the Gospel unveils a radical postcolonial alternative – a vision of absolute otherness.

Envisioning the Other-World

The projection of an other-world, conveyed through the first and final sections of 1.1-2 and 1.18, provides a solid point of departure for a postcolonial reading. This other-world – removed, above, anterior and spiritual – is characterized as a world of 'glory', a sole existing spatial and temporal dimension of reality, a mythological beginning. Such a world has not been constructed in a social or cultural vacuum.

Within the imperial tradition and context of Rome, a rather populous and flexible vision of the other-world is in place. This is a world where numerous deities dwell – a pantheon encompassing a variety of indigenous and assimilated divine figures, where heroic, divinized humans can and do find their way – a suprahuman abode revealing a broad range of divinity as such, and where emperors themselves receive or claim a home – a divine point of origins or destination for supreme rulers of the political world. In contrast, the prologue advances a very different conception of the other-world altogether: all such deities, heroes and monarchs are nowhere to be found; they have all been excluded. Instead, there is but the God of all, one and supreme, though accompanied by another and lesser god, the Word. Such a God is that of Judaism, hence a deity from the colonial periphery. Within the colonial tradition and context of Judaea, however, the vision of the other-world in place allows for the one and only God, surrounded by various gradations of spiritual beings. In contrast, the prologue advances a very different conception of this deity as well: this one and only God has engendered – along the familial lines of a father–son relationship – an only-born god, the Word. This god is portrayed as dwelling in the presence or bosom of God, possessing full knowledge of God and having the power to make God known.

This construction of the other-world bears distinct political ramifications. In the first place, any type of divine foundation or validation is withdrawn thereby from the imperial centre – its authorities and institutions, its practices and beliefs. The God of all is a god not from the centre but from the periphery. This God is not one among many or even the first among many but the one and only God. This God can be known not through the official representatives and channels of the empire but only through the Word. Similarly, divine grounding or justification of any sort is also denied thereby to the colonial periphery – its institutions and authorities, its beliefs and practices. The God of all is a god that has begotten an only-born god, the Word, who alone reclines upon the breast of God and alone serves as God's messenger and revealer. This God is approached, therefore, not through the established delegates or venues of the Jewish 'nation' or ethnos but only through the Word. The introduction thus deprives both Rome and Judaea of all other-worldly sanction of power. The same applies, to be sure, to all other political frameworks whether within the Roman Empire itself or outside of it. All power is vested thereby, over and beyond the God of all, in the figure of the Word.

Such a move on the part of 1.1-18 is profoundly deconstructive and subversive, placing all powers-that-be in the this-world under a new supreme and ultimate power, the power of God. Appeal to the Word in the face of worldly power is thus made possible, and hence all power in the this-world is relativized – delegitimated and decentred. In any imperial–colonial framework – indeed, in any political framework whatsoever – this is a dangerous and momentous move, laying the grounds for an alternative path.

Envisioning the This-World

The configuration of the this-world, undertaken in the central section of 1.3-17, proves quite important as well for a postcolonial reading. This world – roundabout, below, posterior, material – is represented as a world of 'flesh', a spatial and temporal dimension of reality distinct from the world of glory, the mythological beginning, both emerging out of it and in ignorance of it.

To begin with, the prologue attributes all that is, emphatically and without exception, to the agency of the Word, who alone is responsible for the whole of creation and thus of the this-world. As a result, the power vested in the Word is enormously enhanced. In effect, engendered by God, with full knowledge of God and sole revelation of God, the Word engenders, in turn, all that has come to be. As such, all of creation, in principle, stands under and is subject to the power of the Word, just as the Word itself stands under and is subject to God. Thereby, both the imperial centre and the colonial periphery are made subordinate to the Word. Indeed, not only Rome and Judaea but also all powers-that-be as well as all human beings in the this-world lie and should lie under the ultimate and supreme power of the Word. However, quite unexpectedly and inexplicably, the this-world is characterized as in death and darkness, with life and light available only through the Word. Moreover, insofar as grace and truth are said to lie solely in the Word as well, the this-world is further marked as in sin and falsehood. Thereby judgment is passed on the imperial centre and the colonial periphery. In fact, not only Rome and Judaea but also all powers-that-be and all human beings in the this-world stand in darkness and death as well as in falsehood and sin. Such a fundamental situation, and contradiction, can only be resolved through the Word.

This move on the part of 1.1-18 proves more deconstructive and subversive still, depicting the powers-that-be in the this-world as alien to the ultimate and supreme power of the Word of God. Recourse to the Word in the face of worldly power thus becomes imperative, and consequently all power in the this-world is not only relativized but also pronounced estranged – deflated and deracinated. In any imperial–colonial framework – and, again, in any political context what-soever – such a stance is perilous and consequential, pointing the way toward an alternative path.

Envisioning Relations between Worlds
The blueprint of the relationship between the other-world and the this-world, elaborated in the middle section of 1.3-17 through the unfolding of the relation-ship between the Word and the world, adds a key dimension to a postcolonial reading. The way beyond estrangement between the world below and the world above is set forth, but only in view of two radically different options.

To start, the prologue offers a resolution to the situation of estrangement by having the Word of God become embodied, en-fleshed, in the this-world. The only-born god and agent of all creation enters and becomes part of the world below – a human being in the colonial periphery, a member of the Jewish ethnos and a subject of the Roman Empire. As a result, the power of the Word, and thus the power of the God of all, is deposited in a human being from the political margins – a god-man by the name of Jesus, from Nazareth of Galilee. In him the glory of the other-world abides: he alone knows and reveals God; he is the unique dispenser of life and light, grace and truth; he is the agent of all creation. Thereby, in the face of all worldly power, the ultimate and supreme power of the Word is assigned a specific location within the this-world. To this god-man both the imperial centre and the colonial periphery are and should be beholden, as are and should be all powers-that-be and all human beings in the this-world.

At the same time, the presence and revelation of Jesus, the Word of God, in the this-world result in two different and conflicting scenarios regarding the situation of estrangement: on the one hand, an overcoming of such alienation (yielding life and light, grace and truth); on the other hand, transformation into outright opposition (yielding death and darkness, sin and falsehood). It all depends on the reaction in the world below to such revelation and presence. In effect, Jesus divides the this-world into two sides: those who reject the god-man by refusing to believe and those who accept by believing. The former undergo transformation from alienation to hostility, seeking in vain to overcome the god-man; the latter undergo rebirth from God, becoming children of God and members of the other-world within the this-world. Thereby, in the face of all worldly power, the ultimate and supreme power of the Word is further assigned a concrete locus among his followers in the world below. To these children of God both the imperial centre and the colonial periphery, as well as all powers-that-be and all human beings in the this-world, lie and should lie beholden, therefore.

Such a move on the part of 1.1-18 proves even more deconstructive and subversive, revealing all the powers-that-be in the this-world as in opposition to the ultimate and supreme power of the Word of God. Following the Word in the face of all worldly power is thus pronounced indispensable, so that all power in the this-world is not only relativized and declared estranged but also unmasked as hostile – discovered and dislocated. At the same time, power within the this-world is relocated unto a particular human being – the god-man Jesus, and his circle of followers – the children of God. In any imperial–colonial framework – and, to be sure, in any political framework – such a position is at once risky and pregnant, laying out the alternative path.

Prologue as Postcolonial Alternative

In the very midst of an imperial–colonial framework, underlaid by the immensely extensive and enormously powerful imperial context of Rome and with particular reference to the colonial context of the Judaean 'nation' and its governing classes, 1.1-18 raises the question of geopolitics and hence the postcolonial problematic. This quandary the Gospel continues and expands in the narrative that follows. Within the reality and experience of Rome in general and of Judaea and Palestine in particular, 1.1-18 further sets forth the fundamentals of an alternative path – a substitute reality and experience – to be acknowledged, embraced and executed. Its details and consequences the Gospel proceeds to fill out in the remainder of the narrative.

This alternative path encompasses the whole of reality – the other-world of God and the this-world of humans. It is a path laid out in overwhelmingly religious terms, but with immediate and far-reaching ramifications for all of

culture and society alike, including the realm of the political. It is a path that
further extends, in principle, beyond the imperial–colonial framework of Rome
and Palestine in view to encompass all other political frameworks and hence all
human beings in the this-world. This path is not presented simply as an option
among others but as radically different and uniquely superior – the only true
option, in contrast to and defiance of all other existing paths. Consequently, the
substitute reality and experience introduced in 1.1-18 and subsequently drawn
out in the course of the narrative emerge as primordial – all-embracing, all-
surpassing, all-defining.

Within the reality and experience of Rome and Palestine, this path sets up
a rival system of power. Its structure and reach envelop the world above, the
world below and the mode of interaction between the two worlds. With respect
to the other-world, ultimate and supreme power is reserved, beyond the God of
all, to the figure of the Word, the only-born god engendered by God. This Word
is with God, whom it alone knows and it alone reveals. No other figure, divine
or semi-divine, from the imperial–colonial framework of Rome, or any other
political framework, is to be found in such a construction of the world above.
With regard to the this-world, then, ultimate and supreme power is located in
the Word as well. First, as creator of all that is; second, as depository of all life
and light, grace and truth. Without the Word, therefore, all that is – all human
beings and all political frameworks, including that of the Roman Empire and
colonial Palestine – stands in falsehood and sin, darkness and death, in this
construction of the this-world. With respect to cross-world interaction, finally,
ultimate and supreme power is further concretized within the this-world: first,
centred in the figure of the Word made flesh, Jesus of Nazareth; then, extended
onto his group of followers. In this construction of the interchange between
worlds, all attributes of the Word come to reside, first, in a specific human
being (Jesus as Messiah and Saviour of the world), and, second, within his
circle of adherents (the believers as those born of God, the children of God).
Consequently, within the this-world, light and life as well as grace and truth can
only be found in and through Jesus and his disciples. Needless to say, this rival
system of power stands, in principle, over against not just the imperial–colonial
framework of Rome but all political frameworks and all human beings.

With 1.1-18, therefore, a set of key strategies begin to be deployed for the
purpose of dealing with the postcolonial problematic. Primary among them are
the following: displacement and desacralization – the removal of power from all
existing structures and channels in both worlds; replacement and resacralization
– the relocation of power in substitute structures and channels in both worlds;
othering – a portrayal of the outside as chaos: prior to the Word, the world as
utterly devoid of epistemic and moral compass (un-alive and un-enlightened
as well as un-graceful and un-truthful), after the Word, the world as utterly
depraved, morally and epistemically (rejectful, full of hatred, violent); inversion
– a portrayal of the inside as whole: the group as utterly privileged (children of

God, born of God through the Word) and utterly blessed (alive and enlightened, grace-full and truth-full) in epistemic and moral terms. Thus, at the very heart of the imperial–colonial framework of Rome and Palestine, and extending in principle to all other political frameworks, the Johannine response to the question of geopolitics in 1.1-18 is clear. In effect, and despite any appearances to the contrary, it is: the Word of God, who holds ultimate and supreme power in the world above; Jesus, as the Word made flesh, who dispenses such power in the world below; and the followers of Jesus, as children of God, who inherit and transmit such power in the world below. Without question, a postcolonial alternative.

Third Angle of Inquiry
Plotting Jesus: Disclosure and Opposition – A Postcolonial Programme

The plot of the Gospel – what might be generally described as the actual sequence of events, causally arranged, as presented to readers by the narrative (Prince 1987: 71–72) – may be approached from two different but related perspectives: the character of the Gospel as a biographical account or life of Jesus, the Word; and the centrality of the journey motif in the narration of Jesus' life. As an example of ancient biography, the Gospel displays all three constitutive components of the genre: a narrative of birth and origins, in itself optional, consisting of 1.1-18, as already noted; a narrative of the public life or career, comprising the whole of 1.19–17.26; and a narrative of death and lasting significance, also optional, composed of 18–21. As an example of a travel narrative, the Gospel adopts a twofold use of the journey motif: first and foremost, an overarching journey of the Word across the worlds of reality, encompassing the life of Jesus, through whom the Word becomes 'flesh', and involving a 'descent' from the other-world into the this-world and a corresponding 'ascent'; then, within the span of this cosmic journey, a series of geographical journeys of Jesus, the Word, involving a succession of visits to the city of Jerusalem. The narrative divisions resulting from the interaction of these two formal considerations may be further explained and demarcated.

On the one hand, the journey of the Word across worlds is conveyed by means of the narratives of birth and death, although references to it are numerous and widespread throughout the length of Jesus' ministry. This cosmic journey, however, is unevenly narrated. While the element of 'descent', the humanization of the Word, is explicitly addressed in 1.1-18, that of 'ascent', the (re-)glorification of Jesus, is foreseen but not represented in chs 18–20. Such anticipation involves a twofold movement: a series of preparatory events having to do with the arrest and trial of Jesus (18.1–19.16) followed by the portrayal of death and its aftermath of burial and resurrection (19.16–21.25). On the other hand, the journeys of Jesus, the Word, in the this-world shape the narrative of the public life, 1.19–17.26, in terms of four major cycles revolving around

Jerusalem. The first three precede a visit of Jesus to Jerusalem with a journey to Galilee (1.19–3.36; 4.1–5.47; 6.1–10.42). The final cycle (11.1–17.26) introduces a Lazarus cycle of events (11.1–12.11), organized around two visits to Bethany near Jerusalem, as a prelude to the fourth and last visit to Jerusalem (12.12–17.26).

The combined effect of these narrative divisions is a highly dramatic exposition of the fundamental confrontation within Johannine reality as a result of intervention from the other-world in the this-world through the figure of Jesus. The journeys that provide the microstructure for the plot in the narrative of the public life bring out the growing rejection of Jesus in Galilee and Jerusalem as well as the increasing hostility in Jerusalem itself. The overall journey that supplies the macrostructure for the plot comes to an end with the narrative of death, which records the climax of the growing opposition and violence as well as the conclusion of the cosmic journey. By means of the plot, therefore, the Gospel presents a radical postcolonial project – a way of absolute opposition.

Narrative of the Public Life

First Galilee–Jerusalem Cycle

The first round of geographical journeys inaugurates the pattern of travel to the region of Galilee (1.35–2.12) followed by a visit to the city of Jerusalem (2.13-21). While the displacement to Galilee comes across as abrupt and without motivation, the move to Jerusalem is tied to a religious celebration, the feast of Passover. These trips are flanked by sections having to do with the figure of John and his baptismal activity, respectively located in Bethany across the Jordan (1:19-34) and Aenon in Judaea (3.22-36). These sections develop at length the asides on John from the prologue (1:6-8, 15), where he is introduced as a man sent from God and his task specified as giving witness to the Light. Thus, the initial unveiling of Jesus the Word is carried out indirectly as well as directly: while the surrounding accounts of John offer detailed witness to Jesus' identity and role from the outside, the intervening trips of Jesus provide extensive revelation from the inside. The intervention of God in the this-world is thereby portrayed as guided by God (from Isaiah through John), as distinctly peripatetic, and as specifically situated in outlying territories of the eastern empire.

Witness of John. The disclosure of the Word to the this-world begins indirectly, through the witness and work of a figure, John, who not only identifies himself as in fulfilment of the prophetic tradition of Israel but also claims divine appointment and knowledge – a 'voice crying in the wilderness', who will reveal the Son of God to Israel through a baptism of water and will recognize the one in question through a vision, when the Spirit descends and remains upon him. Upon fulfilment of this vision, John identifies Jesus as the

Lamb of God who will take away the sin of the world and who will baptize with the Holy Spirit. Such identification unleashes the formation of a group of followers, with a corresponding affirmation of identity – the Messiah. The import of this first section is significant: the unveiling of Jesus as well as his first followers comes not from official circles of power but from an emissary of God working in the local periphery; Jesus is from the start presented as the bearer of the Spirit of God and the expected Messiah of Israel; and the this-world is portrayed as in sin, with Jesus, in his status as Lamb of God, as the way of deliverance.

First Journey to Galilee. The first trip to Galilee continues the disclosure of Jesus, now directly but still largely within the group of followers. It is a disclosure accompanied by marvellous deeds. The group about him undergoes expansion, with the help of a miraculous display of knowledge, leading to further affirmations of identity – the one about whom the Law and the Prophets wrote; the King of Israel; the Son of God. Their belief in him solidifies as a result of a miraculous transformation of water into wine at a marriage feast, described as a revelation of Jesus' 'glory'. With the first foray into Galilee, therefore, the 'glory' or other-worldly character of Jesus is confirmed, leading to recognition by his disciples of his religious and political status.

First Journey to Jerusalem. The first trip to Jerusalem seemingly takes place as a result of the feast of Passover. The disclosure of Jesus, again accompanied by marvellous deeds, now turns public. Its point of departure is striking. In a visit to the temple, the seat of official power, he takes aim at all the activities surrounding the sacrificial cult, denouncing such a state of affairs as akin to a marketplace and laying claim to the temple as his Father's house, with but an enigmatic statement regarding its destruction and restoration in three days as his defence, identified by the narrator as a reference to his death and resurrection. During the course of his stay, moreover, his wonder-working activities are done in sight of all, eliciting belief in him from many but distrust on his part, given his miraculous knowledge of human beings. Lastly, in a private conversation with a member of the Pharisees and a 'ruler' of Judaea, Jesus unveils an alternative religious and political entity, the kingdom of God, accessible only to those who undergo a process of re-birth, through water and the Spirit, from the world of 'flesh' into the world of 'Spirit'. Such revelation is pointedly expanded: on the one hand, it is belief in the Son of God, whom God has sent into the this-world as a sign of love, that determines salvation or condemnation; on the other hand, such witness is not received, as people prefer 'darkness' over 'light', and the Son of Man will be lifted up. The first sojourn in Jerusalem yields important religious and political developments: Jesus mounts a severe challenge to the temple on the grounds that it is his Father's house, proclaims the existence of a kingdom of God open only to those who believe in him, and presents his coming as a gift of love on the part of God to the world and its sole path to salvation – all alongside forebodings of tragic events ahead.

Witness of John. A withdrawal from Jerusalem to the Judaean countryside leads to a remote encounter with John, as both pursue their respective baptismal activities. In response to his own followers, John expands on the relationship between the two: while Jesus must increase, he must decrease. In the process he expands on Jesus as well: he comes from above and is above all; he speaks the words of God and gives the Spirit without measure; God loves him and has placed all things in his hands. Consequently, those who believe in him will have life and those who do not will suffer God's wrath. Yet, John adds, no one receives his testimony. The import of this concluding section is crucial, as John provides a keen summary of Jesus' identity and role: he is the one in whom rests the full power of God.

Summation. With the conclusion of the first cycle of geographical journeys, the intervention of God is clearly drawn in geopolitical terms. First, with the Word embodied in Jesus of Nazareth, the kingdom of God irrupts in the this-world, marked by deeds of wonder and words from above. Second, within a this-world characterized as in sin, salvation is presented as attainable only through belief in Jesus, yielding incorporation into the kingdom via regeneration from 'flesh' into 'spirit' through water and Spirit. Third, from the beginning Jesus is cast in highly significant religio-political categories of Judaism associated with the end times, with further development of his figure by way of the abiding of the Spirit, the removal of sin from the world, the love of God for the world, and a lifting up for eternal life. Lastly, while no opposition or hostility is yet in evidence against the Word, inklings of an untoward destiny abound, including the characterization of Jesus as the Lamb of God. At this point in the plot, therefore, the kingdom of God has been unleashed and is on the march within the this-world and the imperial–colonial framework of Rome.

Second Galilee–Jerusalem Cycle

The second round of geographical journeys repeats the earlier pattern of travel to Galilee (4.1-54) followed by a visit to Jerusalem (5.1-47). This time, the displacement to Galilee, which involves a detour to the region of Samaria, appears linked to a decision by Jesus to avoid an encounter with the 'Pharisees', as a result of his success in baptizing in comparison with John (4.1), while the move to Jerusalem again takes place in conjunction with the celebration of a religious feast, unidentified (5.1). The intervention of God in the this-world is thus continued by having Jesus the Word return to known terrain for further activity and disclosures, still-unknowing Galilee and receptive-though-questioning Jerusalem, while expanding the process of revelation to Samaritan territory. As a result, the progressive unveiling of Jesus' identity and role retains its highly peripatetic character.

Second Journey to Galilee. The return to Galilee (4.1-3), interrupted by a stay in the town of Sychar in Samaria (4.4-42), now turns into a highly public affair, given the open welcome extended to Jesus on the part of those who had witnessed his many 'signs' in Jerusalem (4.43-45). It includes an open expression of belief in him by a member of the royal court or family – with household in train – as a result of one such miraculous deed of healing (4.46-52). The intervening sojourn in Samaria leads to a fundamental affirmation of Jesus' identity at Sychar, partly as a result of a miraculous display of knowledge regarding the woman at the well and partly on account of his own declarations while in their midst – the Saviour of the world. In the course of his conversation with the woman, Jesus makes it known that he is the gift of God, dispensing the water of life to all; worship of God will henceforth take place not in traditional sacred places but in spirit and truth, for such is the nature of God; and he is the awaited Messiah, who will reveal all. In his ensuing conversation with his followers, he makes further key pronouncements: his mission is to do the will of the one who sent him and fulfil his work, and they themselves are called upon to harvest the results of such sowing. With the second foray into Galilee, Jesus receives a broad welcome, not only among the Galilaeans but also among Samaritans. The sojourn in Sychar in particular yields a series of religious and political affirmations regarding his role and identity: he is the Messiah awaited by the Samaritans and the Saviour of the world; he does the will of the Father and offers life eternal to all; he supplants established patterns of worship through spirit and truth.

Second Journey to Jerusalem. The return to Jerusalem resumes his public activity in the city, but with a restricted focus on a marvellous deed of healing and its ramifications – the reaction of the 'Jews' to this affair and a long exposition by Jesus in return regarding his identity and role. The healing itself, motivated by a miraculous insight into the man's situation and yielding no response from the individual in question other than to identify Jesus to the authorities, provides the trigger for what follows. In effect, the violation of the Sabbath enjoined and the subsequent defence proffered – as the Father works, so does he work – bring about the first instance of rejection and violence: a determination to kill Jesus as a result of both the breaking of the Sabbath and his claims with respect to God. Jesus' rejoinder yields much information concerning his role and identity: the Son does nothing on his own, only what he sees the Father doing, but the Father shows him all that he does; the Father has given all judgment to the Son, so that the Son may be honoured like the Father; the Father has given life to the Son, and he gives eternal life to all who believe in him; many are those who witness to him (John; the works that he does, given to him by the Father;

the Father himself; the Scriptures). Yet, he points out, they do not accept him. Indeed, such defence brings forth much accusation as well: they have neither the word of God nor the love of God in them. The second sojourn in Jerusalem brings about heightened religious and political claims: in the face of a resolve to put him to death by the 'Jews', a group unidentified but no doubt representative of the ruling circles, Jesus claims all power as the Father's Son and hence the same honour due the Father.

Summation. At the close of the second cycle of geographical journeys, the intervention of God emerges in sharp geopolitical relief. To begin with, the spread of the kingdom of God in the this-world continues, through the humanized Word of God in Jesus, with ongoing deeds of wonder and words from above. In addition, all established cultic practices in the this-world are invalidated and replaced by the worship of God in spirit and truth. Further, beyond traditional Jewish claims associated with a figure of the end-times, Jesus receives the title of Saviour of the world, the one who makes all things known and offers life eternal to all. He also expands at length upon his relationship to God: God has entrusted all judgment to him, and all owe him honour as God's Son. Lastly, in Jerusalem a first burst of opposition and hostility breaks out. At this point in the plot, consequently, the ramifications of the kingdom of God in the this-world become increasingly evident, as the world above imposes itself on the world below and a clash between the two worlds begins to surface.

Third Galilee–Jerusalem Cycle

The third round of geographical journeys replicates the established pattern of travel to Galilee (6.1–7.9) with a subsequent visit to Jerusalem (7.10–10.39). This cycle is much more extensive than the first two, taking up the whole of 6.1–10.39, and is brought to an end by a brief segment on John (10.40-42). This unit on John points back to the second account of 3.22-36, and together they serve as a formal framework around the second and third travel cycles. The displacement to Galilee, suddenly introduced and only later explained in terms of the given decision of the 'Jews' to kill him (7.1), covers much physical space, as Jesus moves from the eastern to the western shore of the Sea of Galilee and then throughout Galilee. The move to Jerusalem, linked again to a religious celebration, the feast of Booths, takes up much narrative space, involving two lengthy series of events within the city, punctuated by attempts on his life. Such attempts, in fact, may be construed as the motivation behind the journey to the area beyond the Jordan of 10.40-42. The intervention of God in the this-world is thereby advanced by having the well-known Jesus the Word revisit well-trodden terrain, receptive space in Galilee and dangerous space in Jerusalem. In the process, while still preserving its peripatetic thrust, the ongoing revelation of Jesus' identity and role begins to concentrate more and more on Jerusalem.

Third Journey to Galilee. The third tour of Galilee, fully conducted in the public arena and brimming over with marvellous deeds of all sorts, signals a crucial development in the ongoing disclosure of Jesus the Word in the region. At first, drawn by his many miraculous healings and in direct reaction to the 'sign' of feeding, a large crowd (6.1-15) not only affirms Jesus as the prophet who was to come into the world but also attempts to make him king. Subsequently, in response to extended declarations regarding his role and identity, widespread rejection results – from the 'Jews', many of his 'disciples' and even his 'brothers'; at the end, only a small group of followers remains, described as the 'Twelve'. Jesus' pronouncements are manifold: he is the bread of life, the true bread from heaven, whose food endures for eternal life; those who believe in him, who eat his flesh and drink his blood, will live forever and will be raised up on the last day; he has come down to do the will of God and his words are spirit and life. On the one hand, he specifies, those who believe in him have been given or drawn to him by the Father, and he shall lose not one. They will abide in him and he in them. On the other hand, those who do not believe will have no life in them. In the end, only the 'Twelve' express their belief in him as the one who has the words of eternal life – the Holy One of God. Yet, even among them, one is pronounced a 'devil' – a betrayer. The 'world', Jesus concludes, hates him, because he declares its works as 'evil'. With the third foray into Galilee, the open welcome of Jesus becomes wholesale rejection. Religious and political actions and statements abound. To begin with, Jesus expressly walks away from an offer of worldly 'kingship'. From a world that is evil, nothing but hatred is to be expected. Yet, only in him is the true bread from heaven to be found, and only those who partake of this bread will be raised up on the last day.

Third Journey to Jerusalem. The third stay in Jerusalem, which begins in secret but soon takes a radical public turn, may be formally divided into two large blocks of material, with the attempts on Jesus' life serving as culmination in each case (7.10–8.59; 9.1–10.39). The first block revolves around a series of exchanges with a variety of groups ('Jews', 'Pharisees') in the city, mostly in the temple area. These are marked by popular debates regarding his veracity and innocence, extended revelations concerning his role and identity, repeated attempts to arrest him, and mounting opposition to his pronouncements – all finally leading to an explicit act of violence (8.59). The second block features a miraculous deed of healing and its ramifications, from further exchanges with 'Pharisees' and 'Jews' regarding the resultant violation of the Sabbath to additional disclosures regarding his identity and role – all finally erupting, after a clear temporal hiatus, in another explicit act of violence (10.31-39). Religious
l statements are numerous. Concerning Jesus himself: his teaching
i God, who sent him and whom he knows; he is the light of the
nows where he comes from and where he is going; he is from above
his world; he has come into the world for judgment, that those who

do not see may see and those who do see may become blind; he and the Father are one. Concerning unbelievers: they do not know the one who sent him, God; they are from below and will die in their sin; their father is the devil, a murderer and a liar, and they do as he does; they are not from God. Concerning believers: they will have the light of life; they will know the truth and it will make them free; they will never see death. Throughout, moreover, one finds recurring intimations of a forthcoming departure and return to God – a laying down and a taking up of his life.

Witness of John. While the first attempt on Jesus brings no withdrawal from the city, the second leads him to the region across the Jordan, seemingly for refuge. Not only is the initial baptismal activity of John recalled, but also his witness regarding Jesus is affirmed. The result is widespread belief in Jesus in the region. Thereby the earlier testimony of 3.22-36, especially John's dictum regarding his own decrease in light of Jesus' own increase, is specifically validated in the light of the two intervening travel cycles of Jesus.

Summation. After the third cycle of geographical journeys, the intervention of God appears in stark geopolitical contrast. First, the impact of the kingdom of God in the this-world multiplies, through the enfleshed Word of God in Jesus, with undiminishing deeds of wonder and heightened words from above. Second, for a this-world whose beliefs and practices are all declared as without life and in darkness, it is Jesus alone who serves as the bread from heaven, whose food endures for eternal life, and the light of the world, whose light gives sight to the blind. Third, beyond conceptualizations as Messiah and King as well as Saviour of the world, the claim is now advanced that Jesus and the Father are one. Finally, widespread opposition now rules the day in both Galilee and Jerusalem, while hostility steadily mounts in the city. At this point in the plot, the ramifications of the kingdom of God in the this-world lie in full display, bringing the confrontation between the two worlds to the boiling point.

Fourth Jerusalem Cycle

The final round of geographical journeys, the most expansive of the travel cycles (11.1–17.26), follows a different pattern altogether, given Jesus' stay away from Galilee, an absence best construed perhaps as a result of the rejection experienced during the third visit. Consequently, the focus now shifts almost entirely toward Jerusalem. The Lazarus cycle of events (11.1–12.11) functions as a prelude, and dramatic build up, to the visit proper: in association with the illness of a beloved follower, Lazarus, Jesus travels twice to the village of Bethany, in the vicinity of Jerusalem. The visit itself, while associated once again with a religious celebration, the feast of Passover, is also motivated by Jesus' consciousness regarding the arrival of his 'hour': an opening account of the actual entry and surrounding events (12.12-50) is followed by a long farewell in the company of his followers (13.1–17.26). The intervention of God in the this-world thus begins to move toward its climax by having the now largely rejected and actively pursued Jesus the Word hover around and finally venture into explosively dangerous space, the city of Jerusalem. As a result, the peripatetic unveiling of his identity and role rapidly winds down and shifts toward localized revelation among the disciples.

Lazarus Cycle as Prelude. The cycle of events revolving around Bethany, all conducted in full public view, actually involves two trips. First, in response to a message from Lazarus' sisters, Mary and Martha, loved disciples as well, Jesus returns to the region of Judaea, where a final deed of wonder is performed, the raising of Lazarus, and further disclosures are offered (11.1-54). The latter lead to the former. To Martha, Jesus identifies himself as the resurrection and the life for those who believe in him. To the attending crowds, the 'Jews', he presents himself, via a public prayer to the Father, as the one sent by God, whose requests God always hears and grants. The response is varied: Martha offers a resounding affirmation – Jesus as the Messiah, the Son of God, the one coming into the world; many of the 'Jews' come to believe in him; others bring the news to Jerusalem and the governing authorities, leading to a further and crucial response. In a meeting of the council, 'Pharisees' and 'chief priests' discuss the momentous political ramifications arising from Jesus' activities and attraction. As they envision the destruction of both the temple and the 'nation' by the Romans, the 'high priest' lays down the course of action ahead: the death of one individual over the destruction of the ethnos, formally sealing Jesus' fate. Jesus takes refuge in the village of Ephraim, near the desert (11.54). Second, in light of the approaching Passover, Jesus pauses in Bethany on his way to Jerusalem, where he shares a meal with the family and his followers. A brief pronouncement emphasizes the political dimension of the unfolding events: the anointing of his feet by Mary is defended, against the betrayer's accusation of profligacy, as an anticipation of his burial. When news of this return reaches the Jerusalem authorities, the 'chief priests' extend their plan of action to include the elimination of Lazarus as well.

Initial Events in Jerusalem. The opening round of events takes place in the public arena: an account of the entry as such (12.12-19) is followed by two series of pronouncements – the first occasioned by the wish of 'some Greeks' to see Jesus (12.20-36) and the second without context (12.44-50). Embedded within this sequence of events, a comment by the narrator is to be found, a summary of the public life (12.37-43). The entry reinforces the political stakes at play: a 'great crowd' welcomes Jesus the Word as the King of Israel; both the crowd and Jesus himself play their roles in the regal procession as fulfilment of scriptural tradition; the 'Pharisees' give vent to despair, noting that the 'world' has gone after Jesus.

Such strong political overtones carry over into the first set of declarations: the hour of 'glorification', involving a death unto life and a lifting up, has arrived; the 'world', its 'ruler' overthrown, now stands in judgment; those who believe in the Light will become children of light; those who follow Jesus, who hate their life, will be honoured by the Father and be with Jesus in the other-world. The second set repeats previous claims regarding his relationship to the Father – to believe in him is to believe in the Father; to see him is to see the Father; to hear his word is to hear the Father's word – but foregrounding the political in so doing: while he has come to save and not to judge the 'world', this word of his will stand in judgment 'on the last day'. Lastly, the narrator brings the public life to a close on a strikingly sombre note: on the one hand, widespread unbelief, in keeping with the prophetic tradition of Israel; on the other hand, fear and silence among believers, out of fear for the 'Pharisees' and love for human 'glory'.

Farewell. The second round of events takes place within the circle of followers: a farewell meal (13.1-30) provides the setting for a farewell speech (13.31–16.33) and a farewell prayer (17.1-26).

Farewell meal. The meal itself presents a twofold sequence: the washing of the disciples' feet and the exposure of the betrayal; both contain a sharp, albeit implicit, commentary on power. Regarding the footwashing, the focus is on Jesus' disposition toward and explication of this deed. First, the narrator presents him as fully conscious of both the significance of the moment (it is the 'hour' to depart from the 'world' and return to the Father) and his relationship to the Father ('coming from' and 'going to' God), who has placed 'all things' in his power. Then, Jesus presents the washing as a defining expression of his love, a sign of both proper praxis and ultimate death – a key to his identity and role, therefore, as well as a must for his followers. In effect, the one in whom God has deposited all power exercises such power via service unto and death for others. Regarding the betrayal, the focus remains on Judas as a conduit of the 'devil' and 'Satan' as well as on Jesus' control of the situation. It is Jesus, the all-powerful one, who sets in motion the clash between love and hatred, between the ruler of the world and the all-powerful Word.

Farewell speech. The farewell discourse provides extensive disclosures regarding Jesus' identity and role as the Word of God. Many previous claims are repeated in the process, in ever-varying combinations; others surface here for the first time or in uniquely distinctive fashion. Thus, for example: he is going away to the Father's 'house' – he goes to prepare 'rooms' for the disciples and then he will come back to fetch them, so that they can be all together in the other-world; he is the way, the truth, and the life – no one comes to God but through him; the world hates him because he is not 'of the world' – thereby the 'world' manifests its hatred for God and reveals its 'sin'; the 'ruler of the world' will put him to death – this happens out of obedience to the Father and not because he has 'power' over him. In the end, Jesus declares, he has conquered the 'world'!

The discourse provides extensive instructions for his disciples as well. The following are worth noting: they shall not be left orphans while in the 'world' – the holy Spirit of truth will be sent by the Father at Jesus' request, to be with them forever and teach them all things; they are to love him by keeping his commands, believing in him and loving one another as he loved them – in return, the Father and Jesus will love them, will come to them, and will make their abode in them; the 'world' will hate them because they are not 'of the world' – they have been 'chosen out of the world' by Jesus and have become his 'branches'; they too shall experience persecution and death – this happens because Jesus' 'peace' is not that of the 'world'. In the end, Jesus declares, joy shall be theirs: they shall know Jesus and the Father, do even greater signs, and have whatever they ask for in his name granted by the Father.

Farewell prayer. Through direct address to the Father, the farewell prayer provides further disclosures about both Jesus the Word and the group of follow-ers. Concerning his own identity and role, these pronouncements represent varia-tions on previous claims: God has given him authority over all flesh; he gives eternal life to all given to him by the Father and has lost not one – to know the one true God and the one sent by God, Jesus Christ; before the world came to be, he was with the Father in the world of 'glory'. Given the completion of the work assigned to him by God in the this-world, his glorification of the Father, Jesus asks for glorification. Concerning his followers, these pronouncements constitute variations of earlier disclosures as well: they were of God and were given to him by God, they are not 'of the world' but are hated by the 'world', they have believed in Jesus' revelation and have kept God's word. Given his forthcoming glorification, Jesus asks on behalf of the disciples as well: to protect them from the 'evil' one; to sanctify them in the truth – the word of God; for unity among them all, present and future, so that they may reflect the unity of Father and Son and the 'world' may come to believe; lastly, that they may be glorified and thus be with Jesus and the Father in the world of 'glory'.

Summation. By the end of the final cycle of geographical journeys, the inter-vention of God reaches outright geopolitical confrontation. To begin with, the dissemination of the kingdom of God undertaken by Jesus, the Word made flesh, shifts in marked and ominous fashion from the public to the private domain. The mode of open outreach, here conveyed by a culminating deed of wonder and pointed words from above, both bearing sombre connotations for the time ahead, is replaced by group instruction, involving intensive teaching and detailed provisions for the future. In addition, within a this-world subject to the rule of Satan, all paths to the one and true God are denied except through Jesus, the 'way' insofar as he is truth and life. Further, enormous emphasis is placed on the power of Jesus: as the one who has received all authority from

God and holds all authority over all flesh, he rules over death itself, has cast out the ruler of the world, and has conquered the world. At the same time, it is specified that such power is exercised through un-power, in service unto others and love unto death. Lastly, news from Bethany leads to direct political action among the Jerusalem authorities: a decision is made to avoid destruction by the Romans by putting Jesus to death and a plot is put into effect toward this end. At this point in the plot, the presence of the kingdom of God in the this-world and at the heart of the Roman imperial–colonial framework approaches its logical climax – the final encounter for dominion.

Narrative of Death

With the conclusion of the farewell scene and the move out of the city, across the Kidron valley, and into a garden identified as a common meeting place for Jesus and his disciples, the narrative of the public life yields to the narrative of death. Aside from the opening scene of 18.1-12 and the concluding scene of ch. 21, the focus remains on the city throughout: a series of preparatory events (18.1–19.16) precede the events of the execution and its aftermath (19.16–21.25). Except for the resurrection appearances, which take place within the group of followers, all that transpires is in the public arena. The garden scene represents the point of transition: Jesus' arrest wrests him away from the circle of disciples and throws him into the hands of the opposition, who proceed to bring him back by force to the city. God's intervention in the this-world thus reaches its climax by having the long-sought and now-seized Jesus the Word undergo the full explosion of opposition and violence in the powder keg of Jerusalem, long in gestation and steady in building over the course of his several and ever-longer stays in the city. This detonation, however, is ultimately undone and radically transformed by God's intervention in the raising and glorification of Jesus the Word.

Preparation

The stage of preparation comprises a series of mounting encounters with various high figures in authority. Apprehended by a mixed party involving a 'cohort' of soldiers as well as 'officers' from the 'chief priests' and 'Pharisees', Jesus is taken, first, before Annas, father-in-law of Caiaphas, where an initial interrogation is recounted; then, to Caiaphas, the high priest, with no report of the proceedings; and, finally, before Pilate, the Roman official in charge of Judaea, where a petition for execution is made and a summary trial conducted. In the process, the all-powerful and victorious Jesus undergoes a swift and total demise: questioning as a bound prisoner regarding his claims and doings, physical aggression (an 'officer' strikes him across the face) and torture ('soldiers', upon orders from Pilate, subject Jesus to flogging, a crowning with thorns and bodily blows), sustained verbal and physical ridicule as 'King of the Jews', and a judgment of death despite a finding of innocence, for the sake of political expediency.

At the same time, the disclosures of the captive Jesus reveal him as altogether in control and not at all vanquished: opposition to the chain of events is ruled out as not in keeping with the Father's plan, the public mode of his revelation is vigorously defended, his 'kingdom' is defined as 'not of this world' and the hold of Roman power over him is explained as actually given to Rome from above. All such pronouncements are accompanied by the reiteration of a fundamental claim regarding his 'coming into the world': a witness to the 'truth'. A 'truth', however, that is evident to neither the 'Jews' – who reject him as 'king' in favour of loyalty to Caesar and who seek his death for his claim to be the 'Son of God', nor Pilate – who questions the very concept of 'truth', but only to those who belong to it – those who believe.

Execution

The stage of execution involves death and burial as well as resurrection and appearances. The judgment of death ordained by Rome is formally carried out under the charge of Jesus' status as 'King of the Jews', protested by the 'chief priests' but to no avail. It involves physical abuse (the bearing of the cross), a most cruel mode of execution (crucifixion), despoliation of personal belongings (distribution of clothing) and corpse desecration (piercing with the spear). For Rome, the execution clearly stands as a severe warning to a subject population. This first phase is brought to an end by swift burial in a nearby tomb, given the approaching feast and in keeping with Jewish custom – all facilitated by a disciple of Jesus, marked as a 'secret' follower for 'fear of the Jews'. The vindication of resurrection involves four appearances in all – one to Mary Magdalene, by the tomb; two to the group of the Twelve, in Jerusalem; and one to a group of seven disciples, in Galilee. This second phase brings important pronouncements from Jesus: before Mary, Jesus points to his forthcoming ascent to his, and their, Father and God – the return to the other-world; before the Twelve, Jesus issues a formal charge of sending into the world, bestows the Holy Spirit, and grants power over sin – the continuation of his mission; before the seven, Jesus teaches, through Peter, that love for him and following him entail looking after the believers – a charge ultimately associated with death itself. For Jesus, the execution stands as the conclusion of his personal mission in the 'world' and the commencement of that of his followers under the Spirit.

Summation

At the conclusion of the cosmic journey, which also signifies the formal close of the final geographical journey, the intervention of God stands in full geo-political victory and full geopolitical control. To wit: the climax of the cosmic confrontation is now past; the old world order has been displaced; and the new world order has been installed – in principle, but not yet in practice, for a new phase now begins.

In the first place, with the apprehension and trial, execution and burial, resurrection and ascent of Jesus, the embodied Word of God, the establishment of the kingdom of God in the this-world stands fulfilled and secure. The deeds of wonder and words from above that marked its process of revelation are replaced, as adumbrated through the public ministry in general and the final journey in particular, by the forced arrest and detainment, verbal as well as physical abuse and ridicule, unjust condemnation and ignominious crucifixion, corpse desecration and rushed burial.

In the second place, in a this-world where political intrigue and extreme violence mark the comportment of the ruling elites, both local and imperial, 'truth' and 'glorification' are defined exclusively through the way of suffering and death undertaken by the humanized Word of God in Jesus. In the third place, in and through the nefarious proceedings to which he is subjected by the elites of the this-world, the power of Jesus, the enfleshed Word of God, attains its maximum manifestation: his status as 'king', with a kingdom 'not of this world', is fully acknowledged; the power of Rome, even that exercised against him, is characterized as actually given to Rome 'from above'; his death is represented as the culmination of his mission, the path to his vindication by the one and true God through his resurrection from the dead, and the gateway to his 'glorification' with the Father.

In the last place, the political design of the Jewish authorities unleashed againt Jesus, the Word made flesh, with the pacification of the crowds and the reassurance of the Romans in mind, is brought to fulfilment with the cooperation of the Roman authorities from arrest to crucifixion – a cooperation secured through accusations of seditious behaviour, determined insistence on death, open avowal of submission to the emperor, and strategic insinuations of political repercussions for Pilate.

At the end of the plot, the dominion of the kingdom of God rules supreme over the this-world and the imperial–colonial framework of Rome. Again, however, in principle but not in practice. A second phase of expansion now begins in and through the circle of followers, as anticipated in the private instructions of the final journey: commissioned to go forth into the world; empowered by the Spirit of God; following the way of Jesus via deeds of wonder, words from above, suffering and death as well as vindication and glorification; and holding power over the sin of the world, among numerous other promises and privileges granted. This phase will clearly come to an end with the arrival of the 'last day'; about this cosmic transformation, however, its components and ramifications for both dimensions of reality, precious little is disclosed.

Plot as Postcolonial Programme

Through its adoption of the biographical genre and its framing design and through its turn to travel narrative and its journey motif in the structuration of the narrative as a whole and its central account of the public life, the plotting of Jesus brings to the fore the question of geopolitics and, consequently, the postcolonial problematic. The plot concretizes in historical sequence the postcolonial proposal offered by the story and expands in detailed fashion the postcolonial alternative advanced by the prologue, yielding thereby a gradual exposition of a postcolonial programme through the life and journeys of Jesus.

Through such a mapping of his life and journeys, Jesus, the Word of God, is situated squarely within territories under the control of Rome in one form or another, whether by way of client kingdom or direct rule, and hence within the framework of the imperial–colonial formation of the Roman Empire. The territories in question – involving Palestine and, for the most part, the region of Galilee and the city of Jerusalem within the region of Judaea – lie in the eastern Mediterranean and are closely associated with the 'ethnos' of the Jews. Moreover, in the course of his life and journeys, Jesus, the appointed messenger and unique mediator of the one and true God, undertakes the revelation of the kingdom of God in unrelenting and peripatetic fashion, in the face of the local, colonial authorities of the Jewish 'nation' and the foreign, imperial authorities of the Roman 'kingdom'. This process of revelation entails a succession of expanding sorties in Galilee, with various visits to other areas, alongside a series of ever-longer sojourns in Jerusalem. Through such disclosure of the kingdom of God, Jesus, the Son of God, calls into question, in repeated and escalating fashion, all that has to do with the this-world, whether local or imperial, and promotes instead, in unique and exclusive terms, all that has to do with the other-world. Such a two-edged disclosure results in a progressive portrayal of the religious and political confrontation between the other-world and the this-world that constitutes the apex of the fundamental conflict at the heart of Johannine reality.

Indeed, through its representation of Jesus' life and journeys, the plot traces the steady elaboration, explosive climax and varied denouement of a war of worlds: the kingdom of God, through the figure of Jesus, the Messiah of Judaism and Saviour of the world; the kingdom of Satan, through the provincial elites of the Jewish 'nation' and the metropolitan rulers of the Roman 'Empire'. The denouement is complex but evident. In the first instance, and from the perspective of the 'flesh', the this-world emerges resoundingly triumphant: Jesus is put to death; the proclamation of the kingdom of God is halted; the Jewish ethnos is saved from foreseen destruction by its ruling classes and a provincial political troublemaker is conveniently dispatched by the Roman authorities. In sum, Satan wins the battle and the irruption of God is successfully fended off. Subsequently, and from the perspective of the 'spirit', the other-world stands gloriously victorious: in death Jesus brings his mission to an end, giving way to his vindication through resurrection and glorification; the proclamation of the kingdom of God is taken up by his group of followers, guided and informed by the Spirit; colonial and imperial authorities alike stand condemned by God, as the religious and political disturbance of Jesus continues throughout Judaea and Rome. In sum, God wins the battle, and the resistance of Satan is smashed.

In the end, as a result of such life and journeys, the kingdom of God is made available in the this-world. Those who love Jesus, who believe in his claims and follow his instructions, undergo regeneration as the children of God through the Spirit of God, yielding a life of service and love unto others, of privileged status in the other-world as well as unremitting hatred from the this-world, and of ultimate reunion with Jesus in the other-world of God. Those who hate Jesus, who reject his teachings and commands, go on abiding and finally die in their sin as the children of Satan, giving way to a life of love for the this-world, of hatred for the other-world and condemnation by this other-world, and of ultimate exclusion from the other-world of God. Within the plot, this radical division of human beings continues until an unspecified time, a 'last day', when such a state of affairs between the two domains of reality will presumably come to an end and the victory in principle achieved by Jesus will become a victory in practice. Of such cosmic resolution and its ramifications for both dimensions of reality and corresponding inhabitants, the Gospel, again, remains silent. Beyond question, therefore, a postcolonial programme.

The Fourth Gospel as a Postcolonial Text

In this commentary I set out to pursue the construction of reality in the Fourth Gospel, the Johannine representation of all that is or existence as a whole, from three distinct but related angles of vision: the narrative of events in abstract temporal sequence – its story; the opening narrative unit, at once foundational and summarizing – its prologue; the narrative of events in given causal sequence – its plot. I opted for such a three-pronged approach in order to shed as intense and multifocal light as possible on the Gospel as a discursive intervention within the imperial–colonial framework of Rome and its geopolitical dynamics, wherein it was produced, circulated and consumed. I sought to examine thereby as comprehensively as possible the postcolonial import of the text (within the semantic parameters of the term specified in the Introduction). Such analysis has yielded an intervention that not only is sharply, even painfully, aware of the postcolonial problematic but also mounts a pointed and weighty response to such a problematic. Toward this end, I have argued, the story component bears a postcolonial proposal, the opening component articulates a postcolonial alternative, and the plot component unfolds a postcolonial programme.

John's postcolonial vision posits a reality-wide clash of kingdoms and empires involving the two dimensions constitutive of such reality: the non-material or spiritual other-world, the kingdom of God; the material or fleshly this-world, the kingdom of Satan. This clash is represented as follows:

- Prior to the clash, the vision traces a standing, passive opposition between the two realms of power: the other-world of God remains removed and indiscernible within the this-world of Satan. Beyond such opposition, the myth of origins goes on to lay bare the existence of the other-world by itself and the creation of the this-world through the agency of the other-world – without mention of a rationale for such creation, explanation for the subsequent estrangement of the two worlds, or reference to the figure of the devil and its emergence as ruler of the this-world.
- Regarding the clash itself, the vision offers a direct and deliberate intromission of the other-world in the this-world, characterized as an act of love on the part of God: God sends the Word – creative agent of the this-world and a figure divine, like unto God but subordinate to God – into the this-world with the mission of making God known in the this-world. The resultant humanization of the Word in the person of Jesus of Nazareth – a member of the Jewish ethnos, an inhabitant of the area of Palestine and the territory of Galilee, and a native subject of Rome – unleashes a mighty and decisive battle for power between God and Satan. As Jesus makes known the kingdom of God throughout the kingdom of Satan, utter division ensues: acceptance and following on the part of some, with attention focused on the group of attendant disciples; rejection and hostility on the part of most, with emphasis on the provincial colonial authorities of Jerusalem and the metropolitan imperial authorities of Rome. Such division, while accounted for, remains ultimately unresolved and fundamentally ambiguous – with fluctuation between attribution to human agency, allowing for choice and becoming, and invocation of divine drawing, yielding belonging and unmasking.

  Ultimately, the clash culminates in a formal overturning of the kingdom of Satan by the kingdom of God, attained through the death/execution of God's agent by those of Satan. A complex overturning, therefore: on the one hand, at first and always from the perspective of the flesh, seemingly overwhelming defeat – annihilation of the messenger and elimination of the message; on the other hand, subsequently and always from the perspective of the spirit, indisputably absolute triumph – glorification of the messenger and expansion of the message.
- After the clash, the vision lays down ongoing, active opposition between the two domains of power. The other-world of God is present and at work in the this-world of Satan through the followers of Jesus – spiritualized *in nuce* while in the this-world through reception of the Spirit of God, sent forth by the Word into the this-world to continue the task of revelation, and eventually divinized in full in the other-world as dwellers in the Father's household. The other-world of Satan remains in a mode of counter-attack through its followers, including religious and political elites – in opposition

to the revelation and in persecution of its bearers, seeking to inflict upon them the same treatment accorded their leader. Beyond such opposition, the myth of fulfilment goes on to visualize a final cessation and resolution of the clash between the two worlds and the full victory of the other-world – with no specification of the time or mode of execution, the fate of the evil one and its retinue, or the destiny of the this-world in relation to the other-world.

Given the additional representation of this clash between kingdoms or empires as an encounter between light and darkness, the intromission of the other-world in the this-world may be construed as a journey of the Word of God, Light itself, into the 'heart of darkness'. Seeking to bring the light from above into the darkness below, the Word undertakes, at the behest of and in obedience to God, not only a cosmic journey across the light–darkness divide into the this-world but also a series of geographical journeys within it – localized within the rule of Rome, centred on the subject territories of Galilee and Judaea, and focused on the city of Jerusalem. Such contextualization in general and such escalating and teleological travels to Jerusalem render the latter as the main signifier of darkness in the this-world, both in terms of the local, colonial authorities and their foreign, imperial overseers. To be sure, given the further representation of the clash between the kingdom of God and the kingdom of Satan as involving life and death, grace and sin, truth and falsehood, such journeying on the part of the Word further constitutes a venture into the 'heart of death, sin, and falsehood' – all similarly signified in pre-eminent fashion by the colonial elite of the Jews and the imperial rulers of Rome. Ultimately, however, what applies to Galilee and Judaea, to Jerusalem and to Rome and its vast expanse, applies to the this-world in its totality: all is darkness, without exception, and to it light comes from above; all is death, sin and falsehood, without exception, and to it life, grace and truth come from above. Similarly, what applies to elites and rulers in particular applies to all who do not believe in the Word.

A result of this clash is the clearing of a space for the other-world within the this-world – an 'outpost', as it were, of the kingdom of God in the kingdom of Satan, where light and life, grace and truth, are to be found. Initially, through the presence and activity of Jesus, upon whom the Spirit of God descends and abides; subsequently, through the presence and activity of Jesus' followers, upon whom the Spirit of God is breathed by Jesus and abides forever. In and through both, Jesus and his followers, the Son of God and the children of God, the one and true God becomes known and is made accessible in and to the world. Within this space – amid those re-born of the Spirit, who have gained their sight and live forever, who possess grace upon grace and witness openly to the truth – God dwells and is worshipped. Within this space, mutual abiding and mutual love bind God, Jesus, the Spirit and the children of God together as one. Such a space, tantamount to a 'colony' of the other-world in the this-world, serves, therefore, as a 'redoubt' for resistance to and raiding into the kingdom of Satan. Such a space is also highly complex and thoroughly ambiguous.

It is a space at once colonial and imperial. Clearly, a site of opposition to the this-world, indeed absolute opposition, disrupting the rule and power of Satan exercised through its retinue of allies and followers – a colonial strategy of anti-imperialism. At the same time, such opposition, rooted in the rule and power of God, replicates in significant fashion the constitution and comportment of its target, the this-world – an imperial-like strategy of colonial anti-imperialism. A site of religio-political enthronement and dethronement: within, the sacralization and emplacement of the abode and dominion of God; without, the demonization and displacement of all other religious beliefs and practices as well as political formations and institutions. A site of inclusion and exclusion: within, the children of God, among countless privileges and promises; without, the children of Satan, under condemnation. A site of freedom and hierarchy: a space where the children of God find themselves in freedom from slavery, 'friends' of the Word of God, but in obedience to a hard-and-fast chain of command that flows from God, through Jesus and the Spirit, to them.

A place at once secure and fragile as well. Beyond any doubt, a site of opposition grounded in the cosmic victory attained by God's agent over Satan's agents – a colonial imperial-like strategy beyond dislodgement. Yet, an opposition under siege from the routed but still active forces of the this-world – a highly unstable anti-imperial colonial imperialism. A site of love and hatred: within, the children of God receive and dispense mutual love; without, the children of God suffer hatred. A site of comfort and sorrow: within, the children of God receive whatever they ask of God; without, the children of God stand to suffer, in the way of Jesus, persecution and death. A site of gain and loss: a place where the children of God find themselves branches in the vine of Jesus with God as their gardener, but face, if unfruitful, the dire prospect of removal, withering and destruction by fire.

Through its construction of reality and the ramifications of such a construction, therefore, the Gospel offers, from within the ambit of an unidentified and unplaced, in time as well as in space, Christian formation, a self-conscious and pointed response to the geopolitical problematic perceived at work in the imperial–colonial framework of Rome. Against the mighty empire of Rome and its allies in Palestine, under the overseeing kingdom of Satan, John pits the supreme power of Jesus the Word and his disciples, under the overseeing kingdom of God. Such a strategy of absolute opposition, while no doubt reassuring and perhaps most effective as well for hard-pressed believers, in the end borrows perhaps much too much from its target for its own good.

To conclude, what I have done in this commentary is but to lay out a grand outline of the Gospel's postcolonial vision. It is an outline subject to much refining and nuancing, as units and sections, traits and codes, themes and concerns are similarly examined on a geopolitical key and the findings brought to bear upon such a vision – perhaps by way of revision or expansion, perhaps through complexification or deconstruction. It is also a vision much in need of transactional analysis, calling for interaction with other ideological approaches to the Gospel – comparing and integrating insights emerging from the confluence and application of discourses on gender, materialism, sexuality and race/ethnicity. It is lastly a vision that cries out for critical interchange, involving its religious and political postulates as well as ramifications – a legacy under which we stand, especially those of us who bear the name of Christians, and with which we have no choice but to wrestle. Such considerations remain an urgent postcolonial task for the future.

BIBLIOGRAPHY

Dube, Musa W.
   1996   'Reading for Decolonization (John 4:1-42)', in Laura L. Donaldson (ed.), *Postcolonialism and Scriptural Readings* (Semeia, 75; Atlanta: Society of Biblical Literature): 37–59.
   1998   'Saviour of the World but Not of This World: A Postcolonial Reading of Spatial Construction in John', in Fernando F. Segovia (ed.), *The Postcolonial Bible* (The Bible and Postcolonialism, 1; Sheffield: Sheffield Academic Press): 118–35.
   2000   'Batswakwa: Which Traveler Are You (John 1:1-18)?', in Gerald West and Musa W. Dube (eds), *The Bible in Africa* (Leiden: E. J. Brill): 150–62.
Dube, Musa W. and Jeffrey L. Staley (eds)
   2002   *John and Postcolonialism: Travel, Space and Power* (The Bible and Postcolonialism, 7; London and New York: Sheffield Academic Press).
Loomba, Ania
   1998   *Colonialism/Postcolonialism* (New Critical Idiom; London and New York: Routledge).
Prince, Gerald
   1987   *Dictionary of Narratology* (Lincoln and London: University of Nebraska Press).
Segovia, Fernando F.
   1991   'The Journey(s) of the Word of God: A Reading of the Plot of the Fourth Gospel', in R. Alan Culpepper and Fernando F. Segovia (eds), *The Fourth Gospel from a Literary Perspective* (Semeia, 53; Atlanta: Scholars Press, 1991): 23–54.
   2002   'John 1:1-19 as Entrée into Johannine Reality: Representation and Ramifications', in John Painter, R. Alan Culpepper and Fernando F. Segovia (eds), *Word, Theology, and Community in John* (St. Louis: Chalice Press): 33–64.
   2005   'Mapping the Postcolonial Optic in Biblical Studies: Meaning and Scope', in Stephen A. Moore and Fernando F. Segovia (eds), *Postcolonial Biblical Criticism: Interdisciplinary Intersections* (The Bible and Postcolonialism; London and New York: T&T Clark International): 23–78.

THE LETTER TO THE ROMANS

Neil Elliott

Beneath much of the present ferment in Pauline studies we may detect a fundamental ideological struggle to manage the interpretation of Christian origins. Postcolonial interpreters insist we 'take empire seriously' (Said 1993: 6), but sustained attention to the imperial context of Paul's apostolate has been sporadic, until very recently (see Georgi 1991; Elliott 1994; Horsley 1997). This state of affairs should astound us. After all, Paul wrote during a period when tremendous military might served to perpetuate a 'parasitic' economic system, allowing a Roman elite to 'plunder the provinces on a massive scale' (Garnsey and Saller 1987: 8; de Ste. Croix 1981: 355, 374) – as the empire's advocates readily admitted (see Josephus, *JA* 18.172-77; Seneca, *De Clem.* I.6.1).

In fact, no writing in the New Testament, with the obvious exception of the Apocalypse to John, offers a more striking engagement with Roman imperial ideology than the letter to the Romans. Against the emperor's claim to embody the justice of a new world order, Paul proclaims that the justice of God is now being revealed in the triumphal announcement (*euangelion*) of a rival 'Son of God', the scion of the house of David (Georgi 1991: 85–87). The force of Paul's argument has been blunted, however, by centuries of Christian dogmatic appropriation of the letter that have made it the cornerstone in constructions of Paul's theology. The consequence has been to obscure the role of Roman imperialism in shaping the letter's occasion and Paul's strategic response (Stowers 1994: 1–41; Elliott 1994: 73–75).

Interpretive Roadblocks

Several prevalent interpretive routines present challenges to a postcolonial reading of Romans.

First, although few interpreters today would approve Reformer Philip Melanchthon's characterization of Romans as a 'compendium of Christian doctrine' (1965: § 2.7), the letter is routinely treated as containing Paul's 'basic theological position…more or less completely set forth' (Bultmann 1951: 190), in its 'most complete and complex synthesis' (Segundo 1986: 4) and 'the most sustained and reflective statement of Paul's own theology' (Dunn 1998: 25–26). Even when interpreters recognize a specific situation in Rome as prompting the letter, this is often glossed as the mere occasion for Paul's 'presentation' of his gospel by way of 'self-introduction', as if Romans were a theological brief written to gain support for Paul's mission *elsewhere*. In this way a complex of unstated assumptions regarding the Pauline 'mission', and Paul as a 'missionary', are imported into the letter, despite clear warnings that nothing resembling the phenomenon of 'mission' in the modern imperial age existed in the ancient Roman world. The letter is thus treated as the mere delivery vehicle for a theological 'cargo'. (See discussions by Beker 1980: 11–12, 59–108; Wedderburn 1988; Elliott 1990: 69–104; Donfried 1991; Elliott 1994: 73–75; Hay and Johnson 1995. On the issue of mission, see Keck 1995: 23; Wright 1995: 35; Jewett 1995; compare Goodman 1994: 60–108; Sampley 1995: 112–15. Aune 1987: 219 and Stowers 1986: 114 continue to regard Romans as an 'introduction' or 'presentation' of Paul's gospel.)

Second, the content of that 'cargo' is routinely determined according to one of three fundamentally *dogmatic–apologetic* readings:

According to a 'soteriological' reading, Romans is *Paul's presentation of his theology of God's saving action in the face of universal human sinfulness.* Stendahl (1976) and Sanders (1977) have decisively undermined the classical attempt to oppose a Pauline doctrine of justification by faith to a supposed Jewish doctrine of 'works-righteousness', and thus ushered in a 'new perspective on Paul' (Dunn 1983). Older habits of thought persist, however, evoking a vigorous debate among Latin American interpreters whether Paul's concern for the justice of God has eclipsed his concern for social justice (surveyed by Tamez 1993: 19–43).

In the wake of Sanders' work, many read Romans as *Paul's charter of theological 'universalism'* opposed to the 'particularism', 'ethnocentrism' or 'national privilege' of Israel (compare Baur 1873, 1876). While Western interpreters have hailed this 'universalistic' reading of Romans as a resource for a genuine multiculturalism (Barclay 1996a; 1996b: 14–15), we must beware the tacit assumption that genuine universalism is best represented by the dominant culture, for history has shown that a purported Christian universalism often serves to bolster 'a politics of the eradication of cultural embeddedness' (Boyarin 1994: 218–57; see Fanon 1963: 163). If Paul opposed as 'ethnocentrism' his own people's efforts to maintain cultural identity and distinctiveness against imperial pressures to suppress or obliterate it, how can his theology be construed as 'good news' to marginalized communities today, engaged in similar struggles for survival? Should we not rather affirm traces, in Paul and the movement around him, of a 'stubborn hanging on to ethnic, cultural specificity, but in a context of deeply felt and enacted human solidarity'?

According to a 'sociological' reading, Romans is Paul's *defence of the law-free mission to Gentiles*, against Judaizing pressures *within* the Christian movement. Paul seeks to constitute either a *Gentile* church completely separated from Israel and the synagogue or a *'mixed'* congregation in which Jewish observance is relativized, or even stigmatized as 'weak', behind a veneer of 'equality in Christ'. Though popular (Howard 1970; Stendahl 1976: 1–7, 130; Sanders 1977: 488; 1983: 30–32; Gaston 1987: 6; Segal 1993: 181–83; Watson 1986; Dunn 1998: 340. For critiques see Boyarin 1994: 49–50; Campbell 1991: 122–60; Reasoner 1999: 228–30), this reading runs counter to the rhetorical drive of the letter, which reaches its climax in the admonition to Gentile Christians not to 'boast' over Israel (11.13-32). Against this evidence, many interpreters insist that the letter is *primarily* a critical 'dialogue with Jews' (Beker 1980: 74, 77; Meyer 1988: 1133). The *de facto* result is to conform Romans to Ephesians as a charter for Gentile Christianity's historical ascendancy. This accords with what Richard Horsley has called the 'theologically determined metanarrative' of modern New Testament studies, that is, 'the replacement of the overly political and particularistic religion "Judaism" by the purely spiritual and universal religion "Christianity" ' (Horsley 1998: 154–55).

Third, all these readings tend to isolate the 'theological' argument of Romans from the arena of concrete political struggle. Once the one undeniably political passage in the letter, the exhortation to 'be subject to the governing authorities' (13.1-7), is insulated from any meaningful connection with the letter's overall purpose, it can be accorded an artificial status as '*the* Christian theology of the state', with disastrous results (the 'Kairos' documents: Brown 1990). Removed from its larger context in a praxis revolutionary enough to secure Paul's repeated arrests, arraignments, imprisonments and eventual state execution, ch. 13 has been transplanted into larger theological constructions of the apostle's 'social conservatism' or 'love patriarchalism' (Theissen 1978), alongside constructions (based on the pseudo-Pauline writings) of Paul's indulgence of slavery and the subordination of women (see Jones 1984: 28–63; Elliott 1994: 3–90).

Any politically critical edge to Romans is thus lost. The only remaining interpretive task is to explain the apostle's apparent indifference to the oppression around his congregations, most fashionably by appeal to Paul's supposedly privileged social position (now critiqued by Meggitt 1998). Only recently have feminist voices insisted on an ideological critique of the language of 'obedience' and 'subordination' in Paul's own letters, language which too easily yields service to hierarchical constructions of authority within faith communities today (Schüssler Fiorenza 1987; Wire 1990; Castelli 1991; Briggs Kittredge 1998; compare Sobrino 1993).

Dis-covering Empire

In contrast to the politically obscurantist habits just described, the reading of Romans offered here proceeds from two crucial exegetical insights. First, *the letter is explicitly directed to Gentile Christians in Rome* (1.5-6, 13, 14-15). We must resist the temptation, however useful it has proven to the theological tradition in the West, to 'import' Jews or Jewish-Christians as the letter's 'real' target (Stowers 1994: 22–33). Second, the letter reaches a rhetorical 'climax' in chs 9–11, culminating in Paul's forceful admonition *to Gentile Christians* not to 'boast' over Israel (11.13-32). Rather than setting Romans over against a reconstruction of a stigmatized Jewish theology, then, *we most profitably read the letter as directed against a nascent anti-Judaism among the predominantly Gentile congregations in Rome.* While some scholars refer at this point to 'proto-Marcionism', indicating that the view Paul opposed resembled the theological anti-Judaism of the second-century heretic, I hasten to point out that the doctrine of supersessionism or 'replacement' of the Jews would quickly find a comfortable enough home at the heart of orthodox Christianity. (Here I follow lines of argument in Gaston 1987: 82; 116–34; Elliott 1990: 9–104; Campbell 1991: 1–13, 34–35; Stowers 1994: 22–33; Wright 1995: 59; on supersessionism see Davies 1979; Gager 1985; Simon 1986; Wilson 1995.)

These exegetical observations support a widely accepted reconstruction of the historical situation behind the letter. Moreover, *this reconstruction implicates Roman imperial policy toward a despised minority population, the Jews.* Paul's urgency is probably connected to the aftermath of the emperor Claudius' notorious edict banishing Jews from Rome (49 CE), which would have left Gentiles in the predominance within the capital's Christian congregations. These were decidedly *not* Judaizers, but, to the contrary, individuals 'inclined, not least from social pressures within pagan Rome, to distance themselves' from Judaism (Wright 1995: 35). Paul's warning may indicate that, upon Claudius' death, Jews returning from exile and seeking to re-enter the Christian congregations met resistance and even contempt from these Gentile members. Paul's expression of 'great sorrow and unceasing anguish' for his fellow Jews (9.1) is meant to model the attitude he wishes the Gentile Christians in Rome to adopt (Bartsch 1967; 1968; Elliott 1990: 253–74; Wiefel 1991; Campbell 1991: 201; 1995: 260–61; Wright 1995: 35, 58–59; Sampley 1995: 114. On the social pressures of Romanization see Woolf 1994; 1995).

The issues at stake should not be glossed as merely intramural 'ethnic' tensions within Christian congregations. Claudius' expulsion of Jews from the city was but one episode in a long and consistent imperial policy toward Jews. Since the time of the republic, the Roman aristocracy had looked upon the Jews, with a mixture of suspicion and horror, as the authors of a foreign 'superstition' and 'a persistent "threat"' among their own people' (Cicero, *Pro Flacco* 67; Horace, *Satire* 1.9.69-71; 2.3.281-95; Plutarch, *Superstition* 169C; Juvenal, *Satire* 14.99, 104. On what follows, see Gager 1985; Reasoner 1999; Schäfer 1997; Slingerland 1997). Cicero had set the tone of subsequent Roman views when he decried the intrusion of the Jews' foreign ways as destructive of Roman values and mocked the Jews as a people 'conquered, farmed out to the tax-collectors and enslaved' (*Pro Flacco* 28). The Jewish 'rights' which Josephus celebrated, for obvious apologetic purposes, never prevented successive emperors from expressing a fundamental contempt in outrages against Jewish communities throughout the empire. Roman efforts to be 'tolerant' or 'intolerant' were hardly the point: 'Rome was interested in keeping the urban masses under control' (Rutgers 1994: 71; Gager 1985: 55). Even if – very occasionally – proselytes were to be found in the senatorial class, they risked ostracism or worse: about the time Paul wrote Romans, a prestigious Roman veteran was unable to prevent his wife's arraignment on charges of 'alien superstition', that is, Judaizing (Tacitus, *Annals* 13.32.2).

From the time of Augustus onward, the imperial court cultivated an extensive tradition of vicious anti-Jewish propaganda, probably originating in Greek Egypt. Tiberius' suppression of 'alien rites' targeted Roman Jews especially: four thousand of them were press-ganged to do military service, or die, in Sardinia; the rest were banished from the city (Suetonius, *Tiberius* 36; Tacitus, *Annals* 2.85). Philo blamed the catastrophe in Alexandria (38–41 CE) on the tyrant Gaius's 'indescribable hatred of the Jews'. Jewish homes and shops were plundered, Jews themselves massacred, members of their *gerousia* publicly scourged at the governor's direct order. Not for the last time, an atmosphere of prejudice made the Jews convenient targets for a political conflict among others (Philo, *In Flaccum* 22; *Legatio ad Gaium*; Schäfer 1997: 136–60; Gager 1985: 43–54).

The Jews of Rome must have been aware of the contemptuous reception that the Emperor Gaius accorded the protest delegation led by Philo and of the vicious anti-Semitic propaganda published by the rival Greek delegation. Whatever the cause of the Jewish agitation in Rome, neither it nor Claudius' reaction – in 41 or in 49 – should be seen as aberrations from a 'normal' Roman policy of tolerance toward Jews (Rutgers 1994). (Cassius Dio reports that Claudius forbade assemblies but did *not* expel the Jews [*History* 60.6.6]. Slingerland [1997] and others identify Dio's report with another, earlier incident around 41 CE. We should probably *not* think of Christian or 'messianic' agitation provoking these disturbances. Slingerland's careful discussion of Suetonius' statement, *Iudaeos impulsore Chresto assidue tumultuantes Roma expulit* [*Claudius* 25.4], shows that *impulsore Chresto* probably refers to 'Chrestus' having prompted Claudius' expulsion, *not* the Jews' disturbances, which to Suetonius' Roman prejudices would not have required explanation anyway; that *Chrestus* is probably *not* a confusion for 'Christus', whose name Suetonius probably knows [*Nero* 16.2]; and that Suetonius' failure to identify Chrestus more precisely probably means he presumed his readers would recognize the name [which belonged to a number of prominent Romans]. Nanos [1996: 377, 384] points out that neither Acts [18.2] nor Suetonius nor Dio describe Christians as such being involved in the expulsion.) Nero, who ruled during the years in which Romans was written, had been tutored by one anti-Semitic propagandist, Chaemeron; he was closely advised by another, Seneca – who decried the unnatural influence of 'this accursed race', the Jews, 'the vanquished' who have 'given their laws to their victors' (after Augustine, *City of God* 6.11; Gager 1985: 62).

The Jews' situation was further aggravated by parasitic Roman taxes. These were a chronic complaint of the lower classes, who bore the greater burden of them (Goodman 1997: 83–86, 100–101), but Cicero had set the precedent of shifting the blame for a resented tax burden onto the Jews (*Pro Flacco*). Tax-collectors in Egypt treated Jews savagely, and Jews bore the brunt of popular resentment of Roman taxes there. (According to *Special Laws* 2.92-95, tax-gatherers had resorted to extorting taxes through terrorism, because Jews have left their fields fallow for the seventh year; see also 3.159-63; *Embassy* 199.) We cannot know whether the 'riots' to which Claudius responded in 49 CE might have been provoked by taxation or by the emperor's decision not to investigate anti-Jewish violence in Alexandria, or both. Clearly, around the time Romans was written, Claudius' successor, Nero, confronted a budget crisis and serious public resistance to tax policy, in Rome and elsewhere: he managed to suppress tax riots in nearby Puteoli only by the deployment of Roman troops and 'a few executions' (Tacitus, *Annals* 13.48-51). The problematic exhortation in 13.1-7, including the injunction to 'pay your taxes', may have been meant to deflect just the sort of agitation that has already provoked disproportionate imperial reactions against the Jewish community (Friedrich, Pöhlmann and Stuhlmacher 1976; Elliott 1997).

Significantly, that Israel 'has stumbled' is a perception Paul expects his readers to share, and one he is at pains to interpret rightly (chs 9–11). Indeed, a series of rhetorical questions involving Israel's apparent stumbling punctuate the letter at 3.3, 5; 9.6; and 11.11 (see Campbell 1991: 30–31; Johnson 1995: 216–17; Fraikin 1986: 101).

But how has *Israel* 'stumbled'? While some see here the reflection of a 'theo-logical event', that is, 'the failure of the Jewish mission', it is hard to imagine how the refusal of the gospel *by individual Jews* would alone have led to the perception of *Israel's* wholesale disbelief. It is even less likely that Paul would have embraced this perception, since he expects his readers to acknowledge him as one of numerous Jews who believe in Jesus (11.1-6; 16.3-16).

On the other hand, the perception of *the people Israel as a dishonoured and vanquished race* is amply documented among members of the Roman aristoc-racy, from Cicero to Seneca.

A Preferential Option for the Powerless

It appears, then, that Paul is *not* simply addressing intramural 'ethnic issues' between Jews and non-Jews in order to preserve the unity of the Christian con-gregations (contra Walters 1993). Rather, he confronts the danger that Roman Christians will seize upon the (politically convenient) anti-Jewish prejudice rife in Rome *and baptize it as a theological fact* about Israel in order to interpret the recent misfortunes of the Jews in their midst. And so it must have seemed, *from the perspective of imperial theology*, with its preoccupation with the supremacy of the Roman people over all other peoples (the 'lords of the world': Virgil, *Aeneid* 1.282). Far from combating *Jewish* 'ethnocentrism', in Romans Paul resists what may be called a '*Roman* ethnocentrism', among and around elite members of the Roman churches (Reasoner 1999: 212–15).

Recent interpretation has found decisive clues to the situation Paul addressed in chs 9–11 and 14–15. The 'contempt' toward the weak (*astheneis*) against which Paul warned the powerful (*dunatoi*, 15.1) was a more politically complex phenomenon than a mere difference of opinion among Christians regarding dietary practice (Reasoner 1999). As one of the most distinctive and most despised ethnic groups in Rome, abused for being disproportionately represented among the city's destitute, the Jews suffered, in addition to these insults, the periodic injury of being targeted for expulsion from the city, dispossession of their homes and goods, and the concomitant disruption of family and community life (Rutgers 1994: 64). Those Jews who had evaded police actions, or had returned to the city after Nero rescinded Claudius' expulsion order, might well have appeared a wretched lot, struggling to put together minimally adequate shelter and food for their families. They would have appeared like the targets of vicious satires by Roman aristocrats, ridiculed as 'the weak' (*inferiores, tenuiores*), terms of contempt prevalent in an elite Roman ideology of social status (Horace, *Satire* 1.9.68-72; Juvenal, *Satire* 3.12-16, 296).

Reasoner (1999) has demonstrated that Paul is concerned throughout Romans to promote an ethic of 'obligation' among the 'strong' toward the 'weak' (15.1-2), urging them to 'stand with the oppressed' (*tois tapeinois sunapagomenoi*, 12.16). These terms indicate higher-status Christians, many of them perhaps Roman citizens, tempted to hold in contempt their neighbours whose poverty, low social status, foreign ethnicity and religious scrupulosity (or 'superstition') they regarded as signs of 'weakness'. (On obligation, see Reasoner 1999: 175–99; for a summary characterization of 'strong' and 'weak', 218–20. On 12.16, see Reasoner 1999: 206–207; Lampe 1987: 64; Elliott 1994: 203–204; Wielenga 1982: 83. On heightened religious sensitivity as a symptom of the colonial situation, see Fanon 1963: 55–58 and *passim*.)

This ethic of obligation was potentially subversive of the patronage system, with its careful calculation of relative status. The powerful are to recognize their obligation to the powerless (15.1), and none is to accept any obligation other than 'to love one another' (13.8). (On the revolutionary aspects of Pauline 'mutuality', see Meggitt 1998; compare Fanon 1963: 47–48.) The exhortations in ch. 12 centre around mutualism, a material ethic of mutual interdependence that informs the collection for Jerusalem as well (15.16, 25-28; see Meggitt 1998: 155–64; Horrell 1995). Indeed, this ethic is the rhetorical goal of the whole letter, for as Furnish (1968: 98–106) has shown, in ch. 12 Paul calls his hearers 'to a new life exactly opposite that which he has previously described' in ch. 1. In contrast to the darkened minds (1.21-22), vain worship (1.23), bodily dishonour (1.24) and 'shameless acts' (1.25-27) to which God has abandoned the impious, Paul calls the Christians to present their bodies to God in holiness as their 'spiritual worship' and to be renewed in their minds (12.1-2). This change is possible because of baptism, in which believers are transferred to the service of justice (6.1-19). Similarly, the gift of the Spirit empowers the community toward fulfilling God's will (8.3-11), as 'debtors' sharing a familial obligation (8.12-17).

Since this way of life is truly honourable, just as Paul is 'not ashamed' of his gospel (1.16), so those who live accordingly will live without shame, in holiness (6.19-23). The Romans' holy response to Paul's letter will in turn guarantee the holiness of the 'offering of the Gentiles', which is his sacred obligation (15.14-16). The fulfilment of Paul's apostolic work, securing 'the obedience of nations' (1.4), requires that the Romans fulfil their own obligations in a holy life. The letter is rightly seen, therefore, as constituting 'Paul's *very work with the Romans as mission*' (Sampley 1995: 112–15; compare Elliott 1990: 86–99).

However, how does the strategic character of Romans *as praxis* relate to the seemingly abstract theological arguments in chs 1–8? The traditional apologetic–dogmatic paradigm reads chs 1–8 as Paul's 'presentation' of his gospel of salvation, in pointed contrast to Judaism, and 1.18–3.20 as a 'diagnosis' of a universal 'plight' to which Paul's gospel of salvation (1.16-17; 3.21-31) provides the 'solution' (see Cranfield 1975: 1.107–10; Beker 1980: 78–83; Käsemann 1980: 33–90). Yet, careful study has demonstrated that such a 'diagnosis' would have been generally unconvincing, even unintelligible, to Paul's Jewish contemporaries (Sanders 1977; Räisänen 1983). The diatribal rhetoric in chs 2–3 has confounded efforts to demonstrate a 'demolition of Jewish privilege' (Käsemann 1980). Identifying 'the Jew' as the *target* of Paul's rhetorical apostrophe in 2.1-16 is as 'anachronistic and completely unwarranted' as it is common: this indictment of a hypocritical, boastful person who judges others is stereotypical (Stowers 1981: 110–12). Similarly, the address to 'the Jew' in 2.17-29 is not an attack on presumed Jewish privilege: Paul insists on Israel's very real privileges (3.1-2; 9.4-5). Rather, Paul here calls upon 'the Jew' to bear witness that *all* are accountable before God for their actions (compare 2.12-16; 3.19-20). Indeed, the Jewish interlocutor appears to *assume* premises that are supposed (on the dogmatic–apologetic reading) to be the *burden* of Paul's argument – that 'some have been unfaithful' (3.3), wicked, the objects of divine wrath (3.5), under the power of sin (3.9) (see Elliott 1990: 127–42; Stowers 1994: 159–75).

These passages *were never meant* to demonstrate 'the sinfulness of every human' (Stowers 1994: 192). Some liberation theologians have applied an 'anthropological' hermeneutic here, reading 'the problematic of Judaism' as a cipher for 'religious humanity' or 'civilization' or 'law' (for example, Miranda 1974: 160–92; Segundo 1986: 12–24; Pietrantonio 1986: 12–24; da Silva Gorgulho 1993: 144; Comblin 1993: 476; Gonzáles Faus 1993: 534; see

Nanos 1996: 10–12), but this only perpetuates negative caricatures of Judaism and misses the genuine political thrust of the letter as *a critique of Gentile Christianity*. The boastful hypocritical person who judges others (2.1-16) simply establishes a principle to which Paul will later appeal when he urges the Gentile Christians in Rome not to 'boast' over Israel (11.13-32) and 'the strong' in Rome not to 'judge' or 'despise' the weak (14.3-4, 10, 13; see Stowers 1994: 100–109; Meeks 1987). That all are accountable before God for their actions (2.17-29; 3.19-20) is, similarly, the basis for exhortations later in the letter (14.4, 10-12, 22-23). Paul seeks *not* to explode Jewish presumption, but to distinguish – *for the sake of Gentile-Christian hearers* – between the present plight of *actual* Jews and the ultimate status of God's covenant with Israel.

The Justice of God and the Claims of Empire

A postcolonial reading must attend not just to the topics so useful to traditional theology – 'law', for example, or 'gospel' (Wuellner 1977–78) – but, more importantly, to the subtly pervasive themes of imperial culture, the 'notions that certain territories and peoples *require* and beseech domination' (Said 1993: 9), the politically 'loaded' terms sure to evoke associations to Roman political theology (Georgi 1991: 26–29, 93).

In fact, from the very beginning of the letter, *Paul presents his apostolic praxis as the antithesis of imperial ideology*, developing 'a discourse to counter that of the subjugators' – Esler's phrase (1995). (For what follows, see Georgi 1991: 81–89; Tamez 1993: 93–117; Elliott 1994: 181–85.) The 'Lord' and 'Son of God' whom he serves (1.1-4) is not the *divi filius* of the Julio-Claudian house, descended from the ancient Aeneas – Virgil posed Julius Caesar and Augustus as descendants of Aeneas in the *Aeneid* (1.286-96); opposite panels surrounding the *Ara Pacis* in Rome presented Augustus and Aeneas in sacrificial pose (White 1999: 112; I am grateful to John White for sharing proofs of his work with me). The Trojan heritage was claimed for Nero as well (Calpurnius Siculus, *Eclogue* 1.45-53; *Einsiedeln Eclogues* 1.37-41) and ridiculed in a popular Roman *graffito* (Suetonius, *Nero* 39) – but Jesus, scion of the house of David, is a past king of a now subject people. This rival has been 'confirmed' as Son of God, furthermore, by God's powerful act in raising him from the dead (1.4). No Roman hearer would have failed to contrast that accession in power with the suspicions hanging over Nero's very recent rise or with his deification of the murdered Claudius, his adoptive father, an honour so transparently cynical that the emperor's own counsellor felt comfortable satirizing it – Nero's mother was rumoured to have murdered Claudius with poisoned mushrooms (Suetonius, *Claudius* 44); Seneca satirized the deification of Claudius in his *Autocolocynthosis*.

God had also given Paul a vocation no less staggering in its breadth than the ambition of the imperial house, namely, to secure 'the obedience of faith among all nations' (1.5; 15.18; 16.26), a commission that includes the Christians in Rome (1.5-6, 13, 15-16). White (1999) has shown that the geographic contours of Paul's apostolic commission (15.19-20) reflect the breadth of the *Roman* imperial vision under Augustus – Paul was preceded by the translators of the Septuagint, who had already begun to reconceive the messianic age in terms of the Hellenistic *oikoumene* (Roetzel 1992; 1998: 15–16). The contrast is significant. Augustus boasted of having 'subjected the world' to the *imperium* of the Roman people, graciously preferring 'to preserve rather than to exterminate' any foreign peoples who could 'safely' be pardoned (*Res gestae* 3.2). His propagandist Virgil announced that Augustus had thus fulfilled ancient oracles that the Roman people, 'a race sprung from Jove most high', should 'subject or subdue' the earth (*Aeneid* 1.257-96). Over the next century, provincial intellectuals pretended seriously to debate whether Roman sovereignty resulted from naked power or innate Roman virtue, inevitably reaching the politically correct conclusion, that is, both (compare Philo, *Embassy to Gaius* 310; Josephus, *JW* 2.348-401; Plutarch, *De fortuna Romanorum* 318; Aelius Aristides, *Roman Oration*; Brunt 1978; Nutton 1978; Gordon 1990).

The balance of terror on which the empire rested was obvious enough to most of its subjects, of course – for example, the British rebel Calgacus (Tacitus, *Agricola* 30.3–31.2), or the author of the Habakkuk Pesher (1QpHab); Josephus obliquely hints at the arguments made by the 'many' who 'wax eloquent on the insolence of the procurators' (*JW* 2.348ff.). Occasionally, it was admitted frankly by the Romans themselves – Cicero, for example, acknowledged that the republic rested upon the consent of the elite *and* the fear of the rest (*De republica* 3.41; 5.6) and that Rome's military power had compelled the world's obedience (*Pro Mutena* 21-22); Virgil described the Roman people's vocation as *parcere subiectis et debellare superbos* (*Aeneid* 6.853), which Esler paraphrases as follows: 'Grovel and live; resist and die' (1995: 240). The 'veil of power' (Gordon 1990) held up by civic iconography at the heart of Rome (and, indeed, in every major provincial city) testified, however, that *Augustus* was the 'model priest and benefactor', a paragon of 'religious and civic duty'. Early in his principate, Augustus had abandoned official self-representations as a military conqueror and monopolized the imagery of self-sacrificial piety. He was represented in the *Ara Pacis* complex offering sacrifice in emulation of his ancestor Aeneas. Inscriptions and ceremonials hymned his *pietas* (Gordon 1990; White 1999: 109–13).

This was not merely political posturing. The Augustan age was obsessed with a sense of 'the wickedness of the age', the pre-eminent Roman 'sin' being the recent civil war. The more religious hoped that the blood shed at Actium (31 BCE) had provided ample atonement and were heartened by Augustus' public humility: surely, now, 'any lingering traces' of guilt would be assuaged, and the earth released 'from its continual dread' (Virgil, *Georgic* 1.501-2; *Eclogue* 4.11; Stowers 1994: 122–24). Further, it was crucial to the ideology of the emperor's virtues that Augustus had conquered, not to win glory for himself, but to bring the peoples of the earth into bonds of friendship (*amicitia*) and good faith (*fides*; Greek *pistis*) with the Roman people. Augustan coins and inscriptions thus celebrated *fides* as a virtual Roman monopoly (Georgi 1991: 84). The ideological requirements of the principate determined that the manifest 'courage, clemency, justice and piety' of one man showed clearly that perfect power had been wedded with divine justice (*Res gestae* 31, 32, 34; compare Ovid, *Ex Ponto* 3.6).

Under Nero these themes persisted, even blossomed. Court poets offered exultant 'prophecies' that *Nero* should 'rule the nations' as a god, governing 'peoples and cities' in peace. They could hardly be trusted to govern themselves, after all: a 'vast throng, discordant, factious, and unruly', they were likely to rush blindly to their own destruction without the guidance of the one great spirit who had, with great condescension, taken upon himself the 'massive burden' of empire. Now all sensible people were properly grateful, confessing they wanted nothing more than that their current blessings should continue, and aware that they should be 'free from danger' only so long as they remembered 'how to submit to the rein' (Calpurnius Siculus, *Eclogue* 1.46, 72-73; 4.8; Seneca, *De clementia* I.1.1, 5-9; 3.6–4.2. Josephus held out similarly dismal expectations for Judaean self-government. Tacitus recites a Roman general's warning to rebels in Gaul 'not to prefer insubordination and ruin' to 'obedience and security' [*History* 4.74]).

Suspicions clouded the young emperor's succession, setting different ideological requirements. Nero's propagandists audaciously set themselves to trump even Augustus' claims. In this new and brighter golden age, the forests reeked of incense and sacrificial smoke even more than they had during Augustus' day. Since the 'sin' of civil war was now a remote memory, the requirements on the emperor's model piety were lessened. If 'all had sinned', the great need was no longer for a supreme priest to intercede with the gods but for a god-on-earth to pardon the wicked (Seneca, *De clementia* I.6.3). Nero's propagandists emphasized the distance from the Pax Augusta as an advantage: in contrast to the warrior Augustus, Nero had come to power without bloodshed. (The poets remained tactfully silent about the circumstances of Claudius's death.) Justice and power were again perfectly met in the person of one man, as Nero's 'innocence of wrong' made manifest (Calpurnius Siculus, *Eclogues* 1.45-88; 4.6-9, 82-86, 111-15, 136-46; *Einsiedeln Eclogues* 2.18-22; 4.15-38; Seneca, *De clementia* I.1.3, 5; 6.3; 11.2-3). Seneca hails Nero's *innocentia* and his provision of *securitas, ius, libertas, clementia* (*De clementia* I.1.5, 8-9). As in Augustus' day, the goddess justice ruled throughout the world (*Themis*, in Calpurnius Siculus, *Eclogue* 1.42-45; *Astraea*, in the *Einsiedeln Eclogues* 2.23-4; Georgi 1991: 84–85).

With such vaunts swirling the air, Paul's solemn declarations that *he* is commissioned, by the truly empowered Son of God, to secure the obedience of faith (*pistis*; Lat. *fides*) among the nations, and that *he* thus performs 'priestly service' to God (*latreuein*, 1.9; *leitourgon, hierourgōn*, 15.16), making the nations his 'offering' (*prosphora*, 15.16), cannot but have been heard as a defiant challenge to imperial claims. Yes, Paul declares, the era dawns when God's justice is being revealed. Its ancient heralds, however, were the prophets of Israel, not the purported revelations to Aeneas. Its scion is the anointed from the lineage of David, who arose from a subject people (see 9.1-4; 15.8), suffered a shameful death (see 3.25; 8.3; 15.3) and now by God's power has been raised from the dead (1.4). Paul announces the coming triumph of God (*euangelion*, 1.1) in the name of this rival, 'the Christ' (1.5) – a phrase that has lost none of its political force for Paul (Wright 1991: 41–55) – and brings all nations into a relationship of obedient trust.

Nor does this rhetoric drift into the sphere of the individual spiritual state. Paul declares that the justice of God is being revealed now (1.17), as is the wrath of God (1.18). These two 'revelations' cohere in what is for Paul a thoroughgoing prophetic realism. The wrath of God is *manifestly* revealed – not in any 'secret' or 'hidden' or 'indirect' way, and not as a mere postulate in Paul's proclamation – in an obvious and 'observable situation' (Barrett 1957: 34). (A 'kerygmatic' reading [see Cranfield 1975: 1.107–10; Käsemann 1980: 34–37] makes these complementary themes in Paul's proclamation: the wrath of God is 'revealed' *in Paul's preaching* [the 'diagnosis' of humanity's plight, 1.18–3.20], in preparation for the announcement of God's salvation [the 'solution', 1.16-17; 3.21-26].) God has abandoned the wicked practitioners of injustice, who suppress the truth, to the ever-widening maw of their own arrogance, self-deceit, dishonour and self-destruction (1.24, 26, 28). That claim would be absurd, and Paul's tone 'grossly' and 'thoroughly unfair' (Käsemann 1980: 49; Cranfield 1975: 1.104, 107), if Paul meant to convince his readers that human corruption and immorality *in some general or stereotypic sense* had suddenly become 'revelatory', but that is not his point. Neither can the sexual perversity described in 1.24-27 bear the weight of a 'paradigmatic' or 'extreme' expression of human sinfulness (Martin 1995; against Hays 1986). Some liberation theologians have plausibly found in 1.18-32 hints of an anthropological analysis of social and structural injustice in general, as these are legitimized by 'idolatrous' ideology (Miranda 1974; Segundo 1986; Tamez 1993). More specifically, however, *Paul calls 'revelatory' the paradoxical concentration of idolatry, sexual perversion and all manner of abusive and violent behaviours, precisely in those who publicly vaunt their claim to be wise* (1.22), and thus prove themselves insolent instead (1.30).

While such florid language would be an unbearable exaggeration applied to humanity in general, it makes perfect sense – in fact, it would have seemed rather mundane! – as an allusion to the extreme idolatry, insolence and corruption of the imperial household. Nero's cynical 'deification' of his own uncle, widely rumoured to have been murdered by Nero's own ambitious (and incestuous) mother, might have come especially to mind for Paul's hearers. The whole string of epithets in 1.29-31 could serve as a sort of *Cliff's Notes* to the accounts by Tacitus or Suetonius of the Julio-Claudian dynasty, and Nero's reign of wickedness in particular (compare Paul's language here with Suetonius' report that Nero 'practiced every kind of obscenity, ... defiling almost every part of his body' [*Nero* 29; 33]; Tacitus' reference to the emperor's 'notorious prof-ligacy' [*Annals* 13.45]; and, for an earlier period, Philo's remark that Gaius' unsurpassed offence was to have failed to give fidelity and thanks to God, the supreme benefactor [*Embassy* 8]).

These verses make sense precisely as an inversion of the empire's ideological claims. Paul calls attention to unmistakable, *public* evidence of divine interven-tion in the breathtaking immorality and perversion of the imperial house, rather than in the celebrated virtues or piety of the emperor. Just as God's 'harden-ing' of Pharaoh's heart served to bring God glory (see 9.17), and just as God's 'hardening' of Israel has produced the miraculous gathering from the nations (see 11.7-12), so now God's manifest *punishment* of the impious, handing them over to public shame in the increasingly destructive effects of their own deprav-ity, clearly belies Caesar's claim to embody justice on earth. Thus, by dramatic contrast, the glory of God's justice is revealed!

Genealogy and Hope

Paul declares his obligation to all *ta ethnē* (1.5, 13, 14-15; see 15.15-16, 18-21). His hearers would not have heard themselves addressed (as we hear, and trans-late, the word today) as *Gentiles*, that is, as individual members of a 'generic' category of humans but as members of 'the *nations*' (Stanley [1996: 105-106] points out 'there was simply no such thing as a "Gentile" in the ancient world ... To speak of "Jewish-*Gentile* conflicts" in antiquity is to confuse social analysis with ideology'; see also Stowers 1994: 26, 33; J. M. Scott 1996). Greek and barbarian, the more and less civilized (*sophois te kai anoetois*, 1.15), are equally his charge ('Greeks and barbarians' was originally a Greek trope, eagerly taken over by the Romans. Aelius Aristides repeatedly refers to Rome's subjects as 'Hellenes and barbarians' [*Roman Oration*], as had Cicero; Philo uses the phrase when discussing the Roman imperial reality [e.g., *Embassy* 547]). Paul thus refuses the dishonour Rome imputes to his 'vanquished' people, insisting, in the defiant language of the Maccabaean martyrs, that he is *not* put to shame, for he serves the true Lord who offers salvation in power to *all* who keep faith (1.16). (The declaration, 'I am not put to shame' echoes the defiance of the Macca-baean martyrs, who declared their own honour and 'shamelessness' before the Greek tyrant: *4 Macc.* 5.34-38; 6.20; 9.2; 12.11. The protest of having nothing to put one to shame was frequent in Christian martyrologies [Schottroff 1992]. Esler [1995: 242–45] highlights the central importance of honour and shame in Roman political ideology. On shame and the psychological dimensions of colonialism, see Fanon 1963; Martín-Baró 1994.)

The pointedly political challenge raised here is clearest when set against the hierarchy of the earth's peoples constructed by imperial theology. All peoples were to learn their place in this hierarchy, which descended from the heaven-blessed Romans, whose nature it was to rule, to their more malleable provincial protégés, 'the Greeks', who had graciously given place to their superiors, to, beneath them, all the uncivilized or 'barbarian' peoples who had wisely sought the 'friendship' and 'good faith' of the Roman people, and thus averted annihilation. (For example, Jews figure as least among the earth's peoples in the pro-Roman speech Josephus puts into the mouth of Herod Agrippa [*JW* 2.345-401]. On the Romanization of Greece, see Alcock 1993; on Greek provincials, De Ste. Croix 1981: 344–50; Crawford 1978; Woolf 1994, 1995. On the rhetorical hierarchy of 'worthy and unworthy victims' in modern imperial ideology, see chapter 2 in Chomsky and Herman 1988.) The daily drone of civic ritual and pious panegyric rehearsed the self-evident inevitability of rule by Roman elites and of the 'steep social pyramid' of Roman society. Power and prestige dropped quickly away from a dizzying peak in the Roman orders, through a relatively narrow rank of freedmen and civil servants in the provinces, whose loyalties and obligations lay along the clear channels of patronage (MacMullen 1974; De Ste. Croix 1981: 341–43, 364–67; Chow 1992; Meggitt 1998: 146–49), down to the great masses, whose blind, unthinking movements could only be checked through fear or force. (On 'terror and propaganda' and 'the class struggle on the ideological plane', see De Ste. Croix 1981: 409–52; on civic ritual, Price 1984; on imperial panegyric, consult the 'epideictic' speeches of Dio Chrysostom, Plutarch and Aelius Aristides, and the jingoistic *topoi* offered in the rhetorical forward in the rhetorical handbook *Ad Herrennium*. On 'force and opinion' in modern imperial rhetoric, Chomsky 1991, chapters 4, 12.)

The rhetorical questions in chs 2–3 are ultimately directed to Gentile Christian hearers who know enough of the 'oracles' and 'promises' given to Israel (1.21; 7.1), regarding hopes for a messianic *oikoumenē* (see 3.2; 9.4-5), to compare them with 'facts on the ground' in the imperial capital. It is crucial to recognize that the rhetorical thrust of the argument here, *and* in chs 9–10, is not to establish a 'fact' about Israel's present circumstances – these seem rather to be presumed – but to *interpret* what that fact means for the ongoing covenantal purposes of God. Paul warns Gentile Christians not to reach the wrong conclusion (Stowers 1994: 298–316). Do not conclude that Israel's hopes have suffered shipwreck on the reefs of Roman supremacy – a conclusion unthinkable on Jewish covenantal premises, but *practically unavoidable on the assumptions of Roman imperial propaganda*. It is hardly surprising that Paul must invoke the prophetic–apocalyptic rhetoric of 'mystery' (11.25) to dispel the empire's illusions!

The appeal to the case of Abraham (ch. 4) confirms this analysis. 'Is it in terms of the flesh that we should consider Abraham our forefather?' (4.1: Hays 1985). Paul's concern is to determine what has happened to the promises given to Abraham, promises that raised the prospect of a worldwide *oikoumenē*, the 'inheritance of the earth' (4.13-14). Note that Paul never calls the reality of these promises into question (4.20-21). He insists, rather, that the validity of God's promises cannot be judged against the *present* state of Abraham's genealogical descendants (those *ek nomou*, 4.14; compare *hoi ex Israēl*, 9.6, and *pantes tekna [Abraam]*, 9.7), for the God in whom Abraham believed was precisely the one 'who gives life to the dead and calls into existence the things that do not exist' (4.17), who *thus* can save an apparently vanquished Israel (11.15).

In this light, the currently raging debate about 'universalism and particularism' in early Judaism is beside the point. However 'embarrassing' the political weight of Paul's Christological hope may be to traditional Christian dogmatics (Stowers 1994: 213–26), it is fundamentally rooted in the broad common hope of Roman-period Judaism, where 'ethnicity' mattered far less than a common *politeuma* (Stowers 1994: 283–84; Collins 1983). The hope Paul holds out as the object of Christian 'boasting' (5.1-2) is thoroughly political. It is at once a hope for *nations* (4.18) and for Israel; a hope for the 'liberation from bondage' of the earth's peoples (*eleutheria*, 8.21), indeed of all creation, from the 'futility' and 'ruinous slavery' (*tēs douleias tēs phthoras*) to which it was subjected (8.20-21).

There is not the slightest basis for spiritualizing this language. Interpreters note that Paul's evocation of a tortured and expectant creation in 8.18-25 echoes Gen. 3.17-19. However, while the dogmatic tradition has tended to localize the Adamic drama within the individual psyche (e.g., the troubled doctrine of 'original sin'), the horizon of Paul's eschatological realism includes the sociopolitical. The fundamental opposition throughout ch. 8 (and into chs 9–11 as well!) is between slavery, and the 'spirit of slavery' (8.15, 21), and that 'liberation' (*eleutherōthēnai, eleutheria*, 8.21) that will restore the 'glory' of human beings as 'children of God'. Paul's description of the creation's subjection to 'futility' and slavery draws more directly upon the drama of Exodus: the 'groaning and labouring' of an agonized creation (*systenazei kai synōdinei*, 8.22-24) directly echoes Israel's labour and groaning in Egyptian bondage (see *katestenaxan, stenagmon*, Exod. 2.23-24; *katōdynōn, odynēn*, 1.14; 2.7). In the sharpest possible denial of the empire's realized eschatology – the effusive claims of a golden age of peace and tranquillity on earth – Paul characterizes the present world order as a tortured slave society crying out for divine deliverance (Wielenga 1982: 74–75).

Resurrection and Endurance

Paul speaks of 'tribulation and distress' (8:35), eschatological shorthand for the very real sufferings of the righteous, subjected under foreign domination to 'persecution, famine, nakedness, peril, sword' (8.35). These are *political*, not 'natural' evils: 'For your sake we are being killed all the day long, we are regarded as sheep for the slaughter' (8.36).

The fundamental sin of all imperial ideologies is to confuse hegemonic reach with historic destiny, might with right. Thus, in reviewing the conventional *topoi* of Roman ideology in a set piece attributed to Herod Agrippa, Josephus alternates between a *realpolitisch* assessment of Rome's power (*tēn Rōmaiōn hēgemonian*) and Israel's weakness, on one hand, and, on the other, the mythological corollary that 'Fortune [*Tychē*] has transferred her favours' to Rome and that to Israel 'thralldom is hereditary' (*to hypakouein ek diadochēs pareilēphotes*, *JW* 2.360-2).

Paul is, in contrast, eager to drive a wedge between *present* sufferings and the assurance of *future* glory (8.12-24; 5.2-5). The power of God (1.16) is evident not in Rome's power to destroy but in the power that raised Jesus from the dead (1.4; 4.17, 24). To be united to the resurrection of Jesus is, therefore, to be free from the dominion of sin and death (6.9). Since the 'endurance' Paul encourages (*hupomonē*, 8.25; see 5.3-5) is grounded in the assurance of this same power to raise the dead (8.11; see 5.10), it is no mere acquiescence in the face of adversity. It is, rather, a defiant strategy for survival in the face of seemingly insurmountable oppression. In confidence of this same power to raise the dead, the Maccabaean martyrs suffered torture and by their endurance 'conquered the tyrant' (*hupomonē*, *4 Macc.* 1.11). So, Paul says, those who live by 'the Spirit of the One who raised Jesus from the dead' are free from the 'spirit of slavery' (8.9-17). In this light it is impossible to characterize belief in God's power to raise the dead as mere fantasy, anaesthetizing the oppressed and turning their energies away from real political struggle.

From within the colonial situation, determined as it is by systematic violence, there appears to be no other power than violent force itself (Fanon 1963). It is not unreasonable, therefore, to regard the colonized as facing a simple, clear-cut dichotomy: either violent revolution or accommodating acquiescence. James C. Scott has observed, however, that 'most subordinate classes throughout most of history have rarely been afforded the luxury of open, organized, political activity. Or, better stated, such activity was dangerous, if not suicidal': most revolts have been 'crushed unceremoniously' (J. C. Scott 1985: xv), a truism for which ancient evidence is as abundant as modern (see Dyson 1971). With regard to peasant societies, it is more appropriate, Scott argues, to study 'the constant, grinding conflict over work, food, autonomy, ritual', 'everyday forms of resistance', the accumulation of multiple acts of 'insubordination and evasion' which 'create political and economic barrier reefs of their own'. The struggle between rich and poor is often 'a struggle over the appropriation of symbols, a struggle over how the past and present shall be understood and labeled'. This struggle involves 'an effort by the poor to resist the economic and ritual marginalization they now suffer' and to insist on the minimal cultural decencies appropriate to human dignity (J. C. Scott 1985: xv–xviii). It is on just such contested territory that John Dominic Crossan seeks the figure of Jesus the Galilaean peasant (Crossan 1991).

With regard to Paul, such questions come to a focal point in Paul's admonition to 'every soul' to 'be subject to the governing authorities' (13.1-7). Although some readers of the New Testament speak of 'revolutionary subordination' among the early Christians (Yoder 1973: 193–214; Meggitt 1998: 185–88), it is never made clear why the Roman Empire (or any empire) should have been any more worried by 'revolutionary' subordination than the prosaic, merely accommodating kind. To press the point acutely: however 'subversive' Paul's eschatological rhetoric, does not its heat dissipate into 'pleasantly harmless' myth in the cold wind of political reality? Is all his talk of the 'power of God' merely 'a religious opium' that 'enables a suffering people to endure, by offering private dreams to compensate for an intolerable public reality' (De Ste. Croix 1980: 432; Pixley 1981: 101)? Was Paul that sort of popular leader who represents the colonial power's interests, proclaiming 'that the vocation of the people is to obey, to go on obeying, and to be obedient till the end of time' (Fanon 1963: 168)?

There is very little revolutionary about ch. 13. That should surprise us, given the truly revolutionary tone of what Paul said elsewhere, even in this same letter, about his apostolic responsibilities vis-à-vis the empire's claims (Kallas 1964–65). On the other hand, this is not simply an exhortation to accommodate oneself to the imperial order. Paul's stated attitude toward the ruling authorities is far more reserved than that of other Jews under Roman rule: as Meggitt observes, 'God *orders* them (*tetagmenai*, 13.1), he does not *ordain* them' (1998: 186). There is no enthusiasm here for the divinely apportioned destiny of the Roman people, such as infects Josephus. Indeed, there is no recognition whatsoever of the commonplace – as old as Aristotle – that the world is 'naturally' divided into rulers and ruled, masters and slaves. To the contrary, *every soul* is to be subject to 'the authorities who are presently in charge' (*exousiais huperechousais*, 13.1), a participial phrase remarkable for the modesty of its claim.

Paul's seemingly blithe expectation that the authority will reward good behaviour and punish bad (13.3-4) and thus act as God's servant (*diakonos*, 13.4; *leitourgoi*, 13.6) is marred by two remarks: that the authority 'does not bear the sword in vain' (13.4) and that one therefore must 'fear' the authority – not only in the instance that one does evil (13.4) but because fear is 'owed' to the authority as such (13.7).

These remarks are all the more startling in light of the commonplaces of Roman rhetoric. Propagandists like Cicero consistently held that fear and the threat of force were necessary only for insubordinate and uncivilized peoples. Citizens would naturally yield their happy consent (*De republica* 5.6; 3.41; Elliott 1997). Josephus appeared just as confident that reasonable Jews would embrace Roman rule as the appropriate form of their obedience to God (the exception of the poisonous 'fourth philosophy' proving the rule). Indeed, Nero's propagandists insisted that strategies of coercion belonged to a bygone era. The emperor had come to power without resort to violence, and had thus ushered in a golden age of 'peace…knowing not the drawn sword' (Calpurnius Siculus, *Eclogue* 1.45-65). The weapons of earlier wars were mere historical curiosities (*Einsiedeln Eclogues* 2.25-31). Seneca even had the emperor declare, 'With me the sword is hidden, nay, is sheathed; I am sparing to the utmost of even the meanest blood; no man fails to find favour at my hands though he lack all else but the name of man'. Seneca gushed that so noble a ruler need not fear for his own protection: 'The arms he wears are for adornment only' (*De clementia* 1.2-4; 13.5).

Clearly Paul has a different view. The Roman sword is still wielded, provoking terror (*phobos*), and thus one's posture must be one of 'subjection' or 'subordination' rather than revolt (*antitassesthai, anthistanai,* 13.2). Despite the proximity of the 'riots' that, in Suetonius's view, justified police action against 'the Jews' and of recent unrest over taxes in Rome and nearby Puteoli, we cannot tell from this distance whether Paul in fact considered an attempted uprising to be an imminent danger (although his reference to paying taxes in 13.6-7 has been read this way). Any reasonable Jew could have imagined what the probable imperial response would have been to even modest popular agitation, however.

I read 13.1-7 as part of an ad hoc survival strategy (see Meggitt 1998: 155–78) in an impossible situation, no more – and certainly no less. Paul's 'eschatological realism' – a realism determined by the unwavering conviction that God had raised the crucified Jesus from the dead – was never an *otherworldly* realism. Paul was at least as adroitly political a creature as Philo, whose insistence on discerning the political moment in his allegorical treatise *On Dreams* sounds surprisingly modern. 'When the times are right', Philo wrote, 'it is good to set ourselves against [*anthistanai*] the violence of our enemies and subdue it: but when the circumstances do not present themselves, the safe course is to stay quiet'. Otherwise, one risks sharing the fate of those who have been 'branded and beaten and mutilated and suffer before they die every savage and pitiless torture, and then are led away to execution and killed' (2.83-92).

The modest remarks in 13.1-7, or in the second book of Philo's *On Dreams*, are hardly unusual. Indeed, such 'realistic caution' was required of 'all people of the Empire' (Goodenough 1962: 54–62). What *is* remarkable is how out-of-step this caution would have sounded to ears accustomed to the exultant themes of Roman eschatology. In effect Paul declares: the empire is as dangerous as it has ever been. Nothing has changed. Exercise caution.

There is no fantasy that the powers that be are about to vanish in a miraculous puff of smoke, but neither are they permanent (13.11-12). The Christian's arena of responsibility is much closer, in any event, for the Christian must be diligent for the common good (12.3-21) and fulfil the obligation of mutual love (13.8-10).

The 'hinge' between the 'argument' of the letter, chs 1–11, and the exhortative material in chs 12–15 is the broad exhortation to resist conformity to the world

(12.2). We have seen that this resistance clearly involved, for Paul, a defiance of the empire's ideological insolence, by which it sought to legitimize a brutal rapacity (i.e., to 'suppress the truth', 1.18). As we recognize the mechanisms and legitimizations of imperial domination in our own day, Paul's letter to the Romans provides important guidelines for our own discernment and resistance as we strive for 'the glorious liberty of the children of God'.

BIBLIOGRAPHY

Alcock, Susan E.
  1993   *Graecia Capta: The Landscapes of Roman Greece* (Cambridge and New York: Cambridge University Press).
Aune, David E.
  1987   *The New Testament in Its Literary Environment* (Philadelphia: Westminster Press).
Barclay, John M. G.
  1996a   'Do We Undermine the Law?: A Study of Romans 14:1–15:6', in James D. G. Dunn (ed.), *Paul and the Mosaic Law* (Tübingen: J. C. B. Mohr [Paul Siebeck]): 287–308.
  1996b   *Jews in the Mediterranean Diaspora from Alexander to Trajan (323 BCE–117 CE)* (Edinburgh: T&T Clark).
Barrett, C. K.
  1957   *A Commentary on the Epistle to the Romans* (Harper's New Testament Commentaries; New York: Harper).
Bartsch, Hans
  1967   'Die antisemitischen Gegner des Paulus in Römerbrief', in W. Eckert *et al.* (eds), *Antijudaismus im Neuen Testament?* (Munich: Kaiser Verlag): 27–43.
  1968   'Die historische Situation des Römerbriefes', *Studia Evangelica 4/Theologische Untersuchungen* 102: 282–91.
Baur, Ferdinand Christian
  1873   *Paul: His Life and Work* (vol. 1; 2nd edn; trans. E. Zeller; London: Williams & Norgate).
  1876   *Paul: The Apostle of Jesus Christ* (trans. E. Zeller; London: Williams & Norgate).
Beker, J. Christiaan
  1980   *Paul the Apostle: The Triumph of God in Life and Thought* (Philadelphia: Fortress Press).
Boyarin, Daniel
  1994   *A Radical Jew: Paul and the Politics of Identity* (Berkeley, Los Angeles and London: University of California Press).
Briggs Kittredge, Cynthia
  1998   *Community and Authority: The Rhetoric of Obedience in the Pauline Tradition* (Harvard Theological Studies, 45; Philadelphia: Trinity Press International).
Brown, Robert McAfee (ed.)
  1990   *Kairos: Three Prophetic Challenges to the Church* (Grand Rapids: Eerdmans).
Brunt, P. A.
  1978   'Laus Imperii', in Garnsey and Whittaker 1978: 159–92.

Bultmann, Rudolf
  1951   *The Theology of the New Testament* (vol. 1; trans. Kendrick Grobel; London: SCM Press; New York: Charles Scribner's Sons).
Campbell, William S.
  1991   *Paul's Gospel in an Intercultural Context: Jew and Gentile in the Letter to the Romans* (Studies in the Intercultural History of Christianity, 69; Frankfurt am Main: Peter Lang).
  1995   'The Rule of Faith in Romans 12:1–15:13', in Hay and Johnson 1995: 259–86.
Castelli, Elizabeth
  1991   *Imitating Paul: A Discourse of Power* (Louisville, KY: Westminster/John Knox Press).
Chomsky, Noam
  1991   *Deterring Democracy* (New York: Verso).
Chomsky, Noam and Edward S. Herman
  1988   *Manufacturing Consent: The Political Economy of the Mass Media* (New York: Pantheon).
Chow, John
  1992   *Patronage and Power: A Study of Social Networks in Corinth* (Journal for the Study of the New Testament Supplement Series, 75; Sheffield: Sheffield Academic Press).
Collins, John J.
  1983   *Between Athens and Jerusalem: Jewish Identity in the Hellenistic Diaspora* (New York: Crossroad).
Comblin, José
  1993   'The Holy Spirit', in Ellacuría and Sobrino 1993.
Cranfield, C. E. B.
  1975   *A Critical and Exegetical Commentary on the Epistle to the Romans* (2 vols.; International Critical Commentary; Edinburgh: T&T Clark).
Crawford, M. H.
  1978   'Greek Intellectuals and the Roman Aristocracy in the First Century B.C.', in Garnsey and Whittaker 1978: 193–207.
Crossan, John Dominic
  1991   *The Historical Jesus: The Life of a Mediterranean Jewish Peasant* (San Francisco: HarperSanFrancisco).
Da Silva Gorgulho, Gilberto
  1993   'Biblical Hermeneutics', in Ellacuría and Sobrino 1993: 123–50.
Davies, Alan T. (ed.)
  1979   *Antisemitism and the Foundation of Christianity* (New York: Paulist Press).
De Ste. Croix, G. E. M.
  1981   *The Class Struggle in the Ancient Greek World: From the Archaic Age to the Arab Conquests* (Ithaca, NY: Cornell University Press).
Donfried, Karl P. (ed.)
  1991   *The Romans Debate* (2nd edn; Peabody: Hendrickson).
Dunn, James D. G.
  1983   'The New Perspective on Paul', in *Bulletin of the John Rylands Library* 65: 95–122.
  1998   *The Theology of Paul the Apostle* (Grand Rapids: Eerdmans).

Dyson, Stephen L.
1971   'Native Revolt Patterns in the Roman Empire', *Historia* 20: 239–74.

Ellacuría, Ignacio, sj and Jon Sobrino, sj
1993   *Mysterium Liberationis: Foundational Concepts of Liberation Theology* (Maryknoll, NY: Orbis Books).

Elliott, Neil
1990   *The Rhetoric of Romans: Argumentative Constraint and Strategy and Paul's Dialogue with Judaism* (Journal for the Study of the New Testament Supplement Series, 45; Sheffield: JSOT Press).

1994   *Liberating Paul: The Justice of God and the Politics of the Apostle* (Maryknoll, NY: Orbis Books).

1996   'Figure and Ground in the Interpretation of Romans 9–11', in Stephen Fowl (ed.), *The Theological interpretation of Scripture: Classical and Contemporary Readings* (Oxford: Blackwell): 371–89.

1997   'Romans 13:1-7 in the Context of Imperial Propaganda', in Richard A. Horsley (ed.), *Paul and Empire: Religion and Power in Roman Imperial Society* (Philadelphia: Trinity Press International): 184–204.

Esler, Philip F.
1995   'God's Honour and Rome's Triumph: Responses to the Fall of Jerusalem in 70 C.E. in Three Jewish Apocalypses', in Philip F. Esler (ed.), *Modelling Early Christianity: Social-Scientific Studies of the New Testament in Its Context* (London and New York: Routledge): 239–58.

Fanon, Frantz
1963   *The Wretched of the Earth* (trans. Constance Farrington; New York: Grove Press).

Fraikin, Daniel
1986   'The Rhetorical Function of the Jews in Acts', in Peter Richardson and David Granskou (eds), *Anti-Judaism in Early Christianity*. Volume 1: *Paul and the Gospels* (Waterloo, ON: Wilfrid Laurier University Press): 91–105.

Friedrich, J., W. Pöhlmann and P. Stuhlmacher
1976   'Zur historischen Situation und Intention von Röm 13,1-7', *Zeitschrift für Theologie und Kirche* 73: 131–66.

Furnish, Victor Paul
1968   *Theology and Ethics in Paul* (Nashville: Abingdon Press).

Gager, John G.
1985   *The Origins of Antisemitism* (New York: Oxford University Press).

Garnsey, P. D. A. and Richard Saller
1987   *The Roman Empire: Society, Economics, Culture* (Berkeley: University of California Press).

Garnsey, P. D. A. and C. R Whittaker (eds)
1978   *Imperialism in the Ancient World* (Cambridge and New York: Cambridge University Press).

Gaston, Lloyd
1987   *Paul and the Torah* (Vancouver: University of British Columbia Press).

Georgi, Dieter
1991   *Theocracy in Paul's Praxis and Theology* (trans. David E. Green; Minneapolis: Fortress Press).

Gonzáles Faus, José Ignacio
1993   'Sin', in Ellacuría and Sobrino 1993: 532–42.

Goodenough, E. R.

1962   *An Introduction to Philo Judaeus* (2nd edn; Oxford: Basil Blackwell).

Goodman, Martin

1994   *Mission and Conversion: Proselytizing in the Religious History of the Roman Empire* (Oxford: Clarendon Press).

1997   *The Roman World 44 B.C.–A.D. 180* (New York: Routledge).

Gordon, Richard

1990   'The Veil of Power: Emperors, Sacrificers and Benefactors', in Mary Beard and John North (eds), *Pagan Priests: Religion and Power in the Ancient World* (Ithaca, NY: Cornell University Press): 199–231.

Hay, David M. and E. Elizabeth Johnson (eds)

1995   *Pauline Theology*. Vol. 3, *Romans* (Minneapolis: Fortress Press).

Hays, Richard B.

1985   'Have We Found Abraham to Be Our Forefather According to the Flesh?: A Reconsideration of Rom. 4.1.', *Novum Testamentum* 27: 77–98.

1986   'Relations Natural and Unnatural: A Response to John Boswell's Exegesis of Romans 1', *Journal of Christian Ethics* 14: 184–215.

Horrell, David G.

1995   'Paul's Collection: Resources for a Materialist Theology', *Epworth Review* 22: 74–83.

Horsley, Richard A. (ed.)

1997   *Paul and Empire: Religion and Power in Roman Imperial Society* (Philadelphia: Trinity Press International).

Horsley, Richard A.

1998   'Submerged Biblical Histories and Imperial Biblical Studies', in R. S. Sugirtharajah (ed.), *The Postcolonial Bible* (The Bible and Postcolonialism, 1; Sheffield: Sheffield Academic Press): 152–73.

Howard, George

1970   'Romans 3:21-31 and the Inclusion of the Gentiles', *Harvard Theological Review* 63: 223–33.

Jervis, L. Ann and Peter Richardson (eds)

1994   *Gospel in Paul: Studies on Corinthians, Galatians and Romans for Richard N Longenecker* (Journal for the Study of the New Testament Supplement Series, 108; Sheffield: Sheffield Academic Press).

Jewett, Robert

1995   'Ecumenical Theology for the Sake of Mission: Romans 1:1-17 + 15:14-16:24', in Hay and Johnson 1995: 89–108.

Johnson, E. Elizabeth

1995   'Romans 9–11: The Faithfulness and Impartiality of God', in Hay and Johnson 1995: 211–39.

Jones Jr., Amos

1984   *Paul's Message of Freedom: What Does It Mean for the Black Church?* (Valley Forge: Judson Press).

Kallas, James

1964–65 'Romans XIII:1-7: An Interpolation', *New Testament Studies* 11: 365–74.

Käsemann, Ernst

1980   *Commentary on Romans* (trans. from the 4th German edn; trans. Geoffrey W. Bromiley; Grand Rapids: Eerdmans).

Keck, Leander E.
1995   'What Makes Romans Tick?' in Hay and Johnson 1995: 3–29.
Lampe, Peter
1987   *Die stadtrömischen Christen in den ersten beiden jahrhunderten* (Wissen-schaftliche Untersuchungen zum Neuen Testament 2/18; Tübingen: J. C. B. Mohr [Paul Siebeck]).
MacMullen, Ramsay
1974   *Roman Social Relations 50 B.C. to A.D. 284* (New Haven: Yale University Press).
Martin, Dale B.
1995   'Heterosexism and the Interpretation of Romans 1:18-32', *Biblical Interpretation* 3.3: 332–55.
Martín-Baró, Ignacio
1994   *Writings for a Liberation Psychology* (trans. Adrianne Aron and Sharon Corne; Cambridge: Cambridge University Press).
Meeks, Wayne A.
1987   'Judgment and the Brother: Romans 14:1–15:13', in G. F. Hawthorne and O. Betz (eds), *Tradition and Interpretation in the New Testament: Essays in Honor of E. Earle Ellis* (Grand Rapids: Eerdmans): 290–300.
Meggitt, Justin J.
1998   *Paul, Poverty and Survival* (Edinburgh: T&T Clark).
Melanchthon, Philip
1965   'Römerbrief-Kommentar, 1532', in R. Stupperich (ed.), *Melanchthons Werke in Auswahl* (vol. 5; Gütersloh: C. Bertelsmann).
Meyer, Paul W.
1988   'Romans', in James L. Mays (ed.), *Harper's Bible Commentary* (San Francisco: HarperSanFrancisco): 1130–67.
Miranda, José Porfirio
1974   *Marx and the Bible: A Critique of the Philosophy of Oppression* (trans. John Eagleson; Maryknoll, NY: Orbis Books).
Nanos, Mark D.
1996   *The Mystery of Romans: The Jewish Context of Paul's Letter* (Minneapolis: Fortress Press).
Nutton, V.
1978   'The Beneficial Ideology', in Garnsey and Whittaker 1978: 209–22.
Pietrantonio, Ricard
1986   'Está la justicia enraizada en el Nuevo Testamento?', *Revista Bíblica* 48: 49–119.
Pixley, Jorge
1979   'El evangelio paulino de la justificación por la fé: Conversaciones con José Porfirio Miranda', *Revista Bíblica* 41 (Special issue on *Diakonia tou logou*): 57–74.
1981   *God's Kingdom* (Maryknoll, NY: Orbis Books).
Price, S. R. F.
1984   *Rituals and Power: The Roman Imperial Cult in Asia Minor* (Cambridge: Cambridge University Press).
Räisänen, Heikki
1983   *Paul and the Law* (Tübingen: J. C. B. Mohr [Paul Siebeck]).

Reasoner, Mark
    1999   *The Strong and the Weak: Romans 14:1–15:13 in Context* (Society for New Testament Studies Monograph Series, 103; Cambridge: Cambridge University Press).

Roetzel, Calvin J.
    1992   '*Oikoumene* and the Limits of Pluralism in Alexandrian Judaism and Paul', in J. Andrew Overman and Robert S. MacLennon (eds), *Diaspora Jews and Judaism* (Atlanta: Scholars Press): 163–70.

    1998   *Paul: The Man and the Myth* (Columbia: University of South Carolina Press).

Rutgers, Leonard V.
    1994   'Roman Policy towards the Jews: Expulsions from the City of Rome during the First Century C.E.', *Classical Antiquity* 13.1: 56–74.

Said, Edward W.
    1993   *Culture and Imperialism* (New York: Vantage).

Sampley, J. Paul
    1995   'The Weak and the Strong: Paul's Careful and Crafty Rhetorical Strategy in Romans 14:1–15:13', in L. Michael White and O. Larry Yarbrough (eds), *The Social World of the First Christians: Essays in Honor of Wayne A. Meeks* (Minneapolis: Fortress Press): 40–52.

Sanders, E. P.
    1977   *Paul and Palestinian Judaism: A Comparison of Patterns of Religion* (Philadelphia: Fortress Press).

    1983   *Paul, the Law, and the Jewish People* (Philadelphia: Fortress Press).

Schäfer, Peter
    1997   *Judeophobia: Attitudes toward the Jews in the Ancient World* (Cambridge: Harvard University Press).

Schottroff, Luise
    1992   ' "Give to Caesar What Belongs to Caesar and to God What Belongs to God": A Theological Response of the Early Christian Church to Its Social and Political Environment', in Willard M. Swartley (ed.), *The Love of Enemy and Nonretaliation in the New Testament* (Louisville, KY: Westminster/John Knox Press): 223–57.

Schüssler Fiorenza, Elisabeth
    1987   'Rhetorical Situation and Historical Reconstruction in 1 Corinthians', *New Testament Studies* 33: 175–86.

Scott, James C.
    1985   *Weapons of the Weak: Everyday Forms of Peasant Resistance* (New Haven: Yale University Press).

Scott, James M.
    1996   *Paul and the Nations: The Old Testament and Jewish Background of Paul's Mission to the Nations* (Tübingen: J. C. B. Mohr [Paul Siebeck]).

Segal, Alan
    1990   *Paul the Convert* (New Haven: Yale University Press).

Segundo, Juan Luis
    1986   *The Humanist Christology of Paul* (ed. and trans. John Drury; Jesus of Nazareth, Yesterday and Today, 3; Maryknoll, NY: Orbis Books).

Simon, M.
    1986   *Verus Israel: A Study of the Relations between Christians and Jews in the Roman Empire (135–425)* (New York: Oxford University Press).

Slingerland, H. Dixon
    1997   *Claudian Policymaking and the Early Imperial Repression of Judaism at Rome* (Atlanta: Scholars Press).

Sobrino, Jon, SJ
    1989   'Jesus, Theology, and Good News', in Marc H. Ellis and Otto Maduro (eds), *The Future of Liberation Theology: Essays in Honor of Gustavo Gutiérrez* (Maryknoll, NY: Orbis Books): 189–202.
    1993   'The Winds in Santo Domingo and the Evangelization of Culture', in Alfred T. Hennelly, SJ (ed.), *Santo Domingo and Beyond: Documents and Commentaries from the Historic Meeting of the Latin American Bishops' Conference* (Maryknoll, NY: Orbis Books): 167–83.

Stanley, Christopher
    1996   'Neither Jew Nor Greek: Ethnic Conflict in Graeco-Roman Society', *Journal for the Study of the New Testament* 64: 101–24.

Stendahl, Krister
    1976   *Paul among Jews and Gentiles* (Philadelphia: Fortress Press).

Stowers, Stanley K.
    1981   *The Diatribe and Paul's Letter to the Romans* (Chico, CA: Scholars Press).
    1986   *Letter Writing in Greco-Roman Antiquity* (Philadelphia: Westminster Press).
    1994   *A Rereading of Romans: Justice, Jews, Gentiles* (New Haven: Yale University Press).

Tamez, Elsa
    1993   *The Amnesty of Grace: Justification by Faith from a Latin American Perspective* (trans. Sharon H. Ringe; Nashville: Abingdon Press).

Theissen, Gerd
    1978   *The Social Setting of Pauline Christianity: Essays on Corinth* (trans. John Schutz; Philadelphia: Fortress Press).

Walters, James C.
    1993   *Ethnic Issues in Paul's Letter to the Romans: Changing Self-Definitions in Earliest Roman Christianity* (Philadelphia: Trinity Press International).

Watson, Francis
    1986   *Paul, Judaism and the Gentiles: A Sociological Approach* (Society for New Testament Studies Monograph Series, 56; Cambridge: Cambridge University Press).

Wedderburn, A. J. M.
    1988   *The Reasons for Romans* (Edinburgh: T&T Clark).

White, John L.
    1999   *Apostle of God* (Peabody, MA: Hendrickson).

Wiefel, Wolfgang
    1991   'The Jewish Community?', in Donfried 1991: 85–101.

Wielenga, Bastiaan
    1982   *Biblical Perspectives on Labor* (Madurai: TTS).
    1996   'Called to Be Free: Biblical Approaches to Slavery', *Dialogue* n.s. [Colombo] 23: 32–52.

Wilson, Stephen G.
    1995   *Related Strangers: Jews and Christians 70–170 C.E.* (Minneapolis: Fortress Press).

Wire, Antoinette Clark
    1990   *The Corinthian Women Prophets: A Reconstruction through Paul's Rhetoric* (Minneapolis: Fortress Press).

Woolf, Greg
    1990   'World-systems Analysis and the Roman Empire', *Journal of Roman Archae-ology* 2: 44–58.
    1994   'Becoming Roman, Staying Greek: Culture, Identity, and the Civilizing Process in the Roman East', *Proceedings of the Cambridge Philological Society* 40: 116–43.
    1995   'Beyond Romans and Natives', *World Archaeology* 28.3: 339–50.

Wright, N. Thomas
    1991   *The Climax of the Covenant: Christ and the Law in Pauline Theology* (Edinburgh: T&T Clark; Minneapolis: Fortress Press).
    1995   'Romans and the Theology of Paul', in Hay and Johnson 1995: 30–67.

Wuellner, Wilhelm H.
    1977–78   'Toposforschung and Torahinterpretation bei Paulus and Jesus', *New Testament Studies* 24: 463–83.

Yoder, John H.
    1973   *The Politics of Jesus* (Grand Rapids: Eerdmans).

THE FIRST AND SECOND LETTERS TO THE CORINTHIANS

Richard A. Horsley

Postcolonial criticism, developed primarily in the field of literary criticism, reads colonial, anti-colonial and 'postcolonial' literatures in colonial/imperial and (what I would prefer to call) neo-imperial contexts. Its principal challenge to biblical/New Testament studies is to recognize that the Bible functioned effectively as colonial literature. Bible reading inspired Western European and North American imperialism. It formed the focal agenda of imperial missionary enterprises among colonized African and Asian peoples. After centuries of its operative effects as colonial literature, the Bible is now, for better or worse, entrenched in previously colonized cultures as well as Western imperial cultures. In confronting those effects, postcolonial biblical criticism will surely make its most important contribution by focusing on the imperial/colonial use and abuse of the Bible.

Established academic biblical studies is heavily implicated in the operation of the Bible as colonial literature. As it developed during the heyday of Western imperialism in the nineteenth and twentieth centuries, biblical studies strove ostensibly to understand biblical texts in their ancient/original historical context. Assuming the distinctive modern Western separation of religion and political–economic life, however, theologically determined New Testament studies in particular reduced its focus to religion, understood mainly as personal faith, as separate from political affairs. Also partly because developing New Testament studies was oblivious to its own complicity in modern Western imperialism, it tended to ignore the ancient Roman imperial context in which Jesus and Paul operated and in which the New Testament and early Christianity originated. Indeed, as it developed in interaction with the developing German, French and English national cultures that idealized the Roman Empire and patterned their own elite cultures and educational systems on an idealized ancient Greek humanism, New Testament studies itself tended to idealize rather than criticize Hellenistic and Roman imperialism.

Postcolonial studies is also one of the principal factors now forcing us to acknowledge and explore the remarkable contradiction between standard New Testament/Pauline studies which developed in imperial Western Europe and the letters of Paul, and the Corinthian correspondence in particular, in their broader ancient imperial context. Paul helped catalyse and then addressed letters to fledgling communities of a movement among peoples who had been subjugated by the Roman Empire. His mission and letters in their vision and goals, moreover, pointedly oppose the Roman imperial order. It is thus ironic in the extreme that the letters of the anti-imperial apostle to those subjugated peoples have become the canonical Scriptures of the imperial Western religion that were made to justify, even inspire, the European campaign to propagate the Christian faith among peoples under European colonization and the European imperial expansion with which Christian missionary enterprises went hand in hand.

The standard paradigm in which Paul and his letters, such as 1 and 2 Corinthians, are understood in New Testament studies was the product of Protestant, particularly German Lutheran, theology influenced by wider Western European orientalism. In what has become the most influential work of postcolonial theory, Edward Said (1978: 1–28) exposed the remarkable Western construction of orientalism, especially in modern English and French literature and intellectual history. He demonstrated how, in close relationship with the Western powers' institutionalized mechanisms for domination of 'oriental' peoples, academic fields such as anthropology, history and philology developed a distinctive discourse of a timeless, essentialized Orient that embodied the virtual opposite of the self-image of the West as rational, democratic and progressive, that is, the West's other. In parallel fashion, theologically determined New Testament studies developed a grand paradigm in which Christianity, as the universal and truly spiritual religion, emerged and broke away from Judaism, which had been an overly political and parochial religion. The apostle Paul was understood as the key figure in the dramatic break with the Jewish law, with its particularist obsession with legalism and ritual, and the pioneer of universal and spiritual religion that transcended narrow ethnic boundaries and opened salvation to the Gentiles. Assuming the separation between religion and political–economic life, and the reduction of religion to individual belief, New Testament studies defined Paul primarily as the hero of faith, to the virtual exclusion of political and economic life. Equally important for the collaboration of the European churches in the expansion of European empires, Paul was the paradigmatic missionary, taking the universal faith to the (backward) nations of the world.

Another factor we must take into account in any critical consideration of Paul, particularly postcolonial criticism, is that the establishment Paul, who was read and interpreted to support the institution of slavery and the blatant subordination of women and was instrumental in the reading of the Bible as imperial/colonial literature, was derived from what we now recognize as 'deutero-Pauline' letters (2 Thessalonians, Colossians, Ephesians, 1–2 Timothy and Titus) as well as the 'genuine' letters (Romans, 1–2 Corinthians, Galatians, Philippians, 1 Thessalonians, Philemon). It is in the later letters written by representatives of a 'conservative' branch of the Pauline movement that the most subordinationist declarations are found. These represent a dramatic adjustment toward and a considerable degree of assimilation to the dominant Roman imperial order. Although critical Western New Testament studies distinguished between the original and secondary letters, the resulting picture of Paul was still heavily influenced by (read through the lens of) the later letters that represented one tradition of the results of Paul's mission and earlier letters. After all, established Western Christianity still needed Paul as the founder of a new, universal and spiritual religion. Despite ostensible recognition that his letters were ad hoc communications in standard New Testament studies, Paul is still read as a source for 'Pauline Christianity' and his statements are still taken as authoritative declarations of the 'Christian' faith.

Historical Background of Paul's Mission in Corinth

In order to understand Paul's mission in Corinth and his Corinthian correspondence in their original Roman imperial context, we must consider an unusually broad historical background. In the centuries prior to the time of Jesus and Paul, both the Greek city-states and the peoples of the eastern Mediterranean had come increasingly under the rule of empires. The Judaeans, Samaritans and Galilaeans had been subjugated by the ancient Near Eastern empires of the Assyrians, the Babylonians and the Persians, who established the temple-state and its ruling high-priesthood in Jerusalem as an instrument of imperial rule. Alexander the Great of Macedonia, already in control of the Greek cities, first established 'Western' imperial rule over the ancient Near East. In contrast to the eastern Persian empire, Alexander and his successors imposed Western cultural and political forms onto the subjected cities and established many Western-model cities in the Near East as colonies ruling over the indigenous peasantry. One of the exceptions was their allowing the temple-state to continue in Judaea.

In the two centuries before Jesus and Paul, the Romans relentlessly expanded their control over the eastern Mediterranean by military conquest, destruction of cities and villages, and slaughter and enslavement of subjected peoples. Having bullied a league of Greek cities into war, the Romans destroyed the glorious ancient city of Corinth in 146 BCE. A century later, in 44 BCE, the Roman warlord Julius Caesar established a Roman colony on the site of the former city of Corinth as a means of getting rid of potential sources of discontent among the Roman urban mob: freed slaves, surplus army veterans and displaced country-folk who had migrated into the city (Strabo, *Geogr.* 8.6.23) – somewhat as England in modern times emptied its prisons and barrios of unwanted surplus urban riff-raff and sent them to Australia and other colonies. The rebuilt, colonized city of Corinth quickly became a major commercial centre, because of its strategic location for imperial trade in luxury goods. The Corinth into which Paul and others came in the early 50s CE was thus a melting pot of languages and cultures dominated by the Greek language and Roman-style politics. It was the first large cosmopolitan city to which Paul brought his mission after he left his original base in Antioch.

The movement of Jesus-believers that Paul had joined, of course, took its origins in Roman-dominated Palestine. The Israelite peoples – Judaeans, Samaritans and Galilaeans – had managed to maintain their traditional way of life through centuries of rule by foreign empires. More than any other peoples in the Near East, Judaeans and Galilaeans in particular persisted in mounting serious and sometimes temporarily successful peasant revolts against their Western imperial rulers and the client regimes through which they tried to control Palestine, that is, the Herodian kings and the high-priestly aristocracy in Jerusalem. In addition, the Galilaean and Judaean peasantry produced periodic movements of resistance and renewal headed by popular prophets, posing as the new Moses or Elijah, or popular kings (Messiahs) as the new David. For their part, scribal circles such as the *maskilim*, who evidently produced the book of Daniel, and the priestly–scribal community, who produced the Dead Sea Scrolls, cultivated apocalyptic visions according to which God would soon act to judge/destroy the oppressive foreign empire, restore the people of Israel and vindicate the martyrs who died leading resistance to imperial rule. Right around the time Jesus was born, some of the more activist Pharisees and other scribal teachers organized resistance to the Roman imperial tribute as a violation of the exclusive sovereignty of their true lord and master, God.

Jesus, and the movement he catalysed, following the same patterns as the other popular prophetic and messianic movements, also pursued a programme of a renewal of Israel, in its constituent village communities, against its Jerusalem as well as its imperial Roman rulers. As Jesus also suggested in skilfully avoiding entrapment, it was impossible for Israelite peoples to render to Caesar, since they must render to God, to whom all things belonged. It is unavoidably clear that Jesus and his movement were anti-imperial from the fact that he was crucified, a form of execution the Romans used for rebel leaders in the provinces and the fact that his movement reconfigured itself around Jesus as a martyred leader ignominiously crucified by the Romans but then vindicated by God in resurrection.

Before he ever encountered the Jesus-movement, however, Paul had come to Jerusalem from one of the many communities of Jews that lived in various cities of the eastern Roman Empire. Tens of thousands of Judaeans had been deported from Palestine, taken by earlier imperial regimes as mercenaries or by Roman imperial warlords as slaves. Many, perhaps most, of these diaspora Jewish communities were semi-self-governing, according to their ancestral laws and rituals, through their 'assemblies' (*synagogai*). Jews living in Greek cities and Rome itself had assimilated to the dominant Greek and Roman culture to varying degrees. In the sprawling imperial metropolis of Alexandria in Egypt mystically oriented elites such as explained by the philosopher Philo believed that by acquiring wisdom through the spiritual understanding of Scripture they could attain a transcendent immortality of soul as the truly wise, wealthy, nobly born and ruling spiritual aristocracy.

Most members of provincial elites who were subjected by Rome acquiesced in and became beneficiaries of the Roman imperial order, with its extremely wealthy and powerful families at the very top and the masses of subsistence peasants and urban poor at the productive base of the political economy. Philo's nephew Tiberias Alexander entered the Roman equestrian order and was even appointed governor of Judaea. Similarly, the intellectual elites of subjected peoples assimilated to the dominant culture; like the political–economic elite, they did not continue to cultivate the traditional culture of their origins or did not think of representing the interests of their own people, now subjugated by the Romans. In this respect Philo, and presumably some other diaspora Jewish intellectuals as well, were different. Such Jewish intellectuals created what postcolonial intellectuals might call a hybrid culture and identity. When their people came under attack, for example, Philo wrote a now famous appeal to the emperor Gaius.

Other diaspora Jews were likely oriented more to maintaining a traditional community life guided by their ancestral laws. Many Jews, having come to view the temple as a sacred centre, travelled from their cities in the diaspora as pilgrims to Jerusalem. Some of these 'Hellenist' Jews from the diaspora joined the Jesus-movement in its first few years in Jerusalem, that is, they became politicized in an anti-imperial direction in association with this upstart movement heretofore based mainly among the Galilaean peasants, such as its leaders in Jerusalem (Peter, James, John and James the brother of Jesus). Among the diaspora Jews who quickly became leaders in the movement were Saul of Tarsus and Barnabas from Cyprus, who later collaborated on a mission to diaspora Jewish communities in Cilicia and Cyprus, in which they began to accept non-Israelite peoples into the Jesus-movement. That experience must have helped Paul reach clarity on his own distinctive role in the wider mission of the movement: he was to be the lead apostle to the other, non-Israelite peoples.

It is evident from several of Paul's later letters that his own distinctive mission was an integral part of God's plan for the fulfilment of history. That is, Paul was operating according to a 'master-narrative', the kind of world-historical overview with which postcolonial theorists are uncomfortable. Paul's grand narrative, however, was an anti-imperial understanding of history, not an imperially imposed scheme. The dominant culture – shared, for example, by the later Jewish historian Josephus – understood history, and God's providential guidance, as working through Rome, recently ascended to the heights of imperial glory as the only remaining superpower in the Mediterranean world. Paul, and presumably others in the Jesus-movement as well, understood history as moving not through Rome but through Israel. Indeed, in the Roman crucifixion of Jesus Christ and his divine vindication as the true Lord of the world, God had brought about the fulfilment of the promises to Abraham whereby not only would Israel be a great people on its own land but also other peoples of the world would receive blessings. Now that God had fulfilled God's promises in Abraham's seed (Jesus), other peoples as well as Israel could receive the blessings available in Christ by joining the movement (Galatians 3–4). In the historical context of the Roman Empire, Paul's mission was to spearhead a movement among the peoples subjugated by Rome, a movement based in the history and cultural tradition of one of those subject peoples, Israel, and focused on the Roman crucifixion and divine vindication of the martyred peasant Messiah, Jesus, whose imminent return would mean God's final termination of Roman imperial rule.

After an extended mission among the Galatians and briefer sojourns in the Roman colony of Philippi and the Macedonian town of Thessalonica, Paul launched a more extended, eighteen-month mission in Corinth, the first large, cosmopolitan city he had visited since Antioch. As the new capital of the province of Achaia, Corinth was the centre of Roman imperial influence and control in Greece. The official language of the colony remained Latin, while Greek language and culture steadily regained ground. After Octavian/Augustus defeated his rival warlord Anthony at Actium and had formally established the empire, the Greek urban elite had constructed the burgeoning emperor cult, installing statues of the emperor in the temples to Greek gods, erecting shrines of the emperor in public spaces, building new temples to the emperor as the focal point of the forums at the centre of urban space, and dedicating week-long festivals and games to the emperor. The presence of the emperor, in fact, came to pervade public space. Corinth, like other cities of the empire, was controlled by a small circle of wealthy families who, as the chief clients of the imperial patronage, also sponsored the imperial cult. Democracy was a thing of the distant past, civic assemblies now being merely formal gatherings to hear and honour the elite. Under the sway of the tiny wealthy elite, some perhaps under their paternalistic patronage, the mass of urban residents would have been economically marginal artisans and labourers living close to subsistence level. Since most Corinthians were descendants of former slaves – perhaps the descendants of Syrians and Palestinians enslaved by Roman warlords in previous generations – and other urban riff-raff, virtually none of the ordinary residents of Corinth had any significant social status.

In Corinth, as in other mission sites, Paul formed a team with several other co-workers, such as Timothy, who accompanied him on his mission in other places, Prisca and Aquila, other diaspora Jews who had been expelled from Rome (were they former slaves?), and indigenous leaders who emerged during his mission in the city. Avoiding public spaces and attention, contrary to the common image of the missionary preacher of the gospel, Paul and his co-workers worked in private households, which they pulled together in occasional meetings of 'the whole assembly' for celebration of the Lord's Supper and sharing of prophecies, teaching and discussion. The scenario was far more like organizing cells and local units of a labour movement or anti-colonial movement than like modern European missionary practices. Paul and his co-workers were building a movement, not saving souls or founding a religion, which are modern misconceptions and projections.

Paul's Corinthian Correspondence

After Paul had gone on to Ephesus, he continued his communication with the assembly he had helped establish in Corinth through an exchange of letters. In 1 Cor. 5.9 he mentions a previous letter he had sent, then mentions that the Corinthians had written to him inquiring about several matters/issues. The letter we know as 1 Corinthians is, among other things, a response to the questions they asked in their letter. The letter we know as 2 Corinthians is a composite of several letters that Paul wrote over many months.

Like all of Paul's letters, the many letters to the Corinthians were not formal theological treatises written to lay out doctrine but ad hoc communications about particular issues that had arisen in the community or particular disagreements that (some) members of Paul's assembly in Corinth had with him. The recent resurgence of rhetorical analysis has made us increasingly aware that these letters are Paul's attempts to persuade the addressees (not) to take some course of action or position. It is evident in the Corinthian letters more than in others that there were several, often conflicting viewpoints in the new community that Paul and others had catalysed in the city and surrounding towns. We are in effect listening to one side of a many-sided conversation or argument. However, since Paul often quotes the statements and uses the language of some of those other voices in the Corinthian assembly, we can reconstruct at least some of those other viewpoints. This makes the Corinthian correspondence an unusual resource for investigating the struggles of a fledgling community of a movement among peoples subject to the Roman Empire, both the struggles internal to the community and those against the dominant Roman imperial order. If we, therefore, read Paul's Corinthian correspondence not as authoritative statements of Christian theology but as ad hoc arguments addressing issues with which the community of a nascent movement was concerned, we can catch informative glimpses of the struggles of an ancient anti-imperial movement.

The Corinthian correspondence is also of special importance because it addresses many key issues that must have emerged in the broader 'Pauline' movement. Indeed, 1 Corinthians is the principal letter in which Paul discusses matters such as the Lord's Supper, social and/or spiritual status, marital and sexual relations, slavery, relations with outsiders, community discipline, spiritual gifts and the resurrection. 1 Corinthians is also the letter in which occur the principal passages on which the prevailing view of Paul as a social conservative is based.

Comment on 1 Corinthians

Both 1 and 2 Corinthians are addressed to 'the *ekklesia* of God which is in Corinth'. To translate *ekklesia* with 'church' (i.e., the Lord's house) is seriously misleading, given its connotations of a merely religious community in modern Western societies. In ancient Greek cities the *ekklesia* was the political assembly of adult male citizens who constituted the body politic and gathered to deliberate on social, political, legal and religious matters. The term was used in the Greek translation of the Judaean 'laws' to refer to the 'assembly' of all adult male Israelites, also known as 'the assembly of Yahweh'. Paul's usage throughout his letters has this double meaning of the overall movement or community he is spearheading (in continuity with Israel) as the 'assembly of God' and as the equivalent of, hence replacement for, the assembly in a given city such as Corinth. It thus has connotations both of continuity with and fulfilment of the history of Israel and (over against!) of political opposition to and displacement of the official (and under Roman rule now merely formal) assemblies in the cities of his mission. It sounds pretentious as well as political, and it was.

The basic term Paul uses for his fundamental message, moreover, is not merely a religious term. Before Paul launched his mission, 'gospel' had become the standard term for the 'good news' that the Roman emperor, as the saviour of the world, had brought 'salvation', 'peace and security', and indeed a whole new era of history, to humankind. Again, in using 'gospel' for his basic message, Paul was opposing it directly and pointedly to the gospel of the imperial saviour and salvation. Such opposition to the imperial order occurs repeatedly throughout the Corinthian correspondence and other letters.

In his first long argument, 1 Corinthians 1–4, articulated at the outset in 1.10, Paul's principal concern is that the *ekklesia* maintain unity and concord. In this argument Paul borrows much of the language as well as the theme from Graeco-Roman political rhetoric, which regularly emphasized the importance of concord to the health and welfare of a city or the empire. Paul, however, is applying this political rhetoric to his own assembly. Moreover, insofar as he insists that the assembly of God in Corinth maintain its solidarity in independence and opposition to the dominant order, as will become increasingly evident, he is using the rhetoric of concord in opposition to the imperial order.

In the first several steps of the argument of 1 Corinthians 1–4, it is evident that Paul sees internal conflict in the Corinthian assembly as having to do with wisdom as a means of knowing God (1.17–2.5, esp 1.21). In countering what he sees as a problematic wisdom, Paul presents 'the wisdom of God' (1.21) that he portrays as evident in God's action in history. Thus, 'God chose what is foolish in the world to shame the wise, ... what is weak in the world to shame the strong', and so forth (1.27; see 'nobly-born', 1.26; 'rich ... kings' and so forth, 4.8-10). In the Roman imperial order, these terms refer to the political–economic and social elite whom the Romans supported to control every city and province in the empire.

Paul then says more ominously that the wisdom he speaks 'is not a wisdom of this age or of the rulers of this age, who are doomed to perish, but... God's wisdom in a *mysterion*, which God decreed before the ages for our glory. None of the rulers of this age understood this; for if they had they would not have crucified the Lord of glory' (1 Cor. 2.6-8). Paul here restates his anti-imperial gospel and 'master-narrative' in an 'apocalyptic' nutshell. 'Mystery' was almost a technical term in Judaean apocalyptic literature such as the book of Daniel (see esp. Daniel 2) – for which 'wisdom' was a synonym in the Dead Sea Scrolls – for God's plan for the fulfilment of history that would end the crisis in which a foreign empire ruled over the people of Israel. The apocalyptic visionaries received special revelation that God would judge the imperial rulers and restore the people to independent life directly under the kingship of God. Paul claims to have received precisely such a revelation in his *apokalupsis* of Christ, through which he received his gospel (Gal. 1.13-16), and gives a summary here. The rulers of this age, not being privy to the mystery, had brought about their own destruction by crucifying Christ, whom God had then exalted as the true emperor, 'the Lord of glory'.

In the standard Western scholarly attempts to avoid any political implications, especially anti-imperial implications, New Testament scholarship has regularly read 'the rulers of this age' through the later deutero-Pauline letters Colossians and Ephesians. There any direct political implications of the 'principalities and powers' can be defused by taking them as transcendent cosmic spiritual forces. In 1 Corinthians, however, Paul is not as 'mythological' as modern European interpreters have claimed. He does not need to mention the Roman emperor and his governor Pontius Pilate by name for us to recognize that he is speaking of the actual imperial rulers as those who are doomed to perish in the Christ events through which God is bringing history to fulfilment.

Postcolonial theorists are suspicious of historical grand narratives, such as British colonial histories of India or the Marxist scheme of world history in terms of successive modes of production, and would presumably be uneasy with Paul's apocalyptic scheme of historical fulfilment. Modern Western biblical scholars rooted in the European Enlightenment, of course, are very uncomfortable with Paul's apocalyptic 'mythology' and tend either to 'demythologize' it or, more recently, simply to ignore it. In doing so, however, they throw the political and anti-imperial baby out with the apocalyptic bath water in which it was sustained. In recent decades New Testament scholars have found yet another solution to Paul's problematic apocalyptic perspective. Borrowing the modern functionalist sociology that was developed to serve the cohesion of modern Western (imperial) advanced industrial society, they can reduce Paul's scheme of historical fulfilment to 'language' that was 'functional' for 'Pauline Christianity' in its adaptation to the realities of their world (Meeks 1983). By contrast, the collaborative 'subaltern studies' historians are finally taking seriously the popular anti-imperial movements in India previously dismissed as merely religious fanatics by Western (Enlightenment) historians. Perhaps postcolonial biblical critics can in parallel fashion find reinforcement for their criticism of colonial readings of the Bible, including the imperial master-narrative of New Testament studies, in Paul's anti-imperial apocalyptic master-narrative.

Paul provides enough clues in his occasionally abrupt and sarcastic argument against it for us to reconstruct the other view of wisdom that he sees behind the conflicts in 'his' Corinthian community. Recent critical studies have shown that there is no reason for and no explanation gained from reading later Christian Gnosticism back into the Corinthian assembly and that Paul really gives no indication of 'Judaizers' in Corinth at this point – two of the older explanations of the conflict in the Corinth community. Instead, virtually all of the terms that Paul cites that come from the Corinthians who are attached to wisdom as the means to know the divine parallel those found in Hellenistic Jewish literature, in particular the Wisdom of Solomon 6–10 and the treatises of Philo of Alexandria. That Paul implicates Apollos, who was known as an eloquent Jewish interpreter of Scripture from Alexandria, suggests that the wisdom that had become prominent in the Corinthian assembly was derived from just such an enlightened Jewish mystical theology in a diaspora centre, most likely Alexandria itself. By becoming fully imbued with *Sophia* as the means and contents of salvation (1 Cor. 1.19, 21), the wise soul could attain immortality, a transcendent spiritual status as truly wise, powerful, nobly born, mature, spiritual, rich and kingly (1.26; 2.6, 14-15; 4.8-10).

The characterizations of *Sophia* as the agent of creation and the means of salvation in such Hellenistic Jewish literature also provides the best explanation for the highly uncharacteristic predications Paul makes of Christ in 1 Cor. 8.6, which form part of his argument against Corinthian slogans that 'we all possess *gnosis*' and 'there is no god but (the) One' (8.1, 4), which are also best paralleled in such literature. Further, *Sophia* as the agent and contents of spiritual salvation, which is the true meaning of the scriptural stories of the exodus and wilderness wandering, including the 'rock' and the 'manna' and the 'pillar of fire' as symbols of heavenly Wisdom, provides the best explanation for the uncharacteristic discourse that Paul begins and suddenly counters about 'the cloud and the sea' and 'spiritual food and spiritual drink from the spiritual rock' in 1 Cor. 10.1-4. Personal attachment to and intimacy with heavenly *Sophia* would also help explain the practice of separating from one's spouse and refusing sexual relations behind the Corinthian slogan Paul cites in 1 Cor. 7.1.

This is a very different – and what we would reasonably call religious – way of responding to the rather complete domination of subjugated peoples' lives by the Roman imperial order. It resembles what moderns might call personal spirituality, particularly what has become known as 'new age' spirituality. Paul's objection, in addition to the fact that it was attracting Corinthians away from his own gospel, was that the emphasis on personal spiritual transcendence of the oppressive imperial order seemed to disrupt rather than reinforce community cooperation and solidarity. In any case, we can discern through Paul's arguments that there were two options in the Corinthian assembly for how to respond to the Roman imperial order: on the one hand, attainment of high personal spiritual status and immortality of soul through close attachment to heavenly Wisdom; on the other, Paul's insistence that God had inaugurated the fulfilment of history and the termination of the Roman imperial order in the events of Christ's crucifixion by the Roman rulers and vindication as the true Lord by God. Paul further insists that the existence and solidarity of the assembly in Corinth itself is part and parcel of how God is taking action against the Roman imperial order. That solidarity of the community constitutes his concern in the next several steps of his overall argument in 1 Corinthians.

In the next three or four closely related shorter arguments (1 Cor. 5; 6.1-11, 12-20; 7) and in the next longer argument (1 Corinthians 8.1–11.1), Paul deals with several related issues of potential interactions between the assembly and the wider society in which they are still living, issues of *porneia* (more than simply 'sexual immorality') and *eidololatria* (more than is connoted by 'idolatry'). These were the principal aspects of the dominant Graeco-Roman social–cultural ethos that diaspora Jews as well as Judaeans and Galilaeans in Palestine found utterly unacceptable according to their own covenantal way of life. Jews still solidly grounded in their traditional Israelite covenantal principles, protecting the integrity of the (patriarchal) family, found intolerable the permissive, promiscuous Greek social ethos that allowed well-off adult males free sexual access to their female and male slaves, male protégés and female 'entertainers' as well as their wives. Further, Jews who still held firm in the covenantal principle of exclusive loyalty to their God found it impossible that Jews living in diaspora cities could participate in the sacrifices and meals (to the multiple gods and goddesses) that constituted the multiple overlapping tribal, city and empire-wide bonds that held the imperial social order together. Standard Western interpreters of Paul have seen fairly clearly that Paul appears to give mixed messages with regard to sexual relations and marriage, while they have often misread Paul's arguments on 'meat offered to idols' to indicate that he himself shared the 'enlightened', 'universalist' viewpoint. While Paul is remarkably flexible on matters of marriage, he is adamant that assembly members (of Christ) avoid sharing in rituals that constitute social–political bonds besides those of the assembly itself.

His instructions to the community to take formal action, in an assembly in the power of our Lord Jesus and in the presence of his own spirit, to exclude the man living with his father's wife (1 Corinthians 5) is a vivid illustration of how he expected the *ekklesia* to be a tightly knit body with rigorous internal community discipline. However, they were not to cut themselves off from the rest of the society (from which they aimed to recruit), not to worry about contamination by contact with wicked outsiders.

The next argument, which forbids them taking cases of internal conflict to the civic courts (1 Cor. 6.1-11), makes it abundantly clear that Paul thought of his assemblies as local communities of an alternative society that would take care of its own affairs without interacting at all with the official political order. This would appear to be an extension to the new communities organized by Paul and co-workers of the practices of diaspora Jewish synagogues and/or of village communities in Galilee and Judaea. Similar instructions about handling internal community conflict within the self-sufficient community appear in the Gospel of Matthew (18.15-22) and in the Qumran community (1QS 5-6). Again, in this argument by Paul, we see a vivid illustration of an apocalyptic scenario or master-narrative of subjugated people, currently subject to the imperial order, who will imminently share in the divine judgment of their unrighteous oppressors, as they enter the participatory popular sovereignty of the kingdom of God (1 Cor. 6.2-3, 10-11).

The first half of Paul's discussion and advice regarding marriage and sexual relations is remarkable for that or any age for its unprecedented rhetoric of equality. So remarkable in fact in balancing the usual husband's authority over his wife's body perfectly with the unheard-of assertion that the wife has authority over her husband's body that we may well be suspicious of his motive. Indeed, as Antoinette Wire (1994) has argued, Paul seems to have emphasized the actual and hypothetical cases of men's inability to control their own dangerous tendencies to *porneia* in order to set up his encouragement of women to relinquish their authority and rights to help control their menfolk's dangerous drives. In the second half of the argument, Paul simply reverts to the usual anthropocentric pattern of addressing only the males.

That Paul gives two further illustrations, from circumcised and uncircumcised and slave and free, in a discussion involving male and female signals that this discussion is focused on the social ideal of the Jesus-movement articulated in its baptismal formula: 'There is no longer Jew or Greek, there is no longer slave or free, there is no longer male and female; for all of you are one in Christ Jesus' (Gal. 3.28). This suggests that the movement did indeed intend to be an alternative society that has broken through the principal divisions and power-relations that characterized the kyriarchal Roman imperial order, with its economic base in the enslavement of conquered peoples and women's work institutionalized in the slave-holding patriarchal family, and the (ancient orientalist) Graeco-Roman sense of superiority over Jews and other barbarians. In his argument in 1 Corinthians 7, Paul is clearly compromising the ideal to which he is alluding both by making this special appeal to the women and by using the movement's rhetoric of equality to manipulate them into yielding to his appeal. Otherwise, his advice is quite flexible, stating general principles applicable to different cases, but in every case allowing for exceptions.

Traditional established Christian and modern scholarly reading has consistently twisted Paul's second additional illustration of his 'rule in all the assemblies' to legitimate the established political–economic order of inequality and oppression. In English translations, the King James Version and even the New Revised Standard Version illustrate the self-serving imperialist reading that legitimated slave-holding and formed the traditional establishment scholarly basis for understanding Paul as a social conservative. 'Were you a slave when called? Do not be concerned about it. Even if you can gain your freedom, make use of your present condition now more than ever' (1 Cor. 7.21). The Lutheran doctrine of one's God-given 'vocation' (*Beruf*), of course, supported this reading as a logical illustration of Paul's general rule (7.17, 20, 24): 'Let each of you remain in the condition in which you were called'.

Two considerations, however, make this reading of Paul's illustration from slavery impossible in the context of his overall argument in 1 Corinthians 7. First, the incomplete second half of Paul's statement in Greek lacks a noun, 'If you can gain it, rather use [it]!', which must be supplemented from the closest previous noun, which is 'freedom'. The more correct reading in Greek would therefore be: 'If you can gain [your freedom], avail yourself of the opportunity!' Second, this translation fits the rhetorical pattern that prevails throughout the argument in 1 Cor. 7.1-16. Paul gives a general principle, then offers an exception. Thus, also in 7.17-24 he states his general 'rule in all the assemblies', which he illustrates first from circumcised and uncircumcised, which indeed fits! That is what he was at pains to explain in the letter to the Galatians, that the uncircumcised need not change into Israelites to receive blessings! However, in his second illustration, from slavery, he realizes that he needs to make an exception. According to the social ideal of the movement, there is no longer slave and free! To realize that, then, he had to encourage slaves, if they received the unlikely chance to become free, to seize the opportunity, by all means. As he asserts adamantly in the ensuing argument (7.23): 'You were bought with a price; do not become slaves of human masters'.

The principal proof-text on the basis of which scholars have traditionally claimed that Paul was a social conservative turns out to be a self-interested mistranslation! Since, as he states a few paragraphs later, Paul firmly believed that 'the appointed time has grown short, … the present form of this world is passing away', there was no point in agitating against the slave system on which the whole Roman imperial order was based. That would have been analogous to launching an attack today on multinational, global capitalism, on which the new imperial order policed by American military power is based. Yet, Paul clearly did encourage slaves to take the chance to become free here in 1 Cor. 7.21-23. This parallels his argument in the letter to Philemon – if indeed Onesimus was even a slave and not just a previously ne'er-do-well brother of Philemon – where he urges Philemon none too gently to henceforth treat him not as (if) a slave, but as a brother. There is, however, no point arguing whether Paul was a social conservative or progressive. Both categories are far wide of the mark. He was rather spearheading an anti-imperial movement of communities that

supposedly embodied ideals of an alternative society – although he did regress
a bit with regard to the supposed new equality of women and men.

The long argument of 1 Corinthians 8–10 climaxes in Paul's insistence that
members of the *ekklesia* cannot share in the table of the Lord *and* the table
of demons (other gods/idols). Western New Testament interpreters, viewing
Paul as an enlightened intellectual (like themselves) as well as the hero of faith
versus Jewish parochialism, usually understood Paul as sharing the universalist
Enlightenment theology he ostensibly agrees with at the beginning of the argument (8.1-4). Of course, in his sensitivity to the scruples of the less enlightened
'weak' community members, Paul balanced his enlightened theology with the
ethical principle articulated in 1 Cor. 8.13. The main point, however, was the
new-found freedom of social relationships made possible by the enlightened
theology, as stated in 10.23-30. The habit of reading Paul's letters as lessons
of theological instruction (*pericopes*/Sunday scriptural lessons) and/or separate
theological statements (individual scriptural verses) greatly facilitated such an
Enlightenment theology reading.

With the clarity generated by rhetorical criticism, we can now recognize that,
after 8.1-12 introduces the issue and the seeming digression of 9.1-27 provides
an autobiographical illustration of the principle articulated in 8.13, Paul's argument climaxes in the blunt warning of 10.1-13 and the adamant prohibition of
participation in sacrificial meals stated in 10.14-22, with 10.23-30 as, in effect,
an afterthought on subsidiary related matters.

In Greek and Roman cities, sacrificial meals in temples of the gods were the
principal rituals by which the various overlapping networks of social relationships that made up the social order – families, 'tribes', 'associations', cities,
etc. – were constituted and maintained. They were hardly 'empty' rituals or
'superstitions'. Paul's discussion in 10.14-22 is not simply a 'sacramental
realism', as labelled by certain theologians, but a social–political realism as
well. He insists that in order not to be socially engaged in, socially woven into
the very fabric of, the dominant social order, members of God's new assembly
in Corinth must not participate at all in such sacrificial meals. Here is yet
another powerful indication that Paul understood the *ekklesia* as an alternative
society to the Roman imperial order. Being a member of the assembly was
not merely a matter of theology, of belief in the reality of the One God, but
of exclusive loyalty to that God and the exclusive engagement in the body-
politic of the alternative assembly in which God's new people in the making
was embodied. Participation in the assembly meant a commitment of one's
complete social–political life and simply cannot be compared to the modern
Western theological concept of faith, modern Western religion as individual
belief, or participation in a church as a 'voluntary association' in the typical
North American pattern. Moreover, Paul himself was not a theologian but
a movement leader insisting on exclusive loyalty and solidarity in the local
communities of the movement.

We can also observe at key passages in this argument how, in Paul's attempt to engage the slogans and key symbols of a position with which he disagrees, he constructs 'hybrid' formulations that became central in subsequent (Pauline) Christian Christology. 1 Corinthians 8.6 and 10.4 are the basic 'proof-texts' for (the genuine) Paul's supposed articulation of the pre-existence of Christ (as the second person of the Trinity, in later creeds). Once we recognize that in this and other arguments of 1 Corinthians Paul is engaging, often citing or himself using the slogans and key concepts of (some of) the Corinthians he is trying to persuade, we must also recognize that he has applied to Christ certain predicates that Corinthians, perhaps under the influence of the Alexandrian Jew Apollos, believed about *Sophia*, predicates that are standard in Philo and the Wisdom of Solomon.

In the Hellenistic Jewish spiritual interpretation of the Scriptures represented in Philo and the Wisdom of Solomon, heavenly *Sophia* is understood as the divine instrument of creation and salvation and is identified with the water from the rock and the manna in the wilderness. It is in trying to displace *Sophia* as the object of some Corinthians' devotion that Paul substitutes Christ in the predications they were making of heavenly Wisdom. This results in the predication of Christ as the 'through which are all things' in 8.6 and the identification of Christ as 'the spiritual rock' in 10.4 – that is, that Christ was ostensibly present at the creation and operative in the history of Israel. Otherwise, one looks in vain in the rest of the genuine Pauline correspondence for any indication of the 'pre-existence' of Christ. Paul's rhetorical manoeuvring resulted in what became Christological doctrine of the imperially established church. The emphasis in Paul's own argument, however, comes in the ensuing sentences and steps of his argument, where he first calls on the theologically enlightened Corinthians to let their fellow community members' concerns guide their behaviour outside the community (8.7-13) and then warns those excited about transcendent spiritual realities about the dangers of becoming caught up in the religious/cultural celebrations that engage them in values and social relations that distract them from full commitment to the process of liberation into which God has led them (10.5-13; leading into the climax of the argument, 10.14-22).

In recent years scholars have been divided about whether the short argument in 11.3-16 was originally part of Paul's letter known as 1 Corinthians. Much of the language is as dissimilar to Paul's as it is similar to the later letters, such as Ephesians (and 11.2 forms a natural introduction to 11.17-34, but an awkward introduction to 11.3-16). The chain of ontological subordination, God–Christ–man–woman, in 11.3, 7 – despite the apparent qualification of 11.12 – is particularly foreign to the patterns of thinking elsewhere in Paul's genuine letters. As suggested by its placement after 14.40 in some ancient manuscripts, the sentences currently in 1 Cor. 14.34-35 (not vv. 33b-36, which are placed in parentheses in the NRSV) would appear more clearly to be a later gloss subsequently placed at two different places in the developing text of

1 Corinthians. If either or both of these passages were original to Paul, then he had backed away dramatically from the ideal of 'no longer male and female' part of the ideal articulated in the baptismal formula cited in Gal. 3.28. Neither passage, however, fits well with the rest of the arguments of 1 Corinthians and should probably be taken as later additions related to the development of the deutero-Pauline viewpoint expressed in Colossians, Ephesians and the 'Pastoral' Epistles, which reverted toward the kyriarchal patterns of the Roman imperial order.

In 1 Cor. 11.17-34 Paul scolds the Corinthians for their procedure at celebrations of the Lord's Supper, before repeating the 'tradition' he had taught them (vv. 23-25) as a basis for further admonition. His portrayal of the procedure that he finds unacceptable resembles that at typical Greek and Roman group meals or banquets. Thus, in insisting that there be no divisions and hierarchically differential consumption in the Lord's Supper of the *ekklesia* but rather an expression of the solidarity of the community, he is also insisting that his assembly's celebration be dramatically different from the usual meal patterns in which differences in status were affirmed and embodied. The statement he adds to the tradition, that they 'proclaim the Lord's death until he comes', reminds them again that what they are doing, besides embodying the solidarity of the community, is to 'proclaim' the Roman crucifixion of Jesus as an anti-Roman rebel leader and his vindication in exaltation, from which he will come to terminate the imperial order.

1 Corinthians 12–14 is a sustained discussion of 'spiritual gifts' in general. Yet, Paul is clearly most concerned to persuade the Corinthians that 'speaking in tongues' should be subjected to interpretation in order to make it intelligibly edifying to the whole community, which he argues in ch. 14. In the second step of his argument on spiritual gifts, 12.12-26, Paul borrows a stock metaphor from ancient Roman politics comparing the 'body-politic' to a human body. In Latin literature, the metaphor was used by the elite to persuade the plebeian poor to sacrifice their own interests for the sake of the whole, headed by the wealthy and powerful. Paul's use differs dramatically. He transforms the metaphor into an argument for an egalitarian spirit among the members of the body-politic, such that the ostensibly superior do not claim greater honour and respectability (as in the imperial order), while the ostensibly inferior receive greater honour for their indispensability. In yet another argument for the solidarity of the assembly, he stresses that members of the body-politic should 'care for one another'. Yet, in his next step he ranks the spiritual gifts, that is, leadership of the *ekklesia*, so that apostles (such as himself) are first and 'tongues' are last (12.27-31). The now famous 'hymn to love', full of irony insofar as he adopts the 'high-falutin' style of those he is arguing against, serves to elaborate on his exhortation to take care for one another.

It seems quite possible that the term *glossolalia* is Paul's own invention and that the Corinthian 'spiritual gift' he is concerned about was ecstatic prophecy, in which the spirit-seized person transcended normal social interaction and speech. This would explain Paul's insistence on interpretation to achieve some sort of intelligible message edifying to the community. Paul himself has clearly experienced an apocalyptic vision and had received 'the word of the Lord' as a prophet (see Gal. 1.13-16; 2 Cor. 12.1-5; 1 Thess. 4.14-18). Indeed, he encourages prophecy in the Corinthian assembly. Yet, he insists that all be done for the building up of the body-politic. In his mind and argument, prophecy was to enable the movement to understand, and maintain its struggle within, the historical situation in which it stood. He rejects the more ecstatic form of prophecy as a personal spiritual experience if it brings no intelligible benefit to the community or movement.

In 1 Corinthians 15 Paul presents an argument for, really more of a reassertion of, the reality and importance of resurrection. After establishing what he must believe will be common ground of the movement's basic creedal statement of the crucifixion and resurrection of Christ, he states the problem. Some of the Corinthians simply do not believe in the reality of the resurrection. This should not be at all surprising, considering that most of the Corinthians would have been socialized into a culture oriented to the natural and social–political–economic order, not to historical conflict between peoples and empires. The Israelite culture of Paul was unusual in the ancient Mediterranean world. The intellectual elite and perhaps many or most people in cities such as Corinth probably understood the soul as the true self, attached to the body, by which the soul was involved in corruptibility and mortality. Resuscitation of that corruptible body was hardly an attractive idea: Paul cannot really explain, so he simply reasserts the reality of the resurrection and then creates yet another hybrid conceptualization, what surely must have seemed to those Corinthians an oxymoron of the 'incorruptible' and 'immortal' body.

Especially interesting for postcolonial criticism must be Paul's paragraph reasserting that 'in fact Christ has been raised from the dead' (15.24-28). Paul proceeds to walk the Corinthians though the final events in which history will be brought to a conclusion. The resurrection itself is evidently a restoration or renewal of historical life. What has been difficult for Western rationalist interpreters to grasp is the declaration that apparently the exalted Christ, whom Paul elsewhere asserts is now the true emperor of the world now reigning until he has put all his enemies under his feet (15.25; see Phil. 3.19-21), is imminently to 'destroy every ruler and every authority and power' (15.24). Like 1 Cor. 2.6-8, this is usually read through the lens of the spiritualizing transformations of Pauline thinking in Colossians and Ephesians. It seems rather that in 'every ruler' Paul is referring to the imperial rulers. Then, because he is constructing an argument for the resurrection of the dead, he adds a sentence about a spiritual enemy, Death. In Paul's way of thinking, and in the Judaean apocalyptic tradition in which he was rooted, the resurrection of the dead was not simply a restoration of 'those who have fallen asleep' to embodied societal life. The historical problem for which God's deliverance and resurrection of the dead was the solution was oppressive foreign imperial rule. The resurrection of Christ meant that God had vindicated him after his martyrdom by Roman crucifixion. God had also made Christ the counter-emperor who would imminently destroy the imperial rulers, and his resurrection was the 'first-fruits' or 'down-payment' on the general resurrection, when imperial rule would be terminated once and for all. The thrust of Paul's whole argument in 1 Corinthians, stated explicitly at 15.24, was decidedly anti-imperial.

Comment on 2 Corinthians

2 Corinthians is usually seen as a composite of (fragments of) two or even four or five different letters that Paul wrote to the Corinthians. The simplest division is between 2 Corinthians 1–9 and 10–13; the most complex finds coherent letter fragments in 1.1–2.13 + 7.5-16; 2.14–6.13 + 7.2-4; 8; 9; and 10–13. In these letters, particularly 10–13, often called the 'letter of tears', Paul is clearly in serious conflict with (some in) the Corinthian assembly. As Shelly Matthews (1994) points out, attempts to arrange these letter fragments into a sequence whereby the more conciliatory come last may be suspect, because they are rooted in and result in a picture of the paradigmatic apostle as successfully managing a reconciliation with a cantankerous community and emerging as the unquestioned authority figure. We simply cannot tell from the letter fragments whether genuine reconciliation happened or whether it had anything to do with Paul's arguments in these letters. What is evident from 2 Corinthians, however it is divided up, is that Paul's attempts at persuasion in 1 Corinthians were not particularly effective in bringing the Corinthian assembly into acquiescence in his viewpoint and authority. Paul's Corinthian correspondence, therefore, indicates, if nothing else, just how difficult it was for a fledgling group of people of diverse viewpoints and interests to coalesce into a coherent and disciplined community. The ideal of a cohesive self-governing community may have been derived from the traditional peasant village and/or the diaspora Jewish synagogue. However, in contrast to both village community and diaspora Jewish synagogue, which were comprised of people who already had mutual bonds from belonging to the same community for generations, it was difficult in the extreme to mould a disparate group of people of diverse backgrounds who had wound up in an imperial colony or city as the result of disruption on the part of imperial forces of their previous, more traditionally grounded lives.

The difficulty of forming a coherent community was surely compounded by the multiple and diverse leadership that worked in the Corinthian mission. One factor in the conflict that Paul addressed in 1 Corinthians was that some members of the assembly had coalesced around Apollos, who had clearly taught a devotion to heavenly *Sophia* and an enlightened *gnosis* of God that Paul was not at all happy with. Interpreters of the letters contained in 2 Corinthians often conclude that new 'super-apostles' had come into Corinth after the writing of 1 Corinthians – some sort of 'Judaizers' in an older view, and what have been labelled wonder-working 'divine men' in a more recent construction. A careful reading of the language in Paul's arguments in 2 Corinthians, after gaining familiarity with the way he engages the Corinthian 'spirituals' in the arguments of 1 Corinthians, however, suggests rather a continuity of issues and conflictual positions in the whole Corinthian correspondence.

Conflicts over certain Corinthians' and/or Paul's 'boasting' and over Paul's refusal to accept economic support from the Corinthians for his work among them recur and escalate from 1 Corinthians into 2 Corinthians, where both issues loom large in more than one letter fragment. Paul's lack of eloquence similarly escalates as a contentious issue between the apostle and (some in) the assembly. Certain themes or terms, such as 'consciousness' (not 'conscience'!) and 'ministry/service' (*diakonia*, etc.) are distinctive (while not exclusive) to the Corinthian correspondence among Paul's genuine letters (1 Cor. 8.7, 10, 12; 10.25, 27, 28, 29; 2 Cor. 1.12; 4.2; 5.11; 1 Cor. 3.5; 12.5; 16.15; 2 Cor. 3.3, 6, 7, 8, 9; 4.1; 5.18; 8.19-20; 11.15, 23; etc.). Much of the other language of spiritual status is evidently of the Corinthian 'spirituals' that Paul is citing in his responses in 1 Corinthians, such as the contrast between weak and strong, foolish and wise, poor and rich, humbled and exalted/glorious. Distinctive terms or symbols or transcendent spiritual entities, such as (wisdom as) a mirror (of the divine), the 'image of God', and the Spirit, which figure in the transcendent spirituality that (some) Corinthians learned apparently from Apollos, as mentioned in 1 Corinthians, crop up again in Paul's arguments in 2 Corinthians. In fact, virtually all of the characteristics or claims of what Paul labels the 'super-apostles' – such as being Israelites, descendants of Abraham, ministers of Christ, and proclaiming another Jesus and a different gospel (2 Cor. 11.4-6, 24, 22-23) – fit Apollos, as known from the fragments of information about him supplied in 1 Corinthians and Acts 18. Further, it is not the 'super-apostles' who claim to perform the 'signs of a true apostle', that is, 'wonders and mighty works' (12.12), but Paul himself (e.g., 1 Thess. 1.5; Gal. 3.1-5; 1 Cor. 2.4; Rom. 15.19)! It seems most likely that the conflicts between Paul and (some of) the Corinthians that he addresses in 1 Corinthians had simply escalated, so that he addresses them again and again in his subsequent letters, now collected in what we know as 2 Corinthians.

Much of the argument in sections of 2 Corinthians consists mainly of Paul's self-defence of his ministry. He makes frequent appeals to his weakness and suffering. From the particular instances to which he refers we can piece together a picture of a driven man repeatedly in serious trouble with representatives of the dominant political order. To be sure, he plays his repeated 'run-ins' with the authorities for all they are worth for rhetorical effect with his Corinthian critics, so we must read critically, focusing mainly on specific cases and the tone, for implications of what those 'run-ins' were all about.

In 1 Cor. 4.8-13 his mocking contrast of his own weakness, ill-repute and outright abuse, on the one hand, with the exalted spiritual status of the Corinthian 'spirituals', on the other, includes an allusion to his having been thrown into the public arena, presumably with other prisoners, to entertain the crowds. In 1 Cor. 15.32 he further mentions that in his next mission site he had 'fought with wild animals at Ephesus'. This is not merely an extravagant metaphor for opposition within the nascent assembly at Ephesus. While we should probably not take the reference to fighting wild animals literally, Paul had apparently been confronted by the authorities in Ephesus with the prospect of some such severe punishment.

In 2 Cor. 1.8-9 he mentions the *thlipsis* he experienced in the province of Asia (western Asia Minor): 'We were so utterly, unbearably crushed that we despaired of life itself'. This term, often translated rather vaguely with 'affliction' in New Testament literature (e.g., the book of Revelation), refers to political persecution, official or informal attacks against leaders and/or members of the communities of the movement. His reference to the 'severe ordeal of persecution' that the assemblies in Macedonia (presumably the Thessalonians and Philippians) had undergone indicates that his own arrests or attacks were part of a broader pattern of official or unofficial attacks on the communities of the movement elsewhere, if not in Corinth. It is conceivable but not at all certain that the severe 'persecution' Paul mentions in 2 Cor. 1.8-9 refers to the same incident as in 1 Cor. 15.32 at Ephesus, the provincial capital of the province of Asia. It is clear from Philippians 1–2 that Paul was placed in prison under military guard and on trial, apparently in Ephesus. It seems likely that he was in serious trouble in Ephesus/Asia more than once.

Whatever the precise circumstances, he says that it seemed like a 'sentence of death', that is, based on some sort of official court 'sentence' that placed him in a life-threatening situation. Again, Paul interprets this 'sentence of death' as a (potential) martyrdom for resistance to empire, which would be vindicated by God by resurrection. He repeats the same interpretation in a more general reference to 'affliction and persecution' in 2 Cor. 4.7-23. The focus of his argument is a defence of his ministry. However, by immediately interpreting his own suffering as an imitation of Christ's crucifixion by the Roman rulers and anticipating resurrection as God's vindication of martyrs for resistance to it, he consistently places his experiences of persecution in the broader context of the Roman imperial order, his opposition to which is the reason for them.

In 2 Cor. 6.4-8 Paul mentions afflictions and persecutions in a longer list of sufferings that become more specific at points about 'beatings, imprisonments and riots'. The most specific list, where he seems to be remembering particular cases many of which were official and formal actions, comes in 2 Cor. 11.23-27. As if it were a standard experience for 'apostles' such as himself, he recites that he had undergone 'far more imprisonments, with countless floggings, and often near death. Five times I have received from the Judaeans the forty lashes minus one, three times I was beaten with rods. Once I received a stoning...'. Here is a list of specific incidents in which Paul was formally and/or officially sentenced and corporally punished. Paul here refers to standard forms of official punishment, by Judaean (stoning as well as the thirty-nine lashes) and Roman (rods) authorities. Judaean officials, in Palestine or in diaspora synagogues, precisely in order to retain their rights to self-governance, needed to avoid any appearance of Judaeans disrupting or challenging the Roman imperial order. Paul himself, of course, had earlier been active in rounding up leaders or members of the Jesus-movement as threats to Judaean/Jewish attempts to maintain Jewish traditions and self-government, under the suspicious eye of Roman officials (Gal. 1.13-14; Phil. 3.4-6). The beating with rods was the standard mode of public flogging in Roman cities. Carried publicly before Roman magistrates, the 'rods' were both instruments of coercion and intimidating symbols of Roman power. Paul's reference to 'bearing the marks of Jesus branded on my body' in Gal. 6.17 may well pertain to such corporal punishment by Judaean and/or Roman authorities.

Finally, in connection with Paul's reference to the many times that he was apprehended and condemned to punishment for behaviour threatening to the Roman imperial order, we should note the dramatic and usual – and unmistakably imperial – imagery he uses regarding his mission activities in 2 Cor. 2.14-16: 'But thanks be to God, who in Christ always leads us in triumphal procession, and through us spreads in every place the fragrance that comes from knowing him... to those who are being saved and among those who are perishing'. Paul here borrows the imagery of, and in the process mocks, the great official Roman imperial triumphs. These were elaborately staged public celebrations featuring grand military processions of great Roman warlords and their legions, with huge floats portraying their devastation of enemy cities and lands and displaying captured enemy combatants, including the enemy leader, who was ritually executed at the end of the procession. Such celebrations were meant to portray in great pomp and splendour the utter humiliation and devastation of conquered peoples who had the audacity to challenge the supremacy and military might of Rome. The Judaean historian Josephus provides a lengthy description of the Triumph of Vespasian and Titus over the rebellious Judaeans, in which the enemy general Simon bar Giora, 'king of the Judaeans', was paraded in chains with other rebels and executed to the acclaim of the Roman mob (*JW* 7.123-57).

While often seemingly unaware of, or at least inattentive to, these imperial triumphs, many Western interpreters are bothered by Paul's portrayal here of God as the agent of Paul's humiliation and degradation. The rhetorical effect of this image, however, would be twofold. First, the hearers/readers, who would be only too familiar with Roman imperial triumphs and the devastating imperial conquests that they celebrated, would understand that Roman imperial rule of the world in general, and the cities of Paul's mission in particular, were the actual immediate cause of Paul's humiliation. In addition, the hearers/readers would further see in Paul's attempt to explain his changes of travel plans the constraints of periodic arrests and imprisonment that he was subject to as he moved from city to city. However, by making God the one who is leading Paul in celebration of a triumph, Paul suggests that God is ultimately in control of history and is taking action precisely in Paul's own mission both to deliver those in the movement (from the imperial 'salvation' imposed by the saviour Caesar) and to condemn 'those who are being destroyed' in the divine judgment of the imperial order. The pattern of thinking is the same as in 1 Cor. 1.18, 26-28; 2.6-8. Paul's whole mission, like the Christ events of crucifixion, resurrection and *parousia*, the framework within which it fits and which it imitates, is taking place in the historical crisis in which God is bringing an end to oppressive Roman imperial rule.

Many Western scholars still interpret these passages, in innocuous terms, as Paul's references to being 'socially disadvantaged'. Even Western interpreters who are most aware of the (Judaean) apocalyptic perspective and scenario with which Paul views the world obscure the seemingly obvious political character of these 'afflictions' and Paul's anti-imperial interpretation of them. Paul is caught up in the transcendent apocalyptic war of light versus darkness or God's 'invasion of the cosmos'. In modern terms, Paul's repeated 'run-ins', trials and corporal punishments by the imperial authorities and their local subordinates would have to be described as those of an anti-imperial militant and activist – and one whose anti-imperial activities were international! In 1 Corinthians Paul reminded the *ekklesia* in Corinth that in celebrating the Lord's Supper they were 'proclaiming the Lord's death until he comes', a gesture of defiance and resistance to the Roman 'rulers of this age', who in crucifying the true 'Lord of glory' had become unwitting agents of their own imminent destruction (1 Cor. 11.26; 2.6-8). He portrayed his own mission activities, for which he was repeatedly arrested and punished, to the point of near-martyrdom, as repetitions of Christ's martyrdom and vindication, as analogous acts of resistance to the empire, which God was condemning and imminently bringing to an end in those very acts.

The collection for (the poor among) the saints in Jerusalem that Paul is organizing in 2 Corinthians 8–9 as well as in 1 Cor. 16.1-4 provides a dramatic confirmation that not simply Paul but the wider movement he was spearheading was attempting to embody an alternative society to the Roman imperial order. The *ekklesia* Paul was catalysing was not a religious cult but a comprehensive social movement that had an integral economic dimension, indeed an economic dimension that was international. At the very outset, apparently, the earliest community in Jerusalem led by Peter and others of the Twelve had practised communal economic sharing, perhaps after the traditional pattern of Israelite village communities (Acts 2.44-45; 4.32–5.6). A similar communal economic sharing was practised by the scribal–priestly community at Qumran that left the

Dead Sea Scrolls. When the Jerusalem leaders Peter, James and John agree to allow Paul and Barnabas to expand the movement among other, non-Israelite peoples, the one stipulation was that they should 'remember the poor' (Gal. 2.1-10). The seemingly stock phrase used here suggests that the practice of making a collection among the expanding assemblies of the movement was common and that Paul simply extended it to the new assemblies he catalysed among other peoples. In reciprocal relations with the central assembly in Jerusalem, other nascent communities were to send economic assistance to the poor there. As Paul explains later in Romans (15.27; see Isa. 56.7), the assemblies of the other peoples should 'be of service' to Israel in material goods, since they had come to share in Israel's 'spiritual blessings'. He seems to have a similar reciprocal 'balance' in mind in 2 Cor. 8.13-14.

Paul's passing comment in his instructions in 1 Cor. 16.1-4, that he had given the same instructions to the assemblies of Galatia, indicates that he had taken the collection seriously as an important material as well as symbolic gesture from the outset of his extended mission. That he writes at length about it in 2 Corinthians 8–9 means that he attributed considerable importance to it during the turmoil of his mission in Macedonia, Achaia/Corinth and Asia/Ephesus in the early 50s. By the time he wrote Romans, of course, it may have taken on an added personal dimension as his symbolic 'delivery' to the Jerusalem leaders, as proof of the validity of his mission, about which they were clearly sceptical, before he sought their blessing on extending his mission to Spain in the west (Rom. 15.22-33). To motivate the respective assemblies to donate as generously as they can to the collection, Paul plays them off against one another. He 'boasts' to the Corinthians about how eager the assemblies of Macedonia are, despite their severe recent ordeal in 1 Cor. 8.1-6. He then indicates that he has 'boasted' to the Macedonians about the eagerness of the Corinthians, hence they had better 'come through'. Just to make sure, however, he is sending a delegation ahead to make sure a suitably 'bountiful' gift will be awaiting his own arrival.

Westerners and others who live today in very comfortable economic circumstances probably cannot appreciate the level of poverty at which the vast majority of ancient peasants and urbanites (including artisans and/or those who 'had houses') lived. This is reason for the suggestion of weekly titbits in 1 Cor. 16.1-4. The resources available were extremely limited, yet the communities as well as the 'apostles' attributed great importance to such gestures of reciprocity. It is significant to note Paul's pointed choice of language in 1 Cor. 8.8 and 24. The meaning of *agape* that he had praised, in a style that mocked the prized eloquence of the Corinthian 'spirituals', lay precisely in concrete social-material mutual caring, such as giving to the collection for '(the poor among) the saints'.

Particularly in today's emerging neo-imperialism of global capitalism, which parallels the centralization of resources in the Roman imperial political economy, we should note yet another important dimension of the collection that Paul was administering. Seemingly magnanimous loans by the World Bank or the International Monetary Fund to the poor and 'developing' countries turn out to drain economic resources from those countries and further impoverish their people. Similarly, the combination of the payment of tribute to Caesar by some subject peoples and the expanding patronage system sponsored by the Roman imperial regime steadily drained resources upward to increasingly wealthy local and imperial ruling class. The collection organized by Paul and other leaders of the assemblies forms a dramatic contrast of a horizontal movement of economic resources, in direct opposition to the hierarchical vertical movement of resources in the empire. Besides comprising an 'international' movement of poor peoples, the local assemblies of this movement shared economic resources across the peoples/nations as well as across considerable distances. Such 'international' economic reciprocity was unusual, perhaps unique in the Roman Empire or in any ancient empire.

The collection, moreover, was also to be the occasion of an expression of the 'international' political solidarity of the many local assemblies. As indicated in 1 Cor. 16.1-4, delegates chosen by the assemblies themselves were to bring the resources collected to the assembly in Jerusalem. More than any other issue Paul addresses, the collection for the poor/saints in Jerusalem perhaps can illustrate to modern Western readers, accustomed to the separation of religion and economics, that the movement Paul was helping organize among peoples of the eastern Mediterranean was, in his mind at least, not only in opposition but also a social formation alternative to the Roman imperial order.

In some sections of 2 Corinthians, however, Paul seems to be compromising the Judaean apocalyptic perspective that constituted the key to his anti-imperial mission, as articulated in 1 Corinthians, 1 Thessalonians, Philippians and Galatians. In 2 Corinthians 10–13 Paul appears to be basically continuing the same defence of his own ministry that he had already made in 1 Corinthians 1–4, only more desperately so. In 2 Corinthians 2.14–6.13, on the other hand, he appears almost to be speaking the language of the Corinthian 'spirituals' rather than arguing against their position, as he did in 1 Corinthians.

In 2 Cor. 3.4-18 in particular he seems to adopt almost the same spiritual reading of Israelite Scripture that he warned the Corinthian 'spirituals' about in 1 Cor. 10.1-4, 5-13. He does substitute Christ for *Sophia* in 2 Cor. 3.14 ('only in Christ is the veil set aside'), just as he did in 1 Cor. 10.4 ('the spiritual rock was Christ'). However, in the ensuing statements he speaks positively in the same mystical terms of seeing the divine 'reflected in a mirror', with the mystic transformed into the very 'image of God' that he had denigrated as very temporary in 1 Cor. 13.12. (In the Wisdom of Solomon, which has so many parallels to the special language of the Corinthian 'spirituals', *Sophia* is both 'the mirror' of God's working and 'the image' of his goodness, 7.26.) Paul is surely alluding to Christ in referring to 'the Lord' in 2 Cor. 3.17-18. Yet, in discussion with the Corinthians, the identification of 'Lord' and 'the Spirit' would work in the other direction, since they almost certainly would have identified the Spirit with *Sophia* (as in Philo and the Wisdom of Solomon). In the next paragraph, 4.1-6, Paul continues to adopt the Corinthians' key language and central symbols, such as 'the light of (the gospel of) the glory', 'the light of the knowledge of the glory of God' and 'the image of God' (4.4, 6). The passing identification of 'the image of God' as Christ (in place of *Sophia*) and the passing location of 'the light of the knowledge of God' in 'the face of Christ' seem a bit subtle, compared with the abrupt reversals and dramatic replacements of *Sophia* with Christ in 1 Cor. 8.6 and 10.4. Even when he comes to restate the resurrection in 4.13–5.5, he moves so far into the Corinthians' body–soul dualism of 'inner man' versus 'outer man' and earthly tent or clothing versus eternal nakedness and mortality versus life/immortality that resurrection as a collective historical event that reconstitutes social reality has virtually dissolved into heavenly spirituality.

Paul seems to have accommodated so far toward the Corinthian spirituals' thinking in 2 Corinthians 3–5 that he has moved halfway toward the subsequent spiritualization of his gospel that we see in Colossians and Ephesians.

BIBLIOGRAPHY

Dirlik, Arif
    1997   *The Postcolonial Aura: Third World Criticism in the Age of Global Capitalism* (Boulder, CO: Westview Press).

Elliott, Neil
    1994   *Liberating Paul: The Justice of God and the Politics of the Apostle* (Maryknoll, NY: Orbis Books).
    2002   'Paul's Letters: God's Justice against Empire', in Wes Howard-Brook and Sharon H. Ringe (eds), *The New Testament: Introducing the Way of Discipleship* (Maryknoll, NY: Orbis Books): 122–47.

Fee, Gordon
    1987   *The First Epistle to the Corinthians* (Grand Rapids: Eerdmans).

Furnish, Victor Paul
    1984   *II Corinthians* (Garden City, NY: Doubleday).

Garnsey, Peter and Richard Saller
    1987   *The Roman Empire: Economy, Society, and Culture* (Berkeley: University of California Press).

Georgi, Dieter
    1990   *Theocracy in Paul's Praxis and Theology* (trans. David E. Green; Minneapolis: Fortress Press).

Horsley, Richard A.
    1998   *1 Corinthians* (Abingdon New Testament Commentaries; Nashville: Abingdon Press).

Horsley, Richard A. (ed.)
    1997   *Paul and Empire: Religion and Power in Roman Imperial Society* (Harrisburg, PA: Trinity Press International).

2000   *Paul and Politics: Ekklesia, Israel, Imperium, Interpretation* (Harrisburg, PA: Trinity Press International).

Loomba, Ania

1998   *Colonialism/ Postcolonialism* (London: Routledge).

Martyn, J. Louis

1997   *Galatians: A New Translation with Introduction and Commentary* (Anchor Bible, 33A; New York: Doubleday).

Matthews, Shelly

1994   '2 Corinthians', in Elisabeth Schüssler Fiorenza (ed.), *Searching the Scriptures*. Vol. 2, *A Feminist Commentary* (New York: Crossroad): 196–217.

Meeks, Wayne

1983   *The First Urban Christians: The Social World of the Apostle Paul* (New Haven: Yale University Press).

Meggitt, Justin L.

1998   *Paul, Poverty and Survival* (Edinburgh: T&T Clark).

Pickett, Raymond

1997   *The Cross in Corinth: The Social Significance of the Death of Jesus* (Sheffield: JSOT Press).

Said, Edward

1978   *Orientalism* (New York: Random House).

Schüssler Fiorenza, Elisabeth

1983   *In Memory of Her: A Feminist Theological Reconstruction of Christian Origins* (New York: Crossroad).

Wire, Antoinette C.

1994   '1 Corinthians', in Elisabeth Schüssler Fiorenza (ed.), *Searching the Scriptures*. Vol. 2, *A Feminist Commentary* (New York: Crossroad): 156–95.

THE LETTER TO THE GALATIANS

Sze-kar Wan

The starting point for a study of Paul's Letter to the Galatians is the ethnic tension that infuses every line of the work. Paul wrote to the Galatians because he heard that they had been asked to fulfil the requirements of the Mosaic law, chief among them circumcision, before they could be accepted as full members of the fledgling Jesus-movement. Paul objected. Though the precise reasons for Paul's objection were never spelled out, the Galatian controversy revolved around the issue of ethnicity or, more accurately, how 'Gentiles' could be received into the circle of Christ-followers who had hitherto been 'Jewish'.

I put 'Gentiles' and 'Jews' in quotes, because both, like all ethnic categories, are inherently unstable. They are forever in flux and constantly open to perpetual redefinition. This is true today and was even more true in the first century, when there was no such thing as 'Christianity'. When, for example, the Thessalonians became Christ-followers by 'turning to God from the idols to serve a living and true God' (1 Thess. 1.10), how 'Jewish' were they? The answer, of course, depends on what is meant by 'Jewish'.

If one takes Jewishness to be a primordial given defined by bloodline and kinship, inextricably tied to a particular land, history, language, culture, religion or some myth of origins, anyone failing these criteria are considered outsiders. This is a form of essentialism, which reduces ethnicity to certain irreducible qualities. Entrance into an ethnic group, while not impossible, depends entirely on whether one is able to acquire these essences that define identity. In this view, lines demarcating insiders from outsiders are explicitly drawn and strictly enforced. Ethnic boundaries take on a sacrosanct status, and no one is thought to be able to move or change these boundaries without endangering the putative integrity of group identity. Outsiders could be admitted into the group, if at all, only after taking rigorous steps towards becoming insiders. These steps might include taking part in certain rituals, acquiring a new language or new cultural traits, perhaps even adopting a myth of origin. The degree to which outsiders can embody these defining essences of the in-group identity directly determines whether they would be accepted as full members. If phenotypes are essentialized in group identity by the dominant culture, those who do not have them or have them partially are then branded by insiders as 'unassimilable' outsiders. The same goes for languages, accents, mannerisms, qualities that, unlike phenotypes, could be imitated but often only imperfectly. All these, when used to define in-group characteristics, form a pattern of pseudo-objectivity that gives insiders enormous power over the marginalized and the exoticized. In such a framework, essentialists would consider the Thessalonian Jesus-followers 'Jewish' only to the extent that they could fulfil the full complement of entrance requirements, requirements such as circumcision and dietary requirements that were thought to be defining characteristics of Jewish identity from time immemorial.

But can this ontology of Jewishness or, for that matter, any ethnic identity be maintained? Why privilege one set of characteristics over another in defining group identity? More to the point, *who* gets to set the hierarchy of characteristics and *who* determines whether one has them or not? In other words, while differences are real and observable, the attribution of power to these differences is artificial and manipulable. It is dependent on who does the attribution. That is so because ethnic identity is itself a social construct. It is based on a mutable definition of what group identity ought to be and how to apply such definition. Who is in and who is out can be and often is revised as the group changes over time or acquires new members. In due time, characteristics once thought essential to group identity can be dropped from consideration and new ones added, the line separating insiders from outsiders can be redrawn, and ethnic boundaries can be moved to include the once estranged. (For a fuller discussion of the primordialist and constructivist positions discussed below see Wan 2000b and accompanying bibliography.)

The anachronistic category 'Christianity' in this early stage has long clouded the interpretation of Galatians. Today, it is generally recognized that Paul worked as an apostle within his own Jewish context and that he debated with other Jewish apostles who, like himself, honoured Jesus as the long-awaited Messiah of Israel. The Galatians and others who came under Paul's sway did not convert from Judaism to 'Christianity', as has been maintained in the past, since Christianity as a distinct sociological phenomenon would not come about for another half-century. Rather, they were converted from 'idol-worship' to a Christ-following sect of first-century Judaism. If that is the case, the early Jesus-movement was characterized by a good deal of crossing, as well as moving and redrawing, of ethnic boundaries. If first-century Jewishness was not an essentialistic category or an immutable constant but one that admitted of 'Gentile' participation, the question of boundary-maintenance would need to be revisited in every generation in order for Jewishness to remain vital and viable.

If ethnic identity is indeed a social construct, then the question in Galatians is not whether Paul or his opponents got first-century Judaism 'right' but how they each constructed Jewish identity. The question is twofold. What were the competing definitions of Jewishness proposed by Paul and his opponents? And, how did they negotiate and arbitrate the differences between them? There were, first of all, areas of similarity. Both parties agreed that there should be borders to separate insiders from outsiders. Both advanced criteria by which Gentile Christ-followers were to be incorporated into the Jewish ethnos. Both took faith in or of Christ as integral to their characterization of Jewishness. Yet, they disagreed in two crucial areas: how ethnic boundaries were to be drawn and how power was to be distributed inside these boundaries. In sum, the controversy over whether Gentile Christ-followers should be circumcised was at heart an internal power struggle between different factions within the same Christ-following Jewish sect.

These two visions agree on the necessity of ethnic boundaries. While both allow for the possibility of admitting outsiders, albeit to varying degrees, the first strategy forecloses the possibility of communication with outsiders, while the second holds open the possibility for Gentiles to be persuaded of the supe-riority of Judaism and the pre-eminence of the Jewish ethnos. While the two approaches differ in their attitudes towards outsiders, they both agree on the importance of ethnic boundaries that could distinguish insiders from outsiders. Who is in and who is out is naturally an important question for the ethnocentric approach whose primary goal was ethnic purity, but it was no less important for the universalist, since its version of Judaism, modelled after Hellenistic philosophical systems, was in competition with them. In both approaches, the enduring question was where to draw ethnic boundaries that would best serve group identity in the hostile sea of the empire.

However, the two visions differ in one crucial respect: the locus of authority and the exercise of that authority in the maintenance of group integrity, stability and identity. For the universalist, the resultant ethnos is voluntary in nature. Power would not reside with insiders alone but is negotiated between them and newcomers, and then on the basis of mutable principles governing group identity. These principles are not the exclusive properties of any one group but are located between them, in the interstitial space between contending interests, separating and uniting the old and the new. These principles are, therefore, public in that they convene a platform shared by insiders and outsiders alike, joining them in a common discourse. To put it in another way, the universal-ist impulse is issued from the depths of a diaspora identity, an identity that resembles at once the ancestral and the adopted homes. At the same time, the diasporic identity is different from both as well. It finds the seat of power in the in-between *terra nullius* that simultaneously invites and repulses, so that the diasporic subject belongs to both and none at the same time. The discourse in this in-between land is characterized by ambiguity and double-speak, and its language is double-accented, understood by insiders and outsiders alike but regarded by both as 'fringe' and 'other' (Bhabha's doubleness). Voluntary asso-ciations are intrinsically diasporic. It is, therefore, not surprising to find Paul, in his advocacy for the inclusion of Gentiles, not only defending his universalist stance but also attempting, in the process, to construct a diasporic self.

Conceptions of Jewish Identity in the First Century

First-century views on ethnic identity can be documented in two extreme approaches to the question of Jewish identity and, in particular, the reception of Gentiles.

At one end stood the book of *Jubilees*, which emphasized the need for a strong sense of ethnic integrity by maintaining the historical privilege of the Jewish people and the internal coherence and self-sufficiency of the Jewish belief system. Gentiles were to be assiduously avoided, intermarriage with them strictly prohibited, and worship of their gods severely punished. Disobedience would spell the demise of the Jewish race (VanderKam 2003). Though conversion to Judaism might theoretically be allowed, given the radical break between Jews and Gentiles, the result of that conversion would have meant the abandonment of all things Gentile and the adoption of unique Jewish markers. Little wonder, then, the author of *Jubilees* stressed above all the importance of keeping the Mosaic law, the Sabbath, the dietary requirements, circumcision. Jewishness was seen to be something objectifiable and quantifiable, and the ethnic boundary fixed and rigid. Unless one was willing to embrace all the traits and requirements set forth therein, one could not be accepted as 'Jewish'.

At the other extreme, we find Philo of Alexandria. In his effort to advocate Judaism as the most superior of all systems, he was willing to move the ethnic boundaries to include everyone, be they racially Jewish or not, even to the extent of offering them 'Israelite' citizenship. Since Jews belonged to and participated in the Graeco-Roman world, he argued, Judaism had much to contribute to the cosmopolitanism of its day. It in fact surpassed all other philosophical systems, and its truth was self-evident to all lovers of wisdom (*philosophoi*). 'Israel' was interpreted by Philo as *horatikon genos*, meaning 'a people who see [God]', so that membership in it was open to anyone who wished to achieve a contemplative vision of God and not just to ethnic Jews (although he did concede that the Jews, his kinsfolk, had certain privileges). In so doing, Philo might appear to have blurred the line separating Jews from Gentiles. However, by elevating Judaism to the status of a universal system, he in effect moved the ethnic boundaries to include, potentially, everyone, thus holding out the possibility of making everyone 'Israelite' (Birnbaum 1996).

These two approaches could not be artificially grouped into neat historical camps but represent two contrasting attitudes towards outsiders. Nor, for that matter, should they be seen as mutually exclusive options. It was possible to maintain a rigid ethnic boundary while holding it open to conversion of outsiders, provided they were willing to acquire characteristics that distinguished the Jews from outsiders. Paul's interlocutors in Galatians, in insisting that the Galatian converts follow the Mosaic law, keep kosher requirements, and undergo circumcision, would seem to fall into the essentialist category. This was an outcome of affirming the essential characteristics of Judaism while integrating Christ into one's Jewish self-definition. Paul, on the other hand, was no less Jewish in his own mind, but his universalism led him to the conclusion that ethnic boundaries could be so expanded as to include all humanity, especially the Gentiles. In his apocalyptic formulation, which was a form of cosmic totalism, Paul envisioned Gentiles being grafted into a Jewish world. While it might appear that Paul was compromising Jewish ethnic integrity by transgressing boundaries that governed its ethnos, the new world order of his conception was constructed in Jewish terms. Its centre remained in Jerusalem, and its patterns were recognizably Jewish. The debate between Paul and his detractors was, therefore, one between two competing survival strategies for a minority group in the Roman Empire, and both strategies offered their own visions of the world.

Two Competing Visions of Jewish Identity

Paul never addressed his critics directly in his letter to the Galatians. We are afforded a glimpse of who they were through two sources: Paul's oblique references to their position when he spoke directly to the Galatians, and his first-person narrative of events in Jerusalem and Antioch leading up to the Galatian crisis. While there is no definite proof that his Galatian opponents had come directly from Jerusalem or Antioch, that Paul would preface (if it is indeed a preface) the main body of his letter with such a lengthy account of events connected to these cities strongly suggests that Paul thought they came from there.

Unlike his strategy in Philippians and 2 Corinthians, Paul in Galatians elected not to confront his opponents but to call his readers and hearers to ignore his opponents' message on circumcision. In his appeal, Paul made it clear that, if the Galatians were to opt for circumcision, they would have no part in the Jesus-movement. In stark, emphatic terms, fortified with a double first-person singular, Paul wrote, 'Look, I myself, Paul, am saying to you that if you were circumcised Christ will benefit you nothing' (5.2). The law and Christ were thus rhetorically contrasted as irreconcilable opposites permitting no compromise. Yet, this was likely the result of Paul's *reductio ad absurdum* for the purpose of weaning the Galatians from a perceived seduction. Paul drove a wedge between Christ and the Mosaic law to force his converts to choose between the two, with 'Christ' and 'law' being shorthand for what Paul took to be uncompromising factions in the community. His opponents in all likelihood never set Christ and the law as opposites, but as complementary, irreducible components of Jewish identity. While the Mosaic law was the traditional symbol of the Jewish ethnos, early Christ-followers were equally convinced that Jesus was the long-awaited Messiah through whom God had accomplished and could continue to accomplish great things – for the *Jewish* people. Though they did not deny the possibility of Gentiles entering the Jewish covenant, their primary focus was the traditional role of the Jewish ethnos through which God would bring changes to the world. In insisting that Gentile converts follow the law, they operated on a narrow understanding of Jewish identity based on supposedly well-defined ethnic boundaries.

Paul's first-person narrative of events in Jerusalem and Antioch confirms this observation. In his account of the Jerusalem meeting (2.1-10), Paul emphasized that Titus, though a Gentile, was never compelled to be circumcised (v. 3). Why he was not circumcised, Paul did not elaborate, but his account strongly suggests it was 'the reputed ones' who had the final say. The 'pillars' (v. 9) appear to have been the only ones with the authority to grant the work of Paul and Barnabas the requested legitimacy and to demand of them care for the Jerusalem poor (vv. 9-10). It was they who must have overruled the 'false brothers brought in from the side for the purpose of spying on our freedom' (v. 4), critics of Paul who argued for stricter imposition of the Mosaic law on the Gentiles.

The purpose of the Jerusalem meeting is shrouded in mystery. The author of Acts or his sources concluded that it was convened to resolve the question whether Gentile converts would be required to go through circumcision and keep the dietary laws (Acts 15). In all likelihood, however, that was read back into the meeting, perhaps on the basis of Paul's letter to the Galatians. Paul's own account of the meeting argues against such a view. His carefully worded summary of the meeting in vv. 6-10 makes no mention of circumcision. Instead, it stressed a symmetry between 'the ministry to the circumcised' and 'the ministry to the uncircumcision', a statement repeated several times in a few verses. Paul was much more concerned with reporting how he wrested recognition from the pillars and how the Gentile mission gained independence from Jerusalem. This silence on the matter of circumcision is highly significant, because the meeting was recounted for the purpose of dissuading the Galatians from undergoing circumcision. If the meeting had been convened for the specific purpose of deciding on that question, all Paul would have had to do was simply to cite the resolution verbatim. This Paul did not do. In fact, the only such evidence Paul had to offer was an oblique one: namely, Titus the Gentile was not asked to undergo circumcision in Jerusalem.

Whatever was the original purpose of the Jerusalem meeting, Paul interpreted it as having implications on how Gentiles were to be incorporated into the Jesus-movement. Specifically, the double fact that the pillars did not have Titus circumcised and that they acknowledged the significance of the Antioch efforts at bringing Gentiles into the fold was taken by Paul to mean that the Gentiles could be brought in without the traditional trappings that defined Jewish distinctiveness – that is to say, without the stricture of circumcision, dietary requirements and all such signs and rituals that marked the Jewish ethnos from Gentiles. It was, however, more than a mere matter of putting aside certain ritualism. If that had been the case, Paul could have been accused of simply replacing one set of markers with another, say, baptism. What Paul saw was that when Gentiles were brought into the Jesus-movement, they would decisively change its fundamental make-up, how it would understand itself and how it would mark itself off from outsiders. In other words, Paul saw the universalist logic more clearly than the Jerusalem leaders. The latter operated on an assumption of stability within the Jesus-movement, but Paul understood that, once newcomers were brought into the fold, internal authority would have to be negotiated on inherently unstable and ambiguous principles based on characteristics of the new ethnos.

The seed of controversy between these two competing visions of Jewish identity came to full flower soon after the Jerusalem meeting, in Antioch, in the controversy with Peter and Barnabas over table fellowship with Gentiles (2.11-14). Peter's actions bespeak confusion on his part with regard to the question of circumcision and dietary requirements for Gentiles. Peter had flaunted the kosher food law by eating with Gentiles, presumably meaning Gentile Christ-followers. When James' people showed up to put pressure on the Jews of Antioch to maintain the traditional ethnic markers – for reasons never clearly spelled out; it is possible that, as James Dunn theorizes (1983), political pressure in Jerusalem forced James and the Jewish Christ-followers to show their allegiance – Peter complied and withdrew from the Gentiles, but Paul refused and confronted him 'before them all' (2.14). The public row ended badly for Paul; most if not all the Jewish members of the Antioch con- gregation sided with Peter. Even Barnabas, Paul's erstwhile colleague, turned against him. Paul left Antioch in disgrace, and the Jerusalem–Antioch alliance was complete. (That Paul lost the power struggle is easy to see. If he had not, he would have trumpeted the triumph to the Galatians, since it would have been to his great advantage to do so, and he certainly would not have had to leave the city. On this latter point, the account in Acts is readily corroborated by the letters' travelogues. Paul's bitterness is unmistakable: 'The remaining Jews', as well as Barnabas, took part in what he called 'hypocrisy' [2.13].)

The Jerusalem–Antioch Alliance

The meeting between the two cities forged an understanding that Antioch would 'minister to the uncircumcised', while Jerusalem would 'minister to the circumcised' (2.6-9). This seeming equal partnership, however, belies a tacit agreement that Jerusalem would remain as the centre of the fledgling Jesus- movement, something even Paul grudgingly acknowledged, when he accepted Jerusalem's demand that the Antioch delegates 'remember the poor' (2.10). From the perspective of Jerusalem, this was a power play based on the assump- tion that the upstart Gentile congregations should pay obeisance to the met- ropolitan centre, but that probably was not the understanding of the Gentiles. Under the Roman patronage system, the Gentile contributors to the collection would have interpreted their gift as putting them in a superior, patronal position (Wan 2000a).

The relationship of Jerusalem to Antioch followed a classic colonial pattern. The metropolitan centre exercised dominance over marginalized and peripheralized colonies both discursively and materially. Materially, by demanding tributes and material from the colonies; discursively, by constructing a symbolic universe in which the colonizers occupied the centre while the colonies were reduced to its extensions. The meeting of the two cities took place in Jerusalem, not in Antioch. Delegates from Antioch – including Paul, Barnabas and Titus – had to submit their version of the message for examination, if not in fact for authentication and approval. Paul's use of *anatithesthai* and the concessive clause, '*lest* I run or ran in vain' (2.2) – according to Danker (2000: 74), *anatithesthai* in the middle means 'to lay something before someone for consideration, communicate, declare w. the connotation of request for a person's opinion' – suggests that his message to the Gentiles, the *euangelion,* might have been open to question and controversy. Paul's critics, the 'false brothers' of 2.4-5, failed to carry the day. The leaders granted Antioch a measure of approval, even as they at the same time extracted from them a financial concession. Throughout the proceedings, only Jerusalem was in a position to dictate to Antioch, not vice versa. Jerusalem acted as conservator and preserver of traditional values that it hoped would define the essence of the Jewish Jesus-movement. Once it decided that circumcision and dietary requirements would be central to its ethnic self-definition, it was able to impose this decision on Antioch. In so doing, Jerusalem claimed superiority over Antioch and asserted itself as the metropolitan centre in relation to Antioch and, by extension, all Gentile communities founded under its auspices (for the centre–colony relationship see Said 1993).

Ethnic Binarism as Counter-Discourse

To call Jerusalem the metropolitan centre of the Jesus-movement might seem at first glance ironic, since the city was regarded as the backwaters of the Roman imperium. The military and political centre was Rome; only Rome had the authority to make demands on its colonies, among which counted Jerusalem. Yet, a certain reverse logic gave Jerusalem and first-generation Jesus-followers a sense of entitlement. The apocalypticism of the early Jesus-followers had given them a claim on the whole world. By setting as their goal the conversion of all humanity, the Jesus-followers acquired a totalistic vision of the world that pertained to the whole of humanity. In addition, their self-perception as 'the poor' (2.10) – that is, the eschatological poor – helped produce a discursive logic in reverse that placed them in the centre of this universalism.

For its agenda Jerusalem divided humanity into an ethnic binarism, the circumcised and the uncircumcised, with all non-Jews, now marked 'uncircumcised', becoming objects of missionary efforts. All Jews were likewise marked 'circumcised' regardless of their place of origin and were thus claimed by the centre as subjects. This universal division was repeated three times in Paul's summary of the Jerusalem meeting (2.7-9) and again in his argument with Peter: 'We are by nature *Jews* and not Gentiles who are sinners' (2.15). Though in both instances we only hear Paul, he was clearly aware that he was reporting something that had broad appeals among his fellow-Jewish interlocutors.

What lent strength to this binarism was its simultaneous dependence on two myths – the myth of homogeneity and the myth of difference. By gathering all Gentiles into a collective sameness, the discourse nullified differences that existed among peoples outside the metropolitan centre. All Gentile lands were thus effaced and made blank, awaiting the arrival of the *euangelion*, and that could happen only from the centre. By inscribing all Jews under the label 'circumcised', the discourse similarly smoothed out the surface differences between Jews of all stripes and oriented them in the direction of Jerusalem. Paul's elaborate allegory of the heavenly and earthly Jerusalem in 4.21–5.1, if it was to retain any irony at all, assumed an unstated and hitherto unchallenged centrality of Jerusalem. At the same time, 'Gentiles' and 'Jews' were polarized into opposite camps. With their respective ethnicities made into ontological antonyms, differences between them were essentialized. This was done for two reasons: to define 'Jewish' identity by its putative opposite, 'Gentile' identity, as if both were stable; and to maintain internal control of the very things that distinguished 'Jews' from 'Gentiles'. (According to Mary Douglas [1975], taboos serve a social function of clarifying group boundaries and strengthening group solidarity. This is accomplished by means of constructing the outside space as 'polluted' and the inside as 'pure'. This notion of purity and taboo is needed the most where identity is at its most ambiguous and therefore the weakest. Beliefs of the uncleanliness of the others are designed to protect the 'most vulnerable domains, where ambiguity would most weaken the fragile structure' 1975: 58]. Kosher food laws, for instance, function in Judaism for the purpose of maintaining boundaries between insiders and outsiders. See the general theory of purity and pollution in Douglas 1966 and her application of theory to Leviticus in Douglas 1999.) The Roman imperial discourse was thus revised and appropriated for the use of the Jerusalem Jesus-movement.

The Jerusalem proclamation was a reverse cartography that made lands beyond the centre into a new *terra nullius* to be occupied and written in by missionary efforts issued from the centre. Then, Jerusalem would await the riches and tributes of the Gentiles who would forsake Rome for Jerusalem. In so doing, the Jerusalem leadership inaugurated a subversive act by proclaiming that it is the centre that will oversee the outlying settlements of Damascus, Antioch and all communities founded under their sponsorship (Wan 2000a).

This is indeed a daring bravado by a subjugated people: to reverse the Roman order by privileging the position and status of the Jesus-movement. The lack of political and military power did not prevent Jerusalem from asserting its authority over cultural and religious adherents to the movement. In this regard, the Jesus-movement of Jerusalem paralleled the temple administrators' self-proclaimed centrality over a similarly constructed 'Judaism'. In both cases, self-arrogated authority was based on an ahistorical essentialism that gave the respective metropolitan centres mythical control over their peripheries.

What we witness in the case of the Jerusalem Jesus-movement is the construction of a counter-discourse. Instead of buying into the dominant discourse of its day, that Rome was the divinely ordained centre of the empire, Jerusalem constructed for itself a new discourse that had it as the new centre. To fight the political and cultural controls of Rome, Jerusalem appropriated the master's language and 'worlding' impulses and constructed a competing form of totalism (Terdiman 1985: 3–4). Whereas the dominant discourse might appear stable, controlled, hegemonic and universal, the discourse of Jerusalem, the result of mimicry, appeared no less stable, controlled, hegemonic and universal. Jerusalem arrived at its new position by first destabilizing the imperial discourse, casting doubt on Roman homogeneity by differentiating the circumcised from the uncircumcised, thereby contesting the imperial and dominant centre. With a defiant proclamation, it took over the centre, the seat of the 'circumcised', while the uncircumcised Gentiles were relegated to the periphery and became objects of aid. At the end, Jerusalem created its own 'colonial worlding', a counter-hegemony that ironized and interrogated the hegemonic insistence of the imperial discourse (the language of 'colonial worlding' is that of Spivak [1996]). Along the way, Jerusalem, like Rome, created its own peripheral colonies.

Settler Colonialism

If Jerusalem indeed maintained a colonial relationship to Antioch and a *fortiori* all the Jesus-communities founded under its patronage, the colonial status of Antioch might best be compared to 'settler colonies' (Brydon and Tiffin 1993; Denoon 1979; 1983; Lawson 1995; Matthews 1962). As opposed to a 'colony of occupation', where the majority indigenous population is ruled by an occupying power, a settler colony is one in which the invaders–settlers eventually, over time, replace the indigenes by means of violence, annihilation or, in the case of the Jesus-movement, by cultural and religious assimilation. Prime examples of the former are Nigeria and India; of the latter, Australia, Canada, even the United States, in spite of its enormous military and global power.

To say that the Jerusalem Jesus-movement extended its influence on its colonies with design on replacement is, therefore, no exaggeration. The Jerusalem meeting resolved an issue that was universal: the fate of all humanity – 'humanity' as divided into the circumcised and uncircumcised. Its goal was a totalism that had as its central aim conversion of the world. It is, therefore, not inappropriate to call the missionary outposts in Antioch and other cities 'settler colonies' and the emissaries from Jerusalem–Antioch colonial viceroys dispatched from the centre to claim and govern its colonies. What made this colonial situation vastly different from the classic European model of colonization, which was woven in violence, conquest and above all capitalism, was that the Jesus-communities were voluntary in nature. Adherents could always choose to leave or, more drastically, to dissolve these communities at will. The mode of assertion or entitlement was by persuasion and argumentation rather than by force.

A New Discourse

In settler colonies the identity of the settlers is deeply and disturbingly ambivalent, especially when they are racially and ethnically distinct from the indigenous population. This is an instantiation of the general ambivalence that Homi Bhabha has long articulated:

> The colonial presence is always ambivalent, split between its appearance as original and authoritative and its articulation as repetition and difference... To recognize the *difference* of the colonial presence is to realize that the colonial text occupies that space of double inscription. (1994: 107)

The colonizing power views them as having been displaced from the supposedly pure values of the centre, contaminated by their proximity to the natives ('having gone native') or diluted by miscegenation. They are frequently constructed in the colonial discourse as inferior and 'other', only marginally better than the colonial subjects (Brydon and Tiffin 1993; Denoon 1979; 1983; Lawson 1995; Matthews 1962). At the same time, as representatives of the colonizing power, settlers derive their privileged status over the natives from being members of the master race and from being different from the locals. Thus, two discourses of difference and inferiority function side by side: one giving the settlers privilege because they are different from the natives but the same as their culture of origins; the other inducing subordination because they are the same as the natives but different from those back home. All this results in the settlers' being trapped at once in the contradictory but complementary roles of colonizer and colonized, master and subject. Paul's location in the diaspora as an agent of Jerusalem and Antioch would fit this pattern.

After his departure from Antioch, however, Paul was displaced from Jerusalem–Antioch, the colonial metropolis that now assumed the responsibility of constructing a new discourse to define the norms of the new movement. It is in this place of dislocation and hybridity where we meet Paul the letter-writer. While he was physically displaced from his cultural 'home' of Jerusalem and Antioch, he was also dislocated from its binary discourse on Jews and Gentiles. Situated in the interstice between the representatives of the Jesus-movement and the targeted converts, between the colonizers and the colonized, between 'Jews' and 'Gentiles', Paul's position was one of ambivalence: simultaneously attracted to the discourse of the Jesus-movement of the metropolis and repulsed by its binarism; simultaneously drawn to his 'home' discourse, according to which he occupied the periphery, and to the 'native' discourse endemic to his place of exile, by the logic of which he was the honoured apostolic founder. Among his kinsfolk, he was reviled and marginalized as a law-breaker; in the diaspora, among Gentiles, he was a representative carrying the weight of authority that befits an ambassador or viceroy from the centre. It is in this rich texture of ambivalence and hybrid textuality that we must approach the discursive construct of Galatians.

Paul and the Colonial Viceroys
After Paul left Antioch, he retraced his steps through the Jesus-communities he and Barnabas had founded in their first journey west. The motive for this second trip was never made explicit but is probably not hard to fathom. Paul had seeded these sapling communities, but he did so under the protectorate of Antioch. Now that he had become independent of the metropolis, the ownership of these communities became a matter of dispute. While these communities might pledge their allegiance to Paul personally, which would be the fond wish of the self-conscious apostle, they could just as well remain under Antioch's parental guardianship. So long as the colonial relationship between Jerusalem–Antioch and the new communities remained ambiguous, the latter became, figuratively and geographically, sites of contestation. Paul, therefore, had good reasons to revisit these cities, as did emissaries from the metropolitan centre of the Jesus-movement. These emissaries, dogging Paul's every step after his departure from Antioch, regarded themselves, of course, as legitimate overseers of these new communities, but Paul saw them as meddling outsiders, derisively calling them 'trouble-makers' (1.7). Elsewhere in the extant Pauline letters, the same group in all likelihood stood behind such disparaging epithets as 'dogs', 'doers of evil deeds' (Phil. 3.2), 'superlative apostles' (2 Cor. 11.5; 12.11), 'ministers of Satan' (2 Cor. 11.15). Their concerns? The same as Paul's: to regain and to retain ownership of the new outposts. It remains a controversial point whether these various opponents of Paul cohere into a group with intellectual and socio-logical integrity. I have elsewhere argued that they do, based on Paul's similar characterizations of the group and the identical arguments used to counter their views (Wan 2000c). That said, it should be recognized that the colonial reading of Galatians attempted here is not dependent on whether there were a single or multiple groups of opponents.

If Paul's invectives are to be trusted, these emissaries showed up in Galatia advocating that the Galatians observe stricter adherence to the Torah. This observance was to be crystallized in the Gentile converts undergoing circumcision (5.2-3, 6; 6.12-13; cf. 5.6; 6.15). That they would valorize circumcision is indicative of their Jerusalem–Antioch pedigree. That must have Paul's assessment. Else, he would not have started the letter with an autobiographical section chronicling his ambivalent relationship with the two cities (chs 1–2) or put forward the subversive allegorical interpretation of the Sarah–Hagar story to decentralize discursively 'Earthly Jerusalem' (4.21–5.1).

Paul's reactions to the emissaries were predictably swift and virulent. As a displaced and dislocated exile from the metropolitan centre, he was incensed in particular at three issues. First of all, there was the obvious matter of turf. It was his understanding that the Jerusalem meeting had granted the Gentile mission separate but equal partnership (2.7-9). That might not have been the understanding of Jerusalem and Antioch, but it did not stop Paul from using the proceedings to make his point: the emissaries had violated an earlier argument to divide the mission field between the apostles into 'circumcised' and 'uncircumcised'. Secondly, in adducing his childhood education and his youthful zeal for his ancestral tradition (1.14), a zeal that led him to try to annihilate the burgeoning Jesus-movement (1.13, 23), he hoped to prove his standing in Judaism. If he had questioned the centrality of circumcision, how dare second-rate personnel reintroduce it to his congregation? Implicit in this argument is a certain disdain for the current leadership of Jerusalem and Antioch. Finally, his annoyance was probably informed by anxiety, now that his location in the Jesus-movement has been vacated in the metropolitan hierarchy. Could he still have the confidence to regain his equilibrium and his standing in the diaspora if Jerusalem–Antioch had succeeded in imposing its standard on the Gentile converts? Paul understood the law to be representing not merely casuistic requirements but a master narrative that derived its power from the structure of the Jewish ethnos.

At heart, these issues were really one and the same: which version of the story, going back not only to the Jerusalem meeting but to the very origins of Judaism, should hold sway over the Gentile converts? Make no mistake: the debate was not between a static, rigid form of Jewish ethnocentrism and a supposedly more flexible, more inclusive form of universalism. Rather, both narratives were attempts at restructuring Judaism to accommodate the entrance of Gentiles, though they differed in the roles they assigned them. The Jerusalem–Antioch narrative stressed traditional legal requirements for the purpose of maintaining separation between Jews and Gentiles. In the process, they legislated a binarism between insiders and outsiders. Paul's narrative, too, was a form of binarism turning on the 'faith of Christ'. Paul's narrative was no less ethnocentric than the Jerusalem–Antioch narrative, but it drew the ethnic boundaries around all peoples and nations. Like Philo, who broadened the circle to cosmic universality, Paul proposed to make all 'Gentiles' into 'Jews'. The battle line was thus drawn discursively. At issue was more than just the loyalty of the Galatian converts; it had more to do with the shape and tenor of the dominant narrative.

Paul's strategy in trying to persuade the Galatians consisted of constructing a new discourse along three lines: a new colonial self, a new ethnos and a new authority structure.

Construction of a New Colonial Self

First, he constructed an autonomous self that was, while ambivalent, a hybrid, both similar to and different from the colonizing authorities of Jerusalem–

Antioch. A discourse based on such a constructed self provided the Galatians a paradigm for their own relationship to the centre. Just as he had gained autonomy from the centre, so should and could Antioch. This autonomous self was pursued primarily in his autobiographical section.

He presented himself as an accomplished member of his tradition; indeed, he advanced far beyond his contemporaries. He was so zealous for his ancestral tradition that he was initially an enemy of the Jesus-movement prior to his call to be an apostle to the Gentiles (1.13-14). The account of his former life served an important function: to set himself apart from the Jerusalem faction and to highlight the divine initiative in his calling (1.15-16). Even after his call, Paul reminded his readers emphatically that he had no immediate business with Jerusalem but went instead into Arabia before returning to Damascus (1.17). In his only visit to Jerusalem three years after, Paul said, he had visited only Peter and James, without disclosing the nature of that visit (1.18-19). (The use of *historein* in this connection is deliberate, for the word means both 'to visit' and 'to visit for the purpose of getting information'. This is of a piece with the equally ambiguous *hoi dokountes*, 'those who *appear* to be something'. Both expressions were intended in all likelihood to add irony and subversion to the stated relationship between Paul and the Jerusalem leaders.) Yet, even to this visit Paul attached a qualification: no other person in all Judaea knew him personally, only news of his radical change from pursuer to promoter (1.22-24). In so doing, Paul wanted his Galatian readers to know that he did not trace his apostolic pedigree to the metropolitan centre or that he had been commissioned to be its emissary; rather, his apostleship was divinely ordained through a revelation (1.11-12). One should note especially the repetition of 'not from human beings' or its equivalents in 1.1, 15-16.

In narrating the Jerusalem meeting, Paul took great care to counter the impression that he had been marginalized at the Jerusalem meeting. He claimed to have attended the meeting when he was prompted by a 'revelation' (2.2), lest one should conclude that the Antioch delegation had been summoned to Jerusalem. Paul, however, claimed active agency only for himself, not for Barnabas or any of his fellow-delegates, suggesting that Paul thought them to be Jerusalem lackeys. His use of the first-person singular throughout stands in stark contrast to the passive roles Paul assigned to the others. It was Paul, not Barnabas or Titus, who 'went up' to Jerusalem. It was he, not the delegates, who took Titus to the meeting (the participle *symparalabon* agrees with the subject of *aneben*); Barnabas was mentioned only incidentally, giving the impression that he only came along for the ride. It was Paul, not Barnabas or any of the delegates, who presented to Jerusalem his version of the *euangelion*. In fact, Titus was important to Paul's presentation of the proceedings only because he was not compelled to be circumcised; Titus otherwise disappears from the narrative. Likewise, Barnabas was named as a fellow-recipient of the 'right hand of fellowship' extended by the Jerusalem pillars, but his name always followed Paul's.

Barnabas and Titus were subsumed under the generic 'we' who resisted pressure from 'the false brothers' and who were the beneficiaries of the pillars' concession, but even then the concession came only after the authorities had recognized the Pauline 'I' who was entrusted with the *euangelion* just as Peter was (2.7), who was 'energized' just as Peter was (2.8), and who was given grace just as Peter was (2.9). Even the financial concession Jerusalem received from Antioch (2.10), though issued to the delegates ('*we* remember'), Paul took it upon himself to fulfil ('which very thing *I* was eager to do'). To minimize the appearance that Paul needed and was seeking Jerusalem's approval, Paul acknowledged the leaders only grudgingly. He called them *hoi dokountes* ('those who appear or are reputed [to be something])' four times (2.2, 6[2×], 9), a phrase dripping with irony and ambiguity. The only time he used the full expression *hoi dokountes ti einai* ('those who are reputed to be persons of sub-stance', 2.6), he qualified it with a proverb, 'God takes no account of a person's mask'. At the end, Paul referred to Peter, James and John not as 'pillars', only 'reputed pillars' (*hoi dokountes styloi*, 2.9). In Paul's discourse, therefore, he stood out as the leader whose divine endowment of grace ultimately made him responsible for defending the welfare of Gentiles like Titus. All this contributed a picture of his superiority to his opponents.

His summary of the proceedings was thus a protest of the colonial arrange-ment to which Antioch was willing to submit but which Paul now found objectionable. Paul acknowledged the authority of the 'pillars', but insisted that the agreement had been reached between equal partners and that it granted the Gentile mission recognition and autonomy. Paul let stand the impression that the Jerusalem leaders had granted him authority, but he insisted that it was based on the self-evidential 'grace'. In the allegorical interpretation of Sarah and Hagar (4.21–5.1), he likened Jerusalem, which is to say 'earthly Jerusa-lem', to Hagar the slave woman, while drawing an unmistakable connection between his own divine revelation with the 'heavenly Jerusalem' of Sarah, the free woman who produced for Abraham the legitimate heir. In the end, he suc-ceeded in constructing a parallel locus of authority that aimed at displacing the claimed centrality of Jerusalem.

Construction of a New Ethnos

Paul constructed the Galatians into a 'new' ethnos around a new symbol: in-Christness. This new ethnos was not thought of a new people but really the renewal of an old, since it was built on Jewish and Gentile particularities. Paul's universalism enabled him to re-vision the old Jewish ethnos into a 'new creation' (6.15), the sum total of the Jews and Gentiles but in which Jews and Gentiles would no longer be distinguished (3.28; 5.6). This new ethnos should therefore be autonomous, independent from the colonizing power of Jerusalem.

The Jerusalem–Antioch emissaries advanced a construct that inscribed the Galatians as Gentiles, which is to say members outside the ethnic boundaries of an essentialistic Judaism. The Galatians *qua* converts would then occupy the space reserved for latecomers. Paul, however, advocated an alternative discourse that inscribed the Galatians as the original subjects of Judaism. Far from being latecomers, Paul argued, they were the intended recipients of the original charter established, like Paul's own experience, by divine initiative. The promise given to Abraham, in typical Pauline exegesis, already had all the Gentiles (*panta ta ethne*) within its purview (3.5-9). Just as Abraham was a 'Gentile' convert, from polytheism to the living God much like the Thessalonians, the Galatians, too, have become converts. Just as Abraham was reckoned the patriarch of all Jews by a divine call, the Galatians, too, by dint of their extraordinary, extra-mundane experiences (3.1-4; 4.6) – 'the power of the Spirit' – have been granted the same divinely ordained identity. They, in fact, should have stronger claims to the real or 'Jerusalem from above' than the current Jerusalem, because they had already received the ancient promise of Genesis in their reception of the Spirit (3.14). (I have argued [Wan 2004] that for Paul the 'Spirit' of Galatians is the functional equivalence of 'land' promised to Abraham in Genesis 15.)

This is indeed a daring piece of exegesis, one which would be 'anti-Jewish' if it had not been advanced by a fully fledged Jew who was himself a self-conscious zealot for his 'ancestral tradition'. But if the foregoing colonial situation is correct, then Paul's rhetorical move did not intend to create a new *ethnos* alongside Judaism but inside it. To claim the Galatians as Abraham's descendants (3.29), legitimate heirs not slaves (4.1-7, 28), Paul did not so much create a new people as push the ethnic boundaries outward to incorporate the Galatians, turning them into an Abrahamic people.

Construction of a New Authority Structure

Paul tried to persuade the Galatians that his relationship to them had taken on a new form. He was not a new head, a new viceroy replacing the old; rather, he should be honoured as a new patriarch in an emerging colony. In 4.12-20, Paul issued his customary call to the Galatians to imitate him, but this time by reminding his readers the sort of reception he had received when he first visited them. Even though Paul had first come to the Galatians through an ailment, they did not 'scorn or spit out' their trial (presumably a trial caused by Paul's weakened flesh) but 'received [him] as an angel of God, as Christ Jesus' (4.13-14). The resemblance of this exhortation to his opening salvo to the Galatians in 1.8-9 was no accident but deliberate: 'But if we ourselves or an angel from heaven were to preach a message contrary to that which we preached to you, let him be damned. As we have said already and now I say it again: if someone were to preach to you a message contrary to what you received, let him be damned.' In both instances, Paul compared himself to an angel who might be in a position to preach to the Galatians. In ch. 1, in a rhetorical *tour de force*, Paul even placed himself above an angel: even an angel from heaven could not alter the message that Paul had earlier preached to the Galatians. This, combined with his persistent claim to divine revelation, gave Paul the authority to oversee and supervise his charge. It was this authority that enabled him to warn the Galatians sternly of the danger of falling away if they accepted circumcision from the rival teachers (5.2-12). Paul did this by setting up his own binarism, Christ and the law: 'those of you who are justified by the law have been abolished from Christ, fallen away from grace' (5.4).

Conclusion

The interpretation of Paul, and often his letter to the Galatians, has too often been heavily colonized by Reformation theology. Annexed by an all-too-eager predilection to read 'justification by faith' out of the text, Galatians has too often been singled out for a theological treatment, mined for timeless truths and dogmatic dicta for the ideal readers. The result is a theological *Tendenz* that can best be described as ideological captivity. Even with the recent efforts of trying to evaluate Paul as a Jewish writer, there is the common tendency to essentialize 'Judaism' and 'Jewish' identity, disregarding the political reality and internal tensions within the fledgling Jesus-movement. This has led to two blind spots in the modern reading of Galatians. First, it makes the first-century Jesus-movement into a disembodied, non-ethnic phenomenon abstracted from its concrete roots in a group of people marked by their experience in the empire. They were constructed by an imperial narrative, to which they responded with a narrative of their own. All this happened prior and concurrent to the rise of the Jesus-movement. Second, an essentialized construction of Judaism also tends to make Paul into either a 'Jew' or a 'Christian' without any regard to whether such categories were at all meaningful in the first century. Neither, in fact, was a stable, incontrovertible category; both were open to polemical appropriation by competing claims over Jewish identity. The battles behind the text of Galatians were waged over this very issue.

The postcolonial reading of Galatians attempted here is an experiment to re-evaluate Paul and his critics in the context of an internal debate within a 'Judaism' that felt the constant impingement of the empire and had to construct a vision in response. Here 'Judaism' is understood not as an ontological category but the very bone of contention between Paul and his critics. The Jerusalem–Antioch leaders saw themselves as the centre of the Jesus-movement and thus constructed a narrative that, perhaps too conveniently, bolstered their authority. In their response to imperial pressure, they adopted a rigid ethnic boundary between themselves and outsiders. Paul, for his part, foregrounding his own diasporic identity, elected to embrace a universalism that would extend the 'Jewish' borders to the ends of the earth. Both parties took seriously the reality of ethnicity as it impinged upon the Jesus-movement. Both did so as self-conscious 'Jews'.

BIBLIOGRAPHY

Bhabha, Homi
1994 'Signs Taken for Wonders: Questions of Ambivalence and Authority under a Tree Outside Delhi, May 1817', in *The Location of Culture* (London and New York: Routledge): 102–22.

Birnbaum, Ellen
1996 *The Place of Judaism in Philo's Thought: Israel, Jews, and Proselytes* (Atlanta: Scholars Press).

Brydon, Diana
1995 'Introduction: Reading Postcoloniality, Reading Canada', *Essays on Canadian Writings* 56: 1–19.

Brydon, Diana and Helen Tiffin
1993 *Decolonising Fictions* (Sydney: Dangaroo Press).

Danker, Frederick
2000 *A Greek-English Lexicon of the New Testament and Other Early Christian Literature* (3rd edn; Chicago: University of Chicago Press).

Denoon, Donald
1979 'Understanding Settler Societies', *Historical Studies* 18: 511–27.
1983 *Settler Capitalism: The Dynamics of Dependent Development in the Southern Hemisphere* (Oxford: Clarendon Press).

Douglas, Mary
1966 *Purity and Danger: An Analysis of Concepts of Pollution and Taboo* (New York: Praeger).
1975 *Implicit Meanings: Essays in Anthropology* (London: Routledge & Kegan Paul).
1999 *Leviticus as Literature* (New York: Oxford University Press).

Dunn, James
1983 'The Incident at Antioch (Galatians 2:11-18)', *Journal for the Study of the New Testament* 18: 3–57.

Lawson, Alan
1991 'Cultural Paradigm for the Second World', *Australian-Canadian Studies* 9: 67–78.
1995 'Postcolonial Theory and the "Settler" Subject', *Essays on Canadian Writings* 56: 20–36.

Matthews, John P.
1962 *Tradition in Exile: A Comparative Study of Social Influences on the Development of Australian and Canadian Poetry in the Nineteenth Century* (Toronto: University of Toronto Press).

Said, Edward
1993 *Culture and Imperialism* (New York: Alfred A. Knopf).

Spivak, Gayatri
1996 *The Spivak Reader* (New York: Routledge).

Terdiman, Richard
1985 *Discourse/Counter-Discourse: The Theory and Practice of Symbolic Resistance in Nineteenth-Century France* (Ithaca, NY: Cornell University Press).

VanderKam, James
2003 'The Demons in the Book of Jubilees', in A. Lange, H. Lichtenberger and K. F. Diethard Römheld (eds), *Die Dämonen/Demons: Die Dämonologie*

Der Israelitisch-Jüdischen Und Führchristlichen Literatur Im Kontext Ihrer Umwelt/the Demonology of Israelite-Jewish and Early Christian Literature in Context of Their Environment (Tübingen: Mohr Siebeck): 339–64.

Wan, Sze-kar

2000a   'Collection for the Saints as Anti-Colonial Act: Implications of Paul's Ethnic Reconstruction', in Richard Horsley (ed.), *Paul and Politics: Ekklesia, Israel, Imperium, Interpretation. Essays in Honor of Krister Stendahl* (Harrisburg, PA: Trinity Press International): 191–215.

2000b   'Does Diaspora Identity Imply Some Sort of Universality? An Asian-American Reading of Galatians', in Fernando F. Segovia (ed.), *Interpreting Beyond the Border* (The Bible and Postcolonialism, 2; Sheffield: Sheffield Academic Press): 107–31.

2000c   *Power in Weakness: Conflict and Rhetorics in Paul's Second Letter to the Corinthians* (The New Testament in Context; Valley Forge, PA: Trinity Press International).

2004   'Abraham and the Promise of Spirit: Points of Convergence between Philo and Paul', in Esther G. Chazon, David Satran and Ruth A. Clements (eds), *Things Revealed: Studies in Early Jewish and Christian Literature in Honor of Michael E. Stone* (Journal for the Study of Judaism Supplements, 89; Leiden: E. J. Brill): 209–20.

THE LETTER TO THE EPHESIANS

Jennifer G. Bird

A brief review of the methods employed in postcolonial biblical criticism shows that there are many ways to approach a postcolonial critique of the New Testament writings. In defining my own method, I am quite conscious of my social location and how it impacts on my interest in this area of biblical studies. I read both as a white woman within a male-dominated field and as someone who, having been reared within a United Methodist Church congregation, took a turn toward conservative Christian fundamentalism and then to membership in the Presbyterian Church (USA). I thus come to the task of biblical interpretation with a grasp of various theological reflections or ideologies and, in light of these experiences, am committed to the task of offering liberative critiques and interpretations of the texts of the Christian churches. For this commentary, therefore, I will be reading Ephesians with four specific aspects of the text in mind: (1) resonances with the methods of imperial propaganda, (2) imagery that counters, yet reinscribes, an imperial order, (3) constructions of gender roles that perpetuate the subordination of women to men, which is one of many particular manifestations of imperial order and (4) potential glimmers of hope for a liberationist subversion of the author's own construction.

I would like to begin this postcolonial critique of Ephesians by noting the lack of attention to, or denial of, the political implications of the various aspects of this letter in recent commentaries. Admittedly almost ten years old now, this quotation from Pheme Perkins' work reflects the trend within scholarship that replicates the escapism into the 'spiritual' realm that is contained within Ephesians itself: 'Some have even compared [the language about G*d's plan for humanity in this letter] to claims for the peace created by the Roman Empire. Though there is no clear evidence that Ephesians is concerned with imperial ideology, the suggestion points to the spiritual importance of its message' (1997: 32). I do not wish to indict Perkins' opinions and work. On the contrary, I respectfully draw upon her work, intending to highlight how deeply rooted the preference for a spiritualized interpretation is for many scholars.

Whether or not one finds 'clear evidence that Ephesians is concerned with imperial ideology' is determined by the extent to which one assumes *any* of the writings of the early Christian communities would have been specifically engaging political ideologies. Religion and politics were either inextricably related or separate unto themselves. What does one assume on this matter, and thus how does one read these texts based upon this presupposition? Given recent scholarship on the early Christian movement's response to the Roman Empire, one can no longer responsibly read these texts *without* the political lens in place (Price 1984; Horsley 1997). However, even as I make such a declaratory statement, I am aware that many well-intentioned scholars continue to resist or deny the importance of applying a postcolonial interpretation. This resistance indicates not only the extent to which biblical studies, as generally taught or conceived within many Western locations, is apolitical and thus has lost a significant aspect of the texts' originating impetus, but also the extent to which depoliticizing the biblical texts serves to maintain instead of transform the status quo.

The primary aspect of Ephesians that I will be addressing, and under which fall all other elements of this postcolonial critique, is the counter-empire or kingdom that is constructed within the letter. Since *basil* terminology only appears once within the letter (5.5), I will refer to the realm constructed by Ephesians as a counter-empire. The application of terminology typically associated with imperial ideological pronouncements as well as terminology having to do with the household codes and battle imagery should not be so easily spiritualized but should rather be seen as involving deliberate religio-political claims. That the establishment of such an empire is spoken of within the spiritual or heavenly realms simply expresses an escapist tendency, not an apolitical agenda (Whang 1998: 96).

Empires in Conflict

Reinscribing Empire

From the very beginning of the letter, the author directs the attention of the recipients into the heavenly realms (1.3). For it is in the highest, that is, most powerful, spiritual realms that their G*d and Father dwells, and from there G*d bestows on them rich spiritual blessings. These blessings are part and parcel of their adoption as sons, and we may infer by their role as leaders in this empire that the phrase 'as sons' is key here and includes their inheritance (1.3-11). All of these things have been made possible by the raising of Christ and his seating at the right hand of G*d. Immediately, we can see that what was essential in Paul's non-hymnic writing, the (weak) crucified Christ (Elliott 1997), has been replaced by a risen and all-powerful Christ, who is victorious over all other powers and rulers in the universe (1.19-23). The message of Jesus' identification with the weak has been transformed into a ruling Christ to whom all things, and thus all people, are subject (1.22). Weakness is a human issue and is not an aspect of this ruler in the heavenly empire. In the process of the exaltation of Christ, Jesus loses that which made him human, and his followers are simply trading in one ruler for another!

The members of these communities are already seated above with Christ (2.6-7). Again, their attention is directed to the spiritual or heavenly realm. Are we to understand that they are part of the dynastic rule over this spiritual empire? For whom are they overseers, then? Whatever the case may be, it is clear that the powers of the air that held sway over them before they were raised with Christ are now subject to them. Divine deliverance has turned the oppressors into the oppressed, and vice versa. Thus, the cycle of domination of one power over another continues.

Perkins notes that when 'Ephesians is read over against the ideology of the Roman emperor cult, its encomium to the exalted Christ (especially 2.11-22) appears to copy the style of speeches in praise of the emperor (Faust 1993)' (Perkins 1997: 51). As I noted earlier, she does not pursue the political implications of such mimicry. Whether or not the imitation of the encomium to the emperor here in reference to Christ was done consciously, it added to the construction of the heavenly empire of G*d by establishing the right-hand man to the emperor.

Most dramatically, those who were not members of the *politeia* of Israel (*politeias tou Israel*, 2.12) are now citizens, along with the saints (*sumpolitai*, 2.19), in G*d's household. One might pause to ask, Why 'household' instead of 'kingdom/empire', since citizenship implies the latter, not the former? The image of 'the house of G*d' runs deep in religious discourse. The suggestion of citizenship within G*d's domain, however it is consciously constructed, secures the idea that the household of G*d is a political entity.

In a mixing of metaphors, the author suggests that this house was built upon the prophets and apostles – Christ is not their foundation (Thurston 2004: 106). Instead of the lowly, meek and human Jesus of Nazareth – the Jesus of the grassroots movement in the Gospels, what we have here is the elevated and pinnacle Christ, out of reach of the people. Apparently, the meek may inherit the earth, but the high and mighty rule in the empire of G*d.

Since G*d's empire is in the heavenly realm and Christ's rule is 'far above all rule and authority and power and dominion, and every name that is named', any powers at work in the world have already been conquered. Neil Elliott has suggested that the implication of this realized eschatology is that the Christian communities would withdraw from the world. Perhaps the 'Roman dynasts' would have heaved a collective sigh of relief at this other-worldly empire, thinking that it actually sounds like a 'pleasantly harmless' myth (1997: 178). Not a bad suggestion, it seems to me. Yet, in light of the need to be perceived as not simply indifferent to but supportive of the empire in order to avoid persecution, I would suggest a completely different outcome: a reinscribed submission and subordination to the (temporary) powers of this world. With their true citizenship in a heavenly empire, their dealings on earth matter very little, and thus submission to the ruler of this world's empire, for the sake of peace or the avoidance of persecution, is quite reasonable.

Timothy Gombis has compared the extended thanksgiving and blessing section of this letter to the general structure of ancient Near Eastern divine-warfare mythology, in which the divine king or warrior god is exalted. The typical progression moves as follows: naming a threat, describing the battle/conquest/victory, ascribing lordship due to the victory, building a house or temple to the god and ending with a celebration. Although this format is often a central aspect of apocalyptic material, it is clearly reflected in Eph. 1.20–2.22. Gombis writes: 'The triumphs of Christ over the evil power vindicate the exalted status of the Lord Christ, who announces his victory by proclaiming peace. His people gather to him in unified worship as his temple, which he has founded and is building as a lasting monument to his universal sovereign lordship' (2004: 418).

There can be little doubt that the exaltation of Christ was clearly understood through this section of the letter on the basis of the divine-warrior myth structure present in their consciousness as well as their own honouring and deification of emperors. The exalted Christ is lord over all in his heavenly empire. The fact that this divine-warrior myth is appropriated in this 'moment' in the development of the Christian movement both hints at the need for it – in response to the emperor's claims – and assures the continuation of such beliefs about the emperor, indirectly. The image of the divine emperor Christ depends upon the image and 'reality' of the earthly divine emperor. In this way, moreover, submission within the earthly realms is encouraged by their obedience to the victorious heavenly king or lord.

As we see the practices of exaltation of the emperor ascribed to the Christ and the construction of citizenry within G*d's household, we cannot miss the establishment of a counter-empire. As we will see below, there are other significant pieces of the Roman Empire that are co-opted within this letter, specifically the preparation of an army for battle and the confirmation that the household is the foundational unit of this new empire.

Rebuilding the Community

The building metaphors early in the letter may have been intentionally crafted for the sake of the recipients. While a thorough engagement of the discussion regarding the initial intended audience – a question made relevant by the secondary ascription *en Ephesō* – is not necessary at this time, I would like to point to one possibility that helps to make some sense of the mixed metaphors in the letter. Not only does such usage offer insight, but it also deepens our appreciation of potential socio-political aspects of the letter.

Larry Kreitzer notes that the cities in the Lycus valley, particularly Laodicea and Hierapolis, which were destroyed in the great earthquake of 60 CE (2004: 81–94), are prime candidates as the initial recipients of this letter. Hierapolis was a city full of temples to multiple gods and had several building programmes. It was also a neocorate four times over, that is, a city that held an imperial temple.

The Hierapolis community would resonate well with the content in this letter that speaks of foundations (2.20), temple building and reconstruction (2.20-22), and perhaps even debt cancellation/tax relief. Part of Emperor Augustus' 'creative response' to these cities devastated by earthquakes was to refund their tribute as well as to assign a governor for two years. Tiberius, after him, was equally generous, and minted imperial coins to reflect his efforts: 'restoration of the communities in Asia', 'Tiberius Augustus, Creator/Of the Magnesians at Sipylus'. Tiberius also waived the tribute, or offered exemption from taxes, for five years after the earthquake of 17 CE. The fact that the Hierapolis community was also a daughter of the church in Colossae, whose letter many scholars believe was used in writing Ephesians, only strengthens Kreitzer's hypothesis.

Again, I do not seek to make a definitive claim on this matter. I raise these reconstruction and rebuilding components in order to shed some light on the peculiar language used to describe the *ekklesia* – elsewhere Paul speaks in terms of a body, not a building – and to highlight the emperor's role in construction in this general area and vested interest in the temples in particular. The rebuilding of temples for the worship of the gods and the honouring of the emperor are thus mirrored in this letter, which speaks of building the house of G*d for the worship of this counter-emperor.

What has caught my attention most in Kreitzer's work is the way the imperial aid to these cities was marked, or advertised if you will, on coinage produced either by the emperor or the local people who had received the aid. The use of coinage as a means of spreading imperial propaganda should not surprise us, since it continues to this day. Whether it was in the form of coins or seals, the image of a benevolent emperor spread throughout the region, giving a sense of unity to those under his rule. It comes as no surprise, then, to see the author of Ephesians speaking of the sealing of the Holy Spirit.

A Sacred Sealing

The stamp of a king, his 'seal', served to identify him as both the maintainer of justice and order and the source of authority; it also indirectly referred to the power of his kingdom, which sustained him in his role (Winter 1987: 61–84). When impressed upon a letter or scroll, the mark of a seal confirmed that person's obligation to uphold or follow through on the matter it communicated. It should be noted that the author of Ephesians identifies the stamp of the heavenly empire as the seal of the Holy Spirit: 'After listening to the message of truth, the gospel of your salvation – having also believed, you were sealed in him with the Holy Spirit of promise' (1.13). These people are marked by G*d's Holy Spirit, presumably an indication that G*d has claimed them, and are given the assurance that this counter-emperor will be true to the promise of redeeming them and offering them the inheritance of the empire of G*d. Instead of the emperor's gospel of salvation, we have the counter-gospel of a different deity, whose salvation is far greater than that offered by the Roman Empire.

This adaptation of stamping or sealing imagery was not simply a feel-good assurance of belonging to their G*d but a subversive political move.

Heavenly Citizenship

A part of the issue the author is addressing in this text is that of creating unity between Jews and Gentiles among these communities:

> For he himself is our peace, who made both groups into one, and broke down the barrier of the dividing wall, by abolishing in his flesh the enmity, which is the Law of commandments contained in ordinances, that in himself he might make the two into one new man, thus establishing peace, and might reconcile them both in one body to God through the cross, by it having put to death their enmity. (2.14-16)

Clearly there is, or was, enmity between two groups within this community. Just as an emperor creates 'peace' by imposing a unity of all peoples under his reign and rule, so also the cosmic Christ, ruler over all things, is the peace between factions in the Christian community. Through Christ the two groups have become one, and they are now allowed into the presence of the king, their G*d, and have citizenship within this spiritual domain.

The reference to citizenship in Israel is now trumped by citizenship with the saints in the household of G*d. This supersession is somewhat problematic, given that the foundation of this house was built upon the apostles and prophets (of Israel), yet ultimately seems to erase the identity of Israel altogether. Additionally, there is no getting away from the fact that speaking in terms of citizenship points to a larger matrix of social relations: one is a member of only one nation or empire at a time. No matter what is happening in clashes of ethnic identity within this community, the final struggle is between the emperor and their G*d, and the author of Ephesians makes clear who has already won that battle.

There is an interesting tension, however, between the new empire in the 'heavenly realms' and that of Caesar. The followers of Christ are a minority, but their counter-emperor is victorious over all, thus rules or reigns over all. Just as the Roman emperor sent out men to be in charge of various areas far removed from Rome, so that the many are ruled by a few representatives, so we can see a similar exclusivity at work in the construction of this counter-empire. Again, Perkins brings to light some of the striking implications of citizenship in this new empire: 'Despite their minority status in the world of first-century CE Asia Minor, Christians found themselves the center of God's cosmic design because they belonged to the risen Lord who is exulted over all of the heavenly powers' (1997: 44–45). In order for heavenly citizenship to be reassuring for them as a replacement for their socio-political minority status in this world, it must evoke familiar images of political structures and relations. A simple substitution of 'reign' for 'design' in Perkins' comment makes the point that their G*d was the victorious ruler enthroned in the heavenly realm. For servants/subjects of the victorious emperor, this 'reality' offers comfort and reassurance, but woe to those who do not recognize and participate in this heavenly citizenship. The tension between these two empires, then, is that, in order for the comforting aspect of the heavenly empire to be effective, the earthly empire must continue to exist; consequently, although this counter-empire offers relief from the oppression of Caesar, the same dominant ruling paradigm is inscribed within it.

Those who now have access to the heavenly emperor through the servant Christ have been unified. The enmity that separated them has been removed. As often happens with groups of people today, the source of conflict among them was over which traditions and ordinances were to be followed in their gatherings. In Christ the law is removed, allowing for a new peace, one that is established much in the same way as the Pax Romana is given or established throughout the Roman Empire. In both cases, the act of pronouncing that peace has been won through victory which both makes the peace a reality and imposes the peace upon all. In both cases the 'peace' is won in a realm far removed from the lives of common people, making it an elusive abstraction that can be asserted or denied by those in power. All people are to bow before the Father (earthly and heavenly), from whom all peoples, families or nations receive their name (3.15) and through whom they are all unified. It is not that a new kind of order has been established, just a new version of the same.

Another unfortunate development of this removed empire is that the formerly 'Suffering Servant' of Christ, who came into conflict with the imperial order, is now addressed as the servant of their G*d. The kings' servants, high-ranking court ministers, were endowed with power and status because of their close connection to the king. Paul had referred to Christ as a servant and to himself as a servant of Christ, often in letters written while in prison. A servant who 'takes one for the team' is quite different from the second-in-command servant of the all-powerful king. One must question which kind of servant the recipients of this letter understood Christ to be.

The issue of Gnostic influence within this letter is clearly seen in the third chapter. For the sake of this commentary, I point to it as another indication of the spiritualizing of reality that is taking place in this writing. The focus on abstract concepts such as the *plerōma* and special knowledge serves to place G*d's empire in a realm that is not accessed physically. The terminology of 'fullness' and 'being filled' is sprinkled throughout the letter (1.10, 23; 3.19; 4.10, 13; 5.18) and stands in stark contrast to the emptiness of their former way of life, the emptiness in which the Gentiles still live. In addition to its resonance with Gnostic tendencies, this kind of language might sound comforting to those who are empty, oppressed and spread thinly as colonized peoples. Focusing on abstraction, thus directing thoughts to the spiritual realm, can be a palliative for real, physical discomfort or oppression; it can also, however, engender an escapism that neutralizes the motivation for social change.

Cosmic Ekklesia

Margaret MacDonald sees in Ephesians a self-conscious awareness of the new universal, international movement in the Christian *ekklesia*. 'In presenting a vision of the universal *ekklesia* as a distinct society', she writes, 'the author of Ephesians draws on the history of Israel and Jewish concepts of resistance to the *Pax Romana*' (2004: 443). For her, the political aspect of citizenship – highlighted by terms such as *politeia, ekklesia* and 'aliens and strangers' – must be understood in light of the 'points of contact of the text (in the form of both appropriation and rejection) with imperial ideology' (2004: 422). Without such an ideology already at work for the colonized, the use of such terms would not make sense or have as much import.

This new heavenly *ekklesia*, an assembly or gathering of the *polis*, stands in contrast with Paul's concept of the *ekklesia* as a political gathering of the people 'in Christ', a gathering that would address issues of concern for the citizenry (Horsley 1997: 209). In this case, the realm in which their membership takes effect is the spiritual, cosmic realm. As mentioned above, this spiritualizing move must be seen as a form of escapism and actually serves to create indifference toward earthly political concerns. We should also not be surprised to see that *ekklesia* language is most prevalent in the modified household code section of the letter (addressed below), since the household is the location for the gathering of the citizens of G*d's empire.

Where I disagree with MacDonald is in her assessment of the effects of installing this new empire. 'In contrast to [the emperor's] gospel, however, the preaching of peace in Ephesians does not involve terror, intimidation and military action for those who resist Roman rule; it is the peace that belongs to the *ekklesia* – the peace of Christ (cf. Eph. 6.15-16)' (2004: 439). It seems to me that MacDonald's conclusion regarding the terror, intimidation and military action of the Roman Empire should be a lens through which we view the empire of G*d and the heavenly rule of Christ. This perspective would then highlight the tension between offering the peace of Christ and the imposition of it upon others. Those who, as members of the cosmic *ekklesia*, presume to be members of this new empire may be reassured by the dominance and rule of Christ, but it must be a fearsome thing for those 'outside'. The image constructed of those who continue to live in disobedience and ignorance (4.17-22; 5.5-8, 11-12) does not encourage including them but rather distancing oneself and one's group from such others. So the demonizing of the 'other' continues in this new empire – an act of intimidation at the very least – and sets the stage for violent military attacks once this *ekklesia* is also embraced by the emperor of this world.

A New Empire Writes Back

There is another aspect of this letter that needs to be addressed here, and that is the very document itself. Richard Gordon talks about 'writing as a form of social control' (1990: 189), a practice well used by emperors throughout the ages. The

Roman imperial practices of committing to writing the explanation of various aspects of religious rituals, institutions, symbols and objects lead to the ability to promulgate otherwise 'obsolescent religious categories'. This documentation then not only allows for a connection with the past but maintains the social expectations for general consumption, whether or not they are understood in the first place. So also the production of a piece of writing by a follower of Christ is not merely convenient for communication purposes but also serves as a material manifestation of the ideological vision of control and conformity. That the author intended to counter the Roman imperial ideology only deepens the implications for (un)conscious submission. In the same way that the Roman Empire sustained itself in part by the distribution of written proclamations and orders, the new empire of G*d will be sustained by the writing, collecting and reproducing of the texts from G*d's emissaries.

Gordon also notes the intersection of the senatorial elite and priestly offices (1990: 182–91), which leads to a telling aspect of political life noted here by Livy: the Romans were so preoccupied with the various gods, imbued with piety, 'that it was regard for promises and oaths by which the state was governed in place of fear of the laws and [of] punishment' (Livy 1.21.1; 183). The promises of the deity instill a deeper piety, and thus obedience, than the laws of the land. The ruling elite would be foolish not to channel the piety of the people toward the realms of official governmental control, and what better way to do so than to take on titles or roles within both realms? The priestly senators would then be the vessels of the gods, whose tacit approval of the senators engenders consent to their laws and decrees.

The point of political propaganda was to engender devotion to the Roman emperor's agenda by extolling his benefactions and creating a sense of unity and like-mindedness. Ephesians mimics political propaganda, painting a picture of a new heavenly empire, ruled by a king whose right-hand man, his servant, has conquered all powers, rulers and authorities of this age. The act of committing to writing such religious claims, imbued with imperial terminology, is one of desire to control and to engender conformity within the heavenly empire. Just as the Roman imperial ideology 'succeeds' when it is viewed as common sense, and thus needs no justification, the counter-imperial ideology in Ephesians need not be justified and fits nicely within the 'normative' socio-political structures already at work.

Socio-Political Exhortations: Household Codes

Textual Politics

There has never been a time when matters of the household did not have political import. In such a recent commentary as John Muddiman's, it is a bit shocking to see a scholar dismiss the possibility that Ephesians was written to counter political propaganda or state persecution. His reasoning is as follows: 'Ephesians lacks any call to suffering discipleship on the part of Christians and there is nothing on relations with the state in the section on Christian conduct' (2001: 15). Aside from wanting to discuss why only suffering discipleship would have political implications, I am intrigued by the assumption that something must be directly named in order for it to be present in the text. Household codes are socio-political by nature (Balch 1988); thus, their adaptation in the section on Christian conduct in this text indirectly communicates something to the recipients about relations with the state. Unfortunately, perspectives such as Muddiman's serve to reinforce a spiritualized interpretation of the text, thus unwittingly reinforcing a denial of the connection between family/private matters and politics.

The *Haustafel* section begins with, or comes immediately after, a call to the entire community to 'be subject to one another in the fear of Christ' (5.21). Similarly, the wives are to submit to their husbands as they do to the Lord (5.33), and the slaves are to obey their human masters with fear and trembling (6.5). Although the other typical members of the household are also addressed, their exhortations are not buttressed by obedience out of fear, as we see for the wives and slaves. While there is much within the sacred writings of the Jews, and thus this community, that refers to devotion to G*d in terms of 'fear', that does not necessarily mean that the terminology is positive or helpful. Fear and control go hand in hand. Fearing the power of the emperor is one thing. (Re)importing such fear in the religious realm is simply ascribing the same dominant, and thus oppressive, position to the deity that the emperor has with the people. These may be structures and relations people can understand, and are thus affective, but that does not mean that they are beneficial.

Additionally, we do well to stop and ask why it is that such strong language is used for these two groups of people in particular. The rhetoric of the letter betrays the fear and intention of the author, who seeks to restrain those whose actions could pose the greatest threat to the order and control of this counter-empire. Carolyn Osiek notes the lack of reference to finances in the Ephesians *Haustafel*. While this particular aspect is missing in all manifestations of the *Haustafeln* in the New Testament (2002: 29–39), what makes it of interest here is that it was the women/wives and slaves who were central to the economic productivity of the household. In this construction, then, it is the wives and slaves who are most essential in supporting empire (D'Angelo 1993: 315) – both the Roman and the heavenly; thus, most subject to directives of control. This element that focuses upon the subject producers could be used for a liberationist interpretation. It could be the lens that allows us to envision a reality in which all members are present, valued and given space to share their voice. It could allow us the means to subvert the imperial ideology and replace it not with a counter-imperial system but with one of embodied equality. In context, however, it is clearly not applied for such ends. The unspoken economic aspect of this exhortation, then, becomes part of the grander picture of imperial ideology that is co-opted by Ephesians and thus passed along to the churches thereafter.

It is no coincidence that historians can point to numerous affirmations of the ideals of the Roman family within the speeches of emperors and rhetoricians, since the family/household was seen as the basic unit of the empire. Since the rules of the household are, as Elisabeth Schüssler Fiorenza puts it (1997: 241), 'part of economics and politics, as are religious rites and ancestral customs', the household is key to socio-political control. In effect, as she adds, 'the well-being of the state and the religious observance of the laws and customs of the patriarchal family are intertwined' (1997: 241). Just as the religious and the political are inseparable and foundational realms within Roman imperial ideology, so too are they within the empire of G*d.

Sexual Politics
There is a striking comparison within this section that is particular to the Ephesian *Haustafel*. The Christian community is constructed in terms of two images: the body of Christ and the subject status of a wife (Osiek 2002; Sampley 1971). The intermingling of these images is somewhat problematic, since it sets up the *ekklesia* in terms of both Christ's body and Christ's bride (Mertz 2000: 131–47; contra Applegate 2004: 94). This mixing of metaphors, both of which refer to something a man has control over (body and wife), allows, then, for a similar relational dynamic between men and women within the *ekklesia*. There is something powerful subconsciously communicated by the use of such symbols to name and constrain women in the community. I would say that the assertion of such symbolism points to a deeper power struggle, one that was certainly won by the men in charge. The emergence of the comparison of women to the socio-political entity of an *ekklesia* is something of an 'irruption' in the text (Hennessy 1993: 94); it is not expected and thus should raise a flag for the reader. The women's role here is over-determined, which indicates the power they do embody and the need of the author to keep them under control.

The significant *ekklesia* terminology in this section of the letter (5.23-25, 27, 29, 32) also solidifies the political implications of the community of believers. This *ekklesia* is to be subject to their counter-ruler in the same way that a wife is to her husband and supportive of the counter-empire as the more typical *ekklesiai* are of the Roman Empire. Thus the systemic, androcentric, patriarchal dynamic of marriage is reinscribed within these communities, which, according to some scholars, were initially trying to move beyond such limiting structures. Schüssler Fiorenza's comment on Gal. 3.28 makes this point clear:

> 'No longer male and female' is best understood, therefore, in terms of marriage and gender relationships. As such, Gal. 3.28c does not assert that there are no longer men and women in Christ, but that patriarchal marriage – and sexual relationship between male and female – is no longer constitutive of the new community in Christ. Irrespective of their procreative capacities and of the social roles connected with them, persons will be full members of the Christian movement in and through baptism. (1997: 227–28)

In light of this interpretation of sexual relationships within the Christian communities up to and during Paul's time, the move made in Ephesians not only reintroduces the practice of identifying women according to their marital status but also makes the patriarchal marriage the ultimate, or *only* (Mertz 2000: 147), representation of the church's relation to Christ.

In terms of a postcolonial perspective, this move is problematic because, in countering a Pauline view of sexual relations, which was 'a frontal assault on the intentions of existing law and the general cultural ethos' (Schüssler Fiorenza 1997: 233), Ephesians is in line with the Graeco-Roman cultural values. Just as in the Roman Empire the married (with children) state was encouraged by legislation, now the married state is encouraged, due to its reflection of true Christ-like-ness, in G*d's empire. The ruler(s) of the heavenly empire are to be emulated (in all their power and glory), worshipped and treated with deference. Indeed, everything about the lives of the followers of Christ is to be for glory and honour of their G*d, the counter-emperor. While this may not manifest itself *directly* as a socio-economic exploitation, it is a similar dynamic of subject–ruler as the one in the Roman Empire, where every aspect of their lives was overshadowed and controlled by their subject status.

The household codes have rich material for a postcolonial critique. The construction of gender roles, which imitate the hierarchy of and obedience sought by the empire, the economic concerns indirectly involved in maintaining order, and the socio-political nature of the *Haustafeln* – all make this section an important one from a postcolonial perspective.

Call to Battle

A final aspect of Ephesians that needs to be addressed in terms of a postcolonial commentary is the closing section on the armour of G*d or, as John Lincoln has noted, the 'call to battle' (1990: 432–34) in 6.10-20. Although this armour is fully 'spiritualized' and described in terms of beneficent and loving actions, it is preparing the community for battle nonetheless. They are to put on the undergarments of truth, protect their heart with righteousness, shod their feet with the readiness to share the good news of this counter-empire, carry the shield of faith, wear the helmet of salvation that this imperial ruler brings, and carry the sword of the Spirit, which is the word of G*d (6.10-17). In other words, they are to be prepared at all times to figuratively 'slay' their enemies with the words of their G*d, knowing that their armour, their focus on the realm of the Spirit, will protect them. While some may say that this battle imagery is justified because it is familiar and thus effectively communicates the urgency and intensity of the message, at the end of the day we still have followers of Christ imagining that they are donning armour, preparing for figurative battle for the sake of their heavenly empire. Just because the imagery is now deployed/employed within the spiritual realm does not neutralize the violent, aggressive and bloody battle imagery associated with the use of armour.

Letty Russell poignantly notes the depth of the problematic of the culmination of divine warrior and 'holy' armour imagery within this counter-insurgency:

> With military imagery filling the music of our churches, we have served the Prince of Peace but often have also served the Prince of Darkness, supporting wars of conquest and plunder. Today we can no longer afford the luxury of this militant imagery because we live in a world which is full of violence and on the brink of total destruction. Those who live in nations that shape the principalities of our day cannot afford triumphal hymns. If anyone is to sing hymns, it seems to me it should be the victims of exploitation and oppression as they struggle to claim their humanity. (1984: 125)

The problem she notes, violent battle imagery embedded in Church liturgy, is based upon the language that is present in the texts of the Christian tradition. This particular imagery alluding to battle, victory and relations of ruling and domination was chosen by the author of Ephesians because it made sense; it was part of their daily experience of living in the Roman Empire. In doing so, the author simply turned the violence and exploitation they were subject to into something wished upon their enemies and brought to fruition through their all-powerful and victorious G*d. Some suggest that the oppressed are justified in desiring a world order that puts their oppressors in the position of being dominated. I would say that nothing is gained in this reinscribing of the same oppressive and violent paradigm, except the permanent foothold of violence and justified domination within the Christian tradition.

While I do not like the implications of Martin Kitchen's concluding comments, I do agree with them: 'Ephesians 6.10-20 is therefore also a fitting conclusion to the whole epistle, since it portrays an image of a perfected church, reconciled and renewed, over which Christ rules as Lord; this is the "summing up" of all things' (1994: 127). This image of the *ekklesia* in armour is the 'crowning achievement' of this letter that so powerfully establishes a counter-empire of G*d with devout and obedient subjects. Their lord and master reigns in the new empire-in-the-sky with his battle-ready followers.

Conclusion

The construction of the Christian *ekklesia* in Ephesians is dependent upon the imperial structural and religious ideology for its own relational design and motivation for obedience. The author creates a counter-empire by drawing upon terminology typically associated with imperial claims, decrees and restorative actions. The appropriation of a tool for social control such as the *Haustafel* within the realm of religious discourse further secures the connection between religious and political content in the text. The act of writing for the sake of communication and further distribution, the politically charged content within this religious text, and the people such propaganda is focused upon – all reflect techniques employed to maintain Roman imperial rule. The author of Ephesians constructs an empire that has conquered that of Rome. Yet, the victorious emperor and his empire are thoroughly 'spiritualized', giving the subjects of this realm no reason to seek change within the earthly realm, with its unjust rulers and systems, but rather passive acquiescence to its systems. In fact, in order for their counter-empire to make any sense, the earthly empire must be maintained.

As I discuss with ministry students the problem inherent in a text such as Ephesians, where the earthly empire is simply reinscribed 'in the skies', thus perpetuating the idea that *someone* must be in control, at the top of a power structure similar to a pyramid, I see their frustration at such never-ending cycles of power and domination. What gives them hope is the idea of not simply turning the system on its head but of an alternate way of conceiving power and the ways it is used and shared. This vision gives me hope that a postcolonial critique or commentary might lead to something more than a mere critique of the system, to the construction of liberative spaces and new ways of being in the world. This space may begin with a subversion of the author's own construction and control over the household, in which the people who are seen as most threatening to the counter-imperial order are instead appreciated as powerful. Yet, in this new space power is power-with. Instead of controlling those who 'threaten' the system, the focus is on empowering them to lead the way into new understandings of community and liberation for all people.

BIBLIOGRAPHY

Applegate, Judith K.
    2004   'The Co-Elect Woman of 1 Peter', in Amy-Jill Levine with Maria Mayo
            Robbins (eds), *A Feminist Companion to the Catholic Epistles and Hebrews*
            (Cleveland: Pilgrim Press): 89–102.
Balch, David
    1988   'Household Codes', in David Aune (ed.), *Greco-Roman Literature and the
            New Testament: Selected Forms and Genres* (Society of Biblical Literature
            Sources for Biblical Study, 21; Atlanta: Scholars Press): 25–50.
D'Angelo, Mary Rose
    1993   'Colossians', in Elisabeth Schüssler Fiorenza and Shelly Matthews (eds),
            Searching the Scriptures. Vol. 2, *A Feminist Commentary* (New York: Cross-
            road): 313–24.
Elliott, Neil
    1997   'Anti-Imperial Message of the Cross', in Richard A. Horsley (ed.), *Paul and
            Empire: Religion and Power in Roman Imperial Society* (Harrisburg, PA:
            Trinity Press International): 167–83.
Faust, Eberhard
    1993   *Pax Christi et pax Caesaris: Religionsgeschichtliche, traditionsgeschichtliche
            und sozialgeschichtliche Studien zum Ephesebrief* (Göttingen: Vandenhoeck
            & Ruprecht).
Gombis, Timothy G.
    2004   'Ephesians 2 as a Narrative of Divine Warfare', *Journal for the Study of the
            New Testament* 26: 403–18.

Gordon, Richard
    1990   'From Republic to Principate: Priesthood, Religion and Ideology', in Mary Beard and John North (eds), *Pagan Priests: Religion and Power in the Ancient World* (Ithaca, NY: Cornell University Press): 179–98.

Hennessy, Rosemary
    1993   *Materialist Feminism and the Politics of Discourse* (New York: Routledge).

Horsley, Richard A.
    1997   'Building an Alternative Society: Introduction', in Richard A. Horsley (ed.), *Paul and Empire: Religion and Power in Roman Imperial Society* (Harrisburg, PA: Trinity Press International): 206–14.

Kitchen, Martin
    1994   *Ephesians* (New York: Routledge).

Kreitzer, Larry J.
    2004   'Living in the Lycus Valley: Earthquake Imagery in Colossians, Philemon and Ephesians', in Jiří Mrázek and Jan Roskovec (eds), *Testimony and Interpretation: Early Christology in Its Judeo-Hellenistic Milieu: Studies in Honor of Petr Pokorný* (Edinburgh: T&T Clark): 81–94.

Lincoln, Andrew T.
    1990   *Ephesians* (Dallas: Word Books).

MacDonald, Margaret Y.
    2004   'The Politics of Identity in Ephesians', *Journal for the Study of the New Testament* 26: 419–44.

Mertz, Annette
    2000   'Why Did the Pure Bride of Christ (2 Cor. 11.2) Become a Wedded Wife (Eph. 5:22-33)? Theses about the Intertextual Transformation of an Ecclesiological Metaphor', *Journal for the Study of the New Testament* 79: 131–47.

Moi, Toril
    2002   *Sexual/Textual Politics: Feminist Literary Theory* (New York: Routledge).

Muddiman, John
    2001   *A Commentary on the Epistle to the Ephesians* (New York: Continuum).

Osiek, Carolyn
    2002   'The Bride of Christ (5:22-23): A Problematic Wedding', *Biblical Theology Bulletin* 32: 29–39.

Perkins, Pheme
    1997   *Ephesians* (Abingdon New Testament Commentaries; Nashville: Abingdon Press).

Price, S. F. R.
    1984   *Rituals and Power: The Roman Imperial Cult in Asia Minor* (New York: Cambridge University Press).

Russell, Letty M.
    1984   *Imitators of God: A Study Book on Ephesians* (New York: General Board of Global Ministries, United Methodist Church).

Sampley, J. Paul
    1971   *'And the Two Shall Become One Flesh': A Study of Traditions in Ephesians 5:21-33* (Cambridge: Cambridge University Press).

Schüssler Fiorenza, Elisabeth
    1997   'The Praxis of Co-Equal Discipleship', in Richard A. Horsley (ed.), *Paul and Empire: Religion and Power in Roman Imperial Society* (Harrisburg, PA: Trinity Press International): 224–41.

Thurston, Bonnie B.
2004   'The Pauline Tradition: Colossians and Ephesians', in Dennis E. Smith (ed.), *Chalice Introduction to the New Testament* (St. Louis: Chalice): 96–116.

Whang, Y. C.
1998   'Cohabitation or Conflict? Greek Household Management and Christian *Haustafeln*', in Michael A. Hayes, Wendy Porter and David Tombs (eds), *Religion and Sexuality* (Sheffield: Sheffield Academic Press): 85–100.

Winter, Irene J.
1987   'Legitimation of Authority Through Image and Legend: Seals Belonging to Officials in the Administrative Bureaucracy of the Ur III State', in McGuire Gibson and Robert D. Biggs (eds), *The Organization of Power: Aspects of Bureaucracy in the Ancient Near East* (Chicago: Oriental Institute of the University of Chicago): 61–84.

Linked to the study of the suppressed gospels is the widening understanding of the milieu of early Christianity. Postcolonial studies need to look beyond the limitations of the Jewish-Hellenistic context and pay attention also to the Jewish-Aramaic. The New Testament writings play into and confirm the notion that they were aimed at and tethered to Hellenistic Christianity. They and their interpretation were largely concerned with Hellenistic Christianity and the movement westwards, at the expense of Aramaic Christianity which was closer to Judaism and moved eastwards. Except for three letters – Romans, Corinthians and Thessalonians – the rest were written against those who supported the Jewish form of Christianity envisioned by Peter, James, John and the sons of Zebedee. They were labelled variously – sometimes mockingly, as 'pillars' (Gal. 2.9) or 'super apostles'(2 Cor. 11.5; 12.11); derisively, as 'false brethren' (Gal. 2.1); and even derogatively, as 'dogs' (Phil. 3.2). The only document to record the growth of early Christianity, the Acts of the Apostles, not only neglects Judaeo-Christianity but at times shows an outright antagonism towards it. It duly records the conversion of Western pagans such as Cornelius the Italian, the high-standing Greek women and men at Beroea (17.12), Dionysius the Areopagite, and the woman called Damaris (17.34), but ignores the conversion of non-Western pagans, the exception being the Ethiopian eunuch. The way the author of Luke-Acts handled the disputes between the Hellenists and the Hebrews is an indication of where his sympathy lay.

There are compelling reasons for us to revisit the often neglected cultural milieu in which Christianity emerged. One is that recent research has shown that both African and Asian Christianity grew out of the Jewish-Aramaic background rather than the Jewish-Hellenistic, thus posing a different set of theological questions. Biblical scholarship tends to focus on the Jewish-Hellenistic background and to underplay the Jewish-Aramaic in the formation of early Christianity. The former is seen as progressive, adaptable, tolerant and universal, whereas the latter is portrayed as rigid, backward, bigoted and insular. To survive and to gain status in a strange, imperial environment, Christian faith in its formative years may have mimicked the dominant Hellenistic culture, but the historical necessity and theological need which led to such hermeneutical manoeuvres were of that time. In a changed, democratic and pluralistic theological context, Jewish Christianity presents and poses a different agenda for Christianity outside the West.

The Jewish Christians were the original hybridizers who wished to remain within the Jewish religious parameters and reconfigured their faith in the light of the teachings of Jesus. Paul's universal gospel, which flattened significant ethnic or cultural differences, has become less tenable in a postcolonial context when vernacular identities and values have a renewed lease of life. The culture-specific expressions of Christianity which use the language of Hinduism, Buddhism, Taoism or traditional African religion have become a significant resistant force against a universal form of Christianity which had its origins in Paul and was later perfected by Western Christianity.

The question which Paul faced then was how to make a particularistic and sectarian faith a universal one. His answer was to extricate it from the particularity of its Jewish observances and ceremonies and transfer it into a cosmopolitan setting. Now, in our changed context, the question is how viable is this universal form of Christianity, which is not only tainted by its association with colonialism but also undermines and undercuts local aspirations and orientations. The theological vision Paul forged for a single humanity incorporated under the lordship of the cosmic Christ now smacks of Christian triumphalism in a context where many gods and goddesses are vying for attention. In the face of rapid globalization, culture-specific Christianity acts as an antidote and provides resources to survive. The task is how to construct a hermeneutics based on specific identities without at the same time wallowing in nativistic pride. In this changed theological context, the recovery of denied and misrepresented Jewish Christianity has important implications and supports the postcolonial concern for denied knowledges and agency.

The Post-Mission Context and the Rebirth of Gods and Goddesses
We need to revisit the colonizing monotheistic tendencies present in the biblical narratives and see them against the many-layered polytheistic context out of which they emerged. Monotheism introduced notions of true and false religions and the chosen and the damned. The biblical monotheistic vision which undergirded one faith and one church has to be viewed against the many gods, many faiths and many churches which crowd our religious landscape. Whereas the old cosmic gods were interculturally translatable and nobody questioned their reality or the legitimacy of their worship, monotheism introduced the notion of false gods, idolatry and estranged people. Biblical monotheism itself has to be problematized. As recent Jewish studies have shown, monotheism is much more ambiguous as a reality than one is usually led to believe. Angelology and the doctrine of the Trinity raise awkward questions for the supposed biblical monotheism. The classical two-nature theory about Christ sits uncomfortably within the single-God framework. What is increasingly clear is that there is no such thing as absolute monotheism. In Rodney Stark's view, the great monotheistic faiths – Judaism, Christianity and Islam – are all 'dualistic monotheisms: each teaches that, in addition to the existence of a supreme divine being, there also exists at least one evil, if less powerful supernatural being' (Stark 2001: 25).

Besides its theological incongruity, the political implications of the monotheistic ideal have been disastrous. What monotheism detests is a variety of empires competing with each other. Monotheism provides a vital instrument in strengthening and maintaining a single empire and presents unlimited prospects for transmitting the message which the dominant want to spread. Origen hailed the Pax Romana established by Augustus as paving an uninterrupted way for the propagation of the gospel: 'Jesus was born during the reign of Augustus, the one who reduced to uniformity, so to speak, the many kingdoms on earth so that he had a single empire. It would have hindered Jesus' teaching from being spread through the whole world if there had been many kingdoms' (Fowden 1993: 89). It is this monotheistic vision of a single empire which has provided the vision and impetus to the current American imperium in its task of creating a single world order with a view to spreading its own ideology and economy based on market values.

The polytheistic situation which the early Christians encountered and which shaped the Christian understanding of a single god is different from the current one. Whereas the old Greek and Hellenistic gods and goddesses are dead and gone, we see the thriving of gods and goddesses in our midst. What we are witnessing is a plural monotheism. There is a rejuvenation and rebirth of gods in the plural – the Christian God, the Islamic God, the Hindu Gods and Goddesses – all competing in the marketplace of religious discourse. This is articulated at the popular level by the heroine of the Indian film, *Bombay*. When she, the Muslim wife of a Hindu husband, becomes pregnant and is worried about the financial strain the new addition is going to cause to their already precarious monetary situation, her instinctive reaction is to tell her husband that Allah will look after the child, but she corrects herself with the words: 'Our child has two Gods. They will care for it'.

There is no longer a monotheistic centre which holds everything together. What we are discovering are multiple centres. Monotheism is managed by a rigid thinking which requires stark choices between right and wrong, truth and falsehood. This kind of stark choice is unhelpful to people whose lives are inherently untidy and their experiences marked by messy and mixed-up realities. We live in a culture which does not believe in one morality, or in one set of principles. Our identities are multiple, and we are simultaneously energized and exasperated by this condition. The diverse nature of our modern living and the diverse nature of our experiences of the divine force us to recognize that monotheism and polytheism are two human apprehensions of reality and are not to be seen as alternative claims upon our attention. The biblical notion of monotheism superseding polytheism is no longer hermeneutically tenable. What Regina Schwartz says in the closing words of her book, *The Curse of Cain*, could be a new guiding principle for postcolonial biblical studies: 'It would be a Bible embracing multiplicity instead of monotheism. The old "monotheistic" book must be closed so that new books may be fruitful and multiply. After all that was the first commandment' (Schwartz 1997: 186).

Making Ritual Invisible

Mainstream biblical scholarship has paid undue attention to doctrinal aspects of biblical texts and has been very successful in mining them. But there is an inexplicable scarcity of study of ritual practices in the lives of the biblical Jews or in the formative years of early Christianity. Both testaments record a variety of cultic and liturgical practices which enabled biblical communities to define, clarify and practise their faith. Mainstream biblical interpretation, partly prompted by Protestant influence, is so doctrine-based that it tends to treat rituals and activities related to the temple as a contaminating influence and a primitive form of faith. Analysing some of the literature published after 1988 on the social and religious world during the formative years of Christianity, Jonathan Schwiebert, in a recent article, has been critical of New Testament scholars and the way they have handled early Christian rituals. He has shown that when the Lord's Supper is studied, the term is employed throughout without any suggestion that it refers to a 'ritual' or a 'ritual meal'. Similarly, when baptism is investigated the term is 'maintained with monotonous insistence' without exploring its ritual import. Schwiebert's indictment is that New Testament scholars:

> Create an important *silence*, a kind of tacit and vague assumption that early Christians did not really practice rituals; or, if they did, these were not as important as what early Christians *believed*; or if they were truly important to some early Christians, this represents a later *corruption* from the earliest period; or, if rituals do not signal corruption, at least they were never to be taken as *real* in their own right – they were token symbols of interior realities. (Schwiebert 2004: 12)

There is an underlying assumption within mainstream biblical scholarship which is spurred on and sourced with impeccable Enlightenment values that theory is superior to praxis. Therefore, the tendency is to treat rituals as aberrant, inferior and second-rate in comparison to the doctrinal elements and, more significantly, incapable of enriching the faith. There is an undeclared assumption that the biblical books contain only diverse beliefs, teachings and messages. The acceptance or non-acceptance of these beliefs, teachings and messages are seen as more important than the participation or non-participation in the rituals. For the majority of Asian and African communities, rituals are at least equally important, for they are the outward manifestation of their faith.

Solicited Martyrdom and Spectacular Demonstration of Faith

The survival and the continued usefulness of postcolonialism depends on generating new knowledge about specific ethical and moral issues which have attracted media attention. Two such cases are suicide missions (Diego Gambetta's term, not ideal since it fails to acknowledge the fact of indiscriminate killing) and asylum-seeking.

Suicide Missions

Since the 7 July 2005 bombing in the London Underground, questions have been raised as to what motivates people to venture on undertakings which have such devastating effects. What postcolonialism has to reiterate is that spreading terror and the capacity to annihilate life is not a monopoly of one religion.

Likewise, martyrs as ideal exemplars are not confined to Christianity and Islam. Other leading world religions such as Buddhism and Sikhism have given some form of scriptural legitimacy to such acts. Christianity, too, has its share of those who have killed for noble causes. The mass killing of innocent people is not new either. It has a biblical precedent. The closest we get is recorded in the book of Judges, where Samson acts as an instrument of God, killing both the high and mighty among the Philistines and 3000 ordinary sports-loving people for the humiliation meted out to him (Judges 16). In the New Testament, the only mass killing, the massacre of the innocents, goes some way towards exemplifying the Christian understanding of martyrdom. The Iraqi, Palestinian and London suicide bombers see martyrdom as a way of fulfilling a sacred duty which itself is tied up with the notion of struggle against injustice. *The Acts of Christian Martyrs* (see Musurillo 1972) is particularly significant for the present time for it gives a fascinating description of early Christian martyrdom. Granted that much of the literature is hagiographical, and contains celebratory sermons eulogizing the achievement of martyrs, these writings offer patterns of martyrdom which have certain limited resonances with current events.

For the ancient Christian martyrs, the heavenly kingdom of God was superior to the earthly kingdom of Caesar. For the current Islamic martyr, it is Allah's heavenly paradise which is inherently better than the current secular and materialist world. Both have an antagonistic attitude to empires, which are viewed in dualistic terms and in apocalyptic images. For the ancient Christian martyrs, the enemy was Caesar; for the Islamic radicals, it is the hegemony of the United States, exemplified in President Bush and the conduct of the Israeli government. Compromise with the enemy/empire is unthinkable for one cannot serve two masters. Both present a threat to and judgment on empire: the Roman Empire for the ancient Christians; the American Empire for radical Islamists. Both see their mission as bearing witness – one to Christ; the other to Allah – and refuse to obey orders from earthly powers. Both have an unshakeable belief that their cause will not fail because it is God's and treat their acts as missionary ventures. Both have their aspirations fuelled by a monotheistic vision. Both see death not as a defeat but as a final triumph and a flawless way to enter the next life. Both emphasize that their decision to die was a conscious choice and of their own free will. Both see martyrdom as a valuable means of motivating and attracting potential converts to the cause. Here the comparison ends. Whereas the martyrs die with the hope of a better life for others, the suicide missioners, in promising to improve life for their fellow believers, in the process destroy innocent human lives, including those of believers. As Terry Eagleton put it: 'Suicide bombers also die in the name of a better life for others; it is just that, unlike martyrs, they take others with them in the process' (Eagleton 2005: 23).

Interestingly, ancient and contemporary reactions to such acts are somewhat similar. The suicidal recklessness of early Christian martyrs not only provoked astonishment and disbelief but also prompted exactly the same sort of reaction among pagan Romans as today's Islamic militants have done in the West. The castigation of Christian martyrs as 'simply out of their minds – insane' by Marcus Aurelius and Celsus (Bowersock 1995: 3) resonates with the current widespread assumption that volunteer suicide bombers must be mentally deranged. Just as the Christian martyrs were investigated for their vague criminal activities, the current bombers are accused of having links with the criminal underworld.

The prevailing popular perception that terrorist suicides are the creation of religious fundamentalism is not always correct. The motivation of the Sri Lankan Tamil Tigers is derived not from Hindu values, but is based on language discrimination. Those who blew themselves up in Lebanon in the 1980s were inspired by socialist or communist ideals. The acts of violence are not espoused by some Muslims alone, but are the result of complex social, religious and political pressures. One of the motivating factors which incites martyrdom is empire. Postcolonialism can draw attention to the fact that empires play their part in fomenting martyrdom. In the popular perception, martyrdom is perceived essentially as a religious act sanctioned by ancient texts and undertaken by noble devotees. Such a view insulates these acts from issues of power and imperial geopolitics. The incentive for martyrdom is provided not by sacred texts alone. The presence of empire – the occupation of other peoples' territory, the power and cultural politics of dominating peoples' lives – plays an important part. This is true of both modern and ancient empires. Bowersock has shown that:

> Christianity owed its martyrs to the *mores* and structure of the Roman empire, not to the indigenous character of the Semitic Near East where Christianity was born. The written record suggests that, like the very word 'martyr' itself, martyrdom had nothing to do with Judaism or Palestine. It had everything to do with the Greco-Roman world, its traditions, its language, and its cultural tastes. (Bowersock 1995: 28)

Robert A. Pape, in his study of the grievances that prompt suicide bombers to undertake these acts (a study initiated by the Pentagon), has reached conclusions which will not please the US Defense Department. Studying nearly 315 suicide bombings carried out by Muslims, Tamils, Sikhs and Kurds between 1980 and 2003, Pape concludes that the 'data shows that there is little connection between suicide terrorism and Islamic fundamentalism, or any one of the world religions' (2005: 4). Rather, suicide attacks by each of the groups studied were 'mainly a response to foreign occupation rather than the product of Islamic fundamentalism' (2005: 237). Pape's study has demonstrated that 'religion is rarely the root cause, although it is often used as a tool by terrorist organizations in recruiting and in other efforts in service of the broader strategic objective' (2005: 4). The broader objective of such a spectacular act, 'or its central objective', is to coerce 'a foreign state that has military forces in what the terrorists see as their homeland to take those forces out' (2005: 21).

THE LETTER TO THE PHILIPPIANS

Efraín Agosto

Paul's letter to the Philippians has been described as his most 'friendly' letter to any of his congregations. Certainly, the polemics of the Corinthian correspondence and Galatians are lacking in Philippians, except for the strong word against outside opponents in 3.2 ('Beware of the dogs...!') In terms of his relationship internally with the Philippian congregation, Paul gives thanks for their 'partnership' with him, 'from the first day until now' (1.5). Indeed, while he looks upon departing from this life to be with Christ as 'far better', he would much prefer, he states, to survive a difficult prison term in order to visit once again and minister to the Philippians (1.23-26).

Why did Paul write this letter to the Philippians while imprisoned in a Roman jail (1.7)? No Pauline letter is without some contingent historical and theological purposes. Moreover, Paul's correspondence with the Christian community in Philippi represents a unique opportunity to explore a missive between two subject correspondents – Paul, subject to the abject oppression of a Roman prison, and the Philippian congregation, subject to their status as members of 'an alternative society' in the official Roman colony that was Philippi. In this commentary I offer a reconstruction of the occasion for Philippians, using a rhetorical analysis of the letter, and explore the contours of the imperial status of both Paul and the Philippians, employing the methods and questions of postcolonial biblical interpretation (see Agosto 2002).

A Reconstruction of Philippians Using Rhetorical Analysis

Paul's letter to the Philippians was written sometime in the decade of the 50s or early 60s CE, depending on whether Paul wrote the letter from Rome during his last imprisonment there in the late 50s or early 60s or from an imprisonment elsewhere earlier in the decade of the 50s (on this question see Fee 1995: 34–37; O'Brien 1991: 19–26; Osiek 2000: 27–31; Witherington 1994: 24–29). A rhetorical analysis of the letter helps to illuminate its occasion and reconstruct, to some extent, what might have happened; in this analysis I follow, with slight variation, the work of Duane Watson (1988) and Ben Witherington (1994: 57–88).

Paul begins the letter with an *exordium* (introduction) in which he gives thanks to the Philippians for their ongoing partnership with him and his ministry, even though he has been imprisoned (1.3-11). In the *narratio* of the letter (the statement of the facts), Paul reports on his situation in a Roman prison and his desire to see the Philippians, if he survives an upcoming trial (1.12-26). Then, Paul turns to the all-important *propositio* (the statement of purpose) of the letter, in which he exhorts the community toward unity and steadfastness in the midst of conflict and opposition (1.27-30). Thus, while Paul resolutely faces his own opposition in an imprisoned situation, he seeks to encourage the Philippians to overcome their own situation of conflict and opposition.

In the heart of the letter, the *probatio* (proofs), Paul wants the Philippians to follow certain examples as a response to their situation of conflict (Jesus, Paul, Timothy, Epaphroditus, 2.1-30). Paul also acknowledges the presence of opposition in Philippi and offers an alternative 'discourse' – keeping their 'eyes on the prize', the prize being a 'heavenly citizenship' beyond their current state of conflict in Philippi, a conflict evidently brought about by their faith commitments (3.1-21). Both of these sections (chs 2 and 3) constitute that part of Paul's rhetoric in which he cites examples, both positive and negative, to 'prove' to the Philippians that seeking unity in the midst of conflict – what he asks of them in the *propositio* of 1.27-30 – is both preferable and possible.

Finally, Paul turns to a *peroratio* (recapitulation) of his exhortation to the Philippians, in which he encourages unity, peace and love, not only for the community as a whole (4.4-9) but also, and especially, for two women leaders, Euodia and Syntyche (4.2-3). These women have worked together with Paul on behalf of the gospel and now seem to be divided against each other. Paul exhorts them to unity in such a way that, it would appear, their continuing division could very well threaten the well-being of the entire congregation (see Schüssler Fiorenza 1983: 169–70). In a final *peroratio* to the letter, Paul thanks the community again for their partnership and monetary support of his ministry (4.10-20; cf. 1.3-7). He mentions Epaphroditus, whom he previously praised (2.25-30), as the one who has delivered the Philippian gift. This offering from the Philippians to Paul in prison exemplifies a kind of 'underground economy' that the Pauline mission utilizes over against the imperial political economies (see Horsley 1997: 249–51), a point to which I will return below.

Briefly stated, then, Paul's letter to the Philippians represents as close to a Graeco-Roman 'letter of friendship' as one can find among Paul's letters, a very personal correspondence between himself and his beloved congregation in the Roman colony of Philippi. (On Philippians and letters of friendship see Fee 1995: 2–14; Witherington 1994: 7–10; Osiek 2000: 21–24. Stanley Stowers, however, argues that there are no such letters in the New Testament, although Philippians, along with several other Pauline letters, does have certain features of the letter of friendship [1986: 58–70].) His difficult situation of imprisonment, including the possibility of death, does not preclude ministry to a congregation that has been supportive of the Pauline mission faithfully throughout, especially given the difficult situation that they themselves currently confront.

Paul exhorts them to unity and steadfastness in the face of opposition and cites models of those who have remained faithful in similar circumstances, including himself; his close associate Timothy; a church representative, Epaphroditus; and, above all, Jesus Christ.

A Postcolonial Reading

Postcolonial thinking asks how imperialism, wherever it is found, has affected its colonies. As the postcolonial critic Walter Rodney puts it, 'to be colonized is to be removed from history' (cited in Gugelberger 1994: 582). Postcolonial criticism attempts to write the colonized back into history. It undertakes this task with two fundamental foci in mind: first, postcolonial interpretation studies 'the totality of "texts" [written and otherwise] that participate in hegemonizing other cultures'; second, postcolonial interpretation undertakes 'the study of texts that write back to connect or undo western hegemony' (Gugelberger 1994: 582).

Such concerns can be applied to biblical interpretation. Fernando Segovia, for example, posits three aspects for a 'postcolonial optic' in reading the Bible (2000: 119–32). First, he asks about those signs of colonial domination present in the world of the biblical texts. In the case of the New Testament, it is obvious that these documents emerge from communities immersed in the imperial domination of Rome. The apostle Paul, in particular, founded his communities in the imperial 'colonies' of the Greek East. When reading Paul's letters, including Philippians, we must ask how the overwhelming power and reality of the Roman Empire impacted on the recipients of the correspondence. To what extent did Paul's letters, and indeed all New Testament documents, accommodate or resist the imperial dominance and concomitant colonialism of its context? Second, Segovia suggests that a postcolonial reading of the New Testament revisit historical interpretations of its texts and the methodologies used, especially traditional historical-critical methods, precisely because these emerged in the eighteenth and nineteenth centuries in the context of such colonial powers as Spain, Portugal, France and England. Imperialism, as defined by postcolonial theorists, imposes one dominant country and its culture over another, distant nation, usually for economic purposes. The imperialisms of Spain and Portugal, France and England, from the fifteenth to the nineteenth centuries, generally speaking, all carried with them a missionary agenda as well, and an appropriate biblical interpretation to support both imperialism and missionizing. US imperialism ('manifest destiny') in both the nineteenth and twentieth centuries also contributed to this phenomenon. Segovia argues that the biblical interpretations and historical-critical methodologies that accompanied imperialism should not be left dormant without a close critical analysis.

Thus, given these two initial points, postcolonialism questions imperial domination, wherever it might be found, in both the ancient and modern worlds.

However, Segovia also posits a third set of questions, connected to the role of modern colonial powers. What is the role of 'the children of the colonized', to use Segovia's term, in the whole enterprise of biblical interpretation? As people who have experienced the effects of colonial domination for generations, they are in a unique position to read imperial and colonial reality as integral aspects of the biblical text. Therefore, it is imperative for the profession of biblical criticism to invite and include the children of the colonized in the task of biblical interpretation, those whose parents and grandparents, whose *antepasados* or forebears, experienced imperialism and colonization in generations not too far removed from our own.

A postcolonial focus on the children of the colonized allows for a shift of biblical interpretation from text to reader. Such a shift is legitimate and necessary in our postcolonial era, because the effects of the long colonial history of the West over non-Western cultures, including non-Western minorities in the United States, still dominate the landscape of our world. Readers from non-Western cultures have experienced the effects of imperialism and colonialism and, therefore, have a unique perspective to offer on the interpretation of texts. Providing the children of the colonized access to biblical interpretation makes possible a better, more complete reading of the biblical texts.

In the remainder of this commentary, then, I would like to pursue a post-colonial reading of Paul's letter to the Philippians in light of the issues identified in the rhetorical analysis I have provided. I am a child of colonization, a child, in my case, of parents just a generation removed from the takeover of the island of Puerto Rico in 1898 by US forces as spoils of the Spanish–American war. Given such a social location, how do I read an ancient document from another colonized region, the city of Philippi in the first century of the Common Era, during Roman imperial domination of the Greek East? By means of the rhetorical analysis undertaken, I read Philippians in its historical and literary context in order to attempt some kind of historical reconstruction. Nonetheless, a more complete reading must also engage the 'postcolonial optic', namely, how does this document resist or accommodate Roman imperial hegemony? In addition, I must engage the question of what I bring to the table of interpretation, given my own experience as a Latino child of colonization. What aspects of imperialism in this text do I see that either remind me of my own context or that my own context allows me to see with regard to the ancient text and context?

Aspects of a Postcolonial Reading in Philippians

A postcolonial reading of Philippians by this Latino child of colonialism yields four sets of questions for the text: the context of Paul's imprisonment, the advancement of model leaders, the tendering of heavenly citizenship and the practice of an underground economy.

Paul's Imprisonment

First, the fact of Paul's imprisonment as he writes this letter merits attention. What was Roman imprisonment like and how did it impact upon Paul's letter to the Philippians? Scholars have debated as to whether Paul was imprisoned in Rome or some other location, closer to Philippi, when he wrote this letter. In particular, Ephesus has been presented as a more logical alternative than Rome, given references to frequent travel in this letter and the proximity of Ephesus to Philippi – 300 miles versus 800 for Rome (thus Osiek 2000: 27–30). Others present Rome as the provenance for the letter because of the references to the Roman guard (the 'praetorian', 1.13) and 'the household of Caesar' (4.22) (thus Fee 1995: 34–37; O'Brien 1991: 19–26; Witherington 1994: 24–26). However, given the widespread influence of the empire, including its prison system and bureaucracy, the 'praetorian guard' and 'Caesar's household' (*oikia*, including bureaucracy and servants) could be anywhere, but most especially in major urban centres like Ephesus and Philippi.

Philippi, in fact, held status as a Roman 'colonia', which meant that its residents, many of them veterans of Roman wars and descendants of such veterans, were exempted from taxation, automatically received coveted Roman citizenship and emulated Roman institutions. The concerns that Paul expresses in Philippians for his survival in a Roman prison (1.19-26) cannot be limited to a final imprisonment in Rome. Rather, Roman imperial hegemony, including the terror of prison, extended itself to the provinces and the colonies, especially major economic and administrative centres, such as Ephesus in Asia. (Richard Cassidy [2001: 36–54] describes the varieties and types of Roman imprisonment throughout the empire, although he argues for the traditional view of a final imprisonment in Rome as the occasion for Philippians; Osiek [2000: 30] acknowledges the widespread nature of Roman prison practices, including the use of the term 'praetorian' for any Roman military guard or a provincial Roman governor's residence, thus making the case for a Roman imprisonment of Paul in this instance outside of Rome, perhaps Ephesus.)

In any case, the internal evidence in Philippians points to a difficult imprisonment for Paul. First, a group of opponents preach Christ in Paul's absence but do so without his well-being in mind (1.15-18). Quite possibly, they question Paul's integrity because, after all, he is in prison. Paul 'rejoices' that they continue to preach Christ, but their lack of loyalty to him was undoubtedly a source of disappointment and frustration: 'The others proclaim Christ out of selfish ambition, not sincerely but intending to increase my suffering in my imprisonment' (1.17). Second, Paul's desire for release so he could once again minister to the Philippians (1.19-26) reflects the hardship of an imperial prison. He could very well not be released and face death after the writing of this letter, and he knew it.

Further, Paul's preaching of 'good news' (*euangelion*, a term often used with the 'good news' of an imperial celebration or military victory) about another

'lord' (*kurios*, a term often reserved for the emperor) – on the conscious trans-
position by Paul of the terms of imperial ideology (including *euangelion, pistis*
[faith or loyalty], *dikaiosunē* [justice], and *eirēnē* [peace]) into his Christian
theological language, see Georgi 1997 – probably landed him in jail, where he
faced the possibility of execution. (For a discussion of the 'probable' charge
brought against Paul – *maiestas*, 'treason' – see Cassidy 2001: 55–67; in effect,
his preaching was interpreted as detrimental to the stability of the empire and,
hence, treasonous.) Therefore, in his letter Paul argues that, just as he himself
may have to sacrifice his life as a 'libation' for the cause of the gospel and his
churches (2.17), so should the Philippians continue their faithfulness and unity
for the gospel, in spite of the opposition of enemies in Roman Philippi.

In short, Roman imprisonment, wherever it was, was not pleasant for Paul.
He suffered harsh treatment, confronted the possibility of death, and was challenged for his authority over the churches that he himself had founded. However,
Paul turned these negatives into positives. He expected to be released so that he
could continue his ministry, although he trusted that the gospel would continue
to be preached despite his absence (see 1.12-30). Moreover, and perhaps most
important for our understanding of the overall thrust of the letter, Paul used his
status of suffering as a model for his congregations, including the Philippians.
He expected them to endure and move forward in the midst of their conflict and
opposition, just as he did in his. Roman prison chained him, but not the gospel
message or the gospel communities.

Model Leaders

Along these lines, Paul puts forward valiant examples in the *probatio* of his
letter, namely, Jesus, Timothy and Epaphroditus. Each of them sacrifices something for the well-being of the gospel community. In an empire enamoured with
glory and honour, Paul pictures Jesus as 'emptying himself' of his heavenly
glory for the greater good (2.7). The 'servant' (*doulos*, slave) attitude of Jesus
included taking human form (2.7). In a postcolonial reading, the children of
the colonized would rightly resist any return to imperial servitude and thus
might question any understanding of this text as a call for a 'journey downward'
by all believers at all times. However, in contrast to a hopeless servitude that
lingers generation after generation, Paul highlights the ultimate vindication and
exaltation of Jesus and his followers: 'Therefore God also highly exalted him
and gave him the name that is above every name, so that at the name of Jesus
every knee should bend, in heaven and on earth and under the earth, and every
tongue should confess that Jesus Christ is Lord, to the glory of God the Father'
(2.9-11). Again, Paul employs and transposes the terms of imperial ideology:
Jesus is *Kurios* (Lord), who brings *doxa* (glory) to God the *Patēr* (Father).
This contradicts who and how one expected to be glorified and honoured in the
empire. It is no longer the emperor and other social elites who receive honour
and glory, and no longer by military might. In other words, no crucified car-

penter should expect to receive ultimate vindication and honour, but such is the picture depicted by Paul in this 'Christ hymn' (2.5-11).

Similarly, Paul praises the leadership of both Timothy, who, like Jesus, showed more interest in the well-being of the community than his own (2.20-21), and Epaphroditus, who sacrificed his own health to be with Paul on behalf of his community, the Philippians (2.25-30). These leaders – Jesus, Timothy, Epaphroditus, as well as Paul – showed qualities that went beyond the expectations of typical leaders in the imperial politics of Rome, with their search for glory and honour. The inclusion of Paul's 'co-workers' Euodia and Syntyche in the discourse and Paul's effort to put an end to their leadership rift (4.2-3) also show the unique diversity of Paul's leadership team. Rarely in imperial commendations does one see the commendation of women as community leaders as we do in Paul here in Philippians, but also in his letter to the Romans in the case of Phoebe (Rom. 16.1-2). (On the commendation of leaders in Paul's letters, see Agosto 1996.)

Thus, Paul often commended leaders for their sacrifice and risks on behalf of the gospel community, regardless of their status in the larger Graeco-Roman society. Such practices went against the grain of the leadership practices of the Roman Empire. Indeed, having as a founder a leader crucified on a Roman cross represented the height of 'foolishness' in the eyes of imperial society (see 1 Cor. 1.18-25). Moreover, to name such a crucified founder 'Saviour' (3.20) and 'Lord' (2.11), terms reserved for the Roman emperor, represented the type of challenge that probably precipitated Paul's imprisonment.

Heavenly Citizenship

The goal of heavenly citizenship in 3.20 seems directed precisely at a coveted status throughout the empire but especially in Roman colonies like Philippi, where Roman citizenship was offered, in particular to local political and religious leaders, in exchange for loyalty to the empire. In fact, for its loyalty to him, Octavian renamed the city in his honour in 31 BCE, 'Colonia Augusta Iulia Philippensis', and established it as a haven for his military veterans. Modelled after Rome in its administration, governance and architecture in the period that followed the finding of such favour with Augustus, Philippi flourished economically and politically (Koukouli-Chrysantaki 1998). It is easy to see, then, how a group of believers in the lordship of Jesus the Christ might encounter opposition and persecution in such a setting. If the ongoing well-being of the colony and the colonial leaders depended on cooperation with Rome, any disruptive force – real or imagined, large or small – represented a threat to be dealt with.

The apostle Paul referred to those opposing to the Philippian believers as 'dogs' (3.2). Because of the Jew–Gentile polemical and biographical references that follow in 3.3-6, most commentators interpret Paul's harsh reference to 'dogs' as an inversion of Jewish invective against Gentiles. According to this view, Jewish-Christian opposition to a Gentile Christianity devoid of circumcision and dietary requirements, as in Paul's letter to the Galatians, was present in Philippi as well (see Fee 1995: 285–303; O'Brien 1991: 345–64; Witherington 1994: 83 90; for a different perspective see Osiek 2000: 79–86). However, such an understanding is not without its difficulties. Why is this problem addressed so obliquely in Philippians 3 and not even alluded to elsewhere in the entire letter?

More likely, Paul cites the Jew–Gentile polemic from his other churches with the biographical references of 3.4-6 ('If anyone else has reason to be confident in the flesh, I have more: circumcised on the eighth day, a member of the people of Israel, of the tribe of Benjamin, a Hebrew born of Hebrews; as to the law, a Pharisee; as to zeal, a persecutor of the church; as to righteousness under the law, blameless') as a comparative challenge. Paul and his other assemblies have confronted opposition of various types (including opposition to Gentile inclusion in the family of God), and they have learned that which has true value ('knowing Christ Jesus my Lord' and 'gaining' him, 3.8). Philippian believers in Christ should similarly confront any opposition to their new-found faith, even if it challenges their status as loyal Roman citizens. After all, theirs is a 'heavenly citizenship' (3.20). Paul's opponents elsewhere 'serve as a foil to Paul himself with his own faultless credentials' (Osiek 2000: 81) and ultimately in this context to the Philippian believers so that they might truly 'stand firm in the Lord' (4.1).

Thus Paul challenges the notion of honour by means of earthly achievements, whether in the Jewish law, as in his own case, or in Roman citizenship, as in the case of many in Philippi and throughout the empire. In the Jesus community, honour lies in gaining Christ and God's righteousness, *dikaiosunē*, the Roman value of justice which Paul transposes into a divine value ultimately achieved by faith in Christ, not *fides* ('faith', 'loyalty') in or to law or a political status (3.7-9). In this way, Paul, subtly but firmly, challenges the hegemony of the Roman state, even in matters of religious allegiance. He echoes the gospel adage: 'Render to Caesar what belongs to Caesar, and to God what belongs to God' (see Mk 12.17). For Philippian believers, as for Pauline communities everywhere, their ultimate loyalty is to 'our citizenship' in heaven, from whence 'we are expecting a Saviour [*soter*, another term reserved for the emperor], the Lord Jesus Christ' (3.20). In what must have been a radical departure for any Philippian colonist, imperial Roman citizenship must take second place in such a worldview.

An 'Underground Economy'

Finally, as I have already mentioned, a postcolonial reading of Philippians must explore the 'underground economy' of the Pauline mission. Paul often worked 'with his hands' – at manual labour (see 1 Thess. 2.9; 2 Cor. 11.7) – in order to support his ministry and not depend on the poor in his churches. However, when imprisoned, as he was when he wrote to the Philippians, Paul depended on gifts from his supporting congregations. Indeed, Paul practised *koinonia* with several of his churches, entering into an agreement of mutual benefit with a partner (*koinōnos*) in order to carry out a joint enterprise (Phil. 4.15; cf. Gal. 2.9). (On the Roman law of *societas*, *koinonia* in Greek, and its appropriation in Pauline mission strategy, including with the Philippians, see Sampley 1980.) In Paul's case, the venture was spreading the gospel and establishing communities of faith. For this ministry Paul depended on his own manual labour, on *koinonia* with churches, or on the support of individuals of some financial means within the community, like Phoebe of Cenchreae (Rom. 16.1-2).

Paul also organized a collection for the Jerusalem church from his Greek churches. Thus, he had 'a horizontal movement of resources from one subject people to another' (Horsley 1997: 251). Details about this collection (see 1 Cor. 16.1-4; 2 Cor. 8–9) 'indicate that the network of assemblies had an "international" political-economic dimension diametrically opposed to the tributary political economy of the Empire' (Horsley 1997: 251). Money in the empire flowed from bottom to top and from the margins (conquered territories) to the centre (Rome) by means of extreme and extensive taxation. In Paul's churches, resources travelled to where they were needed to carry out the gospel mission and to 'remember the poor' (Gal. 2.10). Thus, by means of this 'underground economy', Paul once again challenged business as usual in the Roman Empire, even if only within the limits of his small, struggling urban congregations and the widespread missionary movement which founded them.

A Latino Reading of Philippians

After a historical–literary reading, with the help of rhetorical analysis, to establish the probable occasion and purpose of Paul's letter to the Philippians and a postcolonial reading that reflects on four anti-imperial aspects of the letter, I now turn to a more specifically Latino reading. How do we incorporate the perspectives of actual flesh-and-blood postcolonial readers of the biblical text, in this case a Latino reader? Some suggestions follow, necessarily more preliminary than exhaustive in nature.

To begin with, imprisonment was clearly a reality in Paul's ministry (see 2 Cor. 11.23). Roman imprisonment was hellish in every way. It was an instrument of imperial terror and control, even in its 'less severe' forms, as suggested by Richard Cassidy (2001: 37–43). A postcolonial reading of Philippians explores the contours of what it meant for Paul to be a Roman prisoner, but it also explores the use of prison in both colonial and neocolonial settings in our modern and postmodern era. For example, the prison experiences and writings of such figures as the Puerto Rican nationalist leader Pedro Albizu Campos and the African American civil rights leader Martin Luther King, Jr., who modelled his 'Letter from Birmingham Prison' after Paul's prison letters, must be mined to determine aspects of postcolonial reality in our own day. (For a recent study of the religious and postcolonial reflections of Albizu Campos, with reference to King as well, see Collazo 2001: 19–51, 53–58.) More recently, the well-known

Puerto Rican singer and *independentista* or advocate of political independence for Puerto Rico, Danny Rivera, who was imprisoned for protesting the occupation of the Puerto Rican island of Vieques by the US military, described the meaning of his experience in a federal prison as 'estar encarcelado sin ser criminal, simplemente por amar la libertad y la justicia' ('being imprisoned without being a criminal, simply for loving freedom and justice') (2001: 6). Such reflections and experiences as those of Albizu Campos, King, Rivera and many others can bring to light comparative imperial and postcolonial reflections, including those from religious and biblical perspectives. They can help us to read the biblical text from a postcolonial perspective and not a presumptuous 'objective' and 'unbiased' cultural and political stance.

A second avenue of postcolonial dialogue between Paul, Philippians and Latinos and Latinas in the United States involves the issue of leadership. Paul empowered leaders after the model of Jesus, to serve his communities regardless of their status in the empire. Service and sacrifice were the key qualities expected, unlike leaders in the empire, where family ties, social status and wealth were consistently touted as the means for leadership advancement (Agosto 1996: 4–5; for a discussion of the criteria for social status in the Graeco-Roman world and where the earliest Christians stood with regard to these see Meeks 1983: 51–73, who describes this latter situation as a 'mixed bag', not completely reliant on worldly status for leadership recognition within the church). In the US Hispanic/Latino community, including our churches, the children of the colonized have consistently developed our own cadre of leaders from the bottom up, regardless of the credentials and expectations of the larger, dominant society. More and more mainstream avenues of leadership have opened up for our marginalized Latino communities, but the church and other grassroots communities, like Paul's urban communities, continue to serve as a locus of leadership development. In our postcolonial world we must continue to ensure access to leadership opportunity without recreating the oppressive and limiting structures of the colonizers. Similar to Paul's earliest congregations – and unlike later generations of those congregations, as represented by the Pastoral Epistles, which began to limit the role of women and the poor in the exercise of church leadership – our community must keep lines of leadership and authority fluid rather than hierarchical (see Agosto 1995: 103–22; Forthcoming).

Third, like Paul, we must reflect on the issue of citizenship. In 1917 the US Congress passed the Jones Act, which declared residents of the island of Puerto Rico citizens of the United States. The island had been under US control since 1898. The reason for such a move was neither benevolence nor liberation but rather the need for military recruits, given the entrance of the country into World War I. In other words, the question became: Why not send our colonized peoples to the battlefield? (Maldonado Denis 1969: 102–104). The long-term impact of this unilateral legislation has been a source of much intense debate. Many have lauded the easy access to and from the island with respect to the United

States mainland in the search for jobs and better living conditions. However, the elimination of the entity of Puerto Rican citizenship and, therefore, in effect, the concept of nationhood for Puerto Rico has had a negative impact over time. Much like Roman Philippi, citizenship has been a two-edged sword. Residents of the former city-state Philippi could have Roman citizenship and all its benefits with regard to taxation and military security, but their loyalty to Rome had to remain unquestioned. The cost of economic and military security was loss of identity. This resonates very much with the current neocolonial status of Puerto Rico, best exemplified perhaps by the struggle to manage the future of its people and their health on the island of Vieques. As in Paul's exhortation to the Philippians (3.20), so in the Vieques crisis and the subsequent departure of the US Navy from 'la isla nena', the 'baby island', the people of Puerto Rico found an 'über-citizenship' that superseded the technicality of US citizenship and the lack of a defined nationhood. They found a postcolonial voice.

Finally, what of the economic dimensions? Fernando Segovia writes that, at each stage of imperialism in the modern and postmodern era, capitalism has prevailed and dominated the economic landscape, from mercantile capitalism in the fifteenth to eighteenth centuries, to monopoly capitalism in the nineteenth and first half of the twentieth century, to global capitalism from the latter half of the twentieth century to the present (Segovia 2000: 127). At each turn, millions are left behind in any ensuing economic upswings, but especially in the downswings. 'The poor you shall always have with you' seems to be the acceptable mantra of both monopoly and global capitalism.

The need for small, just, 'underground economies', like those mobilized by Paul with his churches, also seems always to be with us. From *cooperativas* in Latin America to the 'sweat equity' of Millard Fuller in Habitat for Humanity, the church seems to be and needs to be on the forefront of these economies. The hegemony of the empire and the urgency of his eschatology undoubtedly kept Paul from larger challenges to oppressive economic imperial practices. His approaches were subtle and subversive, but ineffective on the grand scale. Three hundred years after Paul, the church became part of the state; five hundred years after that, the road to feudalism and monopoly capitalism was well on its way with the church's blessings.

Hopefully, in our own day the cries of the children of the colonized for a more just economic policy will be heeded, especially after the recent debacle of the Enron and World Com scandals, where the ideal of making money at all costs and the belief that 'trickle-down' economics will work even for the poorest of the poor have been proven wrong.

Conclusion

The letter to the Philippians by the apostle Paul, from the middle of the first century of the Common Era, represents a useful model for the effort to incorporate postcolonial theory (texts and readers from imperial settings ought to be in dialogue) in a re-reading of the New Testament (faith documents from an emerging religious community in the midst of a cruel and oppressive empire twenty centuries ago). The political leadership of Philippi, a major urban centre of conquered and colonized imperial territory in the Greek East, sought to ensure the colony's survival by loyalty to Rome. Paul was an itinerant preacher with an urgent message about a founding religious figure crucified on a Roman cross. He established a small, struggling community of adherents to this message, whose loyalty to another *Kurios* severely challenged their expected loyalty to Caesar as *kurios*. Paul's community had all the makings of a postcolonial statement in the midst of an extremely volatile imperial hegemony. It did not go that far, but it is significant that anti-imperial voices within the community and its texts survived centuries of oppression in various forms. This remains a source of hope to postcolonial communities of today.

BIBLIOGRAPHY

Agosto, Efraín
    1995   'Paul, Leadership and the Hispanic Church', in Eldin Villafañe (ed.), *Seek the Peace of the City: Reflections on Urban Ministry* (Grand Rapids: Eerdmans).
    1996   'Paul's Use of Graeco-Roman Conventions of Commendation' (Unpublished doctoral dissertation, Boston University).
    2002   'Paul Against Empire: A Postmodern and Postcolonial Reading of Philippians', *Perspectivas: Occasional Papers* (Hispanic Theological Initiative): 37–56.
    Forthcoming   *Leadership in the New Testament* (St. Louis: Chalice Press).
Cassidy, Richard
    2001   *Paul in Chains: Roman Imprisonment and the Letters of Paul* (New York: Crossroad).
Collazo, Luis G.
    2001   *Espacio para Dios: Desde Albizu Campos hasta Julia de Burgos* (San Juan: Seminario Evangélico de Puerto Rico–Fundación Puerto Rico Evangélico).
Fee, Gordon D.
    1995   *Paul's Letter to the Philippians* (The New International Commentary on the New Testament; Grand Rapids: Eerdmans).
Georgi, Dieter
    1997   'God Turned Upside Down – Romans: Missionary Theology and Roman Political Theology', in Richard Horsley (ed.), *Paul and Empire* (Harrisburg, PA: Trinity Press International): 148–57.
Gugelberger, Georg M.
    1994   'Postcolonial Cultural Studies', in Michael Groden and Martin Kreiswirth (eds), *The Johns Hopkins Guide to Literary Theory and Criticism* (Baltimore: The Johns Hopkins University Press): 581–85.
Horsley, Richard
    1997   '1 Corinthians: A Case Study of Paul's Assembly as an Alternative Society', in Richard Horsley (ed.), *Paul and Empire: Religion and Power in Roman Imperial Society* (Harrisburg, PA: Trinity Press International): 242–52.

Koukouli-Chrysantaki, Chaido
1998   'Colonia Iulia Augusta Philippensis', in Charalambos Bakirtzis and Helmut
        Koester (eds), *Philippi at the Time of Paul and After His Death* (Harrisburg,
        PA: Trinity Press International, 1998): 5–35.

Maldonado Denis, Manuel
1969   *Puerto Rico: Una interpretación histórico-social* (Mexico: Siglo Veintiuno
        Editores).

Meeks, Wayne
1983   *The First Urban Christians: Social World of the Apostle Paul* (New Haven:
        Yale University Press).

O'Brien, Peter
1991   *The Epistle to the Philippians* (The New Interpreter's Greek Testament Com-
        mentary; Grand Rapids: Eerdmans).

Osiek, Carolyn
2000   *Philippians, Philemon* (Abingdon New Testament Commentaries; Nashville:
        Abingdon Press).

Rivera, Danny
2001   *Enamorado de la paz: Diario en la cárcel federal* (San Juan: Editorial
        Makarios).

Sampley, J. Paul
1980   *Pauline Partnership in Christ: Christian Community and Commitment in
        Light of Roman Law* (Philadelphia: Fortress Press).

Schüssler Fiorenza, Elisabeth
1983   *In Memory of Her: A Feminist Theological Reconstruction of Christian
        Origins* (New York: Crossroad).

Segovia, Fernando F.
2000   'Biblical Criticism and Postcolonial Studies: Toward a Postcolonial Optic', in
        Fernando F. Segovia, *Decolonizing Biblical Studies: A View from the Margins*
        (Maryknoll, NY: Orbis Books): 119–32.

Stowers, Stanley
1986   *Letter-Writing in Graeco-Roman Antiquity* (Philadelphia: Fortress Press).

Watson, Duane
1988   'A Rhetorical Analysis of Philippians and Its Implications for the Unity
        Problem', *Novum Testamentum* 30: 57–88.

Witherington III, Ben
1994   *Friendship and Finances in Philippi: The Letter of Paul to the Philippians*
        (Valley Forge, PA: Trinity Press International).

THE LETTER TO THE COLOSSIANS

Gordon Zerbe and Muriel Orevillo-Montenegro

The letter to the Colossians is, in brief, an assertion of Paul's apostolic authority over a (potentially) wayward community not established by Paul himself. Appealing to Paul's special role in the divine management of redemption (1.24–2.5), the letter attempts to maintain or restore a normative understanding of faith and practice within the community in the face of rival perspectives and teachers and seeks, accordingly, to promote social cohesion both within the community and between the community and adherents of the Pauline movement in other locations (e.g., 4.7-17). In particular, the letter contests the apparent inroads of alternative religious perspectives and practices, introduced by rival teachers (2.4, 8, 16, 18), which, in the author's view, aim to ingratiate intermediary cosmic powers and disregard or deny the cosmic supremacy of Christ.

The key themes of the letter in opposing this supposed wayward direction are: Christ is the supreme power of the universe (e.g., 1.13-20, 22; 2.2–3.4; 3.11); and dying and rising with Christ in baptism locates the identity of believers in the heavenly rather than earthly sphere, thus undermining practices promoted by rival teachers. These practices – apparently including circumcision, keeping special festivals, rules for food and drink, ascetic disciplines and mystical experiences – are deemed to be 'from human tradition' (2.8, 22), 'earthly' (3.2), oriented to 'the flesh' (2.18), 'elemental' (2.8, 20), a 'shadow of coming reality' (2.17), 'worldly' (2.20), based on 'philosophy' and 'empty deceit' (2.4, 8), and 'perishable' (2.22). Instead, the author promotes a religious identity focused on a completed redemption which secures a heavenly location (e.g., 1.5, 13-14, 20-23; 3.1-4), on moral conduct and social 'order' (2.5; 3.5–4.1), and on a liturgical life of prayer, teaching, song, thanksgiving and mutual admonition (3.16-17; 4.2-6).

Interpretive Approaches

Colossians is full of passages which either cradle or promote a colonial ideology. The interpretation of Colossians in the European–American, historical-critical tradition has focused on the authorship of the letter, the nature of the teaching opposed in the letter and the identity of these opponents, and the pre-history (origins and redaction) of a possible Christological hymn (1.15-20) and the so-called 'household code' (3.18–4.1). Religiously engaged readings have stressed its spiritual meaning and have likewise avoided the cultural, social and political questions raised by Colossians.

The present postcolonial reading of Colossians, which takes its point of departure from the authors' location and experience in the Philippines, will reflect on the religious–cultural, social and political perspectives of the letter. This reading, while focusing on Colossians, will necessarily take into account the overall authorial figure of Paul and his missionary enterprise and, accordingly, intertextual connections between Colossians and the rest of the letters associated with Paul.

Admittedly, among the circles of Christians in the Philippines committed to the struggle of social transformation toward a more just society and toward cultural integrity, Colossians, along with the entirety of the Pauline corpus, is not a writing of choice. (For a systematic treatment of the 'theology of struggle' in the Philippines, see Fernandez 1994.) For some, the Christological absolutism of Colossians, for instance, is understandable historically from the perspective of survival on the part of a minority movement but irrelevant for a contemporary colonially oriented, exclusivist and triumphalist Christianity. At best, Colossians is seen from the point of view of its ambivalent potential: on the one hand, to embody, legitimate and promote colonial intentions and assumptions; on the other, to confront colonial ideologies and patterns. While a Filipino postcolonial reading will engage in the former, deconstructive reading, it will not do so to the neglect or undermining of an emancipatory reading of the text, particularly given a pervasive elevated view of Scripture in that setting and/or a resulting pragmatic, de facto approach to the authoritative role of Scripture.

Religious–Cultural Perspective: Attack on the 'Other' Religiosity (1.13-20; 2.8–3.4)

With a few sharp strokes the author asserts the supremacy and absolutism of Christ over all other religious and political claimants (1.13-20; 2.8–3.4). These texts have been a powerful tool in the history of the colonial missionary enterprise, a weapon used to reject indigenous rituals, practices and beliefs of colonized and converted peoples. Still today, these texts are used in the Philippines by pastors attempting to curtail the persistence of traditional, indigenous rituals, especially in rural settings. In particular, these texts have targeted earth-based spiritualities of the indigenous peoples and have annihilated their religious functionaries. Almost invariably, Western scholarly commentators either proudly proclaim and sanctify Paul's resistance to 'error' and 'heresy' or refuse to engage the critical religious and cultural issues by resting content to reconstruct descriptively the alternative perspective which Paul opposes. Proposed labels for the 'other' tendency include: Jewish-Christian Gnosticism, a Christianized mystery cult, Jewish ascent mysticism, Hellenistic philosophy (various forms) and syncretistic folk religion.

The words of Filipino pastor Noel Villalba – conveyed through personal e-mail correspondence while discussing the text of Colossians – are very much to the point here:

> Paul was a prisoner of his time. He was compelled to propose this kind of theological understanding as a matter of survival for the young church. Beset with other more tantalizing religious perspectives, the early Christians could hardly have been expected to survive, or so Paul thought, without the strong and explicit assertions he makes here... Now we realize that the survival of Christianity has become its opposite – an expansionist and exclusivist religion that threatens to wipe out Jesus Christ... In the name of Christ, nations all over the world were subjugated. Cultural identities that mark the variety of God's revelation were wiped out. 'Other spirituality' or awareness of God were stigmatized. What is worse is that the colonial brand of Christianity continues to destroy the world today with materialism parading as spirituality through 'Christian capitalism' or 'capitalist Christianity'... The crucial question for us now is how we Christians live with our indigenous peoples and Muslim neighbors.

At the very best, these texts might be read to show an author rejecting merely what is (perceived as) 'oppressive' in any religious–cultural tradition. More appropriate, however, is the reading that these texts, while opposing the mixing of religious traditions, show an author blind to his own syncretized heritage and perspective. Indeed, Christianity around the world is syncretistic in one way or another. Thus, in the Philippines, in the experience of a Christian believer, when the name of Christ is spoken or the Christ icon is seen, it may well be that behind the Christ image is the suppressed indigenous deity whose presence and blessing are desired.

Paul himself is a quite poignant example of 'hybridity', both in his background and in his rhetoric and thought. Writings by or about Paul indicate that he is quite ready to use syncretism and self-conscious cultural accommodation in his proclamation of the gospel (e.g., Acts 14, 17; 1 Cor. 11). Yet, Paul also appears to be uncompromising in rejecting particular Hellenistic religious notions, such as those regarding the afterlife (e.g., 1 Corinthians 15) or when he considers the 'truth of the gospel' to be potentially compromised (e.g., Galatians 1–2).

Finally, despite the prominent figure of Paul within the colonial missionary movement, one might at the very least observe that Paul's own missionary enterprise was quite unlike that of the colonial missionary enterprise. In particular, Paul did not bring with him a dominating culture and religion on the coat-tails of military and political expansion. Instead, his religious convictions grew out of a minority culture experience. One might describe his missionary venture as a redirected, inclusionary 'nativism', growing out of Jewish missionary theology with its monotheistic and universal horizon. Moreover, a softer version of his missionary stance might point to his activity in inculturating his missionary message into various idioms, signifying a fundamental respect for cultural diversity, in engospelling cultures thereby, affirming ways in which various cultural traditions manifest the 'good news' prior to his arrival, and in bridging cultures in settings of cultural contact and mixing.

Social Perspective: Priority of Hierarchical 'Order' (2.5; 3.18–4.1)

The social-integrating intention of Colossians is clear. The letter functions to enhance the social identity and cohesion of the addressed community through reference to: (1) the redemptive reality experienced (e.g., participation in the 'kingdom'; 1.13; 4.11; heavenly status, 1.5; 3.1-4; incorporation and corporate growth in Christ, 1.18, 27–28; 2.6-7, 19; 3.3-4, 10-11, 15); (2) common commitment (1.9-12, 23; 2.2, 5) to a normative perspective ('the gospel, the word of truth', 1.15; 'the mystery now revealed, the word of God', 1.25-26; 'the faith', 2.7); (3) boundary categories (inside/outside, 4.5-6); (4) fictive kinship (1.2; 4.7, 9) and repeated corporate 'we', and 'you', language; (5) the incorporation of 'Gentiles' (1.21-22, 27); (6) moral demarcation from outsiders (3.5-7); (7) internal tension-managing virtues (forbearance, 3.13; forgiveness, 3.13; love, harmony, unity, peace, mutuality, 2.2, 3.14-16; no lying, slander or anger, 3.8-9); and (8) solidarity networks and virtues (e.g., hospitality) beyond the local community (1.6-8; 4.17). Yet, particularly noteworthy here is the preoccupation with hierarchical 'order' (*taxis*, 2.5), sometimes mistranslated as 'morale' or 'harmony', a concern which comes to full expression in the household code (3.18–4.1).

This code has throughout Christian history put Paul 'in the service of death' (Elliott 1994). Its effects in concrete terms are too numerous to imagine – its words of caution uttered at the expense of the powerless (in this text: slaves, women and children). This text is one of the chief planks used to support androcentric, patriarchal and classist perspectives. Indeed, this text gives the prevailing status quo a religious legitimation – the conduct of all three lower positions (but only one of the superior positions) is motivated by religious means (confirming the social legitimating function of religion). In 3.23-24 service to the higher social class is presented as tantamount to serving God, effectively identifying the two, even as the earthly master is distinct from the divine master (3.22; 4.1). Furthermore, 3.20 also romanticizes the idea that all parents desire the well-being of their children and has become a text of terror for many abused children. Finally, the ideology of the code easily ties in with imperial ideology, insofar as the entire Roman Empire was also symbolized as an orderly, hierarchically organized household ruled by a head. There is only a minimal attempt in the Colossians code to moderate the extremes of some versions of the prevailing social code: thus, men are to love, not to rule; similarly, parents must not provoke children, not just rule; lastly, slave masters must treat slaves justly and fairly, not tyrannize them.

Western interpretation of this code – and similar ones elsewhere in the New Testament, such as Ephesians 5.22–6.9 and 1 Peter 2.18–3.7 – has generally concluded that it represents the Christianizing of the hierarchical commonplaces of Graeco-Roman social morality. In addition, mainstream Western interpretation has either trumpeted its contents as indicating the truth that Christianity favours acquiescence and transformation from within, instead of protest or revolution, or admitted to a fundamental social and political conservatism in Paul and his legacy, explaining the code (or the more general conservatism) either as a consequence of his millenarian perspective, as an attempt to reduce antagonism from outsiders, or simply as representing a 'crucial process of adjustment' to its social environment (Barclay 1997). Scholarly explanations typically sanction or rationalize the social effect of these texts, and thus the status quo, or retreat from offering critical judgments in the name of descriptive objectivism, while objecting to approaches influenced by moral predisposition. All of this continues to put Paul 'in the service of death'.

Emancipatory readings of the household code have gone in various directions. In the West feminist interpretation has taken the lead in critically evaluating the content of the code, arguing, for instance, that the code represents a backward movement of the early Christian movement, toward 'love patriarchalism' and away from a 'discipleship of equals' (Schüssler Fiorenza 1983; similarly Johnson 1992). Attempts to rehabilitate Paul's social and gender perspective often rest on a reconstruction of the historical Paul (a Paul not as marred by the extent of social and gender conservatism often imagined), including an outright rejection of the Colossians code as pseudepigraphical (e.g., Elliott 1994). Indeed, where an elevated sense of Scripture is maintained, it may be appropriate to highlight at least the ambiguity or ambivalence of Paul's gender and social perspectives. This could include the highlighting of numerous women in Paul's circle of co-workers and leaders, undoubtedly a reflection of the notion of charisma (e.g., Romans 16; Phil. 4.2-3; Phlm. 2; Col. 4.15; Acts 16.13-15), and of isolated egalitarian references (1 Cor. 7.2-5, 10-16), despite Paul's overall patriarchal framework and ideology (e.g., 1 Cor. 11.2-16). Similarly, Paul's perspective on slavery might take into account rereadings of 1 Cor. 7.17-24 and the Letter to Philemon and Apphia as reflecting something quite other than 'social conservatism' (e.g., Elliott 1994). Finally, some postcolonial readings will involve the 're-writing' of texts. Thus, for example, Mary John Mananzan, a Filipina theologian, has proposed that Col. 3.18-19 should be re-written as follows, 'Husband and wife, love and obey each other', given the persistence of this text in the wedding liturgy. (This citation is taken from a documentary film entitled *Is Your Gender an Issue?*, directed by Ellen Ongkiko and distributed by the Asian Social Institute Communication Center of Manila, The Philippines [1991]; for a sampling of Mananzan's hermeneutics see Mananzan 1998.)

In this connection, the theme of 'new humanity' in 3.10-11 should also be noted. While drawing attention to the social existence of the community as the 'new humanity', apparently in explicating the effects of baptism, the text does temper ethnic and class exclusivism. At the same time, it does not fundamentally call into question the systemic social use of the distinctions highlighted, as the household code confirms. The text seems to rest content with a limited accepting of social differences, without seeking to change the social, political, economic and ideological structures which create and perpetuate those differences. Also interesting is the omission, as in 1 Cor. 12.13 but not Gal. 3.26-28, of a reference to the ending of gender distinctions in baptism. The omission of the male/female pair anticipates the household code that follows, signifying the author's move away from the concrete freedom the gospel offered to women and slaves, in order to protect the church from external charges of social disruptions (Johnson 1992). By omitting the gender issue, the text encourages continuous colonizing of women as 'the other' who must bear the brunt of intersectionality (where issues of gender, class, race/colour, caste and ethnicity intersect) towards invisibility. Thus, 'other' women of colour (Crenshaw 1992), of ethnicity and caste (Bagh 1998; Immanuel 1998), have to bear a double or triple burden within that community of believers.

Quite evocative, however, for postcolonial Christological exploration is the final assertion of 3.11: 'but Christ is all in all'. While one reading of this phrase focuses on the subject Christ in an absolutist sense, another might focus on the predicate, suggesting a more inclusive perspective, through which diverse earthly and cultural experiences also become bearers of Christ. Indeed, if the 'image of the creator' was fully lived out in the 'new humanity', then certainly an inclusive space could be created in one's life and in society so that the rest who are regarded as 'the other' could be fully welcomed.

Political Perspective:
Christ Triumphs over the 'Powers' (1.12-20; 2.9-15; 3.1-4, 11)

Colossians makes the following assertions regarding the 'powers'. All things, notably the powers – thrones, dominions, principalities, authorities – were created in, through, and for Christ (1.16). In Christ, all things, including the powers, hold together (1.17). Through Christ, God was pleased to reconcile with the Godhead all things, including the powers (1.20). Christ is the head of every ruler and authority (2.10). Through Christ and his cross, God disarmed/unmasked the rulers and authorities, making a public spectacle/shaming of them, exposing them in a triumphal procession (2.14-15).

Western scholarly interpretation persists in arguing that these powers are 'spiritual, invisible or heavenly' in character. This is so, despite the acknowledgment that Paul alludes in 2.15 to the tumultuous practice of Roman parades celebrating military victories, in which the defeated are publicly disgraced and led to their execution (see 1 Cor. 4.8-13; 2 Cor. 2.14-16). Further, it is asserted that the political language of 'kingdom' in Colossians (1.13; 4.11) has only a spiritual connotation.

In recent history in the Philippines, both during the Marcos era and afterwards, these very texts (with the omission of 2.15!) have been interpreted concretely to endorse and support those who are currently in power. Indeed, they have been used to support the idea that the colonizers had a right to 'civilize' and 'Christianize' (i.e., subjugate) the colonized peoples, as a way to extend Christ's reign. Reflecting on 1.16, Walter Wink (1984: 64) admits: 'Throughout Christian history the claim that the Powers have been created in and through and for Christ has all too easily been perverted into a justification of the status quo, a rationalization of every current evil, a legitimation of corrupt regimes'. Meanwhile, the otherworldly focus of texts such as 3.1-4 (see 1.5) has been used by colonizers and rulers, or their legitimators, as a tool to manipulate or to divert the people's critical attention away from concrete realities by calling them to 'seek the things that are above, not things that are on earth'. When this is taken alongside such texts as Rom. 13.1-7, it is not at all surprising that Paul is often not treated as an ally in movements toward social justice and cultural integrity. As Mariano Inong, a Filipino ministerial student, asserted in the course of a seminar on Paul, 'the problem with Paul is that he never renounced his Roman citizenship' (similarly Suarez 1981).

A postcolonial reading of Colossians might go in a number of different directions. Such a reading might:

- Provide, through its claim of Christ's sovereignty over all creation and the powers, the ground by which all human projects and claimants to absolutism can be critiqued (Capulong 1994).
- Highlight, following the lead of interpreters such as Wink, that the 'powers' in Paul 'are both heavenly and earthly, divine and human, spiritual and political, invisible and structural' (1984: 100), that they refer to concrete structures as well as spiritual realities.
- Re-read the rhetoric of the text as one that provides a basis for resistance, in the light of being 'filled with the knowledge of God's will in all spiritual wisdom and understanding' (1.9), empowered by God's power to endure with patience (to engage in *hupomonē*, 'persistent resistance', 1.11) the rigorous task of 'naming and unmasking' the powers (Wink 1984), so that the colonized and subjugated peoples move to 'engage' such powers and claim thereby their 'share in the inheritance of the saints in the light' (1.12).
- Understand Paul's victimization by the empire (1.24; 4.3, 10, 18) not as a mistake by the ruling authorities but as a consequence of his resistance.
- Read the notion of the 'reconciliation' of the powers with Christ (1.20) not as a contradiction to the text, asserting the defeat of the powers (2.15), nor

as giving legitimacy to the powers, but rather as presupposing repentance, rectification and forgiveness. For such reconciliation to be effected, the powers should seek forgiveness from those whom they have subjugated and deprived and should divest themselves of their stolen power by giving it back to those they rendered powerless, concretely rectifying thereby the brokenness that resulted from their acts of domination. (It might also be observed that Christological absolutism functions differently here in contrast to its application to religious–cultural matters; see above.)

- Question the listing of 'anger' (3.8) as undesirable behaviour, a response that the colonialist ideology continually tries to suppress in subtle ways.
- Be attentive to the apparent receding of the millenarian framework which predominates in Paul's undisputed letters, a millenarianism with roots in the Jewish reaction to imperial domination. Redemption in Colossians is described especially as completed (1.13, 20, 22, 26; 2.9, 12-15; 3.1-4) and as heavenly (1.5, 27; 3.1-2), but it draws upon Paul's earlier millenarianism, as references to a future horizon of salvation are still evident (1.12; 2.17; 3.4, 6). While any version of millenarianism may be deemed to be politically inexpedient or irrational, millenarian ideology with strong Christian influences in the Philippines has historically fuelled and continues to fuel the struggle against colonial forces (e.g., Ileto 1979).
- See the text's expression of a realized, vertical eschatology – regularly used (as, for example, in the Philippines) to foster an escapist religiosity, in accommodation to the existing unjust regime – as a challenge to claim and reclaim that status of being 'rescued' (1.13), 'reconciled' (1.22) and living life as 'alive together with him' (2.13). Such a reading would be emancipatory in the sense that the text would make the reader realize that God in Christ Jesus and those who lived Christ-like lives have 'disarmed the rulers and authorities', giving courage to the colonized to resist dominating and stifling powers.
- Show, within a more historical framework, that the historical Paul exhibited a far more critical stance toward the Roman imperium than is usually supposed (Elliott 1994; Horsley 1997; Georgi 1991; Wengst 1987). Such an argument is based especially on the following points: (1) the overall millenarian script undergirding Paul's theology, in which the faithful God ultimately restores a creation in bondage to hostile powers, indeed finally vanquishing them (e.g., 1 Cor. 2.6-8, 15.21-28; Rom. 12.21, 16.20; 1 Thess. 5.3; Phil. 2.5-11; 3.21); (2) Paul's regular use of politically loaded terms to describe salvation, the Messiah's work, and the Messiah's community, often with an implicit challenge to Roman imperial claims and propaganda (e.g., Phil. 1.27, 3.20-21; Rom. 1.1-3; terms such as gospel, faith/fidelity, justice/ righteousness, peace, civic assembly [*ekklesia*] and others; see esp. Georgi 1991); (3) passages where the Roman structures are explicitly challenged or unmasked (1 Cor. 6.1-6; 1 Thess. 5.3); and (4) Paul's own experience of

arrest, torture and execution by the empire on grounds of treason, which indicates that Roman citizenship meant nothing for Paul and/or that his citizenship meant nothing to the Romans. Within this context it is Romans 13 – particularly its generalized, commonplace warrants for an apparently situational call for pragmatic political acquiescence – which becomes an anomaly, if not a complete contradiction, seemingly invalidating not only his own experience of arrest, torture and execution but also that of Jesus (see, e.g., 1 Cor. 2.6-8).

BIBLIOGRAPHY

Bagh, Rachel
    1998   'Breaking Barriers in the Family', in Lalrinawmi Ralte *et al.* (eds), *Envisioning a New Heaven and a New Earth* (Delhi: National Council of Churches in India/SPCK): 89–95.

Barclay, John M. G.
    1997   *Colossians and Philemon* (New Testament Guides; Sheffield: Sheffield Academic Press).

Capulong, Noriel
    1999   'Creation and Human Responsibility: Christology and Cosmology (Col. 1:15-20)', in Yeow Choo Lak (ed.), *Doing Theology with Asian Resources.* Vol. 4, *Mission and Human Ecology* (Singapore: ATESEA): 88–94.

Crenshaw, Kimberlé
    1992   'Whose Story is it Anyway?', in Toni Morrison (ed.), *Race-ing Justice and En-gendering Power* (New York: Pantheon Books): 402–40.

Elliott, Neil
    1994   *Liberating Paul: The Justice of God and the Politics of the Apostle* (Maryknoll, NY: Orbis Books).

Fernandez, Eleazar
    1994   *Toward a Theology of Struggle* (Maryknoll, NY: Orbis Books).

Georgi, Dieter
    1991   *Theocracy in Paul's Praxis and Theology* (Minneapolis: Fortress Press).

Horsley, Richard (ed.)
    1997   *Paul and Empire: Religion and Power in Roman Imperial Society* (Harrisburg: Trinity Press International).

Ileto, Reynaldo C.
    1979   *Pasyon and Revolution: Popular Movements in the Philippines, 1840–1910* (Quezon City, Philippines: Ateneo de Manila University Press).

Immanuel, Usha
    1998   'Expectations in Marriage', in Lalrinawmi Ralte *et al.* (eds), *Envisioning a New Heaven and a New Earth* (Delhi: National Council of Churches in India/SPCK): 254–60.

Johnson, E. Elizabeth
    1992   'Colossians', in Carol A. Newsom and Sharon H. Ringe (eds), *The Women's Bible Commentary* (Louisville, KY: Westminster/John Knox Press): 346–48.

Mananzan, Mary John
    1998   'Woman and Religion', in Mary John Mananzan (ed.), *Woman and Religion*

(3rd rev. edn; Manila: Institute of Women's Studies, St Scholastica's College): 3–14.

Orevillo-Montenegro, Muriel
    2006   *The Jesus of Asian Women* (Maryknoll, NY: Orbis Books).

Schüssler Fiorenza, Elisabeth
    1983   *In Memory of Her: A Feminist Theological Reconstruction of Christian Origins* (New York: Crossroad).

Suarez, Oscar
    1981   'The Phenomenon of Power: Biblical and Theological Perspectives', *Tugón* 5 (1): 49–67.

Walsh, Brian J. and Sylvia C. Keesmat
    2004   *Colossians Remixed: Subverting the Empire* (Downers Grove, IL: InterVarsity Press, 2004).

Wengst, Klaus
    1987   *Pax Romana and the Peace of Jesus Christ* (Philadelphia: Fortress Press).

Wink, Walter
    1984   *Naming the Powers: The Language of Power in the New Testament.* Vol. 1, *The Powers* (Philadelphia: Fortress Press).

Zerbe, Gordon
    2003a   'The Politics of Paul: His Supposed Social Conservatism and the Impact of Postcolonial Readings', *Conrad Grebel Review* 21 (1): 82–103.
    2003b   'Constructions of Paul in Filipino Theology of Struggle'. Paper delivered at a Paul and Politics Group session, Society of Biblical Literature Annual Meeting, November 2003.

THE FIRST AND SECOND LETTERS TO THE THESSALONIANS

Abraham Smith

Contemporary proponents of postcolonial criticism usually embrace a broad definition for postcolonial criticism, namely, one that examines the whole complex of imperialism, from its earliest forms within colonization processes to efforts of resistance for political independence to neocolonialism as well (Ashcroft, Griffiths and Tiffin 1989: 2; see Dube 2000: 3). When biblical studies becomes the arena for postcolonial interrogation, biblical scholars seek to proffer 'archival exegesis' of the historical and discursive kind to trace the shadow of the empire within and beyond biblical texts (on 'archival exegesis' see Donaldson 1996). Following Kathleen O'Brien Wicker, I see historical colonialism as 'the political, economic, and social domination of people of less developed countries by those from more developed countries' and discursive colonialism as 'the psychological domination of people through appeals to authority, based on the asserted superiority of one race, gender, class, or culture over another' (1993: 377).

Thus, an array of several interrelated types of criticism becomes possible: (1) interrogations of the shadow of imperialism in the history of interpretation of biblical texts, (2) explorations of the anti-imperialist stances in the biblical writings themselves and (3) critiques of the imperialist tendencies of those same writings whether or not they include tacit overtures or explicit claims against historical and discursive forms of colonization. Because postcolonial criticism proffers sophisticated critiques about constructions of 'the other', moreover, postcolonial biblical studies raises questions about the 'configurations of power' involved in representing 'the other' (on 'configurations of power' see Said 1978: 5). In this regard, strict dichotomies between 'the colonizers' and 'the colonized' are not valid, and many postcolonial scholars decry simplistic essentialist representations that present the two as 'mutually exclusive' (e.g., Suleri 1992: esp. 764; Sugirtharajah 1998: 94).

Thus, with a focus on the construction of 'the other', this commentary proceeds with two sets of discussions: (1) summaries of the contents of each letter and (2) interrogations of various strategies of domination, whether those strategies are substantively sustained in the effective history of the letters, shrewdly resisted by the letters themselves, or strangely advanced by the letters.

Summaries of 1 and 2 Thessalonians

Interpretations that radically contrast 1 Thessalonians and 2 Thessalonians respectively as 'friendly' and 'cold' in tone are neither sound in reason nor suggestive in reading the apparent shadows of empire found in *each* letter. (Against the claim that 2 Thessalonians is cold see Malherbe 2000: 382; see also Aus 1973; Menken 1994: 82. See Philo, *Special Laws* 1.224.)

To begin with, the letters present similarities as well as differences. The former are evident. A case can be made that 1 Thessalonians is written with a friendly yet exhortative style. Expressions of praise and affection abound; fictive-kinship diction flourishes and mutual-admiration notices (1.3; 2.17; 3.6) polish the otherwise psychagogic and paraenetic finish that Paul has put on his earliest extant letter. Yet, no less is true of 2 Thessalonians, despite its so-called 'obligatory' thanksgiving notices ('We must always give thanks', 1.3; 2.13). On the one hand, a litany of thanksgiving and intercessory-prayer notices in both letters are telltale signs of psychagogic care in both: note the repeated thanksgiving notices in both (1 Thess. 1.2, 2.13, 3.9; 2 Thess. 1.3, 2.13) as well as the intercessory prayers (1 Thess. 3.11-13; 2 Thess. 2.16-17) that follow the thanksgiving notices in both (1 Thess. 3.9; 2 Thess. 2.13). On the other hand, acknowledgment of the boastworthiness of the community's steadfastness (2 Thess. 1.4), the prediction of coming relief for the afflicted (1.5-10), and hortatory appeals against enthusiastic agitation (2.1-12) and irresponsible behaviour (3.6-15) – all suggest for 2 Thessalonians as for 1 Thessalonians the same admiration and watchful care of a letter-writer for his recipients. At the same time, the differences are quite telling.

First, compared to 1 Thessalonians, 2 Thessalonians is saturated with unvariegated diction and pleonastic expressions that revel in excessive or redundant coinage (Menken 1994: 30–32). Thus, for example, Schmidt suggests: 'The degree of syntactical complexity in the opening thanksgiving of 2 Thessalonians is unmatched elsewhere in the Pauline corpus and has it closest parallel in Ephesians and secondly in Colossians, two members of the Pauline corpus often considered "pseudepigraphic" ' (1990; see Trilling 1972: 48–65).

Second, unlike 1 Thessalonians, 2 Thessalonians seeks to authenticate itself in the face of other apparently spurious letters (see 3.17).

Lastly, 1 Thessalonians' presupposition of an imminent parousia (1 Thess. 4.13-18) stands in stark contrast to the projection of a return at an unspecified time in the future (2 Thess. 2.1-12).

In the end, the presence of such differences and similarities lies at the heart of the debate about the authorship of 2 Thessalonians, with the scales tipping more for a pseudonymous origin than a Pauline one, at least in the estimation of many scholars.

At the same time, descriptions of the letters as radically different in tone centre attention exclusively on letter-writer and audience and obfuscate the wider imperial context in which both letters were written and to which they apparently offered subtle critique. The single-minded focus on letter-writer and recipients may, moreover, obscure each letter's direct or indirect contributions to the imperial ideological currency in the militaristic codes of their apocalyptic appeals. Thus, the summaries that follow, deduced in part from Smith (2000: 681–84), while they presuppose the differences between the letters, also provide a basis for the interrogation of each letter's construction of 'the other'.

1 Thessalonians
Saturated with military imagery and a rhetoric of group distinctiveness, 1 Thessalonians was written roughly around 50 or 51 CE to encourage a beleaguered Pauline assembly to persevere in its new 'walk' of life (4.1, 12; see 2.12), in consonance with the apocalyptic gospel Paul had preached (1.5; 2.2). That gospel or 'good news' of YHWH's victory over enemies – a concept likely drawn by Paul, according to J. Beker (1982: 116), from Deutero-Isaiah in its LXX form (see, e.g., Isa. 52.7; 61.1) – reorients one's prestige away from peer review to the pleasure of God (2.4; 4.1) and to a distinctive life worthy of God (2.12). Conceivably, in the face of hostility from its own former neighbours (2.14-16), the assembly (in Paul's eyes) constantly faced the temptation to retreat to its former networks of support (see 3.5). For members of the assembly to do so, however, was for them to set their sights on transient forms of prestige and insecurity (5.3). In the diction of military exhortation, then, the assembly is told to 'stand forth' (3.8) and to do what Paul, Silvanus and Timothy did, namely, to use resources of habituation (5.12-22) to encourage persistence in the walk of life oriented to a permanent prestige and security found in a true (1.9), powerful (1.10), generous (4.8) and faithful God (5.24) – not in the conventional order. (On *stēkete* ['stand firm'] as a term of military exhortation see Malherbe 2000: 203.)

2 Thessalonians
As for 2 Thessalonians, also steeped in militaristic diction and a rhetoric of group distinctiveness, two issues are prominent. First, presupposing the continuation of the earlier hostilities as noted in 1 Thessalonians, this writer also evinces a concern for stability (1.4). (Not assumed here is the view that the audience of 2 Thessalonians was *actually* in Thessalonica. All we can say is that the audience of 2 Thessalonians was likely familiar with the contents of 1 Thessalonians. For more on this matter, see Krentz 1991: 52 n. 5.) So, the assembly is admonished to 'stand firm' and to hold tightly to the apocalyptic traditions it received from established apostolic authorities (2.15; see Malherbe 2000: 439). These traditions had the effect, moreover, of distinguishing 'the oppressed from the oppressors, and in the future the elect from the damned' (see 1.5-10; 2.1-12; see Menken 1994: 92). Accordingly, in form and in some of its diction, 2 Thessalonians is strikingly similar to 1 Thessalonians. Second,

a new problem emerges in 2 Thessalonians: the presence of enthusiastic apocalypticists. Not surprisingly, then, the writer deploys apocalyptic material and assumes his audience's acquaintance with it, though the intent is to counter the enthusiastic apocalypticists, not to endorse them. Not surprisingly, moreover, the writer also frequently uses 1 Thessalonians again in a non-enthusiastic way to advocate involvement in the everyday world (Malherbe 2000: 456).

The work thus aims 'to discredit the claims, made in Paul's name, of apocalyptic preachers which were causing alarm within the community (2.2) and social unrest within its ranks (3.6-12)' (Richard 1995: 299). Indeed, with characteristic military coinage, some of the writer's harshest exhortation is reserved to curb the 'social unrest' of a group described as behaving *ataktōs*, persons who 'did not keep step or follow commands' (3.6, 11; 3.7; see Jewett 1991: 69).

The Interrogative Lens of Postcolonial Criticism

Reading the Shadow of Empire in the Effective History of 1 and 2 Thessalonians

Since the formative days of modern critical biblical studies, the traditional conceptual apparatus for understanding Paul and his assemblies was informed both by a Protestant–Roman Catholic debate about personal faith and a racialized reading of world history. That is, in accordance with a Protestant theology informed by Augustine and Luther, Paul was seen as the bold proclaimer of 'justification by faith', while Judaism was seen as a religion of merits, a projection in part based on Protestant views of Roman Catholicism (for a sterling critique see Buell and Johnson Hodge 2004: 239–41; for a 'social' reading of 'justification by faith' see the discussion below on Elsa Tamez). Furthermore, given the racist 'Western imperialist practices' that ranked the 'mental and moral capacities' of human beings in accordance with rigid essentialist taxonomies, 'all under the guise of objective scientific "knowledge" about race, sex, and sexuality' (Buell and Johnson Hodge 2004: 239), Paul was separated from his own native Judaism and assumed to be the creator of a *superior* 'new, universal and spiritual religion', namely, Christianity, while Judaism itself, at least in the tradition of Georg Wilhelm Friedrich Hegel's (and F. C. Baur's) racialized discourse, was seen as the separatist, parochial and *inferior* 'other' (Horsley 2004: 1; on Hegel and Baur see Kelley 2002: 76–77; Barclay 2002: 197). Relatedly, but issuing out of popular circles in the North Atlantic, Paul and the writings attributed to him have been placed in the service of an 'end of the world' discourse, that is, a millenialist, Manichaean and often merely palliative response to assessments of conditions in the world. In either case, much of the radical, anti-imperial dimensions of Paul and his assemblies have been obscured by a discourse that currently undergirds various imperialistic myths of the United States as a nation uniquely chosen by God.

Though neither letter of the Thessalonian correspondence figures palpably in the production of Paul as a proclaimer of 'justification by faith', the apocalyptic rhetoric found in both letters has been deployed in North Atlantic popular readings, though the deployment has either obscured the anti-imperial foci of the selected passages or radically altered the textual terrain of select passages to accommodate crude scriptural gerrymandering. (Care must be taken not to read North Atlantic receptions of New Testament apocalyptic as the prism through which other cultures have read it. On Brazilian receptions, for example, see Woodruff 2002 :127–39.) Two popular imperialist readings of 1 Thess. 4.17 and 2 Thess. 2.3-4, 6-10 vividly manifest this oppositional, 'end of the world' discourse.

Popular Imperialist Reading of 1 Thessalonians 4.17. Paul's reference to a 'snatching up' (*harpagēsometha*) in the clouds (1 Thess. 4.17) likely brought consolation to his beleaguered assembly who had witnessed the death of loved ones. The assembly was assured of the security of the departed ones and that they ('those remaining alive') would be snatched up to join the departed to be with the Lord forever. Thus, neither the hostility from their former neighbours (2.14-16) nor death itself would ultimately disturb the union with the Lord. Furthermore, with the distinctive terms *parousia* ('presence', 2.19; 3.13; 4.15; 5.23) and *apantēsis* ('meeting', 4.17), Paul portrays Jesus' 'coming' or 'return' and the assembly's 'meeting' with Jesus in diction used respectively to describe the advent of an emperor and the ceremonial delegation that goes out to meet him (4.14-18; see H. Koester 1997; also H. Koester 1990: 446; Míguez 1989). Given the use of *harpazein* cognates in consolatory literature of the period, with reference to Fate as a snatching force that separates loved ones from each other, moreover, perhaps Paul uses the expression to represent a twist on typical condolence literature (on this possibility see Malherbe 2000: 275–76). Hence, Paul says: 'Comfort one another with these words' (4.18).

Since the 1800s, however, Paul's 'snatching up' reference has been linked to the doctrine of the 'rapture' (or the 'at any moment coming of Jesus'), a view that was first developed by the British premillenialist dispensationalist thinker John Nelson Darby, next propagandized in the annotations of the Scofield Reference Bible, and then adopted by fundamentalists in the United States. Uprooted from its textual moorings then, 1 Thess. 4.17 became the basis for a belief in a 'secret rapture' (known only to those snatched up) that would safely protect the 'faithful' from the devastation of the so-called tribulation period as described in Mt. 24.21 (on premillenial dispensationalism, Darby and the Scofield Reference Bible see Sandeen 1970). Within the discursive field of US fundamentalism, moreover, 1 Thess. 4.17 was grist for the mill for the development of a nationalist piety supported by hyperpatriotism, antichrist identifications (see below), and paranoia (Fuller 1995; see also Robert Jewett's sterling critique of the 'rapture' concept and its consequences [1979: esp. 139]).

Popular Imperialist Reading of 2 Thessalonians 2.3-4, 6-10. Although some interpreters of 2 Thess. 2.3-4, 6-10 assume the writer is discussing the figure only obscurely known elsewhere as the 'antichrist', neither the Greek word for antichrist (*antichristos*) nor the idea is found in the passage. Actually, only 1 Jn 2.18-19, 22, 4.3 and 2 Jn 7 mention the word 'antichrist' (on the history of the obsession with the idea of the antichrist in the United States see Fuller 1995). In fact, the 'lawless man' figure (aka the 'son of destruction') in 2.3-4, 6-10 is best described as an *opponent of God* (2.4), though Christ is the agent through whom this enigmatic figure will meet destruction (2.8) (for a careful study of the figure in 2 Thess. 2.1-12 see Peerbolte 1996: 63–95).

Also, the writer's 'veiled and obscure' language throughout 2.1-12 further complicates the identification of the 'lawless man' (Thurston 1995: 175). Restraining the revelation of the figure is 'something' (based on the neuter participle, *katechon* [translated in the NRSV as 'restraining', 2.6]) or 'someone' (based on the masculine participle, *katechōn* [translated in the NRSV as 'restrains', 2.7]). Yet, neither the 'someone' nor the 'something' is identified, nor does the writer indicate the necessity for the use of the two different participles to describe the entity that restrains (Wanamaker 1990: 251). Given the writer's desire to refute an enthusiastic brand of apocalypticism and to ensure that the false claim of the nearness of the day of the Lord does not 'shock the ... [assembly] suddenly' or 'repeatedly agitate' them (2.2, 3), moreover, perhaps the vague diction is deliberate (Wanamaker 1990: 238).

Still, these discrepancies and enigmas have not stopped Christian interpreters from the pursuit to identify the referent for the figure, whether one speaks of pre-Augustine referents such as the Roman Empire or post-Augustine candidates such as the pope, 'Napoleon Bonaparte, Adolph Hitler, Henry Kissinger, Mikhail Gorbachev and, most recently, Saddam Hussein' (Fuller 1995: 3; see McGinn 1994). The obsession with identifying the antichrist in the United States, moreover, is in no small way a result of the nation's self-understanding. Given its citizens' view of themselves as 'uniquely blessed by God, they have been especially prone to demonize their enemies' as 'others', as the antichrist or his minions, whether those enemies were the Native Americans (and, subsequently, the Church of England and the English monarchy) in the colonial period, or 'modernism, Roman Catholicism, Jews [especially before the Balfour declaration of 1917], socialism, and the Soviet Union' in the twentieth century, or 'the Muslim world' today (Fuller 1995: 5, 11–13).

Reading 1 and 2 Thessalonians against the Empire

Given the conceptual obstructions in the North Atlantic effective history of the letters that attest to Paul and his assemblies, whether those obstructions appear in critical modern scholarship or popular circles, the political character of Paul and other early Jewish 'resistance' thinkers has not been sharply accented. (In all honesty, a thoroughgoing postcolonial analysis would not only reveal the evidence for a multiple number of religions in antiquity [see Segovia 1998: 58–60] but also broaden 'textuality' to include 'texts' and interpreters [see Segovia 2000].) By contrast, some of the scholarship on Paul in Costa Rica and Argentina seriously considers the political dimensions of Paul's writings, whether one considers Elsa Tamez' insightful re-reading of 'sin' as structural and of 'justification' as 'social' as opposed to 'individual' or the various writings of Néstor Míguez on Paul's use of political diction in 1 Thessalonians (Tamez 1993; Míguez 1989; 1990). Recent studies in the North Atlantic now also read Paul and his assemblies in 'opposition to the Roman imperial order' (Horsley 2004: 3). These studies do not view Paul as a 'rabble-rousing revolutionary', a thesis that could be shortly put to rest with an appeal to Paul's admonitions in Rom. 13.1-7 (Horsley 2004: 3). Given the 'imperial violence' of the period, moreover, the studies also do not infer that Paul made explicit and blunt judgments against the Roman authorities (Smith 2004: 54).

Yet, resistance can take multiple forms, often in indirect ways. Accordingly, attention now is given to the 'arts of resistance' presupposed by or reflected in the correspondence of Paul and his contemporaries. (On the different paths by which resistance might take place see Scott 1990.) One art of resistance was the deployment of *apocalyptic traditions*, traditions that incorporated political diction and presupposed a 'critique of this age and its values', including those of the Roman imperial order (Sampley 1991: 108). Paul's *cultivation of 'assemblies'* (*ekklesiai*) is yet another 'art of resistance', for Paul envisioned a widespread collection of alternative communities that were, in some respects at least, resisting the ideologies of the cultures around them. (On Paul's development of *ekklesiai* as an alternative movement see Horsley 1998: 165.) Yet another art of resistance – and these are by no means mutually exclusive – was the *subtle political critique of local accommodationist practices* that supported the hierarchical values of the Roman imperial order.

Apocalyptic Traditions of Resistance. The apocalyptic traditions deployed by Paul and others were not innocuous statements of doctrine (Horsley 1994a: 96). The apocalyptic view that the time of the present age is short (1 Cor. 7.29), that a crucified Jesus was vindicated through resurrection (Phil. 2.9-11) and that Jesus' resurrection marks the first-fruits (1 Cor. 15.20) of those who have died within the eschatological community is actually a critique of the values of this age. If one therefore views the apocalyptic traditions deployed by Paul as a critique of 'the rulers of this age' (1 Cor. 2.8), it is possible to see counter-cultural diction in both letters of the Thessalonian correspondence, though 2 Thessalonians falls short of mentioning Jesus' crucifixion and resurrection.

Notice has already been given to both letters' use of the expression *parousia* ('coming' or 'presence': 1 Thess. 2.19; 3.13; 4.15; 5.23; 2 Thess. 2.9) to describe Jesus' advent. In 2 Thessalonians, moreover, the writer also describes Jesus' advent as an *epiphaneia* (2.8), a term 'regularly applied to the Julio-Claudians'

(Harrison 2002: esp. 83). Likewise, the attribution of the appellation 'Father' to God could have been deployed in opposition to the imperial establishment, for the term figured in the ideology of Augustus Caesar, as he sought to construe his empire as one large family (D'Angelo 1992: 623). In fact, the use of such terms as 'gospel' (*euangelion*) and 'saviour' (*sōtēr*) in 1 and 2 Thessalonians or any of the letters attributed to Paul could well have suggested 'opposition to the imperial religion of the *pax Romana* [Roman peace]' (Horsley 1994b: 1157; see Tamez 1993: 58).

One could also read the 'peace and security' passage (1 Thess. 5.3) as an 'ironic allusion to the official theology and propaganda of the *Pax Romana*' (Georgi 1991: 28; see Míguez [1990: 60–61], who contrasts the temporary 'peace and security' [5.3] with the faithful God of peace [5.23, 24]). Furthermore, imperial inscriptions that propagandized the eschatological era (or new beginning) of Augustus and his successors throughout the empire overlap with the eschatological terminology of the Thessalonian correspondence: peace, appearance, hope, good news, salvation, joy. (On the first-century use of each of the terms see Harrison 2002: 92.)

When 2 Thessalonians ascribes to Jesus various images that once described the greatness of God as in 2 Thess. 1.6 (cf. Isa. 66.6) or 1.8 (Isa. 66.15-16) or 1.12 (Isa. 66.5), moreover, it reads events in light of an eschatological vision of God bringing justice and a new creation for those who have faced alienation and oppression. The writer seems dependent as well on either Zech. 14.5 or *1 En.* 1.9 for his imagery about *angels* (2 Thess. 1.7), on Isa. 66.15-16 (which speaks about God) for his imagery of a *flaming fire* (2 Thess. 1.8), on the LXX form of Isa. 2.10 (also once a reference to God) for his insistence that both the persecutors and a larger group will be 'separated from the presence of the Lord' (2 Thess. 1.9), on the LXX form of Ps. 89.7 (that is, Ps. 88.8) for his imagery about Christ being *glorified* (2 Thess. 1.10), and on the LXX form of Isa. 66.5 (again a reference to God) as a backdrop for the expression 'that the name of our Lord Jesus may be glorified in you' (2 Thess. 1.12).

Assemblies as Alternative Communities of Resistance. Paul's work was conducted in Greek cities that sought to manage the Roman imperial complex through enhanced relations with 'local benefactors or foreign saviors who provided resources for urban buildings and public welfare' (Smith 2004: 53). Yet, not everyone acquiesced to the Roman imperial order.

Judaean and Galilaean resistance endured for centuries (see Horsley 2004: 6); the Romans were also constantly quelling disturbances in Gaul and Germany (see Mattern 1999: 70) as well as in Northern Italy, Sardinia, Spain, Africa, Britain and even Macedonia–Thrace (see Dyson 1975). Indeed, Rome had to wage four wars against the Macedonians: the first (214–205 BCE) because of an alliance between Hannibal of Carthage and Philip V (Hammond 1968: 8–12); the second (200 BCE) in which 'Philip decisively [was] beaten at Cynoscephalae'

(Goldsworthy 2002: 11); the third (172–167 BCE), the decisive battle at Pydna, when Perseus (the son of Philip V) was defeated and the Roman 'peace' came with the deportation of Macedonian's military officers, the division of the land into four republics, and restrictive laws on inter-republic trade (Hammond and Walbank 1988: 564); and the fourth (149–148 BCE), when Metellus, a Roman commander, quashed the revolt of the Macedonians led by Andriscus (Pseudo-Philip VI), pretender to the throne of the Macedonian King Philip V.

Some resistance to Rome, however, came in the form of alternative philosophical movements 'whose promotion of good living as well as right thinking, philanthropy as well as piety, could involve sharp criticism of the ruling classes' (Wilson 1996: 3). Jewish life was classified as a philosophical movement, and they adopted the classification (Mason 1996: 43–46). Evidence suggests that Paul also shared much with the philosophers of his age (Malherbe 1987), including a psychagogic tradition that entailed a 'communal pattern of mutual participation by community members in exhortation, edification and correction' (Glad 1995: 7); an acceptance of a wide variety of persons, including slaves and women (Glad 1995: 165–72. Philodemus, Glad notes, was a friend not only to his patron Piso but to a number of other persons of different social levels [1995: 172]. Citing cols 7a8-10, 12a5-6, 14a6-10 and 22a-b of *On Frank Criticism*, he shows the inclusion of women, slaves and important individuals as subjects of Epicurean psychagogy [1995 172 n. 48]); and a reformatory ethic in accordance with communal unity ideals and the varying dispositions of a community's charges (Glad 1995: 8). Since these movements were wider than the usually local, voluntary associations, they had the effect of producing a 'viable, oppositional network of shared values across time and space' (Smith 2004: 54).

Both letters to the Thessalonians may be seen, therefore, as documents of moral formation designed to support the shared values of a network of *ekklesiai* in the face of competing values in the larger society. Both letters seek to 'strengthen' (1 Thess. 3.13; 2 Thess. 2.17; 3.3) their auditors in their dispositions and to aid them in 'standing firm' (1 Thess. 3.8; 2 Thess. 2.15). Both letters, moreover, direct the auditors' search for honour to the *ekklesia*'s court of reputation, not that of the other Thessalonians (DeSilva 1994: 49–50).

Anti-Accommodationist Political Critique. According to Mattern, 'international relations for the Romans, were not so much a complex geopolitical chess game as a competition for status, with much violent demonstration of superior prowess, aggressive posturing, and terrorization of the opponent' (1999: xii). Yet, as noted, Rome's imperial dominance in Macedonia and elsewhere in the Greek East was not secured solely through its massive military forces nor only through its extraction of taxes from colonized nations (Mattern 1999: 157). It was also secured through local cultivation of the emperor cult. That is, on their own initiative, local aristocracies built and prominently placed temples, established public festivals, erected statues, minted coins and underwrote games – all to proliferate imperial honour (Horsley 1997: 20). Though anti-imperial sentiment was not uncommon, Rome's subjects, led by the local elite, accommodated themselves to Roman rule because of Rome's unavoidable presence and power.

In first-century CE Thessalonica, the provincial capital of Macedonia, pro-Roman forces were in abundance, because the Thessalonians had long cultivated the beneficence of the Romans. Occasional anti-Roman revolt was initiated by other Macedonians. Thus, according to Dyson (1975: 169–70), 'relations between the Romans and the Bessi [who were also Macedonian] had been turbulent during the Republic'. In the imperial period, moreover, a certain Vologaesus led a revolt in 11 BCE against the Romans and killed Rhasyporus, the son of the Thracian King Cotys. This revolt lasted for three years and was only finally put to rest by L. Calpurnius Piso (the same Piso who was castigated by Cicero but greatly praised by Antipater of Thessalonica). However, epigraphic, numismatic and statuary evidence from Thessalonica give testament to honours given to the Romans.

In the epigraphic evidence, the Thessalonians praised Metellus as a 'saviour' (*sōtēr*) (Collins 1993: 6). Metellus was the Roman commander who quashed the revolt of the Macedonians led by Andriscus (Pseudo-Philip VI), pretender to the throne of the Macedonian King Philip V. Similarly, the quaestor C. Servilius Caepio was attributed the title 'saviour' possibly because he exercised administrative leniency in not requiring 'exorbitant magisterial exactions' (Hendrix 1984: 266).

Coins testify to the praise of Antony and Octavian and commemorate the city's 'liberation' through Antony's defeat of Brutus in 42 BCE (Hendrix 1984: 156). After the famous Battle of Actium (31 BCE), moreover, the city also issued coinage honouring the deification of Julius. The coins, with Julius and Augustus on the obverse and reverse sides respectively, give witness to the 'Thessalonians' awareness of the imperator's status as *divi filius* [son of a God]' (Hendrix 1984: 172). Even after Augustus, some of his successors (from Gaius and Commodus) also appear on the city's coins (Hendrix 1984: 198). An inscription gives witness to a temple of Caesar, while others praise 'Roman benefactors' or Roma in association with Roman benefactors.

An important statuary remain is a partial statue of Augustus that appears to date from the Claudian period. It is significant, if for no other reason, because it is 'the only statue of a very few archaeological phenomena dating to the immediate period of Paul's missional activity' (Hendrix 1991: 117). Thus, it is clear that there were pro-Roman forces among the Greeks and Asians (despite anti-Roman forces as well) and that Thessalonica was not without its pro-Romans, for the city actively cultivated Roman beneficence through its honour of the Romans. (For all of the examples listed I am drawing extensively on Smith [2004: 57–58].)

Given the ubiquity of Roman propaganda as cultivated by Thessalonica's local aristocracy, some parts of the Thessalonian correspondence may now be re-read as critiques of the pro-Roman elite. The letters are not unique in this regard. As shown by Nestor Paulo Friedrich (2002), the Apocalypse of John may be read also as a critique of pro-Roman accommodation. According to Friedrich, in the midst of competition for the support of the imperial cult among the cities of Asia Minor, the small church in Thyatira was encouraged not to cave in to the desires of the *philoiromanoi* in the latter's support of Rome nor to be seduced by the accommodationist teachings of those within the church who wanted to cave in to the policies of Rome as suggested by the pro-Roman forces. The danger John sees in accommodation is that it leads to assimilation and ultimately to apostasy.

In terms of 1 Thessalonians, Paul's reference to 'salvation' (*sōterias*, 5.9; see 5.8) through 'the Lord Jesus Christ' (5.9) may be a pointed attack against the search for salvation through other saviour figures, including Roman ones. Given the 'siege mentality' of Thessalonica, 1 Thess. 5.3 could also be a critique of pro-Romans whose trust in the Roman 'peace' failed to reckon with Macedonia's past history of being invaded repeatedly (Smith 2004: 63–65). (According to Craig Stephen de Vos, the presence of marauders in the entire Macedonian province including Thessalonica up to the beginning of the civil wars and perhaps even beyond 'may have created something of a siege mentality' [1997: 125].) Perhaps 1 Thess. 2.14-16, moreover, is neither an interpolation nor an anti-Jewish statement but Paul's critique of pro-Roman forces in Thessalonica through an analogous critique of pro-Roman forces in Judaea (Smith 2004: 58–62). Paul's admonitions toward self-(community-)reliance and not on the 'outsiders' may be read as directives to the assembly not to do what the elites of the city were surely doing.

With regard to 2 Thessalonians, while we cannot know the location of its audience, the reference to a Lord of peace who gives peace 'in all ways' (2 Thess. 3.16) could be a telling indictment in any city in which elites had perceived the Romans as benefactors to all people. Whatever the location of the audience of 2 Thessalonians and despite the absence of epigraphic evidence for the epithet 'common benefactor' in Thessalonica, the idea of a person (e.g., several of the Roman emperors) as a saviour or 'benefactor of all' was a commonplace. Particularly, we should note the prevalence of the epithet for Rome or Roman benefactors after the demise of the Macedonian monarchy (after 167 BCE), when the Greek East had to 'accept that the balance of power which had existed in the third century was over. [Hence] Rome was the common benefactor because it was perceived as having no rival' (Erskine 1994). Erskine acknowledges the absence of epigraphic evidence for the epithet in Thessalonica (1994: 80). (On the attribution of the epithet for certain Roman rulers from Julius Caesar to Hadrian see C. Koester 1990: 667.)

Reading Reinscriptions of Imperial Relations in 1 and 2 Thessalonians

A postcolonial analysis cannot be content simply to name the anti-colonial emphases of 1 and 2 Thessalonians. One must also ask if the diction and rhetorical strategies used in these texts in some way reinforced 'empire'. That is, did the arguments for the construction of the 'other' in both texts actually reinscribe the empire's hierarchical arrangement of social relations? Thus, the goal here is not simply to interpret the purposes of the texts but to place the texts in the context of the same 'ancient political invective' that Rome used to speak about the 'other'.

Ancient people did not have 'systematic intelligence' reports about another group's 'political, social, and cultural institutions' (Mattern 1999: 70). Deploying cultural stereotypes, the Greeks, for example, relegated all others to the category of 'barbarians' (Mattern 1999: 70). When the 'barbarians' were described, moreover, they were said to be polygamous, 'fierce, cruel, treacherous, disorganized in battle, drunken, greedy for plunder, [and] lacking in discipline' (Mattern 1999: 71, 74).

In time, the Romans also branded 'others' as 'barbarians', especially the Parthians, though the net was cast wide to include other rebellious groups resisting Roman hegemony, such as the Gauls or the Germans (Mattern 1999: 70). Likewise, the Jews often castigated Gentile 'others' with the epithet that these 'others' were sexually licentious and did not know God (Ps. 79.6; Jer. 10.25). In turn, Gentile writers (Hecataeus of Abdera, Manetho, Apollonius Molon, Diodorus Siculus, Strabo, Popmeius Trogus, Lysimachus, Apion and Tacitus) charged the Jews with either misanthropia or xenophobia, both being polemical motifs against ethnographic 'others'. (On the tradition of misanthropia and xenophobia and its varied uses see Schaefer 1997: 173–75. See also Tacitus, *Histories*, 5.5.2; Josephus notes Apion's use of the polemic in his *Against Apion*, 2.121.)

Although Paul critiqued empire, his use of rhetorical strategies for the construction of the 'other' reinscribed the assumptions of empire (Knust 2004: 164). Like others who engaged in invective characterization, Paul's canon of strategies included commonplace androcentric critiques against sexual depravity, greed and lack of discipline.

In 1 Thessalonians, as elsewhere, Paul castigates 'Gentile others' as 'those who do not know God' (4.5), a status he links to passionate lust (*epithumias*, 4.5) and to *porneia* (or sexual immorality). In effect, Paul begins a discussion on refraining from sexual immorality; then, in the course of illustrating how the audience should so refrain, he mentions the Gentiles who do not know God. (For cognates of *porneia* elsewhere in the Pauline corpus, see 1 Cor. 5.1[×2], 9, 10, 11; 6.9, 13, 16, 18[×2]; 2 Cor. 12.21; Gal. 5.19. The Stoic tetrachord of 'troublesome' passions [*pathē*] included 'pleasure [*hēdonē*], desire [*epithumia*], grief [*lupe*] and fear [*phobos*]' (Aune 1994: 126). On Paul's 'othering' rhetoric, see also Schüssler Fiorenza [2000: 45–47].) Likewise, 'competitive greed' (*pleonexia*) is castigated in 1 Thess. 4.6 (on *pleonexia* as 'competitive greed' see Fiore 1990: 137), and the assembly is admonished not to grieve 'as others' (*hoi loipoi*) do in 4.13.

Presupposed in 1 Thessalonians and in invective characterization in general is an ethic of self-mastery, that is, control of passions (Stowers 1994: 57; see Plato, *Republic* 430E–431A), whereby 'Life was viewed as a constant battle, the moral problem of which was excessive pleasure, i.e., enslavement to desire, and the moral aim – as reflected in several anti-passion topoi – mastery over one's desires, though not total abstinence' (Smith 1999: 99). Presupposed here as well, moreover, is a view of self-mastery as a male characteristic. That is, self-control is viewed as a male trait, while its absence is viewed as a female trait. As Stanley Stowers has argued, 'life is war, and masculinity has to be achieved and constantly fought for. Men are always in danger of succumbing to softness, described as forms of femaleness or servility' (1994: 45). With little wonder it is, then, that the self-control directives of 1 Thess. 4.3-8 seem to be addressed to males, not to all the brothers and sisters of the assembly. (The exact meaning of 1 Thess. 4.3-8 is uncertain, though many scholars presuppose here that Paul has bought into the patriarchal assumptions of the times; see, for example, Burke [2003: 195].)

Paul's construction of 'outsiders' in 1 Thessalonians also relies heavily upon a view of his assembly as faithful military recruits in contrast to others who lack discipline and order. 1 Thessalonians is replete with military imagery, whether one considers Paul's 'instruction' (*parangelia*) in 4.2, which connoted a 'word of command given by a superior officer' (Avotri 1991: 75); or the eschatological weaponry imagery in 5.8 (Avotri 1991: 76); or the trumpet sound image in 4.16 (Hanson 1989: 72); or the 'stand forth' diction in 3.8, which Paul used elsewhere to inspire the Galatians (Gal. 5.1) not to be 'undisciplined military recruits who desert, turn away, apostasize (1.6) rather than stand their ground' (Sampley 1996: 118). The eschatological military context of 1 Thess. 5.1-11 also suggests that Paul used the commonplace polemical diction of undisciplined military recruits to view 'the others' (or 'the outsiders') as drunken and sleeping military recruits who were unprepared for surprise attacks. (On this commonplace see Livy 5.44-45; Pliny, *HN* 14.144, 148; Polybius, *Histories* 2.19.4, as listed by Mattern [1999: 205]. Against idleness see Polybius, *Histories* 11.25.7. On drunken or sleepy soldiers see Polybius, *Histories* 8.37; 29.15.1-2.)

2 Thessalonians also adopts the military diction of 1 Thessalonians, whether one considers the *parangelia* of 3.4, 6, 10, 12 or the 'stand forth' diction in 2.15. As aforementioned, moreover, the erstwhile enigmatic *ataktoi* in 1 and 2 Thessalonians should be viewed in light of military-discipline polemics. In 1 Thess. 5.14, the *ataktous* are not idlers, as some scholars have suggested. They are rather persons who 'did not keep step or follow commands' (2 Thess. 3.6-7, 11; see Jewett 1991: 69). It seems here that Paul fosters community regulations for the assembly by indicating the character (a lack of self-control) he elsewhere associ-

ates with outsiders. The same may be said for the use of the *ataktōs* diction in 2 Thessalonians. While the writer insists that this group not be treated as enemies, the characterization of the group as persons who were not *ergazomenous* ('[really] working') but *periergazomenous* ('working around') was a typical slur cast against 'enemies' to show their lack of discipline (Malherbe 2000: 453–54). Thus, in both letters, an internal rhetoric of othering is based on an external rhetoric of othering. In both letters, moreover, the rhetoric of othering presupposes what was considered an androcentric goal, that is, self-control.

Conclusion

Given the interrogative lens of postcolonial criticism, it is possible to see the ineluctable reality of 'empire' in the Thessalonian correspondence (Segovia 2000: 92–93). In part, empire shapes the discourse formations and governing assumptions of all interpreters of the two letters, whether from popular circles or from the academy. In part, empire was critiqued by the letters themselves as marginalized communities faced the incredible and ubiquitous presence of Roman domination. In part, moreover, we do a disservice to the multiple sub-merged communities of the period if we simply accept the various ideologies offered by Paul and the writer of 2 Thessalonians, for they too incorporated the rhetorical strategies of othering used by the dominant culture. Toward the creation of a just world, interrogation at its best then is always an examination of power relations wherever they exist, from antiquity to today.

BIBLIOGRAPHY

Ashcroft, Bill, Gareth Griffiths and Helen Tiffin
  1989   *The Empire Writes Back: Theory and Practice in Post-Colonial Literatures* (New York: Routledge).
Aune, David C.
  1994   'Mastery of the Passions: Philo, 4 Maccabees and Earliest Christianity', in Wendy E. Helleman (ed.), *Hellenization Revisited: Shaping a Christian Response within the Greco-Roman World* (Lanham: University Press of America): 125–58.
Aus, Roger D.
  1973   'The Liturgical Background of the Necessity and Propriety of Giving Thanks according to 2 Thess. 1:3', *Journal of Biblical Literature* 92: 432–38.
Avotri, Solomon Kwami
  1991   'Possessing One's Vessel in 1 Thessalonians 4:4: Marital or Martial Metaphor?' (PhD dissertation, Iliff School Of Theology and University Of Denver).
Barclay, John M. G.
  2002   ' "Neither Jew nor Greek": Multiculturalism and the New Perspective on Paul', in Mark G. Brett (ed.), *Ethnicity and the Bible* (Boston: Brill Academic Publishers, Inc.): 197–214.

Beker, J. Christiaan
>   1982   *Paul the Apostle: The Triumph of God in Life and Thought* (Philadelphia: Fortress Press).

Buell, Denise Kimber and Caroline Johnson Hodge
>   2004   'The Politics of Interpretation: The Rhetoric of Race and Ethnicity in Paul', *Journal of Biblical Literature* 123: 235–41.

Burke, Trevor J.
>   2003   *Family Matters: A Socio-Historical Study of Kinship Metaphors in 1 Thessalonians* (London: T&T Clark International).

Collins, Raymond F.
>   1993   *The Birth of the New Testament: The Origin and Development of the First Christian Generation* (New York: Crossroad).

D'Angelo, Mary Rose
>   1992   'Abba and "Father": Imperial Theology and the Jesus Traditions', *Journal of Biblical Literature* 111: 611–30.

de Vos, Craig Steven
>   1997   *Church and Community Conflicts: The Relationships of the Thessalonian, Corinthian, and Philippian Churches with Their Wider Civic Communities* (Atlanta: Scholars Press).

DeSilva, David A.
>   1994   ' "Worthy of His Kingdom": Honor Discourse and Social Engineering in 1 Thessalonians', *Journal for the Study of the New Testament* 64: 49–79.

Donaldson, Laura E.
>   1996   'Postcolonialism and Biblical Reading: An Introduction', in Laura E. Donaldson (ed.), *Postcolonialism and Scriptural Reading* (Semeia 75; Atlanta: Scholars Press): 1–14.

Dube, Musa
>   2000   *Postcolonial Feminist Interpretation of the Bible* (St. Louis: Chalice Press).

Dyson, Stephen L.
>   1975   'Native Revolt Patterns in the Roman Empire', in Hildegard Temporini (ed.), *Aufstieg und Niedergang der römischen Welt* 2.3 (New York: Gruyter): 138–75.

Erskine, Andrew
>   1994   'The Romans as Common Benefactors', *Historia* 43: 70–87.

Fiore, Benjamin
>   1990   'Passion in Paul and Plutarch: I Corinthians 5–6 and the Polemic against Epicureans', in David Balch, Everett Ferguson and Wayne A. Meeks (eds), *Greeks, Romans and Christians: Essays in Honor of Abraham J. Malherbe* (Minneapolis: Fortress Press): 135–43.

Friedrich, Nestor Paulo
>   2002   'Adapt or Resist?: A Socio-Political Reading of Revelation 2:18-19', *Journal for the Study of the New Testament* 25: 185–211.

Fuller, Robert C.
>   1995   *Naming the Antichrist: The History of an American Obsession* (New York: Oxford University Press).

Georgi, Dieter
>   1991   *Theocracy in Paul's Praxis and Theology* (trans. David Green; Minneapolis: Fortress Press).

Glad, Clarence
1995   *Paul and Philodemus: Adaptability in Epicurean and Early Christian Psychagogy* (New York: Brill).
Goldsworthy, Adrian
2002   *Roman Warfare* (Great Britain: Cassell).
Hammond, N. G. L.
1968   'Illyris, Rome and Macedon in 229–205 BC', *Journal of Roman Studies* 58: 1–21.
Hammond, N. G. L. and F. W. Walbank
1988   *A History of Macedonia.* Vol. III, *336–167 BC* (Oxford: Clarendon Press).
Hanson, Victor Davis
1989   *The Western Way of War: Infantry Battle in Classical Greece* (New York: Knopf).
Harrison, J. R.
2002   'Paul and the Imperial Gospel at Thessaloniki', *Journal for the Study of the New Testament* 25: 71–96.
Hendrix, Holland
1984   'Thessalonians Honor Romans' (Th.D. dissertation, Harvard University).
1991   'Archaeology and Eschatology at Thessalonica', in Birger A. Pearson *et al.* (eds), *The Future of Early Christianity: Essays in Honor of Helmut Koester* (Minneapolis: Fortress Press): 107–18.
Horsley, Richard A.
1994a   *Sociology and the Jesus Movement* (New York: Continuum).
1994b   'Innovation in Search of Reorientation: New Testament Studies Rediscovering its Subject Matter', *Journal of the American Academy of Religion* 62: 1127–66.
1997   'Introduction to the "Gospel of Imperial Salvation" ', in Richard A. Horsley (ed.), *Paul and Empire: Religion and Power in Roman Imperial Society* (Harrisburg, PA: Trinity Press International): 10–24.
1998   'Submerged Biblical Histories and Imperial Biblical Studies', in R. S. Sugirtharajah (ed.), *The Postcolonial Bible* (Sheffield: Sheffield Academic Press): 152–73.
2004   'Introduction', in Richard A. Horsley (ed.), *Paul and the Roman Imperial Order* (Harrisburg, PA: Trinity Press International): 1–8.
Jewett, Robert
1979   *Jesus Against the Rapture: Seven Unexpected Prophecies* (Philadelphia: Westminster Press).
1991   'A Matrix of Grace: The Theology of 2 Thessalonians as a Pauline Letter', in Jouette M. Bassler (ed.), *Pauline Theology.* Vol. I, *Thessalonians, Philippians, Galatians, Philemon* (Minneapolis: Fortress Press): 63–70.
Kelley, Shawn
2002   *Racializing Jesus: Race, Ideology and the Formation of Modern Biblical Scholarship* (London: Routledge).
Knust, Jennifer
2004   'Paul and the Politics of Virtue and Vice', in Richard A. Horsley (ed.), *Paul and the Roman Imperial Order* (Harrisburg, PA: Trinity Press International): 155–73.
Koester, Craig R.
1990   'The Saviour of the World (John 4:42)', *Journal of Biblical Literature* 109: 665–80.

Koester, Helmut
    1990   'From Paul's Eschatology to the Apocalyptic Schemata of 2 Thessalonians',
            in Raymond F. Collins (ed.), *The Thessalonian Correspondence* (Leuven:
            Leuven University Press): 441–58.
    1997   'Imperial Ideology and Paul's Eschatology in 1 Thessalonians', in Richard
            Horsley (ed.), *Paul and Empire: Religion and Power in Roman Imperial
            Society* (Harrisburg, PA: Trinity Press International): 158–66.
Krentz, Edgar
    1991   'Through a Lens: Theology and Fidelity in 2 Thessalonians', in Jouette M.
            Bassler (ed.), *Pauline Theology*. Vol. I, *Thessalonians, Philippians, Gala-
            tians, Philemon* (Minneapolis: Fortress Press): 52–62.
Malherbe, Abraham
    1987   *Paul and the Thessalonians: The Philosophic Tradition of Pastoral Care*
            (Philadelphia: Fortress Press).
    2000   *The Letters to the Thessalonians* (Anchor Bible, 32B; New York: Doubleday).
Mason, Steve
    1996   '*Philosophiai*: Graeco-Roman, Judaean and Christian', in John S. Kloppenborg
            and Stephen G. Wilson (eds), *Voluntary Associations in the Graeco-Roman
            World* (London: Routledge): 31–58.
Mattern, Susan P.
    1999   *Rome and the Enemy: Imperial Strategy in the Principate* (Berkeley: Univer-
            sity of California Press).
McGinn, Bernard
    1994   *AntiChrist: Two Thousand Years of the Human Fascination with Evil* (New
            York: HarperSanFrancisco).
Menken, Maarten, J. J.
    1994   *2 Thessalonians* (London: Routledge).
Míguez, Néstor
    1989   'Lenguaje bíblico y lenguaje político', *Revista de Interpretación Bíblica
            Latinoamericana* 4: 65–81.
    1990   'Para no quedar sin esperanza: La apocalíptica de Pablo en I Ts. como lenguaje
            de esperanza', *Revista de Interpretación Bíblica Latinoamericana* 7: 47–67.
O'Brien Wicker, Kathleen
    1993   'Teaching Feminist Biblical Studies in a Postcolonial Context', in Elisabeth
            Schüssler Fiorenza (ed.), *Searching the Scriptures*. Vol. 1, *A Feminist Intro-
            duction* (New York: Crossroad): 367–80.
Peerbolte, Lietart L. J.
    1996   *The Antecedents of Antichrist: A Traditio-Historical Study of the Earliest
            Christian Views on Eschatological Opponents* (Leiden: E. J. Brill).
Richard, Earl J.
    1995   *First and Second Thessalonians* (Sacra Pagina; Collegeville, MN: Liturgical
            Press).
Said, Edward
    1978   *Orientalism* (New York: Vintage Books).
Sampley, J. Paul
    1991   *Walking Between the Times: Paul's Moral Reasoning* (Minneapolis: Fortress
            Press).
    1996   'Reasoning From the Horizons of Paul's Thought World: A Comparison of
            Galatians and Philippians', in Eugene H. Lovering, Jr. and Jerry L. Sumney

(eds), *Theology & Ethics in Paul and His Interpreters: Essays in Honor of Victor Paul Furnish* (Nashville, TN: Abingdon): 114–31.

Sandeen, Ernest R.
1970   *The Roots of Fundamentalism: British and American Millenarianism 1800–1930* (Chicago: University of Chicago Press): 59–80.

Schaefer, Peter
1997   *Judeophobia: Attitudes toward the Jews in the Ancient World* (Cambridge, MA: Harvard University Press).

Schmidt, D. D.
1990   'The Syntactical Style of 2 Thessalonians: How Pauline is it?', in Raymond F. Collins (ed.), *The Thessalonians Correspondence* (Leuven: Leuven University Press): 382–93.

Schüssler Fiorenza, Elisabeth
2000   'Paul and the Politics of Interpretation', in Richard A. Horsley (ed.), *Paul and Politics: Essays in Honor of Krister Stendahl* (Harrisburg, PA: Trinity Press International): 40–57.

Scott, James C.
1990   *Domination and the Arts of Resistance: Hidden Transcripts* (New Haven: Yale University Press).

Segovia, Fernando F.
1998   'Biblical Criticism and Postcolonial Studies: Toward a Postcolonial Optic', in R. S. Sugirtharajah (ed.), *The Postcolonial Bible* (Sheffield: Sheffield Academic Press): 49–65.
2000   *Decolonizing Biblical Studies: A View from the Margins* (Maryknoll, NY: Orbis Books).

Smith, Abraham
1999   ' "Full of Spirit and Wisdom": Luke's Portrait of Stephen (Acts 6:1-8:1a) as a Man of Self-Mastery', in Leif E. Vaage and Vincent L. Wimbush (eds), *Asceticism and the New Testament* (New York: Routledge): 97–114.
2000   '1 and 2 Thessalonians', in Leander Keck (ed.), *The New Interpreter's Bible.* Vol. XI (Nashville: Abingdon Press): 671–772.
2004   'Unmasking the Powers: Toward a Postcolonial Analysis of 1 Thessalonians', in Richard A. Horsely (ed.), *Paul and the Roman Imperial Order* (Harrisburg, PA: Trinity Press International): 47–66.

Stowers, Stanley K.
1994   *A Rereading of Romans: Justice, Jews, and Gentiles* (New Haven: Yale University Press).

Sugirtharajah, R. S.
1998   'A Postcolonial Exploration of Collusion and Construction in Biblical Interpretation', in R. S. Sugirtharajah (ed.), *The Postcolonial Bible* (Sheffield: Sheffield Academic Press): 91–116.

Suleri, Sara
1992   'Woman Skin Deep: Feminism and the Postcolonial Condition', *Critical Inquiry* 18: 756–69.

Tamez, Elsa
1993   *The Amnesty of Grace: Justification by Faith from a Latin American Perspective* (trans. Sharon H. Ringe; Nashville, TN: Abingdon Press).

Thurston, Bonnie
1995   *Reading Colossians, Ephesians, and 2 Thessalonians: A Literary and Theological Commentary* (New York: Crossroad).

Trilling, W.
    1972   *Untersuchungen zum 2. Thessalonicherbrief* (Leipzig: St. Benno Verlag).
Wanamaker, Charles
    1990   *The Epistles to the Thessalonians: A Commentary on the Greek Text* (New
             International Greek Testament Commentary; Grand Rapids: Eerdmans).
Wilson, S. G.
    1996   'Voluntary Associations: An Overview', in John S. Kloppenborg and Stephen
             G. Wilson (eds), *Voluntary Associations in the Graeco-Roman World* (London:
             Routledge): 1–15.
Woodruff, Archibald
    2002   'Thirty Years of Near Neglect: Apocalyptic in Brazil', *Journal for the Study
             of the New Testament* 25: 127–39.

THE FIRST AND SECOND LETTERS TO TIMOTHY AND THE LETTER TO TITUS

Ralph Broadbent

The Pastoral Epistles, although claiming Pauline authorship, are almost certainly non-Pauline. The various New Testament Introductions set out the arguments for and against Pauline authorship, but the weight of scholarly opinion places them in the post-Pauline era. These letters belong to the second or third generation of Christianity. Various dates have been suggested for their composition, though with no real consensus. Most dates fall between 90 and 120 CE. The contents of the letters would suggest that these dates are not unreasonable. These historical-critical questions are, however, not the focus of concern here. The main concern is to begin to uncover what insights postcolonial theory might throw on these early Christian writings.

The Postcolonial Perspective

Postcolonial theory is perhaps more complex and convoluted, in some of its manifestations, than the further reaches of biblical studies. However, as with all theoretical perspectives, its importance lies less in its more arcane meanderings than in the questions it raises and thus forces biblical scholars to answer, both about the original contexts of the biblical writings and the interpretations which have been placed on them down the centuries. At the risk of oversimplification, postcolonialism is concerned with the issues of power and hierarchy within imperial settings. It is also concerned to contest such power. In the case of the Pastoral Epistles, this arises in two contexts. First, there is the original setting of the epistles within the Roman Empire. What was happening within these early Christian communities and why did they react to empire in the way that they did? Second, there is the question of the hermeneutical decisions made by biblical scholars when interpreting the epistles. It seems clear that these interpretations, particularly during the period of the British Empire, and beyond, were deliberately slanted to bolster that empire and the power and authority of the elite who controlled it. Passages in the epistles which particularly reflect this are those which deal with empire and rulers, slaves, the place of women, the question of male leadership and riches and wealth.

Postcolonial Analysis

On Empires and Rulers

The key texts on the empire and those in authority are 1 Tim. 2.1-2 and Tit. 3.1 (and to a lesser extent 1 Tim. 6.15). Those who rule the empire are to be obeyed, and prayers are to be offered for them. The passages display some sort of accommodating attitude to the Roman Empire and the imperial apparatus. We do not, in general, know enough about the communities in the background of the Pastorals to know why they made this decision of accommodation with empire, in rather sharp contrast to the communities behind the more anti-imperial book of Revelation and such literature as the Ignatian Epistles. The most usual explanation is that the Pastorals represent early Christian communities under the threat of persecution who opted for the quieter life of accommodation rather than risking the danger of persecution and martyrdom. However, as will become apparent below, this explanation may be rather too simplistic.

Staying with these particular passages, several matters are worth noting from a postcolonial perspective.

First, the essentialization of the 'other' by commentators. Out of many examples, we can note that 'the Cretans were notoriously turbulent' (Brown 1917: 110) and that there was a 'Jewish tendency to rise against the Empire' (Lock 1924: 25). These commentarial observations are precisely the point made by Edward Said's *Orientalism*, that the non-Western 'other' has some sort of essential, primitive nature and that this cannot ever be altered, even by becoming part of the Christian community.

Second, the commentators make the general assumption that 'empire' is a good thing. C. K. Barrett, linking the passages to Rom. 13.1-7 and 1 Pet. 2.13-17, claims that government 'is a good gift of God's providence, and Christians should pray for those who practise it' (1963: 49). The ideological point being made, as commentators often also do when discussing the linked passages, is that these rulers or empires or governments, no matter how tyrannical, are appointed by God and that to disobey them or rebel against them is to go against the will of God.

Third, it has been claimed that the Christian practice of prayer *for* the emperor and others rather than prayer *to* the emperor will be, in due course, subversive of the empire as it points to an even higher heavenly authority (Johnson 2001: 196; Collins 2002: 53). While these commentators do not use the theoretical terms of postcolonialism, such as 'hybridity', they are raising postcolonial concerns in suggesting that such subtle changes in how prayers are said can begin to destabilize the imperial powers. Such subtleties have been raised in the works of 'postcolonial' writers as diverse as Homi Bhabha and Frantz Fanon. However, as the two centuries after the Pastoral Epistles saw the gradual metamorphosis of Christianity into the imperial state religion, the idea of the subtle destabilization of empire by prayer alone seems rather ambitious.

Slaves

A similar hope of destabilizing a well-established system of oppression, slavery, lies behind much of the exegesis of the passages on the duties of slaves (1 Tim. 6.1-2; Tit. 2.9-10; and, on slave-traders, 1 Tim. 1.10). The general trend of exegesis is that good behaviour by slaves is the way to commend the Christian faith to those in authority. As more of those in authority become Christians, this in turn will lead to the eventual end of slavery as an institution.

Commentators display little sympathy for the position of slaves in the imperial world. Their main concern is to emphasize the need for submission and the avoidance of any unrest within the Roman Empire. Thus, for example, Ernest Faulker Brown states: 'Had slaves been urged to revolt against their masters, neither masters nor slaves would have been morally bettered, and a civil war of frightful dimensions would have ensued' (1917: 47). The parallels and support given to Britain's empire (and class system) are clear enough. Another interpretive ploy is the spiritualization of oppression. Slaves or imperial subjects have no need to end their enslavement or improve their social position because true freedom is to be found in 'relationship with Christ' (Kelly 1963: 130). Slaves also obtain some sort of 'strength and nobility' (Johnson 2001: 289–90) from serving their Christian masters.

This need for submission and acceptance is not limited only to empires past and present. It also applies to those employed in the modern world. The biblical passages make 'more obvious the duty of all Christian employees of our own age to show complete trustworthiness' (Leaney 1960: 121). It seems as if modern commentators on the Pastoral Epistles are as uneasy with the egalitarian ideals of early Christianity as were the originators of these writings.

Women

It took approximately 18 centuries after the Pastoral Epistles for slaves to achieve the beginnings of emancipation. The struggle for women's emancipation seems to be taking rather longer, with the Pastoral Epistles providing biblical ammunition for those wanting to halt that process under the newly fashionable guise of 'headship'. Postcolonial feminists, such as Gayatri Chakravorty Spivak, have continued to draw attention to the plight of women who, despite the end of empire, continue to be triply disadvantaged on the grounds of gender, race and poverty. Fortunately, in biblical scholarship, a great deal of work has been undertaken in recent years to uncover the full roles played by women in the egalitarian, early Christian communities. Within the Pastorals, important passages for consideration include 1 Tim. 2.9-15; 5.3-16; Tit. 2.3-5.

Not unexpectedly, commentators from earlier times do not hesitate to give full rein to their reactionary views on the place of women. Just three brief quotations will serve to give a taste of mainstream exegesis, and, in reading these quotations, it is important to remember that the whole discussion of the role of women in society and their right to vote were current, hotly debated topics when the commentators were writing. In other words, in their exegesis of these passages (and others), the commentators were making a *conscious choice* and their choices cannot be simply excused as those made by innocent dinosaurs from a past age. So, we are told that in the Fall, 'the woman was deceived, not the man, and this suggests she will be an unfit guide' (Bernard 1989: 48). The author of the Pastorals, in this case Paul, is 'somewhat depreciating ... about women' because he had observed the idolatry in the worship of Artemis in Ephesus which 'was carried on with the wildest orgies, and sometimes with the utter abandonment of shame; and to these rites the women lent themselves even more readily than the men' (Brown 1917: 19). However, should any woman have the time or energy to want to teach in the Christian assembly, she should be warned that 'the strain of public teaching is usually beyond her strength' (Burn 1928: 583). It is also worth noting that commentators, where it suits their purpose, neatly fail to distinguish between the past and the present, thus implying, for example, that as women were not strong enough to teach publicly in the past, the same is likely to be true today. These commentators 'essentialize' women, past and present, as thoroughly as the oriental 'other'.

Such examples could be multiplied endlessly. Their importance in this context is that they have set a pattern for modern exegesis which is still current, despite the best efforts of feminist scholars (both female and male). So, for example, Marshall tells us that 'Misconceived emancipation movements connected with false teaching might require putting temporary restraints on freedom' (1999: 443). One might think that 20 centuries was stretching the meaning of 'temporary' just a little. Yet, this also points to an emerging pattern, both within the Pastoral Epistles and their subsequent, general exegesis. The pattern seems to be that where there are hermeneutical choices to be made, these choices will be made in favour of empire and hierarchy and against those excluded by empire – slaves, women, the poor, the 'other'.

Male Leaders and Wealth
In contrast to the shortcomings of women, male leaders are seen as the norm and the qualities they require are easily defined (1 Tim. 3.1-13). Anyone who aspires to the office of bishop must be the head of a household and well thought of by those outside the church, 'above reproach, married only once, temperate, sensible, respectable, hospitable' (v. 2). He must be capable of managing 'his own household well' and of 'keeping his children submissive and respectful in every way' (v. 4). Similar conditions apply to candidates for the office of deacon (vv. 8-9). Whether v. 11 refers to women deacons or to the qualities required of the wives of deacons is a moot point. Candidates for office are, by

implication and social status, likely to be wealthy, hence the reference to not being a lover of money (v. 4; see also 1 Tim. 6.10, 17).

It is clear that the passage (1 Tim. 3.1-13) reflects some sort of well-understood, fixed schema, and it seems that there are considerable parallels to the qualities traditionally thought suitable for an army general (Lock 1924: 36; Collins 2002: 80). Three things are apparent from this description. First, the writer is encouraging these communities to become much more closely aligned to the norms of empire. Second, only those of a certain social status can aspire to leadership within the community. Third, leadership is reserved, in the eyes of the writer, to men.

Conclusion

The exact origin of the Pastoral Epistles remains something of a mystery. The Christian communities involved are being encouraged to follow the hierarchical rules of empire, with the emperor and other local rulers at the top and women, slaves and children at the bottom. In between come the male leaders of the Christian community. The context, however, reveals that this picture is a disputed one. Women and slaves have clearly played more prominent roles than the author would like. It is possible that the communities concerned have been structured along the egalitarian lines of Gal. 3.28. The intriguing question is why the author (and some important male members of the community?) wants to revert to a more traditional pattern. Is it pressure from outside the community or is it internal pressure? The answer may be a mixture of both. Postcolonial theory has drawn attention to the sheer power of imperial ideology and the need to conform to that force. The letters talk of the importance of being well thought of by those outside the community and that need to conform should not be underestimated. Yet, at the same time, it does seem that the author and some sections of the community may have more personal reasons for rolling back the prominent teaching positions held by women and the equality of status held by slaves. We may well be dealing with the insecurities of wealthy men who see their power being undermined and have made a conscious decision to try to regain their former authority.

However, whatever may be the origins of the letters, there can be little dispute that subsequent interpreters have put them to good use in supporting modern imperial projects. This is particularly so in the case of British commentators supporting the British Empire. The whole ideological tenor of exegesis has been to support the imperial project as being beneficial to its imperial subjects. 'Learned' discussions of empires old and new have carefully airbrushed any negative aspects from view. Good order and the maintenance of hierarchical power have been paramount, and this has had consequences beyond the immediate control of empire, as the exegesis of the epistles has affected women, slaves, the native subjects of empire, as well as the poor working classes at the imperial centre.

This leads to a final important question. Postcolonial criticism sees one of its most important roles as destabilizing current certainties. It points out that the biblical texts are contested texts. In the case of the Pastoral Epistles, it could be asked if they should have canonical status. To put it another way, does the support that the epistles and their interpreters have given to imperial hierarchy over 19 centuries outweigh their usefulness as canonical scriptural texts? Or, on the other hand, is it better to keep them, while being fully aware of their internal shortcomings and subsequent conservative interpretive history, as witnesses to a more anti-imperial, non-hierarchical Christianity? That is the postcolonial dilemma.

BIBLIOGRAPHY

Barrett, Charles Kingsley
    1963   *The Pastoral Epistles* (New Clarendon Bible; Oxford: Clarendon Press).
Bernard, John Henry
    1989   *The Pastoral Epistles* (Cambridge Greek Testament for Schools and Colleges; Cambridge: Cambridge University Press).
Brown, Ernest Faulkner
    1917   *The Pastoral Epistles* (Westminster Commentaries; London: Methuen & Co.).
Burn, Andrew Ewbank and Henry Leighton Goudge
    1928   'The Pastoral Epistles', in Charles Gore, Henry Leighton Goudge and Alfred Guillaume (eds), *A New Commentary on Holy Scripture* (London: SPCK): 573–95.
Collins, Raymond F.
    2002   *1 & 2 Timothy and Titus: A Commentary* (The New Testament Library; Louisville, KY: Westminster/John Knox Press).
Johnson, Luke Timothy
    2001   *The First and Second Letters to Timothy: A New Translation with Introduction and Commentary* (Anchor Bible; New York: Doubleday).
Kelly, John Norman Davidson
    1963   *A Commentary on the Pastoral Epistles* (Black's New Testament Commentaries; London: A. & C. Black).
Leaney, Alfred Robert Clare
    1960   *The Epistles to Timothy, Titus and Philemon* (Torch Bible Commentaries; London: SCM Press).
Lock, Walter
    1924   *A Critical and Exegetical Commentary on the Pastoral Epistles* (International Critical Commentary; Edinburgh: T&T Clark).
Marshall, I. Howard
    1999   *A Critical and Exegetical Commentary on the Pastoral Epistles* (International Critical Commentary; Edinburgh: T&T Clark).

THE LETTER TO PHILEMON

Allen Dwight Callahan

The Colonialism of Postcolonialism

This reading of Paul's Letter to Philemon is informed by the postcolonial situation of the United States, the fruit of white-settler colonialism. The founding colonialism of the United States was, first and foremost, colonialism with colour. It is 'white', the colour Europeans have used to identify themselves over and against those they have colonized or otherwise subordinated. The project of this form of colonialism is, in the words of Priscilla Luján Falcón, 'the physical movement of Euroimmigrants into a non-European land base, state, region, or territory, displacing or eliminating the native inhabitants' (1995: 115). (While such a description is used to mark what she calls 'internal colonialism', it captures the profile of white-settler colonialism as well; the match is no accident, of course, since she is discussing the Mexican experience of what is now the southwestern United States.) Equally important, it is a species of colonialism that permanently settles its colonies. The invasion and displacement of indigenes, if not complete, is permanent. As anthropologist Patrick Wolfe has noted, 'settler colonies were (are) premised on the elimination of native societies. The split tensing reflects a determinate feature of settler colonization. The colonizers come to stay – invasion is a structure not an event' (1999: 2).

These are important distinctions for postcolonial theory. As Wolfe points out, many of 'the native founders of the postcolonial canon came from franchise or dependent – as opposed to settler or creole – colonies. This gave these guerilla theoreticians the advantage of speaking to an oppressed majority on the supply of whose labour a colonizing minority was vulnerably dependent' (Wolfe 1999: 1). Unlike other forms of colonialism – for example, the British Raj in India or King Leopold's Belgian Congo in Africa – settler colonies, Wolfe continues:

> Were not primarily established to extract surplus value from indigenous labour. Rather, they are premised on displacing indigenes from (or replacing them on) the land ... The relationship between Native and African Americans illustrates the distinction particularly well. In the main, Native (North) Americans were cleared from their land rather than exploited for their labour, their place being taken by displaced Africans who provided the labour to be mixed with the expropriated land, their own homelands having yet to become objects of colonial desire. (1999: 1–2)

Settler colonies have tended to import labour to meet their needs and secure an exploitable surplus labour pool. As Luján Falcón puts it: 'The settler colonial state has continually practiced both deportation and importation of labour as a way to provide a solution for economic problems, whether to guarantee large pools of surplus labour or to deter workers from seeking better wages or working conditions' (1995: 17). The mass importation of Africans as slaves in the North American white-settler colonies that were to become the United States is a signal condition of American colonialism, and the legacy of American slavery is a signal feature of the postcolonial gestalt of the United States.

The Post of Postcolonialism

A critical postcolonial reading of a text in such a context must have several features. First, it must recognize the persistence of the colonialist legacy, acknowledging that it is impossible to read the text in question without the after-effects of colonialism. The colonial past and its present postcolonial residue have made pre-lapsarian readings impossible and claims of such readings mendacious. The reading I offer in what follows is one kind of postcolonial reading. It is anticolonialist: it rejects the legitimacy of the colonialist project and seeks a reading of the text that does not advance colonialist interests. There are postcolonial readings that advance the cause of the colonialist project even after the fact; they are neocolonialist readings. They are just as 'postcolonial' as mine. The difference is one of interests. In my reading I seek to give an account of the text that acknowledges the colonialist project – in this way the reading is historical – while rejecting it and, consequently, alternative readings that aid and abet that project.

Onesimus: Colonial Slave

I acknowledge the colonialist legacy by engaging the effective history of the text; that is, I appreciate the history of the text's interpretation as the history of its colonialist effects. This history of Paul's epistle to Philemon begins with the Roman imperialist interpretation of the fourth-century Antiochene preacher John Chrysostom. As I have shown elsewhere (Callahan 1995a; 1995b), John Chrysostom is the author of the interpretation of Paul's letter to Philemon that treats Onesimus as a runaway slave. According to John Chrysostom's creative exegesis, in his *Homilies on the Epistle of St. Paul the Apostle to Philemon*, Paul's letter illustrates that 'we ought not to abandon the race of slaves' and 'that we ought not to withdraw slaves from the service of their masters' (see Schaff 1988: 546). In these homilies the letter becomes part of a biblical apology for slavery. His interpretation was quickly and widely disseminated in the late antique world and continues to be influential in the postcolonial present. John Chrysostom's reading is imperialist: he reads the text as a warrant for the most important power relation of production under Roman imperialism – slavery.

Built upon Chrysostom's pro-slavery reading in the service of white-settler colonialism is the interpretation of the seventeenth-century Puritan divine Cotton Mather, as conveyed in his 'The Negro Christianized' (see Ruchames 1969). Mather appropriates that reading, but in a white-settler colony within an empire: he reads the text as a warrant for the most important power relation of production under British colonialism – slavery, the power relation of production characteristic of the colony. Mather was reconciled to the wretchedness of the slave's life and resolved that efforts must be made to secure for the slave compensatory, beatific afterlife: 'The State of your Negroes in this World, must be low, and mean, and abject; a State of Servitude. No Great Things in this World, can be done for them. Something then, let there be done, towards their welfare in the World to Come' (Ruchames 1969: 63). Mather also resolved: 'A Catechism shall be got ready for them; first a Shorter, then a Larger; Suited to their poor Capacities' (Ruchames 1969: 68). Mather favoured teaching slaves to read the Bible, but 'Until that might be accomplished', he suggested that they 'Learn by heart, certain Particular Verses of Scripture' (Mather 1706: 42–43). Among these select verses were the apostle Paul's several commands to slaves to obey their masters.

This proved to be the classic white-settler view of African slavery in the Americas. To provide theological direction for the conversion of slaves, in 1627 the Spanish Jesuit Alonso de Sandoval published *De instauranda Aethiopum Salute: El mundo de la esclavitud negra en America (On Securing the Salvation of the Ethiopian: The World of Black Slavery in America)*. Sandoval argued that, because the slaves served their temporal needs, Spanish masters ought to see to the eternal salvation of their slaves. Proper religious instruction would insure the slaves a place in the world to come and show slaves that their proper vocation was obedience to their masters. The Jesuit adduced biblical texts, especially those from the letters of Paul, to corroborate his argument for servile obedience (see Hurbon 1992).

Mather commended the Epistle to Philemon, however, not to slaves but to their masters: as John Chrysostom before him, he read the letter as an exhortation for them:

> And those masters doubtless, who use their Negroes with most Christianity, and use most pains to inform them in, and conform them to, Christianity, will find themselves no losers by it. Onesimus was doubtless a Slave: but this poor Slave, on whose behalf a great Apostle of God was more than a little concerned; yea, one book in our Bible was Written on his behalf! When he was Christianized, it was presently said to his master, Philem. 11. In time past he was unprofitable to thee, but now he will be profitable. But many masters whose Negroes have greatly vexed them, with miscarriages, may do well to examine, whether Heaven be not chastising of them, for their failing in their duty about their Negroes. Had they done more, to make their Negroes the knowing and willing servants of God, it may be, God would have made their Negroes better servants to them. (Ruchames 1969: 65)

Because Mather offered his reading in a white-settler colony where slavery was racialized, his reading is a racialized colonialist reading. Not only are the words 'slave' and 'Negro' synonymous, the latter has supplanted the former in the very reading of the Bible, with the word 'servant' as a middle term.

Mather's reading of Philemon became the dominant one in North America, where slavery became indispensable to the settlers' political economy. Paul's letters, 'together with selected passages from some of the other epistles, constituted the most important – and extensively quoted – biblical weapon in the arsenal of the Christian slaveholder' (Wood 1990: 67). Advocates of slavery cherished the Pauline Epistles because specific passages attributed to Paul explicitly endorsed slavery (Smith 1998). Two arguments recur: Paul never takes issue with the institution of slavery, enjoins obedience of slaves; members of early Christian communities, such as Philemon, were themselves slaveholders (Martin 1998). Antebellum pro-slavery apologists came to call the Epistle to Philemon, supposedly a cover letter attending the return of a runaway slave to his angry master, 'the Pauline Mandate' of American slavery. The letter was their biblical sanction for the return of fugitive slaves (Callahan 1997: 1). It showed that members of early Christian communities were slaveholders and supported the return of slaves who had taken flight.

Not everyone was persuaded by this interpretation. In 1833 the Reverend J. Colcock Jones, a white Presbyterian – not a Methodist, as I had earlier identified him (Callahan 1997: 1) – missionary to slaves in Georgia, filed the following report to his mission board:

> I was preaching to a large congregation on the Epistle to Philemon: and when I insisted on fidelity and obedience as Christian virtues in servants, and upon the authority of Paul, condemned the practice of running away, one-half of my audience deliberately rose up and walked off with themselves; and those who remained looked anything but satisfied with the preacher or his doctrine. After dismission, there was no small stir among them; some solemnly declared that there was no such Epistle in the Bible; others, that it was not the Gospel; others, that I preached to please the masters; others, that they did not care if they never heard me preach again. (cited in Raboteau 1982: 139)

Former slave and abolitionist orator Lunsford Lane recalled 'one very kind-hearted clergyman' who lost his considerable popularity among the slaves 'after he preached a sermon from the Bible that it was the will of Heaven from all eternity that we should be slaves, and our masters be our owners'. As a consequence, 'many of us left him, considering, like the doubting disciple of old, "This is a hard saying, who can hear it" ' (Bassett 1925: 14–15, cited in Washington 2000: 333). Slaves openly questioned the interpretations of Paul's letters that sanctioned their suffering, and some cast their vote against pro-slavery exegesis with their feet. Theirs, however, was to be the minority opinion.

The prefatory note to the Epistle to Philemon found in one modern edition of the Bible summarizes the majority opinion: 'The Letter to Philemon, a resident of Colossae in Phrygia, is a model of Christian tactfulness in seeking to effect reconciliation between Onesimus, the runaway slave, and his master, who according to Roman law had absolute authority over the person and life of his slave' (May and Metzger 1962: 1451). The history of interpretation of the epistle is thus the history of this story, the story of Paul the great apostle interceding on behalf of a thieving slave in flight from his noble master. Telling this story, the Epistle to Philemon became the Pauline mandate for slavery under the white-settler slave regime of the United States. This interpretation remains the prevailing interpretation even today, a century and a half after the fall of that regime. The interpretation, now postcolonial, perdures as a neocolonial vestige of the colonial past.

Philemon: An Anti-colonialist Reading

As an anti-colonial alternative, I essay to tell a different story, the story of Paul, an organizer among Greek-speaking Jesus-communities in Asia Minor, who writes a letter attempting to overcome the animus of one of his comrades, Philemon, against another, Philemon's own brother Onesimus. This interpretation is anti-colonial in that it highlights moments in which anti-colonial values and practices are suggested in the text. Essentially, anti-colonial values and practices advance and promote agency without the exploitation that constitutes the project of white-settler colonialism. That exploitation is comprised of several basic elements. The first is a dialectical myth of radical alterity that posits a superordinate white colonial self over and against a subordinate, non-white colonial other. This myth is articulated in the authoritarian pose of the white colonial self with entitlements to the obedience and deference of the non-white colonial other. Devolving from the pretension of entitlements is the discourse of rights, to be distinguished from justice, a discourse of what is right. Finally, to secure their entitlements and defend their 'rights', white-settler colonies use violence and the threat of violence, thus coercing the colonial other to comply with the white-settler colonial regime. All of these elements were characteristic of the white-settler nation-building of the United States.

Concomitantly, there are features of the exercise of agency without exploitation that we may discern in the text of Paul's Letter to Philemon, features antithetical to the exploitation of white-settler colonialism. In this short, diplomatic letter we find an appeal to solidarity instead of *apologiae* for alterity, a rhetoric of indebtedness instead of pretensions to entitlement, a discourse of what is right instead of claims to rights, and persuasion instead of coercion. Though there may be other aspects of the text, this essay will treat only such suggested anti-colonial values and practices.

Paul, the author of the letter, seeks to assert, preserve and protect the solidarity of the letter's principals. This solidarity is love: the word *agapē* and its cognates, which appear in the letter's greeting (v. 1), thanksgiving (vv. 5, 7) and body (vv. 9, 16) are a unifying leitmotif of the letter. Moreover, because the relationship between principals is without entitlements and so resistant to them, there is no moment of coercion. In the exercise of his will, Paul must persuade; he cannot coerce.

In the opening greeting (v. 1) and again in the body of the letter (v. 9), Paul presents himself as 'a prisoner of Jesus Christ'. In this letter the apostle Paul is not, formally speaking, an apostle. Nowhere in the letter does Paul refer to himself as an apostle, as he does in all his other correspondence, nor does he arrogate to himself apostolic prerogatives.

Paul represents himself and the other principals of the letter as colleagues working together in the common project of the gospel of Jesus Christ. These others work neither for nor under Paul, but with him. Paul calls Timothy the co-author of the letter, his 'co-worker', *sunergos*, a term Paul uses in his letters to speak of various associates and occasionally himself (1 Cor. 3.9; 2 Cor. 1.24). The letter addresses Philemon, Apphia and Archippus: none have ecclesiastical titles, and there is no indication that any of them holds an office among 'the saints'. There are no markers of class or caste, status or station. The notion of rank is completely absent here.

Onesimus is Paul's child (*teknon*); he is not his son (*huios*). The former connotes relationship, intimacy and minority, without the authoritarian dimension of the father–son relationship associated with the latter, especially as it was defined in Roman family life under the law and custom of the principate. Though Paul refers to himself as having become Onesimus' father in prison (v. 10), he does not commend himself to Philemon as a father.

Paul's relationship to Philemon is not patriarchal but filial. He entreats Philemon not as a son but repeatedly as a brother. Paul also commends Onesimus to Philemon as a brother. Paul insists that Philemon 'receive him [i.e., Onesimus] no longer as a slave, but more than a slave, as a beloved brother very much so to me, but how much more so to you, both in the flesh and in the Lord' (v. 16). The point here is precisely that Onesimus is not a slave. Onesimus is no longer to be regarded as anything less than a brother. Paul asserts that it is fitting for Philemon to so regard Onesimus because the latter is indeed a brother to the former 'both in the flesh and in the Lord', suggesting that Philemon and Onesimus are blood brothers who have now become colleagues in the gospel.

Paul also presents himself in v. 9 as 'an ambassador'. The ancient Greek manuscripts support the reading of the word 'old man' here, but Bentley's conjectural emendation makes so much better sense in the context of Paul's diplomatic tone (see Metzger 1971). Elsewhere Paul describes himself to the Corinthians as 'an ambassador of Jesus Christ' (2 Cor. 5.20); in Eph. 6.20, Paul is 'an ambassador on a chain'. He is one who seeks to negotiate, to reconcile opposing parties in the light of common interests. He seeks, in short, not to coerce but to persuade.

Persuasion is necessary because Paul is in no position to foist his will upon the other principals. In this letter Paul holds no office; he does not even hold court – he writes the letter because he cannot be physically present. Further, he writes from prison – hardly the place from which to exercise one's prerogatives and predilections. Paul admits all this in vv. 8 and 9, where he begins in earnest his diplomatic appeal on Onesimus' behalf: 'Therefore being forthright to command what is right for you, on account of love I appeal to you all the more'. Paul is not giving orders. Philemon is not the object of the verb 'command' in v. 8: what Paul is bold to command is 'what is right'. He does not declare what is right; he enjoins Philemon to do what is right. Philemon is not the object of a command; he is the object of an appeal. Paul is not in a position to command anything, as he and all the other principals are well aware. The volition of each is decisive here. Thus, commands and appeals must be contingent. Paul's instructions in vv. 17-22, therefore, are couched in the subjunctive mood and the future tense that mark the language of contingency: 'if you consider me a prisoner' (v. 17); 'if he has wronged you' (v. 18); 'I will repay' (v. 19); 'you will do more than I ask' (v. 21).

Paul makes it clear to Philemon that what is on offer is the retirement of Onesimus' debt. What is at issue is Onesimus' indebtedness, not Paul's entitlement. Even Paul's settlement does not entitle him to make demands on Philemon: Paul pays up 'not so that I may say to you that you are also indebted to me yourself' (v. 19). The offer is not a quid pro quo – Paul's benefaction in exchange for Philemon's cooperation. Though Paul is willing to make good any debts incurred by Onesimus, it is not clear that Onesimus in fact has incurred any debt. This too Paul discusses using a conditional clause. Implicitly conditional as well, of course, is Paul's capacity as a man in chains to stand surety for anyone. The only unqualified imperative is Paul's demand for accommodation in v. 22. Even this, however, suggests the contingency of Paul's negotiations: Paul, in prison, can only 'hope that through your prayers I shall be released to you'. Paul may not be free to enjoy Philemon's compliance, let alone enforce it.

Paul's rhetoric treats of the 'ought' and not the 'is' of his relationship with Philemon and Onesimus: not what is, but what is right. Paul asserts that Philemon ought not regard Onesimus as though he were a slave; that he ought to regard him as though he were a beloved brother; that he ought to receive him as though he were Paul himself. Thus, the letter does not affirm that Onesimus is or was a slave. Onesimus is not a slave, and so it is improper for Philemon to treat him as such. Yet, neither is Onesimus a 'beloved brother': if Onesimus were indeed beloved of Philemon, Paul's intervention would be unnecessary. Of course, Onesimus is not Paul: the point here is that Paul wants Philemon to receive Onesimus as though he were Paul.

Conclusion

In his epistle to Philemon, Paul seeks to patch up the frayed network of solidarity that binds together the various principals mentioned in the letter – Paul, Timothy, Philemon, Apphia and Archippus (vv. 1-2); Epaphras, Mark, Aristarchus, Demas and Luke (vv. 23-24); and, now, Onesimus. The letter makes mention of neither apostles nor bishops, but fellow-workers (Philemon, Mark, Aristarchus, Demas and Luke), fellow-soldiers (Archippus), fellow-inmates (Epaphras), brothers (Timothy, Philemon, Onesimus, Paul) and 'all the saints'. Paul speaks of this solidarity with the language of *agape*, a language innocent of myths of alterity, pretensions of entitlement, claims to rights, threats of coercion. It is the language of the co-worker and the comrade, the language of the brother beloved.

BIBLIOGRAPHY

Bassett, John Spenser
    1925   *The Southern Plantation Overseer, as Revealed in His Letters* (Northampton, MA: Printed for Smith College, 1925).
Callahan, Allan Dwight
    1995a   'Paul's Epistle to Philemon: Toward an Alternative Argumentum', *Harvard Theological Review* 86: 357–76.
    1995b   'John Chrysostom on Philemon: A Response to Margaret M. Mitchell', *Harvard Theological Review* 88: 149–56.
    1997   *Embassy of Onesimus* (Valley Forge, PA: Trinity Press International).
Hurbon, Laënnec
    1992   'The Church and Afro-American Slavery', in Enrique Dussel (ed.), *The Church in Latin America 1492–1992* (Maryknoll, NY: Orbis Books): 363–74.
Luján Falcón, Priscilla
    1995   'The Doorkeepers: Education and Internal Settler Colonialism, the Mexican Experience', in Sandra Jackson and José Solís (eds), *Beyond Comfort Zones in Multiculturalism: Confronting the Politics of Privilege* (Critical Studies in Education and Culture Series; Westport, CT: Bergin & Harvey): 113–26.
Martin, Clarice
    1998   ' "Somebody Done Hoodoo'd the Hoodoo Man": Language, Power, Resistance, and the Effective History of Pauline Texts in American Slavery', in Allen Dwight Callahan, Richard A. Horsley and Abraham Smith (eds), *Slavery in Text and Interpretation* (Semeia, 83/84; Atlanta: Society of Biblical Literature): 203–33.
Mather, Cotton
    1706   *The Negro Christianized* (Boston: B. Green).
May, Herbert G. and Bruce M. Metzger (eds)
    1962   *The Oxford Annotated Bible* (Oxford: Oxford University Press).
Metzger, Bruce M.
    1971   *A Textual Commentary on the Greek New Testament* (London and New York: United Bible Societies).

Raboteau, Albert
  1982   *Slave Religion: The 'Invisible Institution' in the Antebellum South* (Oxford: Oxford University Press).

Ruchames, Louis (ed.)
  1969   *Racial Thought in America: A Documentary History.* Vol. 1, *From the Puritans to Abraham Lincoln* (Amherst: University of Massachusetts Press, 1969): 59–70 (Cotton Mather, 'The Negro Christianized').

Schaff, Philip L. (trans.)
  1988   *Homilies of St. John Chrysostom, Archbishop of Constantinople, on the Epistle of St. Paul the Apostle to Philemon*, in *The Nicene and Post-Nicene Fathers* (First Series; reprint; Edinburgh: T&T Clark; Grand Rapids: Eerdmans): 13.545–57.

Smith, Abraham
  1998   'Putting "Paul" Back Together Again: William Wells Brown's Clotel and Black Abolitionist Approaches to Paul', in Allen Dwight Callahan, Richard A. Horsley and Abraham Smith (eds), *Slavery in Text and Interpretation* (Semeia, 83/84; Atlanta: Society of Biblical Literature): 251–62.

Washington, Margaret
  2000   'The Meanings of Scripture in Gullah Concepts of Liberation and Group Identity', in Vincent Wimbush (ed.), *African Americans and the Bible: Sacred Texts and Social Textures* (New York: Continuum): 321–41.

Wolfe, Patrick
  1999   *Settler Colonialism and the Transformation of Anthropology: The Politics and Poetics of an Ethnographic Event* (London and New York: Cassell).

Wood, Forrest G.
  1990   *The Arrogance of Faith: Christianity and Race in America from the Colonial Era to the Twentieth Century* (New York: A. A. Knopf).

THE LETTER TO THE HEBREWS

Jeremy H. Punt

Globally, imperialism, neocolonialism and Eurocentrism are alive and well, and seldom denied, if not always acknowledged as such. The legitimating and totalizing discourse of the Bible and its reception histories are also implicated in these hegemonies of imperialism. Postcolonial biblical interpretation provides the opportunity to investigate this entanglement of the biblical with colonizing discourse and practice. Moreover, a postcolonial reading allows one to search for 'alternative hermeneutics while thus overturning and dismantling colonial perspectives. What postcolonialism does is to enable us to question the totalizing tendencies of European reading practices and interpret the texts on our own terms and read them from our own specific locations' (Sugirtharajah 1998: 16). In Africa, discursive imperialism bolstered by the Christianity project with a co-opted Bible was and is still rife, where 'imperial travelling agents employ texts to subjugate geographical spaces, to colonize the minds of native inhabitants, and to sanitize the conscience of colonizing nations' (Dube 1996: 37).

Against this context, postcolonial biblical interpretation allows one to use biblical texts in an accountable way, to foster geopolitical (Segovia) liberation, to encourage diversity on a global scale while acknowledging the uniqueness and importance of local and indigenous traditions, cultures and nations, and to search for liberating ways of interdependence yet attuning ourselves to issues related to our current sense of globality. It is against this background and with these aims in mind that Hebrews is interpreted, or engaged really, for the sake of what is traditionally called meaning. However, unlike the modernist perception, a postcolonial approach to the meaning of biblical texts would not claim to be objective (neutral meaning), final and prescriptive (definite meaning), or exhaustive of all textual meanings, and it does not necessarily exclude other exegetical or hermeneutical strategies.

The exhortation to the Hebrews is in the form of an anonymous early Christian sermon, with admittedly some epistolary characteristics, and presents an extensive argument on the role of Jesus Christ and his relationship to the Jewish and, in particular, the Mosaic tradition. Jesus is presented as the great high priest whose death and resurrection inaugurate the new covenant. The argument is reinforced by drawing on a number of religious, philosophical and other traditions, prominently and extensively including quotations and exegesis from and commentary on the Hebrew Bible. This led to the particular style and imagery of Hebrews. (The traditional introductory matters – such as date, author, audience or addressees, place of origin and the like – are not dealt with here; see, however, Cynthia Briggs Kittredge's deconstructive approach in arguing for the female authorship of Hebrews [1994: 430–34], which is apparently still burdened by the correlation of a document's authorship and authority.)

As a result of its distinctive character, Hebrews is often accorded a marginal status in the broader canonical context from which it was almost excluded. Such marginality would in itself call for postcolonial investigation and will be attended to in the next section on the contextual character of Hebrews, which is often experienced as annoying. Before doing so, and before the subsequent comments on a few passages and broad themes found in Hebrews, it may, however, be useful to the reader to indicate briefly my understanding of postcolonial criticism and its value in biblical interpretation.

Postcolonial Biblical Interpretation

Why Postcolonial Biblical Interpretation?

> [Postcolonial criticism] will emerge among nations, communities and groups which have been the victims of the old imperialism, and are victims of the current globalisation, and who have been kept away from power, only to achieve an identity which is nurtured and nourished by their own goals and aspirations. (Sugirtharajah 1996: 24)

Postcolonial biblical criticism questions the co-opting of the biblical texts for colonial, imperial and other hegemonic uses. Indeed, Kathleen O'Brien Wicker (1993: 372–73) sees colonial biblical interpretation as marked by the following characteristics: a strong patriarchal perspective; assuming Christianity to be the only true or, at least, superior religion; accepting political assertions in the texts as theologically justified; invalidating readings of the texts in terms of the categories of orthodoxy and heresy; and decontextualizing texts into absolutized injunctions divorced from their contexts. She further describes 'discursive colonialism' as 'the psychological domination of people through appeals to authority, based on the asserted superiority of one race, gender, class, or culture over another' (1993: 377).

Postcolonial biblical criticism searches these documents for 'the gaps, absences and ellipses, the silences and closures, and so facilitate[s] the recovery of history or narrative that has been suppressed or distorted' (Sugirtharajah 1998: 16). A postcolonial approach attempts to deconstruct colonialist interpretation while forging an alternative approach to texts, yet it remains ever alert to the 'continuing, even if transformed, power' of colonialism and imperialism, and their strategies and tactics (Segovia 1998: 51 n. 2). There is, however, an ever-present danger which a postcolonial optic, like all other hermeneutical strategies, needs to avoid: becoming yet another totalizing discourse (see

Segovia 1998: 64). In an ironic way, postcolonialism can become imperialist and hegemonic in its very efforts to privilege the nationalistic, the neglected and the peripheral. Such practices derive from postcolonial comparativist strategies, which sometimes neglect the 'very real differences between cultures and kinds of imperialist oppressions' (Tiffin 1991: xii).

It has been argued that postmodernism and postcolonialism are two sides of the same coin (Boer 1998: 25–26). Postmodernism is properly seen as both cultural phenomenon and socio-economic development – late capitalism – and can therefore be understood as 'an intense dialectical opposition between globalization and disintegration'. Postcolonialism not only exhibits the same dialectical opposition but is actually 'constitutive of the postmodern moment in the first place'. 'In other words', Boer declares, 'the intense dialectical opposition of globalization and disintegration shows up most sharply in postcolonialism, leading to the suggestion that this opposition is a determinative feature of postcolonialism as such'. At the same time, a number of criticisms have been raised against the postmodern project: it tends to posit another 'grand narrative' in the most absolute sense – *itself*; it is often nothing else but a cultural and intellectual neocolonialism – an 'Euro-American western hegemony'; it is largely unconcerned with politics, which limits its effectiveness; it is often as much a rejection of modernism as a subtle reinscription of it (see Bosch 1995: 15–25); it 'fetishes difference' and 'otherness'; it is 'marketed' as 'a general movement which addresses global concerns' and is therefore limited in its ability to address local issues; it is antagonistic towards 'representation' and thus disallows the much-needed postcolonialist post-naive realism; and so forth (Tiffin 1991: vii–xv).

Postcolonial biblical interpretation accepts, with postmodernism, that truth is mapped, constructed and negotiated, and rejects the notion of objective and neutral truth as expressions of political, religious and scholarly power. As far as the Bible is concerned, it is also no longer *the* meaning of the text which is sought after; rather, a multiplicity of meanings is acknowledged from the outset. This includes the revalorizing of the little traditions (Meeks 1986), the hidden transcripts (Scott 1990) of the disadvantaged, marginalized and displaced – the 'other' embodied in women and minorities. A postcolonial reading implies that the Bible itself can no longer serve as 'fetish' but needs to occupy the opposite role of that, namely, it must be re-imagined as a 'diasporic adventure' (Kwok 1998: 186–87). Sugirtharajah puts it as follows: 'What post-colonial criticism will do is to bring out to the front ... marginal elements in the texts, and in the process subvert the traditional meaning. It will engage in an archival exegesis as a way of rememorialising the narratives and voices which have been subjected to institutional forgetting' (1996: 25). It is to be expected that a postcolonialist reading of the Bible will show up sides of these texts not generally allowed before, especially given its alignment with what can broadly be called cultural studies.

Postcolonial Biblical Interpretation as Cultural Studies

Postcolonial biblical interpretation is, in fact, a form of cultural studies and allows, among other things, for taking readers and their involvement in the construction of the text and its meaning seriously. Fernando Segovia (1995: 294–98) describes the three basic dimensions of a cultural critical reading of the Bible as follows. First, the text is regarded, like any contemporary social group, as a socially and culturally conditioned 'other'. In addition, the reader is equally regarded as socially and culturally conditioned, an 'other' to the text and other readers. Third, the interaction between the text and reader cannot be taken as a neutral encounter but as the 'filtering' of the text through (the world of) the reader. Thus, as Vincent Wimbush argues (1993: 129), the 'cultural worlds of readers' determine which texts are to be read, how they are to be read, what they mean – even the meaning of 'text' itself.

Interpretation and meaning, therefore, are the result of an interactive process between reader and text, but never in a neutral way: the text is 'filtered by and through the reader' (Segovia 1995: 296). The reader is primarily seen not as a unique and independent individual but as a member of a distinct and identifiable social configuration, from a social location. In addition to the otherness of the reader and the text, the interaction between the text and the reader (reading) should be understood in terms of both construction and engagement. All attempts at reconstructing the text – regardless of how well-informed or self-conscious they may be – even as the 'other' are nothing but construction. Moreover, as far as engagement with the text is concerned, perceiving the text as 'other' requires *critical* engagement with it, with 'liberation' as goal. Such engagement, furthermore, requires the effort to understand how the text has been interpreted by others (Segovia 1995: 297–98).

In short, cultural criticism allows for the inclusion of other voices in society in the interpretation of the Bible, a 'polyphonic hermeneutics'. However, as far as popular readings are concerned, the warning against a too easy assumption of the 'basic legitimacy of the ordinary readings' should be heeded: 'A cultural studies agenda that defers to popular readings without *emphasizing* the effects of those readings in the social sphere is in danger of repeating and confirming the liabilities of those readings' (Glancy 1998: 476). Caution is in order, however, on both sides. On the one hand, Jennifer Glancy's warning is important: 'Gramsci acknowledges each person as an intellectual, yet also notes that the "common sense" that is the basis of most people's intellectual interactions with the world is an uneven mix of insights, prejudices, contradictions, and images imposed by hegemonic discourse' (1998: 476). On the other hand, far from assuming equality between the power relationships of privileged scholarship and the poor – even for Gramsci's 'organic intellectual' – it is critical to harness scholarly effort to serve the needs of the poor (Rowland 1993: 239, 241). The recognition of other readers, from different locations, put reader, social location and their interaction in the spotlight.

The Importance of the Location of the Reader

> All human utterances occur in a context. And the contexts in which they occur
> modify their meaning. (Lash 1986: 33)

Paraphrasing Nicholas Lash, hermeneutical activity never takes places in the abstract, in theory alone, and is never neutral. The interpretation of the Bible is always done perspectivally, whether the particular perspective or ideology is admitted or unconsciously subscribed to. The Bible is never interpreted *tabula rasa*, insofar as people do not live or exist with empty minds but are embedded in particular historically embodied traditions of convictions and practices. It follows, therefore, that biblical interpretation necessarily concerns very much the identification of the hermeneutical location. Hence, it implies that the influence of the hermeneutical location on the resultant interpretation has to be accounted for (see Punt 1998).

These notions are often expressed with reference to the circular nature of interpretation. This circularity includes the idea that 'all of our judgments are worldview relative and, second, that all worldviews are interpretations and subject to the logic of interpretation' (Westphal 1997: 65). Therefore, in order to understand a particular interpretation, the centripetal force should be investigated: the location or position of the interpreter. (As Stephen Fowl states [1995: 399], 'location is everything', but not only in the sense that it determines the focus of the reading, for example, for an ecclesial rather than academic setting.) Accounting for the interpretive context has to include more than the situatedness of the interpreter in a historical context and linguistic world(s). Any Bible reader is a member of a distinct and identifiable social configuration and belongs to a social location – no matter how hybrid (see Jasper [1997: 29–44] on the 'heterogeneity of human subjectivity [Kristeva] managed by a process of continuous reinterpretation or re-reading of the ebb and flow of language and desire'). Since language is power, the advocacy of a 'politics of location' should be located within 'communities of accountability and structures of responsibility' (Tolbert 1995: 316). Mary Ann Tolbert argues cogently that, instead of focusing on a politics of identity, a politics of location would be more adequate for our postmodern day (1995). Her claim derives from the modern/postmodern debate, and she argues for a 'fluid, shifting, and generally context-dependent' view of identity. It follows that Tolbert stresses location rather than identity as 'essence'. Such location is, again, dependent on 'facts of blood' (social, personal and familial alignments) and 'facts of bread' (national, economic and political matters), which are often at (violent) odds with one another.

The social situation of this study is postcolonial Africa in general and post-apartheid South Africa in particular. To wit: the author is a white male, middle-class and perhaps not yet fully middle-aged, and indigenous to South Africa – one of those whites or 'Caucasian settlers' in South Africa, Zimbabwe and Zambia who 'knows no other home' (Pobee 1992: 28, 58, 164

n. 13). Having been a full-time biblical scholar for 13 years at a historical and still predominantly black institution of higher learning in South Africa *and* involved part-time in the ministry, I share in more ways than one in the postcolonial project. My hybrid, and to some extent diasporic, proud as well as notorious, identity as Afrikaner is informed by a variety of traditions and contexts, including the colonialist West, the black African, and the eastern Malay. Elements of each, in all *its* diversity, can, for example, be observed in my vernacular, Afrikaans.

Much of this commentary on Hebrews was written during the centenary of the South African War (1899–1902), also called the Anglo-Boer War. It was only after a few years that the British succeeded in defeating the Boer republics of Transvaal and Orange Free State through, among other things, Lord Kitchener's 'scorched earth' policy, which claimed the lives of tens of thousands – Boer and Briton, black and white, soldier and civilian, but mostly women and children interned in the infamous concentration camps. As the external colonization of South Africa receded with the proclamation of the union in 1910 and the republic in 1961, the country ironically saw the increasing introduction of internal colonization through racially biased legislation. The latter culminated in a new form of imperialist colonialism, when the devastating apartheid policies were introduced by the National Party government after 1948, which lasted until 1994, when democratic elections in South Africa put an end to white minority rule. However, with the current ruling party's (African National Congress) vigorous campaign for a two-thirds majority in the 1999 elections in South Africa, the decolonized at home as elsewhere seem perpetually at risk of (re)colonizing others.

Hebrews as Contextual Theology: Context

The diasporic character of life for the early followers of Christ is abundantly clear in Hebrews and is given expression in non-traditional language, thought and imagery. It was the contextual nature of Hebrews which led to the nineteenth-century preacher Charles Haddon Spurgeon's teenage feelings on Hebrews – that the Hebrews should have kept the epistle for themselves! Reacting to such notions, some want to reclaim the relevance of Hebrews for today, arguing that it should not be read 'hastily or superficially', for this will lead to a view of its 'themes' as 'antiquated, irrelevant or even esoteric' (Brown 1982: 20–26). Similarly, it is argued that the readers of Hebrews in both the first and twentieth centuries are equally caught up in the 'midst of growing world chaos and powerful cultural pressures to return to a more comfortable past', while trying to keep to their faith in Christ. Whether or not such generalizing identification of the experiences of people divided by almost two millennia is found convincing, it is in any case clear that we have in Hebrews 'flesh-and-blood believers struggling to overcome the stranglehold of past traditions and adjust to the fresh movements of God in their fast-changing world' (Stedman 1992: 9; see Stibbs 1970: 9–12).

Perhaps this perception of Hebrews as 'a book that has clearly lost its relevance it once no doubt possessed' is an attempt to overcome the feelings of modern readers who find it to be 'an irrelevant and almost incomprehensible book' (Williamson 1969–70: 372). (Although admitting that Hebrews is 'in some ways alien to the modern reader', Lindars [1991: 128, 134–35] thinks that its long and sustained argument as well as its rigorism regarding apostasy contributes to the difficulty of reading Hebrews today.) An important reason for this negative evaluation of Hebrews is the influence of many first-century Greek and Hebrew thought-forms, which gave rise to its strange language. Ronald Williamson approvingly quotes Hatch's opinion of 1888 that the Greek theories and Greek usages which have received a Christian form and flavour remain 'in their essence Greek still'.

Hebrews exemplifies the way in which the Christian message is presented as the good news of Christ by incorporating many elements derived from traditions that might have been called heathen and pagan under certain circumstances, and this was accomplished in a way that today might be labelled syncretistic. In Hebrews the attempt seems to be not so much one of 'using the audience's argument or mindset to argue against them' (e.g., Yeo 1991: 3) but rather skilfully exploiting these elements to further its own cause. The difference is perhaps more than just one of emphasis, that is to say, not so much the refutation of existing ideas as reappropriating such ideas for a different purpose. A postcolonial re-reading of Hebrews should, therefore, properly begin by accounting for its contextual character and significance for today. Here, however, a word of clarification is in order: while some scholars would rather refer to Hebrews as 'contextualized *religion*' (e.g., Johnsson 1978a: 107), the term 'contextual theology' in South Africa is generally not perceived as a pleonasm but rather as a laden term, including notions of liberation theology, which featured strongly in the public sphere during the years of the struggle against apartheid.

Contextualization in/of Hebrews

> There is need to engage in a search for fresh idioms in which to express Christian beliefs and to capture the loyalty of modern men [*sic*] *to the Truth as Christ had made us see it and to arrest the drift away from Christianity of those who, seeing it only in traditional dress, do not comprehend it*. (Williamson 1969–70: 376)

The unfamiliar language of Hebrews often provides the first challenge for its contemporary interpretation. It is, however, the corresponding contextual interpretation of concepts in Hebrews in today's often unexplored contexts of biblical studies, and by means of other worldviews than the 'traditional Christian', which can lead to innovative re-readings of Hebrews. Yet, attempts to prove or disprove the dependency of Hebrews on a particular ancient religious or philosophical tradition still abound. Clearly, many similarities with a wide range of first-century traditions and thoughts can be illustrated. (Naturally many differences also exist, as Harold Attridge [1986: 1] contends: 'Hebrews represents a particularly complex case of both the appropriation *and rejection* of that heritage' [emphasis added]; see Punt [1997: 119–43].) On the other hand, avowing or disavowing influence or dependency does not seem to advance our understanding of Hebrews significantly. Hence, while noting and appropriating apparent similarities, it seems more profitable to ask how and especially *why* the Hebrews letter reinterpreted concepts shared with contemporary movements. Whereas the how-question has to some extent featured elsewhere (Punt 1997), the reasons for Hebrews' use of certain thought-patterns and traditions are probably manifold, but – it can be argued – ultimately point in the direction of contemporizing elements of belief in Jesus Christ as Son of God.

Hebrews gives clear evidence of its interpretation of the meaning of Christ for its particular day and age, and environment. (Hebrews is directed at a destination within second-generation Christianity and with certain traditions in place for some time [see 2.3-4; 5.12; 6.1-3; 10.25; 10.32-34; 13.7]; see also, e.g., Johnson 1986: 417–18; Attridge 1989: 12; Stedman 1992: 12; even Calvin 1963: 2. An interesting question is whether the letter is dated post 70 CE, the date of the destruction of the temple in Jerusalem [see Punt 1997: 144 n. 87].) In the attempt to articulate this, it evidently used a number of traditions, intentionally or unwittingly. It shares the terminology, concepts, thoughts and ideas of a variety of diverse and different traditions, movements and groups. Wilson (1987: 27) stresses not only Hebrews' contextualizing of certain concepts and terminology but also that these could indeed be 'taken up and utilized by different writers for very different purposes'. Clearly, there is not 'any one element in the kaleidoscopic Judaism of the first-century Hellenistic world [which] provides the answer to all the questions that need to be asked of its background' (Williamson 1975–76: 236). Without having to enter into a polemic with any particular set of views, Hebrews sets out and accomplishes an effective and thought-provoking interpretation of Christ for its day, an interpretation that is innovative in many respects in the New Testament; as Johnson puts it, 'Hebrews does not advance an interpretation that disputes shared traditions but advances one that builds on the traditions for those able to move to greater insight' (1986: 417).

Given the inevitable contextual nature of theology, an abiding danger is to become overly protective of traditional categories and thought. This trend can be observed also in some approaches to the context of Hebrews. Naturally, the particular disposition on the context's possible influence in the resultant theology or religious practices betrays something of the interpreter's view of what is traditionally known in Christianity as 'revelation', the nature of the biblical writings as 'inspired' or 'sacred' book, and so forth. There is no room here to attend to these very important matters.

Donald Guthrie (1982: 42–43), as a fairly representative example of this tendency, refuses to acknowledge that Hebrews arrived at its interpretation 'through the application of Hellenistic ideas', leading him to contend that Hebrews' approach is 'more biblical' than Philo's and that Hebrews merely expresses its Christian conviction of Christ as the key to the Hebrew Bible in Hellenistic forms! This argument presupposes a Christian tradition that came into existence without the forces and pressures of society bearing in on it and thus moulding – and in the process *changing* – that tradition. Second, to suggest that contextualized expressions of Christian belief are 'unbiblical' only because they do not adhere to the worldview or conceptual framework of traditional Christianity is tantamount to the idolization of the common and accepted practices and beliefs. Finally, the very idea that one can use a particular language and also worldview to express certain ideas without the language and worldview rubbing off on the ideas seems not only naive but also a dangerous oblivion. Therefore, the comment: 'Adaptation of Platonic philosophy to understanding the biblical message of salvation and the soul's progress toward God became an essential part of Christian spirituality' (Perkins 1988: 278), reaches wider than one particular tradition's influence on the development of Christianity.

The presence of diverse available contemporary traditions, including the early Christian, is evident in Hebrews; their innovative and creative use is much in evidence as well. (As was the case with the dominance of Middle Platonic thought in patristic theology, Hebrews also 'reflects the eclectic tendencies of the time and the capacity ... to absorb many other elements and be the integrating framework for new syntheses' [Ferguson 1993: 365]. This, at times imperialist, tendency towards assimilation and integration is one of the reasons for the tenacity and pervasive influence of Christian theology since the first century CE.) Pregeant (1995: 470) balances Hebrews' creativity with its use of the 'wide range of ideas' available. Indeed, in the New Testament Hebrews' uniqueness in language and thought is matched by its character as 'a highly original piece of doctrinal thinking', crafted by its author's 'creative genius' (Williamson 1969–70: 375). ('[Hebrews'] most striking characteristic is the depth and imaginative quality of its reflection' [Hickling 1983: 115]. Allowing for many Pauline parallels, Witherington [1991: 148] nevertheless argues that the author of Hebrews is 'no slavish imitator of anyone, having in fact one of the most creative and original minds among the NT writers'. See Kümmel 1975: 395. For Pauline parallels, see Guthrie 1970: 722; 1982: 43–45; for Hebrews as part of the Pauline legacy, see Koester 1982: 272–76.) Naturally, this should not be taken in isolation from the context or (rhetorical) exigency detected in Hebrews, which was one of 'desperate urgency' (Klijn 1975: 12–13; Lindars 1989: 404).

Interpreted this way, Hebrews provides its modern-day readers with a warrant to repeat its effort anew, to render the writing accessible for the contemporary situation and mind. It implies that Hebrews' use of 'doctrinal constructions' is not compulsory, that is, prototypical rather than archetypal. Pressing his point home, Williamson (1969–70: 375) considers relegating Hebrews to an 'appendix' to the New Testament preferable to leaving it uninterpreted as a 'hindrance and a barrier'. While an 'abbreviation' of the canon – regarding Hebrews – seems in order, in the same vein 'extensions' of the canon are welcomed by Williamson, since the canon 'cannot be considered properly closed until the Holy Spirit has no further truth into which He wishes to lead the Church'. The imperative is to 'attempt to interpret in modern language categories and concepts employed in the Epistle which, because of the nature of life in a modern, western, industrial society, bear no direct relation to those employed in Hebrews' (Williamson 1969–70: 371–76). In many parts of Africa, Williamson finds a 'relevance and importance' for Hebrews which have been lost for Western society, referring specifically to sacrificial practices (1969–70: 375). However, even this apparently parallel worldview might, under scrutiny, also reveal the need for a reinterpretation of Hebrews, contextualized for Africa specifically. This would necessitate an honest evaluation and comparison of the thought-patterns both in Hebrews and different African societies, probably discontinuing simplistic and generalized 'equivalents'.

Ironically, Stedman, who puts so much emphasis on the nature of Hebrews as contextual (1992: 9), seems to insist (1992: 15) on appropriating certain first-century, contextually derived conclusions of Hebrews 'as is' for today and cautions lest 'our cultural context... lure us into practices or deeds that are inconsistent with the new life we have been given in Christ'. This, in short, leads Stedman to insist on the 'parousia', the cross and resurrection of Jesus Christ as 'complete ground of salvation' in contrast and opposition to 'works-righteousness' as a prominent theme, and the portrayal of Jesus Christ as 'high priest' – even after admitting that modern readers 'may lack the Jewish background' – since such themes need not be recontextualized! (Whether the expectation of the imminent return of Christ is still widespread among Christians today is questionable; Stendahl and others have convincingly argued that the contrast between faith- and works-righteousness as commonly understood today was not first-century Jewish but mediaeval Christian and that insisting on the portrayal of Jesus as 'high priest' probably renders the Son of God incomprehensible for most.) On the other hand, but with the irony intact, Williamson denied in his comparative studies the possible influence of Plato (Williamson 1963) and Philo (Williamson 1970), respectively, on Hebrews, although acknowledging the influence of *merkabah* mysticism. Yet, he insists that Hebrews needs to be interpreted in 'modern language', or else one should accept its 'contemporary irrelevance' (1969–70: 375). It would seem, then, that some of those who are willing to affirm the contextual nature of the biblical documents disavow the same process of contextualization today, and vice versa.

Would it not be more appropriate, in admitting to the contextual and contingent nature of Hebrews, to expect the process of reinterpretation to continue for the sake of today's readers of the Bible? Hebrews presents to us an image of early believers who were called to a persistent, unwavering faith, with the call clothed not in traditional garb but in a language and according to a worldview which its addressees could understand and relate to – a 'with-it' translation of the Christ-event for Hellenistic-oriented, 'dissenting-Hebrew' Christians, intent on urging them to greater resilience in their faith. Is the task of theologians, ministers and Christians today any different from that of Hebrews: to engage in the gospel message with people today – rural and urban, rich and poor, from different cultures and subcultures, church-people and those outside the church – in a language and according to a worldview with which people today can identify? The dress of the message is not simply its Bultmannian exterior, the husk containing the kernel, since the message incorporates its medium. In such a way God speaks to us all today, as he spoke to our fathers and mothers in the past (1.1-2).

Hebrews, 'Christian' Traditions and Scripture

> The author inherits an interpreted Bible and makes his own, often original, contribution to the interpretive tradition in which he stands [and] freedom to highlight, and occasionally to de-emphasize, features which do not carry the weight of the main argument. (Ellingworth 1993: 39)

The attempt to account for the distinctiveness of the religious imagination of Hebrews cannot be limited to non-Christian influences. Hickling (1983: 114–15), in his suggestive comparison of a certain section of Hebrews (2.10-18) with the Fourth Gospel, argues that the 'immediate matrix' of the 'theology' of Hebrews was formed by the Christian tradition, to which the author of Hebrews was indebted. This tradition did not only comprise '*credenda* and proof-texts' but also suggested 'a way of attending to Christ and to his relationship with us that was reflective'. Witherington (1991: 146–52) argues compellingly for the influence of Galatians on Hebrews, which he detects in a shared terminology (e.g., the use of *diathēkē*) and a similar use of Hebrew Bible texts (both in choice and technique). He concludes that the author of Hebrews very likely was 'part of the larger Pauline circle' (see Koester 1982), suggesting the name of Apollos as a possible contender. Guthrie (1970: 723), however, concludes that Hebrews is 'as much in line with Paulinism as with the primitive tradition' (see Rissi 1987: 25).

The apologetic position which holds that Hebrews was *predominantly* influenced by 'the mainstream of Christian life and teaching' often relies on questionable assumptions. Notions of 'primitive kerygma' (Lindars 1991: 25) are at times used as though there was a normative as well as monolithic set of doctrines. A 'large, shared body of common traditions' (Attridge 1989: 31) almost certainly existed, but the diverse positions among the different New Testament authors already contradicts a fixed body of doctrines. Lindars

(1989: 405) also argues that the author of Hebrews 'was in close touch with the primitive kerygma'. However, he disputes the contention of an 'Early Catholicism' in Hebrews (as suggested by Grässer, Fuller, Koester; also Conzelmann and Dunn), because, although Hebrews shares certain terminology and ideas with other New Testament writings, the content and use thereof tend to differ – for example, the role of the Spirit, worship, leaders, faith. In any case, it has become common practice to speak of first-century 'Christianity' as a 'Jewish sect', thus contesting notions such as that of the author of Hebrews as 'first and foremost a *Christian*' (Ellingworth 1993: 47), because such a term would probably not have been all that descriptive or meaningful during the first century CE.

Perhaps one should rather acknowledge the claim made by Attridge (1989: 30) that the 'commitment to Jesus' found in Hebrews is 'as important as any of the Jewish [and other] traditions out of which Hebrews has been formed'. Hebrews' position within the tradition of the followers of Jesus Christ is perhaps best detected in the way it appropriated the Scriptures of Israel: 'His [the author of Hebrews] use of the Old Testament is in continuity with what has preceded him in Christian hermeneutics, but unique in his treatment of relationships and implications' (Longenecker 1975: 185).

Similarly, when Graham Hughes (1979: 124–30) refers to Hebrews' faith and its traditions, he does so from the perspective of the author of Hebrews as 'interpreter of Scriptures'. The use of the Scriptures of Israel and their contextualization in Hebrews illustrates how Christians could exploit the thought and views of their time in order to reinterpret Christ for a new and changed situation. Buchanan (1972: xix), for instance, refers to Hebrews as a 'homiletical midrash'; his is probably the most sustained interpretation of Hebrews as a midrash *in toto* on Psalm 110. Koester (1982: 273–74) sees scriptural interpretation as the 'key' for understanding both the layout and content of Hebrews' argument. (For Hebrews' use of the Hebrew Bible, abundant sources exist, e.g.: Combrink 1971: 22–36, with a short bibliography; Longenecker 1975: 158–85; Ellingworth 1993: 37–42.)

Moving from the interpretive thrust detected in Hebrews, Hughes stresses the 'freedom' of the twentieth-century interpreter: 'The freedom of the modern interpreter then lies in his [*sic*] liberty to choose which of these several hermeneutical attempts applies most fittingly to his present situation, always in critical assessment of their own legitimacy as interpretations, and endeavouring to understand as well as he can the factors which have given them their present shape' (1979: 130). Naturally, such interpretation will happen within the Christian tradition, with the aim of exploring more adequate ways of doing theology through which Jesus Christ will become even more of a present reality to people. Indeed, a postcolonial approach to Hebrews provides an important if alternative interpretation of the document.

Commentarial Notes: Texts and Themes

Amid theories of secularization, decanonization and the like, many of the traditional doctrines, practices and beliefs associated with Christianity and its accompanying worldviews are challenged by the world of the twenty-first century. Given this situation, postcolonial interpretation may not be the only hermeneutical strategy which allows for readings of Hebrews similar to those below, but it does ensure a theoretically accountable and adequate approach to these texts. In any case, a postcolonial approach would not want to claim either a unique or exhaustive reading of texts. The distinctive value of a postcolonial reading is situated in the ability to provide a geopolitically justified reading, capable of dealing with both universal–global and nationalist–particularist concerns. Since this project is not a line-by-line commentary, texts and themes which could be important in a postcolonial reading were selected, often going beyond the scholarly consensus of emphasizing Christological and ecclesiological issues as the two prominent concerns of Hebrews.

'Christian' Dualism (1.3; 8.4-5; see 8.1–10.18)

The dualist element in Hebrews holds up Christ as reflection and representation of his glory and being (1.3) and has priests making offerings as part of a religious practice which is only an inadequate representation or shadow of the heavenly (8.4-5). In 8.1–10.18 the superiority of the heavenly reality over the earthly copy is emphasized. Such notions and expressions are typical and constitutive of a Platonic world of thought, with its emphasis on the inferiority of the *mimēma*: *apaugasma* ('reflection', 1.3) – probably the passive sense of 'reflection' rather than the active in the sense of 'radiance', to fit better with *charaktēr*, with which it is paired (for these two possible translations, see Louw and Nida 1988: 175) – *charaktēr* ('direct representation', 1.3); *hupodeigma* ('example', 4.11; 8.5; 9.23); *skia* ('[fore-]shadow', 8.5; 10.1); and *antitupos* ('representation', 9.24). (See Johnson 1986: 420–21; Lindars 1991: 23; Isaacs 1992: 51–55. Guthrie [1982: 43], as indeed do others, calls these 'superficial parallels'.) Louw and Nida (1988) group the concept expressed by these words in the same semantic field: 'Nature, class, example', with the subfield: 'Pattern, model, example, and corresponding representation' and, in the case of *antitupos*, with the subfield: 'Archetype, corresponding type (antitype)'. Only *apaugasma* is put into a different field: 'Physical events and states (Light)'.

The traditional, Christian *dualism* of and even *dichotomy* between spiritual and material, heaven and earth – conceptualized both vertically *and* horizontally – with its implicit or attached notions of value (or lack thereof) confronts the reader of Hebrews head on. Such elements cannot be relativized with reference to the influence of neo-Platonist thought, Gnostic movements or other traditions active during the early formative period of Christianity. The reception history of Christian dualism reaches far and wide and has informed socio-cultural, political and economic debates on issues ranging from human sexuality and ascetic behaviour to ecological concerns and socio-political activism. Christian dualism later found useful allies in the Enlightenment and Renaissance as well as in the Industrial Revolution, with growing disparity in the value accorded to human rationality as opposed to corporeality and its accompaniments. In an increasingly technocratic-oriented global village – where applied knowledge and skills become the sole criteria for determining the value of people and where the Two-Thirds World and their resources, economies and people are further exploited by international corporations – a holistic approach to human life is crucial for fostering a sustainable world.

The emphasis on otherworldliness, often accompanied by a perverse individualist and spiritualist – historical-critical exegesis proves itself inadequate to resolve the meaning of passages such as 10.19-20 and whether *tēs sarkos autou* is a spiritualizing of *katapetasmatos*; see Johnsson (1978a: 107) – approach to Christianity, has in the past regularly been criticized as one-sided. A postcolonial interpretation extends the incrimination to include the co-optation of the ideology of the transcendent, whether spatial or temporal, in justifying injustice, oppression and other imperial and hegemonic practices. In the Christian tradition dualistic beliefs were bolstered by a particular understanding of eschatology which postponed the full *reality* and validity of human life *ad infinitum*, or, at least, until the anticipated end of the world.

In fact, the insistence on the spiritual/material dualism has in the past led to the neglect of, if not opposition to, the materiality of life. In order to recover the spiritual in our age of secularism, the need for materiality within a non-dualist theology should be emphasized (Füssel 1984; Sölle 1984). (Johnsson [1978a: 107] refers to Hebrews' materialistic, in contrast to a moralistic, view of sin.) As important as spirituality is today, it cannot exist in an other-worldly or a-worldly sense. Similarly, religion, theology and faith cannot afford to withdraw from the public sphere, particularly in the Two-Thirds World and amid global pressure to mould and nurture a technological–industrial utopia.

Identifying Jesus Christ
As the culmination of a long line of prophets, Jesus Christ is introduced in the traditional-wisdom opening of Hebrews (1.1-4) as a reflection of God's character. Jesus' close relationship with the creation and sustenance of the world implies his exalted status, superseding the angels.

Son of Man (2.6) and Son of God (10.29). Hebrews refers to Christ with the title *huios anthropou* ('Son of Man'), which in the past was often interpreted with regard to notions of corporate personality or a heavenly figure. In Hebrews Son of Man and Son of God are used in relation to Psalms 8 and 10, psalms of enthronement, and connote Jesus' messiahship. (Pretorius [1982: 8] argues that in Hebrews Jesus is modelled on Moses, moulding a Moses-Christology: Hebrews aims to show how Christ shares in the undisputed authority of Moses, yet, as Son of Man, is also immeasurably more authoritative than Moses.) Yet, Son of Man had definite political implications as well, as 'a king who ruled over a nation and had such power that other kings would be subject to him'. As divine Son, Jesus received all the attributes of a typical or ideal king of Israel. The earliest recorded Son of Man was probably with reference to Judah the Maccabee, who was also a Levite and whose brothers became high priests (Buchanan 1975: 321). Christologically, Hebrews does not refer to the cross and resurrection but rather to Christ's humiliation and exaltation; in fact, resurrection is not mentioned in Hebrews, unless by implication in 11.19, and the cross only once (12.2) (see Koester 1982: 275).

High Priest (4.14–10.18). In the same way as the Hasmonaean kingship and priesthood were defended by appeal to Scripture, Hebrews justifies the sonship of Christ as well as his high priesthood with reference to Psalm 110. Jesus' descent is traced to the royal line of Judah and the order of Melchizedek, thus measuring up to the Jewish requirements of the time. As high priest, Jesus was interpreted in view of the Yom Kippur rather than the Passover festival, as in the Gospels. The significance of Jesus' priesthood is marked by its inclusive scope and finality, its *ephapax*-character, never to be repeated again, and characterized by its mercifulness.

When the metaphor of Jesus as priest is extended and an analogy established between sacrifice and the Eucharist or Mass, and this results in ascribing a special status to the church's clergy, a danger signal sounds. When the universal access to God is discarded through the granting of mediatorial powers to the clergy, the signal becomes even louder. The broader setting consisting of a patriarchal, androcentric cultural context as well as the exclusionist privilege derived from birth makes the situation worse, particularly since numerous such settings, and analogous situations the world over, still exist today. Is it simply a matter of exchanging the superiority of the Levitical priesthood for that of Jesus, or can the priesthood of Jesus function as a liberating symbol, breaking through privileged and hegemonic systems insisted upon by religious orthodoxies?

Jesus Christ as Initiator and Fulfiller of Faith (12.2; see 2.10; 6.10-20). In the exhortation to the Hebrews to endure in their faith, Jesus Christ is the ultimate example (12.2). The Christ narrative is interpreted and shaped to fit Hebrews' scheme: Jesus endured in faith because of the future *chara* (gladness) which awaited him, closely connected to the eventual prize, joining God by taking up the position of honour at his right-hand side. Christ is therefore the primary focus of Hebrews' exhortation to endure, as the perfect example to be imitated by the whole community. He was both *archēgos* ('initiator') and *teleiōtēs* ('perfecter') of faith (*tēs pisteōs*), with the subject genitive not excluding the (also) exemplary nature of his work. Not only is Christ the ultimate example for believers and thus quantitatively different, but there is also a qualitative difference in the portrayal of Christ. His supremacy over the examples of ch. 11 is grounded in assisting people, being a helper, and, as *perfector*, making perfection possible as the 'author' or 'source' (Peterson 1982: 171) for human beings through his death.

Jesus is the initiator, pioneer, trail-blazer (12.2, also 2.10) of existence in faith and is transposed onto Israelite tradition with historical significance. In 1 Cor. 10.3 and Jude 5, Christ is also closely associated with the sustenance of the people of Israel on the journey between Egypt and the promised land. The tone of this tradition is clearly one of admonition, exhorting listeners to faithfulness and endurance, which accompanies the emphasis on the pastoral significance of the incarnation. (Other titles for Jesus in Hebrews include: *apostolos* [3.1]; *archiereus* ['high priest', 3.1]; *prodromos* ['forerunner', 6.20]; *egguos* ['guarantor', 7.22]; *mesitēs* ['mediator' or 'reconciler', 8.6; 9.15; 12.24]; *poimēn* ['shepherd', 13.20] – a clear pastoral notion is attached to these concepts.)

Jesus Christ as the Ultimate, the Final Revelation: Religious Exclusivism (9.1–10.18). Hebrews carries the seeds for what could and has in the past become a flourishing anti-Semitism. It argues strongly against the Jewish cult, questioning its efficacy (daily repetition by priests) and promoting its obsoleteness (Jesus as ultimate high priest replacing others). In the extension of such claims regarding Jesus, is it possible to sidestep the radical position of Hebrews regarding Jesus Christ? He is presented as the final and ultimate revelation of God to humankind. Does this hold true for the Christian tradition, and how does this claim relate to the general debate concerning religious exclusivism today?

The Diaspora of Faith: A Matter for Celebration? (4; 11; 13.1-7)
The very prominent sojourner or pilgrim motif in Hebrews goes beyond the mere dynamic of movement often emphasized in the exhortation. The notion of people on their way, under way, or in limbo conjures up images positive as well as negative. The wandering people of God – *das wandernde Gottesvolk* (for Johnsson [1978b: 239–51] this motif as metaphor for the cult portrayed in Hebrews enables one to read the book 'holistically': it is no description of the cult, but it 'harmonizes and blends with it'. Koester opposes the pilgrim motif of Hebrews to the Gnostic idea of the celestial journey of the soul [1982: 272–76]) – emphasized by Ernst Käsemann, is, for Hebrews, the Israelites in the desert, between the slavery of Egypt and the hope of the promised land. Hebrews puts this powerful ideology to analogical (allegorical?) use in addressing a contemporary community of believers in Christ.

The centrality of the diaspora theme in Hebrews cannot be underestimated, particularly amid our renewed awareness of the liminality of human existence in the globalizing village of a new millennium. In ch. 4 the exodus theme is developed with the image of the people of God in diaspora, in the desert and underway with a *pistei* (in faith) attitude to the promised land (*katapausis*). The centrality and all-importance of faith is even more central in ch. 11, substantiated with references to many precedents in Israel's past. In 13.1-17 Jesus Christ's death 'outside of the camp' and, therefore, outside the realm of religious security (Koester 1982: 276), is provided as the rationale for the constant failure of believers to secure an unwavering stronghold in the world: 'their place in the world is where Jesus has suffered'. Faith will always lead to an uneasy balance in time and space and puts an obstacle in the way of the faithful who are fixated on heavenly salvation.

The diaspora of the faithful theme calls forth a number of warnings. A very strong warning should be directed against relishing the non-belonging of believers, against craving martyrdom, based on an otherworldly focus and a deliberate alienation from the world in a solipsistic dialectic of self-induced estrangement and otherness. The tendency to romanticize or idealize living in diaspora has to be avoided, since it can refer to life in exile, in ancient times the worst form of punishment, even when it is often celebrated today. The idealization of diasporic life occurs when it is prescribed as exemplary, whereas Hebrews asks about the parameters for living in the diaspora. In our world it is important to move beyond images of the spiritual wasteland, to ask rather about life amid globalization. Arowele (1990) contextualizes the pilgrim or sojourn motif in the church in Africa, which experiences pilgrimage and exile as a result, among other things, of poverty, famine, political instability and tribal and racial discrimination. In post-apartheid South Africa the continental diaspora is often met with a strong xenophobia, ostensibly informed by economic constraints, particularly in the area of employment, both formal and informal. As in other parts of the Two-Thirds World, in South Africa the question remains: what happens when pilgrims become settlers, especially if the settlers claim divine sanction for settling the other?

Ambiguous/Dangerous Identities: House of Christ, People of God? (3.1-6). In 3.6 (see 10.21) those who endure by holding on to the confidence and boast of their hope are called the house (*oikos*) of Christ (the antecedent of the relative *hou*). The appeal to be the house of Christ was in the past often transformed into the claim to be the people of God. This notion introduces probably one of the most dangerous images of colonialism and other forms of hegemony in the past, one that seems set to replicate itself indefinitely. The claim by various groups – whether national–political, social–cultural, ecclesial–denominational, ethnic–racial or otherwise – to be the people of God has often led to the worst of abuses. The self-attribution of divine sanction by such groups was in South Africa exemplified by the Dutch Reformed Church's claim, bolstered by the political ideals of Afrikaner nationalism, to be God's chosen people in southern Africa. Other countries, such as the United States of America, provide their own examples of such claims with expressions like being 'a city on a hill' and having a 'manifest destiny'.

When Hebrews uses the term *laos* ('people'), probably under influence of the usual translation for Septuagint's *'am*, it refers to both Israel (7.5, 11, 27; 9.7, 19) and the believers in Christ (2.17; 13.12). Hebrews is not consciously privileging a certain group of people through an 'us–them' hermeneutics and offers no basis for the vaunted claims of Christian groups for exclusive or special access to God. The early believers in Christ are not called the 'new people of God' by Hebrews but rather the 'people of God according to the new covenant' in the context of partnership (3.1, 14). The notion of covenant is important here, with *diathēkē* used 17 times in Hebrews out of its 33 appearances in the New Testament. Hebrews seems unwilling to sever all links in a final way between the people of Israel and God by proclaiming the believers in Christ as the *new people of God*. It leaves the anti-Semitic tendencies found in traditional readings of Hebrews, especially in light of the contentious works-righteousness attributed to Second Temple Judaism and its cultic practices, without any basis. Hebrews' argument is not against Jews or Judaism but against the denial of the salvific significance of Jesus' death, which may have been Gnostic in origin (Koester 1982: 276).

The entanglement of social identity with religion surfaces on a number of occasions in Hebrews. One example is the listing of the six characteristics of the *themelios* ('foundation') of the gospel in 6.1-2, a move which is sometimes interpreted as an attempt to define the essentials for Jewish converts to Christ. These characteristics, however, were part of synagogue teaching and are probably recalled in Hebrews to mediate the tension between the distinctive features of the Christ-believers and principles of faith among Jews against the background of the delayed return of Christ (Peterson 1982: 180). At any rate, in the late first century the lines of demarcation between Jewish believers in Christ and other Jews were still not clear insofar as they existed at all.

The dangers attached to a religion which is all too comfortable in the world will not subside. However, we will have to move beyond notions of the danger of civil religion or questions whether a religion that no longer evokes strong reaction (Kierkegaard) is worth pursuing. The interrelationship of religion and social identity needs to be acknowledged and examined, and Hebrews will be an interesting conversation partner in this regard.

The Arrival: Rest (3.7–4.13)

Is the striving for the prize not contradictory to the diasporic nature of the faith experience? The wandering people of God are underway, but not endlessly or aimlessly, for their goal is the promised rest: running the race and receiving the prize are inseparable. (Yeo [1991] attempts to show how Chinese 'Yin–Yang' philosophy provides a paradigm beyond the influence of the biblical world with which to appropriate the notion of rest as expressed by *katapausis* and *sab-*

batismos as well the idea of movement: Yin is rest, Yang is movement, mutually interdependent and inclusive; similarly, in Hebrews there is a reciprocal relationship between change and rest in the diaspora.) The term *katapausis* ('rest') is used seven times in Hebrews and only once in the rest of the New Testament (Acts 7.49). It appears twice in ch. 3 and five times in ch. 4. The verb *katapauō* is used only four times in the New Testament, once in Acts 14.18 and three times in Hebrews 4. The connection between the promise of God and the promised land is especially clear in ch. 11, where the content of the promise is consistently the promised land. The rest is also connected to the preaching of the gospel (*euangelizomai*, 4.2), with its relationship to the Jubilee (*sabbatismos*, 4.9) – often considered typological of an envisaged utopia.

The eschatology of Hebrews, like that of the Dead Sea Scrolls, expects the fulfilment of the promise to Abraham's children, which would culminate in the restoration of their land (Buchanan 1975: 325–29). The anticipated rest is not spiritualized but presented as material expectation, the physical inheritance of the land promised by God. How do we understand allusions to the restoration of land after the establishment of the state of Israel in 1948? Closer to home in southern Africa, where Zimbabwe's President Mugabe has embarked on what he calls a land-redistribution campaign, and in South Africa, where ten years after democracy all the signs of land dispossession are still in evidence, can Hebrews' concern with land simply be relegated to being a spiritual matter?

Sin and/as Apostasy (6.4-8; 10.26-31; 12.1-15)

Sin is in Hebrews primarily presented as apostasy (e.g., 12.1,4), and thus neither discardable nor pardonable. Sin relates to everything not out of faith, or even that which obstructs faith. This broader conception of sin as engagement in what is detrimental to faith allows one to move beyond the individualizing tendency so often characterizing definitions of sin. Hebrews' view of sin as materialist goes a long way to avoid the shallow moralism found also in Christianity, often impressed upon believers with the accompanying dread of divine punishment and retribution.

The danger of apostasy today is often not, as is common in many theories of secularization, primarily situated in those elements and powers in the world which encumber faith, the obstacles to faithful living, and the downright opposition to faith on various interrelated axes of human existence. Indeed, Hebrews stresses the danger of conformation to the world and its values as one of the greatest obstacles to faith, as *the* problem which initiates and ensures apostasy, which starts out with lameness and lethargy and ends up in abandonment of the faith in God.

In 6.4-6 the reversal of apostates is described as *adunaton*, 'impossible' (see 10.26). The apostasy of those who were enlightened, tasted the heavenly gift, partook of the Spirit, and tasted the good word of God and the powers of the age to come is uncorrectable, because they have again crucified the Son of God and publicly shamed him. There is intense debate whether such apostasy constitutes the unpardonable sin of Mk 3.29 or the sin unto death of 1 Jn 5.16, whether this is an exaggerated warning or merely a hypothetical example to counter spiritual lethargy in its roots, or whether apostasy is an all too real possibility within the Christian community (Bruce 1964: 124).

There is considerable resistance among commentators not to reduce sin in Hebrews to apostasy, as proposed by Käsemann (Peterson 1982: 169). Sin is clearly linked closely to the cult and can well be described as defilement (1.3; 9.13-14, 22-23; 10.22; 12.15; 13.4). Hebrews' notion of sin is evidently collective, non-moral and materialistic (Johnsson 1978a: 106–107). The emphasis on the communal rather than the individual does not eliminate an individualist perspective, which is present in the warnings against apostasy and its consequence of missing the 'rest' (6.4-8; 10.26-31; 12.15-17). The materialistic view of sin does not preclude ethics or morality as espoused in ch. 13. This is, however, clearly set within the perimeters of the community and overshadowed by instructions intent on the maintenance of community, which include: brotherly love, hospitality, concern for prisoners, sexual morality, avoiding avariciousness (13.1-5) and directives for staying in the faith (13.6-19).

Atonement (8.1–10.18)

Hebrews' innovative interpretation of Christ is often related to the interpretation of its position regarding 'the apostolic kerygma of the sacrificial death of Christ'. The effectiveness of Hebrews' teaching in this regard is related to the possibilities it created for further development of Christian doctrine. By relating the sacrificial death of Christ to the 'apostolic' faith, the legitimacy of both this interpretation of Hebrews and later doctrinal developments thereof in Christianity is assumed (e.g., Lindars 1989: 405–406). The cult in Hebrews is thus connected to one of the most powerful metaphors in Christianity, namely, atonement.

The atonement ritual accompanied by the blood of the sacrificial victims, 'which are most distasteful to modern readers' and without relevance for their conception of the work of Christ, finds a resourceful contextual interpretation in Africa. Even though some contemporary Jewish and Greek protest against such practices was registered, Hebrews nevertheless did not spiritualize the sacrificial concept but stressed its dated temporality and inappropriateness for the era commencing with Christ. The purpose of sacrifice seems to be an important aspect in Hebrews, namely 'a means of reconciliation with God' in a very practical way. It is then also claimed that it is exactly this need for *practical expression* ('to objectify their inner conflict of emotions'), felt by many Christians today, that is exemplified by the sacrificial activities of African Christians with regard to their ancestors (Lindars 1991: 132–34).

The doctrine of atonement has met of late, however, with severe criticism, and its claim for biblical support is disputed. The doctrine as a development of the notion that 'Christ died for our sins' (1 Cor. 15.3) is not necessarily its most adequate interpretation. Atonement is accused of being the cornerstone of much of the abuse suffered so often in the history of the Christian church by the marginalized. The doctrine was used too often to justify the maltreatment and brutalization of the other: women, children and those not belonging to the in-group, whether defined along the lines of national, political, cultural, ethnic, gender or sexual difference.

The death of Christ as depicted in Hebrews can be understood in other ways. A Christological appropriation of the Yom Kippur ritual allows one, for example, to de-emphasize Christ's death as 'atoning sacrifice' in favour of viewing it as 'a covenant inaugurating event' (Attridge 1986: 1–9).

Cultic Criticism: The Cult and Its Practices (7.1–10.18). Hebrews is committed to the dissolving of the official cult and its related practices, including the abolishment of the priesthood and the cessation of the sacrificial system. For this, Hebrews uses cultic regulations to argue against it. The hierarchical and powerful religious system was centred on the Jerusalem temple and was underwritten by an age-old priestly tradition. The Jewish cult, with temple and priests, was the mainstay of first-century Judaism, unlike the already biased portrayal in the Gospels of the prominence of the Pharisees, probably the forerunners of rabbinic Judaism. The cultic tradition was conservative and did not allow for change or renewal in cultic practice, to the extent that the claim for its divine sanction was used in the past as refuge from dissenting voices (see Jer. 7.4). After initial resistance to Hellenistic influences, the temple hierarchy later shared power with the Hasmonaean house and promoted Hellenism, and, with the advent of Roman control, it mastered the art of political and cultural negotiation and compromise. The temple hierarchy gained further support from the Herodians in their quest to promote and maintain the system.

The cultic line in the New Testament writings is overshadowed by and rooted in the nomistic tradition, as determined by the law, although Hebrews suggests the opposite (7.12). The cultic tradition flowed from the nomistic but took the shape of a powerful religious and political system, reinforced by an influential priesthood and the powerful Sadducee group. The eventual international recognition of the high priest as political head of Judaea contributed to the width and depth of the authority of the priesthood (Pretorius 1982: 14–16). At a more personal level, Hebrews' emphasis on obedience rather than sacrifices (10.1-18) supports the notion that believers are in the first instance called to praxis in the community.

The continuing control of institutionalized religion through its various institutions has in the past exerted its authority on the socio-political arrangements of humanity as well as on nature. The collusion of organized religion in the political and economic colonization of Africa and other continents is well-known. With the political power of religion still unfathomed, religious movements and institutions need not so much to be reined in and religions to be restricted or banished from the public sphere; rather, questions need to be asked regarding how religious institutions can shed internal hegemonic elements and best contribute to the welfare of the global village, human and otherwise. On the other hand, with renewed interest in spirituality worldwide, the time is ripe for a re-evaluation of the cultic and ritual in the Christian faith and among Protestants in particular. The spin-offs of a renewed appreciation for the value of cultic practices in general will hopefully include a movement away from the denigration of cultic passages in the Bible.

Word of God (4.12)

In 4.12 the word of God is described as alive, living (*zōn*) and active (*energēs*), and sharper than any two-edged sword, capable of probing 'the inmost recesses of our spiritual being', bringing 'the subconscious motives to light' and acting as a judge of people's thoughts (Bruce 1964: 82). Unlike John's Gospel, Jesus himself is not identified as the Logos in Hebrews, and the word of God is better understood as God continuing to speak to people in a variety of forms. The emphasis on the promise (*epangelia*) of God, especially prominent in ch. 11, becomes definitional for God's word and is significantly placed in a context of struggle and suffering. The sustaining power of the word of God is highlighted in the connection of word and promise. The high frequency of scriptural quotes in Hebrews hints at the importance of Scripture for author and audience alike and can be seen as an implicit acceptance of the living voice of God (Peterson 1982: 169). The quotes align Scripture with the utterances of God and to some extent his presence as well, and the Bible would soon enough be equated with the word of God in the Christian tradition.

In Africa the abuse justified by a 'God says' theology (Oduyoye) extends to political, gender and sex, and cultural configurations. The word of God is equated with the Bible, more particularly with a specific interpretation thereof, and claimed as divine revelation and sanction. On the other hand, and amid vast illiteracy on the continent, the mere possession of the Bible is nevertheless considered beneficial, although large sections of text are memorized, turning the Bible once more into *viva vox Dei*. The danger of theology becoming bibliology and of bibliophilia becoming bibliolatry are, however, always lurking in the corners of the African continent.

Faith and Eschatology (10.19–12.3)

Emphasizing the close relationship between faith and life itself, 10.38 quotes from Hab. 2.4 and does so more reliably than in the case of Rom. 1.17 or Gal. 1.13 – Hebrews 10.38 includes the personal pronoun, *mou*, which is aligned to the prepositional phrase *ek pisteos* in the LXX B text but in the A text and the C manuscripts to *ho dikaios*. In Hebrews faith does not relate to a category of salvation and is non-Christological: Jesus Christ did not constitute the content of faith but the beginning and end of faith (e.g., 12.2). Faith is theological, focusing on God and his promises, and not soteriologically oriented. Faith, therefore, relates to sanctification and should properly be constituted in a sociological sense today. Hebrews has a collective view of faith (Grässer 1986), and 11.1 emphasizes faith as certainty, as reality.

The importance of faith and endurance (*hupomonē*) in faith is clear in ch. 11 through the regular use of *pistei* and *kata pistin*. As in the case of endurance, faith is an active notion and relates to doing the will of God constructively, faithfully. The 'well-known definition of faith (11.1)... has become a famous *crux interpretum*' (Koester 1982: 276), with faith explained as a *hupostasis* ('substance' or 'present reality') of the things hoped for. Endurance (12.12-13; see 6.9-12) is expressed with the vivid image of the bodily parts of hands, knees and feet. Endurance is not, first and foremost, a spiritual or rational matter, of making the right decision. It is about putting the listless hands and slackened feet back into action, arresting dormancy and converting it into sparkling health. Such metaphors align well with the emphasis on bodily and spiritual health, currently in vogue.

Our Ancestor Abraham; and Sarah Then? (11.8-19)
As elsewhere in the New Testament writings, when faith is addressed, Abraham is held up as *the* example of enduring faith. Among the *nephos marturōn* ('cloud of witnesses', 12.1), Hebrews singles out Abraham for special attention and narrates his faithfulness, including – the only time in the New Testament – the *Akedah*, Abraham's intended sacrifice of Isaac (see Court and Court 1990: 319). This story resonates well with many elements related to Jesus as only begotten son of God, earlier emphasized in Hebrews.

Hebrews, like Paul in Galatians 4, accords Sarah an important position in describing the history of Israel's faith in God. The translation and interpretation of 11.11 is contested, in particular whether Sarah is the subject rather than Abraham. Contrary to ancient practice and on the basis of her faith (*pistei*), the barren Sarah (*Sarra steira*) is accorded a seminal [*sic*] role in conceiving Isaac. Not only is the link between faith and empowerment emphasized, but also Sarah's faith is put on par with Abraham's faith. She received *dunamin eis katabolēn spermatos*, the 'power to conceive'. (For the debate on whether the phrase *eis katabolen* refers to the male ejaculation of seed or to the female's generative ability, see Bruce 1964: 299–304; Buchanan 1972: 190.)

The emphasis on Abraham as the father of our faith in 11.17-22 presents a fine opportunity to redefine Christianity's claims to uniqueness and exclusiveness, amid its Christological emphasis. The Christian claim made on Abraham as a (the?) father of the faith is matched by the appreciation of Abraham in other religious traditions such as Judaism, Islam and others. Such shared elements, even if differently conceived, may contribute to the initiation of dialogue between religions.

On Discipline: Human Suffering and Divine Punishment (2.10-18; 12.4-11)
The relationship between human suffering and divine punishment has a long
and profound tradition of interpretation. In ch. 12 the initial link with hostility and suffering encountered by believers is found in their identification with
Christ. (The terminology describing Christ's loathing of the cross [12.2] is
reminiscent of that used of the Maccabaean martyrs [e.g., *4 Macc.* 13.1, *ton
mechri thanatou ponon huperephronēsan*, 'they despised their pain to death'].)
The suffering is, on top of it all, presented – or rationalized – as an assurance of
sonship [*sic*] and as contributing to the development of appropriate subjection
to the will of God and is accompanied by an eschatological warrant in the form
of the promise of a reward.

Divine punishment is presented within the ambit of God's fatherhood of
believers (12.5-9). A father had both power and responsibility for his children,
wife and everyone else in his household. His role as father is traditionally
portrayed as benevolent, if stern (see 1 Thess. 2.11), and included instruction
and discipline or punishment, *paideia*. (*Paideuō* and *paideia* focus more on the
forming of proper habits of behaviour, while *noutheteō* and *nouthesia* focus upon
instruction in correct behaviour; *entrephō* appears to focus more on 'continuous
instruction and training in the area of skill and practical knowledge' [Louw and
Nida 1988: 414 n. 45].) According to this model, the father's role was necessarily positive, with its origin in love and its goal of strengthening the character of
the child (see Prov. 23.13). According to the midrashic *qal wahomer* argument,
Hebrews (12.9-11) points out that, whereas obedience to a father's discipline
brings honour grounded in submissiveness as required by ancient society, subjection to God's punishment will bring life itself. The punishment meted out
by God differs from that of a father in motive, goal and method; the divine
intention is sanctification. This corresponds with the contrast between fathers
of flesh and the God of spirits: punishment by the former renders respect; by the
latter, life itself. The discipline meted out by God leads to holiness (*hagiotēs*,
12.10; see 9.13; 10.10) among its recipients, which allows them to approach
God. The argument in 12.4-11 on discipline ends with a practical application
in 12.12-13. Discipline in community is a shared responsibility and communal
effort (see 10.25).

Yet, the contemporary role of the father as *paterfamilias* should be understood
in relation to corresponding notions of imperialism. The household system was
one of the building blocks for ensuring the hegemonic influence of the empire.
The mainstay of the imperial order was the kyriarchal pattern (Schüssler Fiorenza
1994: 7). In the past, explaining human suffering through its equation with divine
punishment became a convenient platform or even rationale for, at best, glossing
over such suffering or, at worst, justifying if not inducing it. The lack of punishment and resultant prosperity, even if only apparent, can be equated with the withdrawal or absence of God from human lives (12.7-8). Indeed, divine punishment
guarantees God's presence and love and legitimates the relationship with God!

This has invariably proved a valuable tool in the legitimation of hegemony and inequity, has led to a lack of resistance to injustice, and has induced self-blame in many victims of abuse. In families, therefore, abusive fathers dispense punishment as a God-given right, oblivious of the resultant physical and psychological damage (see Briggs Kittredge 1994: 447–48).

On the other hand, something of the discipline inherent in sport (athletics and boxing, 12.1, 4-5, 11) might provide a vantage point in the South African context, where calls for moral regeneration and attention to the ethical fibre of society are common. Indeed, in a society as thoroughly soaked in religiosity as its citizens are religiously committed to their sporting interests, Hebrews suggests a valuable angle to address the declining morality in our country as long at it moves beyond moral object lessons.

The rhetoric on instruction and discipline culminates in 12.29, *kai gar ho theos hemōn pur katanaliskon*. Juxtaposing 'our' God with 'a consuming fire' hardly calls up notions of divine pardon, grace and love and is a far cry from 'gentle Jesus, meek and mild'. The rhetorical force is not difficult to understand within the context of Hebrews' larger argument, but it is also, unfortunately, the image of a vengeful, unforgiving, warrior-God, ready to pounce, which can become an immediate metaphor for justifying violent conflict and 'just war' theories. Deciding between the sentimentalist old man with the beard and the fundamentalist violent avenger might not be as difficult as finding a more adequate image for understanding God today.

The Maturity of Believers (5.11–6.8). Considerable attention is devoted in Hebrews to perfection in the sense of progressing towards maturity, with a clear interrelationship between the perfecting of Christ and the perfecting of the believers. However, much divergence of opinion exists on whether Hebrews is concerned about lethargy (5.11, but 6.12), immaturity (5.12-14, but 6.10), or apostasy (6.1-8, but 6.9-12) on the part of the believers. What is clear is that the call for the perfecting of the believers is the opposite of Hebrews' often repeated warning to the believers not to forsake their faith, not to become careless in their faith. The need for perfection among the addressees of Hebrews is increased by their unwillingness or inability to teach others (5.12), their liking for milk instead of solid food (5.1, 3) and their lack of knowledge regarding righteousness (5.13).

The worldwide resurgence of spirituality, if often in non-traditional forms, offers a challenge not only to secularism theories but also to traditional religion. With spiritual maturity much acclaimed today, such spirituality often turns against itself, particularly when it is used to sanction a narrow inwardness, either individually or communally. With rampant globalization as an important catalyst for this, such inversionist temptation to retreat into the nurtured and isolated security of the individual or his/her religious, socio-cultural or political community should nevertheless be resisted.

Conclusion: Hebrews Today

With no sign that globalization as neocolonialist enterprise is abating, or that it will at least become equitable for all, Christian faith in the third millennium is bound to continue its diaspora. On that score alone, Hebrews provides a valuable perspective on the tenuous character of faith and religious expression, amid the continuous reinterpretation of Christ, and proves to be a challenge to the comfort and security of orthodoxy. However, with the distinct dualism in its thought, its cultic focus, its quest for the final rest, and its reference to a people of God, for instance, Hebrews is implicated in the imperialism which often characterized Christianity's past. The merit of a postcolonial reading of Hebrews includes its ability to find liberating strands in the texts, while showing up the text's or its reception history's complicity in imperialist endeavours.

Everywhere, but in Africa in particular, the challenge for biblical interpretation today is to avoid professional idiosyncracies, often aligned with self-centred ambition, which typically prove to be tempting luxuries in both academic and ecclesial contexts. It has become more important than ever to find hermeneutical strategies that will refuse the complacency of nationalist endeavours as well as the neglect of the local in favour of the global. Postcolonial biblical interpretation has the potential to address these concerns and offers a valuable hermeneutical strategy for exposing and countering imperialist, hegemonic readings of Scripture.

BIBLIOGRAPHY

Arowele, P. J.
    1990   'The Pilgrim People of God (An African's Reflections on the Motif of Sojourn in the Epistle to the Hebrews)', *Asian Journal of Theology* 4(2): 438–55.

Attridge, Harold W.
    1986   'The Uses of Antithesis in Hebrews 8–10', *Harvard Theological Review* 79: 1–9.
    1989   *The Epistle to the Hebrews. A Commentary on the Epistle to the Hebrews* (Hermeneia; Philadelphia: Fortress Press).

Boer, Roland
    1998   'Remembering Babylon: Postcolonialism and Australian Biblical Studies', in Sugirtharajah 1998: 24–48.

Bosch, David J.
    1995   *Believing in the Future. Towards a Missiology of Western Culture* (Christian Mission and Modern Culture; Valley Forge, PA: Trinity International Press).

Brett, Mark G.
    1996   'The Ethics of Postcolonial Criticism', *Semeia* 75: 219–28.

Briggs Kittredge, Cynthia
    1994   'Hebrews', in Schüssler Fiorenza 1994: 428–52.

Brown, Raymond
    1982   *The Message of Hebrews* (The Bible Speaks Today; Leicester: Inter-Varsity Press).

Bruce, F. F.
    1964   *The Epistle to the Hebrews. The English Text with Introduction, Exposition and Notes* (New International Commentary on the New Testament; Grand Rapids: Eerdmans).
Buchanan, George W.
    1972   *To the Hebrews. Translation, Comment and Conclusions* (Anchor Bible, 36; New York: Doubleday).
    1975   'The Present State of Scholarship on Hebrews', in Jacob Neusner (ed.), *Christianity, Judaism and Other Greco-Roman Cults. Studies For Morton Smith at Sixty* (Studies in Judaism in Late Antiquity, 12; Leiden: E. J. Brill): 1: 299–330.
Calvin, J.
    1963   *The Epistle of Paul the Apostle to the Hebrews and the First and Second Epistle of St Peter* (Calvin's Commentaries; Edinburgh: Oliver & Boyd).
Combrink, H. J. B.
    1971   'Some Thoughts on the Old Testament Citations in the Epistle to the Hebrews', *Neotestamentica* 4: 22–36.
Court, John M. and Kathleen Court
    1990   *The New Testament World* (Cambridge: Cambridge University Press).
Davies, Carole Boyce
    1994   *Black Women, Writing and Identity. Migrations of the Subject* (London and New York: Routledge).
Donaldson, Laura E.
    1992   *Decolonizing Feminisms. Race, Gender, & Empire-Building* (London: Routledge).
Dube, Musa W.
    1996   'Reading for Decolonization (John 4:1-42)', *Semeia* 75: 37–59.
Ellingworth, Paul
    1993   *The Epistle to the Hebrews. A Commentary on the Greek Text* (The New International Greek Testament Commentary; Grand Rapids: Eerdmans; Carlisle: Paternoster).
Ferguson, Everett
    1993   *Backgrounds of Early Christianity* (2nd edn; Grand Rapids: Eerdmans).
Fowl, Stephen E.
    1995   'The New Testament, Theology, and Ethics', in Joel B. Green (ed.), *Hearing the New Testament. Strategies for Interpretation* (Grand Rapids: Eerdmans): 394–410.
Füssel, K.
    1984   'Materialist Readings of the Bible: Report of an Alternative Approach to Biblical Texts', in Schottroff and Stegemann 1984: 13–25.
Glancy, Jennifer A.
    1998   'House Reading and Field Readings: The Discourse of Slavery and Biblical/ Cultural Studies', in J. Cheryl Exum and Stephen D. Moore (eds), *Biblical Studies/Cultural Studies. The Third Sheffield Colloquium* (Journal for the Study of the Old Testament Supplement Series, 266; Gender, Culture, Theory, 7; Sheffield: Sheffield Academic Press): 460–77.
Grösser, E.
    1986   'Das Wandernde Gottes volk zum Basismotiv des Hebräerbriefes', *Zeitschrift für Neutestamentliche Wissenschaft* 77(3–4): 160–79.

Guthrie, Donald
 1970 *New Testament Introduction* (3rd rev. edn; Leicester: InterVarsity Press).
 1982 *The Letter to the Hebrews* (Tyndale New Testament Comentaries, 15; Leicester: InterVarsity Press).

Hickling, C. J. A.
 1983 'John and Hebrews: The Background of Hebrews 2.10-18', *New Testament Studies* 29: 112–16.

Hughes, Graham
 1979 *Hebrews and Hermeneutics. The Epistle to the Hebrews as a New Testament Example of Biblical Interpretation* (Society For New Testament Studies Monograph Series, 36; Cambridge: Cambridge University Press).

Isaacs, Marie E.
 1992 *Sacred Space: An Approach to the Theology of the Epistle to the Hebrews* (Journal for the Study of the New Testament Supplement Series, 73; Sheffield: JSOT Press).

Jasper, A.
 1997 'Communicating the Word of God', *Journal for the Study of the New Testament* 67: 29–44.

Johnson, Luke T.
 1986 *The Writings of the New Testament: An Interpretation* (Philadelphia: Fortress Press).

Johnsson, W. G.
 1978a 'The Cultus of Hebrews in Twentieth-Century Scholarship', *Expository Times* 89: 104–108.
 1978b 'The Pilgrimage Motif in the Book of Hebrews', *Journal of Biblical Literature* 97: 239–51.

Klijn, A. F. J.
 1975 *De Brief aan de Hebreeën* (De Prediking van het Nieuwe Testament; Nijkerk: Callenbach).

Koester, Helmut
 1982 *Introduction to the New Testament.* Vol. 2, *History and Literature of Early Christianity* (Philadelphia: Fortress Press).

Kümmel, Werner Georg
 1975 *Introduction to the New Testament* (rev. edn; London: SCM Press).

Kwok, Pui-Lan
 1998 'On Color-Coding Jesus: an Interview with Kwok Pui-Lan', in Sugirtharajah 1998: 176–88.

Lash, Nicholas
 1986 *Theology on the Way to Emmaus* (London: SCM Press).

Lindars, Barnabas
 1989 'The Rhetorical Structure of Hebrews', *New Testament Studies* 35: 382–406.
 1991 *The Theology of the Letter to the Hebrews* (New Testament Theology; Cambridge: Cambridge University Press).

Longenecker, Richard
 1975 *Biblical Exegesis in the Apostolic Period* (Grand Rapids: Eerdmans).

Louw, J. P. and E. A. Nida
 1988 *Greek-English Lexicon of the New Testament based on Semantic Domains* (Vol. 1; New York: United Bible Societies).

Meeks, Wayne A.
  1986   'A Hermeneutics of Social Embodiment', *Harvard Theological Review* 79:
           176–86.
O'Brien Wicker, Kathleen
  1993   'Teaching Feminist Biblical Studies in a Postcolonial Context', in Schüssler
           Fiorenza 1993: 367–80.
Perkins, Pheme
  1988   *Reading the New Testament. An Introduction* (2nd edn; Mahwah: Paulist
           Press).
Peterson, David
  1982   *Hebrews and Perfection. An Examination of the Concept of Perfection in the
           'Epistle to the Hebrews'* (Society for New Testament Studies Monograph
           Series, 47; Cambridge: Cambridge University Press).
Pobee, John S.
  1992   *Skenosis. Christian Faith in an African Context* (Mambo Occasional Papers
           – Missio-Pastoral Series, 23; Gweru [Zimbabwe]: Mambo Press).
Pregeant, Russell
  1995   *Engaging the New Testament. An Interdisciplinary Introduction* (Minneapo-
           lis: Fortress Press).
Pretorius, E. A. C.
  1982   'Christusbeeld en Kerkmodel in die Hebreërbrief', *Theologia Evangelica* 15:
           3–18.
Punt, Jeremy
  1997   'Hebrews, Thought-patterns and Context: Aspects of the Background of
           Hebrews', *Neotestamentica* 31: 119–58.
  1998   'New Testament Interpretation, Interpretive Interests, and Ideology: Meth-
           odological Deficits amidst South African Methodolomania', *Scriptura* 65:
           123–52.
Rissi, Mathias
  1987   *Die Theologie des Hebräersbriefs. Ihre Verankerung in der Situation des
           Verfassers und seiner Leser* (Wissenschaftlichen Untersuchungen zum Neuen
           Testament, 41; Tübingen: J. C. B. Mohr [Paul Siebeck]).
Rowland, Christopher
  1993   ' "Open Thy Mouth for the Dumb". A Task for the Exegete of Holy Scripture',
           Biblical Interpretation 1: 228–45.
Schottroff, Willi and Wolfgang Stegemann (eds)
  1984   *God of the Lowly. Socio-Historical Interpretations of the Bible* (trans. M. J.
           O'Connell; Maryknoll, NY: Orbis Books).
Schüssler Fiorenza, Elisabeth
  1994   'Introduction: Transgressing Canonical Boundaries', in Schüssler Fiorenza
           1994: 1–14.
Schüssler Fiorenza, Elisabeth (ed.)
  1993   *Searching the Scriptures*. Vol. 1, *A Feminist Introduction* (London: SCM
           Press).
  1994   *Searching the Scriptures*. Vol. 2, *A Feminist Commentary* (London: SCM
           Press).
Scott, James C.
  1990   *Domination and the Arts of Resistance: Hidden Transcripts* (New Haven and
           London: Yale University Press).

Segovia, Fernando F.
>   1995   'The Text As Other: Towards a Hispanic American Hermeneutic', in Daniel
>   Smith-Christopher (ed.), *Text & Experience: Towards a Cultural Exegesis
>   of the Bible* (Biblical Seminar, 35; Sheffield: Sheffield Academic Press):
>   276–98.
>   1998   'Biblical Criticism and Postcolonial Studies: Towards a Postcolonial Optic',
>   in Sugirtharajah 1998: 49–65.

Sölle, Dorothee
>   1984   'Between Matter and Spirit: Why and in What Sense Must Theology be
>   Materialist?' in Schottroff and Stegemann 1984: 86–102.

Stedman, Ray C.
>   1992   *Hebrews* (The IVP New Testament Commentary Series; Downers Grove, IL:
>   InterVarsity Press).

Stibbs, Alan M.
>   1970   *So Great Salvation: The Meaning and Message of the Letter to the Hebrews*
>   (The Christian Student's Library; Exeter: Paternoster).

Sugirtharajah, R. S.
>   1996   'From Orientalist to Post-Colonial: Notes on Reading Practices', *Asian
>   Journal of Theology* 10: 20–27.
>   1998   'Biblical Studies after the Empire: From a Colonial to a Postcolonial Mode of
>   Interpretation', in Sugirtharah (ed.) 1998: 12–22.

Sugirtharajah, R. S. (ed.)
>   1998   *The Postcolonial Bible* (The Bible and Postcolonialism, 1; Sheffield: Shef-
>   field Academic Press).

Tiffin, Helen
>   1991   'Introduction', in Ian Adam and Helen Tiffin (eds), *Past the Last Post.
>   Theorizing Post-Colonialism and Post-Modernism* (New York: Harvester
>   Wheatsheaf): vii–xvi.

Tolbert, Mary Ann
>   1995   'Afterwords. Christianity, Imperialism, and the Decentering of Privilege', in
>   Fernando F. Segovia and Mary Ann Tolbert (eds), *Reading from this Place.
>   Vol. 1, Social Location and Biblical Interpretation in the United States* (Min-
>   neapolis: Fortress Press): 305–16.

Westphal, M.
>   1997   'Post-Kantian Reflections on the Importance of Hermeneutics', in R. Lundin
>   (ed.), *Disciplining Hermeneutics. Interpretation in Christian Perspective*
>   (Grand Rapids: Eerdmans): 57–66.

Williamson, Ronald
>   1963   'Platonism and Hebrews', *Scottish Journal of Theology* 16: 415–24.
>   1969–70 'Hebrews and Doctrine', *Expository Times* 81: 371–76.
>   1970   *Philo and the Epistle to the Hebrews* (Arbeiten zur Literatur und Geschichte
>   des hellenistischen Judentums, 4; Leiden: E. J. Brill).
>   1975–76 'The Background of the Epistle to the Hebrews', *Expository Times* 87:
>   232–36.

Wilson, R. McL.
>   1987   *Hebrews* (New Century Bible Commentary; Grand Rapids: Eerdmans).

Wimbush, Vincent L.
>   1993   'Reading Texts through Worlds, Worlds through Texts', *Semeia* 62: 129–39.

Witheringworth III, Ben
1991   'The Influence of Galatians on Hebrews', *New Testament Studies* 37: 146–52.

Yeo, K. K.
1991   'The Meaning and Usage of the Theology of "Rest" (Katapausis and Sabbatismos) in Hebrews 3:7–4:13', *Asian Journal of Theology* 5: 2–33.

The Letter of James

Sharon H. Ringe

The assignment to present a postcolonial commentary on the Letter of James tempts one to engage in a polemic against the relatively sparse and often scornful discussion of that document that has been produced by scholars from the dominant cultures of Western Europe and North America. That elliptical literature has had two foci: such historical questions as the identity of the author and of the addressees, the date of the document, and its place among the literary and rhetorical forms of the Hellenistic world; and the theological value – usually assessed to be minimal at best – of the document. Such facts lead Elsa Tamez (1985) to call this an 'intercepted letter' – intercepted by dominant voices in the church and the theological academy captive to the doctrinal norm of Paul's Letter to the Romans as well as by secular authorities and others who reject the letter's indictment of such economic and social elites as landowners (5.1-6) and wealthy merchants (4.13-17).

Introduction

The Letter of James is the first of the 'General' or 'Catholic' Epistles in the canonical order, but it is scarcely a letter at all. In fact, after the superscription (1.1) there are none of the traditional parts of an ancient letter – not even the opening thanksgiving or the closing words of blessing and good wishes. A number of interpreters have asserted that it is more a moral treatise than a theological letter (like those presumably 'model' letters of Paul) and that it is barely a Christian document, since it mentions Jesus only in 1.1 and 2.1. The superscription names 'James' as the sender, but it identifies him only as 'a servant of God and of the Lord Jesus Christ'. The lack of further identification or credentials have led to its traditional association with the brother of Jesus, who came to be identified as the leading spokesperson for the legally conservative Jewish-Christians in Jerusalem (Acts 15). Interpreters thus suggest that this document represents his counsel to those 'scattered' from that place and community into other parts of the Hellenistic world. While that scattering accelerated during and after the Roman–Jewish War of 66–70 CE, it was a process that took place throughout the Second Temple period. For that reason, a form of address appropriate to the early part of the first century (and thus to that 'historical James') would resonate with increasing clarity as the years passed.

Several factors suggest, however, that a metaphorical understanding of both author and addressees would be more appropriate. The principal problem with the literal understanding of author and addressees centres on other problems related to the early date that such authorship would require. The rather late reception of the letter, especially in the Western church where it did not appear on canonical lists until the fourth century, is an important external factor. Its language – both the intricate grammar and such terms as 'the implanted word' (1.21) and 'the wheel of birth' (3.6) – links it to Christian documents from the second century. Furthermore, the artificially imposed epistolary form points to a post-Pauline date, when the positive reception of Paul's letters imbued that form itself with authority and thus served to win a wider and more favourable hearing for the moral arguments the author of this document wished to put forward. In addition, the author employs rhetorical devices like the diatribe form that suggest a thorough immersion in the educational and cultural environment more proper to life in a Hellenistic city near the end of the first century than to mid-first-century Jerusalem.

Perhaps the strongest clue to a late date of origin is the contrast between faith and works in 2.14-26. Such a contrast would have been unheard of in Judaism! In fact, it would likely have become current in the church on the heels of the Pauline concern to separate God's redemptive work in Jesus Christ from any dependence on a person's obedience to Torah. That affirmation was part of Paul's programme to give expression to his own experience of a call from God to bring the gospel to Gentiles who have not first accepted the whole law, symbolized in the sign of circumcision (Gal. 1.11–2.21). The specific language of James' insistence on the coherence of faith and conduct makes sense only as a corrective to an erroneous reading of Paul that attributed to him the separation of 'faith' in some abstract sense from its incarnation in a life of faithfulness (a separation that Paul himself never suggested, as the strong paraenetic emphasis in his letters makes clear). Apparently, by the time the Letter of James was written, 'faith' had come to carry a doctrinal, emotional or intellectual meaning divorced from action. At the same time, the rejected 'works' had come to signify not efforts at self-justification but any moral expression of one's relationship to God. It is that split and the resulting distortion of the meaning of 'faith' as the central dimension of the Christian life, and not the Pauline argument, that the author of James is addressing.

To accomplish the necessary theological corrective to that confusion about the meaning of 'faith', the author of this letter uses the language of the disputed contrast between faith and works as those terms were being used by his audience, not with their Pauline meaning. He then draws on the moral authority of James and the content of traditions about Jesus' own teachings to address the loss of individual and communal integrity that resulted from the split of 'faith' and ethics. This commentary espouses the view that the author opposes not Paul himself but rather a distortion of Pauline theology that has become captive to an ideology and value system of competition, domination and loss of community integrity that reflected the surrounding culture of empire that flourished in the final decades of the first century.

That context of imperial domination is indispensable as a backdrop against which to examine the letter. It is named explicitly in 1.1, where the recipients are identified by the colonial category of 'Diaspora'. Whether they were people who had literally been driven from the land of Palestine as a consequence of the Roman–Jewish War or who had never experienced physical uprootedness from their places of origin, they were certainly living in a land not under the control of their own people. Like their physical or spiritual ancestors in Israel, they had become wanderers or sojourners whose resources fell under the hegemony of others' plans and purposes. At issue for the author is whether they would wander from their theological grounding as well, into a life normed by the world's values instead of by the canons or 'wisdom' of God (5.19). There is no hint in this document that the recipients are suffering explicitly religious persecution; it seems, rather, that in their diasporic existence they are encountering 'trials' (1.2, 12) in the form of the alien values of their surrounding culture and divisions (especially along class lines) that threaten to tear apart the community from within. In other words, those in the community who had found ways to prosper under the systems and rules of the Roman economic and social hegemony appear to be perpetuating its norms in their shabby treatment of and attitudes toward others within the Christian community who were less wealthy or powerful. The author critiques that modus vivendi as incompatible with faith in 'our glorious Lord Jesus Christ' (2.1).

As an alternative set of guidelines for daily living in their context, the Letter of James is related to the wisdom literature of many cultures by its content as well as by the aphoristic forms that express that content. Indeed, the goal of being wise or possessing wisdom frames the first half of this book (1.5; 3.13). Most wisdom literature appears to reinforce and to counsel adaptation to the prevailing norms and values of the culture from which it arises. This document, on the contrary, is linked to those portions of the wisdom literature of Israel's history (such as Proverbs, Job, Sirach and Wisdom) that understand wisdom as the reflection of the nature and will of God. Wisdom is thus linked to sustaining, by one's faith and action, the norms of God in the face of the conflicting agenda of 'the world'. The binary opposition that shapes the thought of James is not defined as a contrast between 'wisdom' and 'folly', such as is often the case in wisdom literature, but rather the contrast between 'true' wisdom and the world's wisdom and values, to which addressees of the letter have fallen prey (5.13-18).

Along with aphorisms and proverbs common to much of wisdom literature, the author uses the literary and rhetorical tools of Hellenistic culture to depict the Christian life as a radical alternative to the value system of its Roman imperial surroundings. The document thereby echoes within the Christian epistolary literature of the late first century the ethos of the Jesus traditions depicted especially in Matthew and Luke. Thus, while James is not focused on Christological affirmations about Jesus, it stands with Jesus in its theocentric worldview and in its affirmation that faith and love expressed in acts of justice are central to faithful life in keeping with God's will. James thus embodies the core of the gospel.

Commentators rarely posit a coherent structure for this document. A notable exception is Wall (1997: 34), who recognizes two introductory statements (1.1-11, 12-21) and two concluding statements (5.7-12, 13-20) that frame three essays on aspects of wisdom: the wisdom of being quick to hear (1.22–2.26); the wisdom of being slow to speak (3.1-8); and the wisdom of being slow to anger (4.1–5.6). Most commentators identify instead a series of topical essays that more or less elaborate on the aphorisms related to personal conduct or behaviour that comprise the first chapter (see, for example, Johnson 1998: 178). Elliott (1993 :72) advances the discussion by his recognition that the various sections or essays are united by the development of wholeness and holiness as ethical categories that express one's commitment to God. That development is carried out through a pattern of contrasts between the indictment of divisions in the community and in the life of the individual and the praise of both community and individual integrity or wholeness. The anthropological affirmation that addresses individual and communal dimensions with a common voice and the ideological affirmation of unity and integrity as the primary values of the religious life are a key to understanding James as a postcolonial document and to reading it with a postcolonial hermeneutic.

Commentary

Three thematically identified categories of texts provide helpful foci to examine James as a postcolonial document and to read it through a postcolonial lens. They deal with economic concerns, speech and language, and the ideology of unity or wholeness.

Economic Issues

James introduces economic concerns in the opening collection of aphorisms (1.9-11) and develops them more fully in three essays (2.1-7; 4.13-17; 5.1-6). The aphorism provides a glimpse into the composition of the community and an insight into the author's attitude toward wealth. Some members of the community (*adelphoi*) are 'lowly' or oppressed (*tapeinoi*), whereas others are wealthy (*plousioi*). This economic diversity fits the context of a city in the Roman Empire and the reality of even the early Christian communities, as can be seen in 1 Corinthians. Both groups are addressed in the aphorism of 1.9-11.

The former can rejoice in being 'lifted up' and the latter in being 'brought low', in a reversal of fortunes reminiscent of the Magnificat in Lk. 1.46-55. At issue is not the encouragement of social or political revolution – in any event not an option in an imperial context, but rather an affirmation of the naturalness of the instability of privilege. The image of the withering flower as a metaphor for the reversal of fortunes or even divine judgment recalls Isa. 40.6-7, as the negative corollary of the divine protection that secures those who trust in God according to Mt. 6.25-34. At issue in these verses is not specific action but rather an appropriate attitude toward or understanding of wealth: at the end of the day, wealth is a false repository of trust.

A similar point is developed in 4.13-17, in language reminiscent of the parable of the Rich Fool (Lk. 12.13-21). Plans to acquire wealth by commercial ventures (4.13) do not secure the future, which remains in the hands of God. This flies in the face of the assurances of the prosperity of the Pax Romana brought with imperial control over much of the then-known world. The arrogance of such boasting is called 'evil' (4.16) rather than simply foolish, and it is equated with the 'sin' of knowing the right thing to do and failing to do it. Verse 15 is the key announcement of a counter-ideology, especially with its use of the title '*kurios*' to refer to God instead of to Caesar as the ultimate authority in one's life and the source of true security.

The rhetoric shifts in 2.1-7 to specific ethical counsel. On the one hand, it relates to proper conduct in the gatherings of the community. Favouritism toward the rich and disregard of the poor is bad church etiquette, as well as contrary to the option of God for the poor, whom God has made 'rich in faith'. Beyond the human attitude all too common in the West that welcomes the visitor to the church who brings an element of prestige to the community, however, this passage confronts fundamental dimensions of the ideology undergirding the imperial context to which it was addressed. First, the purpose of the colonies was to provide wealth to Rome – wealth seized in conquest and garnered in trade. The wealthy person described in this paragraph is one positioned to contribute to that project. A natural temptation would be to stay on the good side of such a person of relative power in the area. Second, the relative valuing of the rich over the poor is a dimension of the honour–shame system that regulated imperial society and determined the relative worth of persons. Along with such factors as legal status, prestige of birth, gender, educational attainment and access to power, wealth was a significant determinant of a person's status in all aspects of life. In this daring paragraph, both of those 'givens' are confronted. Far from being honoured, the wealthy are indicted as oppressors who use even the Roman legal system against other people. Their actions are given the religious charge of 'blasphemy' (2.7). The addressees of this paragraph are not the rich, however, nor are they the poor who have been wronged. The teaching is addressed instead to the members of the church whose minds and hearts have been 'colonized' by the values and ideology of the surrounding society. The author thus speaks with a postcolonial voice in the sense of a counter-weight to those values and that ideology, in the name of the divine option for the poor (2.5) and true faith (*pistis*, 2.1).

The final section dealing with economic issues (5.1-6) moves into an indictment of the wealthy. Their wealth is no longer simply a futile repository of their confidence but rather evidence that testifies against them and harms them (5.3). Their specific offence is that they have defrauded agricultural labourers of their due wages (5.4). In the context of the imperial economy, no situation was more common or more accepted. Agricultural day-labourers were landless peasants who had usually lost their land through the Roman system of taxation and through the imperial monopoly on trade that set the prices they would receive below subsistence levels. Lands would have been sold bit by bit, and family members would have been hired out, and often eventually sold as indentured servants. Totally without power or status, they would have been the members of the society most readily exploited by those who had cast their lot successfully with the imperial economic and social project. These 'winners' in the world's terms are warned that the cries of those they have exploited have been heard by God (5.4). The 'righteous one' (*dikaios*) they have condemned and murdered (5.6) may allude simply to the poor, but more likely the accusation is being escalated to equate their exploitative behaviour with the condemnation and execution of Jesus Christ, the paradigmatic righteous one of the Christian confession. Though the impending judgment and punishment of these wealthy offenders is not specified, its harshness is implied as the ultimate fire they have stored up as a treasure for the last days (5.3). The message is clear: not the Roman project, but rather the divine will, has the final word.

Speech and Language
In a colonial context like that of the Mediterranean world of the first century, one tool and expression of colonization is language. On the surface, the imperial language replaces and eventually suppresses indigenous languages as the obligatory language of commerce and public life. More deeply, euphemisms mask the agenda of domination and conquest. For example, Pax Romana names the enforced tranquillity imposed by the Roman military dominance over the region. The narrative interpretation of the dominant power defines the meaning and significance of events that shape people's lives in ways that come to be taken for granted and thus exercise their power invisibly. In short, 'truth' is reduced to a term of power and language to a device of manipulation.

In contrast, one of the postcolonial traits of the Letter of James is its attention to speech and language as factors in the integrity and wholeness of life that embodies one's 'faith'. Key to this perspective is 1.18, in which the divine nature and purpose themselves are expressed in the effective 'word of truth' by and in which humankind was created. Whether a reference to the creative word of Genesis 1 or an explicitly Christological meaning is intended there or in the reference to the 'implanted word' in 1.21 is unclear. Most likely both are encompassed in the metaphor. In any event, that creative and redemptive power of the divine word undergirds a number of reflections and commandments related to human speech in the remainder of the letter.

Several of the comments about human speech remind the audience of the power of words to do good or to cause harm, especially to the community to which the letter is addressed. Speech is a factor in social cohesion and integrity, in contrast to the disingenuous use of language in relationships of domination. Thus, in 1.19-21 the recipients of the letter are cautioned to 'be quick to listen, slow to speak, slow to anger' as an embodiment of the 'meekness' appropriate to the 'implanted word' and divine righteousness – in other words, to God's nature and purpose. A similar bit of wisdom related to appropriate speaking is in 5.12, which warns the people against explicit oath-taking, in favour of simple truthful speech.

The power of speech is the central theme of the essay in 3.1-12. What appears initially to be a warning about the higher standards applied to those who claim to teach others turns into a warning about the power of speech to direct the whole body. The warning about the power of the tongue to set the character of the whole person recalls Mt. 6.22-23, where it is the eye that is credited with revealing the entire truth about a person. Here the tongue not only defines the individual person, but it also can be responsible for public damage in the community, even while it utters the pious language of prayer and praise (3.9-10). The lack of integrity of the human character underlying such contradictory speech is a significant expression of one's colonization by the practices and values of the society, instead of one's embodiment of a faithful life.

The affirmation about the power of the tongue echoes the double aphorism of 1.26-27. The first half names the negative implication: without control of the tongue, one's religion is worthless. The second aphorism develops a corollary of the first. Religion that is 'pure and undefiled' – in other words, that includes the disciplined speech that has just been mentioned – is also embodied in deeds of mercy and in keeping oneself 'unstained by the world'. The injunction to care for 'widows and orphans' – the paradigm of oppressed and marginalized persons – makes it clear that literal isolation or separation from 'the world' is not the intent, but rather separation from the competing values of the world, which in a person who professes faith in God signifies a life lacking in integrity.

The theme of unity of word and action implied in 1.27 is also the subject of the reflections on hearing and doing the word in 1.22-25. Hearing and not acting accordingly amounts to 'forgetting' and 'deceiving' oneself. The image is drawn from literature of ethical instruction, in which the person gazes into a mirror in order to learn the truth about himself or herself, and then to alter his or her life on the basis of what has been learned. Not to take the step into action renders the exercise futile, just as does hearing without doing. The power of 'the perfect law, the law of liberty' to ground the integrated life the author advocates is introduced in 1.25. While in this paragraph the term is a synonym of 'the word' that is heard, the precise reference must be inferred. Like the word, the law is effective, bringing about what it proclaims. Thus, for this author it is Torah, as 2.8-13 makes clear, but it is also more than that. As Johnson observes: 'In this composition, faith, word, law, and wisdom are not dialectically opposed, but are seen as mutually reinforcing gifts from God' (Johnson 1998: 189). The aphorisms on the integrity of word and action in 1.22-25 thus form the basis for the discussion of the unity of faith and works as the expression of a faithful life in 2.14-26.

A more puzzling reflection on the power of speech is the elaboration in 4.11-12 of the initially simple command in 4.11: 'Do not speak evil against one another'. One might at first hear that as a caution against the betrayal of one's neighbours to those in authority, or against the sort of idle speech or telling of tales that could be used by the authorities to build a case against the neighbours – a common technique of control or manipulation by those in power, where no legal protections exist. Here, however, speaking against others is equated with 'judging' both them and 'the law' itself. 'Evil speech', which might better be translated as 'slander', judges the other by elevating the speaker and lowering the value of the other who is spoken against. It is thus paradigmatic speech of a life ordered on the sort of competition for status and honour that characterized the imperial context in which the letter was written. To engage in slander also 'judges' the law, not of Rome but of God. It thus usurps the place of God, the only true judge, by disregarding the explicit prohibition of such speech in Lev. 19.16 (Johnson 1998: 215). Slander is the verbal expression of one's captivity to values and purposes that contradict the divine values and purposes, and thus is a crucial dimension of a life lacking integrity and wholeness in one's devotion to God.

Ideology
The third cluster of texts sets forth the letter's challenge to the ideology of the imperial context. 'Ideology' is of course a term foreign to this letter. It is used here as a value-neutral term referring to ideas that characterize a group of people, or to assertions, theories and aims that undergird a political, social and economic programme. In fact, the Letter of James posits two competing ideologies, one that expresses the values of the surrounding culture and the other that the author espouses. These ways of perceiving and assessing the world make claims on the people's loyalty, both through their actions and through their verbal professions. The 'tests' – *peirasmoi*, a word which is sometimes translated 'trials' or 'temptations' – referred to in 1.2-4 and 12-16 may refer precisely to this competition for people's loyalty. The language of the text does not identify specific persecutions or hardships that the addressees of the letter are facing, but rather it points to 'one's own desire' as the entry point of sin that threatens them. In other words, the greed and competition for wealth, status and

honour that undergird the structures and values of the Roman imperial project threaten the faithfulness of the addressees of the letter.

One consequence of their seduction by those values is the fracturing of the community. The personal challenges cited in the essay in 4.1-10 affect especially how a person's actions impact on the common life they share. Personal behaviour is of concern to the author, not because of an assumption that there exists a system of divine accounting that will determine God's verdict on the individual but because of a concern for social well-being in a community outside of the hierarchical order of imperial society. The demands of this letter are a far cry from the escapism of privatized and spiritualized religion that can be practised alone and in secret in the face of imperial claims on one's external behaviour. Instead, the obligations of religion itself challenge the imperial values in the social incarnation of different norms. These norms are affirmed to have ultimate validity and eternal value that will be ratified in God's final resolution of the historical struggle in the coming 'Day of the Lord' (5.7-11).

This document thus reflects a second stage of postcolonial reflection that goes beyond a critique of the content of the imperial ideology to posit its own 'single-mindedness' as the definition of wisdom (1.18). The Letter of James advocates a coherence that arises from within the individual, conforming him or her to a wisdom that mirrors the divine reality itself in all realms of life. In language that echoes the Pauline catalogue of 'fruits of the Spirit' in Gal. 5.22-26, the author describes this Godly wisdom that is the antithesis of the world's wisdom which bids at each moment for the reader's allegiance (3.13-18).

Fundamental to a life lived according to divine wisdom is unity and integrity of life on all levels. Along with the integrity of individual and community life, that wisdom is expressed in the integrity of a person's belief and practice, 'faith' and 'works'. That ideological claim made on the readers underlies the author's emphatic rejection of the notion that one could believe or even articulate a 'faith' that does not take on flesh in one's life. If it is the case that such a distortion of the Pauline teachings about justification had made inroads into the community to which this letter is addressed, the author's polemic in 2.14-26 (further elaborated in 5.13-20) needs to be understood as an affirmation of the all-encompassing character of the divine wisdom that brooks no compromise with or refuge in the imperial system, whether in belief or in praxis.

The letter's stress on individual and social integrity stands in sharp contrast to the mere veneer of social unity imposed by the Roman Empire. The drive toward a common language that transcends the diverse tongues of the subject peoples, a common currency to facilitate trade, and a unified economic project directed by and toward the profit of Rome indeed gave an aura of coherence to life in the eastern Mediterranean basin throughout the first century. That apparent unity obscured the underlying cultural diversity and the disparate economic subsystems of the region and thus built contradictions and divisions into every level of individual and communal life, which the imperial project could only seek to mask. The imperial value of unity is not denied by the author we call James, but rather it is taken with literal seriousness, as people are urged to find that true integrity in their grounding in the values that define Godself, as known through Torah, prophets, the counsel of wisdom and the traditions stemming from Jesus.

Conclusion: James as Postcolonial Voice

The letter thus can be called a postcolonial voice, in that its call is for a response to the imperial reality, not by escaping from it through mystery religions or other expressions of an inner or spiritualized religion that the state cannot touch, which splits the invisible (faith) from the visible (action), the religious from the ethical. Such a solution would mean living a double life of fulfilling the rules as necessary or profitable, while, where one can get away with it, one lives another way. In fact, the author appears to recognize the futility of such an effort, due to the insidiousness of the imperial values that can infect the private or inner religion with the same perverted ideology fostered by the public. Instead, the author advocates an alternative integrity that is portrayed as the reality of which the imperial veneer is but a shadow – a reality given its power by its reflection of the divine reality itself, which is a greater power even than Rome.

This letter that made a daring claim in its original context suffered its own domestication or 'colonization' once the heirs of its recipients came to represent the dominant voices in their contexts. As Elsa Tamez has observed, the Letter of James has been 'intercepted' many times. Still, however, its postcolonial challenge persists through the author's affirmation of the inherently destabilizing values of the gospel – parity, community and integrity or coherence of life – that tenaciously resist imperial challenges, whether from Rome or a later day.

BIBLIOGRAPHY

Deiros, Pablo Alberto
    1992   *Santiago y Judas* (Comentario Bíblico Hispanoamericano; Miami: Editorial Caribe).
Elliott, John H.
    1993   'The Epistle of James in Rhetorical and Social Scientific Perspective: Holiness-Wholeness and Patterns of Replication', *Biblical Theology Bulletin* 23: 71–81.
Felder, Cain Hope
    1998   'James', in William R. Farmer (ed.), *The International Bible Commentary: A Catholic and Ecumenical Commentary for the Twenty-first Century* (Collegeville, MN: The Liturgical Press): 1786–1801.
Johnson, Luke Timothy
    1998   'The Letter of James', in *The New Interpreter's Bible*. Vol. 12 (Nashville: Abingdon Press): 177–225.

Maynard-Reid, Pedrito U.
:   1987   *Poverty and Wealth in James* (Maryknoll, NY: Orbis Books).

Nogueira, Paulo (ed.)
:   1998   *Revista de Interpretación Bíblica Latinoamericana.* Vol. 31, *La carta de Santiago* (San José, Costa Rica).

Sleeper, C. Freeman
:   1998   *James* (Abingdon New Testament Commentaries; Nashville: Abingdon Press).

Tamez, Elsa
:   1985   *Santiago: Lectura latinoamericana de la epístola* (San José, Costa Rica: Departamento Ecuménico de Investigaciones). English translation: *The Scandalous Message of James: Faith Without Works is Dead* (trans. John Eagleson; New York: Crossroad, 1990).

Wall, Robert W.
:   1997   *Community of the Wise: The Letter of James* (The New Testament in Context; Valley Forge, PA: Trinity Press International).

The First Letter of Peter

Elisabeth Schüssler Fiorenza

The Christian Testament writing called 1 Peter invites postcolonial interpretation. It is addressed to 'resident aliens' who live in the Roman Province of Asia Minor and represents them as a marginalized group who experience harassment and suffering. Hence, it is appropriate to engage in a decolonizing interpretation of the letter that is at one and the same time a critical feminist interpretation.

A Critical Decolonial Feminist Analytic

Before I begin with the interpretation of 1 Peter, several preliminary remarks are in order. First, I prefer to conceptualize a critical feminist commentary as 'interpretation' rather than as 'reading'. Although many people in the world are not able to read, they are nevertheless able to interpret stories, information, life situations and relations of power and domination. A critical emancipatory biblical interpretation does not presuppose the ability to read but requires conscientization and systemic analysis. In my own work I have elaborated such a systemic analysis of the structures and ideologies of kyriarchal, that is, lord, slave-master, father, husband, elite male domination. Such a critical feminist analysis is practically identical with a feminist postcolonial discourse analysis, insofar as it includes the analysis of colonial–imperial structures and discourses.

Second, since 'postcolonialism has a multiplicity of meanings depending on one's social location' and is 'a mental attitude rather than a method' (Sugirthara-jah 1998: 93), I will utilize a critical-rhetorical method and feminist systemic analysis for interpreting 1 Peter. Unlike a classic-rhetorical or literary-rhetorical analysis, such a feminist rhetorical approach seeks to comprehend 1 Peter not simply as a system of communication, but, with Said, it understands the letter as a 'worldly' historical text embedded in power relations: 'Texts are worldly, to some degree they are events, and, even when they appear to deny it, they are nevertheless a part of the social world, human life, and of course the historical moments in which they are located and interpreted' (Said 1983: 4).

Third, following Chela Sandoval, I will engage a 'doubled' analysis of power, one that metaphorizes power as pyramidal, or more precisely as kyri-archal relations of domination, and one that understands power horizontally as a network of relations of domination or as 'circulating in a sort of electric pinball game movement' (2000: 72–77). Both modes of power, the vertical and the horizontal one, are at work in capitalist globalization. Nevertheless, postmodern consciousness privileges the horizontal mapping of power over the vertical one and thereby occludes how kyriarchal relations of domination still determine people's lives and consciousness. The kyriarchal (or imperial) pyramid of domination is structured by multiple forms of domination – race, gender, class, empire, age and religion – which are intersecting and have multiplicative effects of domination. Hence, a 'dual systems' analysis of domination that conceptualizes patriarchy and colonialism (Dube Shomanah 2000) as two independent systems of power does not suffice.

Sandoval has developed both a theoretical 'topography of dissident consciousness' (equal rights, revolutionary, supremacist, separatist and differential) and a 'methodology of the oppressed' for supporting 'dissident globalization' (2000: 1–2, 53–61, 80–82). This method consists in the following skills: (1) the ability to read the signs of power, (2) the ideology used to deconstruct the sign systems, (3) the method of meta-ideologizing that creates new levels of signification, (4) the method of democratics as a counter-vision and dissident movement in opposition to transnational globalization that crosses all borders, exploits all peoples and colonizes all citizens and (5) a differential movement that allows consciousness to challenge its own perimeters from within ideology. Sandoval likens the 'differential' to a gear of a car that 'permits a new kind of transmission of power' (2000: 184 n. 3).

Fourth, such a mapping of the dual modes of power requires that one move beyond the 'confessional stance' of identity politics and develop a critical method for interpreting the inscriptions of power. Some might object that a critical feminist–liberationist optic and method of interpretation is not sufficiently 'postcolonial' because it has been developed from the social location and theoretical position of a white Western feminist. As far as I can see, this seems to be the reason why the discussion on the optic and method of postcolonial biblical studies has not engaged my theoretical and methodological proposals. I raise this issue because Fernando Segovia (2000) has invited a rigorous theoretical discussion on the emerging field of postcolonial biblical studies.

More importantly, such an objection in terms of identity politics cannot be sustained on theoretical and methodological grounds. The theoretical and methodological difference in the interpretation of both 'Western' and 'Third World' feminists who are located in the Western academy and its discourses cannot be simply marked as the difference between a hegemonic and a subaltern reading as long as they both use a critical emancipatory analysis and methodology of liberation. This is not to deny the importance of social location and theoretical perspective for a critical feminist and postcolonial discourse analysis.

How scholars interpret the overall rhetorical strategy of 1 Peter and conceptualize its rhetorical-historical situation depends on their socio-religious location, which, because of the academic credo of value-detached objectivism, is almost never explicitly articulated and problematized. Since the majority of the commentaries on 1 Peter which I have consulted are written by Euro-American Christian academicians, their readings are positioned in malestream exegetical discourses that valorize and reinscribe the perspective of the inscribed author.

In contrast, a critical, feminist, decolonizing interpretation focuses on the submerged voices in the text to whom the author responds. It begins by exploring, first, the socio-religious location not only of the author but also of the recipients whom the letter addresses. In a second interpretive move it seeks to trace the power relations inscribed in the argument of the letter and attempts in a third step of analysis to reconstruct the rhetorical strategies of the letter and its interpreters. Finally, in a fourth move it attempts to reconstruct the submerged voices and their arguments. It wants to reconstruct and elaborate the submerged emancipatory discourses inscribed in 1 Peter in terms of Sandoval's 'democratics', which seeks to equalize unequal power relations and to ask whether 1 Peter fosters emancipatory dissident consciousness or whether its rhetoric of power strengthens kyriarchal–imperial consciousness and relations of domination.

In short, utilizing the optic of 'dissident consciousness', a kyriarchal discourse analysis and the 'methodology of the oppressed', I will engage a critical-rhetorical analysis for interpreting 1 Peter as a 'worldly' text. In contrast to a semiotic model of interpretation, an agential rhetorical model understands the *world of the text* not simply as a reservoir of signs and of meaning but as a field of power and of action. In contrast to a hermeneutical model of interpretation, a critical, feminist, decolonizing interpretation is not just concerned with the meaning of the text but with the historical agency of wo/men. (This writing of wo/men signifies that the expression wo/men is inclusive of men as well as that the power differences within wo/men and between wo/men can be greater than those between women and men of the same race, class, nation, culture or religion.) Such a critical feminist interpretation seeks, in the words of Nelle Morton, to 'hear into speech' the submerged voices of the vanquished in history in order to empower wo/men who struggle today against domination and for well-being.

Methodologically, it seeks to differentiate the rhetoric of the author from that of the letter by reconstructing and revalorizing the silenced arguments of the addressees and by reading the text against its kyriocentric grain. Since the first level of communication – the historical level of author–audience – and world of 1 Peter are no longer directly accessible to us, a critical-rhetorical analysis always has to begin with the second level, the level of text, before it can move to a reconstruction of the first historical level of the situation to which the letter is a 'fitting' rhetorical response. Hence, I will begin with a critical discussion of the inscribed sender(s) and recipients, which is followed by a classic-rhetorical analysis of the argument structure (*argumentatio*) in order to reconstruct the inscribed rhetorical situation and the submerged voices of those whom 1 Peter silences.

Inscribed Author, Recipients and Socio-political World

1 Peter is not a writing concerned with inner-church polemics or orthodox beliefs, but as a circular letter it is a rhetorical communication between those who live in the metropolitan centre of imperial Rome, which is theologically camouflaged as Babylon, and those who live in Asia Minor as colonial subjects. The inscribed geographical location and socio-political world of the recipients is that of Asia Minor. It is debated whether the place names given in the salutation refer simply to geographical areas or whether they more likely refer to Roman provinces. In any case, Asia Minor had been for centuries colonized and had absorbed Hellenistic language and culture as well as Roman imperial commerce and religion. This communication sent from the imperial centre presents itself as an authoritative letter of advice and admonition to 'good conduct and subordination' in the colonial public of the provinces.

As a communication from the metropolitan centre, the circular letter is cast in the, by then, traditional and 'authoritative' Pauline letter form. Like the genuine Pauline Letters, it elaborates the letter-opening (1.1-2), which in its typical Hellenistic form consists in the simple salutation 'X sends greetings to Y', by qualifying the sender as 'apostle of Jesus Christ' and by characterizing the recipients not in communal–democratic terms as *ekklesia* but in political–individual terms as 'transients' or 'migrants' who have been 'elect' through 'the foreknowledge of G*d the Father', the 'sanctification of the Spirit for obedience', and the 'sprinkling of the blood of Christ'. The letter's address also uses an elaborate, uniquely Pauline form of greeting ('May grace and peace be with you in abundance').

As was the case in Hellenistic letters, the greeting is followed by a thanksgiving (1.3-12), which, as in the Pauline literature, is more elaborate here. In classical-rhetorical terms the thanksgiving functions as a unit of praise (*encomium*). It consists here of a very long and complicated sentence which does not so much teach as celebrate and confess. G*d's mighty acts on behalf of the letter's recipients are praised as saving acts in the past, in the experience of Christians in the present characterized as a time of faith in Jesus Christ and hope, and finally as G*d's mighty acts in the eschatological future. Even the prophets have recognized the grace given to the recipients and even the angels seek to understand the salvation/imperial well-being (*sōteria*) given to them (1.10-12).

Like the genuine Pauline Letters, so also 1 Peter ends with a farewell address in 5.12-14, which summarizes the purpose of the letter as 'to encourage' the readers, 'to testify to the true grace of G*d' and to admonish: 'Stand fast in it!' It mentions those who send greetings ('the elect one in Babylon', 'my son Mark' and Silvanus the transcriber or the deliverer of the letter) and ends with the admonition to greet each other with 'the kiss of love' and a peace wish to all of them (5.14).

Most critical exegetes agree that the letter is pseudonymous and written at the end of the first century CE, long after Peter's execution. The letter claims to be authored by the fisherman–apostle Simon/Peter from Galilee, but this is not likely, because it is written in polished Greek and evidences a high level of rhetorical competence. Hence, the letter is probably a pseudonymous communication that rhetorically claims the authority and tradition of the apostle for its content. In addition, as we have seen, the letter's rhetoric marshals the authority of Paul insofar as it is cast in terms of the Pauline letter form and claims that both Silvanus and Mark, who are known as associates of Paul, are involved in sending the letter. Hence, some scholars have surmised that the letter is written by a Petrine group or school that was concerned with keeping alive Petrine and/or Pauline traditions. In any case, 1 Peter is clearly authored and sent from the centre of the Roman imperium and claims to be a document of colonized persons who as migrants from Palestine lived in Rome.

It is, however, debated whether a woman is mentioned among the senders. The fourth person or figure referred to in 5.13 is that of the 'co-elect one in Babylon' (*suneklektē en Babulōni*), which can be understood as referring to a communal representation of the Jewish 'Christian' community in Rome, to the Roman church, or to a well-known wo/man leader in Rome. Just as exegetes construe the expression 'elect lady' or 'sister' (*eklektē kuria* or *adelphē*) in 2 John 1 and 13 as not referring to an individual wo/man, so also commentators of 1 Peter insist that the expression 'co-elect in Babylon' does not refer to an actual well-known wo/man leader in Rome but that it is a reference to the Roman church or to a figurative representation of this church. If exegetes read 5.13 as referring to an actual wo/man, they have tended to understand 5.13 as referring to Peter's wife.

Judith Applegate has carefully scrutinized the arguments pro and con of understanding 5.13 as referring to a wo/man leader in Rome (1992). She points out that scholars claim it is 'natural' not to think of a particular wo/man leader, although three out of five Christian Testament greetings to and from churches refer to an actual wo/man (1 Cor. 16.19; Col. 4.15; Rom. 16.5). Thus are wo/men eliminated from the sources! Moreover, the expression 'elect' is never used in conjunction with the word *ekklesia* but is used only with reference to individuals (see Rom. 16.13). Hence, Applegate concludes that the recipients must have known who the wo/man leader was mentioned among those who send greetings. If this is the case, then 1 Peter, like the neo-Aristotelian tractates on 'household' management (*oikonomia*), appealed to the authority of a well-known wo/man leader for legitimating his message of subordination. By not mentioning the name of the early Christian woman leader, this appeal remains general enough so that one could not argue against it.

Moreover, it is not clear as to whether wo/men are included among the addressees, since the letter uses grammatically (*eklektoi*) and contentionally (*adelphotēs*) masculine generic or gender-specific terms to characterize the recipients. If kyriocentric (lord, slave-master, father, husband, male centred) language is used here in the generic, inclusive sense, then one can assume that wo/men in general and slave-wo/men in particular were included among the addressees. The reference to well-to-do wives in 3.1-6 supports such a generic reading, because it indicates that 'ladies' were definitely part of the community. However, one could also argue for a gender-specific understanding. Insofar as the behaviour of slaves and wives is mentioned as a special case, the rest of the letter could be addressed to freeborn male citizens only, depending on how one understands the self – the community's understanding of 'brotherhood'.

If *oikos tou theou* in 4.17 is understood as household rather than as temple, then the 'brotherhood' is conceived, at least by the author, as the household of G*d, whose *paterfamilias* is G*d, the father who is also the Father of Jesus Christ (1.2-3), and whose members are 'obedient children' (1.14). The members of the 'brotherhood' have been 'set free' (ransomed like slaves) from 'the traditions of their fathers' (1.18) and are invoking now 'the father who judges all people impartially' (1.17). Although they are like 'newborn infants longing for the pure spiritual mother-milk', no mother of the family is mentioned.

The recipients are addressed as 'beloved' (2.11; 4.12). They are characterized as those who love G*d, whom they have not seen (1.8) but who cares for them (4.12). They are told to greet each other with the 'kiss of love'. They are admonished to have 'genuine mutual love and to love one another deeply' (1.22). In 3.8, which concludes the 'subordination' section, five adjectives characterize the love-ethos of the 'brotherhood' or the 'house of G*d': 'unity of spirit', 'mutual sympathy', 'brotherly (and sisterly) love for each other', 'compassionate kind feelings toward one another' and 'humble mindedness'.

Those who are 'beloved' should become 'zealots of doing good' and, above all, maintain constant love for one another, because 'love covers a multitude of sins' (4.8). Such love is expressed in hospitality, good stewardship 'of the manifold grace of G*d', service with all one's gifts (*charismata*), and speaking the very words of G*d (4.9-11). Christians are to break the vicious circle of violence and 'not return evil for evil' (3.9) but replace slandering and reviling with 'blessing', for they were called to 'receive a blessing', an expression at home in the language world of Judaism, which is underscored by a lengthy quote adapted from Ps. 43.13-14.

A different 'honour code' determines the Christian community or better 'brotherhood', insofar as it distinguishes 'honourable' behaviour toward everyone and toward the emperor from that which is required in the 'brotherhood': 'brotherly love'. However, in the characterization of the community as 'brotherhood', the kyriocentric elite male ethos seems to prevail, insofar as the community is called 'brotherhood', although we know that wo/men were members of the community. The designation of the community as 'brotherhood' could be a conventional reference to social *collegia* and religious associations; it could imply a masculine theological self-understanding, or it could refer to the

Christian community as a patriarchal family or as egalitarian siblinghood. If one understands *adelphotēs* as 'siblinghood' of 'sisters and brothers', who are equally called, holy and elect, rather than as patriarchal family, then one can grasp that it is the author who seeks to reshape the self-understanding of the communities in Asia Minor in terms of the patriarchal *familia*.

The characterization of the recipients is ambiguous in two other ways. It is not clear whether their characterization as transients or migrants (*parepidēmoi*) and as non-citizens or resident aliens (*paroikoi*) is political and establishes commonality between the sender(s) and recipients as colonial subjects or whether it is purely religious asserting that the 'fatherland' of the recipients is in heaven.

First: Key for the understanding of the recipients is their characterization as transients, migrants or foreigners (*parepidēmoi*) and *paroikoi*, which can be translated as non-citizens, resident aliens, settlers or colonials. The *paroikos* lacked local citizenship and belonged to an institutionalized group ranked socially between the citizen population and freed persons. According to Elliott (2000: 94; relying on Rostovtzeff), such 'by-dwellers' were, on the one hand, excluded from major civic offices and honours, had only limited legal protection, and were restricted in commerce, intermarriage and land tenure. Furthermore, they were allowed limited participation in cultic rites but excluded from the priesthood. On the other hand, they, like the citizenry, were responsible for taxes, financial civic support, tribute and military service. Their status therefore was not very different from foreigners, visiting tradespeople, missionaries and migrants (*parepidēmoi*), and they were exposed to suspicion and hostility. In short, the condition of the addressees of 1 Peter as *paroikoi* accounts for much of their suffering. Finally, their characterization as transients of the diaspora characterizes them as Jewish exiles who no longer have a homeland and were often considered as second-class citizens in their host countries.

Yet, by taking colonialism into account, Prostmeier (1990) – also with reference to Rostovtzeff – tells another story. Centuries of Hellenistic colonization of the kingdoms of Asia Minor had produced a deep social rift between the indigenous peoples of Asia Minor and the Greek settlers. In the Roman Empire this Hellenistic 'middle class' took over the imperial administration, commerce and civic institutions. Hence, Rome did not change the basically Hellenistic culture of the cities, which consisted of a rich aristocratic upper class, the new colonial middle class and the group of workers and slaves. While the natives were the majority of the working and 'lower class' people, the colonial settlers and Hellenized natives formed the cultured 'middle class' who were most loyal to the empire.

This new 'middle class' of diaspora Greeks imported their own standards of family and civic life as well as their cultural and political institutions, although they were not an independent political entity. Hellenistic settlers were a privileged class. Their language, knowledge and financial and cultural capital enabled them to take over leading functions in the kingdom–states, although indigenous monarchs tried to prevent the cohabitation and social mixing of colonials and natives. Hellenistic diaspora Jews would have qualified for such colonial 'middle class' status except for their different customs and perceived religious exclusiveness, which earned them the label *superstition*; and their history of militant struggle against Roman imperial occupation.

Hellenistic culture, religions, lifestyle and education were the *sine qua non* for social mobility. This new, educated, propertied 'middle class' – consisting of colonizing settlers, such as former military personnel and merchants, and of the indigenous elite – had the function to vouchsafe the stability of imperial colonial society for which the stability of the household was crucial. In the course of Hellenistic as well as Roman imperial colonization of Asia Minor and the Mediterranean, the discourse on household management (*peri oikonomias*) became an important ideological tool for preserving the stability and unity of the imperial order.

Over and against more 'liberalizing', emancipatory and egalitarian tendencies in Graeco-Roman culture and philosophy, a rich variety of household literature (*peri oikonomias*) appeared that sought to mitigate ethically the rigoristic exercise of domination on the part of the *paterfamilias* through a combination of the motives of fear and love in the sense of fidelity, cooperation and proper relations of domination. The neo-Pythagorean fragments seek to mediate between the urban 'middle class' colonial *oikos*-society and its ideals of virtues and the Stoic axioms of equality, which jeopardize the fundamental principles of the order of household and state. This emancipatory trend resulted in a limited legal equality of freeborn wo/men and some slaves and freed persons in the household, in commerce and in the wider society. In short, the discourse on household management was not just a moral discourse on how the members of the household (*oikos*) should behave but also a part of imperial discourse and political theory, at least since Plato and Aristotle.

Hence, *oikos* does not mean 'home' and nuclear family but designates the household as a social institution which was fundamental for the stability of the colonial empire. Although the English word 'family' is derived from the Latin *familia*, it does not have the same valence. Within the context of the *oikos*-discourse, the designation 'brotherhood' (*adelphotēs*) for the Christian community (2.17 and 5.9) also receives political meaning, since this term was also used as self-designation for political alliances such as *collegia* and mystery-cult groups like the Isis cult. Unlike the private sphere of the household, such religious and political associations were not based on bloodlines and economic interests but on collegiality, solidarity and mutual support, which fulfilled many of the emotional needs that we associate with family.

Foreign religions were permitted by the empire as long as such practices did not provide a threat to political stability. For instance, Tiberius prohibited the Isis cult and Jewish rites, Claudius forbade mass-meetings by Jews because he feared their proselytizing would cause trouble, and Vespasian and Titus demanded a special tax from Jews after the Jewish War. That religion was used in the interest of political stabilization is evident from the increased practice of the emperor cult in the provinces. The cult served to enhance the dominance of local elites, who could show their loyalty to Rome and, at the same time, maintain cultural continuity, since it reflected their ancestral religious values and customs. Pressure to conform would, therefore, come more strongly from the local authorities than from the Roman administration. Thus, the imperial cult functioned as an integral part of the web of power that shaped the fabric of colonial societies and maintained stability and control (Price 1984).

Finally, the proliferation of collegia and political associations presented a constant problem for the imperial administration. Hence, steps were frequently taken to control such groups. It was the fear that such secret organizations would pursue seditious political interests that led the authorities to forbid them. For the recipients of 1 Peter, who were probably known to outsiders as a type of Jewish association, to be labelled in the aftermath of the Jewish War as messianists (*Christianoi*) could be very difficult and provoke harassment, loss of civic standing, suffering, and even pogroms and lynchings.

Second: It is not clear whether the recipients, like Peter, are Jews with a messianic bent – '*Christianoi*', as they are labelled by outsiders – or whether they are Gentile converts. The first interpretation is suggested by the rich Jewish language of the document and was prevalent until around the beginning of the nineteenth century, whereas the second is held by most modern exegetes. 1 Peter's inscribed symbolic universe – expressed and modulated in the language of the Hellenistic Jewish Bible, the LXX – is that of Israel.

The letter's language is saturated with scriptural allusions, quotations and images. The language of 1 Peter remains theocentric. The title '*kurios*' fluctuates between G*d and Christ, whose vindication, resurrection and glorification exhibit G*d's ultimate power for salvation/well-being. G*d is the Father who has chosen them and whose mercy has given them a new birth and 'living hope'. G*d is called the faithful creator and impartial judge of all people who brings the ages to a close. G*d is the one who calls and whose will and 'living word' have saving power. Jesus has been manifested by G*d as the Christ, the Messiah and inaugurator of the end of the ages, who through his innocent suffering and through his resurrection 'has gone into heaven and is at the right hand of G*d with angels, authorities, and powers made subject to him' (3.22, NRSV). This theocentricity of 1 Peter's symbolic divine universe is completely expressed in the language and conceptuality of Israel. Jesus is understood as the Messiah who inaugurates the end of the ages and who functions as mediator of G*d's saving plan and actions.

Although a plethora of metaphors and titles portray the recipients in terms of the covenant people of Israel, the letter neither mentions Israel directly nor does it describe the 'Christian' community as the 'new Israel'. Israel is not yet seen as the 'other' of the community but as its constitutive identity. This is programmatically expressed, for instance, in 1.15-16: 'As the One who called you is holy, even you yourself must become holy in every respect of your lives, because Scripture says, "You shall be holy because I am holy" '. Those who have been born anew are elect and holy, which according to Lev. 29.26 means that they are set apart from all other peoples.

This Jewish self-identity of the 'brotherhood' comes especially to the fore in 2.4-10, which uses a plethora of traditional images to characterize the elect and holy ones as the covenant people of G*d (Exod. 19.6). This section is steeped in the language of the Scriptures and the traditions of Israel and Judaism. It not only echoes themes which have been already introduced previously but also integrates older traditions which are similar to those found in Qumran, rabbinic Judaism and the Pauline Letters.

The following images characterize the dignity and lofty status of the recipients in terms of the traditional attributes of Israel: They are 'living stones', being built into a temple of the Spirit or spiritual house (2.5). They are a 'holy and royal priesthood, a chosen race, a holy nation, G*d's very own people', who have been summoned to tell forth the great deeds of the one who has called them from darkness to light (2.9), an image that could allude to conversion. They, who were once a non-people, are now the people of G*d, who have been graced with mercy (2.10).

However, despite their recognition of the Jewish provenance of the recipients, the abundant scriptural language of Israel, and the theocentricity of the letter, exegetes maintain that the letter is written to Gentile Christians and that the author has appropriated the language and elect status of Israel for the audience. Rather than considering that the community could have still understood itself as a Jewish messianic community living in the diaspora and whose self-identity was determined by the large number of converts in their midst, commentators insist on reading the letter in a colonialist supersessionist way that assumes that it is Christianity and not Judaism that has inherited G*d's promises to the covenant people Israel.

Inscribed Argument, Socio-Symbolic World and Rhetorical Situation

In order to deepen this analysis by tracing the power relations inscribed in the text, I will now first critically discuss the inscribed overall argument in order to further explore the rhetorical situation and symbolic universe of 1 Peter that encompass the entire socio-religious order, consisting of both the inscribed socio-political and the cultural–religious 'worlds'. These two 'worlds' are contiguous and should not be seen as exclusive of each other. For instance, as we have seen, the characterization of the recipients as *paroikoi* can be understood in political–legal terms as non-citizens or as expressing their religious identity as belonging to another world and as being aliens in this world. Because words are not univocal but multivalent, which meaning is intended can only be decided with reference to an overall interpretive framework and method. Hence, whether one pursues, for instance, a social-scientific method or engages in a theological reading will determine one's excgcsis of the overall rhetoric of the letter. Hence, it is important to look in a second step at the rhetorical strategies that are valorized by commentators and constitute their overall rhetorical interpretation of 1 Peter.

First: The arguments of the letter are fashioned in traditional Jewish theological language in terms of authority (pseudepigraphy, references to Scripture [LXX]), analogy (Christ's suffering), example (Sarah), comparison (like newborn babes) and vivid apocalyptic imagery (fiery ordeal, adversary as roaring lion). The overarching image of the letter is that of the 'election' and 'chosenness' of those belonging to the 'brotherhood'. This image is elaborated in three strings of argument clusters (*argumentatio*) pertaining to the notion of 'good citizenship'.

The first *argumentatio* describes in the language of Scripture the recipients' 'high' status as the people of G*d, 'house (*oikos*) of the Spirit' and 'royal priesthood' (1.15–2.10). The second *argumentatio* spells out the 'good' behaviour demanded especially from the subordinate members of the household (*oikos*). It utilizes the socio-political form of the colonial *oikos*-discourse, which is usually called by exegetes 'Household codes'. This *argumentatio*, however, does not begin by addressing behaviour in the household but by prescribing behaviour toward the authorities of the empire. Thus, the *oikos*-discourse is clearly intertwined with the imperial discourse and forms the central part of the overall letter. It is not just a paraenetic strategy among many (2.11–3.12) but is at the heart of 1 Peter's rhetoric. The third *argumentatio* speaks about the necessity of suffering (*pathēmata*) and explains what 'doing good' means for the 'stewards' (*oikonomoi*) of G*d's manifold grace, who are publicly put down, harassed and defamed as Christians, that is, as *messianists* (3.13–4.11).

These three argumentative moves are summed up and amplified in 4.12–5.11 (*peroratio*), which continues to tell the readers to expect difficulties as 'Christians' and to undergo 'honourable suffering' because the end is in view. The 'fiery ordeal' is upon them and 'the time has come for judgment to begin with the household (*oikos*) of G*d' (4.12-19). These admonitions are followed by an address to elder and younger members of the community which spells out the right order of the household of God and is reinforced with the vivid description of the adversary, the disorder-creating *diabolos*, who is compared to a roaring lion seeking to devour everyone (5.1-9). The whole summation ends with a doxology to 'the G*d of all grace', who has called the addressees to 'eternal glory in Christ' and will 'restore, support and strengthen' them in their troubles (5.10-11).

Thus, the argument of 1 Peter moves from an elaboration of the theoretically high but socio-politically precarious status of the recipients to the central part of the letter, addressing the problem as to how to behave in a politically correct manner (doing good) with regard to the imperial–colonial authorities, especially if one is a subordinate member of the *oikos*. The rhetorical strategy then shifts to a more general argument addressing all the intended recipients about 'good' behaviour in public and the 'honourable sufferings' to be expected. Finally, it climaxes with admonitions regarding the exercise of leadership in the 'household (*oikos*) of G*d'. In short, central to the rhetoric of the letter is the image of the household – *oikos*. Its inscribed argument engages the hegemonic socio-political and cultural discourses about household management (*peri oiko-nomias*) and about politics (*peri politeias*) which were intertwined in Graeco-Roman political theory.

Second: The inscribed lofty titles of ancient Israel as the elect people of G*d and the exalted rhetoric and self-understanding of those living in the diaspora contrast greatly with the inscribed situation of their harassment and suffering. This contradiction indicates the rhetorical situation and problem the author seeks to address. As a rhetorical text, 1 Peter, like other rhetorical communications, is engendered by a rhetorical situation to which the letter must be at least a partially 'fitting' response, if it is to be effective.

Moreover, as a particular discourse, 1 Peter, like any other rhetorical discourse, is engendered by a specific situation and an exigence that invites utterance. However, only when rhetoric endows certain events and circumstances with meaning do they become salient as a rhetorical situation. Discourses may describe particular occurrences, but they actually give us more information about the strategies of the speaker/author than about the actual situation. Nevertheless, the inscribed rhetorical situation must have some commonality with the actual situation of the audience, if the author's arguments are to have persuasive power. Hence, it is important to investigate how malestream exegetes define the rhetorical situation and strategy of the author and to ask whether the 'meta-ideologizing' of some of the major contemporary interpretations of 1 Peter strengthens the colonizing rhetoric of the text both by privileging its kyriarchal elements and by reading its egalitarian decolonizing dissident consciousness in terms of a hegemonic kyriarchal consciousness that 'naturalizes' kyriarchal power relations as 'G*d's will'.

The rhetoric of the author(s) characterizes and constructs the rhetorical situation in terms of three rhetorical strategies that are valorized differently by different interpreters: the strategy of suffering, the strategy of election and honour and the strategy of subordination. These rhetorical strategies are not discrete parallel topical areas but work together dialectically to construct the rhetorical situation to which the letter can be understood as a 'fitting' response. The differences in the interpretation of the letter and its function result from the fact that exegetes tend to centralize one strategy and privilege it over the others.

Strategy of Suffering. Exegetes are almost universally agreed that the problem confronted by the rhetoric of 1 Peter is that of suffering. In addition, virtually all recent interpreters agree that 1 Peter does not refer to an empire-wide persecution of Christians but rather describes the situation of the recipients as harassment, social ostracism and slander of Christians on the local level. There is also agreement that the recipients are threatened with suffering because they are Christians.

A close reading of the letter's rhetoric can show that the opening and the conclusion of the letter refer in an almost formulaic way to the suffering of Christ and the Christians. In effect: 1.10 refers to the sufferings and subsequent glory of Christ; 5.1 calls Peter a 'witness to the sufferings of Christ'; 1.6 stresses that the recipients can rejoice in their imperishable eschatological inheritance, even if now 'for a little while' they have had 'to suffer various trials, so that the genuineness of their (your) faith … is tested by fire'; and 5.9 refers to their knowledge that 'the brotherhood in the whole world is experiencing the same kind of suffering'.

Within the letter one can isolate three clusters of 'suffering' that refer to Christ's suffering as paradigmatic for the recipients of the letter. In 2.18-25 the house slaves who suffer unjustly (v. 19) are referred to Christ's example of suffering but not to his resurrection and glorification. The section 3.13-22 begins with a rhetorical question: 'Who will harm you if you are eager to do what is good?' It tells the recipients not to be intimidated, to keep a good conscience 'so that those who abuse you for your good conduct as Christians (in Christ) may be put to shame', and then in vv. 18-22 speaks of Christ's suffering (see also 4.1), resurrection, vindication and exaltation. The section 4.12-19 refers to the 'fiery ordeal' and tells the audience to rejoice because they will be blessed when his glory is revealed if they now share in Christ's suffering. If they suffer in the name of Christ, the Spirit of G*d is upon them. To suffer as a Christian (a messianist) should not be considered a disgrace. The section ends with the statement that the judgment of G*d begins with the household of G*d, asks what will become of those who are ungodly and sinners and then concludes: 'Therefore, let those who suffer according to G*d's will entrust themselves to a faithful creator while continuing to do good'. Suffering and 'doing good', suffering and being called a 'Christian', that is, a messianist, are intrinsically and eschatologically intertwined, just as they are in the example of Christ, the Messiah Jesus.

While I have foregrounded the political understanding of *'Christianoi* = messianists', most scholars do not recognize this political aspect. Hence, they overlook that the author does not present the suffering of the *Christianoi* as an anti-colonial strategy of resistance but rather moralizes it. In addition, it is generally overlooked that in the paraenesis to the slaves the reference to Christ's resurrection and glory is missing, a theological accent that was determinative for the self-understanding of early Christians, who understood themselves as a new creation and *politeuma* because of the resurrection. Finally, insofar as scholars tend to naturalize and historicize the rhetoric of suffering as factual rather than to see it as a rhetorical emphasis of the author(s), they are not able to engage in a decolonizing interpretation of the letter.

The Strategy of Election and Honour. The author's rhetoric of honour, praise and glory, on the one hand, and of slander, shame and disgrace, on the other, has engendered several books and numerous articles that offer a reading of 1 Peter in terms of the anthropological theory of Mediterranean culture. For instance, Barth L. Campbell has analysed the rhetoric of honour and shame and its function in the overall rhetoric of the letter, which, according to him (1998: 106), is summed up in 2.12: 'Conduct yourselves honourably among the Gentiles, so that though they malign you as evildoers, they may see your honourable deeds, and glorify G*d when he comes to judge' (NRSV). While Elliott previously reconstructed the meaning of the letter in terms of sectarian cohesiveness, more recently he has read the 'gospel according to Peter' in the key of honour and shame.

According to this anthropological theory, ancient Mediterranean culture has been structured by the binary dualism of honour and shame. Such an interpretive grid, however, is constructed in kyriocentric terms whereby maleness is associated with honour and femaleness with shame. Moreover, as developed in early Christian studies, this dualistic theory of cultural anthropology has been intertwined with the dualistic assumption of antiquarian historical studies, which insist that the past is totally different from the present. In the biblical studies version of the cultural theory of honour and shame, the present is then represented by modern American culture.

The Mediterranean cultures of antiquity are said to have been group cultures, in which males embody the honour of the group while females embody the family's shame; they are also represented as conflictual in nature, hierarchical and oriented toward status, honour, praise and recognition. Modern American culture, in turn, is construed as an individualistic 'guilt' culture, which, because it is egalitarian, democratic and non-hierarchical, is labelled an equal-opportunity culture. Thereby biblical antiquity is either 'orientalized' and reified as the totally 'other' of modern American culture, or it is romanticized especially by the political Right as the time when the world was still in order, the family was patriarchal and society honoured the ancestral kyriarchal customs and social hierarchies.

Reading 1 Peter with the lens of the honour–shame construct, Elliott understands the attack on Christians as a 'classic example of public shaming designed to demean and discredit the believers in the court of public opinion with the ultimate aim of forcing their conformity to prevailing norms and values' (1994: 170). In response, 'Peter' does not recommend to 'return insult with insult' but rather turns social disgrace into grace by calling for engagement in honourable conduct. The cultural ethos of honour–shame is 'Christianized' and 'theologically rationalized': the essential criterion for honourable conduct is no longer public opinion but the 'will of G*d'. Christ becomes the chief paradigm for and facilitator of such honourable conduct. Honourable conduct has a 'missionary' effect, especially in the case of wives and the whole community, insofar as it persuades the Gentiles to cease their shaming of Christians and instead to give honour to G*d. Finally, suffering itself is understood in a positive light: it is a divine test that, if passed, leads to eschatological honour and glory.

Steven Richard Bechtler (1998) has focused on suffering, community and Christology in 1 Peter in terms of the honour–shame culture in which the letter was written and concluded that the problem of suffering in 1 Peter is the threat to the honour of the community. According to him, the addressees of 1 Peter were attacked, verbally abused and accused of wrongdoing because of their conversion. Such attacks and harassment constituted a threat to their honour and posed a serious problem for their self-identity in a society in which 'one's place was determined by one's socially conferred honour' (Bechtler 1998: 207). Hence, the letter sought to provide a legitimation of their symbolic universe that is able to satisfactorily address the problem of their suffering and social disgrace. The letter accomplished this by constituting the Christian community as an alternative social entity and symbolic universe in which honour is differently understood and allocated.

G*d is the ultimate source of honour and not society. Just as G*d has restored Christ's honour, who has suffered disgrace, so G*d will bestow in the very near future honour on Christ's followers and does so now through the Spirit. According to this theological rhetorical universe, the slanderous accusations of their opponents will result in a loss of honour not for the Christians but for those who dishonour them now. Although Bechtler realizes (1998: 97) that 'most of what has been said ... concerning honor and shame in Mediterranean societies actually applies predominantly to adult males', he does not ask whether, by interpreting 1 Peter in the key of honour–shame, scholars at one and the same time 'masculinize' or better 'kyriarchalize' – since the honour and shame of elite propertied males is at stake – the symbolic universe inscribed in the letter.

The Rhetoric of Subordination or of Being 'Subjects'. The injunction to subordination is used five times in 1 Peter. Four times it addresses a group of people: everyone in 2.13, household slaves in 2.18, wives in 3.1 and younger people or neophytes in 5.1. Only once is it used in a descriptive praise statement, in 3.22, which says that angels, authorities and powers were made subject to Jesus Christ, who 'has gone into heaven and is at the right hand of G*d'. This last statement makes it clear that *hupotassein* expresses a relation of ruling and power. Apocalyptic language and universe meta-mythologizes the kyriarchal order of the empire. Jesus Christ is Lord (*Kurios*), who is the 'right hand' of G*d, the Almighty. However, whereas later times understand church ministry in analogy to Christ's power of ruling, 1 Peter admonishes the elders of the community not to lord it over (*katakurieuontes*) those in their charge.

In a classical-rhetorical analysis the section 2.11–3.12 'emerges as the core of the letter' (Campbell 1998: 231) and could be titled, 'Become Colonial

Subjects/Subalterns'. Since subaltern behaviour of household slaves and wives towards the imperial authorities is the *topos* of the central *argumentatio*, it has been pointed out that the author(s) first combines and advocates here the imperial ethos spelled out in the discourses *peri politeias* (2.13) and *peri oikonomias* (2.18–3.7), then grounds it with reference to the example of the suffering Christ and the matriarch Sarah, and finally moralizes such colonial submission as righteousness and as 'doing good' (3.8-12).

The whole section is introduced with an appeal to 'honourable conduct' addressed to the 'non-citizens and transients' who are hailed as 'beloved' (*agapētoi*). At this point, it becomes obvious that the sender theologizes and moralizes the dominant kyriarchal ethos of Roman imperialism and requests that the subordinates realize and live it in their practices of subordination. The *ratio* and motivation given is missionary: they should conduct themselves 'honourably' so that the Gentiles glorify G*d on the day of 'visitation' (*episcopēs*).

The summons to abstain from human desires (*sarkikōn epithumiōn*) that endanger their lives (*psuchē*) is elaborated and elucidated in vv. 13-17 with the admonition to subject themselves to the emperor as the supreme one and to the governors who are sent by him, that is, to the imperial administration so that these recognize them as doing what is right, honourable or good. The theological justification given here is that such submission understood as 'doing the honourable' is 'the will of G*d'. Here, the elite masculine ethos of 'honourableness' has become 'Christianized'. The overall rhetorical strategy of the letter is summed up in 2.17: 'Honour everyone, love the "brotherhood", fear G*d, honour the emperor!'

Unlike in 2.13, the injunction to the slaves is not stated in an imperatival but in a circumstantial participle grammatical form, which is also used in 3.1, 7, 9 and which indicates that the whole continues the imperatives of 2.11, 13. The 'doing good' of slave wo/men consists in their subjecting themselves even to harsh and unjust masters, so that if unjustly beaten and suffering – if that is G*d's will – they do so for 'doing right'. Christ's innocent suffering is then elaborated as an example for such honourable behaviour in suffering. However, it is rarely noticed that here no reference to Christ's resurrection and glory is made. In a similar fashion freeborn wo/men are told to subject themselves to their husbands, even to those who are not believers. The goal here is the conversion of the husbands, which will be brought about not by their 'preaching' to them but by their proper 'lady-like' conduct of purity and subordination, which is exemplified by the matriarch Sarah, the prime example for female converts to Judaism.

Finally, the 'brotherhood' is not only to be governed by mutual love and support but also by subordination. In 5.5 the 'younger' members of the 'brotherhood', who are either younger in age or [new/recent?] converts, are told to subject themselves to the older, the presbyters. Although the presbyters are admonished at the same time not to exercise kyriarchal leadership, this injunction still indicates that the inscribed argument seeks to fashion the order of the community as one of subordination.

In sum, the Roman colonial cultural rhetoric of subjection advocates the submission of the subaltern migrants and non-citizens in Asia Minor and specifies as problem cases the unjust suffering of household slave women and the marriage relationship between Christian women and Gentile men. Contemporary exegetes are generally embarrassed by this rhetoric of subjection, which has been indicted by feminist biblical studies. Hence, they seek to eliminate or mitigate the problem for modern hearers/readers by translating *hupotassein* with 'accept the authority', 'defer to', 'show respect for', 'recognize the proper social order' or to ' "participate in", "be involved with", "be committed to" ' (Senior 1980: 43–57). Although such an apologetic translation is primarily concerned with 'wo/men' and 'liberal' readers/hearers, at the same time it conceals the elite male character of *hupotassein* and its colonizing function, which in 1 Peter has become 'theologized'.

Reconstructing the Arguments of the Subordinates

Conceptualizing a possible historical resistant consciousness and the argumentative strategies of slave, freeborn and Jewish-Christians or Christian-Jews, that is, messianists, requires a reading of 1 Peter 'against the grain' of its kyriarchal argumentative strategies. Such an interpretation 'against the grain' corresponds to the strategy of 'meta-ideologizing' in Sandoval's 'methodology of the oppressed' or to that of 'telling the story differently'. If, as the classical-rhetorical analysis of Campbell has shown, the centre of 1 Peter's argument is the discourse of *hupotassein*, that is, subjection or subordination, then a critical emancipatory interpretation must, first of all, attempt, again in Nelle Morton's words, to 'hear into speech' the submerged arguments of those whom the subordination discourse seeks to subject. However, such a critical feminist approach, which focuses on the submerged knowledges inscribed in the letter, runs counter to malestream exegesis, which insists on valorizing the hegemonic rhetoric of the author.

First: Because of feminist work, most recent scholarship on 1 Peter is aware of the problematic ethical–political meaning and socio-historical effects in contemporary society and church of 1 Peter's subordination discourse. Commentators tend to focus less on the hermeneutical problem posed by the Jewish language of the letter, the injunction to political subjection, or the use of the example of Christ to pacify suffering slaves, than on the demand for the subordination of wo/men. In response to feminist interpretation, exegetes feel compelled to write a special hermeneutical excursus (Elliott 2000) or to articulate special hermeneutical rules for reading these texts today (Boring 1999).

The rhetoric of how these texts *must* be read is instructive. Over and against those who critically deconstruct the rhetoric of 1 Peter, scholars insist that 'we *must* explore the Bible in its cultural context with an openness to the way that the good news of the past may continue to animate the good news in the present' (Elliott 2000: 599; emphasis added). What is at stake in this scholarly rhetoric is the legitimization of kyriarchal relations of domination as 'good news'.

To illustrate my point: in a blistering attack on my interpretation of 1 Peter in *In Memory of Her* (1983), John Elliott acknowledges that I have 'proposed a markedly different reading of 1 Peter' from that which he advocates in his commentary (2000: 596). However, such a contrasting of our two readings of 1 Peter is rather unequal, since Elliott's tome is 956 pages whereas I have written barely 5 pages on 1 Peter, which, in addition, are part of an overall discussion of the early Christian missionary movement and of the household code discourse in the post-Pauline literature. Most telling, however, is that his emotional rhetoric feels compelled to misconstrue my argument for interpreting the letter from the perspective of those against whom the inscribed writer argues.

Elliott introduces my argument with the claim that it is made on 'the basis of a *fanciful* reconstruction of the Jesus movement' in which I supposedly imagine that '*Jesus overthrew the patriarchal structures* of his society' and inaugurated '*a golden egalitarian age*' (2000: 596, emphasis added). This, he continues, is a '*fantastic premise which, it must be said, lacks any support whatsoever* in the social data (as even acknowledged by other feminists [e.g., Heine])' (2000: 596, emphasis added). Elliott alleges that this 'fanciful' reconstruction determines my interpretation without acknowledging that it is his reading that produces this 'fantastic premise'. Quoting out of context, he misrepresents my interpretation of the letter when he claims that the relapse of 1 Peter into patriarchal thinking was in my opinion prompted by a concern 'to avoid persecution and suffering and to "lessen tensions" between the Christian community and its neighbours' (2000: 597). Using 'relapse into patriarchy' as a criterion, I supposedly then judge all later positions on wo/men in the New Testament in terms of such an erroneous standard.

Elliott then goes on to claim that I '*completely misconstru[e]* the aim of the letter', which, according to him, is 'to affirm the holiness and distinctiveness' of the community and 'to urge holy nonconformity with Gentile modes of thought and life' (2000: 597, emphasis added). At this point, Elliott seems to have forgotten that he himself has argued that it was the author and not the community who 'transposed' the cultural honour–shame discourse into 'a theological key'. By collapsing author and recipients into one he overlooks that a rhetorical process requires at least two voices.

The reason for his 'put-down' of my position appears to be a rhetorical struggle for the allegiance of wo/men readers as the following statement indicates: 'This *sadly erroneous and arbitrary* interpretation of 1 Peter *must be mentioned* not simply because it is an *egregious example of ideologically driven exegesis* but because this study, which on the whole has much positive to commend it, *has had pronounced influence on subsequent feminist commentary* on 1 Peter, leading to a *misreading and undeserved depreciation* of this pastoral letter in general' (2000: 597, emphasis added).

If I single out for discussion Elliott's emotion-laden remarks as an example of anti-feminist rhetoric, I do so not in order to defend my own interpretation of 1 Peter as the only correct one. Rather, I discuss Elliott's attack as an example of how the kyriarchal, elite male discourse of honour and shame is at work not only in the rhetoric of 1 Peter but also in contemporary scholarship when it is confronted with dissident methodological voices. Since according to the construct of the Mediterranean honour code 'shame' is 'feminine' and 'honour' 'masculine', it is important to observe how such masculine 'shaming' works today in defence of its academic status and honour in order to understand its silencing function in the past. Such a historical analogy allows one to see what is at stake in the exclusive focus on the author's rhetoric: his attempt to transpose the hegemonic cultural ethos of submission into a 'theological key' rationalizes it as 'G*d's will' and divine revelation.

Whether one assumes an identity or constructs differences and tensions between the recipients' and the sender's rhetoric decisively determines one's overall interpretation of the letter. For instance, when commentators see a seamless unity between the first and the second and third chains of rhetorical arguments, then they understand the first section to function as a *captatio benevolentiae* that seeks to secure the good will of the recipients to do what the author tells them. Because in and through their conversion they have been given the titles and prerogatives of the people of Israel, the recipients should now, as G*d's people who live in the midst of Gentiles, behave like Christ who suffered innocently, 'do good' rather than commit criminal acts, and love the 'brotherhood' as much as possible, because this is the 'will of G*d'. In short, what draws Elliott's ire is my insistence that the strategy of the author is kyriarchal insofar as it theologically rationalizes the ethos of subjection over and against the different ethos subscribed to by some of the recipients, for example, 'messianists', wives and slave wo/men. It is the focus on this 'different ethos' of the recipients that is at issue in the contest between a critical feminist emancipatory and malestream colonizing interpretation of 1 Peter.

Commentators agree that the context of the letter is one in which Jews and the '*Christianoi*' were seen as seditious and as a threat to the colonial religious, cultural and political Roman imperial 'customs'. The conversion of slave wo/men, freeborn ladies and younger people in which the master of the house did not convert already constituted an offence against the 'ancestral' laws and customs, according to which the *paterfamilias* – like the emperor who was called the supreme father of the empire (*pater patriae*) – had absolute power over his subordinates in the household and determined the religion of its members. Hence, it was generally accepted as a matter of good civil order that slave wo/men, freeborn wo/men and all other members of the household practised the religion of the master and lord of the house.

Since, according to recent malestream commentary, the letter-writer is concerned with 'honour', construes the 'house of G*d' not as temple but as 'household', and advocates submission and the hegemonic ethos of 'doing good' so that the recipients will not be attacked as wrong-doers, he advocates *limited accommodation* to the kyriarchal order of the house and state for missionary purposes, as long as it does not interfere with their 'Christian' calling. One could argue that the author understands the function of 'Christian' calling as preserving messianic self-identity and praxis. However, such an interpretation does not square with his rhetoric of submission to the authorities and institutions of the empire.

If one sees a tension or conflict between the first, second and third strings of arguments, then the ethos of the holy people of G*d stands in tension with the ethos of submission and the socio-cultural hegemonic ethos of 'honour and shame'. This approach sees this tension as provoking a 'rhetorical debate' in the community about what the 'will of G*d' demands. Slave wo/men, for instance, could have argued that it was 'G*d's will' to be treated justly as members of G*d's elect people rather than to suffer patiently the sexual abuse and cross mistreatment at the hands of their masters. Hence, it was justified to run away, if their masters treated them harshly. Freeborn well-to-do wives could have argued that it was their Christian calling to proclaim the 'good news' to their Gentile husbands. If they could not convert them to the lifestyle of the elect people of G*d, it was the 'will of G*d' to separate from them by divorcing them. They could have bolstered their argument with reference to Paul, who supported the 'marriage–free' state of wo/men.

All of the members of the community could have argued that the covenant of G*d demanded that they separate from Gentile society and resist Roman imperial culture, because their 'low class' status as non-citizens and migrants had been changed in and through their conversion. They, now bound together in love and respect, formed a royal priesthood and holy nation, a temple of the Spirit. In consequence, they could not possibly pay obeisance to the emperor, his governors and other cultural institutional authorities. Thus, they advocated a separatist stance which would not totally avoid but maybe reduce harassment and suffering, since they would not have to mix daily with their Gentile neighbours.

This alternative separatist strategy is made possible by a consciousness different from that of the colonial society and culture of Asia Minor. As I have suggested in *In Memory of Her*, such a consciousness, which might have been shared by the recipients of 1 Peter, comes to the fore in a pre-Pauline Jewish (Christian) fragment preserved in 2 Corinthians 6.14–7.1:

> Do not get misyoked (or mismatched) with unbelievers!
> For what partnership have righteousness and lawlessness
> Or what community has light with darkness?
> Or what common lot a believer with an unbeliever?

What agreement is there between G*d's temple and idols?
For we are the temple of the living G*d; as G*d has said:
'I will dwell in them and walk among them;
And I will be their G*d
And they shall be my people.
Therefore come out of their midst and separate
Says the *Kurios*.
And touch nothing unclean.
Then I will receive you,
And I will be a father to you,
And you shall be my sons and daughters,
Says the *Kurios* who holds all power'.
Since we have these promises, beloved,
Let us cleanse ourselves from every defilement of the flesh and spirit
Making holiness perfect in the fear of G*d.

The affinities between this text and 1 Peter are striking. In 1 Peter the self-understanding of the 'siblinghood' that was once a non-people is expressed with traditional language and images: spiritual house or temple, priests offering spiritual sacrifices, elect, holy, 'defilement of the flesh', 'fear of G*d'. Those who were once a non-people are called in political–cultic language 'a chosen race, a royal priesthood, a holy nation, the people of G*d who proclaim the saving deeds and mighty power of G*d' (2.9). They are a 'brotherhood' who have G*d as their father; they are beloved, called from darkness into light. Therefore, they might have believed that they were to separate from the Gentiles, practise *kashruth*, trust in G*d's promises, form a different society from that of the Gentiles, and live a sanctified life as 'non-citizens' and 'transients', in hope of experiencing soon the messianic day of liberation and glory.

If one does not, with the LXX, translate the first imperative of the pre-Pauline text transmitted in 2 Corinthians as mismatch or cross-breeding but with 'mis-yoke' or with 'unevenly yoke together', the anti-colonial political overtones of such an oppositional theological consciousness come to the fore. Since the metaphor of the yoke usually refers to burdens imposed by foreign oppressors (Isa. 9.4; 10.27; 14.25; Jer. 27.8, 11,12; Gen. 27.40; 1 Kgs 12.4), the community might have understood itself in opposition to Roman imperial rule. The most striking adaptation of scriptural texts is the alteration of the promise given to King David in 2 Sam. 7.14: 'I will be a father to him and he shall be a son to me'. G*d's promise of 'sonship' is here changed to include the 'sons and daughters'. The daughters as well as the sons are members of G*d's elect people and royal priesthood.

Scholars have argued that this oppositional consciousness expressed here in the language of Scripture cannot be of Jewish provenance. However, nothing speaks against a Jewish (Christian) origin of this pre-Pauline tradition that seems to inform the theological universe of the recipients of 1 Peter. It seems to fit well into the theology of the (Hellenistic) Jewish (Christian) missionary movement, which conceived of itself as a new creation through Christ's resurrection, as the eschatological people gifted with the presence of divine Wisdom. Both the daughters and sons, both the young and old, both the male and female slaves, are graced with the gifts of the Spirit and have received prophetic endowment (cf. Acts 2.17-18). They are children of G*d, the holy people, the temple-community among whom the Spirit dwells.

In sum, the recipients share with the sender(s) of 1 Peter a common social situation, Roman colonialism, and a common theological universe and consciousness consisting of an 'elevated' religious self-understanding. However, they seem to have disagreed with each other on how to relate this elevated communal self-understanding to their colonial social–political situation. Hence, the author advises 'limited adaptation' in a difficult situation of harassment and suffering, insofar as he counsels opposition only in religious but not in socio-political terms. Some of the recipients, in turn, seem to have affirmed both their status as non-citizens and transients under Roman colonialism and as the elect people of G*d in the diaspora but might have advocated separation from their dominant culture and society.

Withdrawal from oppressive societal structures whenever possible, they might have argued, would reduce conflict and suffering, because it would minimize contact with unbelievers. Slave wo/men seem to have practised this communal ethos of separation by running away from unjust masters and mistresses, whereas freeborn married wo/men may have left their Gentile husbands if they could not convert them. Both actions would have caused problems with the wider society and with the 'master/patron class' within the community itself. If the whole community consisted primarily of proselytes who were now a part of the Jewish messianic opposition against Roman cultural and religious colonialism, they would have been suspected as *Christianoi*, that is, revolutionary messianists undermining the dominant society.

This situation of suspicion would have been aggravated if they continued to honour in their midst as members runaway slave wo/men or divorced wives. Hence, the recipients might have been interested on religious and socio-political grounds to reduce contact with Gentile neighbours as much as possible. This seems to have been the concrete rhetorical problem and situation which the author(s) of 1 Peter sought to overcome by transposing the dominant cultural rhetoric of 'honour and shame', subjection and domination, into a theological key.

Hence, it is likely that the rhetoric of 1 Peter, which demands the subjection of slave wo/men and freeborn wo/men, of the younger and all members of the community to the kyriarchal authorities of colonial Roman society, expresses the interests of the 'owner and patron class' in the Christian community, who felt that their prerogatives were undermined – an interpretive suggestion made by E. A. Judge some time ago. Sent from the metropolis by Jewish colonials living in the heart of the Roman Empire, 1 Peter advocates these interests over and against an alternative separatist strategy that seeks to protect the counter-kyriarchal practices of those doubly marginalized and jeopardized by the hegemonic colonial ethos.

In contrast to a colonializing interpretation of 1 Peter that reinscribes the kyriarchal values of the empire and legitimizes its kyriarchal practices Christologically, a critical feminist decolonizing analysis of the letter deconstructs such a colonialist imperial ethos and revalorizes the emancipatory values and visions that are also inscribed in the letter's rhetoric. It does so in order to open up the understanding of the letter in terms of the radical democratic equality of the people of G*d.

BIBLIOGRAPHY

Achtemeier, Paul J.
   1996   *1 Peter. A Commentary* (Hermeneia; Minneapolis: Fortress Press).
Applegate, Judith
   1992   'The Co-Elect Woman of 1 Peter', in *New Testament Studies* 38: 587–604.
Balch, David L.
   1981   *Let Wives Be Submissive. The Domestic Code in 1 Peter* (Society of Biblical Literature Monograph Series, 26; Chico, CA: Scholars Press).
Bechtler, Steven Richard
   1998   *Following in His Steps. Suffering Community and Christology in 1 Peter* (Society of Biblical Literature Dissertation Series, 162; Atlanta: Scholars Press).
Boring, M. Eugene
   1999   *1 Peter* (Abingdon New Testament Commentaries; Nashville: Abingdon Press).
Campbell, Barth L.
   1998   *Honor, Shame, and the Rhetoric of 1 Peter* (Society of Biblical Literature Dissertation Series, 160; Atlanta: Scholars Press).
Donaldson, Laura E. and Kwok Pui-lan (eds)
   2002   *Postcolonialism, Feminism, and Religious Discourse* (New York: Routledge).
Dube Shomanah, Musa W.
   2000   *Postcolonial Feminist Interpretation of the Bible* (St. Louis: Chalice Press).
Elliott, John H.
   1981   *A Home for the Homeless. A Sociological Exegesis of 1 Peter. Its Situation and Strategy* (Philadelphia: Fortress Press).
   1994   'Disgraced Yet Graced. The Gospel according to 1 Peter in the Key of Honor and Shame', *Biblical Theology Bulletin* 24: 166–78.
   2000   *1 Peter: A New Translation with Introduction and Commentary* (Anchor Bible; New York: Doubleday).
Hill Collins, Patricia
   1990   *Black Feminist Thought: Knowledge, Consciousness, and the Politics of Empowerment* (Boston: Unwin Hyman, 1990).
Morton, Nelle
   1985   *The Journey is Home* (Boston: Beacon Press).

Price, S. R. F.
  1984   *Rituals and Power: The Roman Imperial Cult in Asia Minor* (Cambridge: Cambridge University Press).

Prostmeier, Ferdinand-Rupert
  1990   *Handlungsmodelle im 1. Petrusbrief* (Forschungen zur Bibel, 63; Würzburg: Echter Verlag).

Sandoval, Chela
  2000   *Methodology of the Oppressed* (Theory out of Bounds, 18: Minneapolis: University of Minnesota Press).

Schüssler Fiorenza, Elisabeth
  1983   *In Memory of Her: A Feminist Theological Reconstruction of Christians Origins* (New York: Crossroad).
  1999   *Rhetoric and Ethic: The Politics of Biblical Studies* (Minneapolis: Fortress Press).
  2007   *The Power of the Word: Scripture and the Rhetoric of Empire* (Minneapolis: Fortress Press).

Said, Edward W.
  1983   *The World, the Text, and the Critic* (Cambridge: Harvard University Press).

Segovia, Fernando F.
  2000   *Decolonizing Biblical Studies: A View From the Margins* (Maryknoll, NY: Orbis Books).

Senior, Donald, P.
  1980   *1 & 2 Peter* (New Testament Message; Wilmington, DE: Michael Glazier).

Sugirtharajah, R. S.
  1998   *The Postcolonial Bible* (Bible and Postcolonialism, 1; Sheffield: Sheffield Academic Press).

The Second Letter of Peter

Cynthia Briggs Kittredge

In writing a 'postcolonial' commentary an interpreter enters into the ironic situation of making an authoritative commentary upon a text while using a perspective that critiques the idea of disembodied 'authority'. In a form that has traditionally claimed objectivity and universal applicability, the commentator reads the text from an explicitly particular perspective with specific questions related to her or his own social, historical and theological context. (In her commentary on Romans, Elizabeth Castelli reflects on the feminist critique of the classic understanding of commentary [1994: 274].) Because she has been shaped by and formed in debate and critique of that tradition, the commentator is both 'in and not of the tradition'. Postcolonial perspectives are by definition diverse, and each one is particular and grounded in a particular context.

I comment upon 2 Peter as a feminist New Testament scholar, trained in Western methods of biblical criticism and challenged by the questions brought to texts by postcolonial critics. I am engaged with the text because, as a member of a Christian community, such a text possesses, by virtue of its canonical status, its reading in public worship, and centuries of interpretation, special status and authority. Despite the brevity of the letter and the lack of focused attention on it on the part of many churches, its specific theological claims and its position within the New Testament canon have distinctively shaped the way Christians see their early history, understand the special character of Scripture and define themselves with respect to those with whom they disagree. From this perspective, I will explore in this commentary the interrelated theological problems of religious authority and leadership within early Christian history, the canon of Scripture, and the use of polemical language in religious debate.

Introduction

The Second Letter of Peter is a pseudonymous work written late in the first century CE and attributed to the apostle Peter. It is the second of the two letters under the name of Peter in the New Testament canon. The authorship of 2 Peter was contested in the early church, and it was accepted relatively late in the process of canonization (Eusebius, *Hist. Eccl.* 3.3.4; 6.25.8; 2 Peter is weakly attested in the second century). In the name of Peter, the apostle (1.1), the author writes a letter of exhortation that provides proofs from Scripture in order to uphold the teaching that God judges the wicked. In the form of a testament, the author appeals to tradition and attacks those who question the promise of the Lord's parousia as wicked and immoral 'false teachers'.

Critics have not given 2 Peter the same attention and analysis as the letters of Paul, because they have classified the letter as a representative of the much denigrated 'early catholicism' (Käsemann 1982). Judged inferior to the Pauline Epistles for theological reasons by Protestant biblical scholarship, 2 Peter has interested modern scholars primarily for the evidence it offers for the process of canonization in the author's reference to Paul's letters and the other Scriptures (3.15). Recent studies have analysed 2 Peter within the context of other ancient documents, explored its rhetorical features and reconstructed its historical situation (Bauckham 1983; Watson 1988). Social-scientific perspectives have illuminated the document by understanding the community that produced it with the categories of purity/impurity, honour/shame, group-oriented culture and attitudes toward the body (Neyrey 1993). A reading from Mexico analyses the letter, among other Catholic epistles, as resistance literature. The letter, it argues, functions to encourage hope within a community in the face of the delay of the parousia by asserting that God drives history. Thus, with the participation of faithful communities who actively wait for God, God is said to be accomplishing the complex work of salvation and the restoration of the new heavens and the new earth (Rodríguez 1997).

In order to explore the complex of authority, canon and self-definition that operate in this letter, it is necessary to place the work within the history of early Christian communities represented by the New Testament documents.

Constructing Religious Authority and Leadership in Early Christian History

The second letter of Peter stands at one important point in the debate over correct teaching and legitimate leadership in the early church. Written at the end of the first or beginning of the second century (see Bauckham 1983: 157–58), it joins together the authority of both Peter, disciple of Jesus who was present at the transfiguration, and Paul, author of Scripture (3.16), to define the community against heretics and false teachers. The letter raises the question of how religious leadership was developed, regulated and controlled during the time of the writing of the New Testament and the establishment of the canon. The way the New Testament writings phrase and resolve the question of authoritative leadership is theologically significant, because traditional reconstructions of early church history serve as authoritative models for later church organization. The text constructs authority and history differently than those scholars who view 2 Peter as pseudonymous.

Within the range of New Testament writings, 2 Peter is one example of a later writing of the New Testament that makes Peter and Paul models and heroes of the church and pairs them in such a way as to imply that they hold unified positions. For example, in 2 Peter the author speaks in the name of Peter, near the time of his death (1.13-15), to his followers. In his final words he both condemns false prophets and teachers and buttresses support for his condemnation by commending Paul's letters as Scripture (3.16). With a similar aim, Luke, the author of the Acts of the Apostles, portrays Peter and Paul together as twin heroes of the narrative. Constructing agreement between these two leaders is part of Luke's strategy of depicting compromise and harmony in the idealized Christian community. The first letter of Peter is further evidence for the convergence of Peter and Paul in later New Testament times. 1 Peter employs the letter form, whose authority has increased with the collection of Paul's letters, and expresses Pauline ideas in the name of Peter. References to Peter and Paul in *1 Clement* 5 and Ignatius' *Letter to the Romans* 43 are further examples of the merging of these two authorities (see Koester 1995: 290, 296).

However, other writings of the New Testament provide evidence to contradict this view of a united Peter and Paul. The author of the Gospel of Mark is critical of Peter as a disciple and portrays Jesus' inner circle ambiguously (Struthers Malbon 1983). In the undisputed letters Paul speaks of his independence from the pillars of the Jerusalem church and contrasts the revelatory source of his authority with the human authority of those who followed Jesus in his ministry on earth (Gal. 1.11-17). In 1 Cor. 1.12-13, Paul implies that people claim allegiance to particular leaders including Cephas or Peter. Viewed in light of other earlier writings, the particular way 2 Peter constructs 'tradition' from the predictions of the prophets through the commandment of the Lord and Saviour by way of the apostles (3.2) makes uniform a history that in reality is diverse and conflicted.

Feminist historians have observed that, as the reputations of Peter and Paul shifted from rivals to prime authorities for the developing church, the claim of their apostolic authority eclipsed other traditions, linked with other authoritative leaders. The status of Mary Magdalene as a resurrection witness became obscured as literature that claimed connection with her authority came to be regarded as heretical (Pagels 1979; Kraemer and D'Angelo 1999). While the undisputed Pauline letters give ample evidence of women's leadership – including the deacon and benefactor Phoebe and the apostle Junia (Rom. 16.1-2, 7) – the Pauline tradition of the Pastoral Epistles constructs women as problems within the community and prescribes silence. Interpretation of Paul's legacy with development of Paul's emphasis upon chastity and the leadership of women survives in the non-canonical *Acts of Paul and Thecla* (MacDonald 1983).

The author of 2 Peter contrasts the source of his authority with 'cleverly devised myths' (1.16-17) and links it to his presence on the holy mountain of transfiguration (1.17-18). He emphasizes this experience as one of the 'eyewitnesses' and one who heard the 'voice come from heaven' as confirmation of the prophetic word (1.19). In contrast to authority derived from the empty tomb or resurrection appearance traditions, which might claim multiple witnesses (1 Cor. 15.6), the authority claimed here is limited to the three apostles – Peter, James and John – who are mentioned by the Synoptic Gospels as present at the scene (Neyrey 1980a).

Feminist historians have interpreted the portrayal of early Christian history exemplified by 2 Peter with suspicion, and they have demonstrated that the perspectival history constructed in it has eliminated evidence of women's leadership. They have reconstructed an alternative history of struggle between a spirit/prophecy tradition in which women were active leaders and the model of male authority that became dominant (the one that is represented in 2 Peter), with three divinely chosen men receiving revelation on the mountain and now writing letters denouncing false prophets (Schüssler Fiorenza 1983).

In reconstructing and presenting an alternative historical narrative to the one expressed by early orthodoxy, feminist historians have raised an unresolved question for other interpreters in the postcolonial situation. What is the proper role for reconstructed history as a model or paradigm for the present? In the traditional construction of orthodoxy, theologians or preachers may identify with those whom the texts construct as having been in charge all along, such as Peter, James and John. Relying on the reconstructed history of conflict in early Christianity, women may identify their struggles with those Christians who once had a voice but were subsequently drowned out, as the church developed apostolic orders and adapted to society around it, such as women prophets or traditions around Mary Magdalene. Some interpreters may imagine those theological positions that never got articulated at all. A community whose hold upon power is extremely tenuous may accept the oppositional structure constructed by the text and identify with the community of 2 Peter, surrounded by false teachers and struggling to survive. Such is precisely the approach adopted by Raúl Humberto Luo Rodríguez in his interpretation of 2 Peter (1997). Some critics have questioned whether the whole project of constructing an idealized historical past is of theological benefit for the present (Tolbert 1995). Careful historical reconstruction that provides a nuanced view of a complex web of debate in the early church can allow interpreters to negotiate theological alternatives in light of their present situation.

Establishing the Canon of Scripture

The second letter of Peter indicates that, at the end of the first and beginning of the second century, constructing legitimate traditions of apostolic leadership was closely linked with establishing a canon of authoritative Christian writings. 2 Peter exhibits an explicit awareness of Scripture and the canonical concern of both recognizing particular books as authoritative and prohibiting the writing of additional books (Farkasfalvy 1985–86). By writing in the name of Peter, by referring to this same letter as 'the second letter I am writing to you' (3.1), and by the use of the deathbed testament form, the author places the writing as the last of the authoritative Petrine tradition (Farkasfalvy 1985–86: 4–5). The authority of the writing is phrased as an exhortation to remember the words of the prophets and the apostolic tradition: 'the commandment of the Lord and Saviour spoken through your apostles' (3.2).

Appealing to the authority of 'our beloved brother Paul' (3.14), the author cites Paul as a further support for his exhortation. The phrase 'in all his letters' indicates that to this audience Paul's letters were known as a collection. The author's statement that 'there are some things in [Paul's letters] hard to understand' demonstrates both that the interpretation of Paul's letters was disputed and that the author understands himself to convey the correct interpretation. (Farkasfalvy [1985–86: 9] identifies these difficult statements in Paul to be references to the parousia in 1 Thess. 4.13-18 and other apocalyptic texts in 2 Thessalonians and the Corinthian letters.) The remark that these interpreters twist the interpretation 'as they do the other Scriptures' is the earliest evidence that Paul's writings were considered 'Scripture'. In addition to connecting the letter with Petrine and Pauline authorities, the author is dependent upon Jude, a source that he considers to be part of apostolic tradition. At the same time, he does not quote apocryphal sources directly, omitting Jude's quotations of *1 Enoch*. This interpretation of his source may indicate awareness of disputes about the Old Testament canon (Farkasfalvy 1985–86: 16).

Feminist and postcolonial critics have challenged the appeal to authorities and the definition of Scripture that the author of 2 Peter both assumes and asserts. Because in the process of canon formation the dominant group who became identified with orthodoxy silenced and marginalized voices of women, critical feminist interpretation has transgressed the textual canonical paradigm (Schüssler Fiorenza 1998; 1994: 8–9). By the writing of the Pastoral Epistles, which interpreted the ambiguities about gender roles in Paul's undisputed letters, canon and orthodoxy functioned to exclude women from positions of leadership and authority (King 1998: 34–35). Feminist evaluation of biblical texts makes the liberation of women and other marginalized people rather than canonicity central in interpreting the authority of biblical texts. Both feminist and postcolonial subjects struggle against reading canons imposed upon them in the process of colonization and seek to find their own language and canons (Dube Shomanah 2000: 48–49; May and Meyer 1994). Postcolonial writers have questioned the privileged status of the Bible and proposed to read it along with other world Scriptures. The very idea of canon with which the author of 2 Peter is operating has come under question by postcolonial receivers of the tradition.

Defining Oneself: Use of Polemical Language in Religious Debate

Fierce polemic against false teachers and prophets supports and strengthens the construction of Peter and Paul as legitimate authorities in the tradition and authors of canonical Scripture. The opposing leaders are characterized as 'irrational animals', 'blots and blemishes' and 'waterless springs' (2.12-13, 17). Described as 'indulgent' and 'licentious', they are compared with dogs who return to their vomit and sows who return to wallow in the mire (2.18-22). The demonizing of those who do not represent the correct position is integral to the strategy of this author.

New Testament scholars have interpreted polemical language within its ancient historical and literary setting. Historical critics have read this language at face value and have attempted to describe the positions of the false teachers and identify them with specific groups in early Christianity (Bauckham 1983: 154–57). Sometimes, commentators, by identifying with the authoritative author of a letter and allying themselves against the opponents, have unwittingly reinscribed and intensified the dualism of a letter in their own polemical context (see Castelli 1991; Briggs Kittredge 1998). Recent scholars of ancient rhetoric have tried to understand how such polemical language functioned in philosophical debate (see Neyrey 1980b. Stanley Stowers analyses the 'agonistic character' of Greek friendship [1991: 113–14]). None of these methods in themselves fully address the key question for postcolonial interpretation. For postcolonial criticism, the simultaneous claim to unique authority and the increase in 'othering' language used against enemies raises a pointed theological problem. Dehumanizing rhetoric, when used against others by those with power, results in violence and destruction of those others. Canonized in the authoritative texts of the New Testament, this rhetoric becomes the model/pattern for demonizing opponents and conducting debate.

Research into the historical context and rhetorical conventions of such language has been helpful in contextualizing rhetoric that sounds intense to our modern ears. In the context of ancient debates between philosophical schools in the Graeco-Roman world, the attack upon those who deny divine judgment closely resembles the apology against Epicurean polemics against providence (Neyrey 1980b). Luke Johnson's work on anti-Jewish polemic has emphasized its defensiveness, stereotypical quality and use of standardized Hellenistic *topoi* (1989). The language conventions of the ancient world include calling one's opponents 'hypocritical', 'blind' or 'possessed by demons'. The use of these epithets is simply evidence that the writer considered them to be opponents. In his commentary on 2 Peter, Neyrey has placed the rhetoric of 2 Peter within the group culture's understandings of purity/impurity as well as honour/shame and clarified the sociological function of such language (1993). These studies are useful in helping the modern reader 'hear' ancient polemic as the ancient authors might have meant it and ancient audiences heard it. To read it accurately, modern readers are required to divest themselves of their modern lenses and sympathetically understand those of an ancient and unfamiliar culture. Interpretation is an exercise in bridging cultural difference.

However, placing the New Testament literature in its historical context is of limited usefulness in addressing the theological and practical problems raised by the reception of such texts. When attributed to a revered heroic personage, given apostolic and canonical authority as Scripture, and linked with the more revered Christian tradition, such polemical language gains power far beyond its ancient context. Dualistic patterns of thought and patterns of vilification continue and become ingrained, forming a kind of template of Christian rhetoric against enemies.

A vast difference in perspective between those in power, who can elect whether or not to use this language, and people who have been subjected to, and with, dehumanizing rhetoric accounts for the fact that feminist and postcolonial interpreters assess vilification as a more urgent theological problem (Bailey 1995). Allegations of sexual transgression and comparison with animals have typified polemics against native peoples. Thus, for example, Fray Tomás Ortiz, a Dominican monk on the northern coast of Colombia in 1524, writes of the people in the land:

> The men on the mainland of the Indies eat human flesh and are more sodomistic than any generation. There is no justice among them, they go about naked, they feel neither love nor shame, they are asses, stupid, mad, insane; to kill or be killed is all the same to them; they have no truth in them unless it be to their advantage; they are inconstant; they do not know what counsel is; they are ingrates and fond of novelties; they boast of their drunkenness; they distill wine from various herbs, fruits, roots, and grain; they also get drunk on smoke and on certain herbs that steal away their brains; they are bestial in their vices; neither obedience nor courtesy do the young boys show to the old, nor sons to their father; nor are they capable of learning from doctrine and punishment; they are treacherous, cruel, vengeful, for they never forgive; extremely inimical toward religion, idlers, thieves, liars, and poor and mean in judgment; they keep neither faith nor order; men do not stay faithful to wives, nor wives to their husbands; they are sorcerers, soothsayers, and necromancers; they are as cowardly as rabbits, as dirty as pigs; they eat lice, spiders, and raw worms wherever they find them. (Goodpasture 1989: 23)

Rhetoric in the pattern of 2 Peter continues to be used against those similarly labelled as 'other'. The coincidence of this rhetoric with claims to represent authoritative leadership and scriptural tradition in 2 Peter makes it an extremely powerful rhetorical strategy.

Conclusion

In its reference to a unified history of legitimate leaders whose agreement on critical theological matters is attested in canonical writings and are opposed by lustful and immoral false teachers, the Second Letter of Peter vividly exemplifies the preference for orthodoxy, authority and universality that feminist and postcolonial interpreters have recognized as elements that have operated as powerful conceptual allies in defining women and indigenous peoples as other and discounting them as subjects and actors in that history. As it contributes to the closing of the canon, the letter does not succeed in finishing the story or in silencing the voices of dissent within the tradition. At the same time as the author attempts to re-read and reshape the apostolic tradition for the present generation, the other writings within the canon undercut these claims. Many, many generations later, those from postcolonial contexts who have been named by such rhetoric now build communities to re-read, re-write and challenge the tradition. When read within diverse communities, the polemic of 2 Peter serves as a warning about how to engage in theological debate.

BIBLIOGRAPHY

Bailey, Randall
    1995   'They're Nothing but Incestuous Bastards: The Polemical Use of Sex and Sexuality in Hebrew Canon Narrative', in Fernando F. Segovia and Mary Ann Tolbert (eds), *Reading from This Place*. Vol. 1, *Social Location and Biblical Interpretation in the United States* (Minneapolis: Fortress Press): 121–38.

Bauckham, Richard
    1983   *Jude, 2 Peter* (Word Biblical Commentary, 50; Waco, TX: Word books).

Briggs Kittredge, Cynthia
    1998   *Community and Authority: The Rhetoric of Obedience in the Pauline Tradition* (Harrisburg, PA: Trinity Press International).

Castelli, Elizabeth
    1994   'Romans', in Elizabeth Schüssler Fiorenza (ed.), *Searching the Scriptures*. Vol. 2, *A Feminist Commentary* (New York: Crossroad): 272–300.
    1991   *Imitating Paul: A Discourse of Power* (Louisville, KY: Westminster/John Knox Press).

Dube Shomanah, Musa
    2000   *Postcolonial Feminist Interpretation of the Bible* (St. Louis: Chalice Press).

Farkasfalvy, Denis
    1985–86 'The Ecclesial Setting of Pseudepigraphy in Second Peter', *Second Century* 5: 3–29.

Goodpasture, H. McKennie
    1989   *Cross and Sword: An Eyewitness History of Christianity in Latin America* (Maryknoll, NY: Orbis Books).

Johnson, Luke T.
    1989   'Anti-Jewish Slander and the Conventions of Ancient Polemic', *Journal of Biblical Literature* 108: 419–41.

Käsemann, Ernst
    1982   'An Apologia for Primitive Christian Eschatology', in Ernst Käsemann, *Essays on New Testament Themes* (Philadelphia: Fortress Press): 169–95.

King, Karen L.
    1998   'Canonization and Marginalization: Mary of Magdala', in Kwok Pui-lan and Elisabeth Schüssler Fiorenza (eds), *Women's Sacred Scriptures* (Concilium, 98/3; London: SCM Press; Maryknoll, NY: Orbis Books): 29–36.

Koester, Helmut
    1995   *Introduction to the New Testament*. Vol. 2, *History and Literature of Early Christianity* (2nd edn; New York: W. de Gruyter).
Kraemer, Ross S. and Mary Rose D'Angelo (eds)
    1999   *Women and Christian Origins* (New York: Oxford).
MacDonald, Dennis Ronald
    1983   *The Legend and the Apostle: The Battle for Paul in Story and Canon* (Philadelphia: Westminster Press).
May, Melanie A. and Lauree Hersch Meyer
    1994   'Unity of the Bible, Unity of the Church: Confessionalism, Ecumenism, and Feminist Hermeneutics', in Elisabeth Schüssler Fiorenza (ed.), *Searching the Scriptures*. Vol. 1, *A Feminist Introduction* (New York: Crossroad): 140–53.
Neyrey, Jerome
    1980a   'The Apologetic Use of the Transfiguration in 2 Peter 1:16-21', *Catholic Biblical Quarterly* 42: 504–19.
    1980b   'The Form and Background of the Polemic in 2 Peter', *Journal of Biblical Literature* 99: 407–31.
    1993   *2 Peter, Jude* (Anchor Bible, 37C; New York: Doubleday).
Pagels, Elaine
    1979   *The Gnostic Gospels* (New York: Random House).
Rodríguez, Raúl Humberto Luo
    1997   ' "Wait for the Day of God's Coming and Do What You Can to Hasten It..." (2 Pet 3:12): The Non-Pauline Letters as Resistance Literature', in Leif E. Vaage (ed.), *Subversive Scriptures: Revolutionary Readings of the Christian Bible in Latin America* (Valley Forge: Trinity): 193–206.
Schüssler Fiorenza, Elisabeth
    1983   *In Memory of Her: A Feminist Theological Reconstruction of Christian Origins* (New York: Crossroad).
    1994   'Introduction: Transgressing Canonical Boundaries', in Elisabeth Schüssler Fiorenza (ed.), *Searching the Scriptures*. Vol. 2, *A Feminist Commentary* (New York: Crossroad): 1–16.
    1998   'Introduction', in Kwok Pui-lan and Elisabeth Schüssler Fiorenza (eds), *Women's Sacred Scriptures* (Concilium, 98/3; London: SCM Press; Maryknoll, NY: Orbis Books): 1–4.
Stowers, Stanley
    1991   'Friends and Enemies in the Politics of Heaven', in Jouette M. Bassler (ed.), *Pauline Theology*. Vol. I, *Thessalonians, Philippians, Galatians, Philemon* (Minneapolis: Fortress Press): 105–21.
Struthers Malbon, Elizabeth
    1983   '*Fallible Followers*: Women and Men in the Gospel of Mark', *Semeia* 28: 29–48.
Tolbert, Mary Ann
    1995   'When Resistance Becomes Repression: Mark 13:9-27 and the Poetics of Location', in Fernando F. Segovia and Mary Ann Tolbert (eds), *Reading from this Place*. Vol. 2, *Social Location and Biblical Interpretation in Global Perspective* (Minneapolis: Fortress Press): 331–46.
Watson, Duane
    1988   *Invention, Arrangement and Style: Rhetorical Criticism of Jude and 2 Peter* (Society of Biblical Literature Dissertation Series, 104; Atlanta: Scholars Press).

THE FIRST, SECOND AND THIRD LETTERS OF JOHN

R. S. Sugirtharajah

Questions relating to the date, authorship and original readership of biblical writings are mostly a matter of surmise, or, as C. H. Dodd put it, a matter of piling 'conjecture upon conjecture' (Dodd 1946: lxx). The Johannine Epistles are no exception. My prime concern here is to use the inner rhetorical logic of the narrative content of the epistles to reconstruct the situation and concerns that the first recipients were faced with. In this pursuit, I intend to side with the scholarly opinion which holds that the epistles were closely linked to the Fourth Gospel, that they were quite possibly written by the same person, and that he was part of that community, probably John, the elder, who might have been the beloved disciple. He might have written these epistles from one of the cities in Asia Minor. He must have spent sufficient time in one of the metropolitan centres of the Roman Empire to acquaint himself with one of the early forms of Gnosticism. These conjectures are largely based on similarities in language, style and content that are discernible in the Fourth Gospel and the letters. It is likely that, after the completion of the Fourth Gospel, a great dissension arose among the community, centred primarily on the person and work of Christ, and that the letters, at least the first two, were addressed to this schism in different ways. It is also evident from the narrative that 1 John was a general circular letter, whereas 2 John was addressed to the house church of the chosen lady and her children, and that 3 John was written to an individual called Gaius, urging him to provide hospitality to itinerant Christian missionaries.

Features of Colonial Discourse

It is noticeable that from a postcolonial perspective there are several hallmarks of colonial discourse in the epistles.

One of the characteristics of colonial discourse is the rejection of diversity. Colonial discourse is staunchly wedded to unvarying and exclusive truth and tolerates no dissent or debate. To the regret of the author of these epistles/letters, the majority seem to have gone over to the opposite camp: 'They are of the world, and therefore what they say is of the world, and the world listens to them' (1 Jn 4.5). The epistles exhibit intolerance of this sort of situation and detest any theological contradiction. The author's hermeneutical device for dealing with theological dissidence is to come up with his own definition of Christianity on the basis of his understanding of the person of Christ. The incarnation and the atoning power of the sacrificed Christ become normative and are used as a way of excluding those with divergent views or who hold a different interpretation from his.

When one reads the epistles, especially the first two, one is struck by their harsh tone and intolerant language. Those of opposed views are branded as the sons of Satan, and those who deny that Jesus is the Christ are labelled 'antichrist', a new coinage hitherto unheard of. The New Testament writings speak about false messiahs (Mk 13.22) and false prophets (Mt. 24.24) but not antichrist. The term 'antichrist' is found only in these epistles (1 Jn 2.18, 22, 4.3; 2 Jn 7), and it is clearly the author's own invention. It is the first-century equivalent of the current term 'axis of evil', employed by President George W. Bush to denounce any unruly state which disrupts the American messianic vision. Like 'axis of evil', which is constantly applied to those who question American values and way of life, 'antichrist' is relentlessly applied to those who question the orthodox, received teachings about the Christ. What irks the author is the different and incompatible theology advocated by his opponents. Anyone who accepts and welcomes those with alternative theological ideas is deemed guilty by association and 'has a share in the evil deeds' (2 Jn 11).

In the face of such dissent, the author resorts to a number of hermeneutical strategies which betray colonial intentions.

The first is to appeal to his own credentials as an interpreter. His authority is derived from his having been an eyewitness to the Christ event. He makes his unequivocal claim to this authority at the very beginning of the epistle: 'We declare to you what was from the beginning, what we have heard, what we have seen with our eyes, what we have looked at and touched with our hands' (1 Jn 1.1-3). The appeal to the claims of the preacher seems to have been the recommended position in the New Testament. When confronted with conflicting messages, the advice seems to be, trust your instructor and know from whom you receive the teaching (1 Cor. 15.1-3; 2 Tim. 3.3-14, 4.3). By investing himself with authority, the writer becomes not only the conduit of the message but also a reliable guide. Colonial hegemony is maintained through asserting the master's credibility.

The second strategy is an expansion of the first – to insist on the authenticity of the message. This is achieved by asserting that what is proclaimed is what has been heard from the inception of the community. Going back to 'the beginning' is the author's way of seeking sanctuary and validation in the face of competing theological ideas. His claim is that what he preaches is consistent with the original message. Anyone who deviates from and does not adhere to what he claims as the original teaching is regarded as not 'having' God (2 Jn 9-11). What he is trying to do is to secure certain meanings as valid for all eternity and to stick strictly to his script. By claiming his message as the 'original' word of God, the writer is able to get others to take him seriously. In doing this, the writer exhibits the classic colonial fear of unscripted inventions and improvisations.

The third way of handling dissent is to confer an elected role as God's people on those who are on his side and supportive of his theological position: 'We are of God. Whoever knows God listens to us, whoever is not of God does not listen to us' (1 Jn 4.6). Moreover, this sense of the divine elected status of their discourse is reinforced by the assertion that only they can 'discern the spirit of truth and spirit of error' (1 Jn 4.6), such a status conferring the role of ultimate umpire of disputed meanings. This recruitment of divine elected status simultaneously legitimizes their tenure of power and at the same time inhibits any agitation for a counter narrative.

The fourth strategy is to project an imperial Christ. On the surface, it appears that the epistles do not project an aggressive Christology. The Jesus of the 'I am' sayings that one encounters in the Fourth Gospel is absent from the epistles. However, the author employs a revealing title which is found only in the Fourth Gospel and in 1 John. Here, Jesus is called 'the Saviour of the world' (Jn 4.42; 1 Jn 4.14). This title, as Craig R. Koester has demonstrated, has imperial connotations (Koester 1990). The term, in his view, was exclusively used in the first century of the Roman emperor. Now there is a new emperor, Jesus, who replaces the Roman emperor as the new sovereign, whom everyone should obey. The opponents, who may have come from a Hellenistic background, do not deny that Jesus was a man but dispute that he was the promised Messiah and the exalted claims made on his behalf (1 Jn 2.22). The message to them is that Jesus was more than a Jewish Messiah, he was in fact the Saviour of the world, and they must decide whether they owe allegiance to him or to their own misconceived and narrow understanding of Jesus. Given the history of colonialism, this image of an imperial Christ is a troubling one. In the name of the imperial Christ a number of cultures have been annihilated and countries conquered. It is, moreover, a disturbing title in the context of religious plurality.

The fifth strategy against dissent is to restrict hospitality. Free food and lodging, customarily available to all travelling preachers, with their varied theological ideas, but especially to those less wealthy, is to be offered only to those who teach in line with the author's approved theological position: 'Do not receive into the house or welcome anyone who comes to you and does not bring this teaching' (2 Jn 10). The author limits his generosity to those Christians who side with his understanding of Christian faith. The dissidents within the Christian faith are a menace and a nuisance and deserve no hospitality. The author has constructed his own understanding of the emerging Christian faith and is clearly opposed to any alternative theological opinions. He has misused theological rhetoric and manipulated traditional hospitality in order to bring his opponents to his way of thinking. Recent studies on famine have shown how ruling elites have used food as a weapon to eliminate political opponents. The Ukraine, Somalia and Ethiopia are notable examples.

Finally, the author uses the colonial rhetoric of flattery and threat to divide the community. He cosies up to his supporters by pointing out that 'you are from God' and that 'the one who is in you is greater than the one who is in the world' (1 Jn 4.4), and at the same time he alarms his opponents by saying that 'murderers do not have eternal life abiding in them' (1 Jn 3.15). By asserting his particular dogmatic theological proposals as the benchmark to test the presence of the Spirit, he effectively de-privileges other theological views. At a time when political and religious people try to divide the world into us and them and those with us and against us, the Johannine Epistles provide fresh ammunition.

Silenced Subalterns

The letters are an example of a colonial scenario where the natives are hardly given a chance to speak. The narrative employs the colonial rhetoric of the mute 'other', where the 'other' remains nameless and silent, or, when named, as in the case of Diotrephes, still remains silent. The readers do not get to hear why Diotrephes disputed the author's authority. He might, quite reasonably, have thought that the local leaders were the best people to interpret the tradition, seeing this as a practical way of meeting the local difficulty, namely different and conflicting interpretations. The author, who is so eloquent in putting forward his views, rarely gives his opponents an opportunity to make their case. There is no way of ascertaining what they thought except through the prism of the author's jaundiced view of their theological stance. As in the Pauline Epistles, the opponents are scripted into the discourse with non-speaking parts. As in so much colonial literature, the epistles are narratives where the natives are either spoken to or spoken on behalf of, but rarely where they speak.

Fostering Imperial Ideology through Binarism

The epistles work with a binary thinking which postcolonialism tries to overcome. Colonial discourse sets up contrasting categories to discredit and trap the dissidents – savage/noble, primitive/civilized, advanced/retarded, sane/ unsound, rational/irrational. From the colonial perspective this polarizing way of imagining the world is a valuable ally in maintaining the imperial ideology and reinforcing power relations between the ruler and the ruled. It is a way of shaming and excluding the dissidents. More importantly, such a dichotomous thinking paves the way to introducing the benefits of modernity to subject peoples. The impulse behind this agenda is to civilize and bring into line the unruly people.

This kind of binary framework abounds in the epistles. While the Judaism of the time was unaware of dualism of a metaphysical sort, the writer is fond of a kind of ethical dualism light/darkness, blindness/sight. He speaks of two kinds of reality – darkness and light (1 Jn 2.7-11), two kinds of humanity – children of God and children of the devil (1 Jn 2.28–3.10), two kinds of spirit – the spirit of God and the spirit of antichrist (1 Jn 4.1-6), and two kinds of theological propositions – true and false. This binary distinction helps the writer to justify his theological, imperial mission of dominance and enlightenment. In the colonial rhetoric, the unruly, erratic and stubborn have to be made stable, pliable and complaisant. In the logic of Johannine thinking, the dissidents become like the wild tribes of the colonies who need supervision and control. In other words, like the depraved natives, the theological dissidents have to be uplifted by a thorough dose of true gospel and by light brought into darkness. These dualisms can be and are easily used and abused in the contemporary world.

The Colonial Allegory of the Child

Another mark of colonial discourse is the use of the metaphorical language of the child. The writer of the epistles employs this trope, though in more than one way. Terms such as 'child' (*teknon*), 'little child' (*teknion*) and 'boy/son' (*paidion*) occur nearly 16 times in the three short epistles. It is quite apparent, however, that the concept of child is not a fixed one in the Johannine writings. In the Gospel and 1 John the children of God are part of the family of God, while in 2 John the family of God (vv. 1, 4, 13) includes the whole body of Christians, or, as W. G. Kümmel claimed, in 'my beloved children' the 'entirety of Christendom is addressed' (Kümmel 1966: 307). The image of the child conjures up the impression of a caring, loving and tender relationship between the writer, the aged John, affectionately addressing his audience. Biblical commentators make much of the fact that the new family of God is based not on birth or heritage but on a combination of God's benevolence and the meritorious capabilities of humanity. It is easy to be enticed by the warm and affectionate pastoral tone that runs through the epistles, but postcolonialism reads it differently.

The concept of the father–child relationship is central to Johannine control and domination and is used as a tool to enforce discipline and conformity. In the colonial rhetoric, the child is susceptible to instruction, correction and improvement. For the writer of the letters, those who disagree with his theological position are ignorant and misinformed children, who, through threat, shame, flattery and reason, can be turned into civilized adults, or, in the case of the dissidents, made into orthodox believers. In using the phrase 'children of the devil' (1 Jn 3.2), what the writer implies is that these deranged children are in need of a master with a hand of firmness to control and instruct them. Like the colonial savage, the children of the devil are redeemable if they believe what the master believes and submit themselves to obedience and instruction. Those who have been led astray should be brought back. In the imperial rhetoric, a child must be corrected, otherwise he or she may persist in bad habits, or, as the writer of the epistles would have put it, in bad doctrines. The possibility of adulthood arises only when the dissidents are brought out of the darkness of their child-hood. In addition, the metaphor of the child tends to conceal the inequality of power which exists within a family. The child is made to depend on the father for everything. In the Johannine Epistles, innocence is not seen as an innate quality of human beings but is conferred by the Father who has the power to forgive sins: 'Your sins are forgiven for his sake' (1 Jn 2.12). This innocence is dependent on the heavenly Father. While the image of children conveys a cosy image of a family, in the Johannine reckoning not all have their place in the family. The awkward members are kept at length and denied hospitality and generosity until they learn the colonial virtues of conformity and obedience.

Buddhized Christianity

When one looks at the interpretation of the epistles, it is noticeable from a postcolonial point of view that the hermeneutics of denial is at work, particu-larly among some Western biblical scholars. Biblical scholars raised up with the Eurocentric habit of placing the Johannine writings within a Hebraic or Hellenistic background are reluctant to acknowledge any possible influence of other philosophical or religious traditions. When faced with awkward passages, mainstream biblical scholars rarely look for theological influences beyond the Jewish and Greek milieux.

Orientalists and Indologists of the past and present have been offering evidence of continuous contact between India and the Mediterranean world, and it is being increasingly acknowledged that Buddhist and Christian ideas were exposed to one another. Traces of Buddhism in some of the apocalyptic literature and in the Gnostic writings, especially in Basilides, have long been recognized. Edward Conze, among others, has identified similarities between Gnosticism and Mahayana Buddhism (1970). Egypt seems to have provided a suitable environment for one form of Gnosticism, while a colony of Indians existed in Memphis as early as 200 BCE. Alexandria was ideally placed to receive both spiritual and material wares from India, and it was in this atmosphere that Gnosticism took shape.

One is not looking for verbal correspondences, which are highly unlikely because of the nature of the texts we are dealing with. Both Buddhist and Christian writings were translated texts, and neither carries the exact words of their founder but rather an interpretation or exposition of those words. Biblical scholars are inclined to rely excessively on textual resemblances and philological correspondences as ways of establishing proof of borrowing, and undervalue especially foreign religious concepts transmitted orally through the constant travelling and exchange that marked the period. This literary bias among biblical scholars tends to devalue orally transmitted knowledge. To ask for verbal similarity is too much, but what one looks for are conceptual similarities.

J. Edgar Bruns is one of those who identified the possibility of Buddhist influences in the Johannine writings. His hypothesis was that in a city like Alexandria it is likely that the writer of the epistles would have heard Buddhized teaching of the Gnostics. He wrote: 'On the basis of his own writings [i.e. the writer of the epistles], especially of certain passages in the first epistle, it seems clear to me that the *key to Johannine thought* lies in an understanding of Buddhist concepts' (Bruns 1971: 28; italics original). Bruns identifies at least three theological categories in the Johannine Epistles which are closer to Mahayana Buddhism than to Judaic or Hellenistic categories of thought (Bruns 1971: vii).

One of these is the idea of God. The concept of God in the letters of John, in Bruns' view, could have been the result of Buddhist influence. In the epistles, God does not do anything; but is called light (1 Jn 1.5), love (1 Jn 4.8, 16) and spirit (1 Jn 4.24) as a result of the actions of human beings. The light is nothing but love (1 Jn 2.10-11), and truth is nothing but walking in it. What humans do reveals who God is. God does not exist beyond the empirical world. Hence God does not generate love in human beings; rather, it is the loving that human beings do that generates God, fulfils, extends, perfects Godly love (1 Jn 4.12). There is a refusal to objectify and to imagine God as a fully existent being unconnected to and divorced from human history. It is the love which human beings enact in their ordinary lives which makes God dwell in their midst. It is not a prior awareness of the divine which engenders love.

It is this notion of 'making God's presence through loving on the one hand and loving through the presence of God on the other' which prompts Bruns to claim Buddhist influence in the Johannine Epistles. The love for a person expressed in action is seen as the sole proof of the unseen and unknown God. In the first epistle, the writer claims that 'no one has ever seen God' but goes on to say that 'if we love one another God abides in us' (1 Jn 4.20). It is the act of love which makes the presence of God real.

This act of loving precedes any premediated knowledge of a divine presence or indwelling. Such a notion, according to Bruns, parallels *Prajnaparamitta* ('The Perfection of Wisdom', 'Transcendent Wisdom'), one of the nine sacred works of Mahayana Buddhism: 'The Lord has not fully known the realm of Dharma; for the realm of Dharma is just the Lord' (Bruns 1971: 31). When the writer of the epistles says that 'God abides' in whoever does love, this means that the act of love makes the presence of God. Similarly, the Johannine understanding of 'born of God' resonates with the Buddhist understanding. Just as in John one who loves is born of God and realizes God, so in Mahayana Buddhism the one who exercises perfect wisdom realizes Enlightenment or Buddhahood.

A second Buddhist correspondence found in the epistles is the Johannine doctrine of indwelling (1 Jn 4.4, 15-6), which is comparable to the Buddhist concept of the Buddha nature – a form of knowing within human beings. A third, the writer's idea that Christians have passed from death to life (1 Jn 3.14), is nearer to the Mahayana notion of 'the exercise of wisdom as identical with the state of Nirvana'.

Textual Juxtapositions
Postcolonial contrapuntal reading finds the Johannine notion of love a restricted one. One of the important messages of the epistles is love – 'love one another'. This love does not go beyond the simple love of the neighbour. Jewish thinking did not prescribe love for all people. For instance, one should note Jesus' reluctance to deal with the request of the Syrophoenician woman, or the Samaritan's surprise at Jesus' request for a drink, and the authorial observation of John: 'Jews do not share things in common with Samaritans' (Jn 4.9). Another notable case in point are the words of Jesus himself, which make love a comradely affair, a matter of solidarity among the Jews: 'Greater love has no man than this, that a man lay down his life for his friends' (Jn 15.13). In one of the Gnostic gospels, Jesus tells his disciples: 'Care not, therefore, for the many, and them that are outside the mystery despise'. True, the Synoptics have a reference to loving your enemies. However, the enemy referred to here is not foreign or a political foe outside the community, such as the Roman imperialists. Richard Horsley has demonstrated that the Matthaean and Lukan contexts in which the saying is located indicate local, personal enemies rather than Gentile or political adversaries. The sort of enemy intended is one who spoils crops by sowing weeds among the grain.

On the other hand, the Buddhist concept of *maitri*, loving kindness, is extended to those who are not normally liked. *Maitri* makes no ethnic, caste or religious distinction. *Sutta-Nipata*, for instance says: 'Cultivate an unlimited loving kindness towards the whole world – to those above, below and on all sides of you. Free from hatred, enmity and rivalry' (vv. 149-150). Whereas Johannine, or, for that matter, Christian love is restricted to human beings, the Buddhist love is all-encompassing, including both human beings and the whole created order, and in this sense it is unbounded. Such resonances and references from other textual traditions introduce other possibilities of meaning. Unlike the comparative reading which is colonial, aggressive and judgmental, contrapuntal reading is about seeing connections and being complementary. One neutralizes and destroys; the other connects and fulfils. Such an intertextual reading will enable us to arrive at a fuller understanding of love.

Fusion of Theory and Practice
In spite of the excessive colonial tone of the letters, postcolonial criticism will readily align itself with their insistence on seeking and finding truth, justice and love, not in doctrinal or spiritual categories but in the tensions and conflicts of life. Here postcolonialism will concur with the writer of the epistles that ethical involvement, not theoretical or doctrinal fine-tuning, is paramount. The value of postcolonialism lies not only in its simultaneous repairing of colonial

misrepresentation and defamation but also in engaging in the struggle for a better world. The letters eschew speculation for practical ethical hermeneutics. Whereas in the Johannine Gospel, 'born again' has an individual and spiritual sense, the epistles make it clear that such an esoteric and mystical experience is not about resignation and retreat, but about religious activism, and that it has communitarian and ethical implications: 'Everyone who does justice is born again'(1 Jn 2.29).

The word 'liar' occurs five times in 1 John, and each time it refers to persons who may in some sense be true to their vocation as Christians but who fail to live justly (1 Jn 1.10; 2.4, 22; 4.20; 5.10). The writer is unambiguously clear about those who are born of God and those who are not: 'Anyone who does not do justice is not born of God, nor is anyone who does not love his brother' (1 Jn 3.10). Another Johannine proposition is that 'everyone who loves is born of God' (1 Jn 4.7). The meaning of love is quite apparent. It is not sentimental love but a transformative love which manifests itself in concrete acts: 'But anyone who has the world's goods and sees his brother in need, yet closes his heart against him, how does God's love abide in him. Little Children, let us not love in word or speech but in deed and truth' (1 Jn 3.17, 18).

For the Johannine writer, the status of salvation does not mean an inactive life. On the contrary, those who are saved are expected to 'walk in love' (2 Jn 4–6), 'walk in the truth' (3 Jn 4). Such a praxis-driven Johannine prescription for Christians resonates with the edicts of Asoka which, nearly three hundred years before the emergence of Johannine Christianity, expected the followers of the Buddha to live a life of commitment and compassion: 'A man must walk by *dhamma* if he would become moral. In the immoral there is no walking by *dhamma.*'

For the writer of the epistles, the real and deep meaning of 'truth', 'justice' and 'love' emerges out of the tension in the midst of life, and they are at no stage separated from action. In John's view, there is no need for these great concepts to be translated into action because deeds and words are indivisible and seen as an integrated whole. The writer recognizes the fact that in order to appreciate the words of Scripture one must weave them into the fabric of one's life. In this the writer of the epistle is one with the postcolonial notion of praxis which puts praxis in its proper place, not as a blind obedience to the word or a pretext for authoritarianism, but as a valuable way of integrating words and deeds, and more importantly placing these at the service of the disadvantaged and the unjustly treated.

Postcolonial Ambivalence

Finally, from the postcolonial perspective, the epistles have an element of ambivalence about them. This epistolary discourse contains both imperial intentions and praxiological impulses.

These letters are about self-appointed chosen people determined to reshape the nature of the gospel message on the basis of their own vested perspectives, with a view to extending their own imperial ambition. They are about claiming to advance God's kingdom through the hegemony of one's own theological truth. The epistles are about hermeneutical clashes and conflicting interpretations where both the protagonist and the antagonist believe that they are correct. They are about the manipulation and wielding of power under the cloak of divine authority. They are about restricting God's generosity to a chosen few.

Yet, the epistles are not without redeeming features. At least on two accounts the epistles absolve themselves and embody marks of postcoloniality. One is the thinly veiled presence of Buddhist concepts which disrupt the alleged purity of Christian tradition and make it clear that sacred texts are textual coalitions, and that they do not exist in unpolluted isolation. The intermixture of cultural ideas resists privileging one single culture. At a time when religious fundamentalists claim textual purity, such a conceptual mobility makes all texts alloyed and unchaste. When the idea of interchange between Buddhism and Christian faith was first mooted in the middle of the nineteenth century, Max Müller, who himself was involved in such comparative studies, posed the question: 'Would it make Christianity less true, if Buddhism contained many things which are taught in the Bible also?' Müller himself went on to answer his own question: 'Truth does not cease to be truth because it is held by others besides ourselves' (Müller 1891: 67). The second redeeming element in the epistles is the emphasis on exhortation and engagement being mutually constitutive, which resonates with postcolonialism's urge that ethical involvement is of equal importance to theorizing.

It would be attractive to end on this upbeat note. My fear, however, is that these commendable ideas will be forgotten and the letters will be read and remembered only for the tough signal they send. At a time when international affairs are decided by men who think that the Bible at their bedside provides them with a blueprint for dealing with the current political problems of the world, it is alarming to think that the grim vision of the epistles, which neatly bifurcates the world into good and evil, might play into their hands and be used and abused by them. My anxiety is chillingly captured in Arthur Miller's contentious play, *The Crucible* – a play about those who refuse to obey and conform. In it, the haunting words of the witch-hunter, Judge Danforth, echo the uncompromising tone of the writer of the epistle, an uncompromising tone which is being put to use by the current leader of the free world:

> You must understand, sir, a person is either with this court or he must be counted against it, there be no road between. This is a sharp time, now, a precise time – we live no longer in the dusky afternoon when evil mixed itself with good and befuddled the world. Now, by God's grace, the shining sun is up, and them that fear not light will surely praise it. I hope you will be one of those. (Miller 1968: 85)

BIBLIOGRAPHY

Bruns, Edgar J.
　　1969　　*The Art and Thought of John* (New York: Herder and Herder).
　　1971　　*The Christian Buddhism of St. John: New Insights into the Fourth Gospel* (New York: Paulist Press).

Conze, Edward
　　1970　　'Buddhism and Gnosis', in Ugo Bianchi (ed.), *Origins of Gnosticism. Colloquium of Messina 13-18 April, 1966. Texts and Discussions* (Leiden: E. J. Brill, 1970): 651–67.

Dodd, C. H.
　　1946　　*The Johannine Epistles* (London: Hodder and Stoughton).

Hutaff, Margaret D.
　　1994　　'The Johannine Epistles', in Elisabeth Schüssler Fiorenza (ed.), *Searching the Scriptures*. Vol. 2, *A Feminist Commentary* (New York: Crossroad): 406–27.

Koester, Craig R.
　　1990　　' "The Savior of the World" (John 4.42)', *Journal of Biblical Literature* 109: 665–80.

Kümmel, Werner Georg
　　1966　　*Introduction to the New Testament* (Nashville: Abingdon Press).

Miller, Arthur
　　1968　　*The Crucible* (London: Penguin Books).

Müller, Max
　　1891　　'Christianity and Buddhism', *The New Review* 4: 67–74.

Rensberger, David K.
　　1997　　*1 John, 2 John, 3 John* (Nashville: Abingdon Press).

THE LETTER OF JUDE

Rohun Park

Beneath much of the legacy of colonialism and the threat of neocolonialism that shape the lands of the Far East, there lies the intersection of colonizing desires with religious symbols and structures. Colonial politics have consistently made use of cultic ritual systems, leading thereby to a construction of empire in covert fashion. While such a link between politics and religion has often gone unnoticed, this colonial metonymic metaphor can be seen readily at work in any number of instances – from the emperor cult of Japan, to the recent deification of the national leader in North Korea (Il Sung Kim), to the declarations of President George W. Bush regarding his own person and the country itself. Such variations of the ruler cult function as signifiers for problems involving military occupation, terrorism, religious chaos and regional conflict. Such a multifaceted context involving politics and religion proves significant for a postcolonial reading of the letter of Jude.

Imperial Cultic Presence

It is widely acknowledged that Roman imperial religion proclaimed a divine appointment for the emperors. The emperor was commonly referred to by the title of 'saviour of Rome' and thought to be favoured by divine powers. This belief was instrumental in the creation of imperial authority and thus extended to the use of ritual systems in the local provinces. Hence, as the empire developed, the cultic and civic spheres became united in hybridized fashion. These, however, are not just beliefs and practices of long ago; they extend right into our own times.

During World War II, for example, Shinto shrines throughout Korea promoted the Japanese imperial cult. These shrines functioned, in effect, as centres for imperial propaganda, not only establishing reverence toward the figure of the emperor but also conducting worship services in the presence of his portrait. The emperor evolved thereby into a symbol that embodied the superiority of both the Japanese empire and its people. Indeed, emperors were believed to be direct descendants of the sun goddess. In the process, the colonized villagers of Korea were obliged to close down their own local temples and build new shrines for the Japanese emperor and his clergy. Despite intense local resistence, the emperor cult in Korea enforced, and seemed to achieve, assimilation between the colonized and the colonizers. One result of such assimilation was the forcing of the colonized by the colonizers into military service, either as sexual slaves or as conscripts.

This colonial legacy of Japan still endures today, though in a bizarre sort of way. Thus, the present Japanese prime minister, Junichiro Koizumi, has paid regular visits to the Yasukuni Shrine in Tokyo. This Shinto shrine, founded in 1869 as Tokyo Shokonsha and renamed in 1879 as Yasukuni or 'Peaceful Country' Shrine, was built as a place of commemoration and worship of all those who have died in war for the country and the building of a peaceful Japan. About two and a half million people in all, from the conflicts of the Meiji Restoration to World War II, are enshrined here, their names inscribed on mortuary tablets. Among them, however, are to be found 1068 convicted war criminals from World War II, including fourteen class-A war criminals, among them the wartime prime minister, Hideki Tojo – all secretly enshrined in 1978. As a result, visits by Japanese prime ministers to the site – which began in 1975 and thus prior to this secret enshrinement and include several such visits on the part of Prime Minister Koizumi – have always proved highly controversial, especially in surrounding Asian countries, given the association of the shrine with the history of Japanese militarism and imperialism. In response, Prime Minister Koizumi himself has declared that his visits are solely for the purpose of *praying for peace*: 'I went with various feelings, including wishes for Japan's peace and prosperity … Japan does not rest solely upon the efforts of people living now … Japan stands upon the sacrifices of others in the past' (*China Daily*, 'Koizumi Visits Shrine to War Dead': 1 January 2004).

Although the Japanese colonization of Korea lasted a mere generation (1910–45), its cultic imperial orientation continued in North Korea in the form of the personality cult of its leader, Il Sung Kim (1912–94). Kim was first installed in September 1945 by the Soviets as head of the Provisional People's Committee; initially, therefore, he was not the head of the Communist Party, whose headquarters were in Seoul in the US-occupied south. However, through a series of military campaigns both before and after the Korean War, he was able to establish and re-establish his rule. In order to legitimate his military dictatorship, Kim, following the pattern of Japanese colonialism, constructed his own narrative history and developed a personality cult in which he was declared to be the 'Great Leader'. He was enshrined in the constitution as the country's 'eternal president', and his birthday became a public holiday. From the 1970s on, Kim upheld his power in supernatural fashion, supervising every aspect of life in the Democratic People's Republic of Korea (Suh 1988). Such deification of Kim led the nation to sustain the imperial–colonial legacy as an ongoing experience long after the surrender of the Japanese Empire in 1945.

The infusion of religious faith into imperial politics is thus by no means just an ancient phenomenon but rather one still very much at work in the modern world. A more recent example can be found in the United States itself, in the figure and declarations of President George W. Bush. President Bush has often stated how much he relies on his religious faith for guidance in governance and has further referred to the significant role that prayer plays in the country's military campaigns during the invasion and occupation of Iraq. In fact, not only have thousands of soldiers on the battlefields and occupied zones of Iraq been asked to pray for the president, but also 'prayer warriors' nationwide have organized to provide support for him and other military leaders in Iraq. Further, President Bush has resorted to biblical imagery in describing the United States and its place in the world. This is clear in his remarks to the nation on 11 September 2002: 'This ideal of America is the hope of all mankind... That hope still lights our way. And the light shines in the darkness. And the darkness will not overcome it' (Bush 2002; see Jn 1.4-5, 'And the life was the light of all people, the light shines in the darkness, and the darkness did not overcome it'). It is readily evident as well in his volume of 1999 entitled *A Charge to Keep*, where he recalls bestowing special significance on a specific weather development at the time of his inauguration as governor of Texas: 'The sky was overcast. As I stood to take the oath of office and give my inaugural address, the sun broke through the clouds. The future of Texas is bright, I told the huge crowd gathered on the south lawn of the Texas Capitol' (Bush 1999: 9). Such a frame of reference reveals how what is to all appearances a 'natural' occurrence is viewed by the president as a sign of divine favour, quite in the fashion of Roman emperors, who thought of themselves as similarly blessed in antiquity.

Cultic practices have thus often served as a means for imperial powers to impose their social, cultural and economic order on indigenous peoples. Korea provides another clear example in this regard. In 1882, the year when American missionaries first arrived in the country, the United States became the first Western nation to extract an unequal treaty from Korea (Paik 1929: 59). At the very moment when the treaty was being put into effect, US missionaries stood aboard a US Navy ship. Although such intersection of the religious and political realms has always been a common occurrence, today it is far more disguised, given the modern reduction of religious life to the private arena. Thus, as Richard Horsley argues (2003: 13–44), the more religion becomes separated from political–economic life and its institutions, the more ambiguous this interrelationship becomes.

Nevertheless, imperial domination continues to affect the lives of many colonial and postcolonial subjects. Indeed, such domination has made it very difficult for them to discern the call of God. In this regard, the emergence of Korean *Minjung* theology in the 1970s and the revival of Buddhism in the early 1990s prove highly suggestive. Both movements arose in reaction to Western cultural and political–economic invasion. On the one hand, *Minjung* theology argued that the marginalized, or *Minjung*, should be viewed in the image of the suffering Jesus and redeemed or liberated accordingly. In so doing, *Minjung* theology sought to reassure the marginalized in their lost identities, silenced as they had been, spiritually as well as physically, by the colonial powers. On the other hand, a *Minjung* movement within Buddhism, which began in the late 1970s and continued to gain popularity through the 1980s, led Buddhist activists and students to participate in demonstrations of opposition to the ruling establishment of the country and its American supporters (Mun 2003).

In light of these reflections, a number of questions come readily to the fore in a postcolonial reading of Jude. How should Jude be read in such a multi-faceted context of religion and politics, or, better, how should such a context be addressed in the light of Jude and its teaching in particular? What does the teaching of Jude have to offer to those living under the threat of neocolonialism? Would such teaching serve to foster a new narrative that acknowledges cultural diversity and independence? The answers to these questions are by no means simple. They require a gradual development of alternative ways of thinking and acting. Such alternative ideologies and faith-visions will, in the end, serve to reorder the view of the past, the present and the future among colonial and postcolonial subjects in the midst of their present and troubled circumstances. In what follows, then, I undertake a reading of Jude with decolonization in mind.

Reading Jude for Decolonization

Jude is a brief letter of exhortation written to a community disturbed by the presence of certain 'ungodly' intruders (v. 4). These are presumably itinerant teachers or prophets of the sort common in the early church. Their doctrines and practices are described as at variance with the apostolic tradition received by the church (vv. 4, 17-19). Appealing to their charismatic authority, such teachers are said to disparage the angels, who were regarded as guardians of the moral order (v. 8), and to present themselves as the only truly spiritual people. Their motivation, however, is identified as financial gain (vv. 11-12, 16). They have seemingly succeeded in gathering a following of their own (vv. 19, 22-23). These false teachers and prophets are further seen as threatening to lead people astray by their moral laxity. Such immorality is said to pervert God's order of creation, which Christ enforces, and to deny his lordship, leaving those who sin vulnerable to judgment (vv. 4, 8-16). Thus, Jude argues, they 'reject the power of the Lord and blaspheme the supernatural powers' (v. 8). Jude, therefore, is alert to their presence, condemns their behaviour, and exhorts the believers to remain faithful (vv. 3-4).

In so doing, Jude hints at the wrong kinds of cultic rituals taking place, including idolatrous worship of these prophets, and urges the believers to acknowledge their falsehood. Jude's focus is thus on criticism of the powers that blaspheme the Lord and defile the community. To begin with, he provides ethical instructions for Christian living in terms of the lordship of Christ. Christians are to make a concerted effort not only to advance their individual and corporate spiritual lives (v. 3) but also to remain cognizant of the real dangers of influence by such false doctrines and practices (vv. 22-23). In addition, Jude attempts to convince those who have been persuaded by the false teachers to abandon them and their ways. In order to save members of the community from destruction, he has to convince them that these intruders represent the 'ungodly' of prophecy (vv. 14-19) and are heading for devastation (vv. 5-16).

Jude's purpose is upfront and clear. He also writes out of urgent necessity. His aim comes across most sharply in v. 5, where he writes: 'I want you to remember'. At this point, then, Jude provides a variety of examples of figures from the past who failed to remain faithful and indulged instead in licentiousness. The list is extensive: the disobedience of Israel during the exodus (v. 5), the displacement of the angels (v. 6), the destruction of Sodom and Gomorrah (v. 7), the battle between the archangel Michael and the devil (vv. 9-10), the erroneous ways of Cain, Balaam and Korah (v. 11) and the prophecy of Enoch concerning God's punishment (vv. 14-16). Quite strikingly, all of these examples are drawn from the Palestinian Jewish scriptural tradition. Even *1 Enoch* and *The Assumption of Moses* are cited. One can surmise, therefore, that the intruders against whom Jude is warning must be encouraging some sort of religious and cultural assimilation to the dominant Graeco-Roman culture. Thus, by reminding his readers of disobedient angels and Israelites from the past who engaged in dangerous intercourse with unbelieving Gentiles, Jude may be seen as urging his readers to remain within a Jewish-Christian definition of life and faith.

Hence, Jude underscores the fact that the opponents deny the authority of the law of Moses (vv. 8-10) and, in so doing, the authority of Christ himself (vv. 4, 8). This denial may be based on their claim of prophetic revelation (v. 8). As a corollary of this rejection of authority on their part, the opponents are characterized as immoral (vv. 4, 6-8, 10, 16). Since the situation at hand is perceived as spiritually fatal, Jude pursues an immediate and drastic course of action. For him, these false teachers, given their beliefs and their behaviour, represent precursors of the parousia; consequently, he argues, they, along with their followers, shall be destroyed at its coming (vv. 14-15, 17-18, 23). Jude raises two issues in particular with regard to this wrong kind of spiritual orientation and worship. The first relates to the meaning of 'faith'. For him, 'faith' represents a body of doctrine to be handed on from one generation of Christians to another virtually unchanged, 'once for all entrusted to the saints' (v. 3). The second has to do with morality and judgment. He insists on the reality of divine judgment for those who deliberately defy the moral authority of the Lord and teach others to do so. Thus, in effect, Jude holds that faith in Jesus Christ entails a corresponding way of life: those who acknowledge Jesus as Lord must live in obedience to him. Throughout, Jude strongly affirms the lordship of Christ (vv. 4, 14, 17, 21, 25).

I shall now proceed to examine how Jude relates the addressees of the letter to their socio-historical context in reaction against the intruders. In so doing, I shall pay particular attention to Jude's articulations of faith as well as to the criteria advanced for acknowledging falsehood in their lives and finding spiritual orientation and worship.

Overview of the Epistle

The question of authorship is complex. The letter as such is attributed to Jude (Judas), 'a servant of Jesus and brother of James' (v. 1). The majority of commentators argue for pseudonymous authorship from a later time, while some accept genuine authorship from an early time. Against authenticity, the fine quality of the literary Greek employed as well as the call 'to remember the apostolic predictions' (v. 17) are invoked. These features, it is argued, speak against an early dating of the letter and, especially, authorship by one of Jesus' blood relatives. For authenticity, among other things, the reference to 'the brother of James' is noted, since James, a brother of Jesus (Mt. 13.55; Mk 6.3), was a well-known leader in the early church, who could simply be called 'James' without any risk of ambiguity. Given the importance of James, then, 'Jude' is identified as a brother of the Lord, who opted to present himself in the letter as a 'servant of Jesus'. Were this to be the case, the letter would emerge as one of the earliest writings of the New Testament, derived directly from Palestinian Jewish Christianity (Bauckham 1983; 1990). In the end, however, the data is much too scant to take a firm position in either direction. What is clear is that the author addresses a community disturbed by the presence of false teachers (v. 4).

For a postcolonial reading of the letter, it is not the question of authorship that is important but the socio-historical context behind the indictment of the opposition. Particularly significant in this regard is the urgent situation identified as the occasion for the writing (vv. 2-4). In effect, Jude explains that his letter is not the extended discussion of Christian salvation that he had originally intended to write but rather an ad hoc response to the news that the communities have been infiltrated by a group of itinerant teachers whose lifestyle and message he considers dangerous to his readers. Although Jude is preoccupied with these intruders, he does not provide their identity or the content of their teaching. He accuses them instead of immorality and threatens them with judgment.

'Our only Master and Lord, Jesus Christ' (v. 4)

Jude's condemnation of the false teachers is intertwined with an emphatic statement regarding Jesus' authority: 'For certain intruders have stolen in among you, people who long ago were designated for this condemnation as ungodly, who pervert the grace of our God into licentiousness and deny our only Master and Lord, Jesus Christ' (v. 4). Thus, from the outset, Jude deliberately places Jesus' lordship at the forefront of his accusation. The false teachers are said to deny Jesus' exclusive authority as their Lord, subjecting themselves instead to other lords or exalting themselves as worthy of being worshipped (see vv. 4, 8-16). For Jude, however, believers owe obedience only to Christ for his work in their salvation, a salvation whose completion is based on a lifetime of obedience (v. 21).

It is worth noting in this regard that Jude refers simply to 'Jesus Christ' only in the opening address and greeting of his letter (v. 1). Once he moves into the body of the letter, he always combines 'Jesus Christ' with 'our Lord' (vv. 4, 17, 21, 25). This shift is probably due to a desire on his part to make Jesus' authority explicit, as it is the case with the use of the title 'Lord'. Such emphasis on lordship seems to be connected with the polemic against the false teachers. Thus, Jude's first reference to Jesus' lordship occurs in his summary statement of the danger posed by the false teachers (v. 4), where it takes an emphatic form: 'our only Master (*despotēs*) and Lord (*kurios*)'. Moreover, Jude is concerned throughout with this kind of divine authority. It is such authority that the false teachers reject (v. 8) when they 'deny our only Master and Lord Jesus Christ' (v. 4).

The term *despotēs* was a common designation for the master of the household, who wielded enormous power (*patria potestas*) over family and slaves. By analogy, the term was used as well of state rulers, who held unlimited power over their subjects. In fact, the Roman emperor was referred to as the 'supreme father of the empire' or the 'father of the fatherland'. Since the time of Caesar, the title *Pater Patriae* had been consistently conferred upon the emperor, although Tiberius never accepted it (Hornblower and Spawforth 2003: 1121). This eloquent title was highly suggestive of the protective but coercive authority bestowed on the *paterfamilias*. Likewise, the title *kurios* was commonly used to refer to the Roman emperors. This image of the ruler as lord of the empire served as an ideological basis for the legitimization of the imperial system. Given such a framework, therefore, the authority of Jesus as *despotēs* and *kurios*, as 'master' and 'lord', becomes the grounds for Jude's polemic. In particular, the phrase 'our only Master and Lord' as a whole would not only reinforce the royal and judicial power of Jesus but also convey a strong indication of divinity. It was the kind of phrase used by Jews to confess the exclusive lordship of the one God of Israel and to refuse idolatrous allegiance to other lords. Consequently, Jude's focus is clearly on the present lordship of Jesus over his people (v. 21). This lordship, moreover, bears a strong ethical sense, insofar as moral laxity is said to derive from an irreverent rejection of Jesus' authority and commandments.

Crimes and Judgment (vv. 5-16)

Given Jude's use of Jewish sources, apocalyptic texts and traditions, it would seem that he is working within the confines of Jewish-Christianity, which possessed a vibrant apocalyptic outlook. From within such a framework, then, he advises his addressees to embrace what is good and to disregard what is not. His aim in this regard is, no doubt, to persuade the church 'to contend for the faith', awakening God's promises 'given once and for all' (v. 3), and not to heed the message and practice of the intruders. Again, Jude employs Jewish moral teachings to reject the claims to primacy of his opponents. They are first described by the single and powerful term 'ungodly' (*asebeis*) (v. 4). This is a watchword to which Jude resorts again later on in the letter (vv. 15, 18). With it Jude denounces the opponents as comparable to great sinners of the past and the subject of prophecies of judgment. It is a denunciation meant, again, to strengthen the church in the faith and to preserve its members from impending judgment. For this purpose, Jude draws upon a variety of interpretive resources, which he proceeds to colour with his own pressing concerns. Such a strategy can be readily seen in his appeal to the following traditions as typological:

- 'A people out of the land of Egypt' (v. 5). In the midst of the exodus, which could be seen as a great salvation event, a whole generation of faithless Israelites came to die in the wilderness. They were doomed because of their apostasy (see Numbers 14; Deut. 1.32; 9.23). They rebelled against the divine authority of God. This sin and judgment on the part of Israel becomes a typological example for apostate Christians such as Jude's own opponents and their followers.
- 'The angels who did not keep their own position' (v. 6). In the Genesis story about the 'sons of God' (Gen. 6.1-4), the angels are portrayed as leaving heaven to mate with women. Jude sees this as a clear example of apostasy. By leaving their heavenly location, they subverted God's purpose on earth. They taught humans forbidden knowledge and all kinds of sin, and their children, the giants, ravaged the earth. Hence, these fallen angels are doomed under the earth until the Day of Judgment, and their children are condemned to destroy each other in battle (see *1 Enoch* 6–19). This tradition Jude applies to the false teachers, who deny the authority of the Lord and rise above it.
- 'Sodom and Gomorrah' (v. 7). In the account of Genesis, the Sodomites are depicted as indulging in sexual immorality and pursuing 'unnatural' lust, even with the angels (19.4-11). Their condemnation was thus inevitable. For Jude, therefore, they serve as a further example of apostate Christians, who also transgress the order signified by God's commandments and abandon their loyalty to it.
- 'Woe to them! For they go the way of Cain' (v. 11). Cain represents a primary example of leading others into sin (Genesis 4). For Jude, Cain is not just the first murderer but the archetypal sinner who corrupted the whole race of Adam in the ways of sin. Consequently, just as he is held responsible for his behaviour, so will the false teachers.
- 'Woe to them! ... and abandon themselves to Balaam's error for the sake of gain' (v. 11). According to Numbers, the prophet Balaam accepted Balak's

invitation for the sake of financial gain and was also the source of the advice that led Israel into debauchery and idolatry (Numbers 22–24; 25.1-3). In similar fashion, therefore, Jude presents the false teachers, who are leading others astray, as enticed by the prospect of reward (vv. 11-12, 16) and notes that they shall not avoid judgment.

- 'Woe to them! ... and perish in Korah's rebellion' (v. 11). Finally, Jude invokes the figure of Korah, who led a rebellion against the divine authority of God's commandments (Num. 16.1-35), a classic example of rebellion and dissension in the Jewish tradition (see Ps. 106.16-18; Sir. 45:18-19). For Jude, therefore, Korah becomes a type of the false teachers: just as he and his fellow conspirators perished by divine judgment, so will the false teachers suffer the same fate.

- In the case of the last three examples, a further observation is in order: the use of a woe (*ouai*) oracle (v. 11) conveys a profound sense of pain and anger with respect to those who have gone over to the way of error and who wage such corrupting influence on the community.

In sum, by drawing upon such typological examples, Jude seeks to make his addressees aware of the opponents and their destiny. They are all, he points out, in violation of God's authority and order of creation. Consequently, believers need to acknowledge these transgressions on the part of the false teachers, who continue to lead others into transgression as well.

Warnings and Exhortations (vv. 17-23)

Jude's examples from the Hebrew Bible involve not only sin but also judgment. He cites examples from tradition in order to show his addressees how they can resist the danger of false teachings (vv. 20-21) and how they should seek to rebuke the false teachers and their followers (vv. 22-23). In effect, God has already acted in history. God's acts in the history of Israel constitute snapshots that point forward to God's acts in Christ. God also acts in the time of Jude and against the false teachers and their claims. According to Jude, therefore, believers need to see such acts of God as a type of prophecy regarding the judgment to be rendered on those who pretend to surpass Jesus' lordship. Thereby Jude seeks to warn believers about the ungodly people of the end times in which they are living (v. 18).

Jude's addressees are called upon to identify, on the basis of their behaviour, the false teachers and their followers with the doomed ungodly of prophecy. They are also called upon to acknowledge the fact of judgment. In the end, moreover, the faithful believers must prevail, while the ungodly await their judgment as prophesied. Again, Jude alerts his readers thereby to the danger in which they find themselves. They must acknowledge the influence of the false teachers and redirect their lives in obedience to the gospel. Through recognition of and participation in the typological interpretations offered, believers are to adopt a vision of life with Christ as *kurios* and of judgment against the false teachers and authorities.

In light of the situation and teaching of Jude outlined as well as the inter-action between religion and politics described in the introduction, I turn now for an appropriate alternative hermeneutics to a reading from the Two-Thirds World. Such a move will serve both to approach rituals and cultic practices in a more liberating fashion and to embrace an alternative hermeneutics for decolonization.

Discovering the Postcolonial Optic

In a sermon entitled 'The Dandelion', Jung Young Lee, a Korean theologian, calls attention to the way in which spatial construction is related to the values of colonization or decolonization. The sermon itself is written in autobiographical fashion and from an Asian perspective. It revolves around the presence of a dandelion in the midst of a green lawn.

Lee describes his own reaction when, upon seeing a dandelion growing in a far corner of his lawn, he snatches it from the grass:

> It was golden yellow, like the rising sun, 'why don't I like you?' I said to the dandelion. The dandelion smiled backed at me. It did not say it, but I knew what it tried to tell me. In its smile was the cynical message: 'You hate me because I represent you.' I became so sad that I lost the courage to question anymore. I sat on the lawn under the warm spring sun and looked mindlessly at the lonely dandelion for some time. Gradually my mind was taken far away to my early childhood in Korea. (Lee 1988: 15–16)

The dandelion is thus humanized in the image of a marginal or underprivi-leged person such as Lee himself. Lee has a flashback to a time when he could describe himself as a dandelion. He recalls a story about a struggle between a dandelion and the grass, as the latter claims dominion over the entire area.

In this story a landowner proceeds to garden his yard and comes upon a dan-delion flower. The landowner does not care for it at all and tries to pull it out by its roots. The plant, however, is so deeply embedded in the ground that it breaks instead. During the winter that followed, the dandelion strenghened its roots. The next year, then, the dandelion decided not to display its own yellow colour, having witnessed the hatred of the landowner for such colour in the midst of his green yard. The dandelion sought to conform to the colour of the yard. This decision, however, caused the dandelion to lose the meaning of its existence, for it found it impossible to blend in with the grass. Finally, the dandelion made up its mind to display its true nature, and, after a while, it stretched its stem up toward the sky, bringing forth its yellowness and golden flower.

At this point, Lee comes back to present reality and brings the story to a conclusion as follows:

> I saw the yellow flower that I was holding in my hand... Several days later its head turned white. I took it outside, put it close to my mouth, and blew it as hard as I could. The white seeds went up high in the sky and began to fall down like parachutes all

over the rich green yards. 'Let them live; let them live anywhere they want to live. *It is God's world, and they are God's creatures,*' I said as I watched them. (Lee 1988: 20, emphasis mine)

This sermon reflects the construction of ritual space in relation to the pattern of the colonizing agents and the colonized marginalized. The landowner epitomizes the power and authority the grass could apply to every corner of the land. The grass mirrors the teachers and prophets who claim their space, legitimizing their teachings and practices. The implicated authority is to be inscribed throughout, exerting its pre-eminent influence in order to harness the faith of all believers. In such a context there would be no isolated marginalized and no independent, 'innocent' privileged. The dandelion, however, encourages us to perceive the world in a different way, for 'it is God's world, and they are God's creatures'. The story readily suggests our own lack of awareness of God, who is actually at work in our midst. Jude's criticism of the powers that promote idolatrous worship and endorse moral laxity and cultic assimilation becomes more poignant in this regard. The story seems open-ended, even now.

Conclusion

Many postcolonial critics have argued that colonialism has never really ended but has survived instead in culturally and politically different forms. In like fashion, I would argue, imperial power relations have also remained embedded in religious rituals and symbols. Such infusion and interaction produce a fairly elaborate narrative of subordination. Jude labels such a phenomenon illegitimate by comparing it to 'waterless clouds' and 'autumn trees without fruit' (v. 12). The agents are thus looked upon as intruders, feeding themselves and not caring for others. They claim freedom to indulge their own desire, denying Christ as Master and Lord. Jude, therefore, urges readers to discern such ungodly teaching and their agents, who have perverted the inviolable faith, by providing a vision of God's presence over against the potential for destruction with regard to the intruders. Through such teaching, the community members would release their cultic space from any misappropriation by exploitative power and desires. Such teaching would further serve to acknowledge their corporeal existence as living in God's world. Such acknowledgment and practice, in turn, would enrich and contribute to the world of 'others', saving all from the alleged necessity of waging war against the 'axis of evil'.

BIBLIOGRAPHY

Bauckham, Richard J.
    1983   *Jude, 2 Peter* (Word Biblical Commentary, 50; Waco, TX: Word Books).
    1990   *Jude and the Relatives of Jesus in the Early Church* (Edinburgh: T&T Clark).

Bush, George W.
    1999   *A Charge to Keep* (New York: William Morrow & Company).
    2002   'Remarks to the Nation' (11 September), Associated Baptist Press <www.abpnews.com/abpnews/story.cfm?newsid=1788&action=2>.

Craddock, Fred B.
    1995   *First and Second Peter and Jude* (Louisville, KY: Westminster/John Knox Press).

Hornblower, Simon and Antony Spawforth
    2003   *The Oxford Classical Dictionary* (Oxford and New York: Oxford University Press).

Horsley, Richard
    2003   'Religion and Other Products of Empire', *Journal of the American Academy of Religion* 71: 13–44.

Lee, Jung Young
    1988   'The Dandelion', in *Sermons to the 12* (Nashville: Abingdon Press): 15–20.

Mun, Chanju
    2003   'A Historical Introduction to Minjung Buddhism – A Liberation Buddhism of South Korea in the 1980's', in *Journal of the Korean Buddhist Seminar* (special issue: *Memorial Edition for the Late Professor Kim Chigy*) 9: 239–71.

Neyrey, Jerome. H.
    1993   *2 Peter, Jude* (Anchor Bible, 37C; New York: Doubleday).

Paik, L. George
    1929   *The History of Protestant Missions in Korea, 1832–1910* (Pyeng Yang: Union Christian Press).

Perkins, Pheme
    1995   *First and Second Peter, James, and Jude* (Interpretation; Louisville, KY: Westminster/John Knox Press).

Suh, Dae-Sook
    1988   *Kim Il Sung: The North Korean Leader* (New York: Columbia University).

THE REVELATION TO JOHN

Stephen D. Moore

To ponder Revelation's relations to empire – a predictable preoccupation for a 'postcolonial' commentary on the book – is hardly a novel gesture. Critical scholars of Revelation have customarily read it as the most uncompromising attack on the Roman Empire, and on Christian collusion with the empire, to issue from early Christianity. Historical-critical reflection on Revelation and Rome crystallized in such studies as Leonard L. Thompson's *The Book of Revelation: Apocalypse and Empire* (1990). More recently, Wes Howard-Brook and Anthony Gwyther's *Unveiling Empire: Reading Revelation Then and Now* (1999) has intensified such reflection, and also surpassed it, in the extent to which the authors place the phenomenon of empire fully at the centre of their reading of Revelation, coupled with their intent to read the book as a critique of contemporary as well as ancient empire. In the latter regard, they have been anticipated by (other) liberationist readings of Revelation, notably Allan Boesak's *Comfort and Protest: The Apocalypse from a South African Perspective* (1997) and Pablo Richard's *Apocalypse: A People's Commentary on the Book of Revelation* (1995).

None of the aforementioned works engage with, or even allude to, postcolonial theory or criticism as they situate Revelation in relation to empire. In noting this, I am not purporting to name a failing so much as gesture to a supplementary space, not yet a crowded one, in which the present commentary will seek to situate itself. (The works by Steven Friesen, Christopher Frilingos, Jean Kim and Vitor Westhelle in the bibliography, along with Catherine Keller's *God and Power* (2005), already have at least one foot in this space, but I know of no others.) Before launching into this portion of the essay, however – a reading of Revelation impelled by the colonial discourse analysis of Homi Bhabha – a preliminary fleshing out of Revelation's socio-political context will be in order.

Imperium Romanum

The concept and practice of colonialism are by no means irrelevant to Revelation's historical provenance, as we shall quickly discover. The scope of postcolonial studies, however, is not limited to the phenomenon of colonialism; it also encompasses imperialism (and much else besides, not least decolonization, globalization and neocolonialism). 'Imperialism' here denotes the multifarious, mutually constitutive ideologies (political, economic, racial/ethnic, religious, etc.) that impel a metropolitan centre to annex more-or-less distant territories and that determine its subsequent dealings with them. Although the English word 'imperialism' did not emerge, apparently, until the late nineteenth century and was first used in connection with European expansionism, its etymological and conceptual roots lie in the Latin word *imperium*, which under the Roman republic designated the authority vested in consuls, magistrates and other select officials to exercise command and exact obedience, and in the post-Augustan era was deemed to reside supremely in the person of the emperor. The latter's *imperium*, voted to him by the Roman senate at his accession, extended in principle to all peoples and territories under Rome's dominion.

At first or even second glance, Revelation would appear to be an anti-imperial(istic) text that, in effect, announces the transfer of worldwide *imperium* from the Roman emperor to the heavenly Emperor and his Son and co-regent, the 'King of kings and Lord of lords' (19.16; see 17.14). As Revelation itself phrases this transfer, 'The empire [*basileia*] of the world has become the empire of our Lord and of his Messiah' (11.15; see 14.6-8). The paramount question the present commentary will raise, however (one impelled by the particular body of postcolonial theory it will be harnessing), is whether or to what extent Revelation merely reinscribes, rather than effectively resists, Roman imperial ideology.

Coloniae Romanum

Revelation is explicitly addressed to seven urban churches in the Roman province of Asia (1.4, 11), the westernmost province of the larger geographical region known (confusingly enough) as Asia Minor, which extended from the Aegean to the western Euphrates, thus corresponding roughly to modern Turkey. The history of colonization in Asia Minor extended back to the Hellenizing campaigns of Alexander the Great and his successors, who sowed Greek cities (*poleis*) throughout the region – though several of Revelation's seven cities, notably Ephesus and Smyrna, were Greek colonies well before the advent of Alexander. The extent, indeed, to which the multilayered Hellenization of the region effected a cultural colonization that expedited its eventual absorption by the consummately Hellenized Romans can scarcely be exaggerated.

The English term 'colony' derives from the Latin *colonia* (the equivalent Greek term would be *apoikia*), but it would be misleading to conceive of Roman *coloniae* purely on the model of the European colonies of the early modern period and its aftermath. The classic Roman *colonia* was a civic foundation, which is to say a city or town. Essentially, *coloniae* were civic communities of Roman citizens settled outside Italy and composed mainly of military veterans.

The *colonia* was one of the three principal types of Roman provincial community, all of them urban; the others were the *municipia* (confined mainly to the Latin west, and of lesser status than the *colonia*), and the city or town that was neither an official *colonia* nor a *municipia*, and as such less 'Romanized' than either. The classic unit of Roman colonization, then (in the contemporary sense of the term), was urban, and it was through an infrastructure of self-governing cities that Roman provinces were administered.

What of the province of Asia? Julius Caesar and especially Augustus had each engaged in the settlement of military veterans in various pockets of Asia Minor generally, which is to say that they 'seeded' the region with *coloniae*, but the systematic introduction of new settlers became rare in the post-Augustan period – which begs the question of the precise nature of Roman rule in Asia under the principate.

Contemporary postcolonial discourse frequently distinguishes between *settler colonies*, on the one hand, and *colonies of occupation*, on the other (while acknowledging that many colonies fit neatly into neither category but straddle both at once). Settler colonies (also known as settler–invader colonies) are ones in which the indigenous population is decimated and uprooted, eventually becoming a minority in relation to the majority settler–invader population; the classic modern examples of such colonies would be Australia, Canada and the United States. In contrast, colonies of occupation are ones in which the indigenous population remains in the majority numerically, but is administered by a foreign power; modern examples would include pre-independence India or Ireland.

Which of these two modes of colonization best approximates the situation of Roman Asia? As has already been implied, Asia could in no wise be regarded as a settler–invader colony (using the term colony now in its modern sense); it better fits the colony of occupation model instead. Roman culture was concentrated in the (mainly coastal) cities of the province in contrast to the rural Anatolian interior, which managed to preserve its indigenous character, conspicuous especially in its native languages and religious cults, more or less intact until the third century CE. Even in the cities, however, the Roman presence would have been relatively slight. In general, the number of elite Roman officials allotted to any one province was minuscule relative to the amount of territory to be administered. Asia was one of the 'ungarrisoned' provinces of the empire; moreover, no full legion was stationed there, and what military presence there was tended to be concentrated in the interior. What, then, were the mechanisms that enabled continuous Roman control of Asia?

Hegemony

At this point, another concept commonly invoked in contemporary postcolonial studies may usefully be introduced, that of *hegemony*, in the special sense accorded to the term many decades ago by the Italian Marxist intellectual Antonio Gramsci. Hegemony, in the Gramscian sense, means *domination by consent* – in effect, the active participation of a dominated group (whether a social underclass, say – Gramsci's own principal focus – or a colonized people) in its own subjugation. The attraction of the concept for postcolonial critics is that it serves to account for the ability of an imperial power to govern a colonized territory whose indigenous population overwhelmingly outnumbers the army of occupation. In such cases, the indigene's desire for self-determination will have been displaced by a discursively inculcated notion of the greater good, couched in such terms as social stability (whether in the form of a Pax Romana or a Pax Britannica) and economic and cultural advancement. The more efficient an imperial administration, indeed, the more it will rely on hegemonic acquiescence and the less it will have recourse to material force in the retention and exploitation of its colonial possessions – in which case the neocolonial empires of contemporary global capitalism would represent a quantum leap in administrative efficiency when measured against the relatively unwieldy empires of the past.

The concept of hegemony usefully illuminates the situation of Roman Asia. The province itself originated not in an invasion but in an invitation: Attalus III of Pergamum bequeathed his kingdom to the Romans. It became *provincia Asia* after his death in 133 BCE and expanded in increments over the next half-century or so, gradually assuming the form it would take under the principate. Like any Roman province, the routine governance of Asia depended upon the active cooperation and participation of the local urban elites. The administrative infrastructure consisted of a loose coalition of self-governing cities, each having responsibility for the territorial hinterland attached to it. The mainspring of the complex hegemonic mechanism that enabled Roman governance of Asia, however – economically a jewel in the imperial crown, rich in natural resources, agriculture and industry – was the competition for imperial favour and recognition in which the principal Asian cities were perpetually locked (Ephesus, Pergamum and Smyrna in particular, although the rivalry extended to many lesser cities as well). An important expression of this competition was the city's public demonstration of the measure of its loyalty to the emperor, the ultimate patron or benefactor in relation to whom the city was a client or dependent, and as such in rivalry with the other client cities of the province for a limited quantity of goods and privileges. The principal mechanism in turn for formal demonstrations of such loyalty was the imperial cult, the rendering of divine honours to Roman emperors, living or dead.

Divus Caesar

Officially instituted in 42 BCE, when the Roman senate posthumously recognized Julius Caesar as divine, the imperial cult – to the extent that it can be spoken of in the singular: it was profoundly marked by regional variation, as we shall see – infiltrated the religio-political life of every province in the empire during the Augustan and post-Augustan periods (with the hard-won exception of the province of Judaea). Whereas in the western provinces the imperial cult tended to be imposed by Rome, in the eastern provinces it was a 'voluntary' affair. It could well afford to be. Ruler worship in the east predated Roman expansion, having been catalysed in particular by the spectacular conquests of Alexander the Great. Whereas in Rome itself divine honours were offered as a rule only to deceased emperors (impatient exceptions notwithstanding, notably Caligula, Nero and Commodus), the worship of currently reigning emperors was tolerated and even encouraged in the provinces. What more reassuring token of an apparent willingness to be conquered could a conqueror possibly desire? – even if the provincial imperial cults may, in historical hindsight, also be construed as surreptitious determinations on the part of the emperor's subjects of who and what he was to be for them, thus setting subtle limits on his autonomy in the very act of acknowledging his absolute authority.

From an exceedingly early stage, the local Asian elites enthusiastically embraced the Roman imperial cult, dedication to which became a major vehicle of competition between the leading cities of the province. But it was a highly regulated competition. Delegates of the various civic communities met annually as the Council or Assembly (*koinon*) of Asia in one of the five official provincial cities (Ephesus, Pergamum, Smyrna, Sardis or Cyzicus) in order to conduct the business of the province, a crucial element of which was the organization of the imperial cult. In 29 BCE, a mere two years after Octavian/Augustus' accession to supreme power, the Assembly of Asia had requested and was granted the honour of erecting a provincial temple to Roma and Augustus at Pergamum. The establishment of a cult of Roma and Augustus in Asia and in the neighbouring province of Pontus-Bithynia became a model for other eastern provinces. The cult of Roma or *Dea Roma* (the personification of Rome as goddess) is a particularly telling manifestation of hegemony (again, in the Gramscian sense), since no such cult existed in the capital itself. It was not imposed or even modelled by those at the apex of power, in other words, but was invented by Roman subjects instead (*elite* subjects, however, a point to which I shall return below). A temple to *Dea Roma* had existed at Smyrna since 193 BCE, the first such temple in Asia Minor.

The Assembly of Asia devised still more extravagant ways to acknowledge Rome's intimate and apparently irresistible hold on the destiny and daily life of the province. Early in the principate, the assembly, in consultation with the Roman proconsul of Asia, determined to honour *Divus Augustus* by creating a new calendar for the province that would begin not on 1 January, as in the standard Roman calendar, but on 23 September, the emperor's birthday – again, a signal instance of those nearer the base of the pyramid of power surpassing those nearer the apex (those elites, that is, in the capital itself with physical access to the emperor) in the symbolic performance of subjection. A performance all the more remarkable for the fact that prior to the principate of Augustus the province had suffered acutely under Roman rule, due to rapacious governors, crushing taxes and a disastrously unsuccessful rebellion. The energy and rapidity with which the province of Asia subsequently set about deifying the conqueror and sweeping the sordid history of exploitation under the rug of myth testifies to the unprecedented efficiency of the Roman hegemonic apparatus under the principate – an efficiency that would be almost inexplicable were it not for the fact that the most extravagant expressions of consent to Roman domination of the region arose from the ranks of the local elites, who stood to gain infinitely more from ostentatious displays of acquiescence than the mainly impoverished urban and rural populations whom they purported to represent. Considerable prestige attached to the priesthoods and other offices of the provincial imperial cults – they could, indeed, form the pinnacle of a local political career. Major priesthoods in the imperial cults, moreover – most especially that of annual president or chief priest (*archiereus*) of the provincial assembly – could also form crucial stepping stones to a political career in Rome itself for the select few, or at least for their sons or grandsons.

In due course, therefore, each of Revelation's seven cities, along with others in the province, erected temples or altars to Roman potentates living or dead: Julius Caesar (coupled with *Dea Roma*), Augustus (also with *Dea Roma*), Tiberius (with the Roman senate), Vespasian, Domitian and Hadrian. The leading cities competed for the coveted title of *neokoros*, 'temple warden/caretaker', awarded at the discretion of the senate and the emperor to cities containing an imperial temple with pan-provincial status. Elaborate imperial festivals became a prominent feature of the religious life of the province, enmeshing the populace in a communal symbolic articulation of the omnipresence and immanence of absolute power in the absent person of the Roman emperor, whose arms encircled the civilized world by virtue of the *imperium Romanum*.

Catachresis

How best to situate Revelation in relation to the complex matrix of power relations that determined the religio-political life of Roman Asia? Consummately counter-hegemonic in thrust (in the specific sense in which I have been using the term hegemony), Revelation represents a stunning early instance of an anti-imperial literature of resistance. In shocking contrast to the official prayers offered to the Greek gods of the Olympian pantheon by priests of the local imperial cults for the health of the Roman emperor and the length of his reign (for prayers on behalf of the emperor were more common than prayers addressed to his image), Revelation gleefully predicts the imminent destruction of Rome instead, which it mockingly renames 'Babylon' (14.8; 16.9; 17.5; 18.2, 10, 21), in answer to the counter-prayers offered by Christians to their own god (6.9-11; 8.3-4; see 16.5-7; 19.1-2). In effect, faithful Christians constitute an imperial counter-cult in Revelation, a priesthood (1.6; 5.10; 20.6) dedicated to the Christian Emperor and his co-regent, Jesus Christ, in relation to which the official cult is meant to be seen as a monstrous aberration: worship of a beast that derives its ultimate authority from Satan (13.4, 8, 12, 14-15; see 14.9-11; 16.2; 19.20; 20.4).

This cunning polemical strategy can be construed as a signal instance of what the postcolonial theorist Gayatri Spivak has dubbed *catachresis*, originally a Greek term and rhetorical figure denoting 'misuse' or 'misapplication'. As employed by Spivak, the term designates the process by which the victims of colonialism or imperialism strategically appropriate and redeploy specific elements of colonial or imperial culture. Catachresis, in this sense, is a practice of resistance through an act of usurpation, a creative retooling of the rhetorical or institutional instruments of imperial oppression that turns those instruments back against their official owners. Catachresis is thus also an act of counter-appropriation: it counters the appropriative incursions of imperialist discourse – its institutional accoutrements, its representational modes, its ideological forms, its propagandistic ploys – by redirecting and thereby deflecting them. As a strategy of subversive adaptation, catachresis is related to parody, which can be defined in turn as an act or practice of strategic misrepresentation. In the context of imperialist and anti-imperialist discourse, indeed, parody is best regarded as a species of catachresis.

Parody of the Roman imperial order permeates Revelation, reaching a scurrilous climax in the depiction of the goddess Roma, austere and noble personification of the *urbs aeterna*, as a tawdry whore who has had a little too much to drink (17.1-6). The most fundamental instance of catachresis in Revelation, however, is its redeployment of the term 'empire' (*basileia*) itself. In Asia as in any Roman province, the primary referent of *basileia* would have been the *imperium Romanum*. Revelation, however, far from dispensing with the category of empire altogether in pronouncing upon the divine, retains the imperial model instead (down to its details, as we shall see), but makes certain audacious adjustments to it – most significantly, switching the figure at its centre so that it is no longer the Roman emperor, an exchange which effects a retooling of the entire model, producing a catachrestic realignment of the whole.

God as Caesar: Revelation 4–5

Speculation with regard to the details of this realignment has long been a standard feature of critical scholarship on Revelation. Chapters 4–5, for example, which constitute a notable case in point, have elicited observations such as the following:

- The acclamation, 'Worthy art thou', addressed to God or the Lamb by those assembled around the heavenly throne (4.11; 5.9; see 5.12), was also employed in Roman imperial court ceremonial to greet the emperor.

- The title, 'our Lord and God', likewise used in the heavenly court (4.11; see 4.8; 11.17; 15.3; 16.7; 19.6; Jn 20.28), was also applied to the emperor Domitian (under whose reign Revelation achieved its final form, if the scholarly majority is correct), whether or not he himself demanded it.
- The 24 elders around the throne (4.4) correspond to, among other things, the 24 lictors who regularly accompanied Domitian (lictors being fasces-bearing bodyguards whose number symbolized the degree of *imperium* conferred upon a Roman potentate).
- The elders' gesture of casting their crowns or wreaths (*stephanoi*) before the throne (4.10) corresponds with a form of obeisance frequently offered to Roman emperors.
- The reappearance of Jesus in the guise of a Lamb standing in the presence of the Divine Emperor 'as though it had been slaughtered' (*hōs esphagmenon*, 5.6) acquires added semantic clout from the fact that the image of the Roman emperor officiating at sacrifice was a pious commonplace from the reign of Augustus onwards, almost no one other than the emperor (and his immediate family) being depicted thus in the imperial iconography (sculptures, friezes, coins and imprinted sacrificial cakes) that proliferated throughout the empire (this last being my own contribution to this heady speculative exercise).

And so on.

The multiplication of such parallels by critical scholars has by no means been confined to Revelation 4–5; to a lesser extent, it has extended to the book as a whole. The sheer number of these alleged parallels, taken collectively, probably prohibits their outright dismissal as a product of scholarly mass hallucination: even if any specific parallel can always, of course, be contested, the existence of the general authorial strategy to which they gesture is probably as secure as most fixtures in the gently quaking quagmire of Revelation scholarship. I have relabelled that strategy catachresis here and noted its intimate relationship to parody. That Revelation's representation of the Roman imperial order is essentially parodic, however, has long been a tenet of critical scholarship on the book. In order to disclose what is really at stake in that tenet, and to rethink Revelation's relationship to empire more generally through the conceptual resources afforded by postcolonial theory, we had best turn to the work of Homi Bhabha. But first a final stage set needs to be wheeled into place.

The New Metropolis: Revelation 21–22

One signal advantage of Bhabha's conceptual categories for a reading of Revelation, as we shall see, is that they enable, indeed impel, us to interrogate the metaphysical and ethical dualism that the book attempts to foist upon us as one of its foundational rhetorical strategies: its construction of the Roman Empire as the absolute antithesis of 'the empire of God and his Messiah' (11.15). The success of the strategy is evident from the fact that this binary opposition has been endlessly and unreflectively replicated even in critical commentaries on Revelation.

Within the book itself, this dualism attains its apogee in the construction of the New Jerusalem, a scene in which Babylon/Rome is both absent (because already annihilated) and present (because still required, as we are about to see). The scene concludes with a blessing and a curse: 'Blessed are those who wash their robes, so that they will have the right to the tree of life and may enter the city by the gates. Outside are the dogs and sorcerers and fornicators and murderers and idolaters, and everyone who loves and practices falsehood' (22.14-15; see 21.8, 27). Here, then, is the cartography of paradise (see 2.7), an attenuated, absolutely hierarchized geography of difference, designed to distinguish a (hyper-idealized) 'metropolis' – the New Jerusalem, from a (demonized) 'periphery' – that which until recently was designated 'Babylon' in this book. Revelation's vision of paradise restored (see 22.1-2; Gen. 2.10; Ezek. 47.1-12) is thus the logical culmination of the dualism that has characterized its rhetoric throughout. The cartographic self-representations of the Roman Empire itself, in which the imperial territories gradually shaded over into the barbaric, the chaotic and the monstrous the further one ventured outward from the metropolis, is here countered with what is, in effect, a catachrestic parody of imperial cartography: immediately beyond the walls of the Christian metropolis, absolute alterity begins, with no incremental passage from sameness to difference to act as conceptual buffer (a binary conceit all the more curious for the contradictory fact that out in the negative zone entire nations are apparently poised to pay homage to the new megalopolis – 21.24, 26). In Revelation's hyperdualistic cosmos, then, Christian culture and Roman culture must be absolutely separate and separable (see 18.4). But are they? This is where Bhabha's strategies of colonial discourse analysis can be said to come into their own.

Ambivalence, Mimicry, Hybridity

Much of Homi Bhabha's *The Location of Culture* (1994), arguably the most influential and controversial contribution to colonial discourse theory since Edward Said's *Orientalism* (1978), amounts to a critical interrogation of any conceptual dichotomization of metropolis and periphery, empire and indigene, colonizer and colonized. Bhabha's enabling assumption is that the relationship between colonizer and colonized is instead characterized by *ambivalence*, which is to say simultaneous attraction and repulsion. Basing himself ultimately on the psychoanalytic contention that ambivalence is ubiquitous in psychic processes, Bhabha's presumption is that the stance of the colonized vis-à-vis the colonizer is never one of pure unequivocal opposition – which, by extension, calls a second dualistic distinction into question, that between the resistant colonial subject, on the one hand, and the complicit colonial subject, on the other. For

Bhabha, resistance and complicity coexist in different measures in each and every colonial subject. The complex conjoining of resistance and complicity is nowhere better expressed than in the phenomenon of *colonial mimicry*.

Colonial mimicry results when the colonizer's culture is imposed on the colonized and the latter is lured or coerced into internalizing and replicating it. This replication is never perfect, however – the colonized is never simply an exact copy of the colonizer ('almost the same but not white', is how Bhabha wittily phrases the matter) – nor does the colonizer wish this mimicry to be absolutely accurate, for then the hierarchical distinction between colonizer and colonized, original and copy, would collapse, and with it the linchpin of imperial ideology. Hence the essential ambivalence of the colonizer's injunction to the colonized to mimic him: 'replicate me/do not replicate me'. The injunction, moreover, is fraught with risk for the colonizer: mimicry can all too easily teeter over into mockery or parody, thereby menacing the authority and identity of the colonizer.

The third concept that, together with ambivalence and mimicry, captures the complex psychic interpenetration of colonizer and colonized, for Bhabha, is *hybridity*. In its 'weak' sense, the term hybridity as used in contemporary postcolonial studies means no more than that the contact between colonizer and colonized is constantly productive of hybrid cultural manifestations. Bhabha, however, has given the concept of hybridity a decidedly Derridean twist, seeing it not as a simple synthesis or syncretic fusion of two originally discrete cultures but rather as an in-between space, or 'Third Space', to use Bhabha's own preferred term, in which cultures are themselves simultaneously constituted and deconstructed: the identity of any cultural system only emerges as an effect of its differences from other cultural systems, but the infinitely open-ended differential network within which any given culture is situated radically and necessarily destabilizes its identity even as it generates it. In consequence, no culture can be pure, prior, original, unified or self-contained; it is always already infected by impurity, secondariness, mimicry, self-splitting and alterity: it is always already infected by hybridity.

In order to outline Bhabha's theory in brief, I have had to abstract it from its embeddedness in the analysis of disparate colonial texts and histories – most especially those of nineteenth-century British India, the prime catalyst for much of Bhabha's conceptual innovation – and systematize it to an extent that Bhabha himself, in good deconstructive fashion, has studiously avoided. But he has not been able to avoid scathing criticism. His theory has been prodded, probed and repeatedly contested over such issues as its alleged universalism – its application of 'First World' psychoanalytic categories to 'Third World' psychic processes, and its alleged diminution of agency – its disregard of overt and conscious forms of resistance on the part of the colonized in favour of covert and unconscious forms of resistance. These are serious criticisms and concerns, which I have pondered elsewhere. Without minimizing their significance, I would venture, nonetheless, to suggest that certain of the supple concepts offered by Bhabha, used cautiously and creatively, can enable a reappraisal not only of Revelation's relationship to empire but of Revelation's theology more generally. In what follows, therefore, I will be less interested in proving the theory than in reopening the book.

The Book of Mimicry

The phenomenon of mimicry is endemic to Revelation. The book's representation of the Roman imperial order is essentially parodic, as we have noted, and parody is a species of mimicry: it mimics in order to mock. Do Bhabha's pronouncements on colonial mimicry apply, then, to Revelation's parodic strategy? Yes and no. In contrast to the scenario adduced by Bhabha in which systemic mimicry of the agents and institutions of imperialism perpetually threatens to teeter over into parody or mockery, Revelation presents us with a reverse scenario in which parody or mockery of the imperial order constantly threatens to keel over into mimicry, imitation and replication. Revelation's implicit claim, as commentators never tire of telling us, is that Roman imperial-court ceremonial, together with the imperial court itself, are but pale imitations – diabolic imitations, indeed – of the heavenly throne room and the heavenly liturgy. Commentators also routinely note that the heavenly court and liturgy in Revelation are themselves modelled in no small part on the Roman imperial court and cult (recall our earlier ruminations on chs 4–5) – which means in effect that the 'heavenly' order in Revelation is busily engaged in imitating or mimicking the 'earthly' order, notwithstanding the book's own implicit charge that the earthly is a counterfeit copy of the heavenly.

To venture the latter observation is merely to state the obvious, perhaps. Yet the obvious is not without interest in this instance. Revelation's attempted sleight of hand ensnares it in a debilitating contradiction. Christians are enjoined to mimic Jesus, who in turn mimics his Father ('To the one who conquers I will give a place with me on my throne, just as I myself conquered and sat down with my Father on his throne', 3.21), who, in effect, mimics the Roman emperor, who himself (at least as represented in the imperial cult) is a mimetic composite of assorted royal and divine stereotypes. In Revelation, Christian authority inheres in imitation ('To everyone who conquers and continues to do my works to the end, I will give authority [*exousia*] over the nations, to rule them with an iron rod [see 12.5, in which the same scriptural phrase is applied to Jesus himself] ... even as I also received authority from my Father', 2.26; see 20.4). However, if the Roman imperial order is the ultimate object of imitation in Revelation, then, in accordance with the book's own implicit logic, it remains the ultimate authority, despite the book's explicit attempts to unseat it.

Mimicry and Monstrosity: Revelation 13 and 17

On Revelation's own account, of course, it is Rome, the sea-beast, that is the consummate mimic – the mimic monster – with its ten horns and seven heads

(13.1; 17.3), in imitation of the great red dragon (12.3; explicitly identified as Satan in 12.9 and 20.2), whose own appearance is in turn an imitation of various ancient Near Eastern mythic prototypes. Furthermore, the unholy trinity of Satan, sea-beast and 'false prophet' (for the latter epithet see 16.13; 19.20; 20.10) mimics the holy trinity (strictly lower-case; we are not yet within spitting distance of Nicaea) of God, Lamb and prophetic spirit (for the latter see 2.7, 11, 17, 29; 3.6, 13, 22; see 1.10; 4.2; 17.3; 21.10). In addition to the general structural parallel of two antithetical triads, certain characteristics ascribed to the sea-beast in particular mirror those ascribed to Jesus or God: note especially the Christlike 'resurrection' attributed to the sea-beast in 13.3, 14; also the thrice-repeated declaration that 'it was and is not and is to come' (which crops up twice in 17.8 and again in 17.11, in variant forms), parodying the thrice-repeated acclamation of God as he 'who is and who was and who is to come' (1.4, 8; 4.8). Also notable is the depiction of the land-beast as having 'two horns like a lamb' (13.11). Revelation is engaging in subtle mockery of Satan and his elect agents here, it would seem, implying that they are best seen as distorted reflections of God and his elect agents.

Yet, as we have just observed, Revelation's Deity cannot function as anchor for this mimetic chain, but is instead merely another link in it, being modelled on the Roman emperor – and we have not even begun to consider the extent to which this deity is also a composite copy of Ezekiel's Deity, Daniel's Deity and so on, themselves in turn ultimately constructed on the model of the ancient Near Eastern monarch. If the Roman imperial court is, in Revelation, merely a dim, distorted reflection of the heavenly court, the latter is itself merely a magnified reflection of the former and sundry other earthly courts, so that the seer's vision of heaven occurs in a conceptual hall of mirrors.

Again, this observation smacks of the obvious, I suspect, and as such falls short of profundity. Yet the 'obvious' does not always command acknowledgment. The difficulty of effectively exiting empire by attempting to turn imperial ideology against itself is regularly underrated, it seems to me, by those who acclaim Revelation for decisively breaking the relentless cycle of empire. To my mind, Revelation is emblematic of the difficulty of using the emperor's tools to dismantle the emperor's palace. The seer storms in through the main gates of the imperial palace, wrecking tools in hand, only to be surreptitiously swept back out through the rear entrance, having been deftly relieved of his tools at the threshold.

The Book of Conquest

More than any other early Christian text, Revelation is replete with the language of war, conquest and empire – so much so, indeed, as to beggar description. Note in particular, however, that the promised reward for faithful Christian discipleship in Revelation is joint rulership of the empire of empires soon destined to succeed Rome (3.21; 5.10; 20.4-6; 22.5), a messianic empire established by means of mass-slaughter on a surreal scale (6.4, 8; 8.11; 9.15, 18; 11.13; 14.20; 19.15, 17-21; 20.7-9, 15) calculated to make the combined military campaigns of Julius Caesar, Augustus and all of their successors pale to insignificance by comparison. All of this suggests that Revelation's overt resistance to and expressed revulsion toward Roman imperial ideology is surreptitiously compromised and undercut by covert compliance and attraction. Not for nothing is Rome figured in Revelation as a prostitute – indeed, as 'the mother of whores' (*hē mētēr tōn pornōn*, 17.5): what better embodiment, for the seer, of seductive repulsiveness, of repulsive seductiveness? Empire is the site of immense ambivalence in this book.

Bhabha's controversial intimation is that since colonial discourse is inherently ambivalent, and as such internally conflicted, it contains the seeds of its own dissolution, independently of any overt act of resistance on the part of colonized subjects. With regard to Revelation, however, the scenario is again reversed. Because Revelation's *anti*-colonial discourse, its resistance to Roman omnipotence, is infected with desire and hence with ambivalence, it contains the seeds of its own eventual absorption by that which it ostensibly opposes. (Actually, this too is consonant with Bhabha's theory, since he ascribes ambivalence to the colonized no less than to the colonizer. The logical collapse of counter-imperial discourse, however, under the weight of its own internal contradictions, is not the sort of phenomenon that Bhabha tends to emphasize.) In this regard, Revelation epitomizes, and encapsulates for analytical scrutiny, the larger and later process whereby Christianity, in the Constantinian and post-Constantinian periods, paradoxically *became* Rome.

As various colonial discourse analysts from Albert Memmi to Homi Bhabha have argued, the relationship between colonizer and colonized is best conceived as a mutually constitutive one. In terms of identity construction, the flow of effects is not all in one direction; instead, there is a complex circulation of effects between colonizer and colonized. The metropolis's relationship to the colonies, to take a quite uncontroversial example, becomes a crucial element in its ideological self-representation, and hence in the communal construction of its cultural identity.

Arguably, the post-Constantinian Christianization of the Roman Empire offers the most spectacular historical example of this phenomenon. As a means through which to conceptualize its own unique identity and destiny, metropolitan Roman culture absorbed and internalized Christianity, originally a peripheral, provincial product (although one to whose emergence Rome had already contributed the crucial catalyst by publicly executing its 'founder'). As though anticipating this astounding act of co-option, Revelation resolutely targets *hybridity* and holds up for emulation a Christian praxis that is at once peripheral and pure.

Hybrid Harlotry: Revelation 2–3

The threat of the hybrid is embodied for Revelation in the 'works' and teaching of 'the Nicolaitans' (2.6, 15), the teaching of 'Balaam' (2.14; see Numbers 22–24; 31.8, 16; Deut. 23.4-5; Josh. 24.9-10; 2 Pet. 2.15-16; Jude 11), and the teaching of 'that woman Jezebel' (2.20; see 1 Kgs 16.31; 18.1-19; 19.1-3; 21.23, 25; 2 Kgs 9.22, 30-37). The Nicolaitans are otherwise unknown, apparently; subsequent references to them in the church fathers seem to depend ultimately on Revelation. The names Balaam and Jezebel are symbolic, presumably. The phrase 'the teaching of Balaam' would appear to be a synonym for 'the teaching of the Nicolaitans'. The context further suggests that 'Balaam' is not a code-name for a Christian teacher at Pergamum, although 'Jezebel' would seem to be a code-name for an actual Christian prophet at Thyatira – a Nicolaitan prophet to be precise: the content of her teaching is described in terms identical to that of the Nicolaitans. Like the names Balaam and Jezebel, the practice of 'fornication' with which the Nicolaitans are charged (*porneusai*, 2.14, 20) is probably symbolic, fornication being a common figure for idolatry in the Jewish Scriptures.

The Nicolaitans are best seen as Christian 'assimilationists', who, like their counterparts in the Corinthian church (see 1 Cor. 8.1-13; 10.23–11.1), took a relaxed or pragmatic view of Christian accommodation to certain cultural norms, specifically (to cite the practice that elicits the seer's censure), eating meat in assorted socio-religious settings – whether public settings, such as regular calendric festivals, including those of the imperial cult; or (semi-)private settings, such as banquets or other meals hosted by trade guilds or other voluntary associations or social clubs; or simply eating temple 'leftovers', meat that had been sold in the marketplace after having been sacrificed and partially consumed in the temple cults.

Revelation's stance, then, with regard to Christian participation in the regular civic life of Roman Asia – exemplified by participation in the many cultic and semi-cultic meals that constituted an important ingredient of the 'social glue' of the province – is strenuously anti-assimilationist. This is to say that its stance is also counter-hegemonic (using 'hegemonic' once again in its Gramscian sense): Christians must not enact, through symbolic means, their own subjection to the Roman Empire by participating in the social and religious rituals that collectively prop up the far-flung canopy of the empire and enable it to cast its shadow over the day-to-day lives of the diverse populations under its sway. Revelation enjoins a practice of non-violent resistance to empire instead, a symbolic 'coming out' of empire (see 18.4: 'Come out of her, my people, so that you do not participate in her sins') while continuing to remain physically within it – though whether a coming out to form fully fledged counter-communities (systematic antitypes of standard Asian communities) or a more ad hoc, guerilla-style coming out is unclear.

As such, the main pillars of Asian collaboration with Roman domination, the members of the Assembly of Asia, an important aspect of whose function was the organization and promotion of the imperial cult, as noted earlier, are singled out for special condemnation in Revelation – provided that the land-beast of 13.11-18, assigned with the responsibility of 'making the earth and its inhabitants worship the [sea-]beast' (Rome and its emperors, see 13.1; 17.3, 9), is to be identified as the priesthood of the imperial cult, as has frequently been suggested. The land-beast derives its authority from the sea-beast, but the latter is said to derive its own authority from the dragon, who is Satan (13.4).

Revelation's unequivocal condemnation of collaboration with Rome, however – even (or especially?) collaboration conducted through symbolic (i.e., ritual) means – extends, by implication, to all strata of Asian society, as its denunciation of Christian assimilationism makes clear. But why? Is it because the mortar of empire is inevitably mixed with the blood of its victims (2.13; 6.9; 13.15; 16.6; 17.6; 18.24), so that (to shift the metaphor slightly) those who reap the benefits of empire, however meagre, are, by extension, guilty of the blood that keeps the wheels of empire oiled (17.1-2, 6)? Only fatal casualties of empire, then, could be deemed innocent of its systemic injustices. If this is indeed Revelation's central assertion regarding the mechanics and ethics of empire, it is an utterly uncompromising and unsettling one.

In light of such a stance, the consistent demonization of imperial authority in Revelation becomes yet more comprehensible, as does its denunciation of assimilationist Christianity. In order that Revelation's blanket critique of empire acquire full rhetorical force, the distinction between the agents of empire, on the one hand, and the victims of empire, on the other, must be asserted at an absolute, and hence metaphysical, level, and such a distinction is menaced by any manifestation of Christian hybridity, however innocuous. The Nicolaitans, epitomized by 'Jezebel', embody the threat of hybridity, as we have seen.

Yet, what is the precise relationship between 'Jezebel' and the 'Great Whore', that other female incarnation of iniquity in Revelation (beyond the – presumably coincidental – fact that each name evokes an especially unappetizing fate, that of ending up on the wrong end of the food chain: the original Jezebel is famously devoured by dogs, whereas the whore is devoured by a far more fearsome beast – 1 Kgs 21.23; 2 Kgs 9.30-37; Rev. 17.16)? In other words, what is the relationship between Christian assimilationism and imperial oppression ('And I saw that the woman was drunk with the blood of the saints and the blood of the witnesses [*tōn marturiōn*] to Jesus', 17.6; see 13.15; 18.24) in this book? The whore, it may be said, represents the threat to Christianity from without, whereas Jezebel represents the threat to Christianity from within. The threat from within, however, represented by the spectacle and the spectre of assimilationism, is precisely that the threat from outside is not *purely* external: the outside has infiltrated the inside. Jezebel and the whore represent but two sides of the same (counterfeit) coin in Revelation: on the one hand, an inside that has somehow strayed outside; on the other hand, an outside that has somehow stolen inside.

The Book of Empire

In its concern to maintain intact the binary partition separating imperial metropolis and Christian periphery, Revelation, though passionately resistant to Roman imperial ideology, paradoxically and persistently reinscribes its terms, to the extent that Roman imperial ideology (like subsequent European imperial ideology) can itself be said to have pivoted around an integrated series of dualistic distinctions between metropolis and periphery, civilized and barbaric, and so on (that brand of imperialistic dualism that the postcolonial critic Abdul JanMohamed has aptly dubbed 'Manichaeanism' [1995]). Of course, Revelation maintains the metropolis/periphery binarism only in order to stand it on its head: the hierarchical power relations that currently obtain between metropolis and periphery, Rome and Christianity, are soon destined for spectacular reversal. Activities or ideologies that do not conform to this binary separation are subject to censure or rendered taboo in Revelation. However, the inherent instability and untenability of the binary division comes to displaced expression in the elaborate mimicry that, as we saw, characterizes Revelation's depiction of the 'other' empire, that of God and the Lamb, a mimicry that blurs the boundaries between the two empires until it becomes all but impossible to decide where one leaves off and the other begins. For the divine empire that Revelation proclaims is anything but independent from the Roman Empire. Instead, it is parasitic on it.

In due course, however, the host absorbed the parasite, precipitating the host's mutation into the one monstrosity that the seer of Revelation seems incapable of imagining: an empire that is Roman and Christian at one and the same time. The curious phenomenon of Constantinian Christianity itself bears monumental testimony to the fatal flaw in Revelation's theology. More than any other early Christian text (prior to Tertullian, at any rate), Revelation epitomizes the theo-imperialist orientation that enabled the Roman state effortlessly to absorb Christianity into itself, to turn Christianity into a version of itself, to turn itself into a version of Christianity – notwithstanding the fact that Revelation is also ostensibly more hostile to Rome than any other early Christian text. The flaw inheres in three mutually reinforcing – and inescapably obvious? – features of Revelation (although the obvious is always hedged about with obliviousness, and hence never as inescapable as one would like). First of all, the throne is the paramount metonym for God in this book. Second, the principal attributes of 'the one seated on the throne' are stereotypically imperial attributes: incomparable glory and authority, overwhelming power and punitive wrath. Third, the principal activities of the one seated on the throne and those of his elite agents are quintessentially imperial activities: the conduct of war and the enlargement of empire.

To construct God or Christ, together with their putatively salvific activities, from the raw material of imperial ideology is not to shatter the cycle of empire but merely to transfer it to a transcendental plane, thereby reifying and rein-scribing it. The dearth of non-imperial synonyms for the Christian theological commonplace(s), 'the kingdom (or reign, or rule) of God (or Christ)', even in current theological and pastoral discourse is symptomatic of the extent to which imperial metaphors have maintained, and continue to maintain, a virtual monopoly on the Christian theological imagination – one ultimately unchecked by the cross, I hasten to add, which all too easily folds up to form a throne – creating an imperial divine 'essence' that is extremely difficult to dismantle or dislodge.

Yet there is undoubtedly a place for what Gayatri Spivak, in a related context, has termed 'strategic essentialism'. The envisioning of a cosmic counter-empire presided over by a divine Emperor may serve an important strategic function in struggles for liberation from situations of desperate oppression, as work on Revelation such as that of Allan Boesak or Pablo Richard eloquently testifies. Revelation is eminently well-equipped to speak to such situations; to a greater or lesser extent, it was in such a crucible that Revelation itself was forged (not yet a situation of systematic state-sponsored persecution, apparently, but the seer's intuition that such oppression lay over the horizon was entirely accu-rate). Ultimately, however, if Christian theology is to be intellectually as well as ethically adequate, and as such less luridly anthropomorphic and less patently projectionist, might it not require what Revelation, locked as it is in visions of empires and counter-empires, emperors and counter-emperors, seems sin-gularly powerless to provide: a conception of the divine sphere as other than empire writ large?

BIBLIOGRAPHY

Ashcroft, Bill, Gareth Griffiths and Helen Tiffin (eds)
    2001   *Postcolonial Studies: The Key Concepts* (London and New York: Routledge).
Aune, David
    1985   'The Influence of Roman Imperial Court Ceremonial on the Apocalypse of John', *Papers of the Chicago Society of Biblical Research* 28: 5–26.
    1997   *Revelation 1-5* (Word Biblical Commentary, 52A; Dallas: Word Books).
    1998a   *Revelation 6–16* (Word Biblical Commentary, 52B; Nashville: Thomas Nelson).
    1998b   *Revelation 17–22* (Word Biblical Commentary, 52C; Nashville: Thomas Nelson).
Beard, Mary, John North and Simon Price
    1998   *Religions of Rome*. Vol. 1, *A History*; Vol. 2, *A Sourcebook* (Cambridge: Cambridge University Press).
Bhabha, Homi
    1994   *The Location of Culture* (London and New York: Routledge).
    1992   'Postcolonial Criticism', in Stephen Greenblatt and Giles B. Gunn (eds),

Redrawing the Boundaries: The Transformation of English and American Literary Studies (New York: Modern Language Association of America): 437–65.

Boesak, Allan A.
1997   *Comfort and Protest: The Apocalypse from a South African Perspective* (Philadelphia: Westminster Press).

Friesen, Steven J.
2001   *Imperial Cults and the Apocalypse of John: Reading Revelation in the Ruins* (Oxford: Oxford University Press).

Frilingos, Christopher
2004   *Spectacles of Empire: Monsters, Martyrs, and the Book of Revelation* (Divinations: Rereading Late Ancient Religion; Philadelphia: University of Pennsylvania Press).

Gramsci, Antonio
1992–96   *Prison Notebooks* (2 vols.; ed. Joseph A. Buttigieg; trans. Joseph A. Buttigieg and Antonio Callari; New York: Columbia University Press).

Howard-Brook, Wes and Anthony Gwyther
1999   *Unveiling Empire: Reading Revelation Then and Now* (The Bible and Liberation; Maryknoll, NY: Orbis Books).

JanMohamed, Abdul R.
1995   'The Economy of Manichean Allegory', in Bill Ashcroft, Gareth Griffiths and Helen Tiffin (eds), *The Post-Colonial Studies Reader* (London and New York: Routledge): 18–23.

Johnston, Anna and Alan Lawson
2000   'Settler Colonies', in Henry Schwarz and Sangeeta Ray (eds), *A Companion to Postcolonial Studies* (Oxford: Blackwell): 360–76.

Keller, Catherine
1996   *Apocalypse Now and Then: A Feminist Guide to the End of the World* (Boston: Beacon Press).
2005   *God and Power: Counter-Apocalyptic Journeys* (Minneapolis: Fortress Press).

Kim, Jean K.
1999   ' "Uncovering Her Wickedness": An Inter(con)textual Reading of Revelation 17 from a Postcolonial Feminist Perspective', *Journal for the Study of the New Testament* 73: 83–112.

Levick, Barbara
1967   *Roman Colonies in Southern Asia Minor* (Oxford: Clarendon Press).

Magie, David
1950   *Roman Rule in Asia Minor to the End of the Third Century after Christ* (Princeton, NJ: Princeton University Press).

Maier, Harry O.
2002   *Apocalypse Recalled: The Book of Revelation after Christendom* (Minneapolis: Fortress Press).

Memmi, Albert
2004   *The Colonizer and the Colonized* (Foreword by Homi K. Bhabha; New York: Beacon Press; French original 1957).

Moore-Gilbert, Bart
1997   *Postcolonial Theory: Contexts, Practices, Politics* (London: Verso).

Moore, Stephen D.
  2005   'Questions of Biblical Ambivalence and Authority under a Tree outside
             Delhi; or, the Postcolonial and the Postmodern', in Stephen D. Moore and
             Fernando F. Segovia (eds), *Postcolonial Biblical Criticism: Interdisciplinary
             Intersections* (New York: T&T Clark International): 79–96.

Pippin, Tina
  1999   *Apocalyptic Bodies: The Biblical End of the World in Text and Image* (London
             and New York: Routledge).

Price, S. R. F.
  1984   *Rituals and Power: The Roman Imperial Cult in Asia Minor* (Cambridge:
             Cambridge University Press).

Richard, Pablo
  1995   *Apocalypse: A People's Commentary on the Book of Revelation* (The Bible
             and Liberation; Maryknoll, NY: Orbis Books).

Said, Edward W.
  1978   *Orientalism* (New York: Pantheon Books).
  1993   *Culture and Imperialism* (New York: Vintage Books).

Spivak, Gayatri Chakravorty
  1984–85   'Criticism, Feminism and the Institution' (interview with Elizabeth Gross),
             Thesis Eleven 10/11: 175–87.
  1999   *A Critique of Postcolonial Reason: Toward a History of the Vanishing Present*
             (Cambridge: Harvard University Press).
  1991   'Identity and Alterity: An Interview' (with Nikos Papastergiadis), *Arena* 97:
             65–76.

Thompson, Leonard L.
  1990   *The Book of Revelation: Apocalypse and Empire* (Oxford: Oxford University
             Press).

Westhelle, Vitor
  2005   'Revelation 13: Between the Colonial and the Postcolonial, a Reading from
             Brazil', in David Rhoads (ed.), *From Every People and Nation: The Book
             of Revelation in Intercultural Perspective* (Minneapolis: Fortress Press):
             183–99.

Young, Robert
  1990   *White Mythologies: Writing History and the West* (London and New York:
             Routledge).
  2001   *Postcolonialism: A Historical Introduction* (Oxford: Blackwell).

Postcolonial and Biblical Interpretation: The Next Phase

R. S. Sugirtharajah

One of the lessons of history is that empires rarely disappear completely. They rise and fall but often resurface in different forms. The current military interventions and territorial occupations in the name of democracy, humanitarianism and liberation are signs of a new form of imperialism. As long as there are empires, dominations, tyrannies and exploitations – either rising or resurfacing – postcolonial criticism will continue to have its vigilant role to play. What this end-piece will do is draw attention to some of the issues with which postcolonialism now needs to engage. It falls into two parts. In the first, I will highlight some of the unfinished or unstarted textual work postcolonial criticism has to undertake within the discipline of biblical studies. The second part will focus on a new vocation for postcolonialism which will take it beyond its traditional territory – ritualized theoretical negotiations and niceties, and recover practical projects and recommit itself to addressing crises that affect the contemporary world – the crucial public issues of today which are attracting wide attention and anxiety in the media, terrorist suicide and asylum-seeking.

Widening the Hermeneutical Horizons

All along, biblical studies have been confined to the canonical Scriptures – the eventual winners in the doctrinal battles of the early church. Postcolonial biblical criticism needs to expand the biblical canon and incorporate those diverse texts which were suppressed or excluded in the ecclesiastical power-game of selection and rejection. Some of these texts did not make it into the canon because they contain risqué passages, involving, for example, excessive kissing of Jesus and Mary; include parables populated with dodgy characters; and, more significantly, portray strong women who defy gender typecasting. The discovery of a wealth of early Christian literature at Nag Hammadi in Egypt means that we are no longer dependent solely on the Scriptures accepted by the clerical hierarchy to understand the first 400 years of the church's existence. This range of diverse Christian writings, which are often described as Gnostic and a target of ecclesiastical suspicion and scorn, should be a prime object of postcolonial studies. These excluded or suppressed Scriptures are often interdicted and demonized, but they are the alternative narratives of the nascent Christian movement.

Hitherto, postcolonial criticism has largely confined its attention to the canonical writings which were selected by the church. The selection of the books that went into the canon was largely determined by the political and religious interests of the conservative West. Incidentally, the canon which was first introduced to Asia was the eastern canon, which came with the Nestorians in the fourth century, and not the western one, which was launched much later, during the colonial period, by European missionaries from the end of the fifteenth century. A postcolonial inclination would be to support and recover those writings which lost out in the canonical process and treat them as part of the broader textual continuum.

There are three reasons for this. One, in spite of being dismissed as esoteric writings conveying sacred mystical knowledge, and scorned for their 'weird' theologies, some of them express an anti-imperial stance. For instance, there is an incident narrated in the *Acts of Peter* where a marble statue of Caesar is kicked to pieces by a demon exorcized by Peter (ch. 11). Secondly, some of these writings have hermeneutical value, especially for churches outside Western Christendom. The earliest gospel to reach India was one of the excluded – the Aramaic version of the *Gospel of Matthew*, brought by Bartholomew in the second century, a fact recorded by Eusebius. More important than its arrival, however, are the references to India recorded in some of the other writings which did not make it into the canon. For instance, the *Acts of Thomas* contains a reference to Thomas coming to India. It records a reluctant Thomas who was forcibly sold by Jesus as a slave to work as a carpenter to a wealthy merchant called Aban, the same Jesus who is silent about slavery in the canonical Gospels. The selling of Thomas suggests that collusion between Christianity and the corporate world has been present since its inception. Thirdly, there are the hermeneutical implications of these texts. The *Gospel of Thomas* provides an interesting starting point for Asian hermeneutics. It offers a Christology which portrays Jesus as an exemplary moral teacher, a Jesus which nineteenth-century interpreters like Ram Mohun Roy and Keshub Chunder Sen were trying to fashion in contrast to the overly divinized Jesus introduced to India by the missionaries. It is not the death and resurrection of Jesus which readers encounter in the *Gospel of Thomas* but his wisdom sayings, which have resonance with the Asian wisdom tradition.

From a postcolonial perspective, canonical Scriptures are not the sole conveyors of truth. The suppressed Scriptures make it clear that competing claims and counter-claims were characteristic features of early Christianity. It is important to establish that the early Christian community was not unified but composed of a whole spectrum of different and rival schools of thought. Postcolonial biblical studies should reflect this unsettled character of the early church and question the motives which reject the alternative forms. All sources – canonical as well as non-canonical, and oral as well as written – have played a decisive role in the historical formation of the early church and enlarge our understanding of it.

Pape has identified two causes which trigger and provide motivation for suicide missions: the presence of foreign combat troops which threaten the way of life of the occupied, and the foreign occupier who happens to be of a different religion. Suicide missions happen when foreign troops occupy territories believed to be the homeland of peoples such as Palestinians, Kurds, Chechens or, in the case of al Qaeda, Saudi Arabia, where American troops are stationed. In each of these cases, suicide campaigns were 'driven by essentially nationalist goals to compel target democracies to withdraw military forces from their *particular* homeland' (Pape 2005: 243). Suicide groups are active when another state occupies a region whose inhabitants follow a different religion. The contemporary case in point is the supposedly Christian US forces occupying Islamic Iraq. Pape acknowledges that 'religious difference matters in that it enables terrorist leaders to paint foreign forces as being driven by religious goals' (cited in Blumenthal 2005: 34).

Pape has drawn attention to the speeches of Osama bin Laden, which depict the US occupation of the Arabian peninsula as driven by religious goals, so that it is an Islamic duty to resist this invasion. 'That argument', in Pape's view, 'is incredibly powerful, not only to religious Muslims but also secular Muslims' (cited in Blumenthal 2005: 34).

What postcolonialism has to do is to complicate the idea of suicide missions as the creation of the extreme teachings of religions by shifting and directing discussion from religious orthodoxy and single reading of texts to a highly specific political circumstance – imperialism. It is becoming increasingly clear that we can not understand the phenomenon of suicide missions unless we understand the power and presence of empire.

Asylum Seekers at the Rich Man's Gate

Besides suicide missions, the other messy affair which has preoccupied the European media is asylum-seeking. Postcolonial diaspora studies have chiefly focused on middle-class migrants and captured their in-between status through such terms as hybridity, liminality and multiculturalism and have paid less attention to the plight of refugees and asylum seekers. Nor have they much considered the case of the South and East Asian migrants in nineteenth- and twentieth-century indenture systems. In a world made unstable by political uncertainties, natural disasters and human-rights violations, there is an unprecedented movement of people from the developing world to the developed. In Western discourse over the years, the terminology surrounding refugees and asylum seekers has changed. During the Cold War, those who were seeking shelter from communist persecution – a dissident writer or scientist or a ballet dancer – were regarded as ideologically convenient and 'good' refugees (Moorehead 2005: 28). Those who sought safe haven were few in number and not seen as threatening. But today, those who want to escape political harassment and come to the West are seen as 'bad' refugees endangering the Western way of life. The current heavy movement of people has altered the charitable definition of refugee, which has given way to a narrower and less benevolent one. Now refugees are those displaced peoples who live in camps in their own or in neighbouring countries, while the term asylum seeker is gaining currency to focus on the place to which those seeking sanctuary want to come. Refugees are those who are 'out' there, whereas the asylum seeker is the one who is 'here' wanting a share of Western prosperity or freedom.

Interrogating biblical material for insights into the current problems of asylum-seeking may not be very profitable. Passages in the Hebrew Scriptures deal with strangers and aliens, and biblical characters like Ruth and Esther highlight how outsiders adjust to a foreign environment. But these narratives do not speak to or represent the anxieties faced by current asylum seekers, whose existence and sheer large numbers are the result of a different political and cultural situation. Among those New Testament writings which talk about exiles, strangers and resident aliens is 1 Peter. These terms refer to minority Christians in Asia Minor who were under pressure and were being maligned by the dominant community. There is no scholarly consensus as to the definite usage of these terms in 1 Peter – exiles, aliens, strangers. Whether they are metaphors, or express an actual situation in which these Christians literally and physically found themselves homeless, is unsettled.

Despite the contentious nature of the definition, there are certain parallels between ancient Christians as resident aliens and current asylum seekers. Both feel under pressure. Some, though not all, are seen as professing a strange religion. Christianity, in the case of the Petrine community, and Islam, Hinduism and so forth in the case of some asylum seekers. Both face aggressive hostility and are viewed with suspicion (1 Pet. 2.12; 4.14-16). The British tabloids are full of stories demonizing asylum seekers as exploiting the social-security system and the national health service (Greenslade 2005). But the parallels end there. 1 Peter describes a situation in which the early Christians were a minority and living in a predominantly pagan world. Today, the 'pagans' are the asylum seekers, many from Islamic, Hindu and Sikh communities, trying to find a home in Europe which has strong roots in Christian values. The Christian basis of Europe was recently reiterated by the late John Paul II. On the occasion of welcoming the ten new countries from the old Soviet bloc, the late pope said: 'Only a Europe that does not remove, but rediscovers its Christian roots will reach the stature needed for the great challenges of the third millennium: peace, dialogue between cultures and religions, the safeguarding of creation' (Pope John Paul II, 2004). Like the Petrine Christians, who reduced the 'other' to undifferentiated Gentiles (1 Pet. 2.12; 4.3), their 'adversary the devil prowls around like a roaring lion, seeking some to devour' (1 Pet. 5.8), the Western press labels every one seeking asylum as economic migrants. More alarmingly, 1 Peter offers a dangerous potential to the host countries. The Christians in Asia Minor saw themselves as a 'chosen race, a royal priesthood, a holy nation, and

God's own people' (2.9). Such a claim to a nominated status as God's elect must have provided the marginalized Christian community in Asia Minor with an alternative hermeneutical strategy to affirm their distinctive collective identity. In the changed circumstances when Western countries have become the dominant power, such claims could be seen as exclusionary and imperialistic.

There is another dangerous aspect to the text that could become malign in the hands of the West. The Petrine Christians fostered the dream of the final conversion of the Gentiles (2.12; 3.1-2). In the current situation, Western countries are not talking in terms of conversion in a religious sense but use secular ideals like integration and assimilation. What assimilation or integration means is that if the strangers want to be part of the Western countries, they must embrace Western values and abandon their own rich cultural heritage. Such a reading presents no comfort to the current asylum seekers. Today's asylum seeker is not *paroikos* in the Petrine sense – resident alien, but *xenos* – a complete stranger with little legal security and economic restrictions.

What is becoming progressively clearer is that sacred texts may not be the right place to look for the rights and treatment of present-day asylum seekers. These texts were produced before the current nation states were formed and international understandings on human rights were devised. Asylum in the end is not about what sacred texts sanction, but, as Caroline Moorehead, who studied the plight of refugee and asylum seekers, says, is about 'morality'. Warning that the question of asylum-seeking is not going to go away, Moorehead pleads that the Western governments should find humane ways of tackling the problem: 'In an age of globalization, it is simply not possible to ignore the world's dispossessed. How a state deals with its refugees should be a measure of its social and political health' (Moorehead 2005: 291). The righteousness of a people will be measured by the welcome they extend to strangers, and their capacity to revise their enclosed history, identity and culture through an encounter with the 'other'.

To sum up, then. The interpreter has not only a discursive function but also an interventionist one which is ethically and ideologically committed. Inevitably, interpreter, text and ethical issues are locked in a dialectical relationship. The creative and productive future of postcolonial biblical criticism depends on its ability to reinvent itself and enlarge its scope. It should continue to expose the power–knowledge axis but at the same time move beyond abstract theorization and get involved in the day-to-day messy activities which affect people's lives.

BIBLIOGRAPHY

Blumenthal, Sidney
    2005   'Bin Laden's Little Helper', *The Guardian* (30 September).
Bowersock, G. W.
    1995   *Martyrdom and Rome* (Cambridge: Cambridge University Press).

Eagleton, Terry
    2005   'A Way of Different Death', *The Guardian* (26 January).
Fowden, Garth
    1993   *Empire to Commonwealth: Consequences of Monotheism in Late Antiquity* (Princeton, NJ: Princeton University Press).
Greenslade, Roy
    2005   *Seeking Scapegoats: The Coverage of Asylum in the UK Press* (London: Institute for Public Policy Research).
John Paul II, Pope
    2004   'Europe Must Recognize Its Christian Roots', available online at <http://www.pluralism.org/news/intl/index.php?xref.>
Moorehead, Caroline
    2005   *Human Cargo: A Journey Among Refugees* (London: Chatto & Windus).
Musurillo, Herbert (ed.)
    1972   *The Acts of the Christian Martyrs* (Oxford: Clarendon Press).
Pape, Robert A.
    2005   *Dying to Win: The Strategic Logic of Suicide Terrorism* (New York: Random House).
Stark, Rodney
    2001   *One True God: Historical Consequences of Monotheism* (Princeton, NJ: Princeton University Press).
Schwartz, Regina M.
    1997   *The Curse of Cain: The Violent Legacy of Monotheism* (Chicago: Chicago University Press).
Schwiebert, Jonathan
    2004   'Evading Rituals in New Testament Studies', *The Council of Societies for the Study of Religion Bulletin* 33(1): 10–13.